Counseling in a Dynamic Society:

Contexts and Practices for the 21st Century

Second Edition

Edwin L. Herr

COUNSELING IN A DYNAMIC SOCIETY, SECOND EDITION

10 9 8 7 6 5 4 3 2

American Counseling Association
5999 Stevenson Avenue
Alexandria, VA 22304

Director of Acquisitions
Carolyn Baker

Director of Publishing Systems
Michael Comlish

Copy Editor
Lucy Blanton

Cover design by Media Plus Design

Library of Congress Cataloging-in-Publication Data

Herr, Edwin L.
    Counseling in a dynamic society : contexts and practices for the 21st century /
Edwin L. Herr. — 2nd ed.
        p.   cm.
    Includes bibliographical references and index.
    ISBN 1-55620-205-9 (alk. paper)
    1. Counseling.   I. Title.
BF637.C6H43   1998
158'.3—dc21   98-29307
                                                                                    CIP

For Pat, Alicia, Amber, and Christopher whose personal achievements, love, and support make writing possible and satisfying.

CONTENTS

PREFACE

The purpose of this second edition of *Counseling in a Dynamic Society: Contexts and Practices for the 21st Century* is to examine major categories of social and economic change likely to affect the purposes for, the techniques of, and the settings for counseling into the 21st century. This book is not about the counseling process primarily. It is not about theories of counseling and their implications for practice. Rather, it is about the environment, that is, the social, political, and economic contexts in which individual behavior is shaped and the provision of counseling occurs. Stated differently, it is about the interactions among economic, social, and political environments, individual behavior, policies and legislation, and the form and substance of counseling.

A central premise of the book is that the United States, like most of the nations of the world, is in a transition in which it is undergoing significant transformations in its institutions, behavioral metaphors, and psychological structures. As these elements of the social structure change, so will the ways by which people negotiate their personal identity and live out their self-concepts. The book attempts to synthesize a wide-ranging, multidisciplinary literature that outlines changes in the larger society, both domestic and global—changes that have or are likely to have direct implications for individual behavior and or counseling responses. It provides counselors, counseling psychologists, other mental health practitioners, and counselor educators an overview of the individual problems, their antecedents and behavioral elements, and their contexts about which helping professionals must be knowledgeable in a rapidly changing society.

The book is also incomplete. The changes described here are constantly in a dynamic state; they are systems in flux. Therefore, any book that attempts to capture these changes is likely to be in search of a series of moving targets. It is also likely to be less than encyclopedic in its treatment of the subject. The major and minor challenges discussed here each could be the substance of multiple books and articles rather than chapters or paragraphs. Thus the examination in this book is selective and, indeed, may miss some social, economic, political, or psychological trends that another writer would have legitimately included and given prominence. It is hoped, however, that the serious reader will find the book's bibliographic references a source of opportunities to carry this book's level of analysis to more extensive and specialized levels.

The book's content is presented in nine chapters. The chapters and their contents are briefly described in the following paragraphs.

Chapter 1 suggests that the content of counseling, with whom the counselor works, and the degree to which counseling is seen as a vital and important sociopolitical institution derive from major social, economic, and political themes that affect individual and group psychology. Thus the images, beliefs, narratives, and realities that compose national macrosystems also have ripple effects through the subsystems—community, school, workplace, family—in which people interact with institutions and with other individuals to negotiate their identity, their sense of purpose, their meaning.

Chapters 2 through 6 examine four major challenges that continue to have significant influence on individual behavior and on the perceptions of how counselors should interact with the settings and populations they serve. These are not new challenges in an absolute sense. The seeds, if not the substance, of each of these four challenges have been affecting the psychological environment of the United States and stimulating new conceptualizations of how, where, and when counseling and related interventions should be implemented.

The first of the four challenges that seem likely to have the greatest effect on the counseling profession into the 21st century concerns the ripple effects of the shifting economy and the transformation of the occupational structure in association with the pervasive effects of advanced technology, rising and shifting educational demands, and a global labor surplus. The second challenge comprises the implications of changing family structures, the gender revolution, and child-rearing practices. The third challenge is the growing pluralism of traditions, languages, ethnicity, and race that is the rule, not the exception, in contemporary America. Group definitions such as *majority* and *minority* are undergoing rapid change, and by the year 2000 will describe an America of substantially different racial composition than was true of earlier demographic profiles. Hence the implications for and the practices of counseling will need to be increasingly responsive to cross-cultural issues. The fourth challenge has to do with the changing definitions of *at-risk populations*. Traditional concepts of psychological vulnerability and the etiology of such vulnerability are increasingly seen through the lenses of stress, anger, crisis, and transition and not simply as psychopathology or deficits. Therefore, mental health problems and other challenges to counselors are viewed as dynamic and as encompassing a larger proportion of the population than may have access to counseling interventions.

Chapter 2 addresses specifically the complex issues that relate to the transition of the United States to an information-based, global economy. A central issue in this transition is the pervasive influence of the implementation of advanced technology. The economic climate, international competitiveness, educational content and delivery, the forms of work organization, the processes of career development, underemployment and unemployment, stress levels, the psychology of change, and many other areas of daily and national life are being affected by the myths and the realities of advanced technology. Clearly, the actual and perceived implications of advanced technology affect and are affected by the other three challenges examined in chapters 3, 4, 5, and 6: families, pluralism, and being at risk.

Chapter 3 treats the dramatic shifts in family structures and the gender revolution; this challenge is perhaps less well defined in its effect than is true of the first challenge, the shifting economic climate and advanced technology. However, just as the increasing adaptation of advanced technology is transforming the occupational structure and all of its corollaries, the revolution in family structures and sex roles is transforming the nuclear and intact traditional family into a large number of family patterns. In so doing it is altering forever many of the historical sex-role divisions that have differentiated the roles of men and women. These matters have in turn altered child-care practices, changed the demographics of the workforce, and, in some cases, put at risk the personal identities of both men and women.

The third challenge, the focus of chapter 4, is increasingly clear in its effects on counseling, but a challenge it will be nevertheless. Because America has been for at least three centuries a land of immigrants, it has declared itself a melting pot of the differences in traditions and languages into a common culture and set of beliefs. Although such national purposes remain intact, it also has become increasingly obvious that America is a land characterized by pluralism and regional differences in worldviews, traditions, values, and related matters. The rise in concern for cross-cultural counseling, multicultural sensitivity, and other such matters is one symbol of the growing recognition of and attention to such pluralism. The implications of cultural differences within the American population, however, are probably more profound than has commonly been acknowledged in counseling, in individuals' information processing, in values and belief systems, in communication, and in other arenas. Chapter 4 discusses some of these implications.

Chapters 5 and 6 address the concepts embodied in the term *at risk*, who can be so characterized, and the factors that put children, youth, and adults at risk. As is true in chapters 2 through 4, perspectives are provided about the role and content of counseling in responding to the challenges described.

Chapter 7 departs to some degree from the format established in chapters 1 through 6. It focuses not on challenges external to counseling or on the social, economic, and political mechanisms that shape individual behaviors, but on some of the emerging theoretical and other paradigm shifts. These describe how the content and processes of counseling are shifting to respond effectively to the challenges, settings, and populations described elsewhere in the book.

Chapters 8 and 9 return to the intent of the first six chapters and discuss recurring and emerging challenges that are less pervasive or more vague in their implications for counseling than the four major challenges discussed in chapters 2 through 6. The challenges described in chapters 8 and 9 vary across settings, populations to be served, and professional issues. They differ also in the level and form of speculation selected futurists project about trends likely to grow in importance for counselors in the next decade.

Permit me to thank the many theorists and researchers from whom I have learned as I have labored to clarify for myself the issues and challenges about which I have written here. Many of them are cited; others are not. Let me also acknowledge the word-processing excellence and organizational skills of my secretary, Peggy Repasky. Finally, I thank my wife and children, Pat, Alicia, Amber, and Christopher, for their love, understanding, and personal achievements during the course of this project.

—Edwin L. Herr
State College, Pennsylvania

ABOUT THE AUTHOR

Dr. Edwin L. Herr is Distinguished Professor of Education (Counselor Education and Counseling Psychology) and Associate Dean for Graduate Programs, Research, and Technology, College of Education, Pennsylvania State University. Dr. Herr has served as head of the Department of Counselor Education, Counseling Psychology, and Rehabilitation Services Education or earlier department iterations for 24 years. He has also served as university director of Vocational Teacher Education and director of the Center for Professional Personnel Development in Vocational Education. Dr. Herr received his B.S. from Shippensburg State College and his M.A., professional diploma, and Ed.D. from Teachers College, Columbia University.

A former business teacher, school counselor, and local director of guidance, Herr previously served as assistant and associate professor of counselor education at the State University of New York at Buffalo (1963–66) and as the first director of the Bureaus of Guidance Services and the Bureau of Pupil Personnel Services, Pennsylvania Department of Education (1966–68). He has been a visiting professor, researcher, or coordinator of international conferences in some 20 European universities as well as in Africa, Canada, Japan, and Taiwan. In 1976, he served as visiting fellow, National Institute for Careers Education and Counseling, Cambridge, England. In 1979, he was selected to serve as a research fellow, the Japan Society for the Promotion of Science, Tokyo, from which he lectured at universities throughout Japan. In 1978 and 1981, he served respectively as an Asia Foundation Lecturer and as a Yoshida International Education Lecturer at Japanese universities. In 1989, he served as visiting professor in the Department of Counseling Psychology, the University of British Columbia, Canada, and as the Landsdowne Scholar, University of Victoria, Canada.

In 1984, he was appointed an honorary member of the Swedish National Labor Market Board for his research and conceptual work in career development. In 1986, he was the recipient of the Eminent Career Award of the National Vocational Guidance Association for sustained national and international influence on theory, research, and practice in career behavior. In 1990, he received the Professional Development Award of the American Association for Counseling and Development for national and international scholarship and research on systems of counseling and the 50th Anniversary Professional Leadership Award of the Association for Counselor Education and Supervision for his scholarship and leadership in counselor preparation. For his scholarship and leadership in vocational education, he was chosen the Visiting Scholar of the University Council of Vocational Education for 1990–91. In 1993, he received a Government Relations Award for outstanding achievement in legislation and public policy in behalf of the counseling profession from the National Employment Counselors Association and the American Counseling Association, and he was chosen the Distinguised Scholar for 1993 by Chi Sigma Iota, the Counseling Academic and Professional Honor Society International. In 1995, Herr received the Career Achievement Award from the College of Education, Pennsylvania State University. In 1996, he received a Special Presidential Award and Governing Council Resolution from the American Counseling Association for his Distinguished Commitment to the Counseling Profession, specifically for his "unique and important research and theoretical contributions." Herr has been elected to fellow status in the American Psychological Association (Division 17, Counseling Psychology), the American Psychological Society, the Pennsylvania Psychological Association, and the American Association for Applied and Preventive Psychology. He is a National Certified Counselor and a National Certified Career Counselor.

Herr is past president of the American Association for Counseling and Development, the National Vocational Guidance Association, and the Association for Counselor Education and Supervision. He also served as a member of the executive committee of the International Round Table for the Advancement of Counseling (1976–84) and now serves as a member of the board of directors of the International Association of Educational and Vocational Guidance (1991–present). He is the author or co-author of over 300 articles and 31 books and monographs. He is the immediate past editor of the *Journal of Counseling and Development* (1993–96) and a member of several other editorial boards, including the *British Journal of Guidance and Counselling*.

Chapter 1

THE CONTEXT OF COUNSELING

THE INTERACTION OF BEHAVIOR, INTERVENTION, AND CONTEXT

A CENTRAL PREMISE OF THIS BOOK is that neither counselors nor the problems people bring to counselors exist in a vacuum. In essence, the argument is that neither individual behavior nor the theory and practice that conceptualize, facilitate, and implement the development of (or change in) knowledge, attitudes, and behaviors important in the counseling process occur in isolation from the social context in which they are located. Although each of these emphases—individual behavior, counseling or guidance theory and practice, social context—can be examined in depth and independently, the larger point is that to understand each it is also important to understand how they interact.

The interaction of behavior, intervention, and context has many implications. For example, studying the social context would be of little relevance if it had not been shown to shape and affect individual behavior and the institutions or processes that mediate individual behavior. Trying to understand how events—political, economic—in the individual's social contexts trigger or exacerbate the problems that clients bring to counselors would be of no utility if the motivation for behavior were located only in the intrapsychic structure of the individual and not in the transactions of the individual with the various systems—family, work, school—that comprise the social context. But as we learn more about individual behavior, we have come to understand that such behavior frequently can not be understood if it is treated as though it occurred in a test tube or a cocoon independent from the contexts, the environments, that provide or limit opportunities, achievement images, personal constructs, freedom of choice, perspectives on gender role, or other factors that influence individual or collective identity. From a constructivist view, it is through encounters with aspects of the social context that individuals make meaning for themselves and construct their reality.

The social context is not a unitary phenomenon. It is composed of political, economic, interpersonal, and cultural components that have varying types of relevance for different subpopulations—children, youth, adults, women and men, the abled and the disabled, the rich and the poor—at different times in their development and transitions across the life span. Different societies—whether defined in political or cultural terms—create different metaphors of the personality characteristics they find normal or abnormal, acceptable or unacceptable. Such metaphors define what behavior is to be rewarded and what types of behavior are sanctioned (e.g., self-reliance or conformity, individual or group decision making, assertiveness or deference) for whom. Such metaphors derive from a complex blend of cultural, historical, political, economic, and religious traditions manifested in the set of social and psychological emphases and the network of roles and role expectations in which persons learn and implement their self-concept.

As societal differences are observed and classified, some societies are defined as competitive, and individual action is prized; others are cooperative, and skills in team work and respect for the judgments of others are seen as overarching virtues. Some societies allocate work and rewards on the basis of communal sharing; others on authority ranking or family status or on individual ability and merit (Fiske, 1991). Thus individual behavior within and across societies is a continuous response to transactions within the social context that motivate persons in positive and in negative ways, that allow them to create new meanings and reconstruct old meanings, that affirm them or demean them, that mentor or confuse them, that encourage them to be purposeful, productive, and future oriented, or that create conditions that limit their vision and aspirations to surviving physically and mentally each day or to living within very restrictive boundaries defined by gender, class, or other attributes. In large measure the metaphors that define the psychology of societies, nations, or families are internalized by individuals and used as guides to behavior. The totality of the cultural apparatus of language, symbols, interpretations, social modeling, whether clear or ambivalent, is used by individuals to learn both positive self-attributions and behavior, habits (Covey, 1989), and personal constructs (Kelly, 1955) as well as a range of responses such as anxiety, depression, information deficits, and despair that become the content of guidance, counseling, psychotherapy, or career interventions.

But it is not only individual behavior that occurs within a social context; so also do perspectives on theory and practice. Whether we speak of theories of behavior (human development, abnormal psychology, career development) or of interventions, both are efforts to describe and place into a cohesive view how individual behavior is learned and how it is changed, primarily within particular cultural contexts. Within such contexts, theories and practice focus on what strategies or interventions are effective in facilitating positive learning about the self and about opportunities; on how environments, either at a micro or macro level, can be created that are mentally healthy and that affirm individual worth and dignity; or on how persons should be treated whose transactions with the environment have been so unfulfilling, so bereft of meaning for them, so negative, so limiting that they have internalized such external stimuli and manifested behavior that reflects feelings of low self-efficacy and lack of worth, incompetence, or other forms of psychological, physiological, or behavioral distress or disorder.

It is important to acknowledge that theory and practice, like individual behavior, also are shaped by transactions with the larger society in which they originated and within which they are designed to respond to the metaphors, the historical models, the cultural perspectives by which individual behavior is described and classified. Theory and practice, in addition, are influenced by government policies, legislation, and cultural traditions that influence the form, purposes, and substance of practice. In perhaps an oversimplified sense, theory and practice are always creatures of the historical period and the cultural context in which they are invented and implemented. They have embedded within them, explicitly or inadvertently, the values and assumptions about individual behavior that characterize a particular time and place, a dominant culture, a social context.

Until comparatively recently, most of the best known models of personality development and of counseling, psychotherapy, or career intervention originated in Europe or North America. But at least two phenomena have begun to modify that reality. The first is the rise of multiculturalism, which has brought a special form of criticism to bear on counseling theory and practice. Multiculturalism has raised important questions about the elasticity or transportability of theory and practice generated under a particular cultural tradition (e.g., Eurocentric) to other cultural traditions (e.g., Afrocentric) in which the interactions between personal experience and social context are different. Approaches to multicultural or cross-cultural theory and counseling practice have raised a mirror to the assumptions on which many traditional theories of behavior and intervention rest and raised questions about how such approaches need to be modified to accommodate cultural interpretations of behavior that accent collectivist or group identity rather than individuation; that define the boundaries of normal behavior more fluidly and less sharply than Eurocentric models; that express physical or mental illness differently; that view the use of time or the salience of work as a central factor in personal worth with less emphasis or value; and that view the discussion of individual problems with strangers, rather then family elders, as inappropriate. Emphases on the importance of cultural diversity, both in pluralistic nations like the United States and across national or regional boundaries, as a defining influence in judging the validity of counseling theory and practice and, where needed, in modifying the assumptions and techniques relevant to different forms of culturally mediated personal experience, have begun the long journey to make counseling theory and practice more accessible and more inclusive of persons beyond middle-class Whites in the United States, the United Kingdom, or Europe.

The second phenomenon is the rapidly expanding globalization of counseling, which has a potential effect on counseling theory and practice parallel to that of multiculturalism. Counseling, psychotherapy, and, particularly, career counseling have become worldwide phenomena. As individual aspirations for a better quality of life, for greater freedom of choice and mobility, and for ways to manage stress and anxiety have grown across the developed and developing nations, more of them are instituting systems of counseling or career counseling to address both individual and governmental purposes. In so doing, these nations are making their own adaptations of counseling theory and practice. They may in some cases build from or adopt Eurocentric or North American models, but in other cases, they may build from or adopt indigenous approaches tailored to the particular cultural traditions, political purposes, resources available, or forms of training that prevail in a particular nation at a particular historical period.

Increasingly, legislative actions, position papers, media attention and international forums, and counseling and career services (e.g., career counseling, career education, career guidance) have been identified as vital sociopolitical instruments in facilitating a particular nation's goals. These goals may focus on human resource development, building human capital, matching persons and occupations, developing work identity and career planning skills, serving as a labor exchange, dealing with persons who have been unemployed or who suffer major work adjustment problems, or dealing with persons experiencing mental illness, violence, or disabilities. As a result, multiple conceptual models of counseling and of career interventions are becoming evident in the professional literature as industrialized and developing nations of diverse cultural traditions attempt to conceive and implement theories and practices that meet the needs of their nation at a particular point in time. Nations in the throes of changing political and economic systems have discovered the need for counselor education and counselors, even though neither social conditions nor governmental resource allocations had accented such needs previously. This is true in Eastern European nations (Ritook, 1993), in South Africa after apartheid (Mathabe & Temane, 1993), and in other parts of the world where counseling has not been easily accessible or inclusive. In other nations, changing resources for counseling and changing political, demographic, or economic conditions have altered the way counseling or career services need to be focused or delivered (Pryor, Hammond, & Hawkins, 1990; Watanabe & Herr, 1993). These are not simple matters. Nations approach such matters differently and from varied historical, political, and cultural traditions and economic conditions.

Answers to questions of what should be the shape and substance of counseling change as nations go through different phases in their evolution, as the social context changes, and as the likely effects of counseling as a national policy instrument are assessed and reassessed. Depending on the specific nation, the resources to support counseling, the definitions of which groups should be served, the conceptions of mental health or illness used, the settings in which counseling is provided, and the configuration or substance of counseling services are likely to be classified, articulated, and provided, directly or indirectly, through funds and policies implemented by federal, state, or local governmental units. Just as individual behavior and the nature of counseling theory and practice are affected by the social context, so are the policies and legislative initiatives that give direction to and provide support for counseling services. As a result, counseling services often differ in purpose and content across national boundaries and across cultures.

Major questions concerning the form and content of counseling, guidance, or career services in any nation have to do with the accessibility of such services, who will plan and house them, for whom will they be available, for what purposes, and who will deliver them. These are complicated issues for which the responses are subtly or directly related to the nature and rigidity of the class and caste structure, the value system, the relationship of the individual to the group, the nature of the enterprise system (Super, 1985), the perceptions and importance of mental distress or illness as a social problem, and other factors that are specific to a particular social context. These elements vary from nation to nation and within nations. But whatever the combination, they are the seedbeds for individual meaning. They are the mediators of the available opportunity structure for different groups of people; of the available career paths and mobility factors; of the social metaphors that are translated into policy and into achievement images portrayed by the mass media; of contingencies or reinforcements that shape the individual's cognitive structures, habits, and information-processing mechanisms; of the in-groups and the out-groups of the society; and of expectations for institutional or personal loyalties.

Regardless of its specific focus, the social structure of a particular community or nation creates the circumstances in which people develop as human beings, as workers, as parents. The social structure shapes the possibilities for choice, determines the knowledge available to people about their opportunities, and reinforces the acquisition of specific types of behavior. It is within their physical, social, and cultural environments that people negotiate their personal identify, belief systems, and life course. Such political, social, and economic contexts in which individuality is framed and is lived out change across nations, communities, and families, across racial or socioeconomic groups, and certainly across time. These and many other factors—including the specific content of policy and legislation, the nature of training opportunities, and the magnitude of resources allocated—shape the provision of counseling in each nation. Together these factors accent the transactional nature of human behavior.

Depending upon the needs, resources, and historical point of a nation's development of its own social context and social metaphors, creativity can be seen in how nations address their needs for counseling services and in how they are delivered, such as through telephone hot lines; by distance education using video conferencing; in collaboration with trade unions and other social institutions; in store fronts or other easily accessible locations; by using computer technology or self-directed instruments; by empowering support groups and peer counselors; and as part of a broader set of social safety nets, welfare systems, or other forms of integrated social services. Comparative analyses of how social contexts affect the form and substance of counseling systems are still new and less than comprehensive, although they are expanding in coverage and quality (Watts, 1994; Watts, Dartois, & Plant, 1988; Watts, Guichard, Plant, & Rodriquez, 1993). Reflecting both the unevenness of counseling systems across the world and the energy committed to reporting on them, they tend to report on some parts of the world frequently and other parts of the world not at all (Martin, 1993).

THE TRANSACTIONAL NATURE OF HUMAN BEHAVIOR

The transactional nature of counseling relative to the social context in which it is located is seen in the behavior that people bring to counselors. The content of counseling, the dilemmas people experience, and the substance of the problems with which they have to cope do not typically arise without external triggering events. From a psychological perspective, the personal questions for which people seek help are, in large measure, functions of how they view current social or occupational expectations and opportunities for personal choice, achievement, social interaction, self-initiative, prestige, role differentiation, autonomy, and many other matters. The resulting anxieties, information deficits, or indecisiveness people experience is the content that concerns counselors and related professionals. These dilemmas and conflicts frequently manifest themselves in mental health problems such as depression and in interpersonal dysfunctions within the family or in the workplace. These problems become the concerns of counseling and also form the interactive layers of anxiety and confusion in which such concerns are wrapped. These must be disentangled in the counseling process or, as the constructivists might argue, be reconstructed or transformed in their meaning to the individual.

Watzlawick, Beavin, and Jackson (1967) effectively described the interaction of context and behavior as they discussed pathological communication and paradox in issues of mental health:

> . . . a phenomenon remains unexplainable as long as the range of observation is not wide enough to include the context in which the phenomenon occurs. Failure to realize the intricacies of the relationships between an event and the matrix in which it takes place, between an organism and its environment, either confronts the observer with something "mysterious" or induces him [or her] to attribute to his [or her] object of study certain properties the object may not possess. . . . This becomes particularly obvious when the object of study is disturbed behavior. If a person exhibiting disturbed behavior (psychopathology) is studied in isolation, then the inquiry must be concerned with the *nature* of the condition and, in a wider sense, with the *nature* of the human mind. If the limits of the inquiry are extended to include the effects of this behavior on others, their reactions to it, and the context in which all of this takes place, the focus shifts from the artificially isolated *monad* to the *relationship* between the parts of a wider system. The observer of human behavior then turns from an inferential study of the mind to the study of the observable manifestations of relationship. (p. 21)

Watzlawick et al. (1967) then focused upon the importance to the individual of communication as a primary mediator of individual existence.

> The environment, then, is subjectively experienced as a set of instructions about the organism's existence, and in this sense the environmental effects are similar to a computer program; Norbert Weiner once said about the world that it may be viewed as a myriad of "To Whom It May Concern Messages." . . . Thus, the impact of the environment on an organism comprises a set of instructions whose meaning is by no means self-evident but rather is left up to the organism to decide as best it can. (p. 258)

To understand human behavior and the potential of counseling is to understand that people live in various social, cultural, political, and economic environments. These environments exert influence or apply limits to the conception of sex and family roles, the achievement images likely to be nurtured, the cognitive and interpersonal styles employed, the resources available, and the forms and comprehensiveness of information provided. The mixes of environments through which people move and negotiate their identity are affected by birth order, place of origin, socioeconomic status, history, and many other factors. Such environments are not static. They are constantly changing, and individuals are under constant pressure to receive, interpret, and act upon messages related to personal behavior that emanate from these environmental mixes.

Interpretations of how individuals act on or interpret the environmental stimuli, the "To Whom It May Concern Messages," that originate in the various systems that people occupy—family, school, workplace, community, nation—are the content with which theories of behavior, learning, and personality development are concerned. Such theories tend to emphasize particular aspects of the transactional process between the individual and the social context, giving more or less power to the environment or to the individual to shape behavior. Such theories also tend to add new emphases or become more inclusive of both older and newer behavioral interpretation over time as the institutions of societies strengthen or weaken in their influence on personality development.

Virtually all counseling students have been exposed to a course in theories of personality in which they examined the classic theories of behavior as well as the theorists who created the conceptions of how people grow and develop and of the mechanisms facilitating or impeding change. They are likely to have studied the early philosophies of Locke and Leibnitz and their quite disparate views on the effects of the environment on the individual or the individual on the environment. Locke saw the individual as a tabula rasa, a blank sheet, at the time of birth who then develops as a product of the environmental influences and learning to which he or she is exposed. In contrast, Leibnitz suggested that the individual is born with will, volition, and a sense of purpose that transcend the environment and permit the individual to affect the environment as well as the environment to affect the individual. In an oversimplified way, these two views of the power of the environment and the power of the individual to shape and influence learning, action, direction, and purpose run through extant theories of psychological behavior and of related interventions. Certainly, for example, Locke's views of the tabula rasa generate assumptions that are akin to theories of behavioral counseling and of learned behavior, and Leibnitz's views undergird theories of client-centered counseling; but both views—behavioral and client-centered counseling—see the individual in context, either as a passive recipient of effects or as an active agent seeking self-actualization as he or she sheds the defensive persona that arises from negative environmental interactions.

It can be argued that most theories of personality development and behavioral change and of counseling can be aligned along a continuum that varies by emphasis on the importance of individual or contextual interaction. That is, the theories vary on whether the theoretical accent is on conditioning and imitation as the primary source of learning and identity or on whether the accent is on individual reflection on what has been learned so as to make meaning from the experience and create reality by what is chosen and not chosen. In either case, it is important that counselors understand that persons live and grow in environments—in interrelated communities of persons in their family, school, workplace, church, neighborhood, and nation—in each of which messages about appropriate or inappropriate behavior, winners and losers, and good and bad are constantly fed back to the individual as influences to internalize or sources of information to act on.

Views of the transactional nature of human behavior have been undergoing change as the psychology of human behavior has been increasingly informed by the sociology of human behavior. In a narrow sense, the psychology of human behavior can be seen as primarily concerned with individual actions and their origins and effects. The sociology of human behavior is instead more concerned with the context, with the socializing factors that are related to individual actions and that stimulate and shape or limit them. As these perspectives on human behavior have complemented each other, they have increased the importance of the counselors and counseling psychologists who view human behavior through interdisciplinary lenses that can accommodate the changing conditions in which individuals learn, negotiate, and act out their identity across time—within the contexts of changing family dynamics, life transitions, economic and political shifts, and other phenomena.

This changing interaction between the sociology and the psychology of human behavior can be viewed in historical terms. Through much of human history until probably the last three decades, the formation of individual identity was seen as relatively unconscious, not necessarily reflective, and largely mediated by the socializing effects of the major social institutions of family, school, and church. Whether good or bad in some absolute sense, the social context provided by those major social institutions was still coherent. Opportunities were mediated by the social class the individuals occupied and by the gender, race, and ethnic attributes by which the individuals were characterized. The choices to be made in social and career terms were largely visible, and their likely outcomes in social status and income were clearly defined. The boundaries between family life and the workplace were understandable, and the roles played in each of these arenas were different but not separated by wide psychological and spatial distances. Persons lived and worked, went to school, interacted with their extended family members, and followed religious traditions within neighborhoods and communities that were close in geographic terms. The socializing influences of identity affected most persons similarly, and rules of right and wrong, of appropriate and inappropriate behavior, were the sources of the conditioning and the sanctions that helped persons develop as single undivided personalities (Wijers & Meijers, 1996). But increasingly, in many if not most of the developed nations, the historical effects of the major social institutions have become less powerful, less coherent, and more ambiguous. As the range of choices through which an individual can live out his or her self-concepts and identity has become so comprehensive, the roles that an individual is expected to play so diverse, and the traditional boundaries ascribed to gender, social class, or race so blurred, individuals tend often to perceive themselves as a collection of subidentities rather than crystallized, holistic personalities.

From a psychological perspective, the conditions just described suggest that the socializing forces, which have had such powerful historical effects in providing the conditioning and imitative influences for shaping individual identity and directions, are diminishing in power and clarity. The role of the individual in sorting through such ambiguity and establishing his or her selfhood becomes more important, if not absolutely critical. It is in such contexts that the emphasis on how individuals alone and in concert "actively construct and co-construct meaning out of their life experiences, as opposed to receiving knowledge in pure form directly from the external world" (Rosen & Kuehlwein, 1996, p. xi), becomes central to new theories and new techniques of counseling. This constructivist view holds that meaning and reality are created and not discovered, that counseling involves the reconstruction of old meaning and the creation of new meanings. This process is obviously not one that requires counseling only at one period of life but across the life span because knowledge and meaning are not only constructed and reconstructed over time within a social matrix but also differ across time and across cultures.

Constructivist theory adds new perspective to the counselor's views of the transactions between individuals and contexts, of the personal meaning making that arises, and of the ways to enlarge our understanding of individuals as meaning makers within social contexts through the uses of narratives, stories, and metaphors. Bruner (1986) contended that reality is constructed and organized through two types of thought modes or processes: one, which has historically been defined in the realms of logic and science, is the *paradigmatic* mode, the process of seeking truth through empirical verification; the other is the *narrative* mode, the construction of stories that are played out across time in various contexts. The essence of such a view is found in perspectives such as that of Rosen (1996) who observed

> We are born into stories: the stories of our parents, our families, and our culture. These made meanings, which predate us and develop us upon our arrival into the world, can be constraining, even imprisoning, or they can be freeing and liberating. The personal narrative prototype that we develop over time is not constructed in a vacuum but instead incorporates much that is derived from stories and myths we are born into. (p. 23)

In some circumstances, clients believe that they are living within someone else's stories, being manipulated, and denied their own story, sense of agency, or volition. It is within such perspectives that the counselor needs to clarify the client's narrative and its meaning, and engage as necessary in narrative revision, the construction of alternative stories, and reforming, rescripting, and reconstruction of narratives as warranted.

The notions of social constructivism that have been cited here do not preclude other approaches to counseling, such as cognitive or psychodynamic. Rather they add another frame of reference to understanding the individual's transactions with environments, how the individual construes reality, how the individual constructs schemas or other filters that guide what he or she pays attention to in current interactions with the world. In this sense, constructivism pragmatically acknowledges the importance of the external world and at the same time acknowledges that because of the personal stories or narrative prototypes that influence their construction of meaning from their experiences, individuals are likely to vary in how they conceptualize the external world and their place in it. From this view, people can be expected to vary in their cognitions, affect, and belief systems as they formulate their identity through their daily encounters with a wide variety of contexts that make differential demands for adaptive, differentiated, and integrated behavior. To succeed in such a challenge, the individual needs to be capable of behavioral flexibility as well as have an understanding of his or her identity, the "personal meaning system that is created over the course of the individual's experience with the world and is organized primarily in narrative form" (Saari, 1996, p. 144). In essence, identity is the individual's "personal theory about himself or herself, about the world, and about his or her relationship with the world and vice versa. It is through this personal theory that the individual organizes past experiences and plans future actions" (Saari, 1996, p. 144).

Thus, to return to contextual issues, in relation to how these are construed and reflected in individual identity and action, the counselor needs to be aware that however coherent or ambiguous the external world is to a particular client, it is dynamic and influential. It is the source of messages, stimuli, reinforcements, and behavioral pathways that are dynamic but that nevertheless are comprised of multiple environments with which individuals are in constant transaction.

Effects of Change on Individual Behavior

To extend the notion cited previously that social institutions are in flux and that such realities cause increased problems for individual action, several related perspectives are pertinent. For example, Drucker (1981) noted that within recent history there have been

. . . genuine structural changes in the social ecology, most pronounced perhaps in population structure and population dynamics in the developed countries; but also in the role and performance of old, established, and seemingly stable social bodies, such as governmental agencies or boards of directors, whether of businesses, hospitals, or universities; in the interface between sciences and society; and in fundamental theories that are still widely taught as "revealed truths." (p. vii)

Of major interest to the counselor is how changes in the social ecology affect individuals and what the nature of such interaction is.

Toffler (1970), almost three decades ago, indicated that changes in the social ecology affect the behavior of people exposed to rapid changes in institutions and values. Toffler coined the term *future shock* to describe the shattering stress and disorientation individuals experience when they are subjected to too much change in too short a time. He believed that future shock is manifested in a great range of stress-related problems that have become the foci of much of the research and literature addressed to counselors in the last quarter of the 20th century. He spoke of stress-related physical illness, the deterioration of individual decision making under conditions of "overchoice," the spreading use of drugs, outbreaks of vandalism and undirected violence, apathy, and other forms of social irrationality under the excessive change and stimulation of future shock. Toffler suggested that people have an "adaptive range" below and above which "the individual's ability to cope simply falls apart" (p. 344).

In an echo of the observations of Watzlawick et al. (1967) described earlier, Toffler (1970) contended that

rational behavior, in particular, depends upon a ceaseless flow of data from the environment. It depends upon the power of the individual to predict with at least fair success, the outcome of his [or her] own actions. To do this, [individuals] must be able to predict how the environment will respond to [their] acts. Sanity, itself, thus hinges on [each individual's] ability to predict his [or her] immediate, personal future on the basis of information fed him [or her] by the environment. (p. 350)

But Toffler again contended that the more rapid the change and the more novel the environment, whether we talk in terms of *culture shock* or *future shock,* the more information the individual must process in order to make effective, rational decisions. When the limits of individuals' ability to process information are exceeded, they are likely to manifest sensory or information overload or decision stress. Such overstimulation causes people to feel increasingly harried, tired, and out of control. In turn, people are likely to cope with these conditions by denial, overspecialization, reversion to previously successful adaptive behavior that is no longer relevant or useful, or attempts to simplify unrealistically what is being experienced. "Overstimulation can also lead to confusion, disorientation, or distortion of reality; to fatigue, anxiety, tenseness, or extreme irritability; to apathy and emotional withdrawal" (p. 348).

Every mental health specialist—counselor, psychologist, social worker—has seen the signs in individual behavior that Toffler so prophetically predicted. The issue, however, is how practitioners interpret such signs. Do they attribute such behavior to mental illness and psychopathology? Or to problems of living instigated by environmental overstimulation, excessive novelty, and difficulty in decoding and processing the multitude of data from the multiple environments people occupy—environments that are themselves in flux? Either way, the question of how individuals and environments interact and under what conditions should be at the heart of any therapeutic alliance between counselors and clients.

Individuals and Environments in Dynamic Interaction

A major premise confronting counselors is that people are in dynamic interaction with their environment. According to Kleinman (1988),

> in the anthropological vision, the two-way interaction between social world and person is the source of thought, emotion, action. This mediating dialectic creates experience. It is as basic to the formation of personality and behavior as it is to the causation of mental disorder. (p. 3)

Vondracek, Lerner, and Schulenberg (1986) described such interaction as follows:

> Dynamic interaction means that the context and the organism are inextricably embedded in each other, that the context consists of multiple levels changing interdependently across time, and that because organisms influence the contexts that influence them, they are able to play an active role in their own developments. (p. 37)

These observations affirm that individual-environmental transactions are reciprocal. Each affects the other. To understand individuals' behavior, it is typically necessary to understand the effects of their past and present contexts on their present perceptions of events, possibilities, or their own characteristics. Most people do not operate in uncontrolled, impulsive, or spontaneous ways. Rather they operate in accordance with prior experiences, rules, and guidelines that have shaped their present behavior.

The phenomenological axiom that Syngg and Combs (1949) espoused 50 years ago—that people behave as they perceive—is a powerful construct with implications for humanistic, behavioral, and cognitive approaches to intervention. In essence, this concept indicates that people learn to interpret or perceive the same event or cue differently and that people also bring different behavioral repertoires from which they select responses to similar cues. Thus people can view the same event, interpret it differently, and behave in response to it in opposite ways with widely varying levels of emotion, intensity, and stress. Whereas one person may perceive a particular event as threatening, another can essentially disregard it as unimportant or benign. The reasons for such individual variability in perceptions and responses are complex and are found in both the individual's history and how that history is played out in current behavior.

Goleman (1995) has recently offered the concept of *emotional intelligence* as an explanation for part of the variability in human behavior and its link to our ancestral past. In essence, he contended that

> in a very real sense we have two minds, one that thinks and one that feels. . . . These two fundamentally different ways of knowing *interact* [italics added] to construct our mental life. One, the rational mind, is the mode of comprehension we are typically conscious of: more prominent in awareness, thoughtful, able to ponder and reflect. But alongside that there is another system of knowing: impulsive and powerful, if sometimes illogical; the emotional mind. (p. 8)

Such a view suggests many axioms for understanding individual behavior. One axiom is that all emotions—anger, fear, happiness, surprise, love, disgust, sadness—are impulses to act; they are biological and physiological; and they have come to us from deep in human history. A second axiom, and a very important one from the perspective of this book, is that these predispositions to act "are shaped further by our life experience and culture. For instance, universally the loss of a loved one elicits sadness and grief. But how we show our grieving . . . is molded by cultures. . ." (p. 7). A third axiom is that intelligence is not confined to abilities to make good grades in school or deal with ideas and abstract phenomena. Rather intelligence takes multiple forms, as Gardner (1983) has identified: verbal, mathematical-logical, spatial, kinesthetic, musical, and personal—that is, "interpersonal skills and intrapsychic or intrapersonal capacity to tune into one's emotions." There is room in each of these multiple forms of intelligence for both feelings and for cognition. Goleman (1995), among other psychologists, has suggested that critical to the cognitive applications of the intelligences described here are the personal intelligences, the emotional intelligences that mediate and interact with the rational, the cognitive. Indeed, Goleman has contended that emotional intelligence includes self-awareness and impulse contral, persistence, zeal and self-motivation, empathy and social deftness. Others have called these elements key ingredients in personal flexibility (Herr, 1990). The importance given to these behaviors and their role in dealing with change, in harnessing and managing the potential responses to sensory or information overload or decision stress that Toffler (1970) described, varies across time and across societies. The valuing of thinking or feeling, of cognition or emotion, of head or heart, or of their interaction has been the subject of philosophical, psychological, artistic, and religious debate for centuries and with different emphases on one or the other types of behavior in different societies across time.

Variations in Individuals' Perceptions

It has been noted in many observations across the social sciences that each individual is unique, in part because each is a child of his or her times. Such a statement affirms that a major aspect of individual-context interaction has to do with when an individual was born and what that means for an individual's values and belief systems, as well as for an individual's pessimism and optimism about economic opportunities and other life possibilities. Neugarten and Neugarten (1987), among other researchers, found that the economic and psychological emphases of different historical periods and the accompanying social expectations affect how cohorts of people—those born in the same year or time period—progress through their lives. People's perceptions and expectations are shaped by the social context in which they are born, raised, and live.

Consider, for example, how Americans who have lived through the Great Depression of the 1930s, the patriotism and common cause of the Second World War, the social activism of the 1960s, the material enthusiasms of the yuppie generation of the 1980s, or the dramatic changes in the political structures and belief systems across the world in the 1990s are likely to differ in their interpretation and approach to possible life opportunities. Their views of the social clock—the hypothetical timetable people use to determine when it is appropriate to get married, have children, establish themselves in a work role, become middle aged or old—are likely to differ, creating varying stereotypes of appropriate and inappropriate behavior, and of how to pattern their lives. The degree to which an individual's life pattern tends to be in accord with the social clock of his or her cohort has much to do with how an individual anticipates and acts on the inevitable transitions from adolescence to adulthood and his or her various parental, family, work, and social roles. Thus the timing of life transitions, the ways an individual is expected to cope with them, and their importance are imposed upon individuals by the society's institutions. But the content and importance of transitions also shift across time. Therefore, the expectations or psychological boundaries that guide one generation's behavior are not likely to be the same for the next. As a result, how different cohorts of people interpret and act upon their society is likely to differ, as are the values and commitments they manifest.

Thus we can view any population as constituted of people acting out different individual scripts, patterns, or scenarios shaped by the social, psychological, economic, and technological conditions with which they were more or less imprinted by their family, birthplace, and period of origin. These conditions are experienced differently from family to family, region to region, community to community, and time to time. As such conditions vary, they reflect the decrease of some opportunities and lifestyles and the increase or emergence of others. New social belief systems or value sets ebb and flow as people try to negotiate their personal identity and the rules by which they "expend their lives." Available achievement images, interpersonal behaviors, and related phenomena differ across time and place as well as across groups. They are differently processed, reinforced, and lived out from one socioeconomic group to another, from one cultural group to another, and from one national group to another (Peabody, 1985).

The context for an individual's life pattern and personality is also a function of his or her birth order among siblings in a family. Parental models of child rearing and available resources are likely to change with time, creating different environments for children born and raised at different times within the same family. As parents cope with their own development, their career, or their entrance into or relief from substance abuse or physical illness, their child-rearing practices may create a different environment for children reared at different points along such a continuum.

The examples just cited are intended to show that the course of an individual's development is influenced by when he or she is born; how many others are growing up at the same time and competing for resources or opportunities available (either within a family or a larger community); how sex roles are defined in an individual's historical time; the rigidity with which the roles of children, adolescents, or adults are demarcated and conveyed; and the sharpness, singularity, and focus of the dominant cultural beliefs about achievement, sex roles, success, happiness, individual versus collective progress, interpersonal interactions, and related phenomena. Therefore, whether an individual is born as part of a baby boom or baby bust, in a time of women's liberation and enlightened or repressive attitudes toward racial minorities, in a time of economic depression or abundance, in a family that is intact and healthy or disintegrating, or in a socioeconomic stratum characterized by hopefulness and minimal economic barriers or the opposite, all are elements of both the psychological and the literal opportunity structure within which an individual copes and interacts as he or she forms personal values, interests, emotional intelligence, and personal plans of action. These elements are also the seedbeds for feelings of self-efficacy, self-esteem, and purposefulness, or their lack. As such, these contextual-individual interactions become the mechanisms that influence what psychological issues are likely to arise at what points of history, for what groups, and whether or not they are likely to be brought to counselors or other helpers.

PERSPECTIVES ON ENVIRONMENTAL EFFECTS ON INDIVIDUALS

As is true in virtually any attempt to understand individual-environmental interaction, there are multidisciplinary windows through which we can view such phenomena. One window is social psychology. At least two notions are useful from such a perspective. The first is that of collective personality; the second is that of collective consciousness. *Collective personality* consists of the collective sensations people share in a society; *collective consciousness* consists of the reflections and reactions people share in dealing with these common sensations (Sennett, 1977).

Collective Personality and Collective Consciousness

To take the point further, collective personality is the ability of people to interact with each other, to share sensations, and to perform common actions by virtue of their belief that they share an essential similarity or likeness. Whether the collective personality is really a typical person or a caricature of a collective profile of what a society would like its members to resemble is debatable. But whether exaggerated or not, the collective personality represents what people in a particular society recognize as the common characteristics of the image they share when they speak of an *American,* an *Arab,* a *worker,* a *woman,* or of *we* and *them.* In the sense of our use of the term *social metaphor* at various points in this book to describe the images societies create about themselves, social psychologists argue that societies differ not only in social metaphors but also in the cast of characters and the personality types they create to play them out.

Collective consciousness is the group consciousness of people exposed to the common, if contradictory, impressions of history. Collective consciousness is "like the wax upon which the forces of society leave their imprint" (Sennett, 1977, p. 69). Social psychology is the study of and the testimony to the perception that social conditions can influence emotional experience. Thus two broad areas of inquiry occur in social psychology. One deals with the kinds of images groups form of themselves (collective personality) and the kinds of symbols and values groups share because of their social interactions (collective consciousness) (Sennett, 1977, p. xix). Inherent in such notions is the acknowledgment that different nations, societies, and cultural groups provide different social and psychological conditions for their people as well as information that has varying levels of clarity. Also implicit in such perspectives is the view that personal enmities, fears and hopes, prejudices and illusions, sympathies and antipathies, convictions, articles of faith, and principles are shared in a particular nation, society, or cultural group but that these differ from one such collectivity to another. These realities are at the base of cross-cultural counseling as well as, in global terms, of diplomacy, political negotiation, and conflict resolution.

Through much of recorded history, social scientists have been attempting to find metaphors that capture the essence of a particular time or a particular group. There are many examples: the Renaissance, the Dark Ages, the Age of Enlightment, the Iron Curtain, the Cold War, the Great Society, the American Century, flappers, hippies, Generation X'ers, the Third Wave, the Cult of Efficiency, the Culture of Narcissism, the Great Society, the Age of Discontinuity, the Age of Unreason, the Age of Paradox, the Triumph of Meanness. The reader can undoubtedly think of many others. Many of these metaphors have been titles of books and speeches. But most important, each of these metaphors carries within the processes it attempts to describe a psychology, a social rhetoric, and a particular type of opportunity structure as well as political, legislative, economic, and social forces that have altered the inter- action between individuals and their environments; that have treated persons as means to ends or as the ends for which society was constructed. Some of the metaphors are optimistic; some are pessimistic. Regardless, these metaphors are markers, mental maps that influence, if not guide, individual behaviors; they are often comprised of myths and symbols that link us to our past and shape our percep- tion of the present. When we ask why a culture, a historical period, a generation is the way it is and why we interpret things the way we do, the answer is frequently found in the stories, the narratives from which metaphors emerge and that persons of a particular culture, a particular time, a particular place unconsciously share. Embedded in them are many of a culture's, a nation's, deepest and strongest beliefs and the cues to individuals' perceptions of their social context.

Reich's Morality Tales

A prime example of the myths, the stories, the symbols, the metaphors that persons internalize and from which their identity is developed is found in the work of Robert Reich (1987). He suggested that American history is composed of several morality tales or parables that underlie the collective consciousness of Americans. This is a realm of values, purposes, and visions to which individual behavior is frequently referred in the mass media, biographies, official pronouncements, art, literature, and politics. The body of metaphor or morality tales that characterize any national, eth- nic, or racial group can be used to mobilize public action or to shape individual aspi- rations and behavior. Morality tales and social metaphors help groups define their uniqueness and understand who they are and what they are for themselves or oth- ers. As nations and societies move through their own stages of development, differ- ent aspects of their social metaphors receive more or less emphasis. Nations define their problems in relationship to the prevailing notions of who they are, their origins, and their destiny. Reich suggested that American history and its uniqueness are rooted in four cultural parables:

- **the mob at the gates:** As a function of the flight from older cultures, its immi- grant heritage, America has become "a depiction of a beacon light of virtue in a world of darkness, a small island of freedom and democracy in a perilous sea" (p. 8). This morality tale suggests that Americans are uniquely blessed, the proper model for other people's aspirations, the hope of the world's poor and oppressed. Such a view also suggests that America must constantly be on guard against the mob at its gates lest the forces of darkness overwhelm it.
- **the triumphant individual:** This parable is one of the little individual who works hard, takes risks, believes in him- or herself, and eventually earns wealth, fame, and honor (p. 9). This parable celebrates self-reliance, rugged individualism, the loner and maverick, plainspokenness, getting the job done, determination and integrity, and uncompromised ideals. Perhaps more than any other tale Americans have incorporated as truth is that of the triumphant individual, as often portrayed in heroic literature and films, and as symbolized by the Statue of Liberty.
- **the benevolent community:** This parable depicts the willingness to reach out to others in need, to provide a helping hand, a fair deal, and foreign aid to the less

privileged. The image is one of philanthropy, local pride and self-help, generosity, and the nurturance of community.

- **the rot at the top:** The fourth of America's parables or morality tales reflects its rejection of central authority and the privilege of aristocracy. It is suspicious of powerful elites in which the common people must be alert to corruption, decadence, irresponsibility, and conspiracy against the broader public. From the time of the Founding Fathers to the present, the possibility of the abuse of power has been at the center of governmental checks and balances and the frequent subject of plays, stories, and movies in which the poor but honest man or woman takes on the corporate giant or the big bully and wins.

Whether or not each of these morality tales is appropriate in a period of global interdependence, international competition, and growing group (rather than individual) action is beside the point. These parables give a sense of uniqueness and meaning to our national lives, to our dreams and hopes. They sanction and reinforce some behaviors and reject others. In some ways, these metaphors represent the ideal, what the nation might be, rather than what it is. In such contexts, these morality tales represent tensions between the real and the ideal. They rebuke selfishness, narcissism, dependence, and pretension; and they provide standards by which to examine gaps between aspiration and perceived reality. They represent the content of conversations about the symbols, ideals, and ways of feeling that matter to the members of particular cultures (Bellah, Madsen, Sullivan, Swidler, & Tipton, 1985). They influence the paradigms, the mental maps that persons incorporate to help them interpret who they are and who they should be, that is, the way things are (realities), and the way things should be (values) (Covey, 1989). The American metaphors of individualism, success, freedom, and justice are unique aspects of the building blocks of social character, just as different concepts are important in other cultures.

Individual and Social Interaction

Somewhat analogously to the social psychology notions of collective personality and collective consciousness discussed earlier, Fromm (1962) also discussed the interaction of individual and social character. In his view, societies differ in their structural elements and objectives. Therefore

> . . . it is the function of the "social character" to shape the energies of the members of society in such a way that their behavior is not a matter of conscious decision as to whether or not to follow the social pattern, but one of *wanting to act as they have to act* and at the same time finding gratification in acting according to the requirements of the culture. In other words, it is the social character's function to *mold and channel* human energy within a given society for the purpose of the continued functioning of the society. (p. 79)

Societies, then, differ in both the content of social character (e.g., in the United States, the behavioral components of the four morality tales) and in the methods by which social character is produced (e.g., childhood training, the content of schooling).

Fromm (1962) argued, for example, that societies apply different filters to reinforce what comes to collective consciousness as appropriate behavior or social character. This includes the subtleties and nuances of national language, the logic (e.g., Aristotelian, paradoxical, inductive-deductive) that directs the thinking of people in a particular culture, and the social taboos that "declare certain ideas and feelings to be improper, forbidden, dangerous and which prevent them from reaching the level of consciousness" (p. 121). The social taboos may be overt, as in cultures where right and wrong are clearly delineated and individuals are exposed to public shame or intense personal guilt if taboos are violated; or the taboos may be less clear, and possibly contradictory, leading to diffuse anxiety in some individuals (Reisman, 1961). The social taboos, and their structuring of what should be, also can capture by inclusion or exclusion the national rhetoric and cultural parables described previously. Fromm called these *national ideologies,* and he compared the United States and the Soviet Union. For Americans, he said, the national ideology is that we are religiously free; we are individualists; our leaders are wise; we are good; our enemies (whoever these happen to be at the moment) are bad; and our parents love us and we love them. For the Soviets, the ideology is that we are Marxists; we are socialists; socialism expresses the will of the people; our leaders are wise and work for humanity; and our profit interest in society is a socialist profit interest and different from the "capitalist" profit interest (p. 123).

The point of this analysis of individual and social interaction is that nations, societies, and subgroups provide the environment for varied perceptions of reality, information processing, and personal identity and behavior. Individual behavior, then, is not simply a function of intrapsychic forces, needs, and drives but of complex interactions, transactions, and negotiations between individuals and the multiple environments they occupy.

Multidimensionality of Environments

To understand better the interaction of individuals and environments as the precipitators of counseling problems, it is useful to consider several other notions. One of these is that the environments people occupy are multidimensional. An individual's *life space* is more properly thought of as *life spaces* that vary in their expectations for individual behavior and the influences or limits they impose on such behavior. Such life spaces can be positive or negative or, indeed, benign with regard to their effects on individuals. As Gibson (1979, 1982) suggested, environments also can be viewed as providing *affordances*—objects, events, people—that can provide information, stimulation, or opportunities to those who can perceive such affordances. The contingency term in such a notion is *can perceive.* Although we might argue that it is theoretically possible to formulate a taxonomy of affordances available in different environments and how these might pertain to different individual needs or perceptual systems, it is likely that many individuals will not profit from such affordances because they are not open to the possibilities, fear they cannot fulfill the expectations, or are preoccupied with other matters that narrow their perceptual field.

Although not using the terminology of affordances per se, Bandura (1982) talked about the importance of fortuitous or chance occurrences affecting life paths through the reciprocal influence of personal and social factors. He contended that the personal determinants of the effects of chance encounters are the entry skills, emotional ties, values, and personal standards individuals bring to the encounter. He suggested that the social determinants of the effects of chance encounters include the rewards likely to be associated with the encounter: hearing a particular lecture, reading a particular book, unexpectedly witnessing a particular event on television, the openness of the environment or of the individual to changing his or her life path.

These personal and social determinants also may predispose people to use or not use affordances. Bandura suggested that different groups or individuals furnish different symbolic environments and that for these reasons and others, some chance encounters "touch people only lightly, others leave more lasting effects, and still others branch people into new trajectories of life" (p. 749).

Cabral and Salomone (1990) have extended Bandura's perspectives on how chance factors affect life paths in relation to the interaction of personal and social factors. They offered a number of concepts that extend perceptions of the role of chance in career behavior, individual ability to control or cope with chance, and the relationship between chance and personality. They agreed that

> chance operates on a continuum from events or encounters that are totally unforeseen (a natural disaster, the sudden death of a spouse, or a conversation on an airplane, for instance) to those that are at least in part under the control of the individual (overhearing information concerning a job opportunity during a meeting of a professional organization, or deciding to enter graduate school in a newly emerging field after learning of that field through one's mentor). (p. 10)

However, they added important insights into how people respond differently to unforeseen encounters or events.

Cabral and Salomone (1990) explained the latter in terms of two possible personality dimensions: *locus of control* and *self-concept*. They argued that persons

> with external locuses of control, as well as those who offer empowering-deterministic explanations for their behavior, will be more susceptible to the influence of chance events or encounters. More importantly, these individuals will be less likely to be proactive when chance events or encounters do occur. (p. 11)

In contrast, it could be assumed that persons with an internal locus of control might be somewhat less affected by unforeseen events and encounters, might attempt to control or diminish the uncertainty they represent, or might instead embrace these encounters and events as opportunities to seize and act on. According to Cabral and Salomone, how individuals function in terms of chance is also a function of the individual's self-concept or self-conceptions, which act as filters through which the individual perceives events and people in his or her contexts. Self-conceptions guide and edit information received in memory, serve as cognitive schemata that aid in the definition of people and events, and provide a basis for choice and evaluation. In chance and in other life events, individuals are likely to behave in ways that reinforce and implement their self-concept. The effects of chance encounters and individual choice is an important illustration of individual-contextual interaction.

Person-Environment Fit

In a different, but venerable, approach to the transactional nature of human behavior, it is also useful to cite the line of research and theory related to person-environment fit. Historically, several lines of theoretical inquiry have been devoted to person-environment transactions or fit. They include such perspectives as those of Murray and Kluckhohn (1956) who stated that

> a human being does not grow up in a vacuum: his [or her] development is determined not only by the physical environment as the biologist proved, and by the family envi-

ronment as Freud proved, but, as the massive data collected by the cultural anthropologists showed, by the larger societal and cultural institutions. (p. 4)

Stern, Stein, and Bloom (1956) contended over four decades ago that to understand behavior we must study both the individual and the environment. More specifically, they stated that

behavior represents an ongoing field process. It is the resultant of the transaction between the individual and other structural units in the behavioral field. For convenience, these other units may be referred to collectively as the environment. This *environment* provides a continual source of actual and potential stimulus demands and consequences. (p. 35)

Murphy (1947, p. 867) in his "situationism" construct maintained that human beings respond as situations require them to respond. Whatever their biological diversities, if capable of learning, they will take on the attributes for which the situation calls. Given a changed situation, there is a changed role and consequently a changed personality.

The line of thinking termed *field theory* is concerned with the interaction between the individual and the stimuli present in the environmental context within which he or she is operating at a given moment. This thesis does not negate the fact that individuals have certain biological differences and inherited propensities; it simply minimizes their importance in view of the present stimuli confronting the organism. An example of this is the belief held by Snygg and Combs (1949) that "all behavior, without exception, is completely determined by and pertinent to the phenomenal field of the behaving organism" (p. 15). Out of the phenomenal field, Snygg and Combs differentiated a phenomenal self, which includes all those parts of the phenomenal field the individual experiences as part or characteristic of him- or herself. The phenomenal field, then, consists of the totality of experiences of which the person is aware at the instant of action; an individual behaves as he or she perceives.

Lewin (1951) also applied the concepts of field theory to a wide variety of psychological and sociological phenomena. He considered the person and his or her environment as interdependent regions of *life space*, Lewin's term for the total psychological field. The principal characteristics of Lewin's field theory can be summarized as follows: (a) behavior is a function of the field that exists at the time behavior occurs, (b) analysis begins with the situation as a whole from which the component parts are differentiated, and (c) the concrete person in a concrete situation can be represented mathematically. Lewin defined the field as "the totality of coexisting facts which are conceived of as mutually interdependent" (p. 240). Hall and Lindzey (1957) stated that "Lewin's theory was one of those that helped to revive the conception of [a person] as a complex energy field, motivated by psychological forces, and behaving selectively and creatively" (p. 253).

Mathewson (1955), at approximately the same time, contended that "no individual can be understood apart from his [or her] field. And the field must necessarily include both inner and outer phases or states, or in other words, a complex of interrelated sociopsychological forces" (p. 132). In an even earlier classic view, Murray (1938) argued that it was possible and advisable to classify an environment in terms of the kinds of benefits (facilitations, satisfactions) and the kinds of harms (obstructions, injuries, dissatisfactions) that it provides.

Murray (1938) distinguished between environmental characteristics (reinforcements, norms, expectations), which he labeled *press,* and individual *needs.* His research examined the degree to which specific needs might be gratified or satisfied in particular environments. He also distinguished between *alpha press,* what objective or scientific inquiry suggests are the actual reinforcements or expectancies in an environment, and *beta press,* the subject's own interpretation of the environment as he or she perceives it. Murray called the process of the individual's recognizing what is "being done" to him or her at the moment (that says "this is good" or "this is bad") *pressive perception.* Murray saw this process as definitely egocentric, giving rise almost invariably to some sort of adaptive behavior. Furthermore, Murray believed that the power of a stimulus situation (which may be considered in our terms as an affordance, a chance encounter, or an environment) does not depend on pressive perception but, instead, on *pressive apperception:* beliefs that "the environmental conditions may do this to me (if I remain passive)" or "I may use the object in this or that way (if I become active)." Murray further believed that because the individual is a historical creature, pressive apperception is a consequence of past experiences conjured up as a result of the present image and which, through integration, determines behavior. In Murray's view, if the individual "apperceives" a stimulus or a constellation of stimuli as harmful, or the present environment as uncongenial or unsatisfying, the individual will engage in adaptive behavior designed to permit the person to leave or otherwise diminish the environmental effects.

Holland (1966, 1973, 1985) advanced the notions of Murray and others into a theory of personality types interacting with different environments. Much of his research has been devoted to developing concepts and structures by which to understand and predict the behavior of individuals in different types of work environments. Holland's concepts have been concerned primarily with the career implications of person-environment fit, but the conceptualizations have wider applicability to social and educational environments.

Basically, Holland took the view that an individual's personality is a product of both heredity and environment. As an outcome of early and continuing influences of genetic potentialities and the interaction of the individual with his or her environment, there develops a hierarchy of habitual or preferred methods for dealing with social and environmental tasks. The notion of "modal personal orientation" attempts to describe the most typical way in which an individual responds to an environment.

Holland explicated the notion that individual choice behavior is an expression of personality. Therefore, because people inhabiting specific environments, occupational or educational, have similar personality characteristics, their responses to problems and interpersonal relations are likely to be similar. Thus people seek those environments that permit expression of their personality styles.

The heart of Holland's theory lies in four assumptions promulgated in 1973 (and several secondary assumptions used to refine and extend his theory in 1985):

1. In our culture, most persons can be categorized as one of six types: realistic, investigative, artistic, social, enterprising, or conventional.
2. There are six kinds of environments: realistic, investigative, artistic, social, enterprising, and conventional.
3. People search for environments that will let them exercise their skills and abilities, express their attitudes and values, and take on agreeable problems and roles.

4. A person's behavior is determined by an interaction between his [or her] personality and the characteristics of his [or her] environment. (1973, pp. 2–4)

Microsystem, Mesosystem, Exosystem, and Macrosystem

In a final example of the transactional nature of human behavior, Bronfenbrenner (1979) provided a different, although complementary, view of environment and individual interaction through his conceptual lens. In essence, he defined an individual's environment as composed of four interconnected systems that affect psychological growth. Each of these four structures is conceived of as being a part of the next largest system, starting from the most intimate, in individual terms, to the largest and most encompassing. These four systems, beginning with the one exerting the most direct, developmental effect on the individual's psychological growth, include the microsystem, the mesosystem, the exosystem, and the macrosystem.

The *microsystem* is represented by an individual's family, school or peer group, and workplace. It is composed of the interpersonal relationships, goal-directed activities, and system-defined roles and expectations an individual experiences most directly from his or her context or environment. As defined by Bronfenbrenner, "a microsystem is a pattern of activities, roles, and interpersonal relations experienced by the developing person in a given setting with particular physical and material characteristics" (p. 22). Encompassed in such a system are activities carried on by an individual alone, with others, or by others directed toward the individual. Of major importance are the dyadic relationships in the family system between a parent and child or between siblings, and the larger systems of interactions in a total family unit or a peer group. Also at issue are the role expectations engendered and reinforced within the microsystem. Recent research on the children of alcoholics, on children of disrupted families, on children used as family scapegoats, and on the effects on children of being in the position of leaders or followers in peer groups conveys the importance of the microsystem for psychological development, and indeed as a target for counseling intervention.

The *mesosystem* is seen as linking microsystems with the content—molar activities, interpersonal relations, and role transitions—spilling from one system to the other, particularly the mesosystem to the microsystem. According to Bronfenbrenner, a mesosystem is "a set of interrelations between two or more settings in which the developing person becomes an active participant" (p. 209). Thus what is happening to a child in school or a parent in a workplace is likely to affect the family environment; but perhaps the more important element is the notion of "multisetting participation." In each setting (home, school, workplace, social network, church, community agency), the individual is likely to experience different demands, expectations, norms, and emotional stimuli. Often the public life at the workplace is very different in intent and psychology than are the demands of the private world of marriage or child rearing experienced in the nuclear family. These settings come into serious conflict when the residual effects of one setting affect performance or happiness in the other (e.g., the unhappy worker who berates his wife or children at home). At times it becomes difficult for people to discriminate which behavior is appropriate in which environment.

It is also possible, according to Bronfenbrenner, to think of mesosystems in sequential terms. As an individual moves from one ecological transition to the next (school to work, job to job, employment to retirement), such notions as "intersetting communication" and "intersetting knowledge" reflect how or whether experience and information is useful as the individual attempts to employ it from one setting to the next. What are the effects of value shifts on behavior from one setting to another, from one time to another? As Bronfenbrenner has cogently observed, "Development is enhanced to the extent that, prior to each entry into a new setting . . . the person and members of both settings involved are provided with information, advice, and experience relevant to the impending transition" (p. 217). The question is, of course, how and where do people get information about the likely effects of their transition from one mesosystem to another, the new behaviors required, or the new perspectives that need to be gained? Counseling is one such place. But counseling frequently also is employed because people have experienced faulty or ineffective transitions from one mesosystem to another. In such cases, people need to understand what has gone awry, how to acquire the new images or skills required by the mesosystem transition, how to be more flexible or discriminating in the behaviors they implement in the new setting, how the mesosystems involved are congruent or incongruent in their expectations and demands, and to what degree prior experience is useful in the current situation.

The third system Bronfenbrenner defined is the *exosystem.* Exosystems encompass the indirect effects upon children and adults of what is happening in a parent's or spouse's system. In Bronfenbrenner's definition, exosystems consist "of one or more settings that do not involve the developing person as an active participant but in which events occur that affect, or are affected by, what happens in that setting" (p. 273). Thus it is assumed that there are causal links among the content of exosystems, external events, and the content of microsystems. The logic is straightforward. For example, if a parent experiences sudden unemployment in the workplace, the child will suffer. The child is obviously not an active or direct participant in that workplace, but the economic and psychological turmoil the parent experiences will undoubtedly change the characteristics of the family environment, or the microsystem. It may also change the mesosystem interaction of the child. To illustrate, the effect of the exosystem, the parent's workplace, upon the child's microsystem may be a reduction of the family's economic viability to such an extent that the planned transition of the child from school to college is no longer viable. The child may need to go directly to work to help sustain the family and, therefore, may need to postpone or change the sequential nature of mesosystem transitions from school to college to work, to one of school to work to college, or to one of school to work. Obviously, a whole series of personal identity, information, skills, values, communication, and interpersonal matters has been altered for the child as an indirect effect of the parent's experience in the exosystem.

Not all indirect effects from the parent's workplace are negative or as visible as in the example just used. Rather, the point is that such matters as the parents' discretionary time, social status, autonomy, vacation time, work content, and relations with supervisors may manifest themselves in parental expectations about the children's initiative and independence, views of punishment, expectations about education—or about part-time work, emphases on income or interpersonal orientations, and so on. These in turn will affect the characteristics of the child's microsystem and will be incorporated in the child's values and behavior.

The *macrosystem* is seen as the most encompassing of the ecological systems. It contains the other three systems and is the purveyor of the major cultural beliefs, the morality tales, and the historical traditions or influences of a society. It is the source and sustainer of the social metaphors by which national images of identity are defined and organized, by which ideologies about sex roles, admired personality traits, and appropriate behavioral sanctions are created. It is also the source of cohort effects—the major political, social, policy, and economic contexts that shape personal images of opportunity, security, risk, style, and other matters that affect personal development.

CONCLUSIONS

Chapter 1 has examined the premise that neither counselors nor the problems that clients bring to counselors exist in a political, social, or economic vacuum. Rather, both the form and substance of counseling and of client problems are seen as products of complex transactions among individual behavior, the characteristics of counseling, and the larger social context in which they are located.

Based on this premise, the notion was explored that counseling services in different nations or, indeed, with different population subgroups are likely to vary. A variety of theoretical positions from social psychology, sociology, and differential psychology were examined in an effort to describe some of the mechanisms of individual environmental transactions from the intimate level of microsystem effects to the national level of macrosystem effects. Particular attention was paid to how social metaphors, national morality tales, and cultural parables affect the psychological climate of a nation or a group, concepts of appropriate behavior that ensue, and shifts in these perspectives over time.

Questions of significance to counselors are How do families, communities, and subpopulations influence the behavioral expectations that individual clients hold for themselves? Are these expectations consistent or contradictory? Does the client perceive these expectations with accuracy? Chapter 4 will explore the cultural diversity and pluralism that characterize contemporary America. In that chapter, it will be apparent that although there are social metaphors and cultural traditions of significance to American history, there are also particular social metaphors and cultural traditions of importance to the many ethnic and racial groups that compose the pluralistic American population. Both the so-called majority and minority cultures are heterogeneous in their values and in their traditions. We cannot substitute the Afrocentricity of Black Americans for the history and worldview of Hispanic Americans or Asian Americans. The sets of values, traditions, and worldviews distinguishing each group are diverse and important in their shaping of individual behavior; they are not interchangeable simply because, in the common parlance, each of these groups is labeled a *minority group*. Although people in each of these culturally diverse groups can identify with the aspirations and possibilities of the larger American view of freedom, success, and justice, the ways of their participation in that agenda are mediated by the systems of reinforcements, expectations, and behavioral sanctions intimately tied to the characteristics of their family, race, ethnic group, and sex.

Chapter 2 is intended to help the counselor consider the effects of advanced technology and the shifting economic climate in the United States upon different groups of youths and adults. Advanced technology also spawns metaphors and mythology. Counselors need to help clients understand these effects upon both the psychology of choice and the opportunity structure.

The remaining chapters of the book will explore other forms of individual-environmental transactions as these are affected by changing family structures, changing demographics of the population, and factors that put clients at risk in terms of psychological, career, or behavioral vulnerability. In each of these areas there are matters of substance and of mythology about which counselors need to be knowledgeable. Finally, in each of the chapters that follow, connections will be drawn between the likely effects on clients of the challenges discussed (e.g., advanced technology, shifting family structures, cultural diversity, risk factors) and how counseling and counselors do, can, or should respond. It is intended that analyses of these challenges will help counselors and other readers understand more fully the complexity of the effects of these phenomena upon client behavior, the comprehensiveness of the responses required, and the fundamental importance of counseling in an American and, indeed, world society in transition.

Chapter 2

ADVANCED TECHNOLOGY: CAREER, ECONOMIC, EDUCATIONAL, AND PSYCHOLOGICAL EFFECTS

IF WE WERE TO DEFINE A contemporary social metaphor of the United States, building upon and refining the historical narratives and morality tales described in chapter 1, it will undoubtedly include such words as *dynamic, free, ordered, complex, powerful, resilient, self-conscious, positivist, scientific,* and *technological.* Certainly in the final years of the 20th century, America gives prominence to those last two words, *science* and *technology,* as crucial to this time in the nation's history. They are words that have been associated with strength, power, and leadership in the world community. To some degree, they define the assumptions on which rest the nation's economic policy and its attempts to be internationally competitive. As such, these words, although not interchangeable, have become part of the macrosystem by which the nation's beliefs, traditions, and values are translated into narratives, stories, rhetoric, and images that affect individual behavior and organizational forms.

Just as individuals change their self-concepts over time and space, so do nations. Each decade or so, a new set of terms surfaces and becomes popularly accepted as descriptive of the current national or social reality. For 30 years or more, various observers have characterized the United States as a postindustrial society. They have argued that massive joblessness was about to occur as a result of automation and mechanization in the workplace. However, for most of this period, neither massive nor particularly prolonged unemployment occurred. Rather, the cyclical rises in unemployment reflected temporary factors rather than underlying structural changes in the economy.

Although the United States is now emerging from a period of restructuring and downsizing of the permanent workforce in many large and small corporations, primarily because of the widespread application of advanced technology in the workplaces of the nation, the reality of the matter is that in 1997 rather than experiencing massive employment the unemployment rates of the United States dropped below 5% (to 4.5%) for the first time in 24 years, since 1973. It might be noted that this rate is in contrast to the average rate of unemployment in the nations comprising the European Union (10.8%), with some nations in Europe (e.g., Spain) experiencing unemployment rates beyond 20% ("The Politics," 1997). It might also be noted that the current low unemployment rate has occurred as the United States has undergone a major transition from an occupational structure dominated by manufacturing jobs to a structure increasingly dominated by service jobs. For example, between 1989 and 1993, even though the economy was recovering from a recession and at the same time adding millions of jobs to the occupational structure, the United States lost 1.6 million jobs in the manufacturing sector.

Many names have been given to the structural transition represented by the term *postindustrial society*. Toffler (1980), after rejecting many attempts to name the changes the United States is now undergoing (such as space age, information age, electronic era, global village, technetronic age, superindustrial age), suggested that the magnitude of the present and foreseeable upheaval and transformation is so great that it constitutes a parallel to the two major waves of change that have shaped most of the world's history: first, the agricultural revolution and then the industrial revolution. The result is the Third Wave of civilization, which, among other features, is highly technological and anti-industrial (p. 10).

Whether or not the current transformations in the content, process, and organization of work are equivalent to the effects of the agricultural and industrial revolutions is debatable (Roscak, 1986), but the effects of science and technology in America are wide-ranging and profound. They also are interactive with other important changes in the American and global economies. A glimpse of the magnitude of such changes is inherent in a major study, *Technology and the American Economic Transition: Choices for the Future* (Office of Technology Assessment, 1988), which began with the following observations:

> During the next two decades, new technologies, rapid increases in foreign trade, and the tastes and values of a new generation of Americans are likely to reshape virtually every product, every service, and every job in the United States. These forces will shake the foundations of the most secure American businesses. (p. 3)

The report then outlines further some of the promises of technology in the workplace:

> Technology can replace many of the most tedious, dangerous, and dehumanizing tasks while creating jobs that require more intellectual and social skills. Machines are likely to plant seeds, weave cloth, fabricate metal parts, handle routine paperwork, enter data, and perform a vast number of other repetitive tasks more efficiently and more productively than people. By default, the majority of jobs created in the economy could be those requiring human, and not machinelike skills: designing; tailoring products and services to unique customer needs; teaching; caring; entertaining; promoting; and persuading. Ironically, one result of sophisticated technology may be a workforce whose primary task is dealing with people—as customers or as colleagues. (p. 3)

Although this was an interesting perspective a decade ago and certainly accurate in many respects, the facts seem to be that there are many current jobs in which knowledge of how to apply advanced technology in a variety of industrial and business sectors is prized. In many instances, humans and machines seem to be entering into new partnerships, becoming linked as systems of productivity, in which technology becomes the tool and the human operator is the trouble-shooter, the planner, the creator using advanced technology to extend his or her research, to minimize boundaries of time and space, and to depict, model, and rehearse engineering, pharmaceutical, and business interventions in cyberspace before having to commit tangible assets to try out such possibilities. Many of these jobs will require persons who can deal with people, but they also require more and more people who can deal with ideas in the workplace.

Given the vast potential of advanced technology to transform the American workplace, the next sections of this chapter first examine the characteristics of the growing relationships between science and technology, the definitions and content of high or advanced technology, and some of the myths and realities associated with such processes, and then turn to its specific implications for human behavior and counseling.

THE INTERACTION OF SCIENCE AND TECHNOLOGY

Although science and technology are not the same processes, they are intricately linked in the sense that in contemporary industrialized societies there would be little technology without scientific discovery. Indeed, under current conditions of international competition and corporate economic rivalry, industry in the United States is increasingly poised to translate scientific ideas into forms of technology that can be applied and exploited commercially. As a result, the historic time lag between scientific discovery and its translation into technological forms that can transform the home, the health care system, or the workplace is growing shorter. As new science creates new technology, it also creates new tools for research that keep shortening the cycle from knowledge breakthroughs to their applied technological roles in society, and these in turn initiate new questions, new problems to be solved, new configurations of science, new technologies, and a constant repeating of these interactions as each of the sciences contributes its particular insights to the social need for information and technological application.

Judson (1985) addressed some of the important trends in science as these begin to shape the future:

> Perhaps the most general and one of the most interesting trends is that until recently the scientific revolution and its technological consequences have affected our external or physical environments, whereas in what is to come we can look increasingly for effects on what can be called our internal environment, the social environment. The shift will manifest itself in many ways. To begin with, the physical, geographical planet is filled in and filled up—ever more thoroughly explored and mapped, now increasingly catalogued for exploitation, mined and harvested, and, of course, populated. The world is becoming ever more urban, ever more exclusively human. Thus, the timing is fortunate. The shift from the external environment to the internal, social environment is paralleled by a shift in attention from the highly developed physical sciences to the sciences of social interaction—demography through the neurological basis of behavior through social psychology, all still in their infancy. (pp. 33, 36)

Judson's observations contain some important implications. The first is their accent on the facts that science operates on many different problems simultaneously and that science is composed of a variety of bodies of knowledge that vary in their maturity and unity of perspective. The natural sciences—physics and chemistry, for example—tend to be older in their theoretical and empirical bases than biology. However, in contrast to the adolescence of biology, and in comparison to the maturity of physics and chemistry, psychology is infantile in historical terms. Thus the questions posed by science tend to change as science itself evolves into its differentiated, hybridized disciplines (such as geochemistry, bionics, neuropsychology), and this hybridization will increase in the future as more disciplines are brought together in order to comprehend complex problems (e.g., the interaction of developmental biology with neurobiology and with perceptual and cognitive psychology to understand how language and other information processing mechanisms evolve and function).

A second important implication of Judson's observations is that scientific breakthroughs are unpredictable in their timing, but when they appear, their effects are not simply linear and evolutionary; they are likely to be exponential and revolutionary in their transformation of how we think about certain problems or respond to them. Thus the search for and accomplishment of scientific breakthroughs become international matters of politics, competitiveness, and resource allocation as each nation tries to find a scientific edge that, in turn, gives it a technology different from that of another nation. That edge might be sought in agriculture, in space weapons, in computers, or in myriad other arenas that have potential for carrying with them power, control, economic growth, or other geopolitical outcomes (O'Neill, 1983).

A third implication of Judson's observations is that people live in both external and internal environments. Historically, science has been most attentive to comprehending and mastering the physical environment. The internal environment, mind and emotions, tended to be left to the philosophers and the artists as arenas not susceptible to scientific or empirical inquiry. In the past century, as psychology has become independent of philosophy and spawned its own subdisciplines and empirical methodologies, the internal environments of cognition and emotion, brain chemistry and structure, mental illness and normal development, and the antecedents to behavior and behavior modification have come under the increasing scrutiny of scientists who probe the organic as well as the social, cultural, and psychological effects upon individual and group behavior.

These observations do not suggest that all counselors must become scientists in order to understand the effects of advanced technology on their clients. They do imply, however, that in a society in which the images and effects of science and technologies are so pervasive, it is important that counselors develop at least a personal "metascience"—an understanding of the language and trends in science that are related to the emergence of advanced technology, and the likely effect that such trends will have on either the external or internal environments of their clients. More will be said about this matter later in this chapter. For now, however, it is useful to acknowledge some of the scientific areas that are on the cutting edge of developing breakthroughs and thus likely to alter individual opportunities, occupations, and environments in the future.

Trends in Science and Technology

It is not possible to reflect fully the types of scientific discoveries and technological breakthroughs that are rapidly transforming daily life and, indeed, the characteristics of the occupational structure; but it is possible to identify some of the highlights in these areas that are changing the language of jobs and work. As examples, researchers at the Battelle Institute have identified 10 products that will be successfully produced and used widely by the year 2006 (Millett & Kopp, 1996). These products, in paraphrased form include

1. **genetacenticals:** Advancing research in genetics in combination with creative pharmaceutical responses are expected in the next decade to discover and make available new treatments for osteoporosis, Alzheimer's disease, cystic fibrosis, and, probably, multiple sclerosis and amyotrophic lateral sclerosis (Lou Gehrig's disease) as well as other afflictions. It is likely that individuals will begin to have available smart cards on which their genetic makeup is contained so that physicians will be better able to tailor and personalize medications and other treatments.

2. **personalized computers:** Computers for home and office will be increasingly powerful, personalized, and portable. Such computers are likely to recognize and follow voice commands and be capable of accessing and making available information tailored to specific individual needs in business and in daily life. They will also be capable of shopping, banking, and making travel arrangements with much higher levels of security than now exist.

3. **multifuel automobiles:** Technology by which automobiles may use two or more fuels is likely to be widely available in 10 years. Computer-driven management of such fuels will make it possible to achieve maximum efficiency and meet increasingly stringent environmental guidelines. The fuels used in combination are likely to include electricity, compressed natural gas, hydrogen, and reformulated gasoline as well as vegetable byproducts.

4. **next-generation television:** The digital high-definition television of the future is expected to hang on the wall like a large painting and serve as a computer monitor as well as an entertainment device. It will be interactive with other computers, videoconferencing mechanisms, satellites, and other devices for expanding home office and worldwide communication.

5. **electronic cash:** Smart cards, far more sophisticated than contemporary credit cards, will increasingly be substituted for cash and keys. Such cards will be directly linked to individual bank accounts and will contain a large array of personal biographical and statistical information. Functions that these cards will be able to serve include downloading information from other databases, paying bills, and making international transactions over computers.

6. **home health monitors:** Such devices will increase the ability of individuals to monitor their own health and physical functions. The devices should not only help to decrease medical costs by reducing physician costs for such monitoring but also to promote attention to personal wellness and ensure earlier recognition of symptoms that should be brought to the attention of physicians.

7. **smart maps and tracking devices:** Such mechanisms, based on Global Positioning Systems, information from satellites, and other sources will provide operators of cars, trucks, and boats precise information about their location and precise directions to their destination. These systems, which are now in some aircraft, will be increasingly applied to cars and trucks to provide information about other objects so that collisions can be avoided. The systems also can be

applied to hikers, children, pets, or valuable articles both to maintain information about their location and to deter crime.

8. **smart materials:** Materials with built-in electronic sensors will be able to provide warnings of excessive stress or fatigue in materials that can be communicated to central, monitoring operators. Or the materials could produce color changes or some other indication on automobiles, aircrafts, bridges, and buildings so that inspectors can be warned early of possible problems.

9. **weight-control and anti-aging products:** Based again upon genetic research and a variety of new applications of technology, an array of natural weight-control mechanisms as well as foods with enhanced nutrients and a cure for baldness are likely to help make health maintenance and aging less problematic. Such products may also extend the lives and careers of individuals until their later decades (i.e., their 70s and 80s).

10. **never-owned products:** To an increasing degree in the next 10 years, individuals will be more likely to lease computers and household appliances, in the way they now lease automobiles and trucks. In these contexts, we will buy the functions rather than the products, with the manufacturer or distributor retaining ownership and responsibility for recycling and repairs. Such a trend is likely to be better for the environment and for the safety of products. It is also likely to meet the current concerns that many products are immediately obsolete upon purchase because of technological developments.

These top 10 products identified by the Battelle Technology Intelligence Program experts reflect the continuing merger of science and technology in behalf of new products and processes that promise, for example, to alter the focus of work, stimulate new industrial processes, and create a new vocabulary of work. Obviously, the 10 products cited here are but the tip of an iceberg of worldwide technological development. Among many other products that could also be mentioned are fresh foods that will be safe as a result of irradiation or other processes; simultaneous translation through electronic devices that will interpret languages as one individual talks to another in person, over the telephone, or through computers; bionic prostheses that will replace limbs or reenergize denervated muscles through electronic stimulation; and artificial blood that will replace lost blood in emergency situations. Each of these technological breakthroughs will create new jobs or occupations and diminish others. Their uses will change the opportunity structure and perhaps lengthen the working life and the quality of retirement for many persons.

Many of these products are extensions of major scientific discoveries that have been underway for more than a decade and were identified in 1985 as among the 25 discoveries that would change our lives ("The Next Step," 1985). As is increasingly obvious, they have done so, and readers will be familiar with many. These discoveries and products include those in

- **biomedical sciences:** The merger of science and technology has made possible the genetic mapping of the egg as it is transformed into an organism as well as gene therapy and drug therapy. Other breakthroughs include breeding plants resistant to diseases and of higher nutritional quality in order to increase farm productivity, creating cancers in order to understand what causes them and how treatments may be developed, making replacement body parts from super-strength composite materials, and making computer-driven prostheses.

- **physical science:** Revisions in the theory of gravity and integration of these revisions with quantum mechanics have made possible new speculations about the geometry of space and matter. New space telescopes now can study galaxies billions of years old, compare their formation and change, and more accurately measure distances from earth to other galaxies for purposes of space travel and other interstellar research.

- **evolutionary science:** Research in fossil data has examined changes in species related to habitat changes. Other research has explored the practical effects of transferring genes between species to improve the productivity of animals or plants for foods as well as the possibilities of cloning animals to produce duplicate life forms.

- **mathematics:** The use of computers has made it possible to display geometric or mathematical formulae graphically and to apply experimental mathematics to both linear and nonlinear dynamic systems (e.g., electrical fields, quantum theory, weather, fluid dynamics). The development of new concepts of geometry and dimensionality and their combination with new mathematical formulae have made it possible to construct models of symmetry in the universe, physics, and number theory.

- **neuroscience:** Research studies linking genes, cellular and molecular biology, brain chemistry, and behavior are beginning to map the origins and mechanisms that trigger or sustain basic emotions, drives, and behaviors from the level of genes and molecules to specific nerve circuits and brain systems. As a result, treatments are emerging to enhance certain types of outcomes (e.g., memory) and inhibit others (e.g., depression, aggression). In addition to modifying the application of psychotherapy in mental disorders that are basically organic or chemical, scientists are creating new drugs to treat neurological and psychiatric as well as genetic disorders.

These major categories of scientific breakthroughs, which have indeed changed our lives, are complemented by other, more specifically technological breakthroughs, which have also changed our lives. These include

- **parallel computers:** In order to increase the speed and capability of computers dramatically, multiple microprocessors are being harnessed to work simultaneously on many parts of a complex task. In so doing, the architecture and use of parallel computers are at the point when a billion or more calculations per second are possible for a computer system.

- **the Internet:** Another recent and international linkage of computers, which weds computers, telecommunications, graphics, and knowledge bases from sites around the world, makes access available to users in any setting or geographic location.

- **fiber optics** and **microcircuit chips:** Theoretically, the use of light wave communications through glass fibers will permit the total scope of current telephone traffic in the United States to be carried on a single fiber.

- **composite materials:** In the near future, space transportation will require not only new propulsion systems (e.g., solar power, electric and magnetic thrusts, nuclear power) but also larger vehicles made of extremely light, advanced structural materials so that the economics of carrying equipment, satellites, and people to international space stations and for other purposes can be less costly and more internationally competitive. Many of the emerging needs for light-weight, strong, heat-resistant materials go beyond the capability or the availability of natural resources. Thus new composite materials are being developed from polymers, carbon, and other sources to form synthetic fibers, plastics, and other materials that are stronger and lighter than steel or ceramics. They also require less fuel to make than do steel and related materials.

- **ceramic science:** By using such raw materials as sand and clay and fabricated synthetic materials, ceramic science is providing new materials for manufacturing, building, medicine, electronics, transportation, and other areas. For example, ceramic materials that are strong, light, anticorrosive, and sensitive to changes in temperature, humidity, pressure, and sound intensity are being used in computers, electrical insulators, optical communications, cutting tools, engine parts, and capacitors. Ceramic materials are also being used for electronic, optical, mechanical, or medical purposes.

Many additional categories of technological breakthroughs fuel and extend the application of advanced technology. These include

- **microchip technology:** The development of lighter, smaller, faster, more powerful superchips capable of storing millions of bits of information per chip, an area much smaller than a fingernail, is a technological breakthrough that extends the application of advanced technology and is a subject of intense international competition. Such engineering challenges include the ability to interconnect millions of tiny circuits and transistors on a single chip and to locate hundreds of integrated circuit chips in spaces smaller than the diameter of a human hair.

- **catalysts:** In the production of drugs and vitamins, fuels, fertilizers and pesticides, plastics and adhesives, and every synthetic fiber, catalysts are another important technology. Catalysts create specific and predictable chemical reactions necessary to the selective production of novel and complex chemical products, such as advanced drugs, plastics, fibers, composite materials, and fuels.

- **computer software:** This overarching technology empowers the accelerating conversion of scientific knowledge into advanced technology. The computer as an electronic tool is guided in its operations by a script, typically called software, which represents the program of action the computer executes. Until now, much effort has been expended in miniaturizing computers—making their internal components smaller, more powerful, and less expensive. The decades ahead are likely to see dramatic changes in computer software as commonplace. Natural language (e.g., English) will be used to make software easier for users to understand and implement. Software will be constructed to extend the representation of information on the screen through, for example, 3D graphics, speech generation and recognition, and music synthesis. A further outcome will be the construction of increasingly sophisticated software able to engage in some learning and artificial intelligence, which will increase the qualitative capability of computers as a complement to the quantitative changes of the past several decades.

The scientific and technological discoveries listed here are not exhaustive of all the scientific-technological connections that are shaping the occupational structure of the present and future. Residual breakthroughs from past decades continue to shape the architecture of advanced technology just as the 25 discoveries identified in 1985 continue to shape the technology breakthroughs of the present and the early years of the next century.

In addition to the effects of the increasingly rapid merger of science and technology and its overt manifestations in new products and processes, emerging technologies have their parallel in both the organization and content of work and in the language used to describe jobs and occupations. Indeed, many terms that were coined as recently as the beginning of the 1980s have now become familiar parts of the vocabulary of work and of the classified advertisements describing work availability. For example, microprocessors, sensors, microwaves, lasers, fiber optics, superconductors, ultrasound, interferon, recombinant DNA, digitization, computer-aided design, robots, artificial intelligence, and embryo transfer were described in 1982 by the National Science Foundation as *emerging technologies*. They are now no longer emerging but rather accepted processes in communications, agriculture, health care, transportation, energy development, construction, defenses, consumer goods, and education.

In a similar fashion scientific processes related to the study of work processes and work organization have created new technologies focused on the management and deployment of employees and on ways by which commitment to customer service and quality production can be enhanced. These in turn have led to a variety of workplace practices that were rarely used a decade ago but are now becoming increasingly routine. These workplace practices also have changed the language of work as reflected in such terms as *just-in-time inventories, worker teams, total quality management*, and *quality circles* as well as in such phrases as peer review of employee performance, compensation increases based on a pay-for-knowledge system, employee involvement in a firm's technology and equipment purchase decisions, and job relations (Frazis, Herz, & Horrigan, 1995).

Advanced Technology: Some Definitions

Providing some definitions for the term *technology* will be useful and give coherence to the variety of technologies just described. There are various ways to define *advanced technology* or *high technology*; these terms are typically used interchangeably. But what is the meaning of technology itself? Gerwin (1981) suggested that, "Technology refers to the means utilized to accomplish a task. It may be manifested in machine processes, computer programs, and other explicit procedures, but also in performance programs stored in individual memories" (p. 5). In a broader sense, technology refers to all the ways people use inventions and discoveries to satisfy needs and desires. From early history until the present, human beings have been in a constant age of technology as they have invented tools, machines, materials, and techniques to make work easier or to cope with new physical or social challenges. Thus technology includes both primitive and advanced techniques and tools applied to problems related to physical survival, industrialization, or other purposes.

In essence, there is not one technology but many technologies that stem from different settings, disciplines, applications, or categories of problems. There are industrial, medical, social, computer, materials, agricultural, and other technologies. In historical terms, not all technology is based on science. Certainly, early humans developed tools and techniques to make things happen without having the benefit of science to help them know why things happened. Increasingly, however, science and technology have become inseparable, particularly in areas now defined as advanced or high technology.

High technology typically refers to the "most sophisticated, esoteric, and often the most recently advancing technological knowledge, skills, and hardware applications" (Dyrenfurth, 1984). Minshall (1984, pp. 29–30) applied the term *high technology* both to workplaces and processes:

- High technology signifies high-growth occupational areas in which technological applications are rapidly changing job knowledge and skill requirements in terms of an arbitrary percentage of a worker's useful working life.
- High technology refers to (1) products, processes, and applications stemming from the latest scientific and technological developments, (2) utilization of high-level machine intelligence and information decision capability, and (3) the extension of human manual and intellectual capacities through the use of computer technology and the application of sophisticated physical principles.

Castells (1985) provided a somewhat different view of high or advanced technology. His perspectives probed the underlying characteristics of advanced technology:

> Two features are characteristic of the stream of technological innovation under way. First, the object of technological discoveries, as well as of their applications, is *information*. What microelectronics does is to process and eventually generate information. What telecommunications do is to transmit information, with a growing complexity of interactive loops and feedbacks, at increasingly greater speed and at a lower cost. What the new media do is to disseminate information in a way potentially more and more decentralized and individualized. What automation does is to introduce preinformed devices in other activities. And what genetic engineering does is to decode the information system of the living matter and try to program it. The second feature concerns the fact that the outcome is *process-oriented rather than product-oriented*. High technology is not a particular technique, but a form of production and organization that can affect all spheres of activity by transforming their operation in order to achieve greater productivity or better performance through increased knowledge of the process itself. (pp. 11–12)

The Growth of a Global Economy

The views of and the implementation of different technologies are likely to affect the types and content of work available in this nation and in others. Many of the technologies discussed in the previous section are essential elements of a global economy—telecommunications, fiber optics, worldwide web, digitization, satellites, computers—without which such national interdependence could not occur in the forms that are emerging. The outputs of advanced technologies flow unfettered across national political boundaries. Through electronic transfers multinational corporations can move more currency overnight than many nations have as their total capital resources; work can be done at any time across the globe unrestricted by the time or space of the originating workplace; financial transactions and investments can take place 24 hours of the day; and individuals in one work site can monitor and manage through computers the work being done in other work sites thousands of miles away.

As Rumberger and Burke (1987) stated,

> Today the countries of the world are much more interdependent and are a part of a growing global economy. New technological developments spread much more quickly throughout the world, affecting developed and developing economies alike. In fact, one

basic feature of the new global economy is that developing countries, such as Taiwan and South Korea, now can compete in international markets for very technically sophisticated products like computers and automobiles. (p. 3)

In essence, then, from a global perspective, advanced technology becomes critical at every step of international trade, communications, production, and distribution as raw materials, labor forces, and ideas are integrated into world systems of commercial interaction. Technology now makes it possible to move ourselves or goods to anywhere on the surface of the earth within hours and to communicate worldwide in a fraction of a second (CPC Foundation/Rand Corporation, 1994, p. 5). Thus geographic and political boundaries no longer serve to contain or to centralize work. "Just as pollutants flow from nation to nation, so capital and technological knowledge flow across national borders altering economic sovereignty as they diffuse" (White, 1990, p. 10).

One implication of these observations is that national economies are becoming subordinate to the economies of international trade and to that of regional trading blocs. The latter—as characterized by the European Union (EU), the North American Free Trade Agreement (NAFTA), the Association of South East Asian Nations (ASEAN), the Nordic Council, and other actual or potential alliances—are interim steps in an increasingly integrated global economy. As such, these trading blocs are both restructuring the world economy and the economies of individual nations. But these worldwide economic changes also represent the contexts for other dynamics that affect national occupational structures, the content of work, and new demands being placed upon the human resources in nation after nation.

Knowledge Work

Alvin Toffler, the author of *Future Shock* (1970) and *The Third Wave* (1980), among other important books, has added *Powershift, Knowledge, Wealth, and Violence at the Edge of the 21st Century* (1990) to his trilogy monitoring the social and economic forces shaping societal and individual behavior. In the latter book, he has contended that knowledge has now become the world's prime commodity and its byproduct is the use and acceleration of time—in terms of the speed of capital movements, transactions, and investments; the speed with which ideas are converted into products and processes; and the speed with which plans are translated into action. In his view, knowledge is rapidly replacing cheap labor and raw materials as the primary requisite to effective international competition, to requiring workers to work smarter, and to improving the quality of life within communities and nations.

Toffler has suggested that the nations of the world are being characterized in new ways—not just into the nations of the North and the South, or into those that can be described as communist or capitalist—but into the fast and slow nations of the world based upon their level of technology and development and their ability to function within the quality controls and the accelerated delivery of goods and services expected by the global market. As a result, the economic aspirations of the nations whose technological capabilities are limited and human resources inflexible will suffer in international competition.

Peter Drucker (1993), the international scholar of work organization and management, has professed for some time that knowledge has replaced experience in most of the emerging occupations in the world as the primary requisite for employability. According to him, until quite recently, there were few jobs requiring knowledge. That is no longer true. In the last quarter of the 20th century knowledge has become the economy's foundation and its true capital, and knowledge workers are being sought by employers as assets to be prized so that workplace practices and processes can be continuously introduced, learned, and implemented.

As is apparent in the discussion in this chapter, more and more work is knowledge based rather than physical or manual or based on experience without an understanding of why processes work. For example, the automobile mechanic without a knowledge of the computer and electronic systems that power a car and their diagnoses is unable to repair most new vehicles, primarily because most of them have more computer power than was available in the first generation of satellites or to the early astronauts in their spaceships. But knowledge work has other effects as well. As Bridges (1996) has suggested, when work was primarily physical, it was easy to divide it into separate jobs, with separate job descriptions that clustered in separate departments with separate missions. But knowledge work is not so easy to divide into jobs in traditional ways. Knowledge work is not typically a series of repetitive actions, but rather a sequence of figurative dialogues between the worker and the data, whether the worker is monitoring and trouble shooting a computer-driven lathe or a robot, engaging in computer-aided design, or diagnosing what computer module is not functioning in an automobile. Thus how sharply to define and classify jobs among knowledge workers becomes more difficult and one of the reasons why much knowledge work is done by cross-functional teams of specialists in different knowledge bases.

The implications of the Toffler and Drucker perspectives as well as of those that precede them are that, as we approach and enter the 21st century, the skills of schooling and learning and the skills of the workplace must be increasingly complementary and overlapping. Educational abilities and achievements will become major elements of individual career development. Such a reality puts those with minimal training or capability of learning at the risk of being permanently dislocated or unemployed or constantly on the move to find jobs that they can do. Frequently, racial or cultural minority group members or immigrants tend to experience the most difficulties in dealing with the educational and psychological ripple effects of advanced technology. This is often because they have been underserved in receiving the systematic information useful in planning for such occupational transitions, or because they have lived in locations where educational provisions are not as good as those made for majority culture members, which has thereby placed them at a competitive disadvantage.

Indeed, it has become increasingly clear in national and international development plans and in strategic industrial goal setting that the key factor in a nation's ability to compete in the growing global economy is the quality of its workforce as defined by the literacy, numeracy, flexibility, and teachability that characterizes it. What is also apparent in such a view is the reality that in planning related to identifying, preparing, and supporting human resources, it is insufficient to focus only on the intellectual or social elite of the society. Rather, in the global economy, workforces will be required that have the capability to be productive and purposeful at all levels of the occupational structure from the managerial and professional levels through the skilled and semiskilled levels. Unless a workforce can function with quality and efficiency at the levels of creativity, invention, and innovation as well as at the implementation and application levels, in services delivery and in goods production, the occupational structure becomes increasingly divided into the haves and have nots and is encumbered by an underclass of persons who have neither the skills nor the motivation to be trained and retrained as emerging jobs require new skills and ways of being productive.

What is further suggested is that nations, including the United States, cannot solve their competitive problems by pouring billions of dollars into capital equipment or physical facilities and not into worker training, retraining, and other support systems. As the effects of the implementation of advanced technology in the workplace change how workers and machines interact, change the social psychology and the flow of information in the workplace, eliminate more and more middle management as well as semiskilled and unskilled jobs, and make more possible the decentralization of where work is done across the world, the impact of technological and scientific knowledge on human career development in a world economy takes several significant forms. These include:

- the globalization of the workforce and its increased cross-national mobility;
- a growing global labor surplus, frequently including highly trained and skilled workers;
- organizational transformations in the workplace that are creating new models of personnel development, not just personnel management;
- downsizing organizational personnel to a small core of permanent employees to hold down permanent overhead costs and to incorporate newer forms of advanced technology to increase overall productivity cost ratios;
- the pervasive effects of advanced technology upon the economic climate and the occupational structures of the nations of the world, which means that because of advanced technology, work of a sophisticated nature can be done any place in the world, without respect to time or political boundaries, and that advanced technologies, however defined, change the organization and the language of work, its content, the role of workers, and the skill requirements to engage in work, particularly in those occupations that involve either high technology or technology-intensive occupations;
- the rise of a contingent workforce around the world, which includes temporary employees whose special skills are purchased for limited periods of time but who do not have long-term institutional identification or health and pension benefits and may involve outsourcing to specialized firms of particular departments, functions, or tasks that were historically included within a corporate structure;
- the rising importance of the knowledge worker and of literacy, numeracy, communication, and computer literacy skills as prerequisites for employability and lifelong training in many of the emerging occupations and in the primary labor market;
- the growing concern about "career relevant" schooling by which students can be systematically prepared with the skills necessary in the occupational structure and in other life roles;
- the recent appearance of new government policy and legislation in many countries concerned about the school-to-work transition and a seamless progression from school to employment and effective induction into the workforce;
- the growing awareness of the linkages between positive or negative career experiences and mental health, self-esteem, purposefulness, physical well-being, and

the ability to support and maintain a family as well as perceptions that an individual has life options and can practice an internal locus of control;

- changing demographic trends related to new entrants to the workforce—primarily women, persons of color, and immigrants; and

- collegemania in many countries that has caused an overeducated workforce but one that also experiences skill shortages at the blue collar and technician levels.

In responding to these trends and developing or supporting human resources as national assets, there is more involved than reforming education or making schools and universities more career relevant. Also of major importance is the creation of policies and resource allocations that support such goals, the restructuring of work organizations and how they induct and orient young workers, the stimulation of job creation efforts, and the continuous upgrading of skills over each worker's lifetime (Kuttner, 1990) as well as attention to the psychology of achievement and success that prevails in a given society. Certainly a major component in the evolving systems of human resource development available in any nation is the range and deployment of career services—career education, career guidance, career counseling—and their availability, accessibility, and purposes. These are not simple issues. In a global economy, nations approach such matters differently and from varied cultural perspectives; these approaches also change as nations go through different phases in their own evolution and place different demands on their human resources.

EFFECTS OF ADVANCED TECHNOLOGY ON WORK AND THE OCCUPATIONAL STRUCTURE

The effects of the emerging technologies described previously, however exotic they seem, have profound implications for the workforce. They are changing the jobs available, their locations, and the characteristics of such jobs as well as the broader economic climate. In so doing, they are changing the contexts, content, and vocabulary with which counselors and clients must process the problems and anxieties that result from work-related questions. More about the latter implications will be discussed later. For now, it is important to consider some of the specific effects of advanced technology.

One of these effects is that emerging technologies are changing our economy from one rooted in the so-called smoke stack or sunset industries to one characterized by an increasing proportion of sunrise industries. The first are involved in high-volume, standardized production of durable goods (e.g., automobiles, steel, rubber, furniture). These are typically large, centralized, management-driven, capital- and labor-intensive industries. The second, the sunrise industries, are those that deal much more with generating information and services and applying advanced technology to goods production. Such industries are increasingly concerned with precision and customized manufacturing. They also are characterized by generating or applying information to the services or products they handle, fabricate, or develop. Both sunset and, to a larger extent, sunrise industries are characterized by machines operating machines (e.g., computer-controlled machine tools, the use of robots), bioengineering (e.g., the development of biological organisms to achieve industrial processes such as devouring pollution and creating new medicines), and the wedding of computers or laser optics to communications and other industrial processes. These high-technology applications are, in turn, changing the processes of banking, retailing, warehousing and inventory control, transportation, agriculture, and production. Thus they are changing the nature of work, where it is located, the amount of work available, and the types of training or education required to engage in high technology occupations.

Another effect is that the speed and magnitude of change that is a common feature of contemporary organizations force their leaders to reconfigure the organization, perhaps frequently, in order to profit from these changes or even to survive them. As Bridges (1996) has observed, these changes are usually related to technological developments, and technology is central to them in three different ways:

1. It forces people to learn whole new ways of making things or communicating with each other.
2. These changes make possible, and even force other organizations to keep up with, rapid modifications in products and services.
3. Improved communication means that changes that once were visible only locally are now experienced everywhere at the same time (p. 13).

Such realities, again, affect the organization of work and the necessary skills of the workforce as well as the management of change and the management of technology.

Education and Training Related to Advanced Technology

Hull and Pedrotti (1983) identified six educational implications common to all high-technology occupations:

1. They require a broad knowledge of math, computers, physics, chemistry, electricity, electronics, electromechanical devices, and fluid flow.
2. They involve heavy and frequent computer use, including knowledge of practical applications of programming.
3. They change rapidly and require lifelong learning.
4. They are systems oriented and involve working with systems that have electronic, electromechanical, electrical, thermal, optical, fluidic, and microcomputer components.
5. They require a fundamental understanding of a system's principles as well as practical skills in designing, developing, testing, installing, troubleshooting, maintaining, and repairing the system.
6. They require substantial employee flexibility and adaptability (pp. 28–31).

Whether or not a worker is directly involved in a high-technology occupation or in an occupation in which technology is pervasive in its use for data entry, analysis, and communication, the application of advanced technology throughout the occupational structure is demanding higher educational skills. Part of this phenomenon is related to the facts that automation of work is easiest in low-skilled jobs, and that eliminating many unskilled and semiskilled jobs through technology increases the average education or training required in the remaining jobs or in the emerging occupations.

Such an analysis is somewhat simplistic because many jobs still require only a minimum education. In the future occupational structure, however, more and more unskilled jobs will be eliminated, and an increasing premium will be placed on higher levels of reading, computation, communication, and problem-solving or reasoning skills. An increasing number of employers are extending their conception of basic skills to include self-discipline, reliability, perseverance, accepting responsibility, and respect for the rights of others (U.S. Department of Education/U.S. Department of Labor [U.S. DOE/DOL], 1988). These latter skills are increasingly being defined as "general employability skills" in the United States and as "industrial discipline" in Britain (Herr, 1984). They are important across the spectrum of work and are, in that sense, "very elastic" in their application. These general employability skills do not substitute for the basic academic skills already noted, but they clearly are mediators of how effectively such academic skills will be practiced. Such general employability skills, as contrasted with technical/job-specific skills, tend to be the content of career guidance and counseling.

According to a joint publication of the U.S. Department of Education and the U.S. Department of Labor (1988), "New technology has changed the nature of work—created new jobs and altered others—and, in many cases, has revealed basic skills problems where none were known to exist" (p. 3). New technology, then, has intensified national cries for educational reform and stimulated the need for literacy audits among workers and the need to introduce basic skills training directly into the workplace where such audits show that it is needed.

For 20 years and more, studies have documented the lack of basic skills of many American workers, both new entrants into the workforce and older workers who do not have the learning skills necessary to be taught new industrial or business processes, particularly those involving technological adaptations. These studies have implied that unless more effective workforce preparation can be instituted in schools, in workplaces, and in other organizations, national goals of remaining internationally competitive are in jeopardy. Twenty years ago some studies (e.g., Knowles, 1977) indicated that approximately 40% of the American adult population is coping inadequately with typical life problems (e.g., getting work, holding a job, buying products, making change, managing economic life, and parenting). More recent studies have been less precise about proportions of adults in the workforce, or of young persons entering, with significant academic or technical skill deficits, but there have continued to be studies and national reports that raise serious issues about such problems. For example, the New York Telephone Company, in a major recruitment effort, found that from January to July 1987, only 3,619 of 22,880 applicants passed the examination intended to test vocabulary, number relationships, and problem-solving skills for jobs ranging from telephone operator to service representative (U.S. DOE/DOL, 1988).

More recent analyses have suggested that, in general, firms report that only about 50% of recent high school graduates are qualified for entry-level positions. Inadequate computational and problem-solving skills are among the most serious deficiencies, with the lack of verbal and writing skills also reported as problems. In addition, workers, particularly young workers, exhibit deficiencies in interpersonal skills, a poor attitude toward work, and an inability "to fit in" (Bassi, 1996, p. 16). Part of the problem with such observations is that it is not clear whether there is a growing deterioration of the basic skills of the adolescent population, whether the deficits noted by employers are simply part of their perennial complaints that workers are underskilled and overpaid, or whether these problems are concentrated in certain subgroups of the population. On the positive side, dropout rates among high school students in the United States have been steadily improving, especially for

African Americans, while measures of basic skills (e.g., Iowa Tests of Basic Skills, SATs) of both White and, more comprehensively, African American students have continued to improve (Bassi, 1996).

Part of the issue in an analysis of implications of education and training related to the importance of advanced technology or other skill changes in the workplace of the nation lies with the variation of students' experience in schools and in the degree to which schools are being redesigned to be more career relevant in their preparation of students for employment. Clearly, for example, the United States spends fewer resources on students who do not attend college than other industrialized nations (Educational Testing Service, 1990; Hilton, 1991). These data suggest that schools continue to accent the importance of college preparation as a goal superior to that of preparing persons to enter the workforce, even though there are now pervasive shortages of skilled workers in the United States and a surplus of college graduates (Gray & Herr, 1995).

The findings reported here suggest that the effects of advanced technology ripple throughout many of the society's institutions, but clearly, a functionally literate workforce is a fundamental requirement for successfully implementing advanced technology. Such findings also suggest that the pressure on both youth and adults to possess basic academic skills will necessitate that counselors diagnose problems stemming from inadequate basic academic skills and broker or encourage remedial programs.

The Changing Mix of Jobs

As the complex interaction of science and technology shape the content, processes, and language of work; where work is done and by whom; and the preparation for work, there is a continuous change in the mix of jobs available in the occupational structures of the individual nations seeking to establish their place in the world economy. As already noted (see the list in the Knowledge Work section), there are several major trends apparent in the occupational structures of the most developed nations and many of the developing nations. To reinforce and extend those trends already cited:

1. In general, it has been accepted that a labor force that is characterized by literacy, numeracy, teachability, flexibility, and commitment to lifelong learning is a major national requisite for participation in the changing dynamics and challenges of a global economy.
2. Emerging occupations reflect educational requirements rising to include some postsecondary education but not necessarily college. This phenomenon is a function of the growing need for knowledge workers who can take more responsibility for job decisions, quality management, and adaptation to new work practices.
3. The evolving configuration of jobs in the economy includes the likelihood that machine systems and robots will replace many of the low-skilled and semiskilled production jobs now held by poorly educated or untrained workers.
4. There are rising educational requirements across the economy, although only 20% to 23% of all occupations are expected to require a college degree. However, 34% of new occupations will have such a requirement. Thus there will be major needs for more technically trained persons who have technical education and experience equivalent to that of a community college degree.

5. Because of the widespread use of computers and other advanced technology, there is a devolution of information and the management of information down through worker levels to those actually doing the data entry, and operating and trouble-shooting the machines, with a consequent reduction in the need for middle managers who historically have managed and disseminated such information.

6. Because of the trend toward mergers and downsizing among corporations, many work organizations now have smaller core employee groups that are then augmented seasonally or at other times of need by the employment of temporary or contingent workers and by outsourcing of specific functions to independent contractors. Although opportunities for self-employment and subcontracting are increasing, many temporary workers or subcontractors have little job security or institutional loyalty.

7. The social covenant between employers and employees has historically favored institutional loyalty and seniority in a job, but job security is now based on the skills a worker brings to the job, the currency of these skills, and the efforts of the workers to keep their skills current.

These types of trends in the occupational structure tend to mask the constant churning of jobs as individuals retire or die, as industries and occupations expand or recede, as business cycles and other economic factors change, and as the introduction of technology and other work practices affect the types of workers and skill sets required by both traditional and emerging occupations. Therefore, according to the research of Moskowitz and Warwick (1996),

> occupations that once offered solid careers are in decline, while positions once unheard of are now among the fastest growing. . . . The number of workers employed in any occupation depends in large part on the demand for the goods or services provided by those workers. Over the last decade or so, for example, increased use of computers by businesses, schools, scientific organizations, and government agencies has contributed to large increases in the number of systems analysts, programmers, and computer repairers. However, even if the demand rises for goods and services provided by a group of workers, employment may not increase at all or may increase more slowly than demand because of changes in the way goods are produced and services are provided. In fact, some changes in technology and business practices cause employment to decline. For example, while the volume of paperwork is expected to increase dramatically, the employment of typists and word processors will probably fall. This reflects the growing use of word-processing equipment that increases productivity and permits other office workers to do more of their own typing. (p. 3)

These observations about changes in particular jobs as a function of demand, technology, and other issues are also reflected in the overall growth of jobs in different U.S. industries. For example, in 1996 among 74 specific industry groups, there were great differences in the job picture. Just six groups constituting 25% of total employment contributed almost half (45%) of the total gain in jobs: business services, health care services, special trade construction contractors (e.g., carpenters, plumbers), local government (education), engineering and management services, and drinking places. However, three groups (the federal government, apparel and other textile products, and food processing) combined to lose 158,000 jobs. During this period substantial increases occurred in construction, local government (including public education), wholesale trade, finance, and transportation, but there were also significant reductions in jobs in mining and manufacturing (Goodman & Ilg, 1997). Rather than manufacturing producing the most jobs, service-producing industries will account for most new jobs through 2005 at least. As already suggested, the goods-producing sector will decline in manufacturing and mining. However, jobs in construction, agriculture, forestry, and fishing are expected to experience gains in employment, although these are likely to be replacement jobs—jobs to replace individuals who are leaving the workforce by retirement, death, or career changes—rather than new jobs. These trends continue to show that many of the traditional occupations on which the nation was built and prospered have decreased in job proportion due to the widespread application of technology and the shift of many jobs to nations other than the United States.

To extend these points somewhat further, today more than 50% of the U.S. labor force are white collar or information workers, ranging from executives, managers, analysts, and programmers to teachers, designers, illustrators, and sales representatives to copy writers, statistical clerks, and secretaries. Administrative support workers, including clerical workers of all types, constitute the largest single class of employees in the U.S. labor force—about 18.2% of all employed people in 1996. Since 1950, industrial work has fallen from around 38% of the labor force to about 18% in 1984 and close to 15% in 1997. Just as the large increase in agricultural employment over the last 40 years has been accompanied by a large rise in agricultural output, so also has the decrease in industrial employment been accompanied by a continuing and accelerating rise in industrial output, signifying a long-term shift from labor-intensive to capital-intensive production. The latter reflects the growing effects of "working smarter" in the workplace, widespread attention to and the management of quality, and the pervasive application of technology to production (e.g., numerically controlled machine tools, computer-aided design and manufacture, robotics). As a result, U.S. workers have regained their position as among the most productive worker groups in the world. Finally, since 1960, service work has risen from about 18% of the workforce to approximately one third of the workforce, a growth that reflects the nation's move from an industrial to a service- and information-based economy.

There are other perspectives that enrich the drama of these trends. For example, by 1982, only 3% of the labor force of the United States was engaged in agriculture (and an undetermined proportion of these workers were engaged in agribusiness, which does not typically occur on farms or involve direct production of agricultural commodities), and less than 30% of workers were engaged in the production of nonagricultural goods (mostly manufacturing) (Ginzberg, 1982). By 1997, approximately 1.1% of the U.S. workforce were farm operators and farm managers. These persons were so productive that they fed not only the population of the United States but the citizens of many other nations as well (Bureau of Labor Statistics, 1996). A further interesting statistic is that 19 out of 20 new jobs since 1981 have been in the service sector. Up to two thirds of the new jobs since 1978 have been in three groups of occupations: business services, retail trade (including restaurants), and health care ("The New Jobless," 1988). From 1994 to 2005 total employment is expected to increase by 17.7 million new jobs. Health care services will account for almost one fifth of all job growth from 1994 to 2005. Factors contributing to continued growth in this industry include the aging population, which will continue to require more services, and the increased use of innovative medical technology for intensive diagnosis and treatment. Patients will increasingly be shifted out of hospitals and into outpatient facilities, nursing homes, and home health care in an attempt to contain costs (Bureau of Labor Statistics, 1996).

Several other trends are embedded in this discussion of the changing characteristics of the occupational structure. One is that the terms *manufacturing* and *service* are themselves losing meaning. By the year 2000, the definition of these two apparently opposite terms will have little relationship to the definitions of these terms in 1985. For example, the auto worker on an assembly line in 1980 was still performing the same tasks auto workers had performed for the past quarter century. By 1990, however, the widespread use of robots for welding, painting, shaping, and moving automobiles through an assembly line began to change the role of the assembly line worker to that of a programmer or maintenance-service worker. Though employed in the manufacturing part of the automobile industry, the production worker produces services, not cars. He or she will increasingly handle information, not raw materials or tools per se. Even in high-tech industries that produce advanced technology or in technology-intensive industries that apply high technology to production or services, many more workers are in support roles—secretaries, maintenance workers, security personnel, copy center operators, equipment mechanics, motor pool operatives, drivers—than are directly employed in production or direct service.

Another trend reshaping the American occupational structure is that of transferring what had been American manufacturing jobs overseas. In the March 11, 1985, issue of *Business Week*, the headline story was "America's High-Tech Crisis: Why Silicon Valley Is Losing Its Edge" (Wilson, 1985). The president of Dataquest, Inc., a market research firm specializing in high technology, was quoted as stating that "American industry is becoming a distribution economy, and we haven't even noticed we are in trouble." Americans design products, then move the actual production overseas where labor costs are cheaper. In a short time, others imitate our development and sell the products we designed back to us. Such examples illustrate that advanced technology is a worldwide phenomenon. It has become a focus of worldwide competition and has stimulated American corporations to purchase a larger amount of goods from overseas manufacturers, thus altering the type of jobs available in this nation, increasing the trade import/export deficit, and creating pressures on the economy. These observations reaffirm that America is deeply enmeshed in a global, not a national, economy.

A final trend that summarizes several of the issues discussed in this section has to do again with the characteristics of the American workforce and the concerns of many employers about the quality of the potential employees. Such data come from many sources, including major business magazines. As an example, Simon and Burton (1990) indicated to business leaders in *Forbes* magazine that what has been learned from the late 1980s is that "a poorly educated labor force may cost the U.S. dearly." The authors contended that as the "baby bust" generation moved into the job market in the late 1980s, "companies got a taste of what lies ahead: a shortage of trained and trainable workers." For example, they said, there is a lack of skilled workers for manufacturing, construction, and health care, but "without extensive training, few of these slots can be filled by the unskilled who are out of work in inner cities or laid off from basic industries. If you can't read, you can't do much today, because most heavy lifting is done by machine." Modern industry does not just require bodies; it requires trained minds.

The growing lack of skilled workers in the United States has also been noted on television news broadcasts. For example, a NBC newsclip on January 27, 1996, stated that 56% of manufacturers in the nation are experiencing substantial skilled and technical worker shortages. Many of these employers are now using headhunters to help recruit blue-collar skilled workers; they are not available.

Part of the reason for the shortage of skilled workers in many parts of the United States is the dominant role that college going plays in the nation and the ambivalence of secondary schools about what role they should play in preparing their students for the workforce. The emphasis on going to college in this country has suggested that there is only one way to win: get a college degree. Thus in various studies it has been shown that, when asked, 84% of students in high schools say they plan on going to college or getting a graduate/professional degree; in many places in the country, 70% or more of each high school class actually start to college, and more than 50% of the lowest academic quartile of students in high school say that they have been encouraged by parents and teachers to go to college and they aspire to do so. In 1993, 64% of high school seniors went to 4-year colleges and community colleges, and those attending the latter were typically in transfer, not technical, programs. In contrast, fewer than 4% of high school seniors, when asked, aspired to courses in crafts, precision metal, or specialized repair, although jobs in these areas comprise about 20% of the total job market in the future and are second only to professional and managerial occupations in income. Thus there is a growing mismatch between skill needs and what high school students are being encouraged to do or to aspire to. Overwhelmingly, high school students and their parents place their hopes for a secure economic future in college degrees or, more specifically, in the attainment of well-paid and prestigious occupations as a result of the degrees. In reality, however, only two in three college graduates will find college-level work, or one in two find a job in a profession (Gray & Herr, 1995).

Reflected in the emerging profile of the American occupational structure is that there are more students aspiring to and attending college than ever before in U.S. history, but that there are emerging skill shortages that, for the most part, college graduates will not be able to meet. Employers are not interested primarily in education credentials, but rather in the possession of skills. In particular, college graduates will not displace non-college-degree holders who have specialized occupational skills that they acquired in a vocational school or a community college. Indeed, because of the nature of the work they represent, many employers rank the need for vocational training higher than the need for a college degree. Such needs are reflected both in the characteristics of the U.S. occupational structure and in such trends as the rise of technicians as a new worker elite in the American labor force. Technicians are workers who have specialty technical skills that typically exceed those of traditional skilled workers, and such technicians typically have some postsecondary education but do not require a baccalaureate degree to do their job. *Fortune* magazine has called these persons "a new worker elite who are transforming the American labor force and potentially every organization that employs them . . . the technician is becoming the core employee of the digital information age" (Richman, 1994). According to available statistics, the number of technicians has increased nearly 300% since 1950— triple the growth rate for the workforce as a whole. Part of this phenomena is explained by organizational downsizing in the United States that has reduced the ranks of middle management (usually jobs held by college graduates) and given more power and information to skilled workers through the incorporation of advanced technology. As a result, the typical work organization looks less like a pyramid and more like a football with a large bulge of technicians and skilled workers in the middle.

Technicians appear across industries. They include air traffic controllers, broadcast technicians, computer programmers, dental hygienists, medical technicians, drafters, engineering technicians, library technicians, nuclear medicine technologists, and science technicians. There are many other types of technicians, but they have in common the ability to use increasingly powerful, versatile, and user-friendly technologies to accomplish complex and challenging tasks (e.g., trouble shoot robots, maintain and operate computer and telecommunications networks, perform and evaluate medical tests) that require judgment and skills and that arise from the increasing information-dependent technical work environment. These are skills to which tech-prep programs in secondary schools and community colleges are directed, as are many of the vocational education curricula in area and regional vocational technical schools.

Table 2.1, adapted from Gray and Herr (1995), suggests the variety of high-skill/high-wage occupations in which technicians are the primary job emphasis and for which a baccalaureate degree is not required.

The Social Psychology of Work

In addition to changing the mix of jobs, advanced technology, particularly computer technology, has also changed the social psychology of work. Kipnis (1997) has analyzed three stages of technology—craft, mechanized, and automated—and concluded that technology can affect how people explain their own and others' behavior and the attributions they use to talk about their feelings of competence and satisfaction. In these perspectives, technology defines our world; it both restricts and facilitates the choices we can make, providing great latitude in some instances and almost none in others; and it alters people's mental representations of their options and responsibility for processes and outcomes.

In particular, Kipnis argued that

> technology is altering day-to-day relations between people in dramatic ways. Robots, computers, audio and video entertainment centers . . . are freeing people from the need to depend on each other on a daily basis. With increasing frequency, we are using new technologies, rather than others, to do our work, to provide us with goods and services, to entertain us, and to give us emotional support and companionship. (p. 210)

Thus the implementation of computers has redefined the social role of workers, changed the relationships among workers in organizations, and changed the flow and exchange of information within organizations. For some workers the installation of computers in the workplace has engendered more autonomy, but for others it has imposed new ways of monitoring worker productivity, exerting social or organizational control, and altering employee and management relationships (Jackson, L. A., 1987). In these instances, computer monitoring of worker output may reduce worker pacing of work, decrease autonomy and self-initiative, increase conforming behavior, alter social relationships and communication, and stimulate worker reactions against technology or attempts to circumvent it. Depending upon how computers are designed and implemented in a particular work setting, they can either "de-skill" the

Table 2.1   Worker Elite High-Skill/High-Wage Occupations Not Requiring a Baccalaureate Degree

Craft and construction
 Construction drafting
 Construction project manager
 Heating/air-conditioning technician
 Plumbing/pipe-fitting technician
 Precision welding
 Specialized carpentry and installation
 Specialized interior finishing and installation

Health occupations
 Dental assistant
 Dental hygienist
 Emergency medical technician
 Home health aide
 Licensed practical nurse
 Medical laboratory technician
 Medical record rechnician
 Optometric technician
 Radiology technician
 Surgical technologist

Manufacturing
 Computer-controlled-equipment operator
 Drafting technicians
 Electronics engineering technician
 Electronics lab technician
 Engineering technician

 Manufacturing systems operators
 Manufacturing technician

Service occupations
 Accountant
 Agribusiness sales
 Automatic office manager
 Commercial design
 Computer graphics specialist
 Criminal justice and corrections
 Data processing manager
 Fire fighters
 Law enforcement/protection occupations
 Library technician
 Paralegal
 Professionally trained chef
 Specialty auto mechanic

Technical service, repair, and installation
 Airframe mechanic
 Avionics repair technician
 Biomedical equipment technician
 Computer systems installation and repair
 Electromechanical repair technician
 Telecommunications installations and
  repair

Note: From K. Gray and E. L. Herr, *Other Ways to Win: Creating Alternatives for High School Graduates,* 1995, Thousand Oaks, CA: Corwin Press. Copyright © 1995 by Corwin Press. Reprinted by permission.

worker or enhance the worker's role, or they can change a worker's role from one of high-task involvement to one of monitoring and troubleshooting what the computer does. Such shifts in workers' roles and self-perceptions in relation to computer technology may be positive or negative, enhancing or demeaning.

 One application of computers to work that has received considerable periodic enthusiasm is telecommuting. In such a situation, also called the *electronic cottage,* a worker with a computer terminal at home can perform tasks without being required to be at a central work location daily. Supposedly, such an arrangement reduces, if not eliminates, the travel from home to work each day, makes child care and parenting at home more feasible, and provides other benefits to people involved in telecommuting. However, available research data suggest that because telecommuting essentially isolates workers and removes them from the social relationships most people consider important at work, many workers find that the positive features of telecommuting are offset by the negative effects of isolation or the inability of some workers to structure their work at home. Certainly, not all telecommuting workers view the situation as negative. Those who have high-demand, essentially irreplaceable skills, who can control the pace and style of their work, and who work at home for personal growth reasons may find telecommuting a positive and exciting opportunity. For others, however, the widespread application of telecommuting is likely to foster less optimistic and positive views.

Computers also can alter the flow and the amount of information as well as how it is presented and communicated. As such, the computer can redistribute power in an organization, change decision-making assumptions and processes, and alter specific individual and organizational communication patterns. For example, "When workers use electronic mail, the nature of their interactions shifts. Terminal users lack the nonverbal communication clues, have few norms of interaction, and have developed a communication which is more content centered" (Jackson, L. A., 1987, p. 258).

Helgesen (1996), in discussing the dominant need for knowledge workers in an increasing number of emerging occupations and knowledge organizations, indicated that employees in such contexts are no longer interchangeable ciphers. They are instead knowledge workers subject to continual upgrading—just like the tools they use, which are primarily technological in nature. More specific to the social psychology of work, then, Helgesen observed that

> those in the ranks have at their command powerful technologies that give them access to a depth and range of information that was formerly restricted to those at the top, as well as the means to apply that information directly in their work. Technology is the key here, for by quickly disseminating all kinds of specialized information throughout the organizations, today's sophisticated networks erase industrial-era distinctions between those who make decisions and those who carry them out, between those who conceive of tasks and those who execute them. . . . Power is then vested at every level in today's organization; this is what makes them flexible and lean. (pp. 26–27)

Much more can be said about how technology, particularly computer technology, modifies work environments, communications, and social relationships. In many ways, such issues of social technology are only now becoming the focus of research. Undoubtedly, however, counselors dealing with workers who are experiencing techno-stress, feelings of isolation, de-skilling, or other behavioral manifestations will want to explore in depth the growing literature on computers and the social psychology of work.

A further, less visible trend associated with advanced technology worldwide is a major process of urban-regional restructuring of job availability and population location. The implementation of high or advanced technology frequently alters the environments in which jobs are located and causes some population shifts. These characteristics suggest that the location of high-tech manufacturing is not a random event (Lyons & Luker, 1996). Rather, the geography, the demographics, and the political environment of a location has much to do with its suitability for high-tech manufacturing. Other issues in the location of high-tech industries deserve mention as well. For example, depending upon the type of advanced technology involved, geographic locations must also have the appropriate infrastructure (e.g., water, sewer systems, transportation networks, electricity) in place to satisfy the needs of a particular industry. In many parts of the United States, because of zoning, inadequate resources, or lack of planning, the infrastructure available is unsuitable to the placement of industries that emphasize advanced technology. Again, whereas some geographic problems can be offset by the linkages across decentralized management or production units that advanced communication technologies provide, political, union, and tax structure considerations, the availability of suitable pools of workers, or other matters may preclude implementing high-tech manufacturing in a particular area. As such circumstances evolve, regional differences across the nation increase rather than decrease the likelihood that people in particular regions will experience major differences in occupational opportunities, quality of life, income and cost-of-living differentials, education and training, and other disparities (Deming, 1996). In the views of some observers, technological innovation is the prime mover in economic development, and high-tech or research and development (R & D) industries are the crucial locus of innovation.

> Through relationships with other industries, technological innovations spawn new generations of products as they diffuse through the economy. In addition, some scholars have argued that R & D intensive industry's ability to spawn new products and processes generates a synergistic and quite positive combination of effects at the regional and local levels: rapid and self-sustaining employment growth, dense networks of linkages between firms, rapidly expanding markets, and high rates of new business formation. (Lyons & Luker, 1996, p. 15)

However, these conditions also stimulate migration within and across national boundaries, urban congestion and stress, widening of the gap between rich and poor, erosion of family and community support systems, and changes in family structures. These conditions engender a dilution of feelings of personal responsibility for our fate, a blurring of behavioral sanctions that tend to control individual behaviors, and other conditions that create a seedbed of mental health and career development problems of major importance to the shape and substance of counseling services. More will be said about these matters shortly.

THE OCCUPATIONAL STRUCTURE

However one defines *advanced technology* or *high technology*, it seems clear that technology itself will be a pervasive factor in the future transformation of the American society. Whether we term what is now happening within the economy, the international environment, and the national rhetoric a function of the Third Wave, as does Toffler (1980), or the Next American Frontier, as does Reich (1983), or the Age of Paradox, as does Handy (1994), it is clear that the occupational structure of the future will not be what has prevailed in the past. The environment in which work takes place and the possibilities for work will change. The context for employability will change. And the effects of those changes will vary from one group of youth and adults to another.

One of the problems with the current transitions in the occupational structure is understanding the timing of the changes in work that are likely to occur as well as predicting the occupations likely to emerge, decrease, or vanish. Current perspectives on these matters as they appear in the popular press tend to disagree with available research studies. Although the onslaught and the effects of advanced technology in the future are likely to be dramatic, counselors and other mental health specialists have an obligation to help their students or clients keep such matters in perspective. For example, Levitan and Johnson (1982) reminded us a decade and a half ago that although we have the technology to transform the workplace and to incorporate mechanization of work in great magnitude, even with tax incentives the costs of such dramatic shifts will be enormous and beyond the capability of many firms. Many employers will have to find ways to compete in the marketplace other than by incorporating new or advanced technologies simply because they are available. This reality is likely to cause many firms to give new and creative attention to the use of human resources, which in turn will provide new opportunities for counselors in business and industry. What seems to be happening is that many firms are trying to incorporate technology to increase their productivity and also find new ways to nurture and develop their human resources.

Indeed, the argument can be made that even though technology adaptation has become routine in jobs from the least demanding to the most sophisticated, there are in fact relatively few occupations that can be defined as *high tech.* Such a view stands in contrast to the perspectives of some futurists that a majority of occupations will require sophisticated skills in technology and information processing. In part because of increasingly user-friendly technology, rising educational experiences and technology skills in many entrants to the workplace, and better training in technology, the proportion of high-technology jobs in the occupational structure has remained fairly stable since the early 1980s. Although government estimates of how many jobs could really be considered high tech in content have ranged up to about 13.8% of all nonfarm jobs, the actual calculations of such jobs indicate that about 7.5% of all nonfarm jobs in the U.S. economy could be considered high-tech jobs or occupations (Lyons & Luker, 1996). That figure is expected to remain at about the same level into the early decade of the 21st century.

One way to understand the apparent discrepancy between the attention in this book and in the mass media on the effects of technology in the society and in the workplace and the relatively small number of high-technology jobs or occupations is to understand how government describes high-technology industries and its effects on the labor force. In these cases, *high-technology* is used to refer to those industries where technology is being rapidly exploited or the state of the art in product development is rapidly changing because of scientific or technological breakthroughs. For example, industries focusing on electronics, telecommunications, aircraft, computer and office equipment, and biochemistry or genetic engineering are often cited as high-technology industries.

There are actually several categories of industries dealing with technology. One consists of those that are by the nature of their processes and purposes truly high technology, and another consists of those industries that are technology intensive. Yet another category consists of those industries in which high technology is not a major factor in its own right even though automated and computerized systems may be used to facilitate the products that are the primary thrust of such industries. Researchers from the Bureau of Labor Statistics of the U.S. Department of Labor have added two additional categories within the most technology-oriented industries: R & D-intensive high-tech industries and R & D-moderate high-tech industries (Hadlock, Hecker, & Gannon, 1991). These differences in high-tech industries are determined in part by (a) research and development expenditures as a percentage of the gross product originated by a company and (b) percentage of scientists, engineers, and technicians in the total employment of the industry. Said another way, high-technology industries are those that consider their major business to be the *creation* of high technology, whereas technology-intensive industries are those that significantly *employ* high-technology products even if they do not themselves create such products. Industries that do not fit either of these categories neither create nor significantly employ high-technology products, although there may be selected jobs or processes in that industry that employ high-technology products.

What is sometimes difficult to understand from a career counseling standpoint is that not every job or occupation in a high-technology or technology-intensive industry is a high-technology occupation. Projections differ, but it is expected that only somewhere between 15% and 20% of jobs or occupations involved in a high-technology industry are high-technology occupations. Such language sounds contradictory, but it really is not. The point is that even in industries that create high-technology products (pharmaceuticals, advanced electronics, or telecommunications equipment) most workers are not high-tech specialists such as scientists, researchers, engineers, and computer programmers. They are instead support people such as administrative and clerical workers, truck drivers, and assembly line operators. The ratio of such support people to those in high-technology occupations may range from 20:1 to 5:1. In non-high-technology or non-technology-intensive occupations, such proportions of non-high-technology jobs may be higher in some industries specializing in personal care, in which where there are virtually 100% non-high-technology jobs.

These statistics imply that because high technology and high-technology occupations compose a relatively small proportion of total employment and are not expected to grow significantly faster than the rest of the economy of the occupational structure, it is not likely that high-technology industries on a national basis will absorb large numbers of unemployed and dislocated workers. The further point is that although new jobs and occupations are created by the growth of advanced or high technology, these jobs may expand at a rapid rate but will numerically account for only a relatively small proportion of all new growth in jobs.

Tables 2.2 and 2.3 illustrate several important points for career planning. One is that there is a significant difference between occupations in which there will be the largest amount of job growth through 2005 and beyond and those occupations in which there is likely to be the fastest growth. Table 2.2 depicts the occupations with the largest growth, and Table 2.3 depicts those occupations with the fastest growth.

As we analyze the occupations included in Tables 2.2 and 2.3, several important observations can be made. One is that of the 20 occupations having the largest numerical increase in employment, only one (systems analysts) is clearly a high-technology occupation, although we could make the argument that some general managers and top executives may be engaged in high-technology industries and have come from a high-technology occupation. A second observation is that many of the 20 occupations with the largest numerical growth through 2005 are support occupations with modest requirements for education, relatively large turnover, and lower pay. Included in this category are such jobs as cashiers, janitors and cleaners, retail salespersons, waiters and waitresses, home health aides, guards, receptionists and information clerks, truck drivers, secretaries, child-care workers, general utility maintenance repairers, and nursing aides, orderlies, and attendants. Thus these 12 occupational categories can be filled with persons with a high school diploma or less. Further, of the 20 occupational categories represented, the majority are in service occupations with differing possible uses of technology, but not in technology-intensive occupations. In only four of the occupational categories is a college degree likely to be necessary for employment.

This does not imply, however, that persons in these jobs are not expected to be able to read and write, calculate numerically, have good judgment and interpersonal skills, and be teachable and able to adapt to change in their roles and in the processes

Table 2.2   Occupations Having the Largest Numerical Increase in Employment, 1994–2005

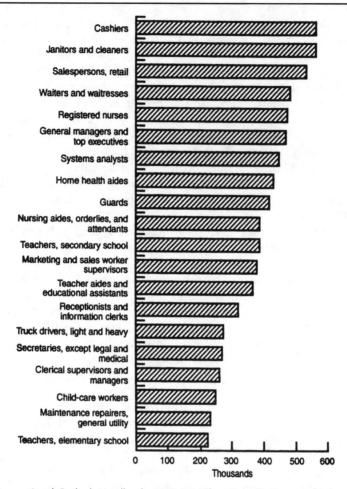

Note: From *Occupational Outlook Handbook, 1996–97,* (Chart 5, p. 3), Bureau of Labor Statistics, 1996, Washington, DC: Government Printing Office.

they use to do their job. Such requisites are becoming important expectations across the spectrum of occupations.

When we turn to Table 2.3, the fastest growing occupations, a somewhat different picture emerges. Four of the 20 occupations are high-technology occupations: systems analysts, computer engineers, electronic pagination systems workers, and operations research analysts. Eight of the 20 occupations are likely to require a college degree, and again, virtually all 20 of the occupations are in service roles, not direct manufacturing. These trends toward service occupations and away from manufacturing occupations are becoming increasingly pronounced and are validating the earlier projections of Personick (1985) that "almost 9 out of every 10 of these new jobs will be added in a service-producing industry (transportation, communications, public utilities, trade, finance, insurance, real estate, miscellaneous services, and government)" (p. 26).

Table 2.3   Occupations Projected to Grow the Fastest, 1994–-2005

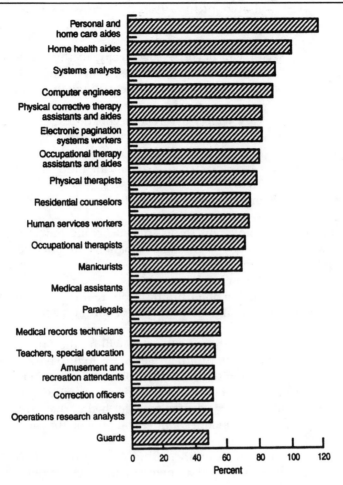

Note: From *Occupational Outlook Handbook, 1996–97,* (Chart 6, p. 3), Bureau of Labor Statistics, 1996, Washington, DC: Government Printing Office.

As the data provided in Tables 2.2 and 2.3 suggest, the continuing dilemma for people exploring job entry and for those considering retraining is to balance the search for occupations among those that have the largest number of job openings, those that have a small number of jobs but the fastest growing opportunities, and those that are declining in opportunity. Such analyses need then to be considered in terms of specific educational requirements, the degree to which specific jobs are available within the geographic boundaries to which an individual has committed him- or herself, and the other traditional factors of an individual's aptitudes, interests, and values.

In more specific reference to the data reported here are some specific trends to the year 2005 that may be of use to consider. These are abridged from the *Occupational Outlook Handbook, 1996–97* (Bureau of Labor Statistics, 1996, pp. 1–6):

- Service-producing industries will account for most new jobs: Business, health, and education services will account for 70% of the growth within services; and health care services will account for almost one fifth of all job growth from 1994 to 2005.
- The goods-producing sector will decline: Specifically, in this sector mining and manufacturing jobs will decline with jobs in construction likely to increase, and systems analysts and other computer-related occupations in manufacturing are expected to increase.
- Employment change will vary widely by broad occupational groups: Professional specialty occupations (which require high educational attainment and offer high earnings) and service occupations (which require lower educational attainment and offer lower earnings) are expected to account for more than half of all job growth between 1994 and 2005.
- The fastest growing occupations reflect growth in computer technology and health services.
- Declining occupational employment stems from declining industry employment and technological change: Many declining occupations are affected by structural changes, resulting from technological advances, organizational changes, and other factors that affect the employment of workers.
- Education and training affect job opportunities: Jobs requiring the most education and training will grow faster than jobs with lower education and training requirements.
- Jobs requiring the most education and training will be the fastest growing and highest paying: Education is important in getting a high paying job; however, many occupations (such as registered nurses, blue-collar workers, supervisors, electrical and electronic technicians/technologists, carpenters, and police and detectives), do not require a college degree yet offer higher than average earnings.
- Jobs requiring the least education and training will provide the most openings but offer the lowest pay.
- Women will continue to comprise an increasing share of the labor force: Women, as a result of a faster rate of growth than men, are projected to represent a slightly greater portion of the labor force in 2005 than in 1994—increasing from 46% to 48%.
- The labor force will become increasingly diverse: The number of Hispanics, Asians, and other races will increase much faster than Blacks and White non-Hispanics; and Blacks will increase faster than White non-Hispanics even though the latter will make up the vast majority of workers in 2005.

Data such as these need to be considered from several perspectives. One is that projections are not absolute realities. Political decisions, economic downturns, war, and other events can alter the trends identified here. Also, even in occupations that are declining there are still opportunities. People retire, die, or take other occupations, thereby creating vacancies for people who really want to be in a specific occupation. Thus even if the long-term future of a particular occupation is less favorable than that of another occupation, these are relative matters that do not suggest an absolute lack of opportunity in a particular industry or occupation.

What is apparent in the trends reported here is that employment opportunities will continue to grow in virtually all occupations from 1995 to 2005. So-called declining industries, those where the proportion of total employment is expected to decline in the future, will actually have more workers in 2005 than in 1995. New jobs will continually be added to the economy, with the result that the civilian work force is expected to grow from 129 million in 1995 to 147 million by 2005. Jobs requiring more education and more complexity, however, will grow more rapidly than occupations requiring minimal education and training. To a large degree, such phenomena reflect the effects of advanced technology, computerization, and automation on the content of work and the requirement for skills that are not easily automated. Another important statistic is that women will account for much more of the growth in the labor force from 1995 to 2005. This attests to the rapid growth of two-worker families in America as well as a growing propensity of all women, regardless of marital status, to enter the job market. This development will be further explored in the next chapter.

Although there is much more that can be said about the specifics of and the changes in the occupational structure and the industries that provide employment to the labor force, these changes in their multiple ways are playing out the effects of many critical forces shaping and reshaping work and the workforce in the United States. At the beginning of the 1990s, Coates, Jarrat, and Mahaffie (1990) identified seven of these critical forces. Some of these have already been identified; several others have not. They include, in paraphrased and abridged form, the following:

- Increasing diversity in the workforce as women move into the executive suite, as Hispanics grow in numbers and influence, and as Black Americans and Asians increase in numbers and in the comprehensiveness of their job placements in the labor market.
- There is an apparent move toward reintegration of work life and home life as corporations adopt new programs to support child care and other family responsibilities of workers, as more work is done from home and other sites removed from the traditional workplace, and as human resource planning increasingly focuses on the worker as a corporate asset.
- The realities of the globalization of the workforce, of technical and scientific competition, and of technological implications related to where work is done has created new challenges for U.S. employers and corporations.
- Human resources planning has assumed new importance and new roles in a changing business and industrial world.
- Given the changing nature of work due to the emergence of new critical skills, training and reeducating for a knowledge-based workforce become new corporate priorities.
- There is a need to address rising employee expectations in the workplace related to health and other quality-of-life issues, and to strike a balance between such demands and their costs.
- Corporate social responsibility related to new forms of social covenants with workers, ethical issues, accountability, and other workplace issues are expanding the needs for new forms of management.

Many of these forces will be revisited in this chapter and in other parts of the book.

Not apparent in these statistics is what these trends mean for individuals and groups. What does it mean for exploration and job seeking? Even though the economy as a whole may be experiencing only a 4.5% unemployment rate, individuals who have not found work are 100% unemployed. How does being in this position affect mental health and self-perception? What are the implications for counselors of the effects of advanced technology on the mythologies and the realities of the occupational structure?

ADVANCED TECHNOLOGY, OCCUPATIONAL TRANSFORMATIONS, AND HUMAN BEHAVIOR

In the first part of this chapter we examined the myths and realities of advanced technology as a social metaphor for contemporary society and as a stimulant to occupational transformation. However, opinions about the rapidity and the extent to which advanced or high technology will alter the content, requirements, and opportunities for work differ. But as an overarching concept, it seems clear that the major problems associated with advanced technology are not scientific or technical problems; they are human problems and problems of "social technology."

There can be no doubt that the scientific and technological creativity is available throughout the world to build newer and more complex machine-machine systems, to miniaturize computer technology, to wed microelectronics and information processing, to alter the way work is done, to mechanize or robotize work, and to amend the interactions between people and machines. Similar changes occur in the biosciences, where we are rapidly achieving the abilities to do things biologically in a controlled manner, such as building biological organisms to accomplish specific industrial tasks, modifying plants and animals through genetic engineering, and significantly increasing our understanding of human biological and biochemical processes. As a function of the latter changes, the whole concept of people's working life span of the future may be different. Some observers believe that people will be provided the nutrition, the medicines, the artificial organs, or the joint replacements to retain their full mental and physical capacities into their 60s, 70s, 80s, and 90s. The traditional working life—leaving school or college at ages 18 to 25, working for 30 to 40 years, and retiring 5 to 10 years—will change. People will instead take a more flexible approach to multiple careers—working at two, three, or four careers, not merely changing jobs or occupations during their working lives. Thus people of the next century may return to school several times for training in a new field at ages as late as 60 or 70. At each of the transition points relating to multiple careers or the significant life events shaping such possibilities, the needs for values clarification, training and retraining, exploration, decision making, information, planning, support, and encouragement are likely to intensify.

These observations make clear that the process of technological change and occupational transformation throws a long shadow. Be they viewed through bioscientific, chemical, or technical lenses, the effects of technological change and economic transitions on each individual in the society of the future will probably be dramatic even if these individuals are not themselves in technological occupations. Such effects also are likely to be different for every youth or adult subgroup of the population. For some people the effects of technological change and occupational shifts will be primarily psychological; for others the effects will be direct and literal.

For children and youth, the combined effects of urbanization, large work organizations, and changes in the occupational structure will impede the process of exploring opportunities and gathering information. As more and more work occurs behind fences and in large organizations controlled by safety, liability, and governmental regulations, it is increasingly difficult for youth to observe and participate intimately in direct observations of work. For a growing number of occupations, direct experience in the workplace is not available, and simulations, reading descriptive material, and interviews with workers are the only feasible exploratory opportunities. When such problems are confounded by rapid shifts in education and training requirements, basic skills needed, and job content, informational sources tend to lag behind and complicate exploration.

For many adult workers, the main issue accompanying technological change in the workplace is obtaining appropriate retraining. Finding out what incentives and opportunities for retraining are available becomes important to such workers, as do concerns about what they should retrain for. Other personal questions concern the degree to which people need to be retrained. Do they need 15% new skills or 100% new skills? Are any of their existing job skills sufficiently elastic to be useful in their new occupations? What are they? How do they recognize and reinforce them? Rather than be retrained, should they seek employment in another location where they might be able to use their current skills? If they become retrained, how will this affect the career path available to them?

Some subgroups of adult workers are likely to have additional questions about their potential vulnerability. For example, women may be disproportionately affected by the effects of technology, particularly information technologies, on clerical work. In both the United States and Canada, clerical work has replaced domestic service as the primary form of female employment (Protti, Shulman, & Kirby, 1985). Aging workers are likely to be concerned about whether their employers will expend the funds to retrain them or whether they will be released. For some minority group members, the issue may be how to retain whatever economic gains they already have made. How do they avoid heightened vulnerability in a time of economic and occupational transition?

For occupationally dislocated adults, the issue may be how to cope with the physical effects of stress-related diseases as well as the psychological trauma associated with the lack of identity, purpose, or income that may accompany unemployment. How will these adults cope with the feelings of victimization, grieving, and helplessness that accompany the loss of self in unemployment? How will they acquire the basic skills that data indicate 20% to 30% of occupationally dislocated workers are lacking (Cyert & Mowery, 1987)?

For other groups, particularly the least educated and new immigrants, the issue will be whether they can cope at all, whether they will be permanently unemployed in the wake of skill changes and work habits they cannot acquire. Clearly, many new immigrants and poorly educated workers are likely to experience multidimensional problems, including functional illiteracy in English; emotional, communication, or interpersonal problems that constrain their employability; dependency on government welfare programs or other types of income transfer that must be replaced by skills of independent living and responsibility for self and family; substance abuse; low self-esteem; child or spousal abuse; marital discord; lack of transportation; inadequate financial or nutrition management skills; or poor industrial discipline.

For the groups just identified and others, the effects of technological change in occupations will influence their feelings about security for themselves and their society, the achievement motives they are likely to pursue, and feelings about their ability to master the opportunities available. The concerns about which such people seek help are functions of how they view current occupational or social expectations and opportunities for personal choice, achievement, social interaction, self-initiative, prestige, role differentiation, and other matters. All of these concerns are likely to change as the choice environment or possibility structure perceived by the individual is altered by the application of new technology. The resulting anxieties, information deficits, or indecisiveness people experience is the content with which counselors and related professionals are concerned. As is suggested later in the chapter, such content may interact with other mental health issues such as depression, panic attacks, and antisocial behavior.

Available data suggest that the emerging structure of the U.S. economy may add new kinds of risk to workers' health and safety:

> Stress resulting from working conditions has become a major health hazard, resulting in stress-related absenteeism and medical expenses that may cost between $50 and $75 billion annually. In addition, alcoholism and drug abuse may be related to job-induced stress. The National Institute on Drug Abuse has estimated that U. S. firms lose $33 billion per year due to employee drug abuse. . . . While uncertainty in the American economy has often been greater, pressures can increase in periods of rapid change. Rapid change in working environments and management practices can lead to stress. Many new office jobs result in increased responsibility without increased authority—a combination that easily leads to stress. Increased use of electronic surveillance equipment may also contribute to stress. (Office of Technology Assessment, 1988, pp. 390–391)

In 1990, an international conference addressed the topic of Work and Well-being: An Agenda for the 1990s. The stimulus for this topic was international recognition that "psychological strain is quickly becoming one of the most prevalent, costly, and debilitating forms of occupational ill-health" (Keita & Sauter, 1992, p. vii). This conference addressed many of the factors relating to job stress and, indeed, work and mental health. The director of the National Institute of Occupational Safety and Health, who was a presenter at the conference, reported that "Today mental disorders are the leading cause for Social Security disability claims in the United States . . . Approximately 1 in 10 workers are suffering from depression, and the cost to society and business is nearly $27 billion dollars annually" (p. 5).

Herr and Cramer (1996) analyzed sources of growing job stress in the workplace and suggested that they include role conflict, inability to perform the tasks demanded effectively, uncertainty or inadequate knowledge about an event or events that require action or resolution, concern about the physical consequences of the work to be done and where it is to be done, participation in autonomous work groups and meeting the productivity expectations of co-workers, interpersonal relations with supervision, work overload and workplace ambiguous roles, work control experienced or exercised, perceived task demands, rewards and punishments in work, and time urgency. In their view, "These stressors, whether perceived or actual, are brought to the counselor as part of the worker's emotional response to the workplace. As such they become the content of career counseling and part of the expanding range of career issues with which counselors are increasingly confronted" (p. 6).

Such content is not static. It is constantly changing because of changes in the occupational structure, the larger society, and the life spaces of clients themselves. Perhaps the major concern for counselors is how their clients perceive what is happening to them and how they feel they can cope with it. How do they label and interpret what they are experiencing? Do they label the stresses associated with change in the work environment as personal inadequacy? Do they label changes in work opportunities as purely economic phenomena, or rather as the playing out of long-range and pervasive changes in the occupational structure itself? Do they see courses of potential action, or do they feel controlled and captured by the onslaught of forced automation and technological adaptation about which they can do nothing?

As suggested in chapter 1 and reinforced in this chapter, counseling is at the intersection, the junction of individual-environment interaction. It does not occur in a political, social, or economic vacuum. As such, it represents a switching mechanism between individual needs and skills and the freedom of choice, available information, and opportunities offered by a particular society or, indeed, a particular locale or work organization. Counseling also represents a mechanism to broker training and retraining opportunities for many workers, both those who are dislocated and those who are interested in enriched occupational opportunities in the future. Counselors can help workers differentiate among forms and structures of employment inside and outside of established labor markets, in government training schemes, in emerging small collectives of workers (who are willing to engage in contract work for firms for which such specialized work may not be economically feasible if their own labor force is used), in entrepreneurial behavior, and in self-employment. Counseling within or outside of business and industry can help workers who are dislocated, unhappy, maladjusted, underemployed, and unemployed with information, support, encouragement, or skill-building approaches that can facilitate hope, reduce feelings of social isolation and unworthiness, and provide stress reduction and management.

Counselor Needs and Roles in a Dynamic Occupational Environment

Within the individual-environment interactions, stimulated by the ripple effects of the science and technology described earlier in the chapter, the emotional aspects of life intensify under the influence of rapid change, and the educational and occupational structures become different and more diversified. Work organizations change. Choice environments change. Social metaphors change. As a result, a series of needs, implications, and issues for counselors emerge.

At the most superficial levels, information about emerging technologies and their effects is important. Counselors working with people affected by technological change need to know about changing requirements of the workplace for different skills and types of employability. Counselors will need to think of person-job fit in new work forms in which temporary work as well as entrepreneurial and cooperative behavior is maximized. It will be important to know about those occupations that are most vulnerable to the replacement of human workers by mechanization and about new occupations being created, the skills they require, and how to train for them. Counselors will need to know about the elasticity of skills as people try to move from occupation to occupation, which in turn are variously affected by technological shifts.

But counselors must guard against allowing themselves or their clients to assume that the world of work will suddenly be transformed into something that has no resemblance to the present. Although new technologies will create many new occupations in the future, the availability of such occupations will be uneven in the timing of their emergence, and therefore, many present occupations will continue to have job openings into the foreseeable future even as the numbers of such opportunities may decrease. Indeed, however different in work mode or use of technologies the occupations of the future may be, current occupations will in many cases serve as the foundation for future occupations. For example, a gene splicer is still likely to be a biologist with a specialty in genetics. A fiber optics technician will probably be related to the physicist of today. Environmental engineers can be specialists in air pollution control, radiological health, solid wastes, industrial hygiene, sanitation, water pollution control, or environmental safety compliance. But they are still engineers, and their conceptual integrity is likely to be rooted in much of what is known today. Although many new occupations will spring from the ranks of existing occupations, it is also likely that there will be expansions in the mergers of intellectual disciplines and in the growth of hybrid occupations such as today's biochemists, geophysicists, and bionicists.

Furthermore, although emerging data suggest that adaptations to microelectronics, information technologies, and other forms of advanced technology do require qualitative differences in worker skills, this does not mean that old skills will become totally obsolete. For example, in Japan, surveys of employees engaged in adapting microelectronics to the workplace have found that workers are required to adapt to changes in working conditions by acquiring a variety of new skills that build on conventional skills. Only 15% of the Japanese enterprises surveyed mentioned the necessity of new skills to replace present skills (Watanabe, 1984). From a psychological standpoint, it is a different matter entirely to learn additional skills than it is to start over from essentially a zero point. Japan's experience suggests that the latter is not the rule even in highly sophisticated microelectronics adaptation. The communication of such insights by counselors to workers and to potential workers will become increasingly important.

The implications for counselors that stem from the effects of advanced technology in the workforce are not confined to needs for different kinds of information about emerging occupations and job content. Counselors also need to rethink how changes in advanced technology affect different groups seeking work. For example, counselors will need to be sensitive to how changes in the employment environment affect persons with disabilities, such as slow learners, the learning disabled, and the mentally handicapped. Will such people experience reduced choices and more vulnerable personal identities as a result of employers' or policymakers' assumptions that the only work skills needed in a high-tech society are intellectual and problem-solving skills? Counselors will obviously hold important roles as advocates for such populations as interpreters of both the myths and realities of advanced technology, and of the characteristics of learning disabled or mentally disabled workers. Counselors will have important roles not only in helping clients with disabilities make meaningful transitions to employment but also in helping employers to foster job redesign, realistic employment and training policies, and work environments that provide opportunity and dignity for such persons.

Another population of growing concern to counselors are the physically disabled. The positive effects of science and technology, particularly medical science, are especially apparent in this population. Forty years ago, a spinal cord injury at the neck resulting in quadriplegia typically meant death within days or weeks because of kidney failure or infection. Now because of medical advances, a 20-year-old with quadriplegia can expect to live to age 62 (over 82% of an individual's expected life span without injury). But what about this person's quality of life, opportunities to work, dignity, and self-respect? As persons with disabilities grow in proportion to the total population because of the advances of medical science, their well-being and effective participation in the workforce will constitute new counseling challenges (Vachon, 1987).

Counselors increasingly will be required to consider the effects of advanced technology at the social level as well as at the individual level. Important questions are rapidly emerging about family changes that may result from using the home as a workplace because of telecommuting, the opportunities to conduct business (e.g., sales, accounting, inventory control) from home through computer networking, and the decentralization of the workplace. Other questions relate to the effects of changes in work times from 9 a.m. to 5 p.m. to virtually anytime during the 24-hour clock when people who have computers at home want to work. And what will be the effects upon the balance of work and leisure and family configurations occasioned by flextime, more dual-career families, and shifts in role differentiation between the sexes? Some of these issues will be addressed in the following chapters. But these are only a few of the types of questions and information requirements associated with the pervasive advances of technology in the society. Other areas need to be considered as well.

As a result of the increasing mechanization of work, more discretionary time is likely to be available for most individuals, although this will vary across the occupational structure. During the past century the average weekly hours of work have decreased from 60 to 40 hours and are now approaching 37 hours per week or less in some industries. These are typically defined as *hours at the workplace*. As such, they obscure the fact that in many of the professional and technical occupations, because of the information handling and abstract aspects of work, the boundaries between working and not working become blurred. Nevertheless, time off the job will probably grow for many segments of the workforce because of the increases in productivity achieved through technological adaptation. A major point of interest to counselors is that such leisure time is not an unmixed blessing to people; its availability differs among people, and the ability to use leisure time without experiencing additional stress or conflict varies widely.

As early as the 1950s, mental health specialists were concerned that leisure time and its use were problematic for many. A.R. Martin, a chair of the American Psychiatric Association's Committee on Leisure Time and Its Use, made the following observation:

> We must face the fact that a great majority of our people are not emotionally and psychologically ready for free time. This results in unhealthy adaptation which finds expression in a wide range of sociopathologic and psychopathologic states. Among the social symptoms of the maladaptation to free time are low morale, civil unrest, subversiveness, and rebellion. (Theobald, 1966, pp. 55–56)

The importance of leisure counseling or education for the constructive use of leisure as a significant professional counseling activity will need to grow as advances in the adaptation of technology continue to affect the balance of work/nonwork time for larger segments of the population.

Brought on by advanced technology, the era of overchoice, which Toffler (1970) described as the result of rapid value and social shifts, is likely to continue to spawn stress-related diseases (which some other observers have labeled *techno-stress*), depression, apathy, and an increase in interpersonal violence. As a result, there will be a growing understanding that problems of dislocation and unemployment breed both physiological trauma and psychological disorders. (The specifics of such relationships will be explored in the next section of this chapter.) Indeed, the behavioral and psychological correlates of techno-stress and future shock may be exacerbated in the future as awareness increases that the nation is really pluralistic in lifestyles, languages, values, and belief systems and that such heterogeneity will expand dramatically in the future. A shifting racial and ethnic balance changes the traditional views many citizens hold of common purpose, language, and motive systems in ways that affect the manner and contexts in which work is done. Chapter 4 will suggest that America has never been as homogeneous in languages, traditions, and beliefs as the melting-pot metaphor suggests, and that the new reality of pluralism requires amendments to how work is viewed, structured, and rewarded in the future. Bilingualism among workers in the future is likely to be more generally prized. Growing interdependence among workers in different settings and with different backgrounds is likely to increase the need for greater attention to conflict resolution, effective communication, and interpersonal skill development in all types of occupations and settings. Counselors will need to understand and be prepared to work with the problems generated by such situations.

A major future issue is that careers are likely to be defined to include not only vertical but horizontal movement in recognition of the need to provide increased opportunities for people to develop new skills, solve different problems, and work with a variety of colleagues without necessarily being promoted within an organization in the traditional sense. Thus occupational mobility will probably be viewed not only as competitive but also as complementary. Such a shift will affect the types of assessment and the kinds of measures necessary in career or employment counseling. New conceptions of work will prize employees' adaptability as well as higher levels of communication, problem-solving, and analytical skills. The generalist who can handle ideas and is flexible and teachable will probably be more prized in the future.

In the future, counselors and other career guidance specialists may work in a field-based way with teams of workers to deal with work adjustment in situ, at its source, rather than in some abstract or vicarious fashion. This tactic could permit counselors to use work as a form of behavior modification and to provide counseling immediately as problems arose at work. Obviously, such techniques can be applied in other work situations. Counselors are increasingly employed directly in business or industry, or as contracted specialists in employer assistance programs, to assist employees who have been referred because of work-related or other problems that interfere with their work and productivity (e.g., chemical dependence, family relationships, bereavement).

The Counselor in the Workplace

Because of a network of factors—the effects of advanced technology, corporate mergers, changing demographics of the workforce, trends toward later retirement, growing worker concerns about the quality of life, economic competitiveness—the view of workers held by business and industry is undergoing change. Workers are being seen increasingly in holistic terms, as people who do not leave their family and personal problems at the door when they enter the workplace, nor leave work problems in the office when they go home. Thus terms such as *employee assistance programs, human resource development, career management,* and *career services* are rapidly entering the vocabulary of business and industry. Workers increasingly are seen as corporate resources to be nurtured, not used up and cast away, and as human capital that needs its own preventive maintenance in the forms of education, training, counseling, and information about mobility within the firm as well as help in preparing for such opportunities rather than encouragement to hop from one job to another across corporations. Employers have learned that hiring and firing workers costs money, time, and productivity. Loyalty of the workforce is at issue just as is the reputation and the public perception of the corporation locally. Closing plants precipitously, laying off workers without regard for their welfare, and fostering high levels of employee turnover bring social costs to the corporation as well as disruption and stress to the lives of the affected workers. In such contexts, more and more corporations are trying to mix high tech with "high touch," the latter being the notion of providing workers with opportunities for personal growth, for further education, and for matching their talent, knowledge, experiences, and abilities to emerging opportunities in the corporation. High touch encourages internal mobility and provides challenge. Corporations can no longer be content with personnel management but must grow in their emphasis on personnel development. As Naisbitt and Aburdene (1985) indicated, powerful trends are at work to transform the business environment and to compel companies to reinvent themselves. One of these major trends is "the shift in strategic resources from financial capital in the industrial society to human capital in the information society" (p. 13).

Examining the most effective companies in the United States reveals that their techniques are not simply altruistic; they have come to realize that the employee's growth and the company's growth are compatible and mutually nourishing (Naisbitt & Aburdene, 1985, p. 54). In implementing such concepts, various companies are engaging in such people-oriented approaches as

- getting more of the most experienced, senior people out of their offices and working with younger talent;
- instituting flexible hours;
- creating an intellectually stimulating environment;
- organizing travel/learning experiences;
- awarding sabbaticals to creative people;
- structuring jobs holistically to stretch, develop, and integrate new skills;
- moving people laterally to develop well-roundedness;
- recreating the role of manager as that of coach, teacher, and mentor;
- redesigning management to include networking and employee/management sharing of responsibility; and
- rewarding and nurturing creativity, independent thinking, and the entrepreneurial spirit within workers at all levels of the organization (Naisbitt & Aburdene, 1985, pp. 54, 56).

Some companies are engaged in an intensive analysis of the fit between new technologies and the companies' organizational context. Such ideas, called *sociotechnical systems design,* are concerned about how management must change and how interrelationships among workers must be altered to integrate new technologies successfully (Davis, 1986).

Hall and his associates (1996) have updated the concepts presented by Naisbitt and Aburdene (1985) and Davis (1986) a decade ago and embedded them in a series of new and emerging concepts that seem almost radical in their implications for the content of the workplace and in their implications for the practice of career special- ists. Because of the rapidly changing workplace structures, contingent workforces, pervasiveness of technological applications in the workplace, and the increase of knowledge workers, Hall and his associates have predicted a reduction in organiza- tional careers and the unfolding of what they call *protean careers*. In contrast to the loyalty, identity, subordination of individual desires to institutional criteria of success, and control of the worker, the protean career is defined differently. It is seen as a career that is driven more by the individual than by the organization. It calls "for frequent change and self-invention and . . . [is] propelled by the desire for psychological success rather than by externally determined measures of success" (p. xi). In addition,

> the protean career encompasses any kind of flexible, idiosyncratic career course, with peaks and valleys, left turns, moves from one line of work to another, and so forth. Rather than focusing outward on some ideal generalized career "path," the protean career is unique to each person—a sort of career fingerprint. (p. 21)

The protean concept provides a different way of thinking about the relationship between the organization and employee: "in the protean career, the person is figure, and the organization is ground. Organizations provide a context, a medium in which individuals pursue their personal aspirations" (Hall & Mirvis, 1996, p. 21). To pursue a protean career individuals will need to be highly adaptable and flexible, possess a depth and variety of skills desired by employers, and have varied work experience as well as a clear sense of self-identity, autonomy, and personal direction so that they are able to self-design much of their personal and career development. They will also need skills in self-assessment and identity exploration, and a commitment to learning how to learn and to continuous learning.

These notions of the individual requirements for a protean career reflect both the changing nature of work organizations and of technology. The argument is that because the life cycle of technologies and products is so shortened, personal mastery cycles related to these processes and products are also shortened. Therefore, "people's careers increasingly will become a succession of 'ministages' (or short-cycle learning stages) of exploration-trial-mastery-exit as they move in and out of various product areas, technologies, functions, organizations, and other work environments" (Hall & Mirvis, 1996, p. 33). Further,

> . . . this protean form of career involves horizontal growth, expanding one's range of competencies and ways of connecting to work and other people, as opposed to the more traditional vertical growth of success (upward mobility). In the protean form of growth, the goal is learning, psychological success, and expansion of the identity. In the more traditional vertical form, the goal was advancement, success, and esteem in the eyes of others, and power (p. 35).

To make such a protean career possible, the work environments that employ such individuals will need to offer opportunities to develop them and to care for them; the work environments will also need to provide meaningful and challenging work that is combined with fairness, good pay and benefits, support, and efforts to meet the needs of the whole person.

The types of work environments in which persons pursuing protean careers will flourish will also provide career services different from those traditionally related to organizational careers. The latter are those discussed through most of the rest of this chapter. In the workplace of the future in which protean careers are possible, a new psychological contract between employer and worker will emphasize not long-term employment guarantees, paternalism, and dependency, but rather training, growing, individual responsibility, empowerment, performing, and working hard (Hall, 1996). In such contexts, employees will be expected to take personal responsibility for maintaining their own learning and development and for their own career moves. Thus the guidelines for career practitioners, counselors, and others who work with employees pursuing protean careers and organizations that support them will

- start with the recognition that the individual owns the career;
- create information and support for the individual's own efforts at development;
- recognize that career development is a relational process and the career practitioner plays a broker role;
- become an expert in career information and assessment technology;
- become a professional communicator about their services and the new career contract;
- promote work planning, not career planning;
- promote learning through relationships and work;
- be an organizational interventionist;
- promote mobility and the value of learner identity; and
- develop the mind-set of using natural resources (assignments, jobs, teams, task forces, committees, feedback, performance review, mentoring, coaching) for development (Hall, 1996, pp. 318–325).

The procedures described by Naisbitt and Aburdene (1985) and by Hall and Associates (1996) may seem utopian, but they are being implemented in several of the most progressive of America's corporations and government agencies (such as General Electric, AT & T, Aetna, Xerox, National Aeronautics and Space Administration, and Government Accounting Office), and other firms are now following their lead. The implementing corporations and agencies have provided assessment centers, career resource centers, and computer-assisted career guidance programs or directories listing all of the education and training opportunities available in the corporation or agency as well as information on, for example, career ladders and requirements for specific jobs and for mobility to supervisory roles. Frequently these companies and government organizations provide career specialists to assist employees with their questions concerning career change and career mobility, work adjustment, and other issues. Certainly such provisions are uneven. Not every employer understands or implements such perspectives, and in many situations workers continue to experience less than enlightened personnel procedures. Even in the most progressive organizations and corporations, changes in management, in supervision, and in views of workers require time, reconfiguration of resources, and new information and support systems for workers and supervisors alike. It is in such environments that the roles of counselors, counseling psychologists, and specialists in employer assistance become increasingly important.

Leibowitz, Farren, and Kaye (1986), for example, contended that a major change is taking place as the focus shifts from career planning programs for individual employees to the broader area of career development within organizations (p. xiii). Such programs are vital, in the authors' judgment, in order to provide "an organized, formalized, planned effort to achieve a balance between the individual's career needs and the organization's workforce requirements" (p. 4). But such programs can also provide mechanisms to support changes in business organizations that are fluid and developing. It is for these reasons that career development as an area of expertise is likely to grow in importance as it plays a flexible and pivotal role in an organization's issues, concerns, and directions. One area of growing importance to which career development programs can offer support is "transformational management." Such a role includes helping

> employees and managers move from traditional formal structures to the less structured approaches of matrix management and temporary work relations; by educating employees to cope with life crises, role transitions, and other types of change; and by designing programs to, for example, overcome obsolescence and help employees enrich their jobs. (p. 275)

Whether in contemporary or futuristic terms, counselors in business and industry can anticipate involvement in a wide range of activities that fall under the rubric of career but tend to push the limits of such a term beyond its traditional meaning. These counselors are likely to be involved in such services as advisement and support for external training, alcohol/drug counseling, retirement planning, leading or initiating support groups for minorities and women in particular work specialties (e.g., in engineering), job separation or outplacement counseling, career exploration and examination of available career ladders, teaching of interviewing or advancement strategies, leading seminars on preparating for supervision or dealing with financial issues, family/marital counseling, working with training specialists to design specific training for groups of workers, coaching middle level managers about ways to facilitate the career development of those whom they supervise, career planning workshops, and development of formal mentorship programs.

In a survey of career development services within Canadian organizations, Bernes and Magnusson (1996) reported that the key goals for these services were to promote job satisfaction, enhance employee productivity, reduce employee turnover, and increase employee motivation. They found that the services available could be classified into three major emphases: career planning, career management, and life planning. In an in-depth study across 30 Canadian organizations with 1,000 to 18,000 employees, they investigated the presence of the career services identified in Table 2.4 within these organizations. Although no organization had most of these career development services, the listing of potential career services in career management, career planning, and life planning in Table 2.4 suggests the range of career services in which counselors in business and industry may be involved. The table also illustrates the reality that there are services provided in some organizations that relate primarily to the needs of the organization, which are typically termed *career management* services, and there are services primarily directed to individual needs, which are reflected in terms such as *career planning* and *life planning* or related terms (e.g., *career development*). In some organizations, there is an integration of services that meets the needs of both individuals and organizations. Ballantine (1993) has advocated the latter perspective in his work with British police organizations, and the research of O'Reilly, Chatman, and Caldwell (1991) has affirmed the view that the greater the fit between the individual and the organization, the higher the job satisfaction and the less the turnover.

Table 2.4 Career Planning, Career Management, and Life Planning Services Investigated by Bernes and Magnusson

Career planning	Recruitment procedures
Informal counseling by personnel staff	Personnel information system
Career counseling by supervisors	Job description and job evaluation
Job performance and development planning	Manpower forecasting
Career exploration programs	Skill inventories
Psychological testing and assessment	Job rotational programs
Career support groups	Flexible working arrangements (work at
Testing and feedback regarding aptitudes,	home, 4-day work week, etc.)
interests, etc.	Communication on training and
Referrals of external counselors and	development options
resources	Communication on job requirements
Training of supervisors in career counseling	Communication on career paths or ladders
Career counseling by specialized staff	Job posting and communication on job
counselors	vacancies
Individual self-analysis and planning	New employee orientation programs
workbooks	Job redesign
Assessment centers for career development	
purposes	**Life planning**
Career planning workshops	Personal financial planning
Informal mentorship programs	Family/marital counseling
Formal mentorship programs	Alcohol/drug counseling
Teaching of advancement strategies	Job separation counseling
	Workshops and communications on
Career management	retirement preparation
Performance appraisal: planning and	Interpersonal skills training
review	Time management
Promotion and transfer procedures	Stress management
Educational assistance programs	Weight control
External training and development	Nutrition
programs	Fitness
Designed training programs	First aid
Management succession and replacement	Preventative health care
planning	Safety
Communication of equal employment	Smoking cessation
opportunity and affirmative action plans	Formal employee assistance program
and policies	

Note: From "A Description of Career Development Services Within Canadian Organizations," by K. Bernes and K. Magnusson, 1996, *Journal of Counseling and Development,* 74(6), 569–574.

In the broadest of terms, the career services that career practitioners potentially engage in, as identified by Bernes and Magnusson, are frequently discharged by using combinations of career development tools. Gutteridge (1985) has classified these in a useful way into five categories. These are (with selected examples) as follows:

1. **self-assessment tools** (e.g., career workbooks);
2. **individual counseling** (e.g., by personnel staff, managers, professional counselors or outplacement specialists);

3. **internal labor market information/placement exchanges** (e.g., job posting, career ladders/career path planning, career resource centers, computerized career guidance information;
4. **organizational potential assessment processes** (e.g., assessment centers, replacement/succession planning, psychological testing); and
5. **developmental programs** (e.g., job rotation, internal or external workshops on human resource development topics, supervisor training, mentoring systems, support groups for selected employees).

Such a classification structure can be useful for purposes of planning the interventions that are most important in a particular workplace, and it can be updated as new tools are introduced. For example, the Internet and intranet might be added to the third category.

A variety of other surveys and opinions have suggested how and why counselors and counseling psychologists should be involved in industry. Leonards (1981) spoke of the appropriateness of counseling psychology's involvement in industry because of industry's emphasis on working with healthy personalities. Leonards suggested that among the roles of counseling psychologists should be counseling for resolution of midcareer issues, for retirement planning, and for specific career development concerns Osipow (1982, pp. 21–22) also suggested a broad range of contributions that counseling psychologists can make in an industrial setting. They include

- helping employees and managers identify hazards in work;
- training people to identify their work styles (especially those that might be deleterious to them) and teaching them how to change;
- clarifying the effects of repetitive work on people;
- clarifying the effects of transfers to new locations, especially if forced;
- helping relieve stresses and strains of the two-career family;
- helping relieve stresses experienced by people employed in boundary-spanning roles (e.g., jobs that require employees to split allegiances);
- helping relieve stresses in people with high interpersonal demands in their jobs;
- preparing employees for retirement;
- helping supervisors deal effectively with the process of job evaluation;
- helping with the special problems of entrepreneurs;
- helping employees deal with the problems of job loss;
- helping with the special problems of small business people;
- helping with the special problems of professionals;
- counseling employees in health care issues;
- counseling to encourage self-help and self-care; and
- performing family counseling.

Clearly, counselors as well as psychologists have roles to play in such areas as

- educating first-line supervisors and managers to current perspectives on job satisfaction, work motivation, and work performance;
- providing information to workers about career paths, career ladders, and the avenues and requirements for mobility within the organization;
- classifying workers with respect to their technical skills and their psychological needs in an attempt to maximize person-job fit with regard to content, supervisory style, and related factors;

- conducting workshops and seminars for workers designed to increase their understanding of their educational opportunities, their employability skills, and their understanding of the organizational characteristics with which they interact;
- consulting with managers about job redesign and work enrichment schemes;
- providing support groups for workers in various types of transitions (e.g., new jobs, geographical relocations, overseas transfers, shifting family structures); and
- providing individual counseling about work behavior and career development.

Another group of primary mental health professionals is emerging in support of career development services in business and industry. Although these persons may be counseling psychologists or counselors, their ranks tend to include social workers. The research of Hosie, West, and Mackey (1993) suggested that in terms of the services offered by agencies engaged in the provision of employee assistance programs (EAP), most are involved in the following five activities: (1) training of managers and supervisors to use EAP services, (2) evaluation and referral (internal or external) of substance abusers, (3) case consultation for supervisors, (4) crisis intervention, and (5) assessment.

It is important to reassert here that different groups of employees experience the stresses and strains of the modern workplace in different ways and respond in many forms. Emotional problems, problem drinking, mental health issues, and family dysfunction all contribute to absenteeism, industrial accidents, excessive use of sick leave, low productivity, and termination. So do feelings of powerlessness and being plateaued in career mobility. Counselors have contributions to make in resolving each of these sets of problems as they learn the language of industry, apply their skills to the problems of adults in transition, and create mechanisms by which workers can acknowledge and respond to an environment that demonstrates that it cares.

The descriptions of the effects of advanced technology and other shifts in the economic environment upon work and workers earlier in this chapter and in the next section accent the reality that personal adjustment and work adjustment exist in a symbiotic relationship. The workplace becomes an environment in which both positive and negative, healthy and unhealthy, and good and bad outcomes are stimulated; an environment in which conflicts, thwarted aspirations, and emotional baggage from life outside the workplace is brought into the workplace to filter and shape an individual's life as a worker. Therefore, career counseling, career assisting, and career intervention in the future will be a much more complex blend of development and remediation, of education and skill facilitation.

But it is inappropriate to argue that the only place where counselors and clients will be affected by advanced technology and economic shifts is the workplace. Counselors in schools and universities as well will have expanded roles to play in preparing youth to anticipate and prepare for the changes in the work environment and opportunity structure that have been depicted throughout this chapter.

Counselors in Schools and Universities

Indeed, within the educational reform movements of many nations, attempts are under way to make schooling more career relevant. Students need help with understanding themselves as well as understanding available opportunities and necessary skills to plan and prepare for work more systematically and purposefully. As the industrialized and developing nations have entered developmental phases in which the relationships between education and work are seen as taking on new and interdependent forms, they have developed approaches to infuse academic subject matter with career development concepts. Now widely available are decision-making courses and experiences; required courses on the principles of technology to help students envision the effects of advanced technology in the workplace and in the occupational structure; career resource centers; expanded contacts between schools and the larger community; work study, work shadowing, and work experience schemes; apprenticeship opportunities; and other career-related mechanisms in communities, schools, and workplaces.

In the United States and several other nations, there has been a major shift over the past decade from the availability of career counseling or career guidance in schools as a random, one-on-one support process to career counseling or guidance as a program that is accountable for specific educational or career-related outcomes. National guidelines and competence statements have been developed to identify the content of these systematic career guidance programs. As a result, major advances have been made in identifying career guidance goals, identifying career guidance resources, and evaluating career guidance outcomes. In general, these comprehensive career guidance programs have been built around what might be described as career development curricula that translate theory and research in career development into curriculum materials designed for use with individuals, small groups, or classroom-size groups. These materials are delivered in career guidance workshops, group approaches, self-directed modules, or in conjunction with computer-assisted approaches. Most career guidance programs are built around specific clusters of career development tasks described in the literature to be most significant at different chronological life periods or at particular transition points. They may involve content designed to stimulate planning, exploration, information seeking, decision making, and self-knowledge. They may involve content designed to facilitate *work context skills* (e.g., skills related to the psychological aspects of the work situation, including employer-employee relations, supervisor-worker relations, interpersonal skills, willingness to follow rules, adaptability, punctuality, pride in work, self-discipline, efficiency); *career management* or *guidance skills* (e.g., job search and interview strategies, constructive use of leisure, personal economics skills, self-knowledge, job knowledge, the use of exploratory resources); and *decision-making skills* (e.g., systematic methods to process information, predict and weigh alternatives, clarify values, examine risk-taking styles, project action consequences) (Herr, 1982). Or, more likely, career guidance programs in schools will use as a framework one of the two sets of competencies described in the following paragraphs.

In the United States, there are many models of "career relevant content" that schools are being encouraged to incorporate into curricula, work-based learning, and career guidance processes. One such model is that developed by the Secretary's Commission on Achieving Necessary Skills (SCANS) in its report *What Work Requires of Schools* (U.S. Department of Labor, 1991). The SCANS report was predicated upon the notion that the workplace of the next century will be significantly, indeed fundamentally, different in organization. In particular, the report suggested that high-wage nations can only continue to be so if they are also high performance, produce the highest quality goods and services, provide greater choices for customers, and utilize more flexible production and automated systems. To accomplish such goals, according to the report, there must be a significant reinvestment in education and training that is directed to producing workers who can think, perform a wide variety of tasks, and assume increasing responsibilities. The report, which outlined important new roles for schools in preparing students to deal with new work organizations in which advanced technology is a significant component, contended that schools should provide five categories of competencies (or workplace know-how) and a three-part foundation of skills and personal qualities. The five competencies recommended for ensuring solid performance are the abilities to

1. identify, organize, plan, and allocate resources such as time, money, materials, and facilities;
2. work with others;
3. acquire and use information;
4. understand complex relationships; and
5. work with a variety of technologies.

According to the SCANS report, the five competencies span the chasm between the worlds of the school and the workplace. These five competencies also involve a complex interplay with the three educational fundamentals on which they rest: basic skills, higher order skills, and the application of selected personal qualities. As defined in the report, demonstrating basic skills means that the student "reads, writes, performs arithmetic and mathematic operations, listens, and speaks;" demonstrating higher order skills shows that the student "thinks creatively, makes decisions, solves problems, visualizes, knows how to learn and reason;" and by effectively applying personal qualities, the student "displays responsibility, self-esteem, sociability, self-management, and integrity and honesty" (pp. 4–5).

Another national approach to connecting schooling to employment is that advanced by the National Occupational Information Coordinating Council (NOICC). NOICC has developed the *National Career Counseling and Development Guidelines* (NOICC, 1988), which include three broad program goals for elementary schools, junior high schools, senior high schools, and adult settings. These program goals include self-knowledge, educational and occupational information, and career planning. These three program goals are, in turn, defined in terms of 12 competencies and a series of indicators for each. The competencies, which must be adapted to individual settings, are

1. understanding the influence of a positive self-concept;
2. skills to interact positively with others;
3. understanding the impact of growth and development;
4. understanding the relationship between educational achievement and career planning;
5. understanding the need for positive attitudes toward work and learning;
6. skills to locate, evaluate, and interpret career information;
7. skills to prepare to seek, obtain, maintain, and change jobs;
8. understanding how societal needs and functions influence the nature and structure of work;
9. skills to make decisions;
10. understanding the interrelationship of life roles;
11. understanding the continuous changes in male and female roles; and
12. skills in career planning.

The SCANS report recommendations, the NOICC *National Career Counseling and Development Guidelines,* and several other possible models are resources for making schools more career relevant through clearly defining needs for and emphases in career guidance and equipping students with the competencies and skills that can help them bridge the transition from school to employment.

Schools that are career relevant can embed the content of the models identified into a series of learning processes that integrate academic, general employability, and occupational skills. The types of knowledge, attitudes, and skills described here need to be introduced in the elementary schools and infused throughout the curricula of the junior and senior high schools in a variety of assessment and exploratory opportunities related to clarifying self-characteristics in relation to educational and employment options, and, for many students, to work-based learning options, occupations or industry-based skill development, and transitional skills for direct entrance to the labor force, postsecondary education, and lifelong learning. These processes are intended to complement—not substitute for—excellence in the acquisition of basic academic skills and to provide a seamless progression of career pathways from school to employment or to further education or both.

Types of learning processes that make schools more career relevant include (Herr, 1995)

- making college and career options known to children beginning in the middle schools if not before; helping them link what they are studying in academic areas to the occupational problems in which that subject matter is relevant or, indeed, critical; helping them to understand that they have options and the skills to address and master them;
- establishing a career guidance system, K-12, that focuses, among other goals, on helping students develop individual career development plans, acquire self-knowledge, and find out about educational and occupational opportunities as well as the ways to explore and choose among them;
- infusing career development concepts into academic subjects to help students understand how course work fits together and forms a body of knowledge and skills related to performance in work and other aspects of life;
- promoting schools-within-schools, career academies, and alternative preparatory academies;
- developing clear expectations for student learning, including the use of competency-based or objectives-based-education (OBE) approaches;
- requiring participation in community service programs for high school graduation. Community or national service can be a mechanism for major career exploration mechanism as well as for acquiring career relevant skills;
- providing educational opportunities acknowledging that not only technical skills but also multilinguality, leadership and social studies skills as well as knowledge of cultural differences, national histories, and the political and economic systems of nations with whom we trade will become increasingly important in international trade;
- focusing on life skills. Secondary schools, including middle schools, should provide training in life skills such as how to form good work habits, how to interact with public agencies, how to hunt for a job, how to behave appropriately in the workplace, how to work in a team, how to complete applications and follow

instructions, and how to look for meaningful employment. Many of these skills can arise from helping young people understand that school is their work and that being punctual, honest, and self-disciplined as well as being able to accept constructive supervision are attributes also valued by the workplace. Many of these skills and others can be gained through a variety of cooperative education and work-based learning opportunities such as summer and academic year internships, apprenticeships, and cooperative work-site training (Massachusetts Institute of Technology, 1990);

- enlarging the availability of cooperative education (which now enrolls about 5% to 10% of all students in high school and college) that structures students' experience in paid jobs that promote learning and extend what is taught in the classroom;
- providing skills certificates for students who have met articulated requirements and demonstrated the certified skills in technical training or other program offerings in high school. Such certifications of skills will undoubtedly increase students use of portfolios for describing their skills, more precise discussion of their skill development experiences, and greater clarity about their achievement of competency-based career development experiences and associated attitudes;
- increasing tech-prep or 2+2 programs;
- modifying the school curriculum to combine academic and vocational courses. Such an approach to an integrated curriculum gives students the benefit of occupational preparation and college preparation at the same time. It also potentially infuses academic courses with the task-oriented, problem-solving, and cooperative learning approaches that have been successful in vocational-technical education. These approaches incorporate the findings of research in the cognitive sciences that suggest that abstract information is often best learned through authentic application in task or problem-solving learning (U. S. Department of Education, 1991);
- expanding the availability of apprenticeship schemes in new ways, beginning in the high schools and providing skill development opportunities during that period in ways similar to those available in several of our competitor nations. Currently, apprenticeships in this country enroll very few students in high school and fewer than 2% of high school graduates, although in Europe, 30% to 60% of employment-bound students are likely to be in apprenticeships following high school (U.S. Department of Education, 1991); and
- ensuring that every student receives help to obtain job placement in ways similar to the placement opportunities for students entering college.

Within this context, one of the human resource dimensions of particular importance with regard to the employers' role in workforce development is how and how much they are involved in job training. In a report to the U.S. Congress (Hilton, 1991), the Office of Technology Assessment concluded that only a few U.S. firms use training as part of a successful competitive strategy, in contrast to firms in Germany and Japan. But however important training is for new workers, heavy investment in training cannot compensate for poor management or misguided product strategies. Nor can training necessarily overcome problems that do not lie with a lack of job-specific skills "but in a surplus of social pathologies—too many people with too little self-discipline, self-respect, and basic education to fit easily into the workplace" ("Training for Jobs," 1994, p. 20).

In addition to the importance of employer on-the-job training as an important aspect of workforce development for either new entry employees or older employees, high-quality supervision of employees in the workplace is also needed. Employer responsibilities in behalf of their role in the school-to-work transition are particularly critical, as illustrated by studies showing that the quality and availability of supervision of work experience has an important impact on the school-to-work transition (Silberman, 1994; Stern, McMillan, Hopkins, & Stone, 1990).

Such programs are being modified to accommodate the needs of different types of populations. Many of these programs are addressed to young people who are experiencing major problems in the school-to-work transition. This issue is a particularly important one because of growing knowledge about the characteristics and issues inherent in this transition. For example, research findings have shown that as a group, young workers enter the labor force gradually rather than abruptly upon the completion of school. A period of trial-and-error experimentation typically precedes complete assimilation into the labor force. Large numbers of teenagers and young adults combine school and work before completing the transition. This process is made possible largely through the opportunity for part-time employment. However, a growing body of research has indicated that beyond a predictable period of trial and experimentation

> . . . joblessness among out-of-school teenage youth carries with it a hangover effect. . . . Those who have unfavorable early labor market experiences are less likely than others to have favorable subsequent experiences, education and other background characteristics held constant. Obviously early labor market experiences are related to subsequent measures of labor market success. They cannot be treated as though they were benign phenomena which simply "age out." (Adams & Mangum, 1978, p. 1)

Additional research has suggested that those who adapt to work effectively must successfully adjust to five different areas: performance, organizational, interpersonal, responsibility, and affective aspects (Ashley et al., 1980). Each of these conditions or challenges can be addressed specifically in comprehensive career guidance programs.

The studies reported here as well as others have indicated that frequent unemployment and other poor labor market experiences during the early years have a damaging effect on work continuity and adjustment later—in part because periods of unemployment represent loss of work experience, information, and skills that may put an individual at a competitive disadvantage in the eyes of an employer and also may have an injurious effect on attitudes toward work. The most serious problems in this regard are found among youths who are both out of school prematurely and out of work. In addition, the major transition problems are frequently experienced by certain groups of minority and other economically disadvantaged youth. Thus the youth population is composed of subpopulations that vary in their ability to master the movement from school to work. Although the reasons are diverse, the need for comprehensive programs of career counseling and career guidance tailored to the needs of these diverse groups is critical and complex.

The U.S. Department of Labor's Employment and Training Administration, in a report entitled *Skills, Standards, and Entry-Level Work; Elements of a Strategy for Youth Employability Development* (1995), has also argued for more employer involvement in the school-to-work transition. Of particular interest in this report is the potential of the secondary labor market as a career development vehicle complementing the variety of activities that can take place in what has earlier been described as processes related to career-relevant schools. The secondary labor market encompasses the entry-level stream of the labor market in which jobs are often part-time and pay the minimum wage. Such jobs are often characterized by high turnover, limited training needs, low skill requirements, routinization, and in many ways a perception that workers are interchangeable. According to the report,

> Secondary labor market jobs are found across a spectrum of industries and occupational groupings. However, they are concentrated in the retail, clerical, and hospitality sectors, especially restaurant, supermarket, and fast-food chains, where many youth have found their first jobs and gained their first formal experience of work. (1995, p. 21)

The recommendations that flow from this analysis (U.S. Department of Labor, 1995) in relation to the employer side of the school-to-work transition, in abridged and paraphrased form, are as follows:

1. **The work side of the school-to-work transition should be more energetically pursued** (p. 4). Unlike technical training in European countries, vocational training in the United States is almost totally a school-based activity. However, the cooperation of employers is essential if these training programs are to connect school and workplace learning effectively. Further, it is important to explore a diverse range of strategies, spanning a wide variety of work settings and industries, so that the potential for integrating real work into the school-to-work system can be fully tested.

2. **Opportunities to leverage naturally occurring work experiences that facilitate adolescents' personal and career development should be exploited** (p. 5). Millions of youth are already involved, because of their own efforts and interests, in real work. In 1993, for example, more than 3 million 16- to 19-year-olds worked part-time, and almost 2 million more worked full-time (Bureau of Labor Statistics, 1994). Obviously, learning does take place in the workplace. However, according to the report, unless work-based learning experiences are deliberately *designed* for learning, they remain deficient as learning environments, particularly for the young and less educated.

3. **Efforts to develop and recognize a full range of workplace certification techniques should be expanded** (p. 5). It appears inevitable in the future that all youth seeking to make the transition from schooling to employment will be required to meet national minimum skill standards. "Yet developing the mechanisms to measure workplace know-how, creating a generalized credential, and convincing a critical mass of businesses [employers] to recognize that credential present serious challenges" (p. 5). However, "the creation of voluntary national competency standards for what workers should know and be able to do is central to the current Administration's workforce development agenda. Such standards would help shape the design of education and training programs and provide youth and adults with portable credentials that would be widely recognized by employers" (p. 5).

4. **A wide range of attainable work-learning opportunities should be made available for disadvantaged youth** (p. 5). Marginal students, and youth who have left school before graduating, are unlikely to find their way into conventional school-to-work models. "Developing *their* potential is a *challenge* that must

be addressed" (p. 5). Fortunately, "an opportunity to do so is indicated by the fact that large numbers of economically disadvantaged and academically at-risk youth are already in the secondary labor market. Efforts to build effectively on their experience there should be recognized as a major policy aim and a critical part of their continuum of education and training programs" (p. 6).

These recommendations add more detail to some of the learning processes that have been identified previously as important to career-relevant schools and to the collaboration of such schools with employers.

A series of national reports has emphasized the need for career guidance and for career counseling to be combined with other activities to address the complex problems that socially and economically disadvantaged youth in a rapidly changing economy face. For example, the Education Commission of the States (1985), in a national report dealing with the growing problem of alienated, disadvantaged, disconnected, and other at-risk youth, recommended "new structures and procedures for effecting the transition from school to work or other productive pursuits. . . . Young people today need more and better guidance than ever before" (p. 26). The report also specified the need for coordinated programs including career counseling, financial assistance, summer jobs, cooperative education options, and role models if such at-risk youth are to be reconnected to schooling and to work. The Committee for Economic Development (1985), in a major report dealing with business and the public schools, strongly recommended that schools provide exploratory programs to assist in career choice, job search, and general employability and employment counseling. The National Alliance of Business (1984), in a major analysis of the nation at work, particularly regarding relationships between education and the private sector, argued for more school-to-work transition programs including job placement assistance, career counseling, cooperative career information activities with business, and counseling about vocational-technical program alternatives to college degree programs (p. 8).

Many of the recommendations of the reports just cited have been echoed and extended in a report entitled *The Forgotten Half: Non-College Youth in America* (W.T. Grant Commission, 1988). This report argued that bridging the gap from school to work should include a mix of action programs. Among them should be monitored work experience, community and neighborhood service, redirected vocational education, incentives (guaranteed postsecondary and continuing education, guaranteed jobs, guaranteed training), career information and counseling (career information centers, parents as career educators, improved counseling and career orientation, community mentors and community-based organizations), and school volunteers.

The National Commission on Secondary Vocational Education in its report, *The Unfinished Agenda* (1984), contended in behalf of guidance services in schools that systematic programs of interest and aptitude assessment, career planning, and occupational information designed to facilitate student curriculum choices must be available to all students. In addition, the report argued that counselor functions need to include cooperative activity with teachers, the use of group guidance techniques, computer-assisted guidance, comprehensive career information systems, and related methods designed to provide career guidance to all students.

As school counselors engage in the many tasks advocated by national reports and, indeed, required by different groups of students (e.g., the college bound, the employment bound, the economically disadvantaged), they are involved in both common and unique tasks. For example, the common tasks school counselors discharge in their work with students include helping them to personalize, apply, and plan based upon the types of career-relevant content and experience suggested as important in the previous paragraph and elsewhere in this chapter. But there are also specific recommendations directed to school counselors working with student populations having needs that are considered to be unique. Among such roles are those relevant to students in the school-to-work transition who are employment bound or who are in such programs as tech-prep described elsewhere in this chapter. In the latter situations, Chew (1993) has recommended the following (in abridged form):

1. Counselors and school districts should implement a comprehensive developmental guidance model for K-12 students emphasizing technical career opportunities.
2. Counselors should provide all students with interest and aptitude assessments (beginning no later than the eighth grade) to help them plan meaningful 4-year educational goals.
3. Counselors can provide school-wide activities that promote the awareness of technical career opportunities.
4. Counselors can provide students with information about community or technical college opportunities.
5. Counselors should give attention to women and minorities by providing them information regarding technical careers.
6. Counselors should assist special-needs students (e.g., learning disabled, physically disabled, teen parents, economically disadvantaged) in making transitions from secondary to postsecondary education.
7. Counselors must have access to appropriate materials and resources that explain the options of tech-prep and technical careers.
8. Counselors should help students develop a portfolio that summarizes their credentials, both educational and experiential.
9. Counselors should utilize career planners with their students. (pp. 32–35)

If we view career guidance as a systematic program of counselor-coordinated information and experiences (Herr, 1995; Herr & Cramer, 1996), the ultimate goal of which is to provide individuals with the knowledge and skills needed to develop realistic career plans and make the appropriate decisions to carry out these plans, there are a myriad processes that can be combined in various ways to serve such goals. The U.S. Department of Labor's Employment and Training Administration (1993, pp. 6, 7), has suggested the following as ways to assist disadvantaged youths:

*   **outreach** to alert students to services;
*   **classroom instruction** to provide an integrated set of planned and sequential curricular activities;
*   **counseling** to help students explore personal issues and apply information and skills to personal plans, which may be offered individually or in small groups;
*   **self-assessment** to provide students with a clearer understanding of their values, skills, abilities, interests, achievements, aspirations, and needs;
*   **career information** that is easily accessible, current, relevant, and unbiased to provide a solid framework on which to base decisions;
*   **exploration activities** and experiences designed to broaden horizons, test interests, and stimulate career planning;
*   **work experience** to offer opportunities to test decisions and develop effective work abilities and behaviors;

- **career planning** activities to help youth learn the skills needed to make decisions and understand the future impact of choices;
- **placement** services to help youth make the transition to school, work, or the military;
- **referrals** to other professional services to allow youth to obtain assistance beyond the scope of the program; and
- **follow-up** activities to provide opportunities to maintain contact and track progress.

Obviously such vital program services can not only be used with disadvantaged students but can also be adapted to the career needs of students in many subgroups.

Although much more deserves to be said about the importance of comprehensive guidance services in secondary schools and in collaboration with community agencies and business and industry in an age of advanced technology, let us turn very briefly to the need for career guidance and counseling in colleges and universities. Research studies of college student populations have continued to indicate that at least one half of college populations feel a need for assistance with career planning or career choice. As a result, career services in higher education have become more comprehensive in their offerings, and these tend to be tailored to the different needs of younger and older students, reentry women, and other nontraditional populations. The era of offering placement services to students only at the end of the college experience has given way to a sequential *process* of career counseling that begins in the first year of college and builds in a sequential manner through the senior year. This process is designed to help students relate job opportunities to majors; to explore their career interests, values, and abilities; to obtain information; to talk to a counselor about career plans; to learn how occupations can affect their future way of life; to gain knowledge of people and places on campus that can help in career planning; to plan college courses that will give more flexibility in choosing among different occupations; and to obtain help in choosing work study, cooperative education, or part-time work that will provide applications of their majors and career exploration.

In broad terms, comprehensive career guidance programs in higher education are providing increased cooperation between academic departments and a central staff of career specialists who provide career advising, career planning, and career counseling. Typically, colleges and universities have used five major approaches in delivering career guidance: (1) courses, workshops, and seminars that offer structured group experiences in career planning, decision making, and job-access skills. Frequently, the topics include occupational information, resume preparation, interview preparation, study skills, values clarification, time management, assertiveness training, decision making, issues faced by special groups, and the career development of women. Increasingly these courses, workshops, and seminars use computer-assisted career guidance programs as adjuncts by which students can explore and clarify self-characteristics, opportunities, and majors; (2) individual counseling; (3) peer counseling; (4) group counseling; and (5) placement.

As both school counseling and career services in higher education are shaped and reshaped to reflect the changes in workplaces and in the requirements of work, they must fully integrate the vocabulary, the content, and the differentiation between myths and realities related to the effects of advanced technology discussed throughout this chapter.

The Counselor and the Unemployed

In the final analysis, advanced technology, changes in worker skill requirements, and shifts in the organization of work will leave in their wake the unemployed. There tend to be limits in all societies to what can be achieved to eliminate unemployment. People in such circumstances frequently experience multiple barriers to employment or reemployment as well as problems that seem intractable. As unemployment rates decrease, people with the most difficult problems become visible as formidable challenges for counselors in schools, in community agencies, and in workplaces.

The transitions in the occupational structure described in this chapter will cause the psychological and transitional consequences for the unemployed to be a continuing concern for counselors in many settings, whether they work directly with the unemployed, or with their children or other family members. At the least, counselors will need to be more knowledgeable about the different types of unemployment, the factors that cause it, who is likely to be affected and why, and how the victims of unemployment can be helped to extricate themselves from such circumstances. A simplistic or unidimensional view of unemployment causes counselors to contend that their profession will reduce unemployment. Although counseling is likely to increase the employability of individuals and, through various schemes of person-job matching, reduce the actual time of unemployment, counseling is, in fact, only incidentally able to create jobs that do not already exist. Thus counselors must not overpromise or create false assumptions among the public or policymakers about what counseling and related services can and cannot do.

Having identified such caveats, however, it is still important to recognize that although the unemployed are not homogeneous in their characteristics or reasons for unemployment, several broad principles can be articulated in working with them. First, counselors will need to help the unemployed understand and anticipate the psychological facets of unemployment, particularly the relationships between jobs, joblessness, and mental health. A growing literature is becoming available about the physiological problems and diseases associated with unemployment and economic uncertainty. Also highlighted is the relationship between unemployment and low self-esteem, mental illness, family discord, and spouse and child abuse. Lichtman (1978), among others, observed an irrational willingness—perhaps even a need—for people to blame themselves for social processes for which they are not responsible. Counselors need to help people develop a transactional understanding of mental health that explores the fact that some problems come from personal, internal dysfunctions, but that many, if not most, are provoked and maintained by external factors such as unemployment, which overwhelm some people but not others. Those who are overwhelmed tend to blame themselves for circumstances they could confront and cope with, though not necessarily control.

Thinking about counseling as a form of preventive therapy or "stress inoculation" is fraught with problems. First, counselors might tend to blame the victim of social circumstances for having negative attitudes or for having chosen unemployment voluntarily or for being part of a particular social group. In addition, some clients have the need to either stigmatize or glamorize unemployment as a lifestyle. Clients must be assisted to gain perspective on unemployment but not to accept it as personally inevitable or as a condition from which they cannot escape.

Second, counselors must help people examine the range of community resources available in the event of unemployment or in order to avoid it. They need to help people see themselves as part of a system, not as social isolates. This requires being aware of services provided by church, education, or social welfare groups as well as those offered by governmental units or the private sector. It is in this context that counselors can help the unemployed to see themselves as social beings operating within a system of social institutions designed to provide experience, skill development, livelihood, and well-being. As the unemployed understand these perspectives, their abilities to be active rather than reactive, and socially conscious rather than individually isolated, are likely to be enhanced.

Third, counselors need to recognize that those who experience unemployment are likely to need more than support. They are people who will probably have multiple problems to deal with, such as transportation, racial discrimination, lack of basic skills, poor industrial discipline, family discord, and drug or alcohol problems. Thus individuals need to be helped to understand the interactive effects of such problems with the condition of unemployment. Counselors can provide basic skill training in many of these areas and information about others. But counselors also can serve as advocates for job needs to employers, community groups, and governmental bodies. In this role, counselors can aspire to be catalysts to stimulate the development of programs designed to create jobs, stimulate selfemployment, and otherwise reduce unemployment.

As these three principles suggest, counselors have many roles to play with the unemployed. Among them are those suggested by Pryor and Ward (1985):

- reduce the psychological effects of unemployment;
- help in job search and improve the chances of obtaining employment;
- assist people to survive unemployment; and
- explore alternative forms of employment.

Pryor and Ward also recommended that in discharging such roles, the following techniques be used: relaxation training, systematic desensitization, assertiveness training, modeling, using video role-play to increase self-presentation skills at job interviews and other situations, psychological assessment, job search skills, and coping with living on unemployment benefits (pp. 4–14). Borgen and Amundson (1984) emphasized additional techniques: effective listening, job search support groups, retraining, reassessment of self and values, early notification of job loss, and early and coordinated intervention for those about to be unemployed.

The concern for the unemployed is becoming more urgent as research studies have demonstrated the linkages between work, mental health, and physiological well-being. Some of the findings that are particularly important for counselor consideration include the following:

- Unemployment tends to be associated with a rising incidence of mental illness, suicides, imprisonments, child abuse, spouse abuse, chemical dependency, and violence (Pryor & Ward, 1985). Other studies have shown that unemployment, fewer hours worked, and business failures are each strongly linked with an increased death rate among those affected; in essence, job loss can lead to early death (Brenner, 1987). Further data have indicated that the experience of unemployment spills over to family members and that spouses report more depression, anxiety, and interpersonal problems as the period of unemployment continues (Shelton, 1985). Unemployment also leads to decreases in perceived competencies, activity, and life satisfaction (Feather & O'Brian, 1986).

- Unemployed persons are likely to experience several major psychosocial problems, such as problems with partners, accusations leveled by family, excessive alcohol consumption, difficulties contacting others, problems looking for work, trouble with government labor offices, loss of status, and a crisis of self-esteem (Kieselbach & Lunger, 1990).

- Extensive research in Canada (Borgen & Amundson, 1984) and in the United States (Schlossberg & Leibowitz, 1980) has clearly linked the experience of unemployment to the experience of grieving and bereavement as originally defined by Kubler-Ross in 1969 and to the role of victim as described by Janoff-Bluman and Frieze in 1983. Thus, in the first instance, occupationally dislocated and unemployed people are likely to go through the stages of denial, anger, bargaining, depression, and acceptance as do those who have lost a loved one. In the case of involuntary unemployment, an individual loses a part of his or her self-concept and the esteem, livelihood, and status that accompany being employed; the grief process addresses such a reality. In the second instance, the unemployed frequently experience psychological reactions similar to those of people who find themselves in the role of victim as a result of rape, incest, disease, or crime. The emotional reactions include shock, confusion, helplessness, anxiety, fear, and depression. Prolonged unemployment frequently is characterized by periods of apathy alternating with anger, sadness, sporadic optimism, few habits of regular structured activities, few meaningful personal contacts, and ominous feelings of victimization, lack of personal power, and low self-worth. None of these characteristics coincide with an ability to readily resume a constructive role in the workforce without counseling or psychological assistance. Such people need at least some type of job search support group to reduce their isolation, receive encouragement, develop more effective job search methods, reassess their interests and abilities, and consider alternate career paths. School counselors may have a major role in helping students understand what their parents are experiencing. As discussed in chapter 1, such situations require counselors and their clients to consider the interactive effects of the macrosystem, the mesosystem, and the microsystem in creating the stresses and strains that both unemployed workers and their family members experience.

- Assumptions that early unemployment is a transient matter that simply ages out is not correct. Unless young people attain some early success in the labor market, they are likely to be doomed to a life of jagged unemployment because of problems of lack of credibility with employers, lack of information relevant to effective job access and adjustment, and a lack of identity as a worker. All of these deficits put them at risk compared to their age cohorts unless they benefit from fairly dramatic and systematic intervention both in terms of economic programs and counseling programs. Schools, employers, and community agencies will need to assume greater responsibility in the future for systematic attention to developing among all youth the necessary knowledge, attitudes, and behaviors that make for an effective school-to-work transition. Meeting such a goal will probably require significant expansion of comprehensive career guidance programs.

- Less obvious, perhaps, than the individual effects of psychological adjustment and stress-related disease that accompany unemployment are the social costs involved. These are the costs of lost worker productivity as well as the costs of providing needed social services to deal with the psychological problems stemming from long-term unemployment. Increases in mortality rates, suicides, imprisonments, mental illness, and child or spouse abuse cost money.

The Counselor and the Underemployed

What is frequently missed in discussions of the unemployed are those who work but are underemployed. International labor statistics define underemployment as a condition where a person's employment is inadequate in relation to specified norms or alternative employment. These statistics also identify two types of underemployment: visible and invisible.

- *Visible underemployment* reflects a condition where an inadequate amount of work exists. That is, the individual works fewer hours than is normal or desired, and would accept additional hours.
- *Invisible underemployment* relates to conditions associated with low income, low productivity, and underuse of personal skills.

O'Toole (1977) referred to underemployment as working at less than an individual's full productive capacity. He suggested that in many jobs a worker's unused potential represents a waste of personal capacity and commitment; the result is that the worker experiences alienation and estrangement from his or her interests, needs, and capacities. The personal and social distress associated with underutilization of talent and skills creates frustration and morale problems that can be a form of social dynamite in their negative effects upon work settings or the larger society. At the least, people who feel that they deserve a better job than they hold suffer from status conflict. As advanced technology is used to replace middle management as well as clerical, semiskilled, and unskilled labor, highly qualified workers often bump slightly less qualified workers from their jobs and push them further down the status hierarchy. As higher levels of skills and capabilities are unused and highly qualified people are underemployed, they are likely to be dissatisfied with their job. In such instances, they have great potential for occupational and social pathology (Herr & Long, 1983).

The implementation of advanced technology in the economic structure has created a new form of underemployment that is only now becoming visible. As the mix of occupations available changes from manufacturing to service industries, and as changes in the organization of work require the displacement of middle managers and others, the quality of life and the earning power of those affected change. For example, the service industries tend to pay roughly two thirds of the annual salary paid in manufacturing industries. Therefore, if a steelworker suffers displacement and finds a job in a service occupation (such as electronics repair), the former steelworker, although still employed, is likely to experience a significantly lower wage and quality of life. Coupled with the loss of seniority rights and the probability of reduced benefits packages, the result is a substantial drop in the standard of living. Similar if not greater disparities are found between former automotive industry or mining workers and the emerging occupations available to them. Research by Flaim and Sehgal (1985) on 5.1 million displaced workers during the years 1979 to 1983 added further concern about such transitions. Most of these displaced workers had lost jobs in heavy industries. This research showed that after 3 years, only 30% of the displaced workers had been employed in equivalent jobs; nearly 30% had to take a pay cut of 20% or more (for nearly half it was 20%); 40% had found no job, only 25% of these were still looking for work, and dominant in the latter group were women and Blacks. Another study by the American Society for Development and Training of Unemployed Middle Managers found that roughly one third of those over 35 find jobs paying less than those they previously held. It takes most of these individuals 5 years to regain their previous salary levels (Rochell & Spellman, 1987, p. 7).

Rochell and Spellman (1987) contended that, as advanced technology increasingly pervades the workplaces of the nation, "for those who want to work and have the skills, technological displacement is not likely to mean unemployment so much as lesser employment—a shift to what work is available—generally at lower pay" (p. 82). Thus "the American working population faces a difficult and contradictory situation. Work will be available, but not necessarily the work people are prepared for and, it appears, not at the wages they are conditioned to expect" (p. 90).

The concern about a lowering of the quality of life and reduced earnings for many Americans is at the heart of the concern for a two-tiered workforce, and a growing distance between the haves and the have-nots of society. The concern is exacerbated by a perception that many occupations are being de-skilled. As the computer is taking over middle-management and clerical tasks for which workers were formerly well paid, former job descriptions are typically downgraded and compensated at a lower level. Indeed, existing studies have suggested that instead of increasing skill requirements, new technologies often replace the skills workers require to perform their jobs (Rumberger, 1987, p. 91). Another phenomenon that contributes to this downshifting of the quality of life is the growing use of temporary or contingent workers, freelancers, and part-time workers employed in small businesses or at home to do specific types of subcontracting for larger businesses. Frequently, these part-time workers get no benefits and must work several part-time jobs to meet their financial obligations. These workers lose much of the control to define their jobs and to participate in decisions about job design or other matters. Although not all freelance and part-time work is at a low level, much of it is parallel to the routine, menial, and tedious work of the severely fragmented assembly line of past history. In any case, part-time work or work at home may increase job autonomy but also increase psychological displacement from the workplace, co-workers, and the other elements of work that lead to self-esteem and affiliation.

Underemployment and the resulting de-skilling, lack of control, downgrading of status, significant reductions in the quality of life, major changes in job content and an individual's knowledge of it, part-time rather than full-time work, and diminished status and self-esteem will not affect all workers or all industries. But the indicators are clear that as certain skills in the workplace are assigned to advanced technological devices, individuals who previously practiced those skills will be affected and potentially underemployed.

Counselors, then, will have a major role in working with the underemployed in ways similar to their work with the unemployed. Counselors will need to provide support, psychological assessment, and assistance to people in reevaluating their self-concepts and needs. Counselors will be asked to help develop avenues other than working to seek self-identity, perform leisure counseling, and help people explore retraining and alternative career paths.

CONCLUSIONS

Chapter 2 has attempted to illustrate the comprehensive transitions and, indeed, transformations in work that are occurring and that will accelerate in the United States into the 21st century. The wedding of science and technology, and the resulting advanced or high technology, have influenced the social institutions, workplaces, and opportunity structures in the United States.

The effects of advanced technology—such as international competition in a global economy, changing skill requirements, and demographic shifts in the workforce—are not isolated or confined to the content of work. They affect where work is done, when, by whom, and for what purposes as well as the levels of stress and anxiety that accompany rapid and wide-ranging change. Thus in the last analysis, the implementation of advanced or high technology in society is not a technical matter. It is rather a matter of human perceptions, skills, and flexibility. It is also a matter of social technologies designed to accommodate the psychological, physical, and educational demands of different groups of youths and adults attempting to explore, choose, prepare, retrain, or adjust to work in a condition of dynamic flux.

The implications for counselors in an age of advanced technology are many. The challenges represented by clients seeking information and support, insight and action planning, and assistance with exploration and adjustment will encourage counselors to become more comprehensive in the techniques used, more programmatic in the use of psychoeducational models, and more cognizant of the connections between career counseling and behavioral health. In such contexts, counselors will become brokers of information, maximizers of opportunity, developers of skills, and collaborators and mentors for larger proportions of the population than they have traditionally served.

Chapter 3

THE CHANGING AMERICAN FAMILY

TO CHARACTERIZE THEIR INSTITUTIONS AND PEOPLE, societies evolve many different metaphors and related ideologies, such as those that encompass sex roles and family structures. The family structure metaphors, which are identified and described through narratives, media images, and social policy, acquire positive or negative social value as they focus societal attention on the nature and impact of family composition and of changes in family dynamics. Factors that affect such values given to family structure metaphors are those related to sex role differentiation, family types and family functions, parenting and child care, and welfare. Also affecting the value are the reflections of these factors in education, in work content, and in organizations.

It is now likely, however, that changes in family structures and their implications for counseling are occurring more rapidly and profoundly than national metaphors and ideologies can capture. Thus in addition to the comprehensive influence of advanced technology on work, social institutions, and individuals described in the previous chapter, a second major challenge for counselors in virtually all settings is the complex nature of the forms of relationships now subsumed under the term *family*. The nostalgic and traditional view of the typical American family unit in which mother, father, and two children coexist in a well-ordered, stable, and loving relationship, with the father the unquestioned breadwinner and the mother the nurturant caregiver, is rapidly fading. Indeed, the nuclear family unit, rather than being the most common family pattern, is rapidly becoming the exception. As a result, both the stresses and strains within families and the changing forms of family life have become increasingly exposed to scrutiny in the mass media and in the professional literature of counseling.

Because of this scrutiny, the fragility of families as well as their fundamental importance to the social fabric are being rediscovered. It has become increasingly clear that some families encourage health and wholeness; others cause stress and pain. The effects of either environment shape both childhood and adulthood, and growing national awareness of these effects is stimulating concerns about the needs for strengthened families as enclaves of love, support, discipline, and spirituality. Questions about the role of parents in sex education, career development, and the teaching of social values of honesty and responsibility are becoming regular features in the popular press as well as in learned treatises.

The reasons for the rapid and comprehensive changes in the family structures of the United States are diverse (Farley, 1996; Sundal-Hansen, 1985). A major reason is certainly economic. Because of worker dislocation, decreasing male salaries (particularly for younger workers), diminishing levels of financial support for and increasing costs of higher education, a devalued dollar, and related trends, it has become necessary for most families to have two incomes in order to maintain their quality of life. Thus two-earner and dual-career families have become the rule rather than the exception. Beyond two-earner and dual-career families, there is the relationship between the salaries of young males and their ability to start and maintain a family. For example, the decline of the manufacturing sector as a major employer has had a particularly devastating effect on those young people with deficiencies in education and basic skills. Historically, there have been jobs in heavy industry—steelmaking, durable-goods production, automotive manufacturing—in which individuals could earn enough to support a family even if they did not have a strong education. However, since 1974, the proportion of young male workers employed in manufacturing industries has declined by one fourth, at the same time that employment in service industries has risen by more than 20%. Perhaps more important, in early 1974, blue-collar craft, operative, and foreman jobs accounted for nearly half (46%) of the jobs held by employed Black men, ages 20 to 24. These were jobs that were frequently unionized and paid above average wages with good fringe benefits. By 1984, these jobs accounted for about one fourth (26.0%) of the jobs held by young Black males, and their decrease has at least indirectly contributed to the expanding number of welfare and father-absent families in this nation. As each new group of young male workers entering the labor market earned lower mean real wages and worked fewer hours annually during the past decade, the percentage of young men 20 to 24 years old who are able to support a family of three above the poverty line has declined from 60% to 42%. A related result is that from 1974 to 1984, the percent of young Black men ages 20 to 24 who were married and living with their spouses dropped from 30% to 9%. Thus as real earnings have decreased, there have been changes in family-formation patterns and increases in the number of single-parent families and children living in poverty (Herr, 1995).

The sexual revolution is another reason for the changes in family structure. As women's access to nontraditional educational and occupational opportunities has increased, women have been entering the professions and technical occupations in unprecedented numbers. Many have chosen to delay marriage or parenting until they have established themselves in careers. For others, the sexual revolution has meant a blurring of traditional sex roles, resulting in equal partnerships in cohabitations, in marriage, and in work in which both husband and wife or partners living together have full-time jobs to which they are committed for reasons of career mobility and advancement, and in support of which they share household responsibilities and child raising. In some still rare instances, the wife may be the major economic provider and the husband the "househusband," primary caregiver, and homemaker. Throughout the remainder of this chapter, a number of new family structures are described that are products of divorce, separation, and widowhood as well as of same-sex orientations, temporary arrangements, or the incarceration or dysfunction of the biological parents.

The increased attention to these shifting family structures and their roles in society has paralleled shifts in how families are viewed in psychology and counseling. The disciplinary lenses through which the behavioral objectives of counseling interventions are viewed are also shifting. We see a movement away from a psychology that attributes all power and all deficits to internal states and to individual decision making and action. In its place there is an affirmation or reaffirmation that people live in collectivities, in environments that reinforce, shape, and model some behaviors and not others. These perspectives validate the importance of seeing families as systems of relationships, roles, and power as we consider their stresses and structures. Thus the family is seen frequently as composing both the context and content as well as the instrument for counseling. The family structure often defines the actors who need to be involved in counseling as well as the context in which roles and relationships are played out. The stresses and strains the family unit, whatever its structure, experiences are frequently the presenting content for counseling.

As views of the family as a system of roles and relationships have evolved in Western psychology, an additional shift in counseling theory and practice has become apparent. There has been a gradual drawing back in psychological literature from the definition of personal maturity as the ability to be independent from the family, to be one's own person, a person whose decisions are self-centered and egocentric. We have gradually come to learn, as Eastern psychology has long expressed, that to be free one must be responsible to others; to be mature is not necessarily to be without gratitude to others or consideration for their needs; to acknowledge the importance of family members to each other is not a sign of weakness, but of strength.

For these reasons and others, the characteristics of the American family as an economic and a social unit, as a molder of values, and as a seedbed for identity are inexorably moving from the back burner to a position of central attention as models of counseling for the future are being defined and studied. Against this background, this chapter explores four major topics: the demographics of family change, perspectives on current and emerging family structures, an overview of family stresses, and some implications for counseling.

THE DEMOGRAPHICS OF FAMILY CHANGE

It has become almost commonplace in the popular press, and in many articles and speeches, to list in some terse fashion proportions and percentages of change in the American population by age, sex, race, income level, number employed, or other social indicators. In one way or another, these demographic variables are relevant to understanding the complexity of the stresses and structures that describe the family in America. Examples of major demographic characteristics pertinent to changing American families will assist this understanding, as will a brief look at how *family* and *household* are defined.

According to the 1990 definition of the family by the U.S. Census Bureau—"two or more individuals related by blood, marriage, or adoption who share a home"— 1980 Census figures indicated that there were approximately 58 million families in the country (Louis Harris & Associates, 1981). By the 1990 Census that figure had risen to some 68 million families (U.S. Bureau of the Census, 1991). Some authorities on the family have anticipated that the definition of family may be, and probably will be in another decade or so, changed to "two or more people joined together by bonds of sharing and intimacy" (Family Service America, 1984, p. 7). Obviously, such a change in the definition of a family will enlarge and shift the focus of the family, and it would also change the current U.S. Bureau of the Census definition of a household as "all the individuals living together in a dwelling unit—a home, apartment, or condominium." Such persons can be unrelated, although in 1990, 71% of households were occupied by families.

Regardless of whether or not such changes in the statistical definitions of family or of household take place, many other demographic trends help us to recognize the pluralism of factors and the magnitude of change now associated with the concept of family in the United States. For example:

- Divorce and more recently rising rates of childbearing by never married women have produced sharp increases in the number of families headed by women without husbands. By the early 1990s about one family in five was of this type (Farley, 1996).
- There has been a steady increase in the numbers and proportions of families headed by men without wives living with them, although in many of these cases the man lives with an adult woman identified as a partner. This phenomenon is producing a new type of family that can be described as a heterosexual but not married couple with children. In 1990, 1.5 million families consisted of a father and his children, but no wife (Farley, 1996).
- For women in Generation X, 37% had married by ages 20 to 24, compared to the 69% married at these ages for parents of the baby boom. Thus it appears that members of Generation X are delaying marriage to record late ages, even though it is expected that 90% of White women and approximately 75% of Black women will eventually marry (Norton & Miller, 1992).
- Given the later marriages of Generation X-ers, and the less likely people are to divorce the older they are when they marry, it is possible that the rising divorce rate is about to peak and may fall to approximately 40% for generation X-ers (Norton & Miller, 1992).
- Although the divorce rate in the late 1980s was high, the remarriage rate was dropping to about half of that of the 1970s, suggesting that the weakening of marriage in the last two decades will be associated with rises in cohabitation (Farley, 1996).
- In 1993, 72% of all teenage mothers were unmarried as compared to 1960 when only 15% of teenage mothers were single (Farley, 1996).
- By 1993, unmarried women accounted for 31% of births (National Center for Health Statistics, 1995).
- Child poverty is a persistent problem in the United States. In 1993, 15.7 million children lived in households with incomes below the poverty line. Childhood poverty is clearly associated with the nation's shift away from two-parent families to lower income single-parent families, usually headed by the mother. Almost one half of all children in mother-only families are impoverished. In 1960, 90% of children under age 18 lived in families with a father and a mother. By 1993, 70% of children lived with a father and a mother. Hernandez (1993) has projected that 53% of children born in the 1970s will live in a one-parent family before their 18th birthday.
- Compared to the period prior to 1965, when a large proportion of mothers remained at home and raised children, contemporary parents increasingly pay

someone else for child care, or they use a barter system with other parents to provide child care while they work (Farley, 1996). Given the availability of free lunches and (increasingly) free breakfasts and changing patterns of child care, many schools have become child-rearing institutions. Further, in some instances, child rearing and child monitoring from early morning (e.g., 7:00 a.m.) until early evening (e.g., 6:00 p.m.) has become a community process combining the work of the school and that of after-school youth-serving organizations (Herr, 1991).

- The termination of a two-parent family or the absence of a father from the home clearly has negative consequences for children (McLanahan & Sandefur, 1994).
- The largest increase in poverty rates in the 1980s was in single-parent families, particularly those headed by a mother.
- In 1994, 61% of married couples had wives in the paid labor force, compared to only 30% of married couples in the 1960s (Farley, 1996).
- A slow but discernible decline in the wages of men, particularly non-college-educated men, has made taking on the financial responsibilities for a family problematic while these men are in their 20s, delaying marriage and giving force to alternative lifestyles including cohabitation as well as births without marriage.
- There is an increasing incidence of dysfunctional parents who remain "in the picture" but are unable or unwilling to nurture their own children. These parents may be substance abusers, victims of perpetration of physical or sexual violence, or sufferers of emotional or neurological disorders that render them incapable of parenting. These particular classes of parents have inadvertently triggered the advent of a grandparent, if alive and available, assuming parenting responsibilities. In the last decade, there has been a 40% increase in these households across the United States, with a disproportionate presence among African American families. The children and youth who become members of these new families are at great risk of psychiatric as well as developmental disorders (Pinson-Millburn, Fabian, Schlossberg, & Pyle, 1996, p. 548).
- The most common American family is now one in which both spouses work.
- The number of married couples who decide to have children has declined; completed family size decreased from 2.4 children in 1970 to 1.7 in 1984 among Whites and from 3.1 to 2.2 children among Blacks (National Center for Health Statistics, 1986a).
- The number of married couples who postpone having children to extend their careers has risen.
- Greater numbers of unmarried couples are living together, although they represent only a fraction (3.1% in 1980; 6.2% in 1990) of all couples living together. In 1990, there were about 18 married couples for every cohabiting one.
- The proportion of never-married women has risen rapidly, especially among young adults, reflecting delayed marriage. The median age at first marriage among women in the United States rose from 20.6 in 1970 to 22.8 in 1984 (National Center for Health Statistics, 1987) and to 24.5 in 1990 (U.S. Bureau of the Census, 1991).
- It is estimated that 56% of recent marriages will end in divorce (Farley, 1986).
- By 1978, the proportion of children under the age of 18 with two working parents had risen to 50%; one working woman out of nine was the sole support of her family. In 1985, nearly half of all women with children under age 18 were in

the labor force, compared with less than 40% in 1970 (Hayghe, 1986). In 1990, more than half of these mothers were in the labor force.

- Attitudes about women working—and about the job of homemaking—have undergone profound changes. The proportion of women in the workforce, particularly wives and mothers, has increased dramatically. Now more than 60% of all married women work outside the home, and most have children under 18. Fewer than 3 out of 10 women are full-time homemakers.

- Working mothers bear particular burdens and pressures. It is working mothers who most emphatically say they do not have time for themselves—by 63% to 36% (Louis Harris & Associates, 1981).

- Perceived changes in the quality of parenting are a greater source of worry than the issue of working parents alone. According to a Louis Harris survey in 1981, almost twice as many family members feel that the effect of both parents working outside the home has been negative (52%) as compared to those who feel it has been positive (28%) for families. However, most feminists and many working women who stress the positive effects feel that the fulfillment for women working outside the home, added financial security, improved family communications, and independence for children outweigh the negative effects on the family.

- In 35% of American households with children at home, parents now supplement their own child care with other childcare arrangements. Nearly half of these households have other family members helping to care for their children, and 23% use paid help in the home. Fewer than one in five households use a day care center. Indeed, only about 10% of working mothers have day care facilities available to them.

- Whereas the number of households containing married couples with children rose by only 4% from 1960 to 1983, one-parent households increased by 173%, and households composed of unmarried couples by 331%. In 1983, households maintained by married couples constituted 6 in 10 U.S. households (Glick, 1984, p. 205).

- Lone parents living with their children represent more than one in five households in 1990. Almost all of these parents are women—of whom two thirds are separated or divorced, one quarter have never been married, and fewer than 1 in 20 are widows. Families headed by women accounted for 8.5 million, or about 15%, of the families in this country in 1980 (Louis Harris & Associates, 1981, p. 204) and about 12 million or 20% in 1990 (U.S. Bureau of the Census, 1991).

- Since 1960, the number of children living with two parents has declined by nearly one fifth, and the number living with one parent—generally the mother—has more than doubled. Most of the children in single-parent households are in transition between residing with two natural parents and residing with one natural parent and one stepparent, because the large majority of divorced and never-married mothers eventually marry (Glick, 1984, p. 204). Around 75% of divorced people remarry, half within 3 years (Family Service America, 1984). By 1990, single-parent and remarriage families constituted about 45% of all families.

- Divorce rates for first marriages are now between 40% and 50%. The incidence of divorce increased from about 14 per 1,000 married women in 1970 to nearly 22 per 1,000 in 1984 (National Center for Health Statistics, 1986b).

- The rise in divorce rates between 1960 and 1980 may explain up to 17% of the rise in labor force participation of women during that period (Johnson & Skinner, 1986).

- By the year 2000, more people are expected to be living in a second marriage than in a first marriage.
- By 1990, 30% of *all* children were in single-parent families, and half of *all* children will have spent some time in a single-parent family before reaching age 18. In the 1980s, almost half of all Black children and a fifth of Hispanic children were being raised in single-parent families (Family Service America, 1984, p. 101).
- Recent U.S. census data suggest that the very norms of childhood are being redefined. In 1955, 60% of American households consisted of an employed father, a mother who remained at home, and two or more school-age children. Thirty years later, in 1985, such families made up only 7% of U.S. households. With the major increase in two-earner families, dual-career or otherwise, estimates now place the number of children who come home from school to an empty house at 4 million. It has been projected that by 1990 there were 6 million such children due to the influx of more mothers into the labor force (Turkington, 1983). These are the so-called latchkey children about whom there is increasing concern that lack of adult supervision will lead to sexual precocity, vandalism, chemical dependency, and other social problems.
- As just suggested, one of the most dramatic changes in family structures is the growing norm of children living with one parent; 59% of the children born in 1983 will live with only one parent at some time before reaching age 18. Many one-parent families consist of teenage mothers who are barely removed from childhood themselves. Of the 3.3 million births annually, approximately 700,000 are to adolescents. Such single-parent family structures, usually female-headed, are the new poverty pockets of the nation. One child in five under age 19 and one child in four under age 6 is poor. Black and Hispanic children living in female-headed households are at the greatest risk of growing up in poverty. Because of the higher rates of poverty and the large number of female-headed households among minority groups, it is likely that the rate of childhood poverty will continue to grow.
- Estimates in the 1980s were that 1.3 million children under age 5 were living with an adolescent parent, and that public aid to teenage parents and their children consumed over $16.65 billion annually ("Studies Target," 1986, p. 1).
- Whether related directly to changes in family structures and stresses or not, teenage homicide since 1950 is up by more than 200% for Whites and by 16% for non-Whites; teenage suicide is up by more than 15% since 1950; arrests for teenage crime for those 18 to 24 years old are up from 18% in 1960 to 34% in 1980; and teenage unemployment since 1961 is up by 35% for non-Whites and 60% for Whites (Education Commission of the States, 1985). Certainly related to the changes in family structures and family stresses is another set of statistics: those that reflect current levels of violence in the family with either child abuse or spouse abuse at issue. For example, the National Center on Child Abuse and Neglect estimates that approximately 1 million children are maltreated by their parents every year; of these 100,000 to 200,000 are physically abused, 60,000 to 100,000 are sexually abused, and the remainder are neglected. Each year more than 2,000 children die in circumstances that suggest or are clearly indicative of child abuse or neglect (Barnett, Pittman, Ragan, & Salus, 1980).
- The data about spouse abuse are somewhat suspect in terms of how much and what type of such violence actually is reported. However, available estimates sug-

gest that one third of all married couples engage in spouse assault (Straus, Gelles, & Steinmetz, 1980), which would involve some 15 to 20 million married couples. Other statistics indicate that more than one fourth of all American couples experience at least one violent incident sometime during their relationship, one sixth experience such an event every year, and 1 couple in 10 engages in extreme physical abuse.

These items describe the substance of a major transformation in the attitudes about and the characteristics of family patterns in the United States. These changes are dramatic and wideranging in their implications for family roles, sex roles, and child development in contemporary society. As subsequent sections of this chapter illustrate, statistics tend to mask the tensions, stresses, and problems inherent in the magnitude of shifts in both the macroenvironment and the microenvironment in which family interaction patterns, parenting roles, expectations for family success, and child-rearing are conceived and played out.

CHANGES IN FAMILY STRUCTURE

Inherent in the demographic shifts in American families are the outlines of both the changes in family structures and the stresses to which they must adapt. A brief analysis of the current characteristics of family structures will provide a useful context for subsequent analyses of changes in these structures.

In considering family structures, it is somewhat difficult to get beyond the notion that there are acceptable alternatives to the traditional, intact nuclear family, to what Goode (1970) called "the classical family of Western nostalgia." It further follows that it is perhaps equally difficult to realize that the family, whatever its form, is a cultural creation, the specific characteristics of which vary across societies and across time as the needs for family units change under the pressures of societal shifts in values and opportunity. Such a view is reflected in the contrasts between the institutional family, dominant in past generations, and the companionate family that is evolving today.

The institutional family

> . . . brings a woman and a man together primarily on the basis of their interdependence and their abilities to perform certain complementary functions. If love, companionship, sexual satisfaction, mutual respect, and happiness are found in marriage, then it is a bonus rather than as a marital right. . . . The institutional family is oriented toward survival, the accomplishment of tasks having to do with production/reproduction, socialization of the young, sexuality, and other functions. (Glazer-Malbin, 1978, p. 11)

The institutional family was predominant in the agrarian society several generations ago when the family lived together and family members worked together to produce goods and perform services. Children were born and raised to promote family survival without much reliance on people outside the household, even though neighbors, kin, and the church did have an influence. In the institutional family, *formal* social relationships predominate, and social interaction is constrained by role expectations. The father is the head of the household and principal breadwinner, and the mother and certainly the children are in different and typically less powerful roles.

The change from the institutional to the companionate family has evolved as technological changes and the organization of urban-industrial society have decreased or changed the functions family members used to perform for each other. As production of goods and services increasingly moved out of the home to the work-place and as birth control was more widely practiced, many of the reasons for tradi-tional family units changed in focus.

In the companionate family structure, personal social relationships rather than formal social relationships and obligations prevail. Although many of the institu-tional functions previously performed in the home are now performed outside the home, mass society tends to bring with it impersonalization and other assaults upon interpersonal needs that the family can counteract in its increasing emphasis upon companionate rather than institutional concerns. In such a context, sexual equality and the women's movement's emphasis on new lifestyles and role modifications can be played out; the desires for personal growth, closeness, and intimacy can find sup-port; and the needs for privacy, property, commitment, safety, and security in an interpersonal enclave can be addressed.

It is obvious that both the institutional family and the companionate family have tensions and frustrations. In the former, perhaps, the stultifying limits of authoritari-anism and rigid role expectations were the major source of family problems; in the latter, the vagueness and ambiguity of interpersonal relationships and personal expectations create stress. Neither of these family forms is necessarily good or bad, nor as absolute or discrete as suggested here. Rather, they both represent the cultural expression of how family structures vary as broader social changes shape and reshape their character and utility.

Although it is not appropriate to make direct comparisons between the institu-tional and companionate description of families and what general systems theory and its various proponents have described as relatively open or closed systems, it is useful to note similarities between these concepts. The terms *open* and *closed* refer to the boundaries of a family system and the effects on the quality and degree of inter-action within the family and between it and the larger environment. The more open the system, the greater the degree of independence and autonomy individual family members experience and the greater their ability is to function in a self-directed manner. The more closed the system, the greater is the difficulty in differentiation, individualism, and separation the individual members experience. The manner in which the family invokes its rules influences the members' perceptions of what is expected, what is appropriate, and what is possible. It also reflects the degree to which a family can deal with critical corrections, changes, and stresses (Herr & Best, 1984).

Clearly the trend in family structures over the past decade or two has been toward increasing pluralism in the forms they take. As compared to the conventional, intact nuclear family, the family forms that have shown the greatest increase are those directly related to increases in divorce (single-parent and stepfamilies), dual-work and dual-career families, single-person households, couples living together in cohabitation without the legal sanctions of marriage, and families in which grandpar-ents raise the children because their parents are too dysfunctional to undertake their parenting responsibilities. Combined with some of the evolving nontraditional family forms, there is a growing trend toward individual freedom of choice with regard to participation or, indeed, nonparticipation in family structures of diverse organization and purpose. Such involvement or noninvolvement and the type of family structure involved entail different forms of stress and different needs for counseling and therapy.

NONTRADITIONAL FAMILY STRUCTURES

As might be assumed from the demographic shifts that affect families and their members, the word *nontraditional* is used frequently in the professional literature to describe current and evolving family forms. In many discussions of the topic, nontraditional is defined "as all living patterns other than legal, lifelong, sexually exclusive marriage between one man and one woman, with children, where the male is the primary provider and ultimate authority" (Macklin, 1980, p. 175). Macklin's review of family forms in the United States and other research studies clearly showed that the majority of the households cannot be characterized as traditional nuclear families. Rather, such family forms as single-parent or dual-career families, persons living alone, and households consisting of nonrelated individuals have grown steadily in number and in proportion to the whole. Undoubtedly, each of these family forms has its own set of stresses. We will hold that discussion until we deal a bit more fully with family structures themselves.

Macklin (1980) identified some nine categories of family forms or lifestyles other than the traditional form just defined. In some cases categories have several variations, and new categories continue to emerge as social metaphors and values about families undergo change over time. In the descriptions of family structures that follow, Macklin's findings, as well as related research pertinent to her categories, are included.

Nonmarital Cohabitation

Although it is still a numerically small proportion of all couple households, roughly 6.2% and 3,510,000 cohabiting couples in 1993, the number of unmarried people living together as a household has more than doubled since 1980. It seems that nonmarital cohabitation is not replacing marriage, but is instead delaying marriage because most people in such arrangements (approximately 90%) intend to marry at some time, although not necessarily their current partner. Indeed, most cohabiting relationships either terminate or end in marriage after a relatively short period of time (6 months to a year or so), although cohabitation has now become the typical way to begin a live-in sexual relationship (Farley, 1996). Thus the absolute number of people who have cohabited at some point in their lives is larger than the number of those who cohabit at a particular point in time. Indeed, several researchers have found as many as five types of nonmarital cohabitation, varying from temporary and casual conveniences to permanent alternatives to marriage. Available research about reported overall satisfaction, communication, sexual satisfaction, decision making, or division of labor has shown few differences between cohabiting and married couples except in the area of commitment.

Voluntary Childlessness

Current estimates are that approximately 10% of all women who ever marry are childless, with about one half of these women choosing not to have children voluntarily. Couples who choose not to have children are for the most part those who are motivated by the disadvantages of parenthood and the responsibilities of raising children, or who decide to engage in interests or lifestyles in which children would be impediments. Fifteen years or so ago, the emerging tendency to delay marriage and childbearing was often associated with the related tendency of women who have not had a child by age 30 to forego childbearing permanently. The latter trend in fertility now seems to be changing that reality. Childbearing is now shifting to somewhat older ages. In the 1980s and into the 1990s, the birthrate increased substantially for women in their 30s. Women in the late baby boom generation, who in their 20s were dedicated to educational attainments and to achieving career growth and earnings, in their 30s are making up for the childbearing they did not do when they were younger. Now childbearing after age 40, rather than after age 30, is rarer but not improbable (O'Conell, 1991). As expected life spans increase, cultural attitudes about appropriate ages for childbearing change, and medical breakthroughs in dealing with problems of fertility and childbearing occur, having children after 40 may become less rare.

The Binuclear Family: Joint Custody and Coparenting

A particularly interesting trend is that of the binuclear family. In this structure, divorce is not seen as a dissolution of the family, but rather as a process that reorganizes and redefines the family. From such a process of redefinition, new models of divorcing families have emerged in which adults continue to practice their parental roles even though the spousal unit has been terminated. The notion of the binuclear family views the child as part of a family system composed of two nuclear households (with varying degrees of cooperation between the two and time spent in each), with or without the parents sharing legal custody (Macklin, 1980, p. 179). Ahrons's (1979) classic longitudinal study of divorced parents who have been awarded joint child custody has shown that the kind of relationship developed by divorced parents who continue to share child-rearing functions is an important factor in determining the effect of the divorce on the child.

The Stepfamily

Families in which one or both of the married adults have children from a previous marriage living permanently with them, traditionally called stepfamilies, increasingly are being referred to as reconstituted or blended families. Such family structures now compose about 10% to 15% of all households in the United States.

The most common stepfamily is composed of a mother, her children, and a stepfather. Research on such configurations has tended to show that stepfathers, compared with fathers in intact families, rate themselves more negatively as fathers and, unlike their wives and stepchildren, rate their stepchildren's happiness as being lower than do natural parents, even though other national research has found few differences between children raised in stepfather families and in intact families (Wilson, Zurcher, McAdam, & Curtis, 1975). Indeed, some research (Duberman, 1975) has found that stepmothers are less likely than stepfathers to establish good relationships with stepchildren and have close relationships with young stepchildren. Here, as in most family forms, there is need for much more empirical research and less reliance on primarily personal and clinical experiences. In particular, there is a need for analyses of the structural and functional differences among the different types of stepfamilies (e.g., families reconstituted because of widowhood rather than divorce, stepfamilies with young children as compared with those with adolescents).

Open Marriage/Open Family

The terms *open marriage* and *open family* have become frequent symbols of alternative family structures in the last two decades. *Open marriage* is descriptive of relationships with realistic expectations, respect for personal privacy, role flexibility, open and honest communication, open companionship, equality of power and responsibility, pursuit of identity, and mutual trust. There is little research on the prevalence of open marriage as a family form. Available research has suggested, however, that the number of such marriages is probably small because of the ego development, personal security, and commitment to personal growth such a lifestyle demands. One study (Wachowiak & Bragg, 1980) reported that open marriage is associated with fewer children, less frequent church attendance, and younger age.

Open marriage as a lifestyle tends to be seen as similar to *open family*. The latter tends to emphasize flexible role prescriptions across age and sex, clear communication with extensive negotiations and decision by consensus, open expression of emotion, and mutual respect (Macklin, 1980, p. 180). Again, however, there are few data suggesting the degree to which *open family* has become a major lifestyle in the United States.

Extramarital Sex

Open marriage and open family as family lifestyles do not equate to the freedom to engage in extramarital sex, although this may be part of the equation in a particular family unit. Nevertheless, there are family structures in which extramarital sex or comarital sex (where two or more married couples share the same domicile and share sexual favors across couples) tend to affect the form family communication and roles take. Data have suggested that for middle-class, educated samples the rate of reported extramarital sex has increased, particularly for women; in general, women who work or volunteer outside the home report higher rates of extramarital sex. Data have not suggested, however, that extramarital sex is necessarily indicative of a poor marital relationship; rather, its significance, which is different for men and women, tends to vary with the stage of marriage.

Within the practice of extramarital sex, there are different degrees of openness among spouses. Some family structures include "swinging," and others can be characterized as a "sexually open marriage."

- **Swinging** has been defined as legally married spouses sharing coitus and other forms of erotic behavior with other legally married couples in a social context defined by all participants as a form of recreational convivial play (Gilmartin, 1977, p. 161). Macklin (1980, p. 182) indicated that the best estimate is that approximately 2% of the present U. S. population has engaged in swinging or wife swapping with about three quarters dropping out each year. Where mutual agreement between spouses exists on the appropriateness of the lifestyle, marriages do not seem to be helped or harmed by swinging, but for those who have dropped out and become ex-swingers, problems such as jealousy, guilt, competing emotional attachments, and fear of discovery by children and neighbors seem to be major issues.
- **Sexually open marriage** is characterized by a mutual decision of the married couple to permit one or both partners to have openly acknowledged, independent sexual relationships with partners who maintain their own residences (Macklin, 1980, p. 182). Available research indicates that participants use such lifestyles as ways to allow both the freedom for personal growth and the security of committed relationships. Problems participants experience tend to revolve around the

need for continuous accommodation and negotiation, jealousy and feelings of possessiveness, loneliness, conflicts over use of free time, and the difficulty of integrating such a lifestyle into a broader social network.

Same-Sex Intimate Relationships

In the last several decades, social values and legal statutes have clearly changed concerning sexuality, whether heterosexual or homosexual, and living arrangements, with or without a formal marriage contract. Several states are debating whether to formally recognize the marriage vows of same-sex partners, and several states have decided to do so or are on the threshold of doing so; an increasing number of corporate organizations are extending health care and insurance coverage and other spousal or dependent benefits to same-sex partners of the employee; and many of the state laws that restricted sexual activity to heterosexual married couples have been rescinded, as have anti-sodomy laws. In some states, gay and lesbian persons are being permitted to adopt children, prerogatives that had been restricted to heterosexual married couples. Although it is not yet clear that gays, lesbians, and bisexuals will be granted all of the opportunities available to heterosexual individuals, it is apparent that there is a trend toward the privatization of sexuality, particularly among consenting adults; and under Civil Rights legislation a series of protections for homosexual lifestyles and alternative sexual orientations that were not present in this nation a quarter of a century ago have been secured.

As homosexual couples and their lifestyles become more open in the society, it has become clear that, as is true for other family structures, there is no one homosexual lifestyle. Nevertheless, according to much of the existing data, the great majority of male or female homosexuals are in stable couple relationships that bear many similarities to those of heterosexual couples. Although there is increasing interest in the homosexual relationship as a family form, with primary focus on the couple or spousal unit, data about the prevalence of such units, the extent of commitment or openness of lifestyle, psychological reactions, and other behavior aspects are only now in the early stages of systematic inquiry.

Multi-Adult Households

Terms such as *multilateral marriage, commune, intentional community, affiliated family,* and *expanded family* are variations on family forms in which more than two adults are involved in child rearing and, perhaps, sexual relationships with more than one adult in the family unit. For example, the Constantines (1973, p. 49) described multilateral marriage as consisting of "three or more partners each of whom considers himself/herself to be married (or committed . . .) to more than one of the other partners." Such units typically consist of four adult partners and their children from preexisting conventional marriages. Generally, the bonds between spouses that existed prior to the multilateral marriage continue as the primary bonds and survive the dissolution of the multilateral units.

There seem to be no reliable data on the number of multilateral family units in the United States. However, communes or intentional communities as a family form were estimated as of 1975 to include 45,000 communities with 755,000 residents (Macklin, 1980). Zablocki's study (1977) of 60 urban communes indicated that many of these were formed to provide social support for the individual or single parent.

Most communes that survive tend to have a high degree of social organization. Thus individual family units tend to experience a shift in the locus of social control from themselves to the communal organization and a loss of control over their life space or territory as well as over their partners. Although parents receive help with parenting, they tend to lose the ability to make and enforce rules that differ from the community norms. Children seem to do extremely well in such communities as they gain expanded adult relationships, rule makers, and rule enforcers. There is little evidence of major emotional damage among children in such arrangements, although there are isolated reports in the mass media of child physical or sexual abuse, and restricted educational opportunities are associated with certain "cult" communes.

Single-Parent Families

As the social values about marriage have weakened during this century, divorce has become almost epidemic, rates of childbearing by never-married women keep rising, and there have been sharp increases in single-parent families. As discussed earlier in this chapter, about 20% of families in the United States are now headed by a single parent, usually a mother. Many of these family units are impoverished both in economic terms and in terms of parental availability. Even when the mother works, many single-parent homes headed by women fall below the poverty line, in part because many women who work still earn considerably less then men; and the mother who works carries all of the parenting and homemaking responsibilities required to maintain the home, thus reducing the time available for individual child care.

One of the variations of the single-parent theme is the steadily rising number of single-parent family units headed by men, in part due to a trend toward the husband retaining custody of his children. Father-only single-parent family units with children have essentially doubled in number since 1975, although still much smaller in number than those headed by women. In 1990, there were some 1.5 million families that included a father and his children but no wife; in about a third of these situations, there was an adult woman identified as a partner. Because single-parent men tend to earn higher income than single-parent women, these-single parent family units are less likely than those headed by women to fall below the poverty line; and because of the rise in cohabitation, single-parent families headed by a father may more likely include an adult woman partner to bring in income and to share in homemaking and parenting tasks.

Grandparents Raising Grandchildren

As suggested earlier in the chapter, this family form represents a transfer of child-rearing responsibilities from an absent or incapacitated parent to an older adult, typically a grandparent. According to the data available, within the last decade there has been a 40% increase in such households across the United States. The precipitating factors in such transfer of child-rearing responsibilities from the biological parents to the grandparents may involve incarceration of the parent, or the parent may experience substance abuse, or emotional or mental illness, or may be HIV positive or suffer from AIDs. Depending upon the circumstances of the absence or the illness of the parent, the children may be at heightened risk of developmental or psychiatric disorders. In some instances, the parent may have engaged in child abuse or neglect.

In general, then, the transfer of parental responsibilities to grandparents takes place in situations in which it has been impossible for parents to assume or continue parenting roles, and thus grandparents, either voluntarily or in other circumstances, have entered the family unit as the principal caregiver for the children and, perhaps, for other family members as well (Pinson-Millburn et al., 1996). According to a study reported by the American Association of Retired Persons in 1994 and cited by Pinson-Millburn et al., "in those households headed by grandparents, about one third have no parent present and reflect an estimated 723,000 midlife and older adults caring for grandchildren" (p. 548).

STRESSES IN THE FAMILY

As reflected in the multiplicity of family structures that now exist in the United States, there are many potential points of stress within and among such structures. Such stresses can be viewed in both macro and micro terms as the sources of stress are identified and analyzed.

If we take the big picture, the macro view of family stresses, there is much to say. Since World War II the United States has experienced wave after wave of significant value shifts. Among them have been those dealing with equality and equity, accountability, quality of life versus material quantity, religion, entitlement, sex roles, sexual preference, sexual freedom, women's awareness, and minority pride. Values in transition obviously have affected social perceptions of family units and perceptions of individuals' places within families.

Shifting values have affected families' commitments to endure and have caused confusion within families about responsibilities, rights, and the appropriate set of values. Some social indicators suggest that value shifts and other changes in society are creating much higher expectations for the family than those held by previous generations. Expectations about sharing, intimacy, and emotional support may be set at too high a level of expectation to be sustained by many people forming families (Family Service America, 1984, p. 10).

The Macroenvironment

In many of the stresses just identified, there is an implicit, if not explicit, concern about how the macroenvironment affects families. Streib and Beck (1980) pointed out the importance of the effects of bureaucracy, pension provisions, service programs, and changes in medical care provisions as elements that bring about family stresses, particularly among older families. Obviously, the macroenvironment, the family-bureaucracy linkage, also can be analyzed in terms of many other areas of potential stress: the home/school relationship, social service/pregnant adolescent linkage, employer/alcoholic family member relationship, or the legal system/divorcing parent linkage. In each of these relationships, the macroenvironment provides a context of stressors that tend to affect different families in different ways.

The macroenvironment, for families as well as for individuals, is the source of images and reinforcements as well as policies at the federal, state, or local levels that affect how families are viewed, the limits of appropriate behavior or structure, or how child abuse or spouse abuse is identified and treated. Such policies and the services they provide are, in turn, responses to the various macrolevel social trends that constitute broad categories of stressors on families.

Family Service America in 1983 surveyed its 270 affiliated family service agencies in the United States and Canada to obtain an inventory of family concerns or stresses. They received responses from 189 agencies serving more than 700,000 families. Although the respondents to the surveys conducted by Family Service America (1984) were of lower socioeconomic groups for the most part, most of the concerns or stresses identified characterize family units at all socioeconomic levels. The concerns that emerged are described in the following sections in paraphrased form (Family Service America, 1984, pp. 72–77). These concerns continue to be important in the 1990s. Where relevant, recent research is added to the findings of Family Service America.

Unemployment. Along with its corollaries, unemployment was found to be the problem most frequently addressed by the agencies. As psychological research reported in the previous chapter has come to show, unemployment is not only an economic phenomenon but also one that is related to physiological stress and stress-related diseases, a rise in suicide and mental illness, spousal and child abuse, chemical dependency, depression, children's irritability, digestive and academic problems, and many other manifestations. Because of its profound effects, unemployment ripples throughout a family, touching every member in one way or another.

Single-parent problems. Also of major concern to family service agencies are single-parent problems. Inherent in such circumstances are feelings of personal vulnerability, frequent poverty, issues of child care, time management, guilt, and personal stress.

Although the largest number of single parents are women, there are also single custodial fathers. Custodial fathers seem to have fewer resources than their female counterparts in the areas of family, peer, and community assistance (Tedder, Scherman, & Sheridan, 1984), although their financial situations are usually better (Farley, 1996). Whereas female single parents have major emotional and economic problems to cope with in relation to child rearing, single fathers also experience difficult times adjusting to their new roles because of the lack of community and personal support, lack of information, loneliness, and poor coping skills in an unfamiliar situation. Some research has indicated that meeting the emotional needs of their children is the area of most concern to single fathers, but other research has suggested that taking care of the physical needs of the children is the major difficulty. Tedder et al. (1984) in their review of the literature indicated that other concerns also tend to be of particular importance to single fathers: "finding good supervision, care, and protection for their children, obtaining information about rearing daughters in a motherless home, knowing what constitutes normal development in children, having the skills to perform homemaking tasks or finding a housekeeper" (p. 181). In addressing such concerns, the research of Tedder et al. (1984) found that support groups with an information-giving/discussion format were useful in helping single fathers deal with the divorce adjustment process. Thus they were able to achieve greater feelings of self-worth, greater separation from their former partners, and lowered feelings of anger toward their former partners.

McLanahan and Sandefur (1994) found that compared to children in stable two-parent families, children who had spent time in single-parent homes had lower grade-point averages and were about as likely to drop out of high school before getting diplomas. Daughters from single-parent families were 2.5 times as likely as daughters from two-parent families to become teen mothers themselves. As compared to children from two-parent families, teenage boys from single-parent homes were 1.4 times as likely to be idle, that is, not enrolled in school or not employed.

Rise in family violence.   Periods of economic instability are often accompanied by a rise in family violence, which is a frequent presenting problem for families. Very young marriages, single-parent stress, unemployment, teenage pregnancies, and alcohol abuse each may trigger child or spouse abuse as family systems bear the brunt of frustration and anger their member's experience.

Incest less hidden.   An increasing issue for those adults who were abused as children, those who now abuse their children, and children now being abused is incest less hidden. As public understanding about this problem grows, its frequency as a family stressor becomes increasingly evident. As more becomes known about the prevalence and the long-term effects of incest, it is evident that it is a widespread family problem. Estimates are that 9% to 16% of all women experience incest before age 18. Incest, as a form of child abuse, includes any type of sexual activity that occurs between a child and a parent, stepparent, sibling, extended family member, or surrogate parent figure (Sgroi, 1982). Depending upon the age of the child and the circumstances surrounding the incestuous relationship, many children exposed to such abuse experience the range of emotional reactions described in the literature on victimization, such as shock, confusion, helplessness, anxiety, fear, and depression (Janoff-Bluman & Frieze, 1983).

The aftermath of such traumatic experiences in an individual's life lead Briere (1984) to describe a post-sexual-abuse syndrome, common among incest victims, that includes such chronic symptoms as dissociation, anxiety, isolation, sleep disturbances, anger, sexual dysfunction, substance addiction, and self-destructiveness. In many instances, incest victims—like victims of rape, spousal abuse, and similar situations—experience significant guilt, shame, low self-esteem, problems with intimacy, inability to trust, and other psychological phenomena. Although the actual events that cause such feelings may be repressed or the links between the experience of incest and the psychological effects may be blurred, the intensity of the psychological and behavioral reactions that persist across time are likely to lead many incest victims to counseling to resolve the conflicts in their emotional life.

Research (e.g., Josephson & Fong-Beyette, 1987) has suggested that counselors can be helpful to incest victims, and that factors related to initial disclosure and exploration of incest are client readiness, direct questioning by the counselor, positive counselor reactions to initial disclosure, and such counselor characteristics as being accepting, validating, encouraging, and knowledgeable about addressing incest experiences in counseling.

> It is recommended that counselors acknowledge and validate the significance of the incest. Incest should be identified as an important trauma that is related to clients' current life difficulties. Perceiving incest clients as survivors who developed complicated coping skills that were actually adaptive to their early environment can help these clients see themselves as survivors rather than as sick or helpless victims. (Josephson & Fong-Beyette, 1987, p. 478)

A shrinking government role.   Assisting families or providing services for families as the government role shrinks results in greater difficulty in locating and using such services, in personal frustrations, and in the exacerbation of the need for legal, medical, and mental health services for many families. Shifting government policies on welfare regulations, particularly the requirement to find paid work within a specific time frame or lose benefits, creates considerable stress on many welfare recipients and on the occupational structure.

Divorce and remarriage. Increasingly open options to many, if not most, people are divorce and remarriage, but they do not occur without psychological and physical costs. Problems of custody of and access to children after divorce, children becoming pawns in hostile divorce proceedings, and issues of child rearing and discipline in stepfamilies as well as questions of identity, divided loyalties, conflicting role expectations, and adjustment to new partners all intensify the difficulties of resolving problems of marriage and remarriage. Linkages also have been made between suicide rates and divorce, suggesting that divorce alters kinship systems, thus decreasing the regulation of the individual ego and increasing the propensity toward suicide (Wasserman, 1984). Other research has demonstrated that all members of a family affected by divorce, including children, have lower mental health and general health ratings than people in intact families. Children who have experienced family disruption and divorce also rate lower in social and academic performance. Finally, this research finds a complex interdependence among divorce, parental stress, children's stress, children's performance, and family physical health (Guidubaldi & Cleminshaw, 1985).

Growing evidence shows that divorce and separation entail developmental problems for children of all ages (McLanahan & Sandefur, 1994; Robson, 1987). As a result of divorce and separation, it is estimated that more than 50% of children born in the 1980s will spend some time in a single-parent home, and that about 25% of all children will be part of a remarried family (Hernandez, 1993). About 47% of second marriages eventually end, and children again face a readjustment in family patterns.

The effects upon children of divorce are not favorable. Robson's (1987) summary of the literature on the topic suggested that children of divorce are overrepresented in psychiatric populations and show higher rates of delinquency and antisocial behavior, neurotic symptoms, depression, conduct disorders, and habit formations such as sleep disturbances than children in intact homes. In nonclinic populations, the children of divorce also demonstrate significant maladaptations as compared with children from intact families. "The children are more dependent, disobedient, aggressive, whining, demanding, and unaffectionate. . . . [They] have generalized feelings of anxiety and helplessness and lower self-esteem. They perform less well on a variety of social and adjustment indices" (p. 2).

Robson (1987) also reported that children at different ages from infancy through college react to divorce and separation in ways that affect their development. For example, "children under age 5 tend to regress in their development, showing feeding difficulties, toileting problems including soiling, smearing, and enuresis and frequently disturbed sleeping patterns" (p. 3). These children also frequently manifest intense separation anxiety—fear of being left alone or being abandoned by both parents. Anger, fear, depression, and guilt are commonly seen in children of divorce at preschool and kindergarten ages. School-aged children (ages 6 to 8) may deny the separation or difficulties with it, but they also may exhibit depression and anxiety. They may be extremely hard to control and often have temper tantrums. They may use tactics such as refusal to go to school or noncooperation as ways to try to get parents back together again. Older school-aged children (ages 9 to 11) may experience loyalty conflicts between parents and become overly dependent on one or the other parent. They may demonstrate shock, surprise, denial, incredulity, and disbelief. They may come to reject one parent as they become enmeshed in the custody battle and, indeed, reject those parts of their life that were particularly associated with that parent (e.g., participation in sports). They may experience a decrease in self-esteem and in their social and academic functioning.

Adolescents (ages 13 to 18) sometimes take on so many responsibilities for siblings or for household chores that they are forced to mature too quickly. Thus they lose their adolescence and do not resolve the normal adolescent developmental tasks expected of them. Adolescent girls who have experienced the absence of a father through separation may change in their interaction with men, seeking attention and acting out sexual behavior. Lacking intact parental guidance and discipline, adolescents may experience mental health problems, weak judgment, poor interpersonal relationships, and difficulty in perceiving their life in the future. College students (ages 18 to 22) experience stress, changed interactions with their parents, anger, worry about their parents' future, anxiety about their own future marriages, and feelings of loss of a family home. Such findings were supported by Lopez's (1987) comprehensive analysis of the effect of parental divorce on college student development.

Robson's (1987) analysis has suggested that the younger the child when divorce or separation occurs, the more vulnerable and the more disturbed future behavior will be. Nonetheless, it is clear that children at all developmental ages are affected by such experiences, and the residual of the feelings and cognitions associated with divorce and separation endure for an extended period of time, perhaps throughout adulthood. Indeed, in an analysis of two large national studies conducted 30 years apart, Kukla and Weingarten (1979) concluded that coming from a nonintact family of origin affects psychological well-being in adulthood. They further concluded that children of divorce are more likely to experience vulnerability to stress, weaker investment in the parental role, and more instability in their own marriages.

Finally, children living with single parents, primarily mothers, after divorce accounts for the recent rise in childhood poverty (Farley, 1996).

Remarriage families. The term *remarriage families* is frequently used as a synonym for an array of new terms in the American vocabulary that describe families, such as *blended, recoupled, reconstituted, merged,* and *reorganized* (Hayes & Hayes, 1986). Typically, such marriages include at least one parent who has been previously married and probably has children. Indeed, both parents may previously have had children who may now be a part of a blended or reconstituted family. Such arrangements bring with them a variety of psychological issues that are different from those likely to be experienced in first marriages. In remarriages, either or both spouses still may be mourning the loss of the first relationship, trying to understand what went wrong, trying to establish who was to blame, experiencing problems of self-acceptance and acceptance of new roles and responsibilities, renegotiating roles and relationships with family and friends, and transforming the relationship with the a former spouse (Garfield, 1980). But in addition, one or both spouses may also be coping with the transition from single-parent status to newly remarried status, with the expectations their remarried status brings. The latter may involve dealing with new stepchildren or worrying about how their own children are going to cope with a new stepparent. They are trying to create a set of relationships for which there is no history.

For the children, remarriage also can be fraught with dilemmas and confusion. At the least, remarriage disrupts the cognitive and social world of a child who had been living with a single parent after having lived in an intact, nuclear family. The reconceptualization of who one is within this new mix of a stepparent, a parent who is now the spouse of a new parent, and possibly a new set of stepsiblings; new grandparents; a changed relationship network; and perhaps a new geographic location takes time and energy for any child even when the outcome is positive. Obviously the child, like the parent, still may be mourning the loss of the previous family constellation or a previous parent and may feel anger, jealousy, guilt, apprehension, conflicting loyalties, abandonment, powerlessness, and many other emotions that are neither vocalized nor clearly understood. McLanahan and Sandefur (1994), for example, reported that for many children whose family of origin was disrupted by death or divorce, the presence of a stepparent or a grandparent does not make up for the loss of their own father.

Hayes and Hayes (1986) suggested that remarriage families have at least four general categories of concerns with which counselors can help: roles and relationships, feelings and fantasies, rules and regulations, and external forces. Within these categories of concerns are the implications that remarriage families have to create a history, a set of traditions, that is uniquely their own; that roles each family member plays must be negotiated, clarified, and supported; that expectations, realities, or fantasies must be sorted out and worked through; that a shared strategy of discipline must be put in place; and that systems by which the remarriage family has contact with the absent, former spouse(s) and how children interact with the separated parent(s) become very important. Hayes and Hayes (pp. 6–7) indicated that in working with remarriage families, counselors can help by

- encouraging family members to relinquish myths they may hold about the remarriage family;
- helping members to understand the entire family system, its differences from their past families, and the involvement of nonfamily members in the system;
- teaching members more effective communication skills;
- helping members, especially children, to mourn the loss of previous relationships and encourage the development of new relationships;
- providing a forum in which members can work out their relationships with one another and with quasi-kin, especially the absent parent;
- offering structured programs of parent training and lists of readings that family members can use as self-instructional devices;
- informing members of the latest research findings and clinical evidence that may be helpful to them in the reorganization process;
- identifying the tasks of parenting and the relationships that are necessary to enact those roles; and
- running groups for remarriage parents in the community or for stepchildren in the schools.

Blurred male and female roles. Continuing to cause conflict and confusion in many families are blurred male and female roles. Matters of dependence and independence, role expectations, women entering the workforce and men being unemployed, and responsibilities in dual-career families for child care and homemaking represent major sources of stress in many family units. One of the issues of blurred male and female roles is the matter of balancing sex and work roles. Whether married or single, women and men must negotiate a personal identity in which views of sex role and views of self as worker are compatible. Cook (1985) described this balancing process as requiring consideration of self-perceptions of masculine and feminine personality characteristics; attitudes about ideal self and ideals for other people; distinctions between behaviors and skills a person possesses and those he or she actually is willing to use in various settings; and perceptions of environmental demands and rewards for behavior. Each of these categories may involve discrepancies or conflicts for particular individuals in one or more areas, leading to feelings of incompatibility between sex roles and work roles. These conflicts in turn may lead to dissatisfactions with the compromises required to resolve sex-role/work-role discrepancies, confusion, or distress. In such instances, counselors have important roles to play in assisting individuals to identify their conflicts and to bring into better balance their perceptions of the various aspects pertinent to sex roles and work roles.

The inability to balance role behavior in the family and in the workplace has been found to foster severe depression in both employed women and in homemakers. At the root of these problems are disagreements within the family about roles and dissatisfaction with the tasks women feel required to undertake in the home. Whereas depression and dissatisfaction are present for both employed women and homemakers who experience such role disagreements with their husbands, employed women exhibit less severe depression, apparently because of the offsetting economic and intrinsic benefits from work. Homemakers have no similar outlet or compensating mechanism for their feelings of dissatisfaction and depression (Keith & Schaefer, 1985).

Depression and loneliness. Affecting family members of all ages, but particularly acute among teenagers, young adults, and the elderly, are depression and loneliness. Where financial hardships, little hope for the future, powerlessness, and social isolation are at issue, they breed depression and loneliness. So, too, do geographic relocation and occupational mobility as factors that separate family members for indefinite or extended periods of time.

Difficult career decisions, work adjustment problems, and underemployment or unemployment also have the propensity to stimulate anxiety, loneliness, depression, and other mental disorders as well as to intensify or amplify stresses within the family that evolve from economic uncertainty, reduction in the quality of life, generalized tension, and role transformations (Herr & Cramer, 1996; Spokane, 1989).

Problems of the aged. Health and emotional problems, loss of family, loneliness, and needs for companionship and for transportation are among the problems of the aged. Concerns about decreasing independence and loss of ability to care for themselves are the major problems. Similarly, middle-aged children of the aged find themselves caught in the emotional dilemma of trying to be a parent to their children and to their elderly parents at the same time. Drains on financial and emotional resources can increase family vulnerability and tension.

Pregnant, unmarried adolescents and associated concerns. Among the concerns of pregnant, unmarried adolescents are many that relate to keeping their babies, whether or not to marry, financial resources, medical care, foster care, and continuing schooling as well as many other matters that put family units at risk.

Alcohol and drug abuse. Across age and sex groups alcohol and drug abuse is increasing. There is a marked increase in such abuse by adolescents and even younger children. Heavy drinking in families often is associated with unemployment. Drug abuse, including the misuse of prescription drugs, is a growing problem among the elderly, and there is a growing problem of cocaine and other drug use among young professionals and other young married couples.

Alcohol abuse and other types of substance abuse have also been found to be associated with family patterns that are thought to contribute to the maintenance of substance abuse (West, Hosie, & Zarski, 1987). One of 35 families in which one member of the family was hospitalized for substance abuse was found to be highly interdependent and fearful of the separation and individuation of family members. This leads to maladaptive patterns of family interaction, including significant problems of boundary setting between spouses and children. Furthermore, the substance abuser, if a child, is likely to be "triangled" into the spouse's relationship, possibly forming a coalition with one parent against the other, or serving as the focus of spousal communication about unresolved intimacy or conflict problems (Minuchin, 1974). Frequently, the result is a hierarchy reversal in the family in which the substance-abusing child becomes more influential in determining family interactions and communication patterns than either one or both parents. Counselors working with such families need to assess family communication patterns, existing triangles, and potential hierarchy reversals so as to help the family restore appropriate role boundaries and to return the parents to an executive position in the family. To accomplish these goals, counselors need to engage in a systems-oriented approach to family counseling as well as in educational interventions designed to help family members consider the assumptions and possibilities underlying both the actual and the ideal family dynamics to which they are committed.

Parent-child communication problems. Family units continue to be stressed by parent-child communication problems, whether the mediating factor is parents' inadequate listening skills, financial pressures that limit the time and energy available to spend with children, confusion about disciplinary measures, or other parenting skills. Parent-child conflicts frequently become parent-parent conflicts and thereby permeate the family structure, creating environments of ongoing hostility and tension.

Dual-career families. Numerous problems plague dual-career families. For example, in the two-earner working class family that has bought into the American dream of material acquisition and the credit card culture, the loss of a job held by either the man or the woman is likely to plunge the family into financial disaster and cause all types of family stresses. If it is the man who loses his job and his wife becomes the breadwinner, the shift in roles can be traumatic. The wife may gain a new sense of self-worth, but the husband loses his, causing a variety of tensions in the family. Some family tensions arise because the woman's career outdistances the man's in the dual-career family, or because of conflict about whose career is more important and under what criteria geographic moves should be made that would cause one spouse to follow the other. As noted previously, dual-career families frequently experience problems in time management, logistics regarding child care and children's medical emergencies, and housekeeping issues relative to which parent will deal with which role in maintaining the family structure.

Hodgson (1984), a family therapist who works with dual-career families, suggested using a number of therapeutic techniques to help such couples determine ways to reduce some of their problems. Some of her suggestions, in paraphrased form, are as follows:

1. Use a "caring days" form in the counseling session in which the counselor can ask the husband and wife to generate a list of 10 to 15 specific behaviors that the other could do to show caring. The form is then kept at home, and each spouse logs the occurrence of caring behaviors on a daily basis.
2. Convene the whole family at least once in the counselor's office to explore ways to divide chores in an equitable manner and thereby alleviate division of labor conflicts.
3. Train the couple in communication skills, relationship enhancement, or problem solving to help them deal with the time crunch and the reduced conversation they experience.
4. Help the couple to negotiate the exercise of power in family decisions in ways that help them "to visualize the ways decisions are currently made, the ways that they would like them to be made, and the ways they agree to apportion decision-making authority in the future" (p. 50).
5. Expose the dual-career couples to other couples sharing the same types of stresses and conflicts through books, popular articles, and dual-career workshops that identify common problems and teach joint decision-making and communication skills.
6. Provide education about effective child-rearing practices or hold parenting workshops.

Although there are stresses and tensions in dual-career families, it is inaccurate to assume that there are no strengths in such structures. The benefits of a dual-career marriage have been enumerated by Wilcox-Matthew and Minor (1989). These include feelings of self-worth, accomplishment and control from work roles, more roles in which to define success, marital solidarity, higher standard of living, child-care support policies in some employing organizations, and more egalitarian roles, among other positive outcomes. In general, dual-career marriages offer the advantages of enhanced identity of the wife, increased income, greater intellectual development, and higher self-esteem. Men benefit too from less sex-role stereotyping. Research studies (e.g., Knaub, 1986) have indicated that both parents and children rate their perceptions of the dual-career lifestyle positively. They tend as well to perceive their families as high in family strengths, particularly with regard to concern, respect, and support. Nevertheless, there are primary problems of time constraints and needs for coping strategies in the areas of successful negotiation and conflict resolution.

Much of the conflicting evidence about the effects of dual-career families on the psychological or physical health of children is a function of methodological flaws in many of the studies as well as of inconsistent study of the effects of dual-career families on different groups of children and youth. Lewis and Cooper (1983) criticized many studies for not taking into account family interactions or the circumstances surrounding both the family and the availability, use, and characteristics of day care. Silverstein (1991) suggested a halt to the attitude of negativism that pervades many research studies about maternal employment and its effects on child care and family unity, and instead, she recommended a search for those positive elements that make these functions work effectively. Bennett and Reardon (1985), in studying data about dual-career families and particularly about working mothers, suggested that the potential harm done by mothers working is not severe, and that negative effects, particularly for boys, may be reduced if several factors are present or accommodated. These factors include choosing day care that is stable, stimulating, and warm. Involvement of the father is increasingly considered important in child development, especially in dual-career families. According to Bennett and Reardon, specific actions that can be taken to enhance the experience of boys in dual-career families are to (a) encourage the active participation and support of the father, (b) try to make the mother's job as satisfying as possible, and (c) be aware of the potential problems and offer special attention to boys in dual-career families. In a major synthesis of the existing research on the effects of paternal employment on infants, preschoolers, and adolescents, the following conclusions were drawn by Herr and Cramer (1996, p. 568):

1. When the child is enrolled in high-quality day care, the intellectual effects are neither harmful nor helpful, except for children who grow up in a high-risk environment. For these children, quality day care actually seems to help to maintain or to raise IQ scores.
2. Maternal employment does not seem to alter the emotional bond between mother and child.
3. Maternal job satisfaction seems to be positively related to development in preschoolers.
4. There is no convincing proof of any negative effects of maternal employment on preschoolers. At the least, maternal employment seems to do no harm.
5. Maternal employment probably has a positive effect on a daughter's career involvement and commitment. When combined with such factors as educational and occupational status, sex-role ideology, and parental encouragement, maternal employment leads to a decrease in a daughter's sex typing and to more assertive career planning.
6. Adolescent children of working mothers do not seem to experience any proven, consistently harmful effects.
7. Female adolescents may react somewhat differently to maternal employment than do male adolescents, primarily in relation to daughters choosing less traditional careers and increasing their emphasis on career planning.

When counseling for dual career couples is appropriate, it needs to be seen primarily as lifestyle counseling. The intense interaction between family and career for both men and women requires that they analyze and understand life roles, Further, many marriages, perhaps most, have relationship issues that may be intensified in the dual career family. Thus counseling in this context frequently must focus on changing spouse needs and identity, the shifting balance of power, competition, and continual revision of the initial marital contract. Sekaran (1986) identified five dilemmas facing dual-career couples that are likely to be reflected in the content of counseling: (1) role overload because of redistributed homemaking responsibilities, (2) identification with traditional gender-based roles, (3) role-cycling problems of timing (such as when to have children), (4) network problems leading to social isolation, and (5) environmental sanctions caused by clashes with traditionally imposed values. To combat these dilemmas, Sekardan suggested counseling that emphasizes helping dual-careerists to define self-concept and self-identity, to explore value orientations and develop functional values, to equalize power distribution and role sharing in the family, to define success, to manage stress, to establish new functional behaviors, and to develop appropriate skills.

Latchkey children. As suggested earlier in this chapter, one of the major corollaries of the rise in dual-career and two-earner families has been the growing visibility of so-called latchkey children. This term refers to children and youth, unsupervised by their parents, "who care for themselves before or after school, on weekends, and during holidays while their parents work" (Robinson, Rowland, & Coleman, 1986).

In general, research studies have not kept pace with the numbers of latchkey children and the circumstances involved. Indeed, the available research is mixed in its analysis of whether self-care by children is good or bad. For example, on the positive side, some research has shown that latchkey children are prone to become more independent, self-reliant, resourceful, and better informed about procedures for dealing with their own physical well-being than children who are supervised after school by adults or by older siblings (Long & Long, 1981; Stroman & Duff, 1982). On the negative side, some research has suggested that latchkey children left in self-care frequently report nightmares and high fear levels (fear of noises and fear of the dark) (Long & Long, 1981). One longitudinal research study examined 1,000 former latchkey children and their parents. Most of these subjects were members of minority groups (Long & Long, 1983). These researchers found that one half of the adults who were former latchkey children were still afraid to be alone. Furthermore, it was found that many of these adults experienced residual feelings of loneliness, boredom, resentment toward parents, fears, social isolation, and a tendency to enter occupations oriented around things instead of people. The explanation for these findings, in contrast to other studies that found no high levels of fear among latchkey children (Galambos & Garbarino, 1983), seems to depend on where the children reside. For example, children who live in high-crime areas where violence, drug abuse, and related conditions predominate are likely to experience fear when they come home to an empty house and must supervise themselves. In contrast, children who live in rural, suburban, middle-class, or affluent neighborhoods considered to be safe are not likely to be fearful.

The one constant that seems to be evident in the research on latchkey children and their parents is the parents' ambivalence about such arrangements. Even when parents feel they have no choice but to leave the children under self-care because of the expense or lack of child care or transportation problems, more than 50% of the parents surveyed were concerned about leaving their children at home alone after school. In addition, many experienced embarrassment and guilt, and they tended to underreport that their children were latchkey children (Long & Long, 1983).

Counselors may work with either latchkey children or their parents. Or they may work in behalf of latchkey children. For example, counselors may take the initiative to help their communities implement programs to assist latchkey children, such as developing an after-school telephone hot line for latchkey children, matching elderly caregivers with young latchkey children, encouraging local police and fire fighting agencies to provide programs for children on safety considerations in the home, promoting after-school activities and sports events conducted by community social services, and encouraging schools to run late buses for children whose parents work until late afternoon. Direct counseling services to latchkey children may involve addressing their feelings of self-confidence, security, or specific fears; it also may involve creating support groups for such children to help them consider their attitudes about self-care and to share the ways they handle such experiences. For parents, counselors can create opportunities to inform them of the various options and alternatives available for their children, form parent clusters whose schedules might permit rotation of child caregiving, and provide support groups and information for parents to help them deal with their apprehensions about leaving their children alone.

The Microenvironment

When we combine the problems of the dual-career family with those of the stepfamily or blended family, other tensions can enter the compound, including residual guilt for a failed first marriage, divided loyalties for natural children and stepchildren, parents' unresolved communication or identity issues, stepparents' overreactions to children's needs, and anxieties about failing as a spouse or parent a second or third time. In the single-parent structure, depression, loneliness, anxiety, poverty, overinvestment by the parent in the children, enmeshment, and a lack of clarity about the role boundaries of parent and child are major problems. If we overlay any of these family structures with extramarital sex, multilateral adult structures, or same-sex coupling, we may find problems of jealousy, possessiveness, poor communication, sexual dysfunction, fear, incompatibility, and many other forms of stress, the roots of which may be in the macroenvironment. The actual playing out of the problem, however, occurs in the microenvironment, the intimate network of role relationships and interactions that makes up the specifics of the family, whatever its particular form.

It was on the microenvironment—the activities, emotions, and interactions in the individual family—that most of the research activity dealing with families was focused until recently. For example, some past research focused on the antecedents to family crisis and postcrisis adjustments; other research was concerned with such elements of family stress as the importance of the decision-making process in the management of stress, the systematic assessment of family hardships, parental coping strategies and their effects on child launching, retirement, and widowhood. As research on how families adjust to and cope with stress continues as a major and important issue, considerable attention is being paid to the major forms of stressors on families, whether they be normative and predictable, or unusual, unexpected, and transitory. Lipman-Blumen (1975), for example, developed an elaborate scheme to examine the extent of stress in a family system. Other researchers have studied such factors affecting family adjustment to stressors as family members' personal resources (financial, health, educational, psychological), the family system's internal resources (family adaptability and cohesiveness, management of family resources, problem-solving ability), social support (kin, friends, neighbors, self-help groups, community agencies), and coping (McCubbin et al., 1980) as well as cohesion and adaptability (Maynard & Olson, 1987).

Although each of these dimensions of family system reactions to stress is important, it is perhaps the family's ability to perceive accurately the stressors it faces and then to manage the various dimensions of family life simultaneously—to achieve balance in its coping behavior—that is most central to a microenvironment view of the family structure in action. Coping, in such a perspective, includes

(1) maintaining satisfactory internal conditions for communication and family organization, (2) promoting member independence and self-esteem, (3) maintenance of family bonds of coherence and unity, (4) maintenance and development of social supports in transactions with the community, and (5) maintenance of some efforts to control the impact of the stressor and the amount of change in the family unit. (McCubbin et al., 1980, p. 135)

The ability to understand how the family perceives and copes with stress, how to strengthen the relationship system, and how to empower the family to manage its resources effectively in any or all of the coping categories just identified becomes fundamental to counseling interventions.

COUNSELING APPROACHES TO THE FAMILY

Although counseling of families, as compared with individuals, is a relatively recent emphasis for mental health practitioners, it is nevertheless a rapidly growing area of interest and importance. Family counseling has been advocated in the schools, in rehabilitation settings, in employee assistance programs, in community agency settings, and in virtually every other context in which counselors are engaged. In its emphasis on the treatment of relationships within the core social institution, the family, family counseling has increasingly become the treatment of choice for a wide variety of problems such as child abuse, learning problems, juvenile delinquency, adolescent eating disorders, chemical dependency, and sexual dysfunction. Whether described as marital and family therapy, conjoint family therapy, or conjugal relations or family counseling, the techniques and the problems at issue are being explored by all types of mental health practitioners—counselors, psychologists, psychiatrists, and social workers—and being applied to all types of relationships, including gay and cohabiting couples, single-parent and reconstituted families, and intact nuclear or multigenerational families at all stages of relationships (e.g., premarital, divorce, reconstituting family structures).

Within such a context of growth, the actual theoretical perspectives of family counseling are still relatively limited in their conceptualizations and in the specific focus of intervention. For the most part, existing approaches to family counseling have not yet become rigid but are still open and dynamic. Although the major unifying theme for family counseling is treating problems within a relationship context, models tend to emphasize many subelements or targets. Various classification schemes have been proposed to provide some typology of family therapy or counseling approaches. There are those, for example, that stress psychodynamic or systems approaches (Guerin, 1976), biopsychosocial or ecological approaches (Myerstein, 1981) and those that compare cultural and experiential approaches (Levine & Padilla, 1980; McGoldrick, Pearce, & Giordano, 1982). There are also a variety of approaches to integrating concepts of family, such as cohesion, adaptability, and communication, toward which therapy might be directed (Olson, Russell, & Sprenkle, 1980; Olson, Sprenkle, & Russell, 1979), and the resulting family types that emerge from the different combinations and magnitudes of these three elements. For example, Maynard and Olson (1987) described a circumplex model of family systems built around the concepts of cohesion and adaptability that permits the assessment, identification, and treatment of 16 specific types of marital and family systems and 3 more general types. Within such perspectives, several major approaches to family counseling have evolved as the foundations on which contemporary models are built. These are briefly summarized in the following list.

- **Psychodynamic family counseling** focuses on intrapsychic selves, unconscious dynamics, conflicts of family members, and how these interlock to create disturbances in family members (Getz, 1987). Ackerman (1958), Framo (1976), and Bowen (1978) are included among the psychodynamically oriented therapists. The content used to pursue insight and growth within the family consists of the emotional life of the family constellation, the scapegoating of a symptomatic client as a function of unresolved family conflicts, the unconscious dynamics that remain unresolved from the parent's family of origin and that are recreated and projected into the current family, and the needs for self-differentiation among family members who are enmeshed in intense interdependence within the family.

- **Structural family therapy** focuses on how the subsystems that constitute families are connected and how the arrangements that govern family transactions are structured. Intervention focuses on promoting structural viability by establishing a clear generational hierarchy, clarifying and changing coalitions, and promoting semipermeable boundaries among subsystems. This approach does not explore and interpret the past but attempts to modify the present. Minuchin (1974) and his associates are seen as the primary progenitors of this approach.

- **Strategic family therapy** includes a blend of Minuchin's work with communication theory (Haley, 1976) and paradoxical relabeling (Selvini, Palazzoli, Boscolo, Cecchin, & Prata, 1980; Watzlawick & Weakland, 1977). It focuses upon the ways problems are labeled and the behaviors used to solve such problems in the family. Families are helped to reframe or relabel problems, and they are provided directives composed of strategically planned behavioral tasks designed to change family behavior and to improve the functioning of the family organization.

- **Experiential family therapy** is an existential orientation to having families experience their own irrationality and "craziness" (Whitaker, 1977). Changed behavior in the family occurs as individual members' self-esteem, communication patterns, and family rules are explored and altered (Satir, 1964).

- **Social learning approaches** combine operant learning and social exchange theories, general systems theories, and attribution theory. Such an approach focuses on interaction patterns, problem solving, and other specific behaviors in family systems (Vincent, 1980).

- **Relationship enhancement** is a psychoeducational model designed to teach couples or families specific problem-solving skills. The participants learn to express themselves in constructive ways to avoid arousing defensiveness and hostility in others and to interact with each other with understanding and acceptance. Participants learn nine sets of behavioral skills or modes of behavior: expressive, empathic, discussion/negotiation, problem/conflict resolution, self-change, helping others change, generalization, teaching/facilitative, and maintenance skills. In studies comparing the relationship enhancement approach to traditional discussion-oriented treatments, relationship enhancement was found to enhance communication, general relationships, and marital adjustment (Guerney, Vogelsong, & Coufal, 1983; Ross, Baker, & Guerney, 1985).

These approaches are obviously neither mutually exclusive nor exhaustive—nor does any one have a clear-cut advantage across different types of family problems. In their individual ways, each of these approaches attempts to treat the family as a system rather than treating a symptom the family experiences collectively or only one member manifests. Just as is true in other applications of counseling and therapy, approaches to family counseling are moving toward specifying which approach or mode of treatment is likely to be most effective for each type of family or group of clients experiencing specific sorts of problems. In addition, as in most other forms of counseling, family counseling is also generating preventive and enrichment programs designed to avoid major stresses and crises by promoting structured communication skill building and other forms of relationship enhancement. Such approaches can be used to help families of different structural types anticipate and perceive stresses as expected and controllable.

A major issue for the future is how and where counselors will receive the training they need to conceptualize and implement family counseling. Will such training be random or systematic? Will it be linked to other emphases in counselor education or stand independently?

Another major issue for counselors results from both the concerns of training and the concerns of practice. It has to do with how behavior is viewed in terms of its locus and its purpose. Traditionally, regardless of the psychodynamic model used, many counselors and psychologists viewed psychological difficulties as intrapsychic matters. The task was to alter the problem that was located within a client's head, or to modify internal states that were manifested in symptomatology. Although such premises continue to be viable for some psychological problems, contemporary views of family counseling shift the focus from symptoms to strategies that people use to cope with their relationships with others. Such approaches seek to affirm that many psychological maladjustments are not biological or intrapsychic but social and interpersonal. In this perspective, symptoms are not viewed primarily as modes of coping with instinctual forces but as methods of dealing with the vagaries, rigors, and interpersonal confusions of daily living. The struggle for the counselor and the clients is to discover and act upon more effective ways to cope with social situations. This is a different view from that, for example, of a psychoanalytic persuasion, which sees family problems as the sum of the disturbances in the individuals involved. Rather, in the emerging, major family counseling perspectives, not one of the individuals involved is necessarily seen as a villain; instead it is assumed that the problems involved are found in the communication and interaction patterns of the system as a whole.

Families are basically interpersonal constellations in which the effects of interaction among the participants become the content of concern. Family counseling assumes that this content is better understood and dealt with in situ, in the family group, than by isolating each participant in one-on-one counseling and assuming that when these individuals are regrouped the interpersonal dynamics will be improved. The notion of a family system suggests that there is a chemistry of relationships and interacting subsystems in which matters of communication, cohesion, adaptability, and resource management come together in unique ways. Individual actions in such a view do not simply spring forth out of some internal mechanism, but are, at base, responses to the actions of other family members. Thus analyses of such dynamics and responses to them are much better effected if parents and children or whoever else makes up the particular family structure are engaged simultaneously in the process of treatment. The focus then becomes the present and the future rather than a reworking of the past; the identification and building of strengths within the family structure rather than the excising of some pathology; and the development of skills by which family members can more adequately cope with each other.

Finally, we come to a counseling implication as powerful as that of viewing families as systems of interaction that need to be seen holistically if intervention is to be effective. That is, "that family structures are not simply personal arrangements among family members. They are manifestations of the values of the cultural group to which the family belongs" (Aponte, 1982, p. 8). Therefore, if counselors are to assess, treat, and communicate effectively with a family they must be sensitive to their own and the family's cultural roots. Families of different ethnic backgrounds do not define the same phenomena as problems nor do they express their caring or pain in the same ways; they differ in what they consider to be acceptable solutions to problems, in the kinds of individuals they usually turn to for help, and in the types of family patterns and expressive behaviors their cultural experiences reinforce. Thus in the midst of increasing attention to the counseling implications of cultural pluralism, therapies have been developed with little attention to the matters of cultural variability, the sustained residual of ethnic values and identifications on individual and family behavior, and the effects of common cultural history and traditions on communication and family rituals vis-a-vis dating, marriage, child rearing, work, or retirement. As McGoldrick (1982) has contended, "Ethnicity is a powerful influence in determining identity. . . . Just as individuation requires that we come to terms with our families of origin, coming to terms with our ethnicity is necessary to gain a perspective on the relativity of our belief systems" (pp. 6–10). Indeed, family properties such as their views about intermarriage among persons of different cultural traditions or ethnicity may require identification and redirection. In such roles as well as those for mediating between the family and the larger society, the counselor may need to be a "culture broker" (p. 23) who helps families to recognize their own ethnic values, to strengthen those values that are adaptive, and to recognize conflicts that result from different perceptions and experiences of ethnicity. In addition, counselors must realize that treatment approaches and counseling theories also have inherent cultural values that frequently are filtered through the counselor's own ethnic and value lenses. Ultimately, family counseling requires the counselor not to be an anthropologist or sociologist but, rather, a person who appreciates the variability in values, traditions, and patterns that become mediators of family systems and, indeed, of the effectiveness of counseling.

There are other family problems that could be addressed here but space limitations preclude addressing them in depth. Suffice it to say that problems for which family counseling is indicated could include impending interracial marriage, families with a disabled child, families with an abusive member, families with a depressed or suicidal member, families with an elderly member with dementia or Alzheimer's disease, or families with a member who is HIV positive or has AIDS. Each of these concerns are issues likely to challenge a counselor at some point in her or his career. As such, they are amenable to the various family counseling approaches mentioned in this section. But as in other type of counseling content, it is necessary for the counselor to learn as much as possible about the issues, content, and possibilities associated with each of these problems (Fenell & Weinhold, 1996) and to apply the family counseling model most likely to be facilitative in each case.

Other Counseling Problems Associated With Families

Not every problem that has relevance for the family or originates within a family structure necessarily requires family counseling or therapy. Some problems may need to be addressed primarily by an individual within the family and a counselor. For example, working or not working after childbirth may be one such concern. Using a subjective-expected utility model of decision making, Granrose (1985) suggested ways counselors can help women with such questions as whether or not to work after childbirth. In such circumstances, counselors may need to explore the relationship between the way clients frame the questions and the intentions they formulate. Counselors also may need to help women examine the relative value of financial rewards, personal ambitions, and child welfare as key determinants of intentions and behavior. Exploring the relative strength of guilt and resentment of working or of staying at home is important as a context to identify emotional conflicts that may prevent adopting a rational plan. Thus counselors need to help clients consider the decision and perceived consequences associated with their intentions to work or not work after childbirth and to prepare for the resulting eventualities.

Single Parent as Peer

Another concern in which counseling is focused primarily on one family member is the situation in a single-parent family when the parent becomes a peer and intergenerational boundaries and role expectations between the child and the parent are lost. In such cases, because most single-parent families are headed by women, the mother typically is the focus of counseling. In such instances, the counseling may address several emphases. The mother may need to be helped to reassume the maternal role and to be taught or reminded of the appropriate expectations for a child of a given age so that the son or daughter can be given the sanction again to be a child. The mother may need help in working through feelings of guilt and apprehension about reinstituting discipline. She may need to explore the likelihood that her perceptions and emotions concerning her ex-spouse and the divorce may not be those of the child and therefore need to be differentiated from the child so that mother and child can behave in accordance with their separate identities. In addition, the mother will probably need some help with stress management, self-esteem, and the skills of independent living. Although the counselor's role in this situation is primarily to empower the mother to reassume her role, the counselor may want to refer the child to another counselor or work with the child independently of the mother. The focus of counseling with the child would probably include legitimizing the child's thoughts about the divorce, about his or her parents and the parents' new friends, and about his or her a sense of identity as well as about any feelings of anger, anxiety, and sadness that might be present (Glenwick & Mowery, 1986). In most instances, the single mother can profit from support networks to replace her marital relationship in order to avoid leaning too heavily on her children for emotional support (Hodgson, 1984).

Patterns of Time Use

It is likely that many single parents who do not have problems with their child-rearing roles or with intergenerational boundaries may have other problems for which counseling may be helpful. One of these is priority setting and time management. As might be expected, patterns of time use in single- versus two-parent families differ when parents are employed. As compared with unemployed single parents and married employed and nonemployed mothers, single employed mothers spend the least time on household chores and on recreation; they also spend the least time on personal care of all groups except employed mothers in intact family units. Obviously, for many single parents and, indeed, some employed mothers as well, such time allocations as just identified can induce guilt, frustrations, and other stresses for which counseling can be useful (Sanik & Mauldin, 1986).

Female Participation in the Workforce

The participation in the labor force of married women with children is not always for the same reason nor is it always seen as positive. Avioli (1985) studied the labor force participation of married women with infants who elected to be employed immediately after childbirth as compared with those who remained out of the labor force for 3 years after giving birth. Four distinct patterns emerged characterizing the White employed wives, Black employed wives, White housewives, and Black housewives. Overall, White employed wives seemed to be working because of an interest in being in the labor force, seemed to be comfortable with their employment status, had substantial feelings of personal efficacy, and had husbands who were supportive of their employment. In contrast, the Black employed wives seemed to be working because of financial need, had a history of being employed and planned to continue to work full-time, and were as likely to be employed with or without their husbands' approval.

In comparison to the White employed wives, White housewives tended to show little attachment to the labor force. They claimed to have substantial feelings of personal efficacy and, consistent with their employment status, reported that their husbands opposed their working.

The Black housewives tended to be the most stressed group of wives. Although they had high financial need and planned to work, they were constrained from entering the labor force by lack of work experience, high local unemployment, and the practical problems of having more children than the other comparison groups. Unlike their White counterparts, Black housewives did not seem to derive a feeling of competence from their housekeeping and child-care activities, but rather had a relatively low level of personal efficacy.

Within the limits of this research, it is suggestive that working women with children and those who wish to work but cannot do so vary in the stresses, purposes for working, and feelings of personal efficacy they associate with labor force experiences. Thus different female married populations have different needs for counseling and support. In some cases, the issues are feelings of self-worth and power; in others they are matters of labor force access, time management, and child care; in some groups all of these factors may be present.

Beyond such perspectives, it seems useful to recognize that counselors need to help working mothers clarify and understand the implications of several other perspectives. For example, as Etaugh (1984) suggested,

> Many of the stresses they are experiencing are due not to their own shortcomings but to external pressures arising from family and employment systems. . . . Role conflicts and

role overload experienced by working mothers are caused not by their inadequacies, but by the press of more demands than most people can handle effectively. The family counselor can help working mothers in setting priorities. (p. 32)

Children of Divorce and Separation

Counselors in schools and in other settings increasingly are instituting individual and group counseling for children of divorce and separation. Frequently such counseling provides these children with opportunities to express and clarify their feelings of loss, anger, conflicting loyalties, anxiety about the future, and related matters. Although not all children experience significant trauma as a result of their parents' separation or divorce, many do. Wallerstein (1980) found that one third of the children in a research study were still distressed and unhappy 5 years after their parents' separation. Wallerstein (1984) found in another study that children who are 7 or 8 years of age when their parents divorce may harbor fantasies that the parents will reunite as long as 10 years after the separation.

Because children exposed to the divorce of their parents exhibit different levels of psychological vulnerability and distress, counselors can engage in multiple levels of intervention. One of these is primary prevention. In such roles, counselors can provide educational and group counseling activities for children and, indeed, separately for parents to examine divorce, the changes in role relationships that ensue, feelings of loss, guilt, or lessened self-esteem that accompany it, ways to maintain communications with a separated parent, coping skills, stress management, and related issues. In addition to an educational approach or primary prevention, counselors also can take more direct approaches to intervention, including making early identification of children of divorce who are at high risk for maladaptive response to their parents' separation; conducting group programs or individual counseling to address directly loneliness, fears of separation or abandonment, feelings of guilt, worry about custody decisions, loss of family or of a specific parent, parental dating, family violence, or posttraumatic syndrome in the case of children who have been "kidnapped" by one parent; and leading clinical groups that use play therapy, creative drama, or other techniques that allow for acting out of fantasies and feelings and promote problem solving (Robson, 1987).

Grandparent as Caregiver for Children

The reasons for the transfer of parenting responsibilities to grandparents varies from family unit to family unit. Whether the biological parent is present or absent, addicted to substance or physically ill, unwilling to take responsibility or mentally disordered, incarcerated or suffering from HIV/AIDs will define the types of interventions the counselor is likely to use. In either case, the counselor may need to deal separately with the children in the family where the grandparent is the caregiver and with the grandparent her- or himself. Certainly, for counselors in school or other community settings, identifying children being raised by grandparents and offering services to them and to their grandparent caregivers may be difficult to achieve. Determining whether the parent or the grandparent has legal custodial responsibility for the children becomes a critical issue as it relates to who needs to be informed and can authorize treatment of the children.

Beyond these issues, the interventions with either the children or the grandparents may take many different forms. For example, as suggested by Pinson-Millburn et al. (1996), it may be useful to provide counseling for the children related to the bereavement and loss they experience because of an absent or ill parent and, perhaps, skills training related to drug education, substance abuse, and issues of being a child of an alcoholic (COA). The grandparents may need to deal with stress of the unexpected disruption of their previous lifestyle as they negotiate the transition to being the caregiver for children again, the problems of grandchild management, and their feelings of bereavement about their own child's illness or irresponsibility. The grandparents may need substantial help in identifying and accessing the legal or financial resources they need to acquire in behalf of their grandchildren even though they do not have legal custody of the grandchildren. It is quite likely that both children and grandparents could profit from stress management and, possibly, participating in support groups dealing with loss, substance abuse, stress, or other emphases. The grandparents also might profit from skill training in parent effectiveness communication and in child management. Counselors in schools might also stimulate recognition of grandparent roles through, for example, a "Grandparents' Day" at school or working with parent-teacher associations to develop grandparent support groups.

Members of an Alcoholic Family

At certain points in the treatment of alcoholism, particularly in aftercare when the alcoholic is recovering and the family is being rebuilt, it is undoubtedly the treatment of preference to engage in family counseling. Prior to that time, however, it is likely that each member of the family needs individual counseling to help him or her understand the addictive process and how it has affected his or her life. Because alcoholism breeds total family dysfunction, each of the family members, including the addicted person, is likely to have played a role in enabling the addiction or in adapting to the family dysfunction in ways that permit survival.

Current perspectives on the alcoholic family have come to view a variety of roles as essential within the family system where alcoholism is the primary problem. Among the roles are those of the dependent (the addicted person), the enabler, the hero, the scapegoat, the lonely child, and the mascot. In a single-child family, that child may play all of the roles except that of dependent and perhaps enabler. In multiple-child families, however, it is likely that children at different places in the birth order will take on different roles. With each of these roles come problems of interpersonal relationships, anger, guilt, stress, low self-esteem, loneliness, and other mental health problems that need to be sorted out and explored in a one-on-one or possibly a peer group relationship. If such sorting out does not occur, it is very likely that the children of alcoholics will carry into adulthood the deficits in social skills, feelings of low self-worth, or other negative behaviors with which they lived and grew up in their family. They need to know that what they experienced was not under their control, to understand the process of addiction, and to examine and act upon the areas of arrested development they experienced as they played the family roles that became theirs because of birth order or other events.

Wegscheider (1981, p. 173) indicated that although the particular problems, stresses, and self-concepts of each of the alcoholic family members are different, there are primary care goals of similar importance to each family member. These goals are to

- let down the wall of defensiveness;
- let the pain emerge;

- begin to experience some positive feelings;
- accept the family illness and the individual's part in it; and
- make a personal commitment to an ongoing recovery program for the family and for him- or herself.

Battered Women

Although family therapy or family counseling may be the treatment of preference in the family where spousal abuse is occurring and the family is still together, individual counseling of battered women or group counseling with other battered women is likely to be the appropriate intervention when the woman has left the home. The magnitude of spouse abuse or the battering of women is difficult to determine precisely. At the beginning of this chapter it was indicated that probably up to 40% of families engage in family violence involving spouses. In addition, the literature has indicated that the problem of abused or battered women is prevalent in all socioeconomic and occupational levels of society (Straus, Gelles, & Steinmetz, 1980; U.S. Commission on Civil Rights, 1978). Walker's research (1979) on battered women of diverse ages, races, religions, and educational and socioeconomic levels suggested that they share a number of common characteristics:

- low self-esteem;
- a belief in all the myths characteristic of battering relationships (e.g., "I must have done something to deserve this," "This man needs me," "He will change," "He was drunk when he did it," "It is a man's right to strike his wife and children");
- a belief in traditional values regarding the family, home, and sex-role stereotypes;
- acceptance of responsibility for the abuser's action;
- feelings of guilt and denial of terror and anger;
- passive behavior and inability to manipulate their environment to protect themselves;
- severe stress reactions with psychosomatic complaints;
- use of sex to establish intimacy; and
- a belief that they are the only ones who can resolve the issue.

Other researchers have suggested other characteristics that extend or overlap with Walker's research findings. They include insecurity and isolation, a conviction that the spouse or partner will reform, economic depression, doubts about getting along in a hostile world, and fear of the stigma of divorce.

Certainly, when battered women first leave the relationship they need crisis intervention and support. They need to be helped to cope with the transition to singleness, the implications of divorce, the care and protection of their children, and protection for themselves. Beyond this initial phase, however, battered women need to be helped to deal with their feelings of low self-worth, their passivity, and the need to move from a state of emotional, psychological, and economic dependence on the abuser toward a state of personal and psychological empowerment and economic independence. Such goals require a comprehensive counseling strategy that may include attention to divorce and singleness counseling, parenting education, reentry counseling, cognitive restructuring, and career development (Worell, 1980). Ibrahim and Herr (1987) offered a group model of life-career counseling especially designed for battered women. The model includes the phases of

- *inner preparation*—dealing with loss of the relationship, with general fears of the world including fear of testing their potential, and with life skills in the world of work;
- *intensive family involvement*—dealing with the needs of children or other remaining family members and with changes in the family system;
- *vocational experimentation*—preparing women to enter the world of work; dealing with occupational fantasies; using guided imagery and role play to try on new roles; examining difficulties they might face on the job; providing training in communication and problem-solving skills;
- *vocational planning*—focusing on self-appraisal and the choices and options available; applying decision-making skills; and formulating realistic career plans;
- *vocational implementation*—providing support during implementation of job choice and induction; dealing with new fears and anxieties; providing stress management skills;
- *vocational analysis*—sharing of how implementation plans are going, what was successful and what was not;
- *vocational resynthesis*—reevaluating career goals after 3 to 6 months; reassessing or reaffirming career directions; and
- *vocational development resource*—using the women who have completed the previous stages and who are now engaged in work and disengaged from their previous battering relationship as resource persons, role models, or group leaders for women just beginning the group counseling process.

The model Ibrahim and Herr proposed can be used not only in group contexts but also as the content for individual counseling. In either case, the individual phases can be elongated or shortened depending on the needs of the women involved. In any case, the insights, activities, information, and support involved must continually focus on strengthening self-esteem, increasing assertiveness, and providing the skills by which the women can achieve economic independence.

Battered Men

For many reasons—stereotypes about men and women and their power differentials, feminist views of battered women—women have been identified in the mass media and research studies as the victims of physical assaults by men and family violence, but the reality is that men are often battered by women as well (Shupe & Stacey, 1987). The data about the number of battered men compared to the number of battered women are not very reliable, in part because men are less likely to report the minor slaps and kicks that apparently women do report to authorities (Steinmetz & Lucca, 1988). In addition, men tend to be reluctant to report such abuse because of the stigma and weakness it suggests. Generally accepted figures have indicated that there are ratios of about 1 in 12 or 1 in 13 abused husbands to abused wives (Steinmetz & Lucca, 1988). Other studies have suggested that for less violent forms of spouse abuse, husbands and wives are nearly equal in most respects.

Spousal abuse against men has not been the subject of many studies, but a basic irony is that in many popular cartoons, movies, and historical documents, men are depicted as being dominated by their wives and slapped and punched. The responses to these aspects of popular culture are typically humorous, probably because they are thought to be inconsistent with reality—which is that men are not helpless victims or weak or wimpish as portrayed in newspaper cartoons and in other media. Nevertheless, from the available evidence, husband battering is not a new phenomenon nor is it one without serious consequences. Obviously battering by men or women in a family context, where there are children, implements the power of social modeling and social learning for these children by suggesting that such violence is all right within the home and by leading to imitation by the children as they have their own families and perpetuate the battering of their spouses and their children. For example, in one study of 400 battered women, 28% reported that they had battered their own children, and 55 said they did so because they were angry at their husband (Walker, 1984).

When violent behavior between husbands and wives is analyzed, it appears that wives exceed husbands in "hitting with something." Men batterers tend to use their fists; women tend to throw or hit with ash trays, bottles, hot liquids, and other objects. When differences of physical strength between men and women batterers are equalized by women, some researchers have suggested that both genders commit similar amounts of spousal homicide. Browne's research (1987) found that 75% of reported injuries occurred to women; however, comparisons of U.S. and Canadian statistics on domestic homicides indicated that respectively, 38% (U.S.) and 30% (Canada) of all homicides involving spouses are committed by women.

Because so much research attention has been placed on male batterers, there is relatively little attention to the psychological profile of female batterers of men. In one study, Bland and Orn (1988) studied violent females in Edmonton, Canada, and found that some 31.2% of them had a diagnosis of antisocial personality, depression, and/or alcoholism. Other research studies have tended to suggest that male battering often occurs while families are experiencing unemployment and economic deprivation (Finkelhor, 1983) and among younger females (ages 18 to 34) (Brinkerhoff & Lupri, 1988). Sommer, Barnes, and Murray (1992), in a study of 452 married or cohabiting females in Winnipeg, Canada, found that some 39.1% (or about 4 in 10) of these women engaged in some form of abuse as a way of resolving conflicts with a male partner or husband, and that the female spouse abuse is best predicted by age and personality characteristics. That is, "a female abuser may be characterized as a young woman who is highly anxious, emotional, worrisome, prone to drug and/or alcohol dependence but at the same time is tough-minded, uncaring, insensitive to others, and antisocial." This profile, according to Sommer et al., supports the notion "of the increased likelihood of abuse occurring among women who have difficulty maintaining relationships due to personality deficits" (p. 1321). A further but weaker finding was that alcohol consumption did have limited ability to predict partner abuse in women.

Several observations seem relevant concerning the men being battered by females. These men are under direct or more subtle pressure to keep the abuse and any physical injuries to themselves because if they do not, they will be perceived as weak, as unable to "handle their woman" and assume the dominant role in the family unit. In essence, husbands being beaten contradict gender norms; thus it is difficult for the mass media or the general public to imagine men being physically victimized by women. According to Lucal (1995), "our image of what it means to be a man militates against the inclusion of an image of husbands in positions of dependency (physical, economic, etc.) that lead to victimization by their wife" (p. 107). As a result of these images and the lack of media or researchers to consider battered men as a serious social problem, men in this situation have few resources to turn to for assistance. Among the resources for women are support groups, crisis hot lines, shelters, and women's resource centers that make provisions for personal safety, individual and group counseling, and other forms of assistance. No such parallel resources are available for men, although counselors sensitive to men's issues as they are becoming visible in contemporary society can play significant roles in assisting men who have been and are being battered.

CONCLUSIONS

Chapter 3 has provided an overview of how the changing American family represents the second major challenge for contemporary and future counselors. There seems little doubt that problems in the family carry residual effects in the communication patterns, feelings of self-esteem or their lack, role differentiation, and other facets of individual development that subsequently are manifested by behavior in the workplace, school, or other social arenas.

The factors affecting family structures and the comprehensiveness of the forms they take are diverse. They come from economic sources, cultural traditions, and shifting perspectives on the roles and purposes of families in contemporary American society. As the society has become more specialized in the functions different social institutions play, many of the historical instrumental roles of the family—to produce goods, perform services, and propagate and rear children as a means for the survival and interdependence of the family unit—have been diluted and changed. Reasons for the existence of family units have changed from those of survival to those of personal and companionate social relationships. Because the latter occur for many reasons and can be met in many structural forms, family patterns have become more diverse, and the frustrations and stresses of family living have changed as well. Confusion about expectations for families and criteria for their success have created new tensions and discomforts for people within families and those contemplating creating a family.

Both the macroenvironment, the linkage between the family and the larger society, and the microenvironment, the patterns of intimacy, relationships, and communication within the family unit, are the sources of stressors with which members must cope. In some instances, such stressors are economic; in other instances, psychological. In some cases they lead to or are associated with substance abuse, child or spousal abuse, ineffective family relationships, problems with intimacy, family health, or divorce and reconstituted or blended families; in other cases, they suggest a lack of balance in family coping behavior or appropriate social support.

As the multiple stressors affecting families have become more apparent, so have the needs for the provision of counseling that is tailored to the unique characteristics of the relationships, coping mechanisms, cohesion, and adaptability of different family types. Such needs have stimulated several major approaches to counseling that emphasize differing theoretical or process dimensions related to family intervention. In addition to approaches that stress working with families as interacting systems, there also are problems that surface within families but require individual counseling, at least at certain developmental points. Depending on the specific circumstances, these might involve single parents having difficulties with intergenerational boundaries and role relationships with their children, children of divorce and separation, individual members of an alcoholic family, or battered women.

Finally, it seems clear that family counseling and therapy are not confined to a specific setting. The stresses and strains associated with family living are of concern to the school counselor, the counselor in the workplace, or the counselor in a community agency, in independent practice, or within a religious institution. Family stressors and the ensuing problems will remain a challenge to counselors in all of these settings and across populations of children, youth, and adults.

Chapter 4

PLURALISM AND CULTURAL DIVERSITY IN THE AMERICAN POPULATION

IN AN ATTEMPT TO DEFINE THE cultural characteristics of the United States, we frequently hear terms like *land of opportunity, melting pot, heterogeneity, equality, democracy,* and *individualism* used as images, if not axioms accepted without qualification. These terms have been incorporated into our national psyche as realities, not as ideals or even as sets of assumptions that sometimes may be at odds with other sets of assumptions within the cultural fabric of the nation. The egalitarian premise of the American creed that "all men are created equal" has been translated into the notion that "all people are pretty much alike" (Peabody, 1985, p. vii). Although these two premises do not necessarily follow, treating them as interchangeable permits us to avoid addressing the cultural differences that so obviously are a part of the demographics of the current and emerging American population. In addition, it is possible to rationalize that not acknowledging cultural differences restrains us from practicing stereotypical or discriminatory behavior toward people from different cultural backgrounds. The problem is, of course, that in practice discrimination and stereotyping continue despite official policies intended as egalitarian and democratic. It is for these reasons that Americans now benefit from civil rights legislation and protection from discrimination in employment, education, or housing because of age, sex, disabilities, sexual preferences, or racial background.

Cultural diversity and pluralism in traditions and beliefs are not negative aspects of American culture; they represent who we, as Americans, are. We are not a group of homogenized people from common stock. We are a land of immigrants who have brought with us to this nation, regardless of when we arrived and under what conditions, assumptions, traditions, worldviews, and cultural constructions. These perspectives carry their psychological residual from the behavioral expectations, group interactions, values, and information-processing mechanisms of the cultural norms in the nations, societies, or tribes that are the ancestral legacies of individual Americans. Even the only nonimmigrant population in the United States, the Native American Indian, was not and is not monolithic in cultural background. The Indian tribes or "nations" that have been in place in this country since before the foreign settlements more than 5 centuries ago differed then as they do now in religious orientations, languages, sex roles, methods of economic and physical survival, and other behavioral norms (Benedict, 1934; Trimble, Fleming, Beauvais, & Jumper-Thurman, 1996).

When we overlap the cultural distinctiveness of Native American groups with the cultural diversity of past and continuing waves of immigrants to the nation from Europe, Africa, Latin America, Asia, and the Middle East, it becomes apparent that the implications of such pluralism must continue to share a larger part of the national agenda in the planning for and the provision of social services, including counseling, in the future.

A major challenge in counseling stems from the fact that for most of its history in the United States, the assumptions and the techniques of counseling have ignored cultural differences or treated them as unimportant (Clark, 1987). Thus counseling models have treated primarily intracultural phenomena, not intercultural phenomena. In essence, theories and practices have tended to take a universalistic, idiographic, or *etic* view (Draguns, 1996) of human behavior rather than acknowledge the cultural distinctiveness of most people in the United States, a primarily *emic* or nomothetic view.

The danger in a predominantly etic view of counseling and of behavior is that not acknowledging cultural differences among people—that explain variations in verbal behavior, interpersonal interactions, work ethic, individualism, or group identity—makes it easy to resort to one approved model of behavior. This view assumes that the role of counseling is one of reinforcing this target model and associating any behavioral deviation with a deficit model. The latter, then, suggests that perspectives or activities different from those in the universalistic, majority, or target model are inferior or abnormal. Such a point may be extended to locating the deficit, abnormality, or inferiority within the individual rather than within the model of normal behavior used, and to giving inadequate attention to how individual environmental transactions are culturally mediated. Thus individuals who may be acting quite appropriately within their cultural traditions or within the intergenerational, residual effects of such traditions, may be characterized as behaviorally aberrant if viewed from different cultural perspectives.

A further danger of an etic view of counseling is a belief that after an individual has been in a particular culture for several years, previous belief systems and culturally mediated behaviors will have been purged and the individual's behavior will then be guided by the norms of the adopted, current culture. However, cultural heritages are not extinguished easily. McGoldrick, Pearce, and Giordano (1982) in their classic book, *Ethnicity and Family Therapy,* emphasized in persuasive terms the continuing, intergenerational effects that family background transmits or reinforces. An individual's orientation to the past, present, and future; how an individual views and interacts with strangers and people beyond the family boundaries; how an individual interprets his or her obligations and responsibilities to others; how an individual views work or marriage or child rearing; what an individual defines as a problem and an appropriate array of solutions; or how an individual copes with a cultural identity are all affected by the values of that individual's ethnic heritage. Such ethnic traditions and their original roots in other nations, cultures, or social structures persist for long periods of time in people's concepts of who they are and the behavioral norms to which they subscribe. These factors shape behavior, and they lay a base for the interactions that are likely to occur in a counseling relationship whether it occurs one on one, in a group setting, or within a family therapy context.

THE INTERACTION OF CULTURE AND CHARACTER

Different cultural traditions and histories give their members particular worldviews or perceptual windows on events. As Kluckhohn (1962) suggested more than a quarter of a century ago, every culture has a structure of expectancies. In essence, cultural differences are differences in the human experience, differences in general conceptions "of the human's place in the universe and of factors that cause human beings to act and interact in the way they do" (Horner & Vandersluis, 1981, p. 33).

Culture can be and is interpreted in many different ways by authors examining different aspects of human behavior. Linton (1945, p. 32) suggested that culture "is the configuration of learned behavior and results of behavior whose components are shared and transmitted by a particular society." Culture is sometimes defined in terms of that part of the environment that is created or shaped by human beings (Herskovits, 1948). Such a view encompasses art, work and other physical or tangible artifacts of a culture. This is a classic anthropological or archaeological view of culture. Sowell (1994) has refined that view of culture by focusing "on those aspects of culture which provide the material requirements for life itself—the specific skills, general work habits, saving propensities and attitudes toward education and entrepreneurship—in short, what economists call human capital" (p. xii). Sowell argued further that

> A particular people usually has its own particular set of skills for dealing with the economic and social necessities of life—and also its own particular set of values as to what are the higher and lower purposes of life. These sets of skills and values typically follow wherever they go. . . . both emigrants and conquerors have carried their own patterns of behavior—their cultures—to the farthest regions of the planet, in the most radically different societies, and these patterns have often persisted for generations or even centuries. (p. 1)

In this view, cultural differences are persistent among groups of persons even in the face of oppression or significantly different values, skills, or beliefs held by a majority group. "Cultures," Sowell said, "are not erased by crossing a political border, or even an ocean, nor do they necessarily disappear in later generations which adopt the language, dress, and outward lifestyle of a country" (p. 2). Sowell further contended that cultures involve attitudes as well as skills, languages, and customs.

Attempts to measure cultural differences between groups by attitude surveys, however, miss the crucial point that culture is expressed in *behavior*, not lip service. "The values of a culture are revealed by the choices actually made—and the sacrifices endured—in pursuing some desired goals at the expense of other desired goals" (Sowell, 1994, p. 10). As McDermott (1980) suggested,

> Somewhere in between the general makeup of human nature and the specific makeup of each individual lie certain qualities that have been acquired and assimilated. They represent culture—the values, beliefs, and ideologies held by members of the various ethnic groups as fundamental and necessary for effective social function. (pp. 1–2)

Triandis (1972) focused not on the physical properties of culture but on those less tangible aspects of which McDermott speaks, and which are described by Triandis as subjective culture. This "culture in our heads" is composed of the shared experience and knowledge of a self-perpetuating and continuous group, and it comprises much of what an individual experiences as personal reality. As Draguns (1996) suggested, subjective culture "is absorbed in the process of socialization rather than actively taught and effortfully acquired. The components of subjective culture, in the form of perceptions, expectations and other cognitions, are acquired unobtrusively over a lifetime of incidental learning" (pp. 2-3).

In essence, cultures are similar to maps or to templates that provide rules of behavior and perceptual cues to their members. These guides shape what members are likely to attend and give meaning to, their views of right and wrong behavior, and their forms of self-perception and self-expression. "Every culture attempts to create a universe of discourse for its members, a way in which people can interpret their experience and convey it to one another" (Barnlund, 1975, p. 16).

Cultures attribute meaning to psychological and physical events and in so doing reduce ambiguity and increase predictability for their members. They provide structures or classification mechanisms for sorting and interpreting the constant profusion of signals and messages from the environment every individual experiences each day. Attributions of meaning allow an individual to respond selectively to environmental stimuli and to structure these stimuli and manage them in preparation for action. Culturally mediated interpretations and predispositions ultimately end up in an individual's cognition as assumptions and symbolic representations of a world that is, in the last analysis, unique to each individual, but is, in a less specific sense, unique to different cultures.

In a heterogeneous society such as that of the United States, many people are in constant interaction with and possibly in transition between at least two cultures. They must balance values and beliefs commonly shared in the dominant, national culture with those predominant in the subculture, the racial or ethnic group of their family of origin. In addition, in a constantly interacting society in which immigrant populations are introduced constantly and social change occurs rapidly, two processes are always in motion: assimilation and accommodation. *Assimilation* is the dominant group's incorporation of the values of a new group so that the group fits into the existing social network. *Accommodation* occurs when a new individual or group adapts to the existing or dominant group values by changing in order to continue to live with the dominant group (McDermott, 1980, p. 224). Societies differ in how hard or soft boundaries between cultural groups are and the degree to which these boundaries overlap or are sharply defined. In either case, members of a cultural subgroup tend to retain the core of their traditional cultural identity whether it emphasizes shame (Asian) or guilt (European) as sanctions to promote the behavior expected in a specific cultural group.

According to a number of observers, culture and character are inextricably linked (Bellah et al., 1985). This, of course, is not a new perspective. Plato described it. So did Saint Augustine. Some 200 years ago Alexis de Tocqueville (1969) described the mores of the American people, which he occasionally called *habits of the heart,* and talked about how the traits of the society—its religious traditions, emphasis on family life, local politics—resulted in a characteristic unique in Western society at the time. For him, that characteristic was individualism. He was the first to describe this trait.

He believed that individualism explained how Americans made sense of their lives, how they thought about themselves and their society, and how their ideas related to their actions. It is in this sense that national social metaphors and rhetoric create behavioral expectations, attributions of the power of internal or external events, and expectations of the importance of the state, the group, or the individual as the focus of behavior.

Different cultures use different social sanctions to induce people to adhere to or embrace as their own the predominant beliefs that characterize their nation or group (Riesman, 1961). For example, the propensity of the United States has been to characterize itself as a nation in which individual achievement is unfettered by any cultural constraints and success is purely a function of how hard and how long an individual works. The belief that every person can be president or can rise from poverty to riches if he or she wants to enough and works hard enough gives little credence to the cultural obstacles to be overcome in such a quest. This is the stuff from which dreams come and achievement motivation is manufactured. Whether or not the statistical probabilities of being president, becoming rich, or, indeed, hitting the $10 million lottery are at all reasonable, such presumptions, emanating at the level of the macrosystem, identify individualism and purposeful action as the motive fuel of success. In the process, such a belief downplays the role of restraints in the environment that may impede progress and success. One result of such a context is that it causes some people to engage in self-blame if they fall short of an idealized goal.

Social goals or beliefs differ across countries and groups. Watts (1981), in comparing the evolution of career development in Britain and the United States, reinforced this point.

> It is intriguing that theories of career development in the U.S.A. have been so heavily dominated by psychologists whereas in Britain the contributions of sociologists have been much more prominent. The dominant focus in the U.S.A. has been on the actions of individuals, while in Britain indigenous theoretical work has been more preoccupied with the constraints of social structures. . . . The failure of the American social structural evidence to have much influence on career development theory seems to be due basically to cultural and historical factors. From the beginning of its independent existence, the U.S.A. has been formally committed to the proposition that all men are created equal. As a result there is belief that the individual controls his [or her] own destiny; that if he [or she] has appropriate abilities and if these can be appropriately developed, his [or her] fate lies in his [or her] own hands. (p. 3)

These perspectives remind us that decision making, the development of self-identity, and life chances do not occur in a vacuum. They occur within political, economic, and social conditions that influence the achievement images and belief systems on which individuals base their actions. They occur within different cultural constructs that reinforce certain types of behavior and try to extinguish others. They occur within different processes to assist the individual to deal with questions of cultural identity, achievement, illness, and other areas.

Cultural constructions of achievement images and belief systems also vary across time within the same nation. An example of such shifts is particularly apparent in the meanings attributed to work. Maccoby and Terzi (1981) suggested that there have been four major work ethics throughout American history and that elements or residuals of each of these coexist today: the Protestant ethic, the craft ethic, the entrepreneurial ethic, and the career ethic. In addition, they contended that a fifth ethic, that of self-fulfillment, is rapidly emerging as a major motivation to work. The point of such observations is that "each work ethic implies a different social character, different satisfaction and dissatisfaction at work, and a different critique of society" (p. 165).

According to Maccoby and Terzi (1981), the Protestant ethic stimulates a drive to work for the glory of God and for personal salvation and does not tolerate unethical and undisciplined behavior. The craft ethic encourages an orientation to "savings and self-sufficiency, to independence and self-control, and to rewards on earth. The craftsman is most satisfied by work which he [or she] controls, with standards he [or she] sets" (p. 165). The entrepreneurial ethic promotes risk taking, boldness, the exploitation of opportunities and people, and a dislike of the bureaucracy, red tape, and regulations that stifle free enterprise and personal initiative. The career ethic represents other-directedness, a striving to get ahead and to become more attractive and valuable in the marketplace, and the survival of the fittest rather than seniority and loyalty as the prime requisite of promotion and reward. The emerging ethic of self-fulfillment represents a quest for challenge, growth, and work that is not so consuming that it denies a place for family, community, leisure, and other aspects of life. This profusion of work ethics affirms that both those who are in the process of choosing work and those who are engaged in work represent a pluralism of purpose and motivation.

Such beliefs create behavioral expectations, define acceptable boundaries for psychological action, and provide, however subtly, criteria by which people from different cultural traditions judge themselves against a social norm or are judged by others. Such beliefs not only influence views of work but also affect the ways people express mental health symptoms, treat illnesses, raise children, or operate from an internal or external locus of control.

In this context it is important to consider the implications for counseling that result from the changing demographic composition of the American population. The reality of pluralism in ethnicity and racial characteristics, regional value differences, and the diversity in lifestyles in different populations are all challenges to conventional counseling approaches. With this in mind, the importance of cross-cultural counseling, bilingualism, and notions of abnormality versus cultural distinctiveness will be considered. At this point in our professional history, Pederson, Draguns, Lonner, and Trimble (1996) have reminded us that

> The role played by culture has increasingly come to be recognized in all aspects of counseling, from assessment to intervention. . . . There is general agreement that the cultures of both the providers and the users of counseling services influence the counseling process both pervasively and profoundly (Pontoretto, Casas, Suzuki, & Alexander (1995). Cross-cultural counseling has been recognized as the "fourth force" in counseling, coequal in its relevance and impact to the three traditional "forces" of psychoanalytic, behavior modification, and humanistic counseling (Pedersen, 1990, 1991). . . . Cross-cultural counseling does not abrogate, or even compete with, the three established theoretical orientations. Instead, it extends each of these frameworks and makes them, optimally, more applicable and realistic in contemporary multicultural contexts. (pp. vii–viii)

Before turning to a consideration of counseling per se, and particularly models of cross-cultural counseling, it is useful to consider further how the demographics of the American population relate to cultural characteristics and then to consider the likely effects of cultural diversity.

THE EMERGING CULTURAL DEMOGRAPHICS OF THE AMERICAN POPULATION

The U.S. population is now composed of people from some 100 ethnic groups, about 50 of which have sizable populations. The United States is a nation of immigrants.

Unlike many other parts of the world, the White population has been in the majority and people of color have constituted the minority cultures. Obviously, that is not true in all parts of the nation: Some cities and states are populated primarily by persons of color, and this is increasingly the case in many areas. Further, in some parts of the United States enclaves of ethnic populations continue to speak the language they brought to this nation and to celebrate the major cultural traditions and rituals from their countries of origin.

Among the 15 major nations contributing to the growing immigrant/ethnic group population in the United States from 1980 to 1990 were seven Central and South American countries and seven Asian countries. First ranked was Mexico (2,161,000). Other Central and South American countries (in order of number of immigrants) were El Salvador (fourth, 336,000), Cuba (eighth, 187,000), Dominican Republic (ninth, 185,000), Jamaica (eleventh, 155,000), Guatemala (twelfth, 151,000), and Colombia (fourteenth, 145,000). The Asian nations were the Philippines (second, 431,000), Vietnam (third, 343,000), Korea (fifth, 298,000), China (sixth, 288,000), India (seventh, 245,000), Taiwan (tenth, 157,000), and Japan (thirteenth, 150,000). The fifteenth nation was the USSR (132,000). When these rankings of the U.S. immigrant population in the late 20th century are compared with the top 15 nations pre-1950, it is interesting to note that in the earlier period Mexico was fourth (161,000), and China and the Philippines were ranked thirteenth and fourteenth (28,000 each). There were no other Hispanic or Asian nations represented; all other nations were Western European (Farley, 1996, p. 165).

There are today in the United States four major racial/ethnic or linguistic minority groups: Hispanic/Latino, Asian American/Pacific Islander, Native American, and African American. Two—Hispanic/Latino and Asian American/Pacific Islander—are rapidly growing. One—Native American—is growing but not as much or as visibly. The largest minority group is African American.

Hispanic/Latino

The first of the two most rapidly growing ethnic groups consists of Spanish-speaking Americans, who number more than 21 million people, or more than 8.7% of the American population. Included among the Hispanic or Latino populations are major concentrations of people from Mexico, Puerto Rico, Cuba, Dominican Republic, Guatemala, El Salvador, Colombia, and other Central and South American countries. Today, the United States has the fourth largest Spanish-speaking population in the world. The Mexican population of Los Angeles is second only in size to Mexico City. The population of Miami is about two-thirds Cuban in origin (Naisbitt, 1984, p. 274). Miami in 1990 had the largest foreign-born population of any U.S. city of a million or more persons (about 34%). Los Angeles was second with about 27% (Farley, 1996). Given the unnumbered additional Spanish speakers who are immigrant workers or who do not have official resident status in the United States but enter the country on a periodic basis to work in the agricultural and food service industries, the estimates of the number of Spanish-speaking people and their resulting impact on the social services, schools, and other social institutions of the United States are undoubtedly understated.

Both the rate of immigration to the United States and the fertility rate of Hispanic families (twice that of Whites, 30% higher than that of Blacks) have led demographers to estimate that the Hispanic population will exceed the African American population in numbers in about the first decade of the next century (Oxford Analytica, 1986, p. 37). Both populations are likely to number about 33 million at that time out of a total population of about 280 million. The Hispanic immigration to the United States, both through legal and illegal avenues, will contribute most of the U.S. population growth into the next century. Indeed, the level of Hispanic immigration exceeds that of the peak migration to this nation before the First World War. In general, most Hispanic immigrants are poor and ill educated by U.S. standards (Farley, 1996, p. 236; Oxford Analytica, 1986, p. 38). Therefore, they tend to enter low-paying jobs that others in the workforce shun. This situation perpetuates double employment ladders or possibility structures for Whites and Hispanics in many parts of the United States, particularly in California and other parts of the Southwest.

As population growth continues among Hispanic Americans, so will their political power in many sections of the United States. The current tensions in states that are trying formally to acknowledge that English is the official language will continue as Hispanic growth changes political patterns. Pressures to recognize language and cultural rights more effectively, improve employment opportunities, and change foreign policy relationships between the United States and the Latin American and Caribbean nations will influence these political patterns.

Several factors have combined to keep Hispanic immigrants separate from other population groups and have slowed their assimilation into the majority culture. These include the Hispanic population's tendency to continue to use Spanish as the dominant language in the family and (frequently) in the workplace, the continuing commitment to Hispanic culture and history within self-sufficient Spanish-speaking communities, the influence on individual and family behavior of Latin American Catholicism, the historical importance of male dominance, and low levels of intermarriage (Oxford Analytica, 1986, pp. 39-40).

Asian Americans/Pacific Islanders

The second of the most rapidly growing ethnic groups in the United States is Asian Americans and Pacific Islanders. They now compose about 7 million, or about 2.8%, of the U.S. population (Farley, 1996, p. 215), and since 1980, there has been a 111% increase in foreign-born Asian Americans and Pacific Islanders in the nation (p. 165). In the past Asian Americans have been divided among those of predominantly Chinese, Japanese, Philippine, or Korean ancestry. Since 1975, however, about 700,000 refugees have come from Southeast Asia, primarily from Cambodia, Laos, and Vietnam. This large influx of refugees and immigrants has changed the demographics of Asian Americans and is challenging findings previously reported on stable Asian American populations (Sue & Sue, 1987).

The Asian American population today is composed of more than 29 distinct subgroups who differ in language, religious background, family interaction patterns, and other characteristics that distinguish them from each other and from Whites and other minority groups (Yoshioka, Tashima, Chew, & Murase, 1981). For example,

65% of Asian Americans are foreign born and (like almost all Indochinese) do not speak English as their native language; yet the average Japanese American is both U.S. born and speaks English as his or her native language. For another example, the refugees from Southeast Asia (unlike Hispanic immigrants who have tended to be absorbed into existing Spanish-speaking communities in the Southwest, South, Southeast, and Northeast) have been dispersed under various government programs to places where "unemployment, social isolation, family estrangement, a new language, racial tension, and other barriers to their leading a normal life are commonplace" (Owan, 1985, p. v).

Because of the traumatic events in Southeast Asia that precipitated refugee status in the United States, there is a high prevalence of chronic depression and chronic psychosocial maladjustment among these refugees.

> It is associated with a variety of problems, including unemployment, illiteracy, cultural isolation, loss of religious practice and personal meaning in life, ignorance of American society, widowhood or singlehood, solo parenting, a generation gap, untreated major depression, and similar psychiatric and psychosocial ills. (Westermeyer, 1985, p. 87)

The refugees, like other immigrants who have permanently left their homelands, are likely to experience the feelings of loss of a cultural identity, feelings that have been found to be similar to those described by Kubler-Ross (1969) in people undergoing the bereavement and grief associated with the loss of a loved one (Sardi, 1982).

Native Americans

The third minority group that is growing in size but is not as large or as visible as the Hispanic/Latino and Asian American/Pacific Islander groups is the Native American or American Indian population. Now numbering about 1.9 million people, or about 0.8% of the total American population (Farley, 1996, p. 215), Native Americans are distributed among some 20 major tribal groups and are dispersed on reservations as well as within the majority culture of the Southeast, South, Southwest, North Central, and Northwest parts of the nation. Native American populations, like other populations, vary in language, religious traditions, culture, and patterns of interpersonal interaction. Intermarriage with other minority populations or with Whites is limited, and the historical reality of the Indian reservations as separate enclaves has kept many Native Americans totally separated by language and geography from the majority culture or even other minority cultures. The resulting social isolation, rejection, and lack of opportunities have frequently been associated with unemployment, chemical dependency, suicide, and serious mental health problems. The answer to these problems is not necessarily assimilation into the dominant culture, which some Native Americans would not want, but rather greater support from the government or the private sector to help create reservation economies by which Native Americans can find identity, opportunity, and purpose while respecting their cultural heritage.

African Americans

The fourth—and largest—minority group is the Black American or African American population. According to the 1990 Census, 29.1 million Blacks compose about 11.8% of the American population (up from 11.1% in 1980) (Farley, 1996, p. 215). Although Blacks are dispersed across the nation, they also are concentrated more heavily in some areas of the nation than in others. For example, "in the Northeast, for every 100 persons of Hispanic origin, there are 210 Blacks; in the North Central states, 590; in the South, 370. But in the West, Hispanics outnumber Blacks by 50%" (Oxford Analytica, 1986, p. 35). It is projected that by the year 2000 the nation's African American population will total 35 million and be concentrated in five states: California, Florida, Georgia, New York, and Texas. Of major consequence to the identity of many Black Americans is their history of intense racial and ethnic prejudice and discrimination. They also have experienced unemployment, underemployment, single parenthood, physical health problems, and stress-related diseases in higher proportions than have most other populations in the United States with the exception of Native Americans. Nearly 40% of Black Americans in the United States live at or below the poverty line (Farley, 1996).

As minority groups increase in number and in proportion to the total American population, the practical effect is a lessening of any historical propensity that encourages uniformity, and an increasing credence to the notion that the melting-pot concept must give way to a celebration of cultural diversity or at least a responsiveness to it. It is also becoming clear that a simplistic notion of majority and minority cultures no longer captures the reality of cultural interaction. The historic problems of Whites and Blacks in an either-or adversarial situation leading to discrimination and other problems is becoming diffused and more complex. There are tensions among minority groups as well as between minority group members and Whites. As the number of non-English-speaking minority groups grows, at least of groups where English is not the first language, bilingualism among Whites becomes prized and spurs many Whites to search for their own roots in a growing awareness that White society is itself culturally heterogeneous and on the verge of becoming a minority proportion of the population in many areas of the United States.

Regional Diversity

Counselors obviously have played and will play many roles in facilitating awareness of and effective responses to cultural differences among people. Those differences are likely to be more pronounced and of varying content from one part of the country to another. Specific counselor responses will be examined later, but it is useful to recognize that the growing differences from region to region of the United States are likely to have implications in their own right for the training and professional interventions of counselors. These differences may require individual counselors to specialize in the treatment of clients from specific ethnic groups; the cultural differences among minority groups will make it difficult for any given counselor to be sufficiently sensitive to and knowledgeable about the cultural characteristics of all groups. Indeed, the growing cultural diversity may require the rise of group practices of counselors who have expertise in dealing with different ethnic populations, or the collaboration of translators or interpreters in working with the counselor and client who do not share the same language or cultural history. It may ultimately require a renewed attention to the importance of indigenous paraprofessional counselors who can provide direct services to selected minority clients under the supervision of professional counselors. The continuing argument that only Blacks should counsel Blacks, homosexuals should counsel homosexuals, and women should counsel women will need to be tested comprehensively to either validate or reject it. But even if such a concept is found to be invalid for all minority or culturally different groups, training more bilingual and minority counselors should be a national priority for the foreseeable future.

Statistics depicting concentrations of different minority groups in different regions of the country are too general to be useful, but they do serve to reinforce the notion that counselors in different parts of the nation are likely to have more opportunity, if not the explicit need, to work with clients of specific cultural backgrounds. Although minority group members may be small in numbers compared to the majority group, they tend to be clustered in ways that magnify the importance of their numbers dramatically. Cluster groupings occur by city and by state. For example, "the cities of greatest Spanish influence in America are Los Angeles, New York, Miami, Chicago, and San Antonio; the states are California, with 4.5 million Spanish speakers, Texas, with 3 million, New Mexico, with 476,000, Arizona, with 441,000, and Colorado, with 340,000" (Naisbitt, 1984, p. 277). Certainly, the influence of Black Americans is dominant in such major cities as Atlanta, Chicago, Detroit, Philadelphia, and Washington, DC. By region, Black Americans vary from constituting 25% of the population in the South Atlantic states, including more than 33% of the population of the state of Mississippi and almost 70% of the population of the District of Columbia, to approximately 2% in Vermont and roughly 3% in the Dakotas, Idaho, Maine, and Montana. Native Americans, a much smaller population group overall, vary in concentration, for example, from less than .2 of 1% in Vermont to 6% of the population in Arizona, New Mexico, and Oklahoma. Asian Americans vary from constituting 5% of the population in California to .3 of 1% in Maine. Hispanic Americans vary from constituting approximately 30% of the population in New Mexico, and 20% in California and Texas, to .5 of 1% in North Dakota and .7 of 1% in Minnesota (U.S. Census Bureau, 1980).

These data from the 1980s are interesting markers of concentrations of minority populations in the United States, but they, too, are in flux. For example, in the 1980s the internal migration of Blacks and Hispanics changed in specific ways. Blacks are now leaving the North and returning to the South. As reported by Farley (1996), "Blacks are no longer moving into Chicago, Detroit, or New York" (p. 319). These cities have experienced net migration declines of 5% or more in their Black populations since 1985. Historical centers of Black population—Atlanta, Dallas, Norfolk, Richmond, and Washington—are now key destinations of Black internal migrants in the United States. Orlando, Florida, is emerging as another such destination as are Minneapolis, Sacramento, and San Diego. These three cities are evidence of increasing Black dispersion nationally, particularly for college-educated Blacks for whom there is a national job market. In addition, the concentration of Black populations in many central cities is beginning to change in relation to a clear trend toward Black suburbanization. Clearly, there are several patterns of distributions of Black families across cities and suburbs. Some older cities are overwhelmingly Black while their suburban rings house few Blacks. Detroit is a prime example of the phenomenon, but in cities like Atlanta and Washington, which have overwhelmingly Black populations in their central cities, it is the suburban rings in which the Black population growth is increasing most rapidly. In some older southern metropolises, such as New Orleans, Memphis, and Richmond, there is a fairly high representation of Blacks in both the central city and the suburbs.

Hispanics, both foreign-born immigrants and internal (or interstate) migrants, are increasingly choosing to live in metropolitan areas. For the past several decades, Los Angeles, New York, and Texas metropolitan areas near the Rio Grande—major points of arrival for Hispanics—have been gaining in Hispanic immigrant populations from abroad. However, these cities have been experiencing recent declines in Hispanic interstate migrants, who instead are being attracted in large numbers to cities such as Las Vegas, Orlando, Phoenix, and Tampa. But the primary attraction for Hispanic migration in the early 1990s is Miami. Indeed, in the early 1990s, Dade County, where Miami is located, earned the distinction of being the first large county in the United States with a Hispanic majority.

If we assumed that the mix of cultures is different from one ethnic, racial, or religious group to another, then in general it is possible to hypothesize that there are regional variations in values, work ethics, religious beliefs, and other characteristics of greater or lesser importance to different population groups. Where greater heterogeneity of cultural groups exists or where major concentrations of certain ethnic populations are clustered, the normative worldview or social metaphors on which people operate are likely to be different.

Garreau's fascinating book, *The Nine Nations of North America* (1981) suggested this reality. He has formulated a view that the North American continent and its offshore islands can be divided into nine different regions or "nations within a nation," not on the basis of political boundaries but on the basis of variations in culture, history, problems, resources, opportunities, and people. Garreau, in drawing his map of these nine hypothetical nations, acknowledged that when we look at the United States or North America in total it is almost impossible to understand the nine boundaries, but when we factor in conditions such as energy resources, unemployment, inflation, water policy, and the characteristics and traditions of the people who have migrated to and now occupy the different regions, we find that events, issues, policies, and concerns are perceived and valued differently from one of the nine regions to another. Terms like *self-sufficiency, pride, teamwork, achievement, freedom, self-reliance,* or *duty* conjure up different meanings in the high plains of Montana and on the streets of New York City or Miami.

In psychological terms, regional differences may be useful to help understand not only "where a person is from" but also "where a person is coming from"! If an idividual's identity is shaped by his or her origins, regional differences help clarify why people born and raised in this vast nation understand and label events and processes differently and behave differently. Such an affirmation does not imply the absence of common values shared by Americans, but rather that it is also possible to hold separate values and "see or make interpretations" that are different from those of other Americans. Trying to understand the origins of such perceptual sets across ethnic, racial, and sex groups is at the heart of cross-cultural counseling. Indeed, the viability and the validity of cross-cultural psychology rests upon the belief that "members of various cultural groups have different experiences that lead to predictable and significant differences in behavior" (Brislin, Lonner, & Thorndike, 1973). Regional diversity, and the ensuing effects upon individual behavior, is a new and relatively untapped lens on such phenomena.

Garreau, in explaining his views, asked us to consider

> . . . the way North America really works. It is Nine Nations. Each has its capital and its distinctive web of power and influence. A few are allies, but many are adversaries. Several have readily acknowledged national poets, and many have characteristic dialects and mannerisms. Some are close to being raw frontiers; others have four centuries of history. Each has a peculiar economy; each commands a certain emotional allegiance from its citizens. These nations look different, feel different, and sound different from

each other, and few of their boundaries match the political lines drawn on current maps. Some are clearly divided topographically by mountains, deserts, and rivers. Others are separated by architecture, music, language, and ways of making a living. Each nation has its own list of desires. Each nation knows how it plans to get what it needs from whoever's got it. Most important, each nation has a distinct prism through which it views the world. (1981, p. 112)

The nine nations Garreau suggested are as follows:

- **New England:** Bounded by New Haven (CT), on the south and Burlington (VT), and Albany (NY), on the west, it includes Boston (MA), New Hampshire, and Maine as well as Nova Scotia, the Maritime Provinces of Canada, Prince Edward Island, Labrador, and Newfoundland.
- **The Foundry:** Bounded on the west by Milwaukee (WI), Chicago (IL), and Indianapolis (IN); in the south by Cincinnati (OH), and Washington (DC); in the north by Green Bay (WI), and Sudbury and Ottawa, Canada; and on the east by Albany (NY), and New Haven and Bridgeport (CT), it includes Pittsburgh, New York City, Columbus (OH), and Wheeling (WV).
- **Dixie:** Includes the area south of Indianapolis (IN), Cincinnati (OH), and Washington, DC; east of St. Louis (MO), and Fort Worth, Dallas, and Houston (TX); and north of Fort Myers (FL). Included are New Orleans (LA), Tampa (FL), Atlanta (GA), Charleston (WV), Louisville (KY), and Raleigh (NC).
- **The Islands:** Miami is the capital of this region, which includes southern Florida, Cuba, Puerto Rico, Jamaica, Haiti, the Dominican Republic, and all islands south to and including Venezuela and Colombia.
- **Mex America:** Bounded on the northwest by Sacramento (CA); on the west by Los Angeles; on the northeast by Austin (TX); and on the east by Houston (TX). It includes Phoenix (AZ), Albuquerque (NM), Tijuana and Chihuahua, Mexico, and San Antonio (TX).
- **Ecotopia:** This region is bounded on the south by San Francisco (CA), and follows the Pacific Coast in a thin strip through Seattle (WA), Vancouver, British Columbia, and Juneau (AK) and is bounded on the north by Anchorage (AK).
- **The Empty Quarter:** This region is bounded on the south by Las Vegas (NV), on the east by Denver (CO), and proceeds north through Salt Lake City (UT), Boise (ID), and Spokane (WA), to Fairbanks and Barrow, Alaska. It includes the vast plains in Canada in which Edmonton, Alberta, is located.
- **The Breadbasket:** This region is bounded on the south by Houston and Austin (TX); on the west by Denver (CO); on the north by Regina and Winnipeg, Canada; and on the east by Dallas and Fort Worth (TX), Tulsa (OK), St. Louis (MO), Indianapolis (IN), Chicago (IL), and Sudbury, Canada.
- **Quebec:** This region is located entirely in Canada. It begins in the south at Ottawa and Sherbrooke and continues north and east until it is bounded by the Empty Quarter on the west and New England on the east.

Whether or not the names or the projected boundaries of each of these regions seem comfortable, they will probably stimulate images, sensations, and perspectives that will help clarify the differences they symbolize and the perceptual lenses or prisms through which many of their inhabitants view the world. The point is that each of these regions attracts different kinds of inhabitants, social arrangements, power, money, expertise, opportunities, and cultures. These become part of the psychology, the cognitions, and the values of the people who grow up and live in these locations.

These regional differences in where minority populations are migrating or how regional differences in North America continue to evidence variation in attitudes about self-reliance, education, job opportunities, individualism, and other matters have potential implications for the content of counseling and the recipients of counseling. For example, counselors in suburban rings where migration of African American students is accelerating, or in areas of the nation where Hispanic population growth is rapidly expanding or where immigration from Southeast Asia is concentrating will be immersed in cross-cultural counseling, prepared or not. Whether the counselor is in the school or in community agencies or in independent practice, the need to view clients with sensitivity to their cultural origins and belief systems, to their aspirations, to their heterogenity, to the political, economic, or family factors that stimulated their mobility within the United States or their immigration from abroad becomes a prime requisite in the world of pluralism and cultural diversity that is the United States.

Socioeconomic Diversity

Before discussing some of the specific meanings that cultural, if not regional, differences hold for people, it is useful to consider a different form of culture from that which rests primarily with ethnicity, race, sex, or national ancestry—namely the cultural differences that emanate from economic circumstances and social class. Although economic and social class often interact with race and gender, it can also be viewed through other lenses. Rich and poor people may both be White, but it is unlikely that the fact that they share ancestral roots in England or Scandinavia allows them to view the world or its opportunities in the same ways. Poor people are not simply rich people without money. Their values, risk taking, sense of self, sense of power, and focus on the past, present, and future are all conditioned by the environment in which they find themselves. Mitchell (1983), as a function of work at the Stanford Research Institute, described nine American lifestyles that characterize the American people.

The resulting typology was derived from national sampling in the United States and has been applied to the population of a number of other nations to examine the differences in the proportions of people in the lifestyle emphasis in each nation and the variance such differences create in elements of national character. The values and lifestyles (VALS) typology used is composed of four comprehensive groups that can be divided into nine lifestyles, each defined by its distinctive array of values, drives, beliefs, needs, dreams, and special points of view (Mitchell, 1983, p. 4). The four groups and nine life styles are

- the need-driven group—survivor lifestyle, sustainer lifestyle;
- the outer-directed group—belonger lifestyle, emulator lifestyle, achiever lifestyle;
- inner-directed group—I-am-me lifestyle, experiential lifestyle, societally conscious lifestyle; and
- combined outer- and inner-directed group—integrated lifestyle.

In succinct terms, *the need-driven group* consists of those who are struggling to meet their basic needs. The survivor subgroup constitutes about 4% of the United

States population. Its members are very poor, typically elderly, poorly educated, lacking in self-confidence, depressed, and essentially unable to take advantage of the work opportunities that might help them improve their position. The other need-driven subgroup, the sustainers, are likely to be somewhat better off financially but still live on the edge of poverty and frequently engage in the underground economy rather than the secondary or primary labor markets. They tend to be angry, resentful, and rebellious. About one fourth of this group are looking for work or work only part-time. Few of these people get much satisfaction from their work, which is primarily in machine, manual, and service occupations. People in this lifestyle category make up about 7% of the United States population. Although these people have not given up hope and seek financial security and economic improvement (many are hardworking and ambitious), they frequently have a difficult time finding opportunities because they are often immigrants without good English skills, minority persons with poor educational backgrounds, or single parents on welfare or with marginal incomes.

The outer-directed group typology includes about two thirds of the American adult population. The belonger subgroup is the biggest in this typology, about 35% of the population; the emulator subgroup makes up about 9%; and the achiever subgroup, 22%. In a collective sense these are the people who dream the American dream, and many within their typology also live it. As the name of the typology implies, outer-directed people pay considerable attention to what others think, to what the media say is important, to the visible, tangible, and materialistic aspects of life. The belongers according to Mitchell's research, are likely to be highly patriotic, conventional, happy, aging, and quite traditional members of the middle class. They want to fit in, not to stand out. They follow the rules and cherish their family, church, and job. They need acceptance and are dependent and conformist to get it. They tend to live in small towns and rural areas, not large cities. The emulators tend to be younger than the belongers and much more intense in their striving to be like those who are richer and more successful than they are. They are hardworking, ambitious, and competitive. They are not likely to have completed college, although they may have attended college for 1 or 2 years or graduated from technical school. Thus they are not likely to achieve the highest levels of professional, technical, or administrative occupations for which they strive, although, of course, some do. Many, however, experience rejection and feel that the system has been unfair and that their primary ambitions have been frustrated. Frequently this results from a mismatch between their goals and their abilities or preparation. They ask much of themselves and of the system, nevertheless, and they often take great responsibility to achieve success. The achievers are the members of the outer-directed group who have made it. They are the people the emulators hope to be. They are typically gifted, hardworking, self-reliant, successful, and happy. They usually live a comfortable and affluent outer-directed life. They are generally middle-aged, self-assured, and prosperous leaders and builders of what is considered the American dream. Very few of these people are members of minority groups; for example, approximately 2% are Black. Many of the achievers have attended college and graduate school. They are often self-made successes, and are politically and socially conservative.

The inner-directed group typology includes the I-am-me lifestyle subgroup that characterizes about 5% of the adult population and the experiential subgroup that constitutes about 7% of the population. As contrasted with the outer-directed group, the inner-directed group members are oriented to how they feel internally about different aspects of their life as compared to what other people or external systems suggest that they should feel. Thus their attitudes toward their job, personal relationships, spiritual matters, and other daily satisfactions become preeminent to them. Many of these people are active in social movements. They are less driven by money and social status than are members of other groups. They tend to have excellent educations and frequently hold good jobs of a professional or technical nature. Inner-directed people are likely to have been raised in relatively prosperous, outer-directed families where they were relatively satisfied with material comforts and no longer feel driven to acquire them as a sole raison d'etre.

Within the inner-directed group typology, the I-am-me and the experiential lifestyle subgroup members tend to differ in some ways. Although both are likely to be younger than the outer-directed group, the I-am-me subgroup members tend to be in a turbulent stage of transition from outer-directed values and characteristics to those that dominate the inner-directed classification; there is considerable anxiety as they give up what have been secure and comfortable lives for more uncertain, contradictory situations. These are people in the throes of seeking out new lifestyles, new ways of life, new personal identities. They are, on balance, energetic and active participants in whatever they undertake. In some contrast to the I-am-me subgroup is the slightly older experiential subgroup. For this latter subgroup, action and interaction and direct, vivid experience with people, ideas, and events is their driving force. These people tend to be independent, self-reliant, excellently educated, and hold high-level technical and professional positions. They are concerned with quality-of-life issues, natural rather than artificial products, spirituality, and skepticism. They are participative, self-assured, interested in personal growth and learning, and socially sensitive. The last lifestyle within the inner-directed typology is the societally conscious subgroup. Members of this subgroup have attained positions of influence and status and do not need to display them or be driven by economic motivations. They tend to be people of excellent education, liberal politics, and affluence who hold professional or technical jobs. They are generally self-confident and independent subgroup, tend to believe that the economic and social systems of the country need an overhaul, and try to make such changes by participating in the "system" and having their say. They are likely to be conservationists and ecologists who prefer simple living and frugality rather than ostentatiousness.

The combined outer- and inner-directed group, the final lifestyle typology, consists of those who Mitchell's research suggested are the integrated types. These people, estimated to make up 2% of the population, combine outer-directed and inner-directed styles into an integrated outlook on life. They tend to adapt easily to existing norms and mores and have a fully developed sense of what is fitting and appropriate. They find ways to balance work and play, to combine close relationships with people with the motivation to accomplish. These people are likely to be middle aged and above, well educated, and working in well-paid occupations in which they can either lead or follow when action is required.

Mitchell's research indicated that groups with different lifestyles or values view life, work, and social interactions through lenses that vary with regard to their security-insecurity, self-concept, expectations of life, freedom of choices, and related phenomena. These windows on life are associated with different behaviors, motive systems, and expectations in all facets of life. People of different social classes or levels of affluence essentially "march to different drumbeats." The social stratum they occupy is likely to be directly related to the type and comprehensiveness of information they receive and the levels of reinforcement of certain types of behavior directed to them by the dominant culture or by people of other social classes.

Social class, like ethnic and racial characterization, functions as "a boundary mechanism operating to regulate family relationships, friendship networks, courting, recreational patterns, usage of language, expectations, and, of course, opportunities" (Johnson, 1981, p. 79). The breadth of an individual's culture or social class boundaries has much to do with the choices that can be considered, made, and implemented. As Moynihan (1964) pointed out, the circumstances in which poverty flourishes produce a distinctive milieu that conditions the social responses, educational attainment, vocational ambition, and general intellectual level of the overwhelming majority of those raised within it. As stated earlier, poor people are not simply rich people without money. Their life space, possibility structures, levels and types of reinforcement, models, information availability, and social resources all differ as a function of their social status (Herr & Cramer, 1996). Within this culture of poverty, poverty itself becomes a great crippler of the career and personal development of many people (Lee, 1988).

Kleinman (1988), synthesizing a large volume of research on social relations, cultural meanings, and mental illness stated quite directly that

> human misery of all kinds is greater among the poor, the oppressed, the helpless. . . . Most disorders—including a wide range of medical disorders—have their highest prevalence rate among the poor and disadvantaged. . . . In this sense, they can also be viewed as socially caused forms of human misery, which physicians euphemistically gloss over as life problems. (p. 61)

In many ways, the development of individuals is like the development of nations. Throughout the past 30 years, it has become conventional wisdom to classify nations as the most developed, developing, and the least developed. Such a scheme suggests a linear relationship between a nation's level of industrialism and the levels of affluence or life chances its people experience. Although it is a useful scheme for some sorts of classification, this notion obscures the view that within nations, we can identify individuals and groups of individuals who could be described as the most developed, developing, and the least developed. Such differences exist even in the most affluent countries of the world, such as the United States, where groups and individuals are more or less advantaged depending upon the resources they have available, their social support systems, knowledge and basic academic skills, command of the dominant language, and understanding of the cultural norms that govern the society. Where a given individual is located on such a continuum suggests how that individual's behavior and vision of the world will be narrowed or broadened based upon the personal needs that are dominant. However much an individual wishes to pursue opportunities for affiliations or information, if he or she has to struggle to survive physically, it is these basic survival needs that govern his or her behavior. It was Maslow's (1954) early work in personality theory that helped counselors understand that individual basic needs can be viewed in a "hierarchy of prepotency." The prepotent needs are the more demanding of attention by the individual, more insistent than the other needs further up the hierarchy. Until the more primitive needs are relatively satisfied, the other needs are not likely to dominate or motivate behavior. As originally arranged by Maslow in the order of potency, the most demanding first, the basic needs are

8. the need for self-actualization;
7. the need for beauty;
6. the need for understanding;
5. the need for information;
4. the need for importance, respect, self-esteem, independence;
3. the need for belongingness and love;
2. the safety needs; and
1. the physiological needs.

In general terms, motivation of behavior directed to meeting the needs at the higher levels rests upon being able to take the lower and more basic survival needs for granted. It is difficult for an individual to be motivated by a need for beauty if he or she is starving. Nor is an individual likely to be principally motivated by a need for affiliation and good interpersonal conditions if his or her basic security is constantly under threat. Thus in cross-cultural counseling we have to be aware of ethnic and racial differences at one level but, certainly, also of the socioeconomic level; that is, we need to be assured that the individual is able to meet his or her basic needs or is, instead, preoccupied by a category of needs beyond which the individual seems unable to move. What an individual attends to in his or her environment and the value attached to it is likely to be associated with culture and with affluence, with advantage and with disadvantage. Although these factors may be relative in their effect across groups in any population, a given individual may experience them as absolutes: "I am poverty-stricken," "I am hopeless," "I am unloved," "I am unable to find shelter or food," "I am alienated." Such perceptions are extremely powerful in organizing and stimulating an individual's behavior. In what has been described as the "culture of poverty," occupied by generations of welfare recipients as well as by many women with teenage pregnancies, people with a lack of power and hope, people of poor education and basic academic skills, and people exposed to racism and cultural prejudices are likely to experience these conditions as important barriers to growth and mobility. These people tend to be locked into a permanent underclass in which the limits on the level and range of opportunities are restricted. Factors such as poverty, poor education, and racism combine to affect negatively the self-concept, ambition, motivation, self-efficacy, and the energy or the perceived utility of engaging in long-range, future planning (Lee, 1988).

OTHER CULTURALLY DIFFERENT GROUPS

Depending upon our perspectives on cultural diversity or pluralism that depart from race, ethnicity, socioeconomic, or linguistic differences, we can also think about groups whose lived realities can often create a cultural milieu that is different from that of other groups in the society and, as such, also makes them candidates for the sensitivity in counseling that is inherent in cross-cultural approaches. We can make this argument for many women who have experienced cultural contexts that are different from men or for persons with disabilities whose psychological and behavioral environments are different from those experienced by the larger population for whom living with disabilities is not a reality or a significant factor in their worldview.

Women

It is appropriate in this context to indicate that women in this society, and in many others throughout the world, have been fighting throughout this century and beyond for their voice, for power, for economic parity. Whether as members of minority groups or of the dominant culture, they have struggled against an array of indignities that frequently have led to personal or collective issues of low self-esteem, role conflict, physical or sexual abuse, limited or fragmented educational or career development, stigma and discrimination, filtered information about opportunity and choice, and emphases on their deficiencies compared to men, not their strengths. Their struggles for inclusiveness and significance beyond childbearing and maternal roles have found many women, similar to racial and linguistically diverse groups, at risk for unemployment and underemployment, single parenthood, different forms of mental disorder (e.g., depression), poverty, psychological or identity issues, and violence and abuse in ways unlike those experienced by men. In increasing numbers, as they try to function both as homemakers and as employed workers, many women find themselves with feelings of insecurity, stress, and inner conflicts about their personal identity, their sense of multiple obligations, their values, their wishes, their freedom of action, and perhaps about their perceived lack of marketable skills.

In essence, many women often react to and internalize stereotypes or models that treat women as objects, as victims, as passive recipients of socialization that does not respect, advocate, or promote their strengths, skills, and contributions within a set of social circumstances that gives them the "confidence to accept themselves and to know that they are good enough just the way they are." As such their culturally different experiences, their worldviews, their voices (Gilligan, 1982) have not generally been considered as important enough or distinct enough to warrant the types of cross-cultural counseling appropriate for more sharply defined racial or linguistically different groups. In a grossly simplified way, this is a definition of personal dignity denied and a refutation that women's experiences can be considered culturally different from those of men.

Persons With Disabilities

At another level, aside from persons of color in this nation, there is probably no group that has had to fight so diligently for dignity as persons with disabilities. The recent Americans With Disabilities Act is a legislative mechanism designed to provide greater access to economic and social opportunity for persons with disabilities, to recognize their potential and actual contributions to the larger society, and to acknowledge their significance as workers, family members, and citizens. This legislation attempts as well to address the reality that persons with disabilities are victims of social stigma, just as other populations suffer the effects of sexism, ageism, or racism. But many observers suggest that a handicap—physical, intellectual, emotional, sociocultural—may not be a disability unless the person feels him- or herself less adequate than others, either in general or in a specific situation. Thus the problem of having a disability is not simply that of being significantly underemployed and poor—although disabled persons are both significantly poorer and unemployed at two or three times the rate of nondisabled persons (Daniels, 1985)—but, perhaps more important, the problem for persons with disabilities is often one of self-perception. In a society that values physical wholeness, athleticism, youth, and beauty, how do persons with disabilities feel about themselves? What stereotypes from the able-bodied population are internalized as valid about the inferiority, incompetence, or worthlessness of the disabled? What loss of dignity, of personal significance, does a person with disability experience, internalize, and act on? Although such attributions undoubtedly vary greatly, the psychological implications of disability are difficult. Given the wide variation in types of disability and the levels of their severity, the needs of this minority population are wide-ranging and divided into various cultures (e.g., the deaf culture) that are significantly different from those of populations without disability. Thus it seems fair to suggest that the majority culture often does not recognize that persons with disabilities frequently are embedded in cultures that have their own metaphors and language systems (e.g., the hearing impaired and the use of signing; the visually impaired and the use of Braille).

If space were not limited, we could extend this notion of cultural diversity among and between various populations more fully. If we did so, included would be the aging and the frail elderly; physically, sexually, and emotionally abused children; persons who have suffered religious persecution; victims of HIV/AIDS; persons of alternative sexual orientations; children of alcoholics; and persons addicted to chemical substances. To the degree that persons in any of these groups cluster together in residential areas or for support or political purposes, the environments in which they live, their language systems, metaphors, and beliefs create culturally distinct systems that often are reactive to that of majority cultural beliefs imposed upon them or proactively reflect the diversity of these groups within the pluralism of the larger society.

Within any of the cultural groupings identified here, it is likely that the individual straddles more than one cultural belief system, and that how the individual sees him- or herself as a male, a female, young or aging, an African American, an Asian, an abled person or a person with disabilities is related to the individual's cultural heritage. In the next section some further elements of cultural diversity will be explored.

PERSPECTIVES ON CULTURAL DIVERSITY

To return to the basic issue of the existence of cultural diversity is to become more precise about the differences in such cultural diversity and the effects upon behavior that result. As Roe (1956) suggested, "Although behavior is almost always motivated, it is also always biologically, culturally, and situationally determined as well" (p. 25). Such cultural and situational determinants take many forms: universal, ecological, national, regional, local, and racio-ethnic (Vontress, 1986).

A major question is whether ethnic groups have separate and distinct cultures. On the basis of face validity as well as other more empirical data, it seems clear that Spanish-speaking and Asian Americans do have distinctive cultures. Increasing attention to perspectives on Afrocentrism as the cultural element important to African Americans is providing perspective on how Black Americans are influenced by cultural attributes different from those of White Americans.

A concept helpful to understanding differences among ethnic and other culturally different groups is the notion of subjective culture introduced earlier in this chapter. Jones and Thorne (1987) suggested that "subjective culture is a group's characteristic way of perceiving its social environment. People who live near one another, speak the same dialect, and engage in similar activities are likely to share the same subjective culture" (p. 490).

Obviously, there is within-group variability among people in a subjective culture based upon such factors as socioeconomic and educational level, gender, or disability. It is also true that the intensity of interaction among subjective cultures is likely to transform them. In the process, some distinctive ethnic characteristics may persist whereas others may disappear. But it is likely that ethnic cultural distinctiveness can be found to some degree within each cultural grouping or subjective culture. It may appear in individual self-concepts, a defensive use of ethnic identity, social alienation, feelings of powerlessness or lack of social control, or in commitment to an internal or external locus of control. Further, such perspectives are likely to differ depending upon how recently an individual has arrived in the United States, the level of contact with the community of origin or immersion in a cultural enclave, the level of education, and other factors (Munoz, 1982).

Cultural effects apparently occur not only at the level of an ethnic community or subjective culture but also in national terms. Tomlinson (1991), in considering the effects of globalization and cultural imperialism around the world, has contended that

> national identities are not cultural belongings rooted in deep quasi-natural attachments to a homeland, but, rather, complex cultural constructions that have arisen in specific historical conditions. There is a "lived reality" of national identity but it is a reality lived in representations—not in direct communal solidarity. (p. 84)

Such a concept seems to be validated by Peabody (1985) who has summarized his research in a book describing national psychological characteristics. His research compared psychological characteristics among the Americans, Austrians, Czechs, Dutch, English, Filipinos, Finns, French, Germans, Greeks, Hungarians, Irish, Italians, Northern and Southern Europeans, Russians, Southern and Eastern Europeans, Spanish, Swedes, Swiss, and Turks. He also summarized other major works that examined intercultural diversity across national groups. On balance, his work has suggested that when national psychological characteristics are compared, there are partial differences rather than complete differences among groups. Some behavioral manifestations tend to overlap across nations, whereas others are quite distinct. Another tenet of his study was that national characteristics are created by historical developments and therefore they can and do change over time. Some national psychological characteristics change rapidly under the onslaught of technology, for example, or occupation by foreign troops, whereas other national character changes are much more subtle and gradual.

If, then, there are national differences in psychological characteristics, what are they and how can they be described? In essence, what traditions and belief systems are immigrants to this nation likely to bring with them from their nations of origin? What cultural concepts are likely to endure across generations among families from selected national origins?

Peabody and his research colleagues in the several nations with which his study was concerned used scales composed of trait adjectives to differentiate national groups on the basis of such major behavioral sets as tight versus loose control over impulse expression, and self-assertiveness versus unassertiveness. The varieties of trait adjectives composing the 14 scales used in his study assessed both descriptive and evaluative dimensions of national character. Pairs of adjectives such as thrifty-extravagant, inflexible-flexible, inhibited-spontaneous, cooperative-uncooperative, cautious-rash, opportunistic-idealistic, and peaceful-aggressive are exemplars of the substance that alternately went into factor loadings and studies of variance among native and out-of-country observers. Specific research results suggested that judgments, especially judgments by out-groups, tend to exaggerate the homogeneity within a group; out-group judgments tend to be more polarized and in-group judgments less polarized. Similarly, judgments may exaggerate the descriptive consistency between different characteristics. Out-group judgments tend to show more descriptive consistency, and in-group judgments less. In-group judgments may be based on conscious experience; out-group judgments are more dependent on manifest behavior.

Perhaps the most striking result of the Peabody (1985) study was the finding that psychological characteristics of the national groups that were the targets of the investigation are distinguishable and consistent (p. 57). Space and purpose here do not permit an analysis of the specific psychological characteristics found in each of the national groups or their similarities or contrasts with those in other groups. Suffice it to say that the national groups tended to have comparative differences on the basis of (1) social relationships, (2) social rules, (3) control of hostility, (4) impulse control, and (5) authority and hierarchical relations. Clearly, the variations in how each of these differences is reinforced and portrayed in a particular nation are internalized by many, if not most, of the individuals in that national group. Thus modal behavior for one national group is likely to be different from that for other groups. Indeed, the rules for interaction or action in a situation are largely cultural with respect to private and public relationships, the formality of communications, and the intimacy or spontaneity by which such relationships are conducted (p. 31).

In relation to the many forms of global mapping (Buell, 1994) of national and cultural differences that are underway across the world, many researchers, like Peabody, are trying to place into some type of taxonomic or classification structure the ways by which nations differ in their psychological characteristics, work-related characteristics, or values. One of the better known efforts in cross-cultural psychology is that of Hofstrede, a Dutch psychologist, who has offered four dimensions or factors on which nations differ (1992). These tend to overlap with the findings of Peabody's study. They include (1) individualism-collectivism—whether individuals in a particular nation are socialized to see themselves as a self-contained, autonomous, entity pursuing idiosyncratic goals and aspirations or, instead, as individuals embedded in a lifelong network of relationships (for example, family) to which individuals' choices are referenced, shaped, and often determined; (2) power distance—how a particular nation deals with acceptance or rejection of inequality in status, income, or power; (3) uncertainty avoidance—by which nations differ in their concerns for rules, traditions, and rituals or spontaneity, improvisation, and flexibility; (4) masculinity-femininity—in which the roles of men and women are sharply differentiated and overlap is minimal or in which such roles are virtually interchangeable, at least in work and social contexts. Typically, attributes prized and associated with dominant masculine cultures are performance, production, and achievement; in contrast, cultures that are conceived to be feminine emphasize caring, comfort, security, and happiness. Obviously, counseling directed at the different points on the four continua of Hofstrede's model are likely to emphasize different counseling content (e.g., the self vs. relationships; freedom of choice vs. choices limited to an individual's social or economic status; predictable choices vs. subjective uncertainty as a decision-making model; performance vs. compassion). Such continua represent the forms of difference in worldview and in the resulting behaviors that are often associated with cultural diversity and with the different national psychological characteristics to which Peabody's research was directed.

Such differences in the continua of characteristics on which national cultures vary can also be seen reflected in the values that different nations emphasize. Super and Sverko (1995) studied value patterns related to work importance and work orientation, among other value sets. The 10 countries that were represented in the study included Australia, Belgium, Canada, Croatia, Italy, Japan, Poland, Portugal, South Africa, and the United States. Across these national samples 18 value patterns were ranked in importance and compared. The findings suggested that there are notable cross-cultural similarities in values, but that "each country tends to create a pattern of values with a somewhat unique emphasis on what is important in life" (p. 234). In terms of cross-national similarities in values, it was found that in all countries in the study, the fulfillment of personal potential or self-realization is an extremely important life goal for the majority of the subjects. Personal development, ability utilization, and achievement were among the highest values ranked in all countries, but at the lower extreme, the willingness to take risks, as well as the desire for authority and prestige, were of little importance everywhere (p. 351). Even so, it was found that value sets were clustered differently in three groupings of nations that shared certain traditions and geocultural similarity within the cluster but differed in these characteristics from the other two cultures. A brief summary of these findings for the three cultures follows. The three clusters were labeled the *New World, Europe,* and *Japan.* The New World cluster included sample subjects from Australia, Canada, South Africa, and the United States. Europe included Belgium, Croatia, Italy, Poland, Portugal, and some Australian subjects. Japan included only Japanese subjects. The distinguishing characteristics among these three clusters included, for the New World countries, a value pattern implying a drive for upward mobility, material success, and prestige, with less emphasis on the less worldly aspects of life. Role salience was characterized by the importance attached to work and homemaking. For the Europe cluster, the primary characteristics were high valuation of relationships and understanding among people, a tendency toward an autonomous lifestyle, and strong rejection of authority. For the Japanese cluster, the distinguishing characteristics were high valuation of aesthetics and creativity and a relatively low rating of all other values, especially of values indicative of upward mobility and material success.

In a more limited but equally interesting comparison of American and Japanese cultures, Barnlund (1975) found, for example, that the proportion of the self that is shared with others, the public self, and that which is not shared with others, the private self, differs in these two countries. In the analyses by several instruments designed to probe the communication patterns of the Japanese and Americans, the cultural profiles that the Japanese attributed to themselves included such descriptions as *formal, reserved, cautious, evasive,* and *silent.* Americans described themselves and were described as *frank, self-assertive, spontaneous, informal,* and *talkative.* People in the two nations were found to differ in the topics discussed in ordinary conversation, the people with whom they were discussed, and the level of disclosure in face-to-face communication. "The Japanese rarely reported talking in more than general terms on any topic to any person. Americans, on the other hand, disclosed on all topics to all persons at deeper levels" (p. 143). The two national cultures also differ in what they view as essential for personal growth and development. Americans view the need for interpersonal interactions and deep verbal involvement as essential prerequisites to expanding maturity and developing a productive personality. The Japanese in Barnlund's study view silence as essential as speech in the cultivation of personality.

> Meditation and contemplation are respected not because they imprison the mind, but because they free it. . . . Those who continually give out, who can always provide some statement, can have little energy left for taking in, for noticing or assimilating the world outside themselves. (p. 151)
>
> Every society creates some entity or unit that serves as a psychological center of the universe for its members, the ultimate source of meaning and the locus for the interpretation of events. In some it is the individual. In others it is the work group. In still others it is the extended family (sometimes including even ancestors). It is this psychic unit that mediates all experience, that provides the incentive and frame for all behavior. . . . In the United States and in most western cultures, this psychological unit is the solitary human being. . . . To preserve this sense of personal uniqueness and personal identity, the individual must often stand apart or even stand against other members of his [or her] family, office, neighborhood, or nation. . . . In Japan, the critical psychic unit may enclose not merely the person but all others who make up the nuclear group. It is this group that becomes the measure of all things; its identity must be asserted and defended above all. (pp. 153–154)

As will be discussed in the next section, the psychological entities, the social metaphors, that cultures create to define their uniqueness and to which their members are to give allegiance are also the sources of emotional disorder, stress, and pathology. In Japan, for example, people tend to be less clear and specific about their self-concepts or about their individual characteristics than Americans. Japanese psychiatrists report that because of the intense subjugation of individuality to group identity, many of their patients experience a sense of "no-self": they feel that they have not "possessed their self," and they do not appreciate the importance of their existence (Barnlund, 1975, p. 155). The human personality and the social structure are interlocking systems. Individual acts are framed within a cultural imperative.

Roots of Intercultural Diversity

Obviously, the historical influences on cultural diversity have diverse origins and timing. The Protestant ethic and the Calvinist traditions with regard to work and achievement have had similar influences for Americans and the English as compared with the lack of such influences on the French, or Italians, or Russians. However, the first two groups have been influenced by the Catholic and Latin traditions much more than have been the Americans, English, or Germans. The Russians and Germans have been imbued differently with supra-individual goals, communal feelings, and solidarity. This is true of many other groups. These characteristics can be conceived as relating to the contrasts between *Gemeinschaft* relationships and *Gesellschaft* relationships, and the transitions between these relationship clusters as nations have evolved from primary, peasant, tribal, small community social orders to more complex, impersonal, secondary, socially differentiated interaction patterns (Lipset, 1963; Parsons, 1951). On one hand, *Gemeinschaft* relationships are likely to be particularistic, ascriptive, and broad. In such a model, family and friends are treated differently from other people, standards of treatment of people are applied differently, people are related to and ascribed status in terms of their birth not their actual performance, and relationships tend to be broad and communal. On the other hand, *Gesellschaft* relationships are more likely to be characterized by universalism in standards applied to people regardless of background, people are more likely to be treated in relation to achievement or performance rather than their ascribed status, and relationships are more likely to be limited than broad.

When we turn away from European and Christian traditions to Asia, to the Chinese and to the Japanese, we find the major influences of Confucianism, Buddhism, and the code of Bushido. Here we find family fidelity, self-discipline, social bonding, and public and private virtues that are different in behavioral manifestation from those found in the national character of European nations.

From research across national psychological groupings, we find that national groupings are not only political units, but psychocultural shapers and reinforcers of behaviors culturally distinctive, at least in part, from those of other national groupings. Vaizey and Clarke (1976) suggested that nations create social metaphors as the bases for personality characteristics, child-rearing practices, education, and other social functions. Concepts such as the *socialist personality* used in formerly communist nations to define behavioral traits that youth and adults should try to emulate are not simply slogans; they are filters of information, sanctions of conduct, psychological boundaries, and seedbeds for value formulation. As Gestalt psychology and, more recently, the work of the cognitive therapists have demonstrated, human perception and judgment are determined by the organization and, indeed, the availability of information from the outside world. As Syngg and Combs (1949) stated many years ago, an individual behaves as that individual perceives. The fact is that an individual is taught what to perceive and how to behave, and these teachings are different across societies. "These differential schedules of reinforcement result in cultural differences in perceptual selectivity, information-processing strategies, cognitive structures, and habits" (Triandis, 1985, p. 22). According to Triandis (1972), cognitive structures may be best summarized by different elements of subjective culture such as categorizations of experience and associations among the categories, attitudes, beliefs, behavioral intentions (self-instructions about how to behave), norms, roles, and values.

Learning about self and about others is at the core of perceptual psychology and cultural differences (Christensen, 1985; Draguns, 1996; Linton, 1945). Indeed, Draguns (1996) has contended that the "self has emerged as a central construct in cross-cultural psychology" (p. 11).

> From the perceptual viewpoint, learning is the discovery of personal meaning, and is an outgrowth of the kinds of differentiations the person makes in the process of development. Although the individual is selective in the personal meaning placed on his/her discoveries, the culture to which (s)he is exposed determines the perimeter of the perceptual field, within the societal context. Through socialization processes and interaction with significant others, the individual learns not only who and what (s)he is, but also acquires values, taboos, moral precepts, and beliefs about different ethnic, racial, and socioeconomic groups, which are prevalent in the particular culture. (Christensen, 1985, p. 66)

Therefore, how we behave toward people and things is a direct outgrowth of how we have learned to perceive them as a function of cultural models.

Culturally Diverse Perspectives on Mental Health and Values

In the sense of convergent and discriminant validity, it is useful to look for other types of confirmation that cultural diversity exists in terms that matter to cross-cultural counseling.

One form of evidence of cultural diversity lies with the way in which psychological disorders are viewed across national groups or cultures. Draguns (1985) reported that

> while large-scale multicultural investigations have demonstrated that the same major disorders occur in a variety of very different cultures, . . . a wealth of research reports have documented the operations of cultural influences upon the manifestations, course, and outcome of psychological disorder. (p. 55)

For example, the experience of personal guilt in depression is predominant in countries with a Judeo-Christian heritage but infrequent or atypical in settings with other religious traditions. In schizophrenia, ideational and paranoid symptomatology is characteristic of countries at a high level of economic development and high rates of literacy. Catatonic manifestations are prevalent in many traditional, rural, and nonindustrialized settings (Draguns, 1995, p. 56). Similarly, among American ethnic groups many class-related and culturally and religiously based differences in psychiatric symptoms also have been observed (Dohrenwend & Dohrenwend, 1974). Thus it is possible to argue that "the same basic patterns of psychopathology exist around the world (i.e., in similar forms) but that these psychopathological conditions are influenced by cultural values (i.e., to yield dissimilar content)" (Westermeyer, 1987).

Sue and Sue (1987) reported that Asian Americans seek treatment only when disorders are relatively severe and that those with milder disturbances do not turn to the mental health system. Part of the reason for such findings lies with the facts that there is much stigma or shame associated with emotional difficulties among Asian Americans, and that mental illness—or the failure or weakness of an individual—is considered a disgrace to the family unit. In addition, Asian Americans are likely to feel that mental illness is associated with organic or somatic variables, and they tend to present somatic complaints when having psychiatric problems. Refugees from Southeast Asia display similar behaviors and tend to describe depression and psychological stress in somatic terms such as headaches, insomnia, general aches and pains, heart palpitations, fatigue, and dizziness (Nguyen, 1985).

In a major review of studies of depression in Asians, Marsella (1980) found that depression and how it is experienced vary as a function of sociocultural factors; some cultures do not "psychologize" depression and, therefore, do not show the psychological and experiential symptoms usually associated with the disorder in Western societies. Marsella also found that assessment methods are culture specific and need to be more attentive to somatic symptoms in non-Western countries. Further, the prevalence of specific psychiatric disorders has been found to vary by ethnicity, sex, and age. For example, Karno et al. (1987) reported on a comparative study of psychiatric disorders among Mexican Americans and non-Hispanic Whites in the Los Angeles area. They found that non-Hispanic Whites reported far more drug abuse or dependence and more major depressive episodes than did Mexican Americans. Mexican American women infrequently abuse or become dependent on drugs or alcohol at any given age. Dysthymia, panic disorders, and phobias are somewhat more prevalent among Mexican American women over 40 years of age compared with both non-Hispanic White women over 40 and Mexican American women under 40 years of age. It was found that antisocial personality is predominantly a disorder of young men of both ethnic groups. Furthermore, when utilization of mental health services by Mexican Americans and non-Hispanic Whites was compared, it was found that Mexican Americans with mild mental health problems reported significantly fewer visits (in the order of one half as many). When mental health disorders are severe, however, there seems little difference in the use of mental health services by Mexican Americans or non-Hispanic Whites (Hough et al., 1987).

Kleinman (1980), a psychiatrist trained in anthropology, performed extensive cross-cultural studies on medicine and psychiatry, particularly in Taiwan. His work focused on three major elements: illness experiences, practitioner-patient transactions, and the healing process. One of his major conclusions was that

> . . . in the same sense in which we speak of religion or language or kinship as cultural systems, we can view medicine as a cultural system, a system of symbolic meanings anchored in particular arrangements of social institutions and patterns of interpersonal interactions. In every culture, illness, the responses to it, individuals experiencing it and treating it, and the social relationships relating to it are all systematically interconnected. . . . These include patterns of belief about the causes of illness, norms governing choice and evaluation of treatment; socially legitimated statuses, roles, power relationships, interaction settings, and institutions. . . . Patients and healers are basic components of such systems and thus are embedded in specific configurations of cultural meanings and social relationships. They cannot be understood apart from this context. (pp. 24–25)

Furthermore, beliefs about sickness, the behaviors exhibited by sick people, their treatment expectations, and the ways in which family and practitioners respond to sick people are all aspects of social reality in a particular culture. In this sense clinical practice, the range of clinical phenomena in a particular culture, and conceptions of illness are cultural constructions, systems of symbolic reality, not entities with absolute, unequivocal reality across all people and cultures. These culturally mediated symbolic realities enable individuals to make sense of their inner experiences. They help shape personal identity in accordance with social and cultural norms. In this view, symbolic meanings influence basic psychological processes such as attention, state of consciousness, perception, cognition, affect, memory, and motivation (p. 42).

In a more recent work, Kleinman (1988) examined psychiatric diagnoses and treatment within the context of cultural and social differences worldwide. He reaffirmed that although some mental health problems have universal characteristics, others tend to be culture-specific. For example, anorexia nervosa, agoraphobia, and dysthymic disorders occur in some societies but not in others, and if they do, patients experience different symptoms and precipitating events. In addition, bodily complaints, as is increasingly evident in the literature on stress, can be symptoms of personal, social, and even political distress—behavioral translations, if you will, of the transactions between the individual and social or life events. These perspectives argue that culturally different groups follow distinctive paths to counseling or other mental health assistance and that they arrive there at very different points in the course of their mental health disorders or problems in living, experience greatly divergent types of involvement with their family members, and respond to psychiatric or psychological treatment in different ways.

The work of Barnlund (1975), Hofstrede (1992), Kleinman (1980, 1988), Peabody (1985), Super and Sverko (1995), and others leads to the conclusion that a major factor in intercultural differences is value sets. Much has been written in the counseling literature about how values influence, indeed, permeate, counseling and psychotherapy, theories of personality and pathology, the design of change methods, the goals of treatment, and the assessment of outcomes (Bergin, 1985, p. 99). Less has been said about the extension of this point to the receptivity to different approaches to counseling or to the provision of mental health services in different nations (Herr & Niles, 1988; Levinson & Haynes, 1984). Thus, although research in crosscultural counseling attests to the importance of value differences between culturally distinct people and the effects these have for the counseling process in microlevel terms, such differences can also be addressed at the level of nations in macrolevel terms. The latter give us insights into differences in the provision of counseling across nations as well as into the transportability of counseling theory and practices across national boundaries.

As suggested previously, terms applied to national groupings—East and West, Communist and non-Communist, developed and underdeveloped—are not only geographical or political referents. They also summarize the groupings of economic, psychological, and political characteristics that, however imperfectly, distinguish nations from each other on the bases of how their citizens are viewed, the idealized achievement motives or values to be espoused, and the social metaphors to be pursued. Because counseling and mental health services are promoters of values (London, 1964), national governments vary in their support for various expectations of such services. Depending upon where nations are in their own industrial or sociopolitical development, they may perceive counseling as a means to facilitate social or individual goals, to facilitate the development of human capital for achieving certain state goals, to enforce gatekeeping or social control, to maintain the status quo, or to promote self-actualization and personal growth (Watts & Herr, 1976).

In pluralistic societies such as the United States, there may be a mix of social and individual expectations for the outcomes of counseling services, particularly as they are provided to different population subgroups. Beyond that point, however, it is fair to state that the provision of counseling services is significantly affected by the characteristics of the society in which these services are found. In this sense, in every nation counseling, career guidance, psychotherapy, and other mental health services are sociopolitical processes that reflect the values individual nations hold about helping its citizens with various types of personal, career, or psychological problems. But counseling provisions also vary because, in essence, every counseling approach is a form of environmental modification that carries political overtones through the assumptions and value sets inherent in it.

If the cultural characteristics of a nation and the value sets inherent in a particular counseling approach do not match, that counseling approach is not likely to have adherents and is not likely to be successful in that particular nation. As Reynolds (1980), among others, reported, Western psychotherapies have a particular way of looking at and processing human behavior; Eastern psychotherapies have a different way of defining and intervening in behavioral norms. One set of therapies is not necessarily a substitute for the other because cultural value sets and assumptions make some forms of counseling and psychotherapy ineffective or unacceptable in nations or cultures different from those in which such interventions were formulated. For example, psychoanalytic therapy has not acquired much clinical popularity in Japan despite its rather wide acceptance in Europe and lesser but substantial support in the United States. The explanation seems to lie with the fact that psychoanalytic theory prizes behaviors such as individuation, self-consciousness, and independence from parents as therapeutic outcomes. These are not the behavioral norms of Japan for example, where Confucianism, the code of Bushido, Buddhism, and related philosophical guides to Japanese behavior emphasize the values of family unity and respect, loyalty to others, subjugation of individualism to group identity, self-discipline, and gratitude to others.

A similar comparison of East and West in the acceptability of therapeutic models is found in the work of Yiu (1978) in Taiwan. Her research accented the view that Taiwanese Chinese culture prizes interpersonal relations, group identification, and family bonds but deemphasizes the individual expression of feelings. Such a frame of reference obviously conflicts with middle-class American tendencies toward self-disclosure. Speaking to the transportability of counseling theories, Saner-Yiu and Saner (1985) contended in their research that the value assumptions embedded in counseling approaches derived from an individualist culture (e.g., the United States) are in conflict with the value assumptions in a collectivist nation (e.g., Taiwan). Others addressing counseling in African and in Middle Eastern nations (Shanhirzadi, 1983) have indicated that many assumptions taken for granted in some cultures, such as "I consciousness, rights to private life and opinion, individual initiative and achievement, the forms and content of interpersonal relationship" (p. 488) are simply not shared across cultures.

Although much more deserves to be said about the subtleties or the overt differences that distinguish cultures, it is sufficient for the purposes of this chapter to contend that culture and social class are significant considerations for counselors (Vontress, cited in Jackson, M.L., 1987). Indeed, in cross-cultural counseling they are preeminent issues that must be acknowledged and responded to if the cultural differences between a counselor and a client are not to become barriers to effective communication and mutual understanding.

CROSS-CULTURAL COUNSELING

The term *cross-cultural counseling* (or *multicultural counseling*) has evolved to summarize those therapeutic techniques designed to be sensitive and responsive to cultural differences between counselors and clients. By definition, cross-cultural counseling involves "any counseling relationship in which two or more of the participants are culturally different" (Atkinson, Morten, & Sue, 1979, p. 7) or, said somewhat differently, is "counseling in which the counselor and client differ as a result of socialization in unique cultural or racial/ethnic environments" (Locke, 1990, p. 18). An even broader notion of cross-cultural counseling was provided by Pedersen (1978): "If we consider the value perspectives of age, sex role, lifestyle, socioeconomic status, and other special affiliations as cultural, then we may well conclude that all counseling is to some extent cross-cultural" (p. 480). Vontress (cited in Jackson, M.L., 1987) suggested that "cross-cultural counseling refers to counseling in which the counselor and the client(s) are manifestly different due to socialization acquired in distinct cultural, subcultural, raciocultural, or socioeconomic environments." As suggested throughout this chapter, the needs for more attention to cross-cultural counseling will intensify and expand as a major challenge to counselors in the future. In order to meet this goal, however, cross-cultural issues important in diagnosis, appraisal, and counseling must be identified and addressed.

In general, techniques in cross-cultural counseling are recent and more theoretical than empirical in their substance. There has been little research on how clients from different cultures present different profiles of concern or behavior in the counseling situation, although there is a growing descriptive and anecdotal literature about such matters. VanZijl (1985), for example, from extensive counseling with clients of different cultural backgrounds, suggested that the following barriers to communication may be present in the counseling relationship. They include, in paraphrased form, the following:

- **transference:** A client of a minority background may react to a counselor of a majority background with resentment, distrust, and hostility because of negative experiences the client may have had with people from the majority culture in the past.
- **countertransference:** The counselor may project onto the client negative feelings that he or she may have experienced with people of the client's cultural background. Or a counselor may exhibit what Vontress (1976) described as the "Great White father" syndrome—a desire to both demonstrate power and authority as well as the image that the counselor is not like all the other majority group people the client may have previously known. Finally, the counselor may be overly sympathetic and indulgent to clients from other cultures and in the process act in a condescending or patronizing manner.
- **resistance:** Because clients may expect counselors to tell them what to do, they may behave in a passive and nonverbal manner. Because of cultural constraints or a lack of trust of the majority counselor, culturally different clients may be reluctant to engage in self-disclosure.
- **value orientation:** Culturally different value orientations may manifest themselves in many ways in the counseling relationship. The client may operate with a "present orientation" that deemphasizes planning for the future. A lack of time consciousness may devalue punctuality, meeting time schedules, or notions such as "time is money." Respect for age may cause an older client not to give attention to a youthful counselor, or a younger client to view an older counselor as a person of infallible judgment and wisdom.
- **language:** A counselor's lack of fluency in or understanding of the cultural nuances important in the client's language may cause miscommunication and inaccuracy in messages given and received.
- **nonverbal communication:** Cultures vary in meanings associated with space (physical closeness) and body language. What is normal and appropriate in one culture may evoke hostility or sexual feelings in people from another culture.
- **high levels of anxiety:** When a client from one culture tries to function in a very different one, he or she may experience a level of culture shock that causes anxiety and inhibits communication because the individual has lost familiar cues to reality.
- **ignorance:** The counselor may suffer from a complete lack of knowledge of the client's culture and, therefore, make inferences about behavior that are inaccurate and constitute barriers to communication.

- **expectations of the client:** Depending upon their cultural background, clients may expect the counselor to serve as a parental figure, or they may expect to engage in a formal relationship with an authority figure who will give direct advice.
- **cultural stereotyping:** The counselor may react to the client as a cultural stereotype, not as an individual. Assuming that all members of the same racial, ethnic, or cultural group share the same values, needs, goals, and abilities, the counselor operates not in terms of cultural sensitivity but in terms of cultural bias.

Ibrahim (1984) applied the work of Kluckhohn and Strodtbeck (1961) to an existential view of cross-cultural counseling. Basically, Ibrahim contended that the skills needed for direct service to clients across cultures include two emphases: (1) an initial understanding of the client's worldview and how it relates to the worldviews held by the client's specific cultural, ethnic, and racial group; and (2) the provision of skills important in intercultural communication including both verbal and nonverbal content of messages sent and received. These two emphases, then, apply to five existential categories among which cultures differ in their values orientations:

1. **the relation of people to nature (people-nature orientation):** In essence this orientation has to do with the terms of survival in the environment adopted by different cultures. Does this particular client come from a culture that believes in living in harmony with nature? Subjugating and controlling nature to meet the needs of people? Accepting the power of nature and how it controls people?
2. **the temporal focus of human life (time orientation):** Is the client embued with a past, present, or future time orientation? Is life viewed as finite or eternal?
3. **the modality of human activity (activity orientation):** Is the client's activity expressive-emotional, detached and meditative, or action-oriented? In which of these ways does the client seek personal meaning and through what specific mechanisms within this activity range?
4. **the modality of human relationships (relational orientation):** How does the client view social relationships or social isolation? Does he or she view such relationships in terms of clearly drawn lines of authority, including rights according to rank and well-defined subordinate-superior relationships? in terms of collaterality, the personal as independent and dependent at the same time? As individualistic, autonomous?
5. **the modality of human nature (good/bad/immutable):** The fundamental question here is How does the client feel about him- or herself and about other people. Are people viewed as basically evil, neutral, a combination of evil and good, or basically good?

Ibrahim's intent is, essentially, to help counselors recognize that there are different worldviews, culturally mediated, that influence feelings about self and others. These five categories provide counselors a paradigm by which to understand culturally different clients within the context of universal existential categories.

Another cross-cultural paradigm is based in perceptual psychology (Christensen, 1985). The fundamental notion is that to understand and effectively implement cross-cultural counseling attention must be paid to the perceptions and understandings of the counselor and of the client as well as of the counseling process in a social context. Overlaid against these three components of cross-cultural counseling are the perspectives from perceptual psychology. In this view

> . . . the perceptual field is defined as the entire universe, including the self, as experienced by the individual at a given moment. This "private map," by which the individual lives, is his/her "reality," although experience as perceived may not correspond to any objective reality. All systems of the perceptual field are interrelated so that a change in one affects all other parts of the system. (Christensen, 1985, p. 65)

Both the counselor and the client, in this view, have their own private maps of the self, or self-concept, and the values attached to it; relationships with significant others; a worldview of their place in society that reflects past, present, and future orientations as well as their status with regard to being a part of a majority or minority culture; and a universe view that provides for personal meaning, spirituality, and a sense of people' s relationship to nature, time, space, a deity, or cosmic force. Counselor and client are also likely to have their own private map of what counseling is, how the counselor and client should relate to each other, and its purposes.

Private maps of clients and counselors of what counseling is, what counseling content can be disclosed and dealt with, and what cultural rules apply to how the interaction between counselors and clients should occur are probably always present to some degree in every counseling relationship. But they are likely to be amplified in situations where counselor and client differ in gender, in race, or in ethnicity. Such differences are likely to be of particular moment when the counselor's private map of counseling is oriented to an activist, cognitive approach to counseling that values client action, individuation, and independence from the family, but the client's orientation is passive, nonassertive, and communal. Clients from African backgrounds, some Asian nations, and other collectivist cultures may be included in the latter category. So, too, may Native American or (as Canadians term native peoples of North America) Aboriginal or First Nation clients (France & McCormick, 1997).

Restoule (1997), in an extended discussion of providing counseling services to Aboriginal clients, has observed that Aboriginal peoples (including Native Americans) are a very diverse group of people in terms of their tribal affiliation, customs, languages, beliefs, and lifestyles. Counselors who work with North American native peoples sometimes assume that all Aboriginal people are homogeneous. They are not; and such assumptions can lead to misunderstanding the complexities of the individual and the tribe to which the individual belongs. As a result

> . . . it is always important to consider each individual as an individual first and foremost, and then to consider . . . tribal background. . . . However, there is also a set of behaviors or "rules" that hold some universality for all Aboriginal peoples . . . [and] seem to be present in all tribes of North America because Aboriginal people had to develop certain rules in order to survive against the environment. (p. 13)

These rules or ethics of behavior constitute at least part of the content of the private maps of Aboriginal clients that counselors who work with them must understand if they are to be helpful.

In the case of Aboriginal, First Nation, or Native American clients, the rules of behavior that guide their interaction with counselors and constitute their private maps of behavior include the following:

- **rule of noninterference:** Everyone should respect the rights and choices of each individual. "Aboriginal people believe in recognizing an individual's independence, and they view any attempts at giving advice, coercion, persuasion, or instruction as undesirable behaviors" (Restoule, 1997, p. 14).

- **rule of noncompetitiveness:** The emphasis is on noncompetitiveness or cooperation, rather than on "showing up" another member of the group, in order to promote the good of the family, clan, or tribe over the individual.
- **rule of emotional restraint:** Self-control of potentially destructive emotions, such as hostility and anger, is stressed.
- **rule of sharing:** Individuals are encouraged to share their possessions with others in order to promote the survival of the family, clan, or tribe so that nobody in the group is seen to be better off or more powerful than anyone else. Such behavior also promotes values of equality and democracy.
- **rule of time:** "Many Aboriginal people are found to take their time in doing things and consider their actions very carefully before acting" (p. 14). In part, this is true because they are concerned with the present and getting things done in a rational order rather than being concerned with the future, which is seen as egoistic. Such an approach to time is also seen as a way of keeping interpersonal relationships in a harmonious balance.
- **rule of gratitude and approval:** Because in traditional and in historical terms the best is expected from everyone in the tribal group, gratitude and approval are not verbalized and compliments are not given. The rationale for this behavior is that giving approval to a member of a group will "single the individual out as being more desirable than others in the group" (p. 15).
- **rule of modeling:** "In Aboriginal communities group members are shown how to perform a certain duty rather than *told* how to perform the duty" (p. 15). Such behavior promotes group cohesiveness because the teacher does not purport to know more than the student but through his or her actions conveys useful and practical information that the student then has a choice of adopting or rejecting.
- **rule of respect:** Respecting others is very important, and is magnified when it is a person of wisdom, an elder. Respect is shown to a person of wisdom by *not* looking him or her in the eye, lest this look be considered confrontational, but "rather by keeping the eyes downcast and occasionally glancing at the individual" (p. 15).
- **orientation to extended family:** Most Aboriginal people have a strong connection with extended family members in part because they taught them how to survive and kept them well when they were too young to care for themselves.

The rules of behavior that Native American and other Aboriginal clients incorporate to varying degrees, depending on where they live and their degree of assimilation into the majority culture, represent both the private maps of appropriate behavior from which they operate and the context within which counseling can proceed. Thus according to Restoule (1997), there are special issues that should guide the provision of counseling and psychological services. These include using "a holistic method which combines culturally sensitive clinical practice with traditional healing methods" (p. 16) and working in cooperation with elders or medicine men or women who have the abilities and knowledge to perform healing services (e.g., healing circles, sweet grass ceremonies, and sweat lodge ceremonies). In so doing, the counselor is not simply directing counseling inventions to the individual but to the family and the community.

These several notions affecting the counselor-client-counseling relationship result from culturally mediated experiences that shape the content and the conscious awareness of the private maps interacting at any moment in cross-cultural counseling. The counselor sensitive to cross-cultural issues must consider the multiple frames of reference—self, significant others, place in society, personal meaning, the meaning of counseling—that are likely to affect client behavior in the counseling relationship and the potential communication barriers that may be operating. In cross-cultural counseling as in other counseling conditions, a counselor-generated atmosphere of mutual trust and acceptance is vital if the client is to be enabled to share his or her feelings and perceptions of concerns. Beyond such a reality, however, many culturally different clients will perceive themselves to be—and will, in fact, be—members of oppressed minorities. In such cases counselors will have to have the capacity and be willing "to experience the pain, vulnerability, anger, frustration, helplessness, and fear of the client" (Christensen, 1985, p. 78).

Beyond such general perspectives on cross-cultural counseling, there are more specific recommendations in the literature dealing with the nature and the emphases of therapeutic interventions for different cultural groups. Although no counselor can be a specialist in all of the culturally different groups that now reside in the United States, counselors should read as widely and gain as much experience as possible pertinent to the major ethnic, racial, religious, socioeconomic, or other culturally defined groups with whom they are most likely to work. A typology of the specific cultural characteristics of each of the culturally different groups in the United States that are relevant to cross-cultural counseling is beyond the scope of this chapter, but there are many in-depth analyses of the mental health problems, behavioral characteristics, expectations of counseling, and counseling techniques likely to be useful with different minority or ethnic populations. Among them are the following:

Axelson, J.A. (1985). *Counseling and development in a multicultural society.* Belmont, CA: Brooks/Cole.

Dudley, G.R., & Rawlins, M.R. (1985). Psychotherapy with ethnic minorities [Special Issue]. *Psychotherapy, 22*(3).

France, M.H., & McCormick, R. (Eds.). (1997). First Nations Counselling [Special Issue]. *Guidance and Counseling, 12*,(2).

Jones, E.E., & Korchin, S.J. (Eds.). (1982). *Minority mental health.* New York: Praeger.

Lee, C.C. (Ed.). (1995). *Counseling for diversity. A guide for school counselors and related professionals.* Boston: Allyn & Bacon.

Leong, F.T.L. (Ed.). (1995). *Career development and vocational behavior of racial and ethnic minorities.* Mahwah, NJ: Erlbaum.

Levine, E.S., & Padilla, A.M. (1980). *Crossing cultures in therapy; Pluralistic counseling for the Hispanic.* Monterey, CA: Brooks/Cole.

Marsella, A.J., & Pedersen, P.B. (Eds.). (1981). *Cross-cultural counseling and psychotherapy.* New York: Pergamon Press.

McDermott, J.F., Jr., Tseng, W.-S., & Maretzki, T.W. (Eds.). (1980). *People and cultures of Hawaii: A psychocultural profile.* Honolulu: University of Hawaii Press.

McFadden, J. (in press). *Transcultural counseling* (2nd ed.). Alexandria, VA: American Counseling Association.

McGoldrick, M., Pearce, J.K., & Giordano, J. (Eds.). (1982). *Ethnicity and family therapy.* New York: Guilford Press.

Owan, T.C. (Ed.). (1985). *Southeast Asian mental health: Treatment, prevention, services, training, and research*. Washington, DC: U.S. Department of Health and Human Services, National Institute of Mental Health.

Pedersen, P.B. (Ed.). (1985). *Handbook of cross-cultural counseling and therapy*. Westport, CT: Greenwood Press.

Pedersen, P.B. (1994). *A handbook for developing multicultural awareness* (2nd ed.). Alexandria, VA: American Counseling Association.

Pedersen, P., & Carey, J.C. (1994). *Multicultural counseling in schools. A practical handbook*. Boston: Allyn & Bacon.

Pedersen, P.P., Draguns, J.G., Lonner, W.J., & Trimble, J.E. (Eds.). (1996). *Counseling across cultures* (4th ed.). Thousand Oaks, CA: Sage.

Sue, D.W. (1981). *Counseling the culturally different*. New York: Wiley.

Triandis, H.C., & Draguns, J.G. (Eds.). (1980). *Psychopathology handbook of cross-cultural psychology*. Newton, MA: Allyn & Bacon.

The conceptual and research literature found in these references and in other sources indicates that groups that differ on the bases of sex, minority, or socioeconomic status are likely to experience problems or concerns that are unique. Some of these groups and problems have already been cited in previous sections of this chapter. An additional example concerns the disorders prevalent among women but not seen to be of major importance when providing psychotherapy to men. According to Hare-Mustin (1983), disorders of high prevalence in women but not adequately treated in the psychological or intervention literature are marital conflicts, hysteria, agoraphobia, reproductive problems, physical and sexual abuse, depression, and problems associated with eating. The point is that "if psychotherapy is to help female patients, therapists must become aware of sex differences where they do exist and refute assumptions about sex differences where they do not exist" (p. 95). Obviously, in addition, counselors must avoid sex bias and sex stereotyping in diagnostic labeling and in providing treatment.

The literature on stress is extensive and includes Smith (1983). She examined racial differences in relation to their function as stressor stimuli, external mediating forces, and internal mediating forces, the three factors typically defined as the sources of the general level of stress individuals experience. In turn, according to Dohrenwend and Dohrenwend (1979), stressor stimuli are events that cause stress by disrupting or threatening disruption of an individual's activities. External mediating forces are environmental factors—such as money, family, and level of social support—that act upon individuals; internal predictors of stress include personal values, life expectations, general feelings, and physical and psychological dispositions.

Within each of the three sets of factors, Smith (1983) analyzed the role of race in relationship to stress. For example, as a source of stressor stimuli, race becomes associated with out-group and in-group phenomena. Out-group status is associated with three forms of rejection: verbal rejection, discrimination, and physical attack. Minority status in a culture may also lead to social isolation, marginality, and status inconsistency or status ambivalence. There may be role conflicts between the majority culture assertions of superiority versus subordination for minority group members. Such role conflicts may be intensified by the proportion of racial minorities in particular locations. For example, where they are "tokens," racial minorities are likely to experience increased visibility, and indeed, their behavior may be viewed as symbolic of their racial group, thus casting them into a highly pressurized situation. Research data indicate that although racial differences alone do not account for the prevalence of mental illness, they certainly can be related to the incidence of depression, somatic complaints, alcoholism, and antisocial personality disorders.

With regard to race and external mediators of stress, Smith (1983) reported two classes of social stress: (1) social class membership, and (2) social support. In the first, she found an inverse relationship between social class and psychological symptomatology. Because racial minorities tend to be poorer than members of the dominant culture, there are also likely to be stresses in turning their educational achievement and credentials into appropriate earning power. This is true for African Americans, for Asian Americans, and for Hispanics. In social support, the second class of external mediators of stress, Smith found that not having friends or family nearby and available in times of need can be particularly problematic for immigrants and for members of racial minority groups who are dispersed and separated from social or family networks.

With regard to internal mediators of stress, racial minorities also differ in their locus of control and vulnerability to stress. Locus of control can be defined as internal or external. Poor people, who are exposed to the continuous effects of racism and discrimination, are likely to experience high levels of stress, feelings that control of their lives comes from external sources, and learned helplessness. Obviously, such social and psychological assaults upon the individual will affect another internal mediator of stress, the self-concept, in negative ways. To the degree that minority group members internalize as self-hatred the racism and discrimination directed at them by the dominant group, their self-concept will be low and mentally unhealthy.

Against such a context, Smith (1983) suggested a cross-cultural counseling model that she identified as a Stress, Resistant, Delivery (SRD) model. This model posits that in counseling minorities the counselor should follow three basic steps:

> (1) identify the source(s) of stress a client is facing; (2) analyze the mediating (both external and internal) factors of stress and the stress-resistant forces within an individual and within the culture from which an individual comes; (3) decide upon a method of delivering services to clients. (p. 573)

Within these steps, Smith also suggested several counseling phases, which include finding the common reference point, educating the client about his or her symptoms and about what counseling entails, locating hope within the client, locating the injury to the self, reparenting in service of the ego, reworking the trauma, healing the wounds and getting on with self-improvement, and helping the client move to an ideal stage.

McFadden (in press) has advocated a Stylistic Model for Transcultural Counseling that embodies many of the elements advocated by other theorists in the field. This model provides a frame of reference for understanding the client and for counseling across cultures while allowing counselors to develop their own eclectic style in implementing the model. Stylistic counseling, as conceived by McFadden, is developed around three dimensions—cultural-historical, psychosocial, and scientific-ideological—and nine cubical descriptors that undergird the three major dimensions. Within these cubical descriptors, the types of descriptors that may affect the unique frame of reference for a particular client include

ethnic/racial discrimination	media influences
ethnic/racial identity	historical moments
ethnic/racial relations	mind building
dynamics of oppression	politics
psychological security	cultural traditions
logical-behavioral chains	human dignity
value system	economic potency
self-inspection (self-concept)	leaders and heroes
individual goals	perception of others
family patterns	relevant programs
personality formation	language patterns
meaningful alternatives	self-development
monocultural membership	institutional goals.
social forces	

Although not all of these descriptors will be relevant to every client, they represent the content of counseling that evolves as the counselor and the client work through, in turn, each of the three main dimensions of the model. For example, the first dimension, *cultural-historical,* "focuses primarily on how people themselves relate to their own heritage, how they perceive themselves in a broader social context, and how they envision their cultural norms perpetuating themselves over time in the larger social context." The second dimension, *psychosocial,*

> relates specifically to the psychological framework, the formation of a mind-set of how a person's psychic influence affects his or her scope and development, such as in the case of a person's interaction based on how the person sees his or her own cultural heritage. The social component of this dimension relates primarily to the dynamics of interaction between and among people, whether it is within or outside of one's cultural constellation.

The *scientific-ideological* dimension of counseling evolves from the interaction of the counselor and the client in the first two dimensions. "It is geared toward making things happen—in other words, a developmental process of empowering an individual to function—given that there is a support system whereby the client becomes optimally productive."

The principles on which McFadden's view of stylistic counseling rests take many forms. Among the most important are that stylistic counseling requires the counselor to develop a genuine concern and commitment to the client's best interest regardless of cultural differences, an ability to open and maintain effective cross-cultural channels of communication, and an attitude that each client has a unique cultural experience. Thus "stylistic counseling requires that the counselor's role becomes that of an agent and helper within the scope of the client's frame of reference."

Guidelines for Cross-Cultural Counseling

Counselors who are engaged in cross-cultural counseling recognize that many points of reference need to be considered when working with culturally different clients. Some of the factors involved are racial or ethnic background, socioeconomic class, country of origin, bilingual/ bicultural status, cultural expectations about counseling and mental distress, types of stress experienced, family status, social resources, and internal-external locus of control/internal-external locus of responsibility. Sue (1981) collapsed these and many other factors into four areas of most concern when counselors and clients are of different ethnic cultural traditions. These are

1. **barriers:** The four major classes of possible cultural conflicts or miscommunication, according to Sue, are language, class-bound variables, culture-bound variables, and nonverbal communication styles. Counselors must be alert to the presence and to the implications of these as they affect goal setting and the creation of trust.

2. **relationship and rapport factors:** Basically the counselor must be seen as credible by the client. This status depends upon the client's perceptions of counselor expertness and trustworthiness. These two outcomes also depend on the psychological mind-set the client brings to the relationship. What are the expectations the client holds for information and for how he or she will be treated with regard to the counselor as an authority? In addition, the more similar in background and experiences the counselor and client are, the more likely credibility and rapport will be achieved. Furthermore, the psychological development of the client with regard to his or her security with a racial identity and his or her experiences of oppression will be a major factor in the substance and the effectiveness of the cross-cultural counseling that takes place.

3. **cultural identity:** How counselor and client perceive and understand the client's views of and behavior regarding concepts of internality/externality of control will be important to what happens in the relationship. Perceptions of having control of life or being controlled by it operate as the frames of reference or windows through which events are interpreted and acted upon. Whether or not the client views him- or herself as having responsibility for what happens in life is likely to determine whether or not the client views planning, skill development, and training as making sense or not.

4. **the culturally skilled counselor:** According to Sue (1981), the culturally skilled counselor is one who is able to use differential approaches with different clients. A counselor sensitive to each client's language, values, class, and other culturally different characteristics will seek the most appropriate techniques available to meet the client's goals.

Henkin (1985) provided a set of suggestions primarily oriented to counseling with Japanese Americans. They tend to have broad generality, however, across culturally different populations. These guidelines, in abridged form, are to

- establish a clear-cut structure for the counseling process;
- explain the counseling process;
- allow the client to ask questions about the counselor and the counseling process;
- allow yourself as a counselor to ask culturally relevant questions;
- establish your own role clearly;
- be patient;
- refrain from making assessments as long as possible;
- ask your client about family and community relationships;
- provide assurances of confidentiality and honor them;
- find out about your client's prior counseling experience;
- restate your understandings of your client's statements frequently;
- bear in mind that some problems brought to a counselor do not indicate client pathology;
- be aware of the degree to which Japanese Americans may have internalized their cultural treatment; and

- work to counter your client's notions of personal fault, which may simply be internalizations of external issues (pp. 502-503).

The last three of the guidelines Henkin provided relate to what Draguns (1981) defined as the *autoplastic-alloplastic dilemma* in cross-cultural counseling. This term refers to the concept that, "in coping with the environment, all humans respond either autoplastically, by changing themselves to accommodate the external circumstances, or alloplastically, by imposing changes on the world at large" (p. 8). Put somewhat differently, it is important in cross-cultural counseling, as indeed in all counseling, to distinguish problems within the individual from those in the environment. Although many counselors have been trained to look for sources of client problems inside the person, among minority clients the sources of the problem are frequently racial discrimination, social disadvantage, poverty, and other phenomena these clients may have internalized but for which they are not responsible. The problem is that unless the counselor is culturally sensitive to the effects of victimization, learned helplessness, and similar incorporation of what are primarily external deficits, the counselor is likely to focus on what may be seen as an internal deficit when it is, in fact, the result of social marginality, discrimination, and related phenomena.

The notions of the autoplastic-alloplastic dilemma are echoed in the view of the pluralistic counseling espoused by Levine and Padilla (1980) for Hispanic clients. These perspectives also have wide generality to other cultural groups because the therapeutic approaches have been found to be culturally adaptive.

1. The therapist should ascertain whether a client's problems are due primarily to intrapsychic or to extrapsychic stress. If extrapsychic stress is predominant, therapy aimed, for example, at social action and the alleviation of discrimination and poverty may be appropriate. If intrapsychic conflict is most basic, introspective or behavioral therapy is the treatment of choice.
2. The therapist should expect less self-disclosure from Hispanics than from clients of other ethnic groups. It will be the client's responsibility to differentiate between personal privacy that is culturally sanctioned and psychological resistance.
3. The therapist should employ a different style of nonverbal communication with the Hispanic client. The therapist should attempt to greet the client as soon as he or she arrives, shake hands, and sometimes embrace the client. The therapist may sit closer to the Hispanic than to the Anglo or Black client.
4. Family counseling should be emphasized. Treatment modalities that facilitate action and interpretation of family interaction, such as psychodrama and role processing, are vital tools. (p. 256)

Draguns (1981) contended that cross-cultural counseling is not "counseling as usual." Although relationship variables may be common across all sorts of counseling with all types of clients, the culturally sensitive counselor must accommodate the cultural sensitivities and uniqueness of the person sharing the counseling relationship. In a general summation of advice to cross-cultural counselors, Draguns suggested the following:

Be prepared to adapt your techniques (e.g., general activity level, mode of verbal intervention, content of remarks, tone of voice) to the cultural background of the client; communicate acceptance of and respect for the client in terms that are intelligible and meaningful within his or her frame of reference; and be open to the possibility of more direct intervention in the life of the client than the traditional ethos of the counseling profession would dictate or permit. (p. 11)

Draguns (1996) has attempted to summarize what he considered emerging points of consensus among theoreticians, researchers, and practitioners of cross-cultural counseling. In abridged form, his suggestions are as follows:

- "First, the techniques or activities of counseling have to be modified as they are applied in a different cultural milieu."
- "Second, complications in the counseling process tend to increase as the cultural gulf between the counselor and the counselee is widened."
- "Third, conceptions of counseling or, more generally, interpersonal avenues of helping are related to the culturally established modes of self-presentation and the communication of distress."
- "Fourth, complaints, presenting problems, and reported or communicated patterns of distress differ across cultures."
- "Fifth, norms and expectations, especially pertaining to coping with external and internal stress, are also subject to variation across cultures." (pp. 8–9)

Therefore, according to Draguns (1981), "A basic component of counseling experience that remains constant across cultures is a trustful and open relationship between the counselor and the counselee. A major tool for the development of such counseling is the counselor's empathy with the client" (p. 16).

Implicit, if not explicit, in Draguns' summary of emerging points of consensus about cross-cultural counseling is the importance of behaving in ways that are as consistent as is possible for the counselor with the client's cultural traditions. From that perspective, it is likely that cross-cultural counselors may be more active in their communications with the client than they might ordinarily be. In addition, they may involve the client's family more than would otherwise be the case. Such views are consistent with Draguns (1981) notion of using culturally relevant reinforcers in cross-cultural counseling.

The views are also consistent with the extensive cross-cultural work of Leininger (1985), who has suggested that caring for people of different cultural backgrounds is "essentially a new or different way for counseling and health personnel to assist people. It is a shift from a largely unicultural to a multicultural approach in human services" (p. 107). *Transcultural caring*, according to Leininger, means the deliberative and creative use of cultural-care knowledge and skills to assist people in attaining their well-being and to help them live and survive in diverse and changing contexts. It means knowing explicitly cultural-care beliefs, values, and lifeways and using such knowledge in culturally specific ways to help people (p. 107).

> Care is culturally constituted and takes on meaning according to cultural beliefs, values, and practices of different cultures in the world. . . . Care meanings, characteristics, and cultural manifestations differ among cultures primarily due to social structure, cultural values, beliefs, and environmental contexts. (pp. 108–109)

In her studies of 35 cultures, Leininger has identified 42 care constructs that are of particular importance within different cultures and thus become important aspects of the therapeutic process or context. For example, in her research, Leininger reported that "Vietnamese in the United States saw *family sharing* of material goods and nonmaterial ideas with the family as extremely important to them" and as a key care concept. Counselors should be expected to try to keep the family together so that such sharing could occur. A corollary caring concept was respect for the family and for elders as part of any therapy regime. In some contrast, Appalachian Americans saw direct help, trust, and respect for how they dressed, talked, and looked as primary elements of a caring relationship. Such culturally defined caring constructs will, of course, have implications for the counseling theory and processes used and whether we engage primarily in individual counseling or family counseling. In either case, however, knowledge of these care constructs and attempts to incorporate them in our interactions with a client are indicators of dignifying the client by valuing his or her heritage.

Herr (1993), in reviewing cross-cultural counseling emphases that reflect the counseling goal of facilitating dignity in clients, offered the following suggestions:

- In keeping with the teachings of Dr. Martin Luther King (1963) and, indeed, the expectations of some ethnic cultures, counseling should be conceptualized as a gift of time and concentrated attention from the counselor to the counselee. Its fundamental goals are to convey a sense of hope to the student or client; to affirm that he or she is significant, valued, a person of dignity; and to suggest that the negative conditions that stifle his or her life chances can be changed. Such a view overlaps to some degree with the earlier conceptions of client-centered counseling that there are conditions essential to the creation of a therapeutic relationship: unconditional positive regard, empathy, congruence. These conditions provide a haven of security and trust so that the client can explore in depth mixed and ambivalent emotions, real-self/ideal-self incongruence, and their potential for growth. Although the relationship variables need to demonstrate respect and caring, there are a variety of cognitive approaches that fully support the analyses of external barriers to dignity and how they might be dealt with as well as provide the types of social and planning skills by which these barriers can be circumvented.

- As cognitive behavioral approaches are used to assist in strengthening dignity, cross-counseling emphases will need to acknowledge that most problems of dignity are multidimensional. The approaches need to be focused on ego-building and strengthening of self-esteem, but some persons will need assertiveness training and a reassessment of their support systems and social resources. Many persons will need financial support, educational and career planning, occupational and educational information that neutralizes limitations or stereotypes on opportunities that are available, retraining, job skills, and psychological support as they try on new perspectives of self and of opportunity or of living substance free. Some persons will need family counseling, others marital or couples counseling. Some will need help with stress or anger management. Others will need to develop crucial life skills for successful living within whatever functional limitations they now face. They will need to redefine their capacity and potential, not only their loss and limitations. Some people will need help to examine their motivation and the specific personal goals, emotions, and personal agency beliefs that relate to their motivation; to examine the effects of distorted or irrational thinking upon their emotions and behaviors, in order to free them to take charge rather than simply react to things that happen to them; and to learn cognitive flexibility so they can go beyond either-or thinking, and can recognize choices, alternatives, and limitations within their control. As suggested by Arrendondo (1992, p. 10), many women and others need, in essence, processes by which they can "rewrite their life scripts about disempowerment."

- Counselors must recognize that many of the problems that occur between a counselor and a student or client are a function of language-use barriers. This is certainly a major issue when clients are linguistically different, but it is also true that a person whose feelings of personal dignity are fragile or nonexistent may be experiencing and using a different language than the counselor—who may be experiencing transference (countertransference problems), resistance, differences in nonverbal communication, differences in expectations for the counseling process, a lack of knowledge of the client's culture, and differences in values ascribed to certain forms of client behavior (VanZijl, 1985).

- Counselors often have been trained to look for problems inside the person; however, in working with persons on issues of dignity, the sources of the problems, the indignities to which they have been exposed, are frequently racial, sexual, or age discrimination; physical or psychological abuse, economic disadvantagement or poverty; or opportunities denied that they may have internalized but for which they are not responsible. Thus unless the counselor is sensitive to the effects of victimization, learned helplessness, social marginality, discrimination, and related phenomena as primary processes to be identified and worked through, the counselor may be ascribing internal deficits to what, in fact, are deficits in psychological environments or ecological problems that have been owned as personal responsibility.

- With respect to barriers that reduce dignity and bring cross-cultural clients to counseling, the counselor must be clear to help the client differentiate that although these barriers are a problem for the client, they are not the client's problem. Being exposed to social stigma, discrimination, and prejudice does not mean that the client has a deficit or is inferior. Rather it means that the client needs to be helped to examine and activate his or her personal resources and support systems to confront and surmount the emotional arousal or the reduced sense of agency that he or she feels. Cheatham (1990) has put this issue well when he talked about the need to empower Black families: "Empowering the client through therapeutic intervention means transcending the unintended adjustment to the disability and dysfunctional conventions of the "dominant" culture. It means assisting the client to validate his or her sense of self-efficacy and ability to productively confront and dismantle disabling events" (p. 388).

- Counselors must understand that cross-cultural psychology seeks to broaden our vision and deepen our insights. As Segall, Dasen, Berry, and Poortings (1990) have suggested,

  > viewing the tremendously varied beliefs of other persons helps us to avoid two errors. We become less likely to project ourselves upon them (egocentrism) or to imagine smugly and incorrectly that men, women, and children think and act like our neighbors and peers (ethnocentrism). (p. xiii)

We must understand and avoid the problems of communications, language, values, and other factors that may make the counselor-client relationship less safe or productive than it should be. Several chapters in this book have talked about various minority groups being denied dignity and having barriers to dignity imposed upon them because of exploitation, discrimination, segregation, or denial of racial or ethnic pride. As a result of these experiences and the cultural traditions from their nations of origin that are reinforced across generations, the history and beliefs of African Americans, Native Americans, Hispanics, and Asian Americans are distinctly different from each other and from the dominant culture. We cannot substitute the Afrocentricity of Black Americans for the history and worldview of Hispanic, Asian, or Native Americans. Any approach to develop the perceptions and the reality of dignity for each of these groups comprised of persons of color requires awareness by the counselor of the cultural diversity within and among these groups, its potential impact on the elements of motivation and their expression—personal goals, emotional arousal, personal agency beliefs—and with regard to interactions with the counselor.

But it is also important to recognize that cultural differences exist beyond those associated with racially or linguistic diverse groups and include those with disabilities and those who are poor. Although the latter are not always considered as distinct cultures, like the cultures defined in racial or linguistic terms, they, too, reflect differences in belief systems, information processing, worldviews, representations of normality, and individual or group reference points for behavioral models. They create and reinforce cultural templates or cognitive maps by which to attribute meaning to psychological and physical events in order to reduce ambiguity and increase predictability for their members. They provide structures and classification systems by which to attend to, sort out, and interpret the signals or messages from the environment that come to every individual each day.

If the counselor is to function effectively with culturally or linguistically diverse persons, it is important that the counselor have sufficient knowledge about the cultures at issue to reinforce cultural pride, provide respect for the history of the group involved, and be sensitive to potential communications or values issues. The counselor also must be alert not to impose the assumptions of Eurocentric theories of counseling on persons from racial, ethnic, or linguistic groups whose cultural systems, family values, worldviews, self-disclosure, achievement metaphors, verbal expressions, and affiliation models (not necessarily increased individuation but rather group affiliation and collectivist identity) are different from those idealized in many Northern European cultures. Counselors and clients are likely to come from sociocultural, sociohistorical, and psychophysical backgrounds in which the inventory of enabling and disabling events is different. It is difficult for a White American to comprehend fully the perceptions, belief systems, and subtle or overt messages received by a Black client, and it is equally difficult for an abled counselor of any race to comprehend fully the pain, isolation, inconvenience, and anxiety of a person with disabilities. Undoubtedly, similar analogies could be drawn between a counselor who is AIDS free, young, heterosexual, or male attempting to understand and facilitate the growth, development, or change of a client who is HIV positive, frail elderly, homosexual, or female. As physicians are charged to "do no harm" to patients, counselors must equally commit themselves to a credo that says "do not add indignity" in counseling but instead respect, enable, and empower clients as persons of dignity, regardless of their social history.

Within such a context several alternatives seem imperative. One is that

> ... the challenge for the helping professional is to be aware of, and sensitive to the ... client's distinctiveness both as a cultural being and as an individual apart from his or her cultural membership and to utilize that awareness to develop, *with* the client, understanding of the client's expectations and needs. (Cheatham, 1990, p. 381)

Following on that principle is the need to provide sensitive, committed, and appropriate collaboration and counseling that value and respect the client's cultural context. As Cheatham, among others, has indicated, "Respect for what is important and culturally relevant to the client is prerequisite to effecting a successful helping intervention" (Cheatham, 1990, p. 382). Such a prerequisite condition is also essential to strengthening feelings of dignity, significance, importance, and self-respect in the client. "Self-concept apparently is not fixed; rather, it is altered by one's experiences and by one's perceptions and management of those experiences" (p. 383). To be accorded an environment in which hope, trust, caring, and respect are the prime ingredients is to be in an environment in which self-conceptions of personal significance can flourish. This is true whether we speak of the school or the counseling office, the family environment or the workplace.

• Cross-cultural counseling also embodies several other concepts worth brief note. One is that theories that emphasize client responsibility or self-disclosure rather than ways of mastering environmental stigma and obstacles may be less useful than those approaches that emphasize stress reduction and performance-based social functioning and use psychoeducational and other skill-based models. When performance-based approaches are used, it becomes important not to demean the counselee's existing social skills that may have cultural antecedents and have been adaptive for particular purposes. Instead, new ways of functioning within the expectations of a dominant culture may be seen as alternative sets of competencies that give the client greater power to discriminate under what conditions or cultural circumstances such alternative task approach skills, self-observation generalizations, or actions might be used (Krumboltz, 1979). Such approaches need to be seen as ways of increasing individual power and self-esteem. In addition, it seems important to help the client identify or inventory and make plans to use available resources and support systems for resolving immediate dilemmas as well as for fostering a longer term sense of an internal locus of control, that is, for fostering in the client, a sense that he or she is not without support, not a social outcast, or not a person for whom the present and the future are disconnected and not susceptible to planning.

As the counselor and the client engage in the development of any set of skills—anger management, stress reduction, goal settings capability and context beliefs, assertiveness—a performance or social learning approach is not likely to be an abstract, theoretical, or philosophical dialogue but rather more of a psychoeducational model in which educational processes, exercises, and homework are linked to such psychological techniques as simulations, role-playing, behavioral rehearsal, modeling, and feedback. Such models need to be seen as increasing the individual's range of competencies rather than being reflective of his or her deficits, pathologies, or illnesses. A competence model essentially asserts that individuals, youths or adults, have adaptive potential and competencies that can be developed by mental health professionals through strengthening individual coping skills, self-esteem, and social support systems. Such a perspective challenges the counselor to provide the client with culture-relevant and culture-specific reinforcers as affirmation that the processes of development, acquisition of performance-related behaviors, and change are useful and important. By so doing, the counselor assists "the client to validate his or her sense of self-efficacy and ability to productively confront and dismantle disabling events" (Cheatham, 1990, p. 388). Such a view also diminishes the frequently well-intentioned but paternalistic view that culturally different persons are helpless or without means.

Cross-Cultural Appraisal

Within the broad context of cross-cultural counseling, an area worthy of concern is testing, appraisal, or assessment. Because this chapter is not oriented to specific techniques per se, assessment will only be touched upon to note that it is an area that deserves much more attention than can be provided here.

Depending on the assessment tools used by a particular mental health worker— for example, tests, clinical assessments, inventories, self-ratings—the basic assumption is that these appraisal techniques must be oriented toward

> understanding how individuals construe their experiences, their predicaments, their lives. . . . Psychological problems cannot be studied, let alone treated, without a fundamental respect for the person and without a constant effort to grasp the experience of the person. . . . Behavioral approaches, especially the newer cognitive behavioral treatments, have increasingly emphasized the importance of the inner thought processes of the subject. Psychodynamically oriented practitioners have traditionally underscored the importance of personal interviews to provide background data that will contextualize and personalize the results of other, often more structured, tests and procedures. (Jones & Thorne, 1987, pp. 491–492)

The problem with culturally inappropriate or insensitive assessment techniques is that they may lead to misdiagnoses, inappropriate therapeutic plans, and treatment failures (Westermeyer, 1987). Easy solutions to such problems have not been forthcoming. Rather, assessment of culturally different clients should be considered carefully in terms of what will be gained from the use of standardized instruments over what may be acquired from structured interviews or other indicators of performance or attitude.

If client assessment is to be undertaken, the counselor should be diligent in seeking instruments that have been validated for use with the client's cultural group. An excellent treatment of both qualitative and quantitative appraisal and assessment in cross-cultural counseling has been provided by Lonner and Ibrahim (1996). Readers interested in this topic are referred to this source, particularly the later chapters of the book in which testing is discussed with reference to the differences between technical validity and social validities and the value sets involved.

Ethics in Multicultural Counseling

Another area worthy of concern within the broad context of cross-cultural counseling is ethics. In large measure, however, the professional codes of ethics that define standards of behavior for counselors have not yet fully articulated how multicultural issues may affect ethical behavior. Ivey (1986) suggested that such conditions prevail because ethical codes, like counselors, are encapsulated or limited by views that result from Western culture and, therefore, are not sufficiently sensitive to culturally different clients. He suggested several steps to rectify such a situation. In paraphrased form, these are as follows:

- The issue of multicultural awareness should be placed at the center of professional codes of ethics, and it should be a starting point for counseling practice.
- The issue of multicultural practice should be the core of publications and research journals.
- A long-term program of public and professional awareness should be initiated to make counselors aware of the implications of clients as cultural beings.
- Ethical codes and practice should be made more open for involvement with the public.

The underlying importance of ethical codes that are sensitive to multicultural or cross-cultural issues, as well as of using assessments that are culturally sensitive, is summarized in the observations of Pedersen and Marsella (1982):

> A serious moral vacuum exists in the delivery of cross-cultural counseling and therapy sources because the values of a dominant culture have been imposed on the culturally different consumer. Cultural differences complicate the definition of guidelines even for the conscientious and well-intentioned counselor and therapist. (p. 498)

They also stressed that the problem with ethical guidelines is that they are based upon mental health assumptions and processes that were conceptualized or created in one cultural context and are used in a different context without validation.

It is fair to suggest that although they may not be in full compliance with Ivey's recommendations, professional organizations are working diligently to incorporate the particular ethical issues associated with cross-cultural or multicultural counseling into their ethical standards. Since 1988, the American Counseling Association has incorporated a variety of statements into its Code of Ethics that are intended to address the importance of counselor sensitivity to protecting the rights and dignity of culturally diverse clients as well as to ensuring that culturally diverse clients have access to new technologies and tests that do not discriminate against them in their procedures or content. The American Psychological Association has provided *Guidelines for Providers of Psychological Services to Ethnic, Linguistic, and Culturally Diverse Populations* (APA, 1993) in which psychologists are cautioned to be aware of their own cultural background, biases, values, attitudes, and personal worldview and to provide counseling, assessment, and research practices that are appropriate to clients, employees, or trainees from other cultures (La Fromboise, Foster, & James, 1996).

The problem at this point in our professional history is not with the content of ethical codes, but with whether counselors or psychologists know what is in the ethical codes of the professional organization with which they identify and are trained both in terms of ethical standards and of engaging in effective models of cross-cultural counseling.

Culturally Relevant Training

In the near term, creating culturally relevant training programs and reducing the unevenness in the quality of the training that currently exists are considerable challenges. It is unlikely that culturally skilled counselors can exist in the numbers required without a dramatic increase in the number of culturally relevant counselor education programs across the United States. Copeland (1983) contended that counselors cannot be expected to understand and be able to work with culturally different clients unless they are exposed to at least four components: consciousness raising, cognitive understanding, affective components, and skills components. These might be delivered through separate courses, or through interdisciplinary, integrated, and area-of-concentration models. Vontress (cited in Jackson, M.L., 1987) argued that because cross-cultural counseling is multidisciplinary, the effective counselor must be schooled in philosophy, psychology, anthropology, sociology, languages, and the life sciences. Sue, Akutsu, and Higashi (1985) suggested that three important elements for cultural competence include knowledge of clients' culture and status, actual experience with these clients, and the ability to devise innovative strategies.

Ponterotto and Casas (1987) elicited nominations of the leading cross-cultural training programs in the United States. Nine such programs received three to eight nominations from a panel of 20 professionals, who had met a set of criteria indicating they were competent to identify such programs. The similarities in the nine programs included having at least one faculty member sensitive and outspoken in behalf of multicultural issues, requiring at least one course in multicultural issues, attempting to infuse multicultural issues into all program curricula, and attempting to include racially diverse faculty members and students. Obviously, locating nine multiculturally sensitive training programs out of the nearly 500 counselor education and counseling psychology training programs in the United States is an inadequate response to a major counseling issue and must be rectified immediately.

Typical training proposals for systematic approaches to multicultural competency include

- a triad model (Pedersen, 1981) that involves role-playing cross-cultural counseling with three persons. One student assumes the role of counselor, a second person plays a client from a different culture, and a third person tries to highlight cultural gaps, unique cultural values, and their effects on the cross-cultural interaction at issue. Such an approach tries to maximize the student counselor's sensitivity to the internal dialogue of the culturally different client. It also tries to maximize the counselor's skill in perceiving a problem from the client's perspective, recognizing resistance, reducing personal defensiveness, and recovering after making a culturally inappropriate remark or gesture.
- a multistage cross-cultural course (Parker, Valley, & Geary, 1986) that includes in sequence an assessment of the student's level of knowledge and increased sensitivity toward minority group members; exposure to multicultural experiences including touring an ethnic community or spending time in the home of an ethnic family; and making small-group presentations of multicultural issues.
- a cross-cultural awareness continuum (Locke, 1986; Locke & Parker, 1994) that is used as a frame of reference for training educational personnel, including counselors. This continuum includes seven levels of development from self-awareness to acquiring skills and techniques appropriate to cross-cultural counseling. The levels in sequence include self-awareness; awareness of one's own culture; awareness of racism, sexism, poverty; awareness of individual differences; awareness of other cultures; awareness of diversity; and skill/techniques.

CONCLUSIONS

Chapter 4 has examined the dimensions and directions of cultural diversity or plural-ism in the United States. Clearly, the proportion of minority group members in the American population is growing in absolute numbers as well as in political, social, and economic influence in the nation. Rather than a nation of homogeneous tradi-tions and beliefs, the United States is a mosaic of values, work ethics, worldviews, communication patterns, and meaning systems. Although all Americans, regardless of their nation of origin or their particular ancestral roots, share a common commit-ment to freedom, justice, and equal opportunity, they also experience cultural differ-ences in how they view individual achievement versus loyalty and subordination to a group, the use of time and space, religious commitments, and life values and goals.

In essence, it is the cultural differences between counselor and client, rather than the shared values, that stimulate the growing need for culturally sensitive coun-selors and cross-cultural techniques. Cross-cultural implications are pervasive for counselor understanding and communication with clients, the use of assessments, ethical behavior, and training. In either independent or collective terms, these ele-ments of cultural differences will become increasingly important challenges to coun-selors in all settings throughout the United States.

Chapter 5

SPECIAL POPULATIONS AT RISK: CHILDREN AND YOUTH

A MAJOR CHALLENGE FOR COUNSELORS NOW and in the future is the changing definition and the quantification of who among the diverse populations of the United States is at risk. Who is at risk of being physically ill or abused, experiencing mental disorders, taking on antisocial behavior, being economically disadvantaged, or experiencing other forms of negative psychological, social, physical, or economic life events?

Chapter 5 and 6 will address these questions for children, youth, and adults. As suggested in previous chapters, factors that put people at risk are not mutually exclusive. People who experience unusual amounts of stress from losing a job or being constantly thwarted in their efforts to become part of the social mainstream are likely to manifest physical symptoms and stress-related disease, mental disorders, chemical dependency, family difficulties and, possibly, abusive behavior. These behaviors are typically interactive and indicate that most of the problems of psychological vulnerability people experience are really multidimensional in their influence. They trigger ripple effects that flow through the interpersonal systems of which they are a part. For example, when a family member becomes an alcoholic, or mentally ill, or unemployed, such a condition affects a wide array of people with whom that family member comes in contact. In the vocabulary of alcoholism, the spouse or child of an alcoholic or substance abuser may become codependent, or they may become scapegoats or objects of abuse, or they may in some other way be caught up in the network of problems, dysfunction, or negativism that may evolve from or surround the primary person at risk.

There are several ways to consider the notion of people being at risk. One is to consider which groups in the population are most at risk of suffering personal vulnerability to mental disorders and related factors. Another is to consider how the definitions of special populations at risk are changing and on what basis additional

173

groups are being identified as being at risk. A third way is to identify risk factors, the environmental, social, or personal characteristics that put people at risk. In epidemiological terms, "a risk factor is a condition which increases the likelihood of a person developing a particular disorder" (Lobel & Hirschfield, 1984, p. 28). A fourth way is to consider counseling approaches that may be targeted to groups or individuals at risk as well as other strategies beyond counseling that counselors may orchestrate or advocate. This chapter will combine each of these dimensions of individuals or groups at risk in the analyses that follow.

SPECIAL GROUPS AT RISK

Although it is ultimately an individual who is at risk, membership in so-called special groups tends to be seen as increasing the likelihood that an individual will be exposed to the number or severity of factors that lead to behavioral disorders, problematic behavior, or a particular disadvantage. Frequently, federal and state legislation serves to identify specific populations who are to receive or be eligible for some set of services designed to ameliorate their being at risk, vulnerable, or of special status. Depending upon the legislation at issue and its purposes, special populations at risk may be described as persons with disabilities, the socially and emotionally disabled, the mentally retarded, the economically or emotionally disadvantaged, single parents, prisoners or ex-offenders, dislocated workers, individuals of gay or lesbian orientation, Vietnam veterans, the aging and the elderly, and members of specific minority, racial, or ethnic groups. Within these groups at risk there may be other subgroups of people at even greater risk because they are suicidal, functionally illiterate, poverty-stricken, exhibit type-A behavior, and so forth. When legislation identifies and targets certain groups to receive special services and resources, it is typically because members of such groups are seen as potential or actual problems to themselves or to others. Further, as understanding of the interaction of external events and of individual behavior has enlarged, it has become apparent to lawmakers and to mental health professionals that certain groups have heightened vulnerability to stress, crises, and personal turmoil at certain life transition points.

In essence, the notion of a special population is a way of suggesting that individuals in that population are more at risk or more vulnerable to psychological, interpersonal, and economic difficulties than people outside that population. Definitions of special populations change as legislative purposes change and knowledge about psychological definitions expands. Thus the definition of persons at risk is dynamic and not absolute. Many people move into and out of at-risk populations as their environmental conditions, resource and support systems, or age changes. For example, a White male worker who has had a stable job and good health may not ever have been included in an at-risk population until he suddenly loses his job at age 50 because the major employer in his hometown closes the plant where he has worked since he was 18 years of age. Suddenly, he enters an at-risk population whose vulnerability to a drop in self-esteem, stress-related disease, chemical dependency, ageism, and economic disadvantage becomes real. Or, consider the woman who—after graduating from high school immediately marries, raises a family, and concentrates on being a homemaker—suddenly becomes a widow at 48 years of age. In an instant her psychological and financial status changes, as does her sense of personal identity, her interpersonal network, and her need to enter the labor market without the experience or the skills immediately available for occupational entry. She has entered an at-risk population in which dealing with grief and bereavement, loneliness, financial insecurity, identity confusion, and a lack of functional skills may place her at risk of mental disorder, a psychological crisis, or a variety of economic problems.

Definitions of At-Risk Groups

Perry indicated in 1982 that, "the delivery of relevant services to special populations has been a focus of mounting concern within the helping professions, in national legislation, and in the heightened awareness of these populations themselves" (p. 50). A basic premise of this chapter is that the concerns Perry identified almost two decades ago will continue to be important to counselors as far as we can see into the future.

Perry indicated that the concept of *special populations* can be defined in several ways. In a restricted sense, special populations can be defined as the most underserved members of our nation. That is to say, these people are special because they experience limited access to counseling and other mental health services, and the services they do receive frequently are not relevant, in social or cultural terms, to what they need.

In a broader sense, however, populations can be defined as *special* from either a social or historical perspective or from a life-span or developmental perspective. According to Perry (1982), the first category comprises all those special populations for whom

> . . . historically and at present, cultural stereotypes, the legal system, processes of socialization, and corrosive social stigma operate to provide a negative social-psychological ecology: women, racial and cultural minorities, the elderly, the handicapped, learning-disabled or gifted children, and other groups such as the mentally ill, the incarcerated, and persons of alternative sexual orientation. The second major category consists of persons who are at significant points of transition and stress in their lives. Thus these changing "developmental" special populations are cross-sections of the population at times of family planning, pre- and postnatal care, early childhood support and day care systems, school entry screening, school-employment transitions, illness and death in the family, separation and divorce, career transitions, periods of unemployment and retirement. (p. 52)

These definitions of special populations suggest the following:

- The risk factors by which special populations are defined differ. Some special populations are special because they have been exposed to historical, social, legal, and educational inequities that have placed them at risk of not gaining access to the educational, social, and economic institutions that would allow them to acquire the personal competencies, self-confidence, and mentoring available to other groups. Therefore, their life chances and possibility structures have been restricted or constrained because of the stereotyping and bias they have experienced related to their disabilities, race, sex, sexual orientation, ethnicity, age, or other group membership characteristics. Other populations are special because at certain developmental or transition points they have experienced psychological or physical trauma, crises, or other conditions that have caused them to be unusually prone to extraordinary stress, abuse, or other emotional and behavioral disorders.
- Because the risk factors affecting special populations are variable, the counseling and other services available must be tailored to the different categories of risk. In

some instances, the treatment of preference is primary prevention; in other instances, intense, individual psychotherapy is the preferred intervention. Sometimes the role of the counselor is a consultative one; sometimes direct services are required. Depending upon the etiology and maintenance of the risk factors involved, self-help groups, deliberate psychological education, or support networks may be the most appropriate treatments.

• Some people are at risk because of historical, social, legal, and educational inequities as well as developmental or transition problems. In other words, they are in both categories of risk, not just in one or the other.

Perspectives on At-Risk Factors

As antecedents to risk, there are factors that predispose people to vulnerability or being at risk. Sometimes clusters of factors are involved; sometimes there may be one factor (e.g., a physical disability, racial background) that becomes encumbered with layers of prejudice and bias and ultimately internalized by the individual as part of his or her self-concept.

In terms of physical health risk factors, it has become common knowledge that widely practiced personal habits such as smoking, alcohol abuse, dietary excesses, sedentary lifestyle, and coronary-prone behavior patterns contribute in substantial ways to disease incidence (Rosen & Solomon, 1985). Risk factors in psychological health are probably more complex and varied. Depending on the risk group, they involve such social variables as education, marital status, religious participation, social integration, employment status, and stress. Mechanic's (1985) research suggested the presence of such risk factors in the use of psychiatric services as low psychological well-being, self-description of unhappiness, degree of worry about specific life problems, and low self-esteem. He found these factors related to three aspects: (1) body sensations, symptoms, or feelings different from those ordinarily experienced; (2) social stress; and (3) cognitive appraisals of what a person is feeling (p.13).

In a broader context, Evans (1985) applied a social learning model to explanations of adolescent smoking behavior. This model suggests that both the social environment and "personality" determinants contribute to the complex of psychological predispositions related to smoking. Perhaps more important for our purposes is that such a model suggests examples of where risk factors can appear or what can shape them along the process that finally is manifested not only in an outcome such as smoking but also in mental disorders, chemical dependency, and other phenomena.

Specifically, Evans, in his model of adolescent smoking behavior, indicated the presence of such factors as

• general social environment, including smoking-related behavior, and expressed attitudes of peers, siblings, parents, respected adults, and media figures;
• interpersonal or personality factors such as low self-esteem, dependency or powerlessness, and frequent rewards for imitative behavior; and
• psychological predispositions including smoking-related attitudes, beliefs, values, expectations, and learned behaviors.

These three factors in turn lead to a negative or positive attitude regarding smoking and, ultimately, to behavior, that is, to refraining from or engaging in smoking.

Another broad view of risk factors relates to the prevention or the treatment of alcohol abuse. According to Nathan (1985), influences on drinking, including alcohol drinking, include genetic and prenatal factors, interpersonal and environmental factors, psychological, psychiatric, and behavioral factors, and sociocultural and ethnic factors. These influences on drinking, in turn, can operate at societal, institutional, community, family, peer group, and individual levels; influences on drinking, moreover, derive from social norms, social controls, access and availability of beverage alcohol in the society in question, the drinker's personal disposition and behavior patterns, etc. (p. 37)

Such paradigms indicate that negative and positive factors can appear in individuals' general social environment, in their personality or intrapersonal structure, and in their psychological predispositions. As negative factors appear in such elements of an individual's life space, he or she becomes increasingly at risk to engage in or to be excluded from certain behaviors or opportunities. Models of such paradigms also suggest where the points of intervention on risk factors should be: the mass media, family, public policy, the individual's self-concept or sense of self-worth, individual beliefs, values, or learned behavior. Depending on the problem at issue, any or all of these points of intervention may need to be considered.

Dryfoos (1997) has discussed the concepts of *high risk* and *low risk* for adolescents and described the sets of factors that cluster to place adolescents in a high-risk category and those factors that are preventive and likely to predict low-risk behavior. Her definition of high risk is "having the attributes of a young person with low probabilities of gaining an education, getting a job, effectively parenting, or being able to participate in the political process" (pp. 18–19). An extensive review of studies that predicted failure in school, in the community, and in the workplace suggested a series of attributes of high-risk youth. These factors tend to co-occur, occur together in a "package." For example,

. . . substance abuse is closely related to delinquency. . . . Heavy alcohol, smoking, and marijuana use appears to co-occur with early unprotected intercourse and multiple partners. . . . Violent behavior is highly related to other negative outcomes such as substance use and unprotected sex. . . . The link between delinquency and being held back in school appears as early as first grade. (pp. 27–29)

Dryfoos (1997, p. 38) suggested that the factors that frequently co-occur and that predict categorical high-risk behaviors include such attributes as the following:

- Family
    lack of supervision
    lack of attachment and bonding
    parental substance use
    abuse and neglect
    absence of cultural resources
    frequent moving
- School
    low expectations for success
    little commitment to education
    being behind in school
    low grades
- Community
    poverty

gangs
access to guns
- Individual
susceptibility to peer influences
lack of social competency
tolerance of deviance/unconventionality.

Other terms for risk factors may be *etiologic factors, predisposing factors,* and *specific culture, age, and gender factors.* Each of these terms is used, for example, in the third edition of the *Diagnostic and Statistical Manual of Mental Disorders (DSM-III)* (American Psychiatric Association [APA], 1980), in its revised edition, the *DSM-III-R* (APA, 1987), and in the most recent edition, the *DSM-IV* (APA, 1994). The *DSM-IV* tends to integrate risk factors into the description of a particular disorder and integrate the identification of risk factors under any one or several headings including predisposing factors, family factors, specific culture, age, and gender features, prevalence, associated features, or other such headings. Predisposing factors as used in the *DSM-IV* include etiological factors that are primarily biological or primarily psychosocial or some combination of both. As an example, under predisposing factors for mental retardation (p. 43) are included the following: heredity, early alterations of embryonic development, pregnancy and perinatal problems, general medical conditions acquired in infancy or childhood, environmental influences, and other mental disorders. In a further example, risk factors for post-traumatic stress disorder (p. 591) are cited as including family psychiatric illness, parental poverty, traumatization in childhood, early parental separation, childhood behavior disorder, neuroticism, introversion, previous psychiatric disorder, other adverse life events, and being female.

Looked at from a different perspective, the *DSM-IV* also identifies psychosocial and environmental problems that affect the diagnosis and treatment of mental disorders. Although not cited as risk factors per se, they are seen as problems relating to the context in which a person's difficulties have developed. As such these problems may play a role in the initiation or the exacerbation of mental disorder, and they also may develop as a consequence of a person's psychopathology. Examples of the categories of psychosocial and environmental problems that counselors and other clinicians may need to be aware of under such a rubric are problems with the primary support group, educational problems, occupational problems, housing problems, economic problems, problems with access to health care services, and problems related to interaction with the legal system/crime.

In large measure, the *DSM-IV*, like its earlier editions, provides assistance to counselors in organizing their diagnoses and assessments of clients around a multiaxial system that classifies five types of information. Information about psychosocial and environmental problems just described is actually the type of information collected and analyzed on Axis IV of the classification system. The other categories of information include Axis I and Axis II that "constitute the entire classification of mental disorders and other conditions that may be the focus of clinical attention; the other axes are used to describe medical and psychosocial problems and adaptational level" (Fong, 1995, p. 635). More specifically, Axis I describes categories of acute states that are typically the primary presenting problem of the client. Axis II tends to be more descriptive of the traits that characterize the Axis I disorder, including the specific symptoms, the chronicity or long-range stability of these traits, defense mechanisms, and the maladaptive responses at issue. Axis III is used to report current general medical conditions that are potentially relevant to understanding and management of the mental disorders. For example, the panic attacks that brought the client to the counselor (Axis I) might be related to the worry and uncertainty about the future associated with a recent diagnosis of a cardiac problems (Axis III) as well as concern by the individual about losing his or her job and experiencing the associated financial problems (Axis IV). Finally, Axis V is a General Assessment of Functioning (GAF) Scale that allows the counselors to assess the level at which the client appears to be functioning at the time of evaluation. The GAF Scale extends from 0 (inadequate information) to 100 (superior functioning).

As suggested here, the *DSM-IV* as well as the earlier *DSM-III* and *DSM-III-R* have been of significant assistance in helping counselors understand the complexity of mental disorders, their assessment, and the variety of factors that interact to influence or to stimulate the course and severity of mental disorders. Many of these factors lie outside the individual, in a range of psychosocial factors that may trigger problems or predispose individuals to being at risk.

Psychosocial stress factors typically are seen as interacting with predisposing factors (characteristics of an individual that can be identified before the development of a disorder that place him or her at higher risk for developing the disorder) in defining the conditions of being at risk or of vulnerability as it is used in this chapter. In a sense, predisposing factors frequently serve as thresholds for vulnerability that, when exceeded, are manifested as a disorder depending upon the presence and severity of specific psychosocial stressors. The potency of psychosocial stressors depends on when these stressors appear in the individual life cycle and the meaning those stressors hold for a given individual. Obviously, given the same stressor, people respond differently. Aspects of the individual who experiences a psychosocial stressor vary and affect how the event is emotionally and cognitively processed.

The intent of this chapter is not to engage in an in-depth analysis of the research on at-risk factors but rather to sensitize the reader to the notion of special populations at risk, the complexity of the issues, and the changing perspectives on populations of increasing concern to counselors because of their particular vulnerability and the need for responses to that vulnerability.

Although it is not possible to deal at length with all of the populations potentially at risk, the following sections address some of the major concerns related to children and youth. Such concerns represent problem areas that counselors in different settings are likely to encounter. In chapter 6, the characteristics of and problems associated with at-risk adults will be discussed.

CHILDREN AND ADOLESCENTS AT RISK

Preschool Children

Researchers and behavioral scientists have been concerned for many years about identifying preschool children who, because of genetic predisposition or intense environmental stresses, run unusually strong risks of developing mental problems in adulthood. Research studies have concluded that many psychiatric disorders begin when persons are quite young. Although symptoms of many psychiatric disorders do not appear until adolescence, the likelihood is that there may be predisposing factors in early childhood that set the stage for the rise of fully developed disorders several years later (Robins, Locke, & Regier, 1991). Rolf (1985, as quoted in Isenstein and Krasner, 1988), among other investigators supported by the National Institute of Mental Health, theorized that very young children do show symptoms of behavior disorders, which, if identified, could be treated with early intervention techniques designed to prevent these early behavioral disorders from developing into adult psychopathology. To these ends, Rolf and others have been developing a high-risk profile that is useful in the early identification and selection of children for individualized treatment. Out of this research has come the consensus that the most vulnerable children are

- those with deviant parents, especially parents with psychotic and criminal histories;
- those with chronic aggressive behavior disorders;
- those who have suffered very severe social, cultural, economic, and nutritional deprivations; and
- those who have physical, temperamental, or intellectual handicaps (Isenstein & Krasner, 1988, pp. 2–3).

In response to such findings, over the past decade or more there have been increasing efforts to provide both pre- and postnatal services to families who have been defined as high risks because they meet such criteria as experiencing poverty, or mother of young age, or single-parent status. The rationale for such provisions is that "at the earliest stages of development, a child's risk is inextricably linked to the mother's or caretaker's behavior and well-being" (Murray, Crierra, & Williams, 1997). These types of services attempt to avoid children being born with low birth weight, or with other birth trauma, or infected by drug addiction or HIV, through providing expectant mothers with parent education about basic health and nutrition during pregnancy and about the importance of refraining from substance abuse and other risky behaviors during that time, and then after birth assisting the mothers to become engaged in parent education about infant development and to gain access to other health and human service programs available as well as relevant support groups. Other programs have tried to provide services from social workers related to access to medical, financial, and support services; to the reduction of parental stress that can be manifested in behaviors that damage the social adjustment of children; and to positive family functioning and a supportive emotional climate in the home. Further approaches to reducing the conditions that place preschool children at risk have been preschool enrichment programs like Head Start, summer preschool enrichment programs prior to kindergarten, and others that focus on social and congnitive skill development prior to entering the elementary school years. Each of these efforts are directed to providing at-risk children the early identification and developmental assistance to offset or prevent potential problems once they enter elementary school.

Once preschool children who fall into at-risk categories are identified, the further consensus is that individualized interventions should be designed that are preventive of future behavioral disorders. From a preventive standpoint, the intent of intervention is to help these children build up their resistance to environmental stressors, give them better methods of coping, and increase the flexibility of their behavioral repertoires. In order to achieve such outcomes a variety of interventions are of possible use. They include, in broad terms, special day care or preschool curricula, consultation, referral, direct child contact, parent and family contact, and advocacy and follow-through. With respect to day care or preschool curricula, social, intellectual, and physical competencies can be developed through graded series of play and work activities, practice of socially acceptable behavior, skits, visits to community sites (e.g., fire stations, police stations, churches, stores) that reinforce the value of socially acceptable behaviors, games, sports, dancing and rhythm exercises, cooperative activities with other children, formal instruction designed to stimulate creativity, verbal comprehension, critical thinking, and sensory discrimination.

As suggested previously, often, if not always, intervention with high-risk children requires intervention with high-risk parents that may take the form of parenting education, counseling and support in child rearing, instruction in nutrition and management of resources, and therapy directed at the parents' own psychiatric, alcohol-related, or other problems. However, research studies have strongly indicated that early intervention directed at the child alone or at the parent alone is not as effective as education intervention programs combined with home-based visits to educate parents about developmentally appropriate behavior. Such research also demonstrated that how actively a family participates in an intensive, early intervention program directly affects the developmental outcomes for high-risk children. Active participation is especially beneficial for children whose mothers have low IQ scores. Further, it has been found that grade retention in elementary school can be reduced by almost 50% by early educational interventions and that the benefits of continuous educational intervention over the first years of life last at least until early adolescence (Ramey & Ramey, 1993).

Further, high-risk children frequently experience multiple problems. That is, they may simultaneously require speech and language therapy, socialization with other children, play therapy, behavioral modification, and other direct intervention. Thus counselors involved will need to engage in direct intervention, parent intervention, and referral to or coordination with different professional specialists and agencies.

Childhood Depression

High-risk children may also experience clinical depression. *Clinical depression* is a term that covers a large range of affective disorders that vary in their causes and in their intensity, severity, and duration. Typically, clinical depression is associated with a depressed mood, the "blues," feelings of rejection or isolation, and a loss of interest in usual activities. Symptoms also may include appetite, weight, or sleep disturbances as well as hyperactivity or lethargy, anxiety, crying, slowed thinking, suicidal tendencies, and feelings of guilt, worthlessness, and hopelessness. Although the symptoms of depression in adolescents are similar to those in adults, clinical depression may occur even in infants, and it certainly occurs as well in prepubertal children. In infancy, a depressive condition. called the *nonorganic failure to thrive syndrome* has been identified in which babies with the condition are found to be unresponsive to external stimuli such as eye contact, tend to cry weakly, refuse food, sleep excessively, and seem apathetic (Lobel & Hirschfield, 1984). The immediate cause of such a syndrome seems to be inadequate care in the environment. Thus as just suggested, such babies may have parents who are themselves at risk, troubled, unable to cope, and as a result, they put their children at risk of depression and other mental disorders.

In prepubertal and adolescent clinical depression, various factors are likely to be implicated. It is possible that in some instances childhood depression may be a function of genetic predisposition and be associated with children of parents with a major problem of diagnosed depression. It is also true that viral disease, some malignancies or other illnesses, and some medications can cause depression. All of these can be considered risk factors for some children. The more common predisposing factors to depression in children are, like those for adults, stressful events: loss of a parent or sibling, illness, divorce, a move to a new community or a new home, teasing from peers, lack of friends, a bad experience with a teacher, or ineptness in sports when they are an important part of an environment. Usually in young children, the treatments of choice are not psychotherapy or medication unless the depression is severe. Rather, what is usually indicated is the need to change the child's environment in order to increase his or her self-esteem, promote friendships, provide more attention, or resolve school difficulties (Lobel & Hirschfield, 1984). As children become adolescents, episodes of clinical depression may, in fact, warrant medication, psychotherapy, or other adult treatments. The point here is that some portion of the population of children, perhaps as much as 10% to 12% (Lobel & Hirschfield, 1984), can experience levels of stress, clinical depression, or psychopathology that put the children at high risk for subsequent problems in adolescence and adulthood.

The consequences of depressive symptoms and disorder during childhood are significant because in addition to the increased risk of depression in later life, childhood depressions also can cause concurrent disruption in effective functioning in many aspects of childhood, increased risk for suicidal ideation and attempts, and the tendency for depression to co-occur with many other problems and disorders including anxiety, disruptive behavior disorders, substance abuse, social problems, and other associated impairments (Compas, Connor, & Wadsworth, 1997).

Elementary School Children At Risk

High-risk preschool children are frequently unidentified or untreated. They enter elementary school and subsequent educational levels carrying the seeds of vulnerability that are likely to blossom into academic underachievement, suicide, dropping out of school, antisocial behavior, or other manifestations. These behaviors are not exclusive to preschool children at high risk; other children are at risk as well. We have alluded to some of the issues that put children at risk in chapters 3 and 4 as we spoke of the changing family as well as cultural diversity. Within those contexts, Hodgkinson (1985), in his review of demographic trends, indicated that educators and counselors are likely to work with increasing numbers of children with the following characteristics:

- premature at birth;
- born to a teenage mother;
- born to parents who were not married;
- come from single-parent households;
- come from blended families that result from remarriage of one original parent;
- come from poor households;
- are minorities;
- have not participated in Head Start or similar preschool programs; and
- have working parents and could be described as latchkey children.

Although not every child with these risk factors is necessarily vulnerable to mental disorders or academic underachievement, research has not been favorable. More and more studies have suggested that children with one or more of these characteristics are likely to perform poorly in school.

Students At Risk, Elementary and Secondary

Students at risk include elementary and secondary school students who, on the one hand, run the risk of not acquiring the knowledge, skills, and attitudes needed to become successful adults and, on the other hand, behave in ways that put them at risk for not graduating from high school. The negative behaviors at issue include "not engaging in classroom and school activities, using drugs and alcohol, committing disruptive and delinquent acts, becoming pregnant, dropping out, or attempting suicide" (Pennsylvania Department of Education, 1987, p. 1). A further use of the term *students at risk* relates to children whose family background and home and community conditions, such as poverty or low parental education, are associated with low achievement and the lack of success in school. Undoubtedly, within these definitions of students at risk are a number of children whose profiles in preschool would have been defined as high risk. The pool of such children gets larger as environmental stresses accumulate.

Students at risk are of major concern to parents and teachers. For example, in one major study of schooling in 38 school districts around the nation (Goodlad, 1983) teachers ranked highest the problems of lack of student interest, lack of parent interest, and student misbehavior. Clearly, student development is complex. When it is impaired by student misbehavior and the disinterest of both students and parents toward school, the tasks of learning become compromised until other problems in the student's environment are resolved.

Drug Use

Data from national surveys by the National Institute on Drug Abuse (Mathias, 1997b) about drug and alcohol use among students reflect another facet of students at risk. These data are more fully discussed in chapter 7, but suffice it to say here that marijuana, tobacco, and alcohol use have continued to increase among students, and they appear to be used by younger children. For example, marijuana use has increased by 250% among 8th graders and by 150% among 10th graders since 1991. In 1996, in national surveys, some 11.3% of 8th graders and 20.4% of 10th graders reported having used marijuana in the previous 30 days. Among seniors surveyed, 21.9% reported that they had used marijuana in the past 30 days and 4.9% reported smoking marijuana every day. Cigarette smoking was found to be on the rise for 8th graders, 21% of whom smoked, and for 10th graders, 30.4% of whom reported that they smoked. With regard to the use of alcohol, 9.6% of 8th graders, 21.3% of 10th graders, and 31.3% of 12th graders reported that they had been drunk in the past month, and larger percentages of students reported the use of alcohol in the past 30 days: 26.2% (8th graders); 40.4% (10th graders); and 50.8% (seniors).

Although marijuana, cigarettes, and alcohol were the primary substances of preference for junior and senior high school students in 1996, it is worth noting that other substances were reported as used by 8th and 10th graders, although in much smaller percentages. For example, 5.8% of 8th graders and 3.3% of 10th graders reported using inhalants in the past 30 days; 1.9% and 2.8% used hallucinogens; 1.3% and 1.7% used cocaine; .8% of each grade level used crack cocaine; .7% and .5% used heroin; and 4.6% and 5.5% used stimulants. These data suggest that it is likely that some students use multiple substances; some may only use one or two. These data also suggest that because of cost or accessibility, the use of substances varies across grade levels. But in each of these grade levels, such substances are available, and a rising proportion of 8th, 10th, and 12th graders use such substances. Indeed, research findings have indicated that although the majority of young people still disapprove of using illicit drugs, the intensity of disapproval has grown weaker as has the view of drug use as dangerous. For example "between 1991 and 1995, there were significant declines in perceived harmfulness of trying marijuana (from 40% to 29% among 8th graders, from 30% to 22% among 10th graders, and from 27% to 16% among 12th graders) and in perceived harmfulness of trying cocaine (from 56% to 45% among 8th graders and from 59% to 54% among 10th graders)" (Dusenbury & Falco, 1997, p. 51).

In 1984, the Pennsylvania Department of Education surveyed 10,683 high school students from 10 school districts in the state with the following selected results: students who reported spending more time on academic activities also reported using less drugs and alcohol; students who reported being heavy users of cigarettes, beer, marijuana, stimulants, depressants, and cocaine also reported dissatisfaction with school and their teachers, lower grade point averages, and less self-confidence (Pennsylvania Department of Education, 1987). These findings on the co-occurrence of substance abuse and other behaviors that reduce academic and psychosocial performance have been supported by other national studies (Dusenbury & Falco, 1997).

Conduct Disorders and Antisocial Behavior

Students at risk are also likely to be involved with delinquent acts. Data from the Federal Bureau of Investigation (1983) indicated that, on the average, 14.2% of 14- to 17-year-olds are arrested annually and that this figure tends to fluctuate very little from year to year. Indeed, the data indicated that children under 18 years of age accounted for approximately 16.8% of all arrests and 30.5% of all "serious crime" arrests. In a study of delinquent behavior in two birth cohorts, one of 10,000 boys born in 1945, and a second of 13,160 boys and 14,000 girls born in 1958, Tracey, Wolfgang, and Figlio (1985) found that one third of each of these cohorts had had at least one episode with the police before they were 18 years of age. They found that within these youth cohorts there were between 7% and 8% who could be considered chronic offenders, and that many of these youth had begun to commit delinquent acts when they were 7 to 9 years of age. On balance, this research found that youth involved with police were 2.5 times more likely to be male than female, from unstable homes, with fewer years of schooling, and with records of lower scholastic achievement. In another study of youth who engage in delinquent behavior, Gottfredson, Gottfredson, and Cook (1983) found that such youth tend to have weak attachments to parents; feel alienated from any social order and do not respect rules of law as having validity; dislike school, are frequently truant, and expend little effort on school work; associate with delinquent peers; and experience low self-esteem or a delinquent self-concept.

The prevalence of antisocial behavior is difficult to estimate because not all children who engage in such behavior are arrested or come into contact with legal authorities. In general, estimates of the rate of conduct disorders among children tend to range between 4% and 10%, with about one third to one half of all referrals of children to outpatient clinics related to aggressiveness, conduct problems, and antisocial behavior (Kazdin, 1987, p. 16). Kazdin (1987) indicated that unlike many other childhood disorders, antisocial behavior is not age specific, tends to be relatively stable over time, and children do not simply grow out of it.

> Conduct problems in childhood and adolescence portend later problems in adulthood including criminal behavior, alcoholism, antisocial personality (i.e., continued conduct disorder), other diagnosable psychiatric disorders, and poor work, marital, and occupational adustment. . . . Antisocial behavior is not only stable over time *within individuals* but also *within families*. Antisocial behavior in childhood predicts similar behaviors in one's children. The continuity is evident across multiple generations. Grandchildren are more likely to show antisocial behaviors if their grandparents have a history of these behaviors. . . . Antisocial behavior has been identified as one of the most costly of mental disorders to society . . . [because] a large proportion of antisocial youths remain in continued contact with mental health and criminal justice systems well into adulthood. (p. 17)

The onset of conduct disorders and antisocial behavior appears to occur quite early. It is not unlikely that the median age of referral of children for antisocial behavior is 8 to 10 years of age, causing this phenomenon to be of particular concern to elementary school counselors. But it is also true that some of the corollaries of conduct disorders may occur even earlier. For example, in the *DSM-III*, Oppositional Disorder—a pattern of disobedient, negativistic, and provocative opposition to authority figures—is characterized as having its onset as early as 3 to 18 years of age.

As described by Bloom (1996), the antisocial behaviors that youth engage in range from what is normal, but possibly obnoxious,

> . . . to the pathological (e.g., setting fires, destroying property, attacking innocent victims), to responses to aggression from others (such as some running away behavior). They can include verbal aggression and physical aggression; individual behaviors and collective actions; and problems at home and problems in school, work, and the community . . . for some, these severe and persistent antisocial actions—termed *conduct disorders*—represent significant problems that carry over into adulthood. (pp. 136–137)

Kazdin (1987) has indicated that "many different terms have been applied to denote antisocial behavior including acting out, externalizing behaviors, conduct disorder or conduct problems, and delinquency" (p. 11). Hawkins (1997), as a result of an extensive review of the research literature, has suggested that several factors have been shown to predict health-risk behaviors during adolescence. For example,

> . . . extreme economic disadvantage or poverty has been shown to increase risk for . . . crime. . . . Studies in different countries and cultures have shown that persistent physically aggressive behavior in the early elementary grades (includes fighting and bullying) predicts later crime, violence, and substance abuse . . . [and] independent studies have found both academic failure and low commitment to schooling to increase risk for later substance abuse, delinquency, school dropout, teen pregnancy, and violence. (pp. 279–280)

As just noted, some children and adolescents will exhibit violent behavior, and it will contribute to an overgeneralized concern that adolescents are violence prone or troubled. In fact, there is an escalating rate of youth violence, and it has become more lethal. Fox (1996) has reported that the homicide rates of youth ages 14 to 17 increased by 172% from 1985 to 1994. Such a statistic seems consistent with the frequent and dramatic reports of youth gang warfare, of children killing their parents, or of children killing other children. The good news is that although the lethality of youth violence has increased, the proportion of youth committing violent crimes or the frequency of youth violence has apparently remained essentially the same since 1980. In fact, violent offenders constitute a small percentage (4% in 1980 and approximately the same in the 1990s) of juvenile offenders arrested (Elliott, 1994; Federal Bureau of Investigation, 1981) and a very small percentage of all juveniles. Many, but not all, of these children will have been previously identified as children at risk or as juvenile delinquents. In any case, violent behavior can occur in school, in the family, in the workplace, or in other community settings. Just as is true of other forms of behavior, "violent behavior occurs within a social context that includes both antecedents and consequences" (Roth, 1985, p. xiii). Thus certain risk factors predispose youth and adults to violent behavior.

Violent individuals, another category of children at risk, manifest both a psychology and a social psychology that must be understood and addressed if behavioral change is to be facilitated. Violence, like most human behavior, is multifactored; rarely is there a single cause for a person's violent behavior. Psychological, situational, medical, and other factors may be implicated in any particular instance of violent behavior. Monnhan and Klasson (1982) proposed that violent behavior often emerges because of an interaction among stressful life events, a person's cognitions and affects, and a person's behavioral coping responses. In sum, "violence does not occur in a vacuum but in response to psychological, social, and environmental stress" (Lion, 1985, p. 41). A first step for the counselor and other mental health workers is determining what the stress is and whether it can recur.

A wide range of categories of risk factors is associated with the presence of violent behavior in children and adolescents. These factors, as adapted from reviews of diagnostic and treatment issues concerning violent juveniles reported by Lewis (1985), Lion (1985), and Kazdin (1987), include the following:

- Social, familial, medical, cognitive, and psychiatric factors often combine to contribute to a particular act of violence.
- Although most violent juveniles come from family conditions of social deprivation, it is apparently not the social deprivation per se that triggers violence; it is important to be mindful that most people raised in social deprivation do not behave violently.
- Within conditions of family social deprivation, risk factors for juvenile violent behavior are the presence of past physical abuse; a psychotic parent; severe central nervous system injury from beatings, blows to the head, being thrown down steps; or psychotic and organic symptomatology.
- Delinquents tend to come from chaotic family situations of family discord that may lead to broken homes and to parents' failure to supervise and discipline their children properly. In addition, in contrast to nondelinquents, delinquent juveniles are much more likely to have parents who have been psychiatrically hospitalized as manic-depressive or schizophrenic. Antisocial children are frequently found to have fathers who themselves have learning or behavior problems. Thus at one level it is apparent that many violent juvenile offenders suffer psychopathology that has genetic, inherited, or physiological underpinnings.
- Whether or not they themselves are psychopathological, a large proportion of children and adolescents, perhaps 75%, have experienced physical abuse at the

hands of their parents or parent surrogates. Violence tends to beget violence as children imitate behaviors they have experienced. They may displace their rage at being brutally mistreated by their parents to other children or adults with whom they come in contact. They may be inordinately suspicious of others. Physical abuse frequently leads to brain damage, neurological deficits, psychomotor seizures, minimal brain dysfunction, and other injuries to the central nervous system that reduce the child's ability to control aggressive impulses or that are manifested in epileptic seizures or a variety of learning and behavioral problems associated with brain damage. Severe physical injury can lead to psychotic behavior, hyperactivity, or episodic violence.

- Children who have been severely abused may develop paranoid tendencies, excessive wariness and suspicion, thinking disorders, or perceptual problems that lead to misinterpretation and miscommunication about events that result in violent reactions.
- An adolescent or an adult who was treated cruelly as a child can grow up with a lack of interpersonal warmth, become aloof to the suffering of others, be indifferent to hurting others, and be prone to excessive discipline of children or pets. These people learn coping styles and adaptations to violence they may use with others, including their own offspring, later in life.
- Violent adolescents and adults are typically characterized by low self-esteem resulting from parental deprivation or alcoholism. Low self-esteem in antisocial adolescents or adults frequently is combined with little tolerance for introspection and considerable projection to external causes and people for their problems. They convert any criticism into externally directed rage, lashing out at others in physical and verbal outbursts.
- A host of toxic factors has been associated with violent behavior. Abuse of hallucinogens, LSD or PCP, amphetamines, barbiturates, and inhalants such as glue fumes has been associated with aggression and homicidal behavior. Alcohol remains the most frequent toxic substance linked to violence.

As suggested by the multiple risk factors associated with violent behavior, assessment of the specific etiology or stresses associated with the violent behavior a particular individual displays is critical. Following such assessment, however, treatment will probably need to be multidimensional. Medication may be necessary to control aggressive impulses. If so, the medication will need to be highly individualized. Anticonvulsants, antipsychotics, or antidepressants may be indicated in particular cases. Educational interventions in response to learning disabilities or other learning problems will be important for many violent youth. Psychotherapy and group counseling frequently will be used for most delinquent and violent youth. And of major importance, either through therapeutic interventions or in other ways (e.g., Big Brother/Big Sister programs), most violent, seriously delinquent adolescents need at least one adult relationship that is steady, stable, caring, and understanding. They need someone who cares about their successes and is dismayed about their setbacks. Without such an empathic, emotionally supportive relationship it is unlikely that violent, delinquent adolescents will be motivated or able to change their behaviors. Even where multiple forms of treatment and support are available, it is likely that many of the risk factors identified as associated with violent behavior will be chronic and incurable; at best, they will be able to be controlled and the incidence of violent behavior significantly reduced. Some of these youngsters will never be able to return to their original family or to function within the normal school environment. Instead, they will require a residential setting, a group home, or other structured and, perhaps, secure environments where their self-control and increasingly independent behavior can be monitored and supported.

Adolescent Depression

Just as clinical depression is, as discussed, a major risk factor in preschool children, it occurs as well in elementary school children and in adolescents. Estimates of the number of adolescents who experience depression vary: some are that it occurs in 6% to 7% of the adolescent population, with some 3 to 6 million adolescents suffering from various forms of depression, often unrecognized and untreated (Forrest, 1990). Part of the explanation for the latter is that depression in adolescents may be different in some of its manifestations than it is for adults. In addition, depression in adolescents co-occurs with many other problems and disorders, including anxiety, disruptive behavior disorders, and substance abuse. In some ways, this co-occurrence with other problems masks the presence of depression as a major factor in the disorder even though it significantly increases the levels of interacting social problems and types of impairment (Compas et al., 1997). For example, several researchers believe that depression is an extremely important—if not the most common—factor in adolescent suicide (Compas et al., 1997; Hafen & Frandsen, 1986).

Whatever the percentage of adolescents who experience depression, the sadness, depressed mood, irritability, loss of interest in normal things, inability to concentrate, insomnia, and other symptoms of chronic depression are painful, and they impair a student's normal development. Such symptoms of depression in adolescence or earlier are predictive of increased risk of depression in adulthood, suicidal ideation, and other problems of mental distress.

Current perspectives on adolescent depression are that it is a depressed mood state, a syndrome or cluster of intercorrelated symptoms, and a psychiatric disorder. The primary diagnostic criteria tend to be criteria used in the *DSM-IV* for adult depression and, more particularly, for a major depressive disorder and dysthymia (Compas et al., 1997). To meet the criteria for depression, a child or adolescent should experience five or more of the symptoms specified in the *DSM-IV* for at least a 2-week period at a level that differs from prior functioning, and at least one of the symptoms should include either (a) depressed or irritable mood or (b) anhedonia. For a major depressive episode or a dysthymic disorder, the symptoms should include five or more of the following for the same 2-week period: depressed mood most of the day, nearly every day, or for children and adolescents, irritable mood; markedly diminished interest or pleasure in all or almost all activities most of the day, nearly every day; significant weight loss when not dieting or weight gain, more than 5% of body weight in a month, or decrease or increase in appetite every day; insomnia or hypersomnia nearly every day; psychomotor agitation or retardation nearly every day; fatigue or loss of energy nearly every day; feelings of worthlessness or excessive or inappropriate guilt nearly every day; diminished ability to think or concentrate, or indecisiveness, nearly every day; recurrent thoughts of death (not just fear of dying), recurrent suicidal ideation without a specific plan, or a suicide attempt or a specific plan for committing suicide (p. 327).

Although the symptoms of depression for children and adolescence may be apparently less intense than those of adults, they are markers of increased risk of the development of a major depressive episode or of dythymia, a somewhat milder form of depression, or of a chronic depressed state. For a diagnosis of Dysthymic Disorder, in addition to depressed mood or irritability, only two of the following need be present: poor appetite or overeating, insomnia or hypersomnia, low energy or fatigue, low self-esteem, or poor concentration or difficulty making decisions (Compas et al., 1997). Such clusters of symptoms in children or adolescents need to be taken seriously and treated as do related symptoms of other mood disorders such as Bipolar (Manic-Depressive) Disorder.

Knowing the general characteristics of depression in children and adolescents permits the school or community counselor to be alert to and include such possibilities in his or her assessment of children using such processes as the student's self-report of symptoms, the student's observable characteristics and behaviors, the self-reported clinical history of the disturbance, and a physical examination by a doctor and a family history related to the disturbance (Forrest, 1990). Obviously, parents and teachers are important participants in such processes as observers and reporters.

Following an assessment that suggests the presence of depression or other mood disorders, the counselor needs to coordinate some system to monitor the child's or adolescent's behavior, to provide counseling support, and to place the student into such educational or support programs that will focus on building self-esteem, cognitive restructuring, decision making and problem solving, teaching interpersonal communication skills, depression awareness training, goal setting, physical exercise, relaxation and stress management, and medication (Forrest, 1990).

In addition to individual counseling and other school- and community-based approaches to treating depression in adolescents, Rice and Meyer (1994) have reported on a psychoeducational intervention program to prevent depression among young adolescents. Their intervention program teaches adaptive emotions, and cognitive and behavioral responses to stressors or challenge. In addition, the program attempts to bolster intrapersonal and interpersonal buffers to challenge. Their model is based upon the assumption that the manner

> . . . in which adolescents adjust to situational and developmental challenges or stressful life events and hassles (e.g., parental divorce, the onset of puberty) is determined by the internal and external resources available to adolescents. Internal resources refer to aspects of the individual such as coping skill, intelligence, and perceived locus of control. External resources refer to interpersonal sources of support and guidance such as satisfying relationships with parents and peers. (p. 145)

In this model, the psychoeducational program consists of 16 sessions, each about 40 minutes in length. Each session of the program focuses on a particular social skill, coping method, or challenge, and uses experiential activities (e.g., role-playing, small-group problem solving, cooperative and competitive games). These activities allow the students to practice specific problem-solving methods and apply these strategies to specific developmental challenges that are frequently aspects of adolescence (e.g., peer pressure, making and keeping friends, problems in the family, shyness, self-esteem). Although there was variability in the effectiveness of the activities used in various units of the program from school to school, the data available suggested that such a psychoeducational model could be very useful as a school-based intervention in preventing adolescent depression.

Teenage Parents

Another category of students at risk are those who become sexually active and pregnant as adolescents. There are now more than 1 million teenage pregnancies annually, with 94% of the mothers who do not have abortions keeping their babies, and about 50% of these mothers becoming pregnant again in 3 years. Teenage mothers tend to give birth to children who themselves become teenage parents. Because teenage mothers frequently come from families in poverty, their babies often suffer from low weight, poor nutrition, and, in some instances, drug addiction at birth. The rate of live births among teenage mothers is lower than among older mothers. The rate of teenage pregnancies is related to the amount of adolescent premarital intercourse, which is, in turn, related to a large number of risk factors, including peer pressure, sexually active friends, living in an urban setting, poverty, low success in school, low educational expectations, use of drugs and alcohol, lack of knowledge about human anatomy and sexuality, low self-esteem, feelings of alienation, and engaging in disruptive acts (Bloom, 1996; Chilman, 1980).

Adolescent pregnancy continues to rise as children and adolescents become sexually active at earlier ages. Research studies have suggested that 27% of girls and 33% of boys are sexually active by age 15, with studies of urban minority youth indicating that the median age of onset of sexual activity may be as low as ages 12 to 14. African American youth have been found to become sexually active at younger ages than White youth, and boys at younger ages than girls. In addition to unwanted or unintended pregnancy, the earlier and longer period of sexual activity in many children and adolescents increases the risks not only of pregnancy but also of sexually transmitted diseases and HIV infection. Such research studies have suggested that young adolescent girls are likely to have sex with older boys and men, which exposes them to more likelihood of sexual activity with intravenous drug users, persons with multiple partners, and partners not using condoms (Sagestrano & Paikoff, 1997). Because so many of the young men and women who become sexually active at early ages are embedded in social contexts in which substance use, delinquency, school drop-out, and other at-risk behaviors are prevalent, intervention programs tend to be focused on giving such youth a sense of hope and purpose for the future, skills training in academic achievement, life planning and goal setting, career planning and job placement, personal counseling, family communication, and sex education (Sagestrano & Paikoff, 1997).

Huey (1987) suggested that the invisible or forgotten half of the teen pregnancy phenomenon is the unwed fathers. His review of the research literature indicated that these young men are just as confused, afraid, and anxious as the young women they impregnate and that they often face a lifetime of frustration. Unlike the frequent stereotypes of unwed fathers, most teenage fathers do care about what happens to their children, and they need opportunities to explore their concerns and feelings. Huey described a group counseling session for unwed fathers in which they were helped to focus on their three Rs: rights, responsibilities, and resources. Using both outside experts and intense group discussions, the unwed fathers explored their own feelings, including their guilt and frustration, their responsibility for the pregnancy, contraceptive use and planned parenthood, their legal and emotional rights and responsibilities, present and future options, problem solving and decision making, and available resources and their use. Huey found that just as teenage mothers need assistance and support, so do unwed fathers; becoming a father during adolescence has serious consequences for individual development, and teenage fathers are not psychologically prepared for their new role. Indeed, without help they are at risk of dropping out of school, not furthering their education, and becoming an economic drain on society.

Child Abuse

Another large at-risk population is composed of children who have experienced abuse by their parents. According to Cooney (1988), it is possible to divide child abuse into three categories that are not necessarily mutually exclusive: emotional abuse, physical abuse, and sexual abuse. Each of these forms of abuse may be present in the life of a single child. Each also puts the child at risk for other immediate problems such as violent or antisocial behavior, dropping out of school, mental disorders, stress-related disease, or, in the case of sexual abuse, possible teenage pregnancy. The child who is abused is also at greater risk of becoming an abuser of his or her own children.

Child abuse has many specific manifestations and is a complex phenomenon. As Cooney effectively described, each form of child abuse tends to be associated with developmental problems for the abused children that vary with the intensity, severity, and duration of such abuse. Cooney (1988) differentiated the three major forms of abuse as follows:

- *Emotional abuse* implies a pattern of continual attacks on a child's self-esteem, self-confidence, sense of belonging, or safety. The child who is emotionally abused may be the recipient of constant criticism, threats, or embarrassment. He or she may be a scapegoat, treated as an unwelcome intruder in the family (p. 3).
- *Physical abuse* is the nonaccidental injury of a child by a parent or caregiver (p. 5).
- *Sexual abuse* is not limited to sexual intercourse; sexual abuse encompasses a range of sexual activity including genital exposure, fondling, forced touching, inappropriate kissing, oral sex, and intercourse. Typically, sexual abuse occurs over a period of years with gradual escalation of sexual demands. If intercourse occurs, it is likely to begin in puberty or prepuberty (p. 7).

The extent of child abuse is difficult to know precisely. Waterman and Lusk (1986) reported that one out of four girls and one out of four or five boys will be sexually abused before reaching age 18. Data from the work of other observers (Finkelhor, 1979; Russell, 1982) suggested that 9% to 16% of all girls experience incest before age 18. Incest in this context is seen as a form of child sexual abuse that includes any type of sexual activity between a child and a parent, stepparent, sibling, extended family member, or surrogate parent figure (Sgroi, 1982). Alter-Reid et al. (1986) reported that the children at highest risk for incest are those with stepfathers. A stepfather is six times more likely to abuse a daughter sexually than a biological father.

Ogilvie and Daniluk (1995) reported on the particular problems associated with mother-daughter incest. Although sexual abuse by mothers against daughters is apparently far less than that which occurs between fathers or stepfathers and daughters, mother-daughter and, to apparently a lesser extent, mother-son incest does occur. Mother-daughter incest is particularly difficult for the victim because this act violates a variety of cultural taboos related to the nurturant mother. Ogilvie and Daniluk's research suggested that daughters abused by their mothers experience additional shame and stigma because the abuse they have endured is out of the ordinary. In addition, identity development of women who have experienced mother-daughter incest appears to be impaired as to the processes of physical and psychological boundary setting. Further, the victims of such mother-daughter incest are likely to be fearful of the intergenerational abuse of their own children and the degree to which they can provide effective and healthy parenting.

In an important review of the research literature on incest, Josephson and Fong-Beyette (1987) indicated that the experience of incest is linked to subsequent psychological problems including the inability to trust, low self-esteem, self-hatred, passivity, sexual identity conflicts, impairment of sexual functioning, feelings of isolation, guilt, shame, and somatic complaints. They reported the presence of a pattern of behavior, which Briere (1984) described as a post-sexual-abuse syndrome, that is common to incest victims and includes dissociation, anxiety, isolation, sleep disturbances, anger, sexual dysfunction, substance addiction, and self-destructiveness. Many of these problems continue into adulthood, by which time many women have repressed the link between the difficulties they are experiencing and the incest or sexual abuse that occurred earlier. At a different level, it has been reported that a high percentage of adult prostitutes have disclosed being victims of childhood sexual abuse (Kempe & Kempe, 1984). Shapiro (1987) described a high relationship between incest, self-blame, and self-mutilation. Many victims of incest abuse drugs and engage in suicide attempts.

Cooney (1988) suggested that "the effects of sexual abuse vary depending on the duration of the abuse, the age of onset, and the closeness of the relationship of the victim to the abuser" (p. 7). Thus at different developmental ages different behavioral indicators in children who experience sexual abuse may be observed. Prior to age 6, for example, some children may seem very withdrawn, whereas others may indicate sexual knowledge, make sexual overtures to others, or display behavior that seems too advanced for their years. These children may also commonly exhibit depression and anxiety, stomachaches, headaches, involuntary bowel movements, bed-wetting, and sleep disturbances. Older sexually abused children, ages 6 to 12, may seem to be distracted or daydreaming; they may feel different from their classmates and thus be loners or seek older children as friends, they may dress in a seductive manner beyond that expected of their age; or they may experience anxiety, depression, and low self-esteem. In adolescence, sexually abused children may run away from home, become abusers of drugs and alcohol, attempt suicide, or act out in a sexually promiscuous manner.

Physical abuse of children may occur independent of sexual abuse, or both may occur together. The number of children who are injured or die from physical abuse by their parents or caregivers is hard to estimate. Frequently injuries occur to the brain or central nervous system of young children who have been violently shaken, struck, or thrown against a wall or hard object. O'Brien (1980) estimated that 7 to 15 children die each day in the United States from such injuries. Physically abused children not only experience bruises, burns, broken bones, and internal injuries, but they also suffer emotional effects that ultimately translate into behavioral indicators. Preschool age abused children may appear shy and withdrawn, tense and fearful, overcompliant, lacking in spontaneity—or hostile and aggressive, cruel to other children, and destructive of their belongings. Abused children at ages 6 to 12 may become bullies, exhibit learning problems, or be so anxious as to experience impaired speech and motor performance. They also may be overly withdrawn around adults of the same sex or adults who resemble their abusers. Many physically abused children tend to internalize these experiences as meaning that they are bad children who deserve the punishment they receive. Frequently the result is a low sense of self-worth, self-esteem, or efficacy that is reflected in poor social relationships or poor academic achievement. The negative self-image and self-blame incorporated by many physically abused children tends to be strongly internalized by the adolescent. Such children may still be trying desperately to please the abusing parents who have found them so unsatisfactory, they may stay away from home to avoid parental abuse, or they may run away from home.

Emotional abuse pervades the presence of either physical or sexual abuse, but it can also occur independently. Psychological assaults on a child's esteem or self-confidence probably occur in most families on a spontaneous and nonreoccurring basis. Parents feel guilty and try to make amends to the child for the behavior. Emotional abuse, however, tends to be a constant pattern indicating that the child is unworthy, inferior to a sibling or to another child, or unacceptable. Depending upon the severity of the abuse, the developmental age at onset, and the duration, the behavioral effect may be a lack of opportunity to develop self-confidence or self-worth. Such children may find it difficult to relate to other children or to adults, may become agitated or withdrawn, or may manifest shyness or poor socialization skills. In severe cases of emotional abuse, preschool and older children may manifest severe emotional and affective disorders and need to be placed in special education programs or other therapeutic environments (Cooney, 1988). As emotionally abused children age, they may treat other children as they have been treated at home, as scapegoats or with threats. They may find it difficult to accept positive feedback or to allow others—children or adults—to befriend them. By adolescence, many such children will have been labeled *troublemakers* or *potential drop-outs* because of poor achievement, low motivation, or hostility to those in authority. Or they may simply fade into the masses and become essentially invisible, drifting along without recognition or personal attachment to the school or anyone in the school.

The implications of the different forms of child abuse for counselors in schools and in community agencies are diverse. In virtually all states, counselors are required to report suspected or actual abuse to state and local agencies concerned with child protection and welfare. The precise reporting requirements differ from state to state, but reporting has legal precedence over the counselor's obligations to maintain confidentiality for either the child victim or the abuser. The counselor also has a role in the prevention of child abuse through a variety of possible activities. Cooney (1988, p. 10) suggested "parent education for teen and adult parents, parenting classes for children and adolescents, self-esteem workshops and groups for parents and children, assertiveness training, and training in problem solving." Counselors can also serve as advocates for community after-school programs, emergency child-care centers, and hot lines for parents who are afraid they will abuse their children or who feel so stressed that they feel they are out of control and may take it out on their children.

Counselors also have important therapeutic roles. They may provide parental retraining individually or in groups to help parents find alternative ways of communicating with their children other than through abusive behavior. They may implement such parenting programs as Systematic Training for Effective Parenting (STEP) or Parent Effectiveness Training (PET). Counselors may refer abusive parents to such groups as Parents Anonymous. Many abusive parents who were abused themselves are simply imitating how they were disciplined. They learned a style of parenting that needs to be unlearned and replaced with more positive parenting. Many of these parents need to learn techniques of anger management, and most need help with their own feelings of self-esteem and self-worth. Many parents need help to cope with their unresolved feelings about their own parents' expectations of them. They frequently need help with stress management, family conflicts, or work problems to avoid such stress from spilling over on their children. For abused children themselves, counselors can develop after-school and in-school programs designed to build their self-esteem, to buffer them from parental abuse, and to increase their positive interpersonal and communication skills. In addition, both individual and group counseling are vital to reduce child and adolescent self-blame and guilt for the abuse suffered. Counselors frequently need to engage classroom teachers and other adults in creating environments that are positively reinforcing for abused children and provide encounters with adults who are caring and supportive of the children. Counselors may also engage in family counseling to try to rebuild the family-child bond as a way of protecting the child from further sexual, physical, or emotional abuse. In cases of incest, Josephson and Fong-Bayette (1987) recommended that

> . . . counselors acknowledge and validate the significance of the incest. Incest experiences should not be minimized even when they were unsuccessful attempts or occurred one time or infrequently. Incest should be identified as an important trauma that is related to clients' current life difficulties. Perceiving incest clients as survivors who developed complicated coping skills that were actually adaptive to their early environment can help these clients see themselves as survivors rather than as sick or helpless victims. (p. 478)

Children of Alcoholics

Although often not thought about as child abuse per se, parents' alcoholism may lead to children's low self-esteem and other psychological problems, including vulnerability to alcoholism in later life. In chapter 3, problems of children of alcoholics are discussed within the context of dysfunctional families and in chapter 8 in relation to alcohol and substance abuse. Those discussions will not be repeated here.

Suffice it to say briefly in this chapter that children of alcoholics are at risk. As has been cited throughout this chapter, the characteristics of the family of origin can provide a positive or negative environment for child development. In their negative sense, they can create problems that predispose children to be at risk for a variety of problems. Growing up in an alcoholic family also puts one in an at-risk environment. As we found in our discussions of violent behavior, alcoholism in the family can lead to physical abuse of children that can, in turn, lead children to behave violently toward others. Alcoholism in parents also is associated with alienation, suicide, and other phenomena.

Children of alcoholics must cope with a unique set of difficulties (Lewis, 1987). The alcoholic dependence of one or more family members creates a disequilibrium in the family that tends to be reflected in a set of roles that are fashioned by a child's relationship to the alcoholic family member. Where one parent is the abuser, the other parent is likely to try to care for the alcoholic parent, and in so doing be diminished in his or her capacity to provide for the children. The consistency of parenting may be undependable or episodic. Children may find it difficult to find personal support in the family and may seek it in peers or elsewhere beyond the family.

As suggested in the growing literature on children of alcoholics, some children blame themselves for their parents' problems. Some may try to take over the parenting responsibilities for maintaining the family or rearing their siblings. These children may become overly responsible, reliable, and controlled. They may lose touch with their own childhood needs. Other children may become the scapegoats or the focus of parental abuse. Others may try to distance themselves from their parents' behavior.

Counseling children of alcoholics needs to deal with where children who have adopted different coping styles are in their development. For children who are not receiving support and affection within the family or feel isolated within that context, counseling may need to help them reach out to others. For children who are afraid to acknowledge their feelings, counseling needs to provide them the opportunity to express these feelings and to deal with them. Children who think their life is unique and unusual may need to be involved in a support group of other children of alcoholics or referred to Al-Anon or other such organizations. Some children of alcoholics need to understand the mechanisms of substance abuse and what addiction does to their parents as a way of reducing their feelings of personal responsibility for their parents' behavior. These children need support to build self-worth and self-esteem.

The effects of being a child of an alcoholic are multidimensional and enduring. Counselors need to be alert to the signs of being at risk in children and adolescents and sensitive to the individual and group counseling responses that can respond to such conditions.

The School Drop-Out

Certainly a major outcome of the various risk factors children and youth experience is dropping out of school. It is perhaps the most well-documented but the most intractable of statistics. Again, just as teenage mothers tend to spawn teenage parents themselves, school drop-outs put their own life chances and those of their future children at increased risk of economic and educational disadvantage and related mental health problems.

Depending on how the statistics are calculated and on what cohort group they are based, roughly 15% of all those who start school do not graduate. In a major analysis of the longitudinal data available in the High School and Beyond national data set, Ekstrom, Goertz, Pollack, and Rock (1986) found that a variety of risk or predisposing factors differentiated those who dropped out of school from those who stayed in school. The differences included the following: drop-outs were disproportionately from low socioeconomic families and from racial or ethnic minority groups; drop-outs tended to come from homes with weak educational support systems (e.g., few books and other study aids, mothers with lower levels of formal education and lower levels of educational expectations for their children, parents less likely to be interested in or monitor the child's in-school and out-of-school activities); drop-outs as sophomores reported less interest in school, attended classes less regularly, were less likely to feel popular with other students, were less likely to participate in extracurricular activities, were less likely to have plans to go to college, were more likely to report spending time outside of school "driving around" and going on dates, and reported working more hours per week. Of the girls who dropped out of school between their sophomore and senior years, 23% cited pregnancy as the reason. Like other groups at risk, school drop-outs are the products of multiple risk factors.

In the past decade, the promotion of academic success in children and the reduction of school drop-outs has become a major national health goal (Hawkins, 1997). The reason for such a national policy is that it is clear that academic success in children and adolescents is associated with social and emotional wellness. As described in this chapter, teenage pregnancy, substance abuse, and many other risk factors are associated with low academic achievement and having little sense of direction or purpose. Therefore, the lack of academic success compromises positive social and emotional behavior and positive future aspirations, and often results in problem behavior, including leaving school prematurely. The solution, complex though it is, is not to see school drop-out as solely an academic problem but one in which academic, social, and emotional competencies are interactive, need to be reinforced in effective schools, and seen as an important priority in the implementation of programs in school counseling by which to facilitate personal responsibility and academic purpose and skills as well as social and emotional maturity.

Suicide

The ultimate expression of being at risk is attempting or committing suicide. Unfortunately, the U.S. suicide rate continues to accelerate. According to Kalafat (1997),

> Suicide consistently ranks as the second or third leading cause of death for adolescents between 15 and 19 years of age. Between 1960 and 1990, the suicide rate for 15- to 19-year-olds more than tripled from 3.6 to 11.3 per 100,000. . . . From 1980 to 1992, it increased, among persons aged 15 to 19 by 28.3% . . . and among persons aged 10 to 14 by 120% (0.8 to 1.7). (p.175)

As other data have suggested, however, the incidence of suicide attempts by adolescents is much higher than successful completions. The Centers for Disease Control and Prevention (1995) reported that in 1993, according to the National Youth Risk Behavior Surveillance, 22.9% of females and 15.3% of males had made a suicide plan during the previous year.

Suicide and adolescent depression are linked, and some 15% of adolescents who suffer major episodes of depression are likely to commit suicide. Put another way, it is estimated that 50% to 80% of youth who commit suicide each year have some type of depressive disorder (Tugend, 1986).

A review of the factors involved in adolescent suicide (Pennsylvania Department of Education, 1986) indicates involvement of

- external stress (e.g., school achievement, fear of nuclear war, community violence);
- physical and psychological changes(e.g., stress associated with dating, sexuality, drugs, and alcohol);
- breakdown of the family unit (e.g., increasing divorces, working parents, mobility, and decreasing role models and support networks);
- responsibilities and privileges (e.g., increased responsibility and privileges with too little adult guidance); and
- inaccurate perception of death (e.g., the inaccurate portrayal of death in the movies, television, and music).

Checklists and sets of risk indicators with a variety of emphases have been developed to create profiles of the person likely to attempt suicide. In summary form, these include

- **sex**: Men commit suicide more often than women, although more women than men attempt suicide.
- **age**: In general, as age increases, suicide risk increases. However, the suicide rate for men tends to level off after age 35 but does not level off for women until after age 70.
- **race**: Whites have a greater suicide risk than do non-Whites except in the case of young male Blacks, for whom the rate is about twice that for young male Whites.
- **socioeconomic status**: The lower the socioeconomic status the higher the suicide rate is likely to be, although suicides occur at all socioeconomic levels.
- **marital status**: Single persons are twice as likely as married persons to commit suicide; the suicide rate for widowed and divorced persons is four to five times higher than that for married persons.
- **previous suicide attempts**: The risk of suicide increases with a history of previous suicide attempts and as suicidal ideation continues to endure over a long period of time. The lethality of suicide attempts also is related to whether other family members or close friends have attempted or committed suicide. Young people tend to imitate in close proximity the suicides of others in a community or school. Such suicidal impulses following a successful suicide by one person are seen by some observers as a form of contagion (Phillips, 1985).
- **character and lifestyle of the individual**: Alcoholism, drug abuse, psychotic behavior involving bizarre or highly lethal suicidal ideation, living alone, and refusing help are important risk indicators. So is the effect of significant losses—death of a loved one, divorce, separation, broken relationship, loss of a job, money, status, or self-esteem.
- **symptoms**: Depression, anxiety, panic, helplessness, hopelessness, despair, and sleep disruption are all symptoms of major concern in suicidal ideation. Sleep disruption can be a particularly important indicator because it is likely to increase depression, and it may be a function of hallucinating—perhaps from drug dependency, overuse of stimulants, or depressants.
- **factors to consider when evaluating emergency risk**: Does the person have a definite plan by which to commit suicide? Is the method available? Is the method reversible (e.g., planning to jump from high places or use of a gun is typically irreversible; taking pills is usually less lethal because there is a chance for reversibility)? Has a time been set for the attempt? Has the person given away possessions or finalized certain social or business affairs?

We can conceive the counselor's role with suicidal clients in terms of several points of involvement. One is prevention; a second is intervention, usually of a crisis nature; a third is postvention, working with attempters or survivors (Fujimura, Weis, & Cochran, 1985). Each of these stages has its own concepts and techniques. In *prevention*, for example, it is necessary to be able to recognize the person's pleas for help before a suicide attempt is made. This involves understanding the risk factors, symptoms, and other behavioral clues for identifying persons at risk. This may require, in the case of schools particularly, instituting and monitoring a referral system of teachers, peers, and parents who have been educated to be sensitive to the signs of potential suicide victims and to refer those at risk. Prevention may also involve a suicide education program, as part of a counseling outreach scheme, to help students understand the feelings and factors involved, the resources for help that are available, and the support systems that can be devoted to suicide prevention. Either the counselor or others in the referral system need to be sensitive to the patterns of verbal and nonverbal communication that frequently give clues to suicidal ideation and, if not confronted, may suggest a rejecting or uncaring attitude to the suicidal individual. At the level of individual counseling, prevention encompasses helping the youth or adult client deal with the predisposing or risk factors and the psychological and situational stresses that could lead to a suicide attempt. Within this context, the counselor's role may be to help the client discover options other than suicide to cope with his or her perceived problems.

Intervention is likely to involve interrupting a suicide attempt that is about to occur or is occurring, or dealing with the immediate result of an unsuccessful attempt. Typically this requires crisis intervention techniques designed to assist the individual to regain a sense of control over his or her life. Intervention may require a multidimensional approach to deal with all of the symptoms that are operating at the moment (e.g., depression, panic, drug overload, physical injury). It may be necessary to cooperate with parents or others to place the person into psychiatric hospitalization, or to use other referral sources (e.g., a crisis intervention team) to deal with the immediate self-destructive ideation or behavior. The counselor who works with a young person exhibiting suicidal symptoms but who has not made an attempt may engage this client in a suicide contract by which the person makes a signed, concrete commitment not to attempt suicide prior to contacting the counselor or another referral source (e.g., a crisis or suicide intervention center). A contract is a tangible expression of caring by the counselor and a commitment to be available and render assistance as needed. A contract also buys time in which to help the client come to terms with the predisposing factors that place him or her at risk, consider options other than suicide to cope with the stresses that have led to the contemplation of suicide, and find access to other resource and support systems that may be of assistance.

The third stage of counselor activity suggested by Fujimura et al. (1985) is that of *postvention*. Counselor behavior in this stage may vary according to need. For example, postvention may involve the aftercare, monitoring, and in-depth counseling of a person who has attempted suicide but not completed the act. Postvention also may be directed to the parents, spouse, classmates, or other survivors of a person who has successfully committed suicide. Because of the possibilities of a copycat, imitative, or contagious effect among adolescents when one of their classmates commits suicide, school and community counselors frequently are required to work with immediate classmates, teachers, and the larger school community in the aftermath of a death. Alexander and Harman (1988) described how they were involved in a middle school following the suicide of a 13-year-old student. In this instance, the counselor, working from a Gestalt therapy perspective, focused on helping the student's classmates to say their good-byes to their deceased classmate, and to express their feelings of personal isolation, hopelessness, and despair as well as their feelings of anger, betrayal, resentment, guilt, grief, confusion, sadness, and emptiness with specific regard to the student who committed suicide. The students were encouraged to speak to the empty seat of the dead student as a way of saying good-bye, letting go of him, and experiencing the collective responses to the death in the present rather than letting the death gain romanticized attraction. Students in each of the classes the dead student had been enrolled in were encouraged to address his empty seat by telling the dead student what they would have liked him to know and how they would have wished to help him if they had known of his suicidal intentions. Students who did not wish to engage in such an overt display were encouraged to write their good-byes to the student or to look at his seat and imagine saying their good-byes to him and telling him what they would have liked him to know. In art class, the students were encouraged to depict their feelings in some artistic representation.

Following these classroom interventions, the counselor encouraged students to engage in either individual, dyadic, or small group counseling. As a result of the expressed needs of several students, a long-term group with weekly sessions continued for the remainder of the school year. This group provided a supportive and caring environment for students who felt guilty because they had not anticipated and prevented their classmate's suicide or who felt highly vulnerable to engaging in such behavior themselves.

Another approach to dealing with loss and group survivorship after a suicide was described by Zinner (1987). In this case, the student who had committed suicide had been a member of a nine-student sixth-grade class in a small private school. The counselor was a consultant brought into the school the day after the suicide and prior to the funeral. The assumption in this circumstance was that "the early actions of professionals or of group leaders themselves can bring the appearance of strength and reassurance to a situation that is unanticipated and overwhelming" (p. 499). It can provide the surviving classmates and teachers permission to vent a wide range of feelings and to engage in a group ritual of coping with the suicide loss. In this school, the counselor engaged members of the suicide victim's class in reviewing the life of the deceased and the death. In the first step, the children could review shared anecdotes about the deceased, lessen tensions, and include the professional as one of their group. In the second emphasis, the children were helped to understand the details of the death so that secrets and rumors would not divide the classmates. While dealing with these matters, students were encouraged to speak of their anger at the suicide or their guilt or extreme emotional reaction to the death. Students also were helped to anticipate what would occur at the funeral and to attend it as a part of their leave-taking. They were encouraged to engage in some symbolic act that expressed their response to the victim. In this case, they bought a toy cat, decorated with the school colors, to be placed in the casket in order to reflect the suicide victim's love for animals and to be part of their leave-taking of the victim. The children planted an azalea bush at the parents' home as a remembrance of the child who died, and the sixth-grade graduation ceremony included a remembrance of the boy. Finally, the consultant helped the principal and faculty to engage in an *academic autopsy*, a term used by death educators to describe the evaluation of actions taken subsequent to a particular death or crisis. The key questions in such an activity include, "What could have been done to prevent the death? What actions taken after the death seem appropriate and meaningful in hindsight? What actions might be modified or added in the future should there be another crisis?" (Zinner, 1987, p. 301). Such questions lead a school to develop a response plan tailored to the characteristics and needs of a particular setting.

School Programs for Students At Risk

Although suicide is the most dramatic of the problems of students at risk, in this chapter a range of other problems has been identified that require focused and systematic school-wide intervention. Teen pregnancy and parenting, alienated youth, underachievement, violence, truancy, and drug abuse all require efforts directed at identifying students at risk, isolating and intervening in the predisposing factors, and mounting sustained follow-up activity. Most of these programs are multidimensional and require teams of professionals to provide the services required. The Pennsylvania Department of Education (1987) identified some exemplary programs in the state targeted to different groups of students at risk. The sections that follow describe four of these programs.

Truancy intervention program. The Philadelphia public schools have implemented a Counseling or Referral Assistance (CORA) Truancy Intervention Program (TIP) designed to assist students with high absentee rates to establish a positive direction in their life. The program is based on an intervention counseling model in which guided group discussions are a primary strategy. Students attend six weekly small group sessions (day or evening). Families are invited to participate, and when they do, students and parents participate in several sessions together. The group sessions in the program include the following areas for discussion: self-esteem, communication with family and at school, decision making, peer pressure and drug and alcohol use, career exploration, problem solving, and values. In addition, counselors conduct assessments designed to reveal specific student needs that may be academic, physical, or psychological. Students are then assisted to find appropriate support services targeted to their specific needs: reading, speech and language, drug and alcohol abuse, teen pregnancy, and psychological counseling. Each student in the program explores alternative strategies for improving school attendance and develops an attendance plan of action.

Program for alienated youth. The goal of this counseling program for disruptive or withdrawn youth in the Montoursville schools is to improve students' self-concepts and perceptions of school, and to strengthen students' commitment to the conventional social goals and activities schooling represents. The improvement of student achievement is an intermediate objective that is expected to result from an improved self-concept and improved social bonding. This program serves approximately 20 students at any one time, primarily through individual counseling, tutoring, and crisis intervention. One counselor is responsible for this program and employs such strategies as

- tutoring and coaching on classroom assignments and occasional peer tutoring;
- counseling based on reality therapy and Adlerian psychology;
- instruction in social skills and problem solving;
- value clarification exercises;
- after-school tutoring;
- lunchtime basketball practice and other after-school sports activities, on an occasional basis;
- Systematic Training for Effective Parenting (STEP) course for parents; and
- parent conferences.

The students in this program are also supported by regular school counselors, to whom they are assigned for scheduling and testing, and by community resources as needed.

Adolescent parenting program. Any pregnant student or student parent in the Gettysburg Area schools may participate in the Gettysburg Adolescent Parenting Program (GAPP). The program is districtwide, implemented by a team composed of the director of pupil services, director of counseling, school social worker, home economics teacher, school nurse, school counselors, and school psychologist. When a student enters the program, the GAPP team prepares an individual graduation plan (IGP). The plan is designed to meet the specific needs and goals of the student, but contains formal life skills coursework in addition to basic skills subjects. The program contains seven parts:

1. Formal coursework in human development, basic and advanced culinary skills, and infant and toddler laboratories are provided.
2. Infant and toddler laboratories provide day care for the children of the adolescent parents and provide opportunities for mothers to learn child care and development. The children are taught gross and fine motor skills, language development, socialization, and cognitive development. Mothers are taught to interact effectively with their children and care for their needs.
3. A full-time social worker provides support and individual and group counseling to students; liaison with the community and referral services, including medical treatments for mother and child; and attendance monitoring.
4. Career counseling, both individual and group, is provided to help students plan for work or further schooling after graduation.
5. Personal counseling is provided by any member of the team to assist students in dealing with problems they may experience with the father of their child, their family, their self-concept, and other related matters.
6. Health care services are provided to monitor and coordinate the medical needs of individual students.
7. Transportation to the program is provided for mothers and children.

The fathers of the students' children and their families can participate in any part or all of the program. In addition to the ongoing academic program of the school that leads to graduation and the seven-part adolescent parenting program, other support services involved are the housing, welfare, and health departments as well as drug and alcohol abuse, family planning, Joint Training Partnership Act, and child services.

Student assistance program. The major goal of this Student Assistance Program (SAP) in the Quakertown high school is to create a system of early identification, intervention, referral, and aftercare for students who exhibit all forms of at-risk behaviors. These behaviors include suicide, alcohol and drug abuse, defiance or belligerence, truancy, pregnancy, and eating disorders (anorexia and bulimia). In addition, the system is designed to identify youth who may suffer from all forms of abuse and neglect, or from malnutrition. SAP is an intervention system that trains school personnel to identify and refer high-risk students who seem likely to benefit from the community's health and mental health treatment system. High-risk students are identified and referred by staff personnel who complete an extensive behavior assessment form. This form is a 105-item checklist and includes an inventory of behaviors that may be noted for individual students under each of the following categories: academic performance, school attendance, disruptive behavior, atypical behavior, physical symptoms, illicit activities, extracurricular activities, home problems, and additional crisis indicators (e.g., suicide, threats, victim of rape or abuse).

Once a student has been referred with a completed behavior assessment form, the first order of intervention is a Student Assistance Case Management Group. This team, which consists of school counselors, administrators, nurses, a psychologist, and representatives from the core team, receives the behavior assessment form and provides a first-level assessment of the student's needs. If a support person assigned by this team cannot help a student resolve a problem, the student is then referred to the Student Assistance Care Team. The latter includes a district central office administrator, counselor, nurse, SAP coordinator, and teacher. This group establishes and maintains school-based crisis intervention policies and procedures regarding early identification and treatment referrals. This group also coordinates parent involvement in the range of interventions possible with outside agencies, such as community drug and alcohol agencies, health and mental health resources, the YMCA, and hospital adolescent programs.

Under the assumption that early intervention in the lives of children and families will lead to the prevention of child and adolescent high-risk, self-destructive behaviors, SAP emphasizes major training efforts involving

- staff training (to foster skill development in crisis identification, appropriate intervention/prevention, and referral processes to out-of-school treatment) that includes in-service training for all faculty, large-group problem-solving theatre performance, and on-site consultation for individuals and small groups;
- student training that includes small groups for peer referral, large-group problem-solving theatre performance, and classroom programs; and
- parents' training that includes all-day workshops and local cable television instructional programs on crisis identification and problem solving.

CONCLUSIONS

Many other examples than those mentioned in this chapter could be cited of risk categories affecting children and youth and how counselors might intervene in them (e.g., Bloom, 1996; Weissberg, Gullotta, Hampton, Ryan, & Adams, 1997). The risk category examples provided, however, suffice to illustrate the growing concern about and the content of programs designed to help children and youth at risk, which will be a part of the major challenges for counselors well into the foreseeable future. It seems clear that any programmatic design for counselor training or for skill application needs to include concepts and strategies to enable counselors to be sensitive and responsive to at-risk factors or behaviors. At the least, such training of counselors needs to provide them awareness of and skills in applying interventions that increase individual strengths, decrease individual limitations, increase social supports, decrease social stresses, increase resources and decrease pressures from the environment (Bloom, 1996). Hopefully, an end result will be optimizing the development of children and adolescents.

Because many of the seeds of personal feelings of vulnerability are first planted in childhood and adolescence, notions of children at risk in these age groups overlap with adults at risk. The next chapter concentrates on the latter.

As previous chapters have suggested and Chapter 5 has amplified, advanced technology, changing family structures, and pluralism and cultural diversity combine with other individual and group factors to put children and youth at risk of becoming physically ill or abused, experiencing mental disorders, taking on antisocial behavior, being economically disadvantaged, or experiencing other forms of negative psychological, social, and physical life events.

Two general categories of special populations were described in this chapter. The first category uses social/historical criteria; the other life-span/developmental criteria. The first category of special populations is composed of people who, because of social stigma and bias, cultural stereotypes, or legal or institutional barriers have been denied full access to opportunities or services in the society. The second category of special populations is composed of people who are at significant points of transition in their lives and are attempting to cope with the stress, uncertainty, and indecision that may accompany such status. Certainly, many children and youth are special populations who fall into at-risk categories that vary from clinical depression, through physical and sexual abuse, to suicide. The seeds and symptoms of at-risk behavior begin early for many children and continue through adolescence into adulthood. Although sometimes organic, the more frequent causes of child and youth at-risk behavior is poor and inconsistent parenting, poverty, negative peer pressure, and substance abuse.

Chapter 5 has described a range of counselor responses and school programs that have been found to be effective in dealing with at-risk problems among children and youth. Later chapters will describe other techniques and interventions that will also be of value in providing counseling and other forms of therapeutic interventions for children and youth.

CHAPTER 6

SPECIAL POPULATIONS AT RISK: ADULTS

MANY OF THE PROBLEMS THAT PUT adults at risk begin in childhood and adolescence if successful intervention does not occur. Children who have been depressed, abused, or who are chronically violent or chemically dependent continue to exhibit such behavior in adulthood. Adults who were abused or brutalized as children tend to imitate this behavior in their own parenting and in their approach to others.

Beyond the outcomes of violence in childhood, other forms of being at risk in the early years of youth and adolescence also continue into adulthood. For example, teenage and unmarried mothers have difficulty staying competitive with their cohorts in education or at work. Because of the additional time and resources required in child rearing and because of the discrimination they may face in their own family and in the larger community, teenage parents are more likely to settle for less education and training than they might have planned. Similarly, they have more difficulty gaining access to and maintaining a place in the workforce than people who are not encumbered by the problems engendered by early pregnancy, single parenting, and the environment that surrounds such circumstances. At best, their potential employment and occupational status falls behind that of others, and the possibilities of financial insecurity, unemployment or underemployment, and stress-related problems tend to accompany them throughout adulthood. Obviously, such conditions are likely to be reflected in the nutritional, psychological, and educational environment in which their children are reared. Adolescents and young adults who are chemically dependent are likely to give birth to children who are themselves addicted. Adolescents who have poor early labor market experiences are likely to continue to have jagged work histories in adulthood.

Without extending this litany of the continuity of risk status from one stage of life to the next, from adolescence to young adulthood and beyond, it might be noted

205

that adults also face other issues that put them at risk. One of these is minority status in the society. As was suggested in chapter 4 and at the beginning of chapter 5, being a member of a racial minority potentially sets an individual apart in the society and places him or her at risk of encountering discrimination, racism, and other barriers to the fullest realization of his or her potential or to equal access to jobs and education. A similar situation exists for persons with disabilities and, in some cases, older citizens who may experience other forms of discrimination. Sexual preference or orientation may lead to additional bias and discrimination. Such group characteristics as ethnicity, race, disability, age, and sexual preference represent factors that may be defined as putting those so characterized at risk. Not all members of a particular group necessarily share the same amount of vulnerability. Many other factors may compound the degree of being at risk. For example, poor education, functional illiteracy, chemical abuse, single parenthood, and ex-offender status may add to or exacerbate the difficulties that any group already at some risk may experience.

Beyond drawing attention to the special circumstances of adults who face discrimination because of some form of group identification that tends to amplify their risk factors, the past decade or more has shed increasing light on the nature of transitions as times of heightened vulnerability. Transitions caused by job loss, separation and divorce, retirement, or the loss of a loved one are only some of the many points in life when people who had not formerly been at risk suddenly become so. Indeed, transitions may, in fact, be crises for some, times when the aggregate of stress factors in their lives has grown beyond their psychological resources to cope.

In essence, the factors that cause adults to be at risk can be chronic, sudden and time-limited, or both. Chronic factors that place adults in jeopardy of psychological, physical, financial, or educational difficulties include deficits in academic skills, membership in a racial minority group, physical disability, poverty, mental illness, age, sexual orientation, and chemical dependencies. Acute, sudden, or time-limited transitions that put people at risk include the death of a spouse or loved one, sexual difficulties, pregnancy, incarceration, financial problems, major personal injury or illness, involuntary unemployment, returning to or leaving schooling, or retirement. In a sense, these factors suggest that being at risk may be a dynamic condition that may affect any person at some point in his or her life, or it may be a chronic or "fixed effect." Indeed, the dynamic quality of the mental health of adults is reflected in research findings that suggested that one or more of the psychiatric disorders in the *DSM-IV* have been experienced at some time in their lives by 32% of American adults. Some 20% of American adults were found to have had an active disorder, defined as a disorder for which criteria had been met at some time in the person's life, and at least one symptom or one episode had been present in the year prior to the interviews on which the research was based. As a result, estimates are that one in five Americans has an active psychiatric disorder that may vary in severity and frequency, from mild to severe and from chronic to episodic (Robins et al., 1991). Such active disorders are related to various constellations or clusters of risk factors in adults just as they are in children and adolescents.

The remainder of the chapter will discuss some of the categories of being at risk into which adults may fall. This analysis is certainly not exhaustive of all possibilities nor of all possible combinations of risk factors, but it will identify some of the major groups about which counselors must be aware.

CHRONIC RISK FACTORS

Poverty and Homelessness

Among the major factors that make people vulnerable to stress, anxiety, and a host of other difficulties is poverty. Poverty may be more generally described as the lowest level of the socioeconomic spectrum, or it may be described as a condition in which people must survive on an annual income of less than $15,700 in 1995 (Farley, 1996, p. 65) for a family of four. However poverty is described, it is a condition that places people at extreme risk of early death, malnutrition, educational deficits, inadequate employability skills, chemical dependency, and psychological and physiological disorders.

As poignantly portrayed in the theater and in literature, and as discussed in chapter 4 of this book, poverty has its own culture. In its extreme and chronic phases it extinguishes ambition and breeds hopelessness, powerlessness, and dependency; it cripples or stifles social mobility, educational achievement, and skill development. Poverty affects the individual's self-concept, self-esteem, and feelings of self-efficacy. It perpetuates itself and robs people of opportunity.

Poverty sometimes occurs on a cross-generational basis; it becomes chronic within certain families. People who are poverty stricken may still be employed. In other words, they may work in unskilled jobs, in stoop labor, or in jobs that pay meager wages with no additional benefits. The economic existence of the poor is so insecure that if they lose a day's or a week's work because of illness they may be pushed into such dire circumstances that they cannot afford food or housing. Some of the most poverty stricken in the society are the elderly who live on very small fixed incomes from Social Security or pensions. Many of the poverty stricken are from racial minority groups, are chronically unemployed, or are able to find employment only periodically and temporarily, or have skills that permit them only menial and poorly paid work. Many of the latter have families but not homes.

> These families are not drifters. More than one fifth of our homeless are employed. Very often they are working parents—one or both of whom hold jobs. But their combined earnings never total a month's rent and a matching security deposit with enough left to buy food. As a result, they are rent-poor, forced to live in overpriced, often substandard lodgings and left with little for life's necessities as they struggle to keep their families united. Some must scatter to survive—with the children living perhaps in various dwellings or the fathers barred from the premises of residences provided through public assistance to mothers and children only. (Whitemore, 1988, p. 5)

The National Coalition for the Homeless estimated nearly 10 years ago that the nation's homeless include some 3 million people, nearly 500,000 of whom are children (Whitemore, 1988). In 1995, it was estimated that the "precariously housed"— those who were just below or just above the poverty line and spent more than one half of their meager incomes for rent—had increased by another percent over what was true in the 1980s (Farley, 1996). Some of these people live in temporary, government-subsidized housing, some in shelters, some with relatives, and some on the streets. The environment for child rearing and for nurturing self-respect and hope is not present in such circumstances. Thus children in such families typically do not do well in school, experience significantly more depression than more rooted and affluent children, and develop serious deficits in social skills.

At the beginning of the Kennedy presidency, Michael Harrington (1962) wrote a book entitled *The Other America*. That book, which has now become a classic, described the plight of the poor in the early 1960s and portrayed their lives of despair and misery. This book played a major role in stimulating President Lyndon B. Johnson's War on Poverty, which in turn spawned an outpouring of federal legislation designed to provide financial aid and training to the poor as a way of breaking the poverty cycle. Obviously, as we look at the plight of the poor three and a half decades later, the problems of poverty still exist but they are changing in some ways. For example, the stereotype of the poor as composed principally of unemployed inner-city minority people or mothers on welfare trying to care for large numbers of children born out of wedlock does not include those who have become labeled the *hidden poor*. These are the poor who are working and have families. Most of these people, whose annual cash income for a family of four is below approximately $15,700, the official poverty line, are White, with one or more members working. About 14.5% of Americans are classified as poor; about 40% of the poor are children. These poor tend to be divided evenly between the central cities, suburbs, and rural areas.

The *welfare poor*, the underclass with which most stereotypical views of poverty seem to be associated, have essentially stabilized in size, but the number of *working poor*, the so-called hidden poor, has grown rapidly. The estimate is that there are now 9 million poor adults who work, most of whom are in the prime working age of 22 to 64. "In 1986, 2 million Americans worked full time throughout the entire year and were still poor—an increase of more than 50% since 1978" (Whitman, Thornton, Shapiro, Witkin, & Hawkins, 1988, p. 20). Part of the problem these families face is that the existing welfare and tax systems do not reward the impoverished for working. For example, a mother on welfare typically qualifies for Medicaid, child-care subsidies, food stamps, and public housing. A mother who is poor but works typically does not qualify for or use such social services. As a result, in many states, a mother with two children is actually better off financially on a combination of welfare and food stamps than is a mother who works full-time at a minimum wage job. Under the most recent changes to federal and state welfare laws, such conditions are now being changed, but the results are yet to be determined.

In a series of interviews with the working poor, Whitman et al. (1988) found that most have no health insurance and constantly worry about the effect an illness or accident may have on them or their dependents. Also common among the working poor is the absence of a sense of ease or leisure. Having to wear secondhand clothes and drive rattletrap cars contributes to a feeling of living on the margin at all times. Many of the working poor are also the *new poor*—those who have been machine operators, farmers, and others and have lost their jobs because of plant closings or economic downturns. Some of the working poor are migrant workers; others are illegal aliens whose survival in this nation depends on their taking low-paying jobs, frequently on a part-time basis, for which health insurance and other benefits are unavailable.

The effects of poverty rest somewhat differently on the welfare poor, the working poor, and the new poor. Such effects are also somewhat different in rural areas where there is a greater sense of community support and shared conditions and generally lower prices than in urban areas. Wherever poverty exists, however, it breeds frustration and stress. These, in turn, cause family fights, drinking and depression, feelings of being hemmed in and not in control of one's destiny, limited prospects for youngsters, functional illiteracy, high rates of teen pregnancies, intellectual stunting, and narrow horizons.

Minority Group Membership

As discussed in chapter 4, the reality of pluralism in the United States stems from the large numbers of people who belong to different minority groups. If we talk in absolute numbers, in some major cities and in other geographical locations people classified as minority group members—Blacks, Hispanics, Asians, and Native Americans—are really in the majority. Across the nation in general, however, people classified as minority group members have not gained the power, fiscal resources, or access to educational and occupational opportunities to permit them to compete equally with those in the majority culture. Thus considering minority group membership as a risk factor does not imply that minority group members are inferior or inadequate compared to majority group members. Risk, in this case, refers to the likelihood that purely because of their status as members of a minority group, people are less likely to be able to meet their full potential, to be equitably served in education and by social services, or to have the same opportunities and incentives for achievement that majority group members experience.

According to Perry (1982), "Blacks, Hispanics, Asian Americans, and Native Americans have long been foremost among the underserved, with higher incidences of unemployment, mental and physical illness, and mortality in adults and youth" (p. 54). These conditions stem from discrimination, language and cultural discrepancies, poor nutrition, inadequate education, and other factors that place minority group members at risk for unemployment and underemployment, feelings of powerlessness, and loss of hope. Minority status, particularly for African Americans, is also related to imprisonment. Glaberson (1990) reported research that indicated that nearly one of every four young African American men (20 to 29 years of age) in New York State is in a state prison or a local jail, on probation or on parole. Even more dramatic, the number of young African American men in custody on any given day (45,000 out of 193,000 in New York State) is double the number of African American men enrolled in all the colleges in this state. This pattern is reflected across the nation, particularly in inner cities. Over 50% of young urban African American men were unemployed in the 1980s, worked part-time jobs involuntarily, or earned poverty-level wages (Lichter, 1988).

In many urban areas, the employment situation has worsened for African American men and women. In part this is because former manufacturing and other employment opportunities have been moved to suburban and other locations to which public transportation is not available, and the nature of the work itself has changed in ways that disqualify many minority youth who do not have the requisite occupational or educational skills. Taylor (1990), for example, contended that

> . . . industrial decentralization, combined with structural shifts in city economies from centers of goods producing or manufacturing activities to higher order service-providing industries has severely affected the employment opportunities of inner-city African Americans, especially the job prospects of poorly educated African American youths. . . . Such structural changes have substantially reduced the number of unskilled and semi-skilled jobs in those industries that have traditionally attracted and economically upgraded previous generations of African Americans. (p. 7)

Clearly, there are significant relationships between job availability and types, the skills of minority persons, and the ability to maintain a home and children. As suggested previously, many at-risk poor White and African American youth are employed, or underemployed, in part-time and low-paying jobs, which limit their ability to anticipate having or adequately supporting their own family. As one of the results of such conditions, there has been a continuing rise in single-parent families, absentee fathers, and teenage pregnancies. Much of the burden of the dislocations and job transitions occurring across the nation has now fallen on the youth and the young adult (ages 16 to 24) populations. For example, in the late 1980s, the unemployment rate for teenagers was about 16% for all teenagers, more than 32% for African American teens. For workers 20 to 24 years of age, the unemployment rates were slightly less than 7% for Whites, 11% for Hispanics, and 20% for African Americans. The real median income of families headed by a 20- to 24-year-old fell 27% from 1973 to 1986; the percentage of 20- to 24-year-old males able to support a family of three above the poverty level dropped by nearly a quarter from 88.3% in 1973 to 43.8% in 1986. The rate of that decline for African Americans in the same age group was twice as high (W.T. Grant Commission, 1988).

Within any minority or majority group, there are subpopulations likely to be at particular risk because of a combination of negative social and psychological factors, economic insecurity, and other reasons. Given some of the information on populations most susceptible to unemployment and underemployment, it is no surprise that many authors are concerned about Black men as a group at particular risk (e.g., Parham & McDavis, 1987). Some of the reasons for such characterization include high rates of unemployment, poor education, inadequate health care facilities, discriminatory judicial processes, lack of adequate legal representation, racist police practices, incarceration (42% of the inmate population in the United States is Black) (Staples, 1982), and frontline military combat duty in Vietnam, Grenada, the Persian Gulf, and other conflicts.

There are other risk factors for Black men, however. Parham and McDavis (1987), in their review of the existing literature, suggested that Black men as a group have a shorter average life expectancy (64 years) than any other group. Black youths have a 50% higher probability of dying before age 20 than White children, and from different causes. The two largest causes of death among White youths are accidents and cardiovascular disease; among Black youths, the primary causes are homicide, drug abuse, suicide, and accidents. Black men now have a higher rate of cancer, especially lung cancer, than any other group in the United States primarily because Black men smoke more cigarettes than men in any other age or sex group in America. Black men also have been found to have a more serious problem with alcohol abuse than is true of White men, White women, or Black women. The consequences of alcohol abuse ripple negatively throughout the personal and social lives of Black men and are related to the high rates of homicides, arrests, accidents, assaults, and physical illnesses (Harper, 1981). Davis (1981), among others, reported that the suicide rate for Black people, and particularly young Black men, has been increasing steadily since the 1960s. Although the average suicide rate for Blacks is still below the national average, the increase in these rates is dramatic, and if it continues at the present levels, will soon exceed the national average. Tseng and Streltzer (1997) contended that the relatively lower levels of suicide among Blacks compared to Whites is consistent with the collective culture of Blacks and with the identification of an external negative force against which African Americans feel they must fight (p. 367).

The profile presented here of the experience of many Black men is one characterized by intense stress, tension, hostility, internalized anxiety, frustration, and resentment. The causes of these are discrimination, the pressures of functioning in educational systems or business and corporate structures dominated by Whites, and the perceived need to compromise their Blackness to incorporate behaviors and values acceptable to the majority culture. Clearly, in such circumstances, many Black men pay a high emotional and physical price as they try to cope with achieving a personal identity, a family life, educational success, and economic security and advancement.

Parham and McDavis (1987) suggested a wide range of recommendations by which counselors in schools, colleges and universities, mental health agencies, and other settings can provide both indirect and direct services to Black men. These recommendations, in paraphrased form, include those for providing

- seminars on parenting for Black parents to help them attend more systematically to the developmental issues and problems of their male children;
- counseling groups to help Black men develop more positive self-concepts and to identify with available role models;
- career counseling to help Black men gain more confidence in their abilities and skills and to help them understand and prepare for career opportunities;
- outreach counseling services, in cooperation with Black churches and community organizations, directed to developing value systems and support groups to strengthen Afrocentricism, principles of collective survival, and ways to help young Black men resist actions such as suicide, homicide, and drug abuse;
- formal programs to help young Black men build strong family lives, develop leadership skills, or communicate effectively their academic expectations to teachers and others; and
- support systems, stress management programs, and other services for upwardly mobile Black men to help them deal with the pressures of their jobs and their identity crises.

Besides Black men, many other minority groups also experience frustrations and stress that deserve more attention from counselors in the future than has been true in the past. Hispanic populations in the United States have also been underserved. Today, Hispanics are one of the two most rapidly growing ethnic groups, and current predictions are that sometime early in the next century, Hispanics will be the majority minority group in the United States. Indeed, as already noted, by the year 2000 or shortly after it is anticipated that the Hispanic population in the United States is likely to match or exceed the African American population in the United States. The Hispanic population, which includes persons of color, is comprised of persons from a variety of Spanish-speaking nations—Latinos, Chicanos, Mexicanos, Puertoriquenos, Dominicanos, Colombianos, and others—and is not so much racially different as linguistically diverse.

The United States is now the fifth largest Spanish-speaking nation in the Western Hemisphere (after Mexico, Argentina, Colombia, and Peru). With the long-term effects of the North American Free Trade Agreement, the border between the United States and Mexico and potentially several other Central and South American nations will essentially be erased for purposes of trade and worker mobility. As this occurs, the Spanish language and associated cultural traditions will be integrated into an even larger portion of the life and transactions of the United States. But through most of the 20th century, until the present time, most Hispanic immigrants and residents have been poor and ill-educated by U.S. standards. Those whose native language is not English tend to complete fewer years of schooling and drop out more frequently than their White counterparts. This situation is slowly changing as many Puerto Rican, Cuban, and other Hispanic populations have come to the United States as educated and often professionally trained persons. Nevertheless, in comparable terms, Hispanic populations have tended to enter and remain in lower paying occupations and attain less education with more drop-outs than other minority groups. Also of interest in terms of being at risk is the observation that the symbiotic relationship between work and mental health is particularly evident with Hispanics (Knouse, Rosenfeld, & Culbertson, 1992). The effects of job discrimination, unemployment, underemployment, and other work-related factors have a significant impact on the general mental health of Hispanics. Within this context, it is clear that the availability of Spanish-speaking counselors, the availability of occupational and educational information and opportunities that reinforce economic mobility and other services that are culturally sensitive have been limited for many persons of Hispanic background, perpetuating limited access to opportunities and requiring Spanish-speaking persons to adapt to the dominant culture rather than find mechanisms that reinforce cultural pluralism, that is, mechanisms that celebrate the richness of culture, value their heritage, and reflect these characteristics into counseling strategies. For example, Hispanics, in general, prefer a direct, concrete counseling style; thus in culturally sensitive counseling for Hispanics, roles and expectations within the counseling dyad should be clear and explicit.

The other of the two fastest growing ethnic groups in America includes Asian Americans and Pacific Islanders. Like Hispanics, Asian Americans and Pacific Islanders are frequently treated as though they comprise one homogeneous group. Obviously, they do not. But in that process, their cultural identify is demeaned, and their personal dignity and their uniqueness are obscured. They come from different nations, with different religious, language, and cultural traditions. They also vary in their recency in the United States and in their use of English as well as in other matters.

In general, Asian Americans seem to have achieved educationally at a high level, compared to other minority groups, but there are unpublicized aspects of Asian Americans, such as that a large percentage of them have little or no education, that they have sociopathic groups within their communities, and that they are underemployed (Sue & Padilla, 1986). Beyond such factors, there are others that may affect the social integration and mobility of some Asian Americans. For example, Leungs (1993) research suggested that Asian American adolescents, more than is the case with Whites, may prematurely constrict their career choices based on perceived prestige or sex type factors. In essence, they may ignore variables such as their personal interests and aptitudes in deference to the prestige of an occupation. Further, it is generally accepted that Asian Americans tend to be less assertive in social situations, and that feelings of anxiety and guilt may inhibit their assertiveness (Zane, Sue, Hu, & Kwan, 1991). Against such perspectives, Fernandez (1988), in addressing the counseling of Southeast Asian students, suggested that it is inappropriate to counsel these students in modes that require introspection, reflection, and extreme client verbalization. Behavioral approaches seem more appropriate. Another suggestion is that because Asian American individuals are not likely to make decisions without the advice and consent of their families, counselors should work toward family cooperation in support of counseling and the decision-making process. Based on this suggestion, Evanoski and Tse (1989) provided groups of Chinese and Korean American parents with culture-specific, bilingual career awareness workshops that used bilingual role models and bilingual materials and community settings familiar to these parents.

Finally, Native Americans are among the most underserved of all minority groups despite extensive evidence that their levels of stress, substance abuse, suicide, and feelings of hopelessness are of epidemic proportions in some tribes and reservations. No minority group in the United States has experienced deeper prejudice or limits on their mobility than Native Americans. Many live on reservations; others live in towns near reservations; still others live among the majority populations. Like other minority populations, Native American nations and tribes are heterogeneous, each with a rich heritage and unique character. Nevertheless, they have been the frequent victim of stereotype, myth, and oppression, extremely underserved with mental health services, and often lacking in awareness of opportunities available to them or for which they could qualify. As a result, in addition to their mental health problems, Native Americans have extremely high unemployment rates, enter a restricted range of occupations, often live under very difficult physical conditions, have lower feelings of self-efficacy than Whites or Hispanics, and lack confidence in their ability to compete academically or technically (Herring, 1990; Lauver & Jones, 1991).

Counseling with Native Americans needs to focus on strengthening the self-confidence of clients, developing active problem-solving skills, and doing so within the context of the choice strategies and religious experiences supported by the notions of community as defined by Native American tribal culture. Some data have suggested that perhaps more than other minority groups, Native Americans are more likely to prefer a counselor who is also Native American (Bennett & Big Foot Sipes, 1991); however, an adequate number of trained Native American counselors is not yet available.

Other groups at risk are immigrant populations. Depending on why and how they came to the United States, they may have severe health problems, language difficulties, educational and occupational deficits, and lack of information. Initial adjustment problems stem from considerable feelings of loss from leaving loved ones behind or mourning the loss of a cultural self and identity in their homelands. Indeed, many immigrants undergo significant loss of social status.

Chapter 4 discussed counseling skills necessary to deal with culturally diverse populations. Suffice it to say here that counselors working with minority populations should, above all, possess the generic counseling knowledge, skills, understandings, abilities, and behaviors thought to be appropriate to any helping relationship. They must be conscious of how their own attitudes and values impinge on counseling specific ethnic and racial groups. They must be aware of the cultural traditions and contexts from which their clients come but not assume a stereotypical perspective that these clients are bound by such backgrounds. Counselors must work to separate their clients' socioeconomic deficits from problems based on race or ethnicity. Counselors must help minority clients find ways to cope with discrimination without internalizing its effects as valid for them. Further, counselors must be prepared to help minority clients analyze lifestyle and career options and to take action based upon goal-setting and problem-solving strategies.

Women

Women also constitute a minority group subject to risk factors. As reported in other chapters as well as here, women tend to be more at risk of unemployment and underemployment than are men, they are more likely to be single parents than are men, they experience different forms of mental disorder (e.g., depression) than men, they are prone to violence and abuse (e.g., sexual assault and rape) in ways different from men, they are more likely to be in poverty than men, and they experience psychological pressures or identity issues that differ from those of men.

It is certainly appropriate to reemphasize here that women in this society, and in many others throughout the world, have been fighting throughout this century and beyond against an array of indignities and risk factors that frequently have led to personal or collective issues of poor self-esteem, role conflict, physical or sexual abuse, limited or fragmented educational or career development, stigma and discrimination, filtered information about opportunity and choice, and emphases on their deficiencies, not their strengths. Their struggles for inclusiveness and significance beyond childbearing and maternal roles have found many women, similar to racially and linguistically diverse groups, at risk of unemployment and underemployment, single parenthood; of different forms of mental disorder (e.g., depression), poverty, psychological or identity issues; and of violence and abuse that are different from those experienced by men. In increasing numbers, as women try to function both as homemakers and as employed workers, they find themselves with feelings of insecurity, stress, and inner conflicts about their personal identity, their sense of multiple obligations, their values, their wishes, their freedom of action and, perhaps, a perceived lack of marketable skills.

In essence, the issue here is that women often react to and internalize stereotypes or models that treat women as objects, as victims, as passive recipients of socialization that does not respect, advocate, or promote their strengths, skills, and contributions. As noted in chapter 2, women are entering the labor force in rapidly growing numbers. Many women do so deliberately and positively as part of a dual-career family. Other women, however, after having completed a child-rearing stage of their life, are reentering the work world after a long period of time or are entering it for the first time. Many women enter the workforce out of economic necessity. They are either single parents who have no choice but to work to support themselves and their children, or they are married women who must become part of a two-earner family in order to maintain the economic integrity of the family. Many women enter the labor force because they feel that this society does not condone their desire to be a homemaker, and they want to resolve their identity confusion and ambiguity about their self-concept and a work role. Many of the women in any of these groups may feel considerable insecurity, stress, or a variety of emotions and uncertainties that put them at risk of psychological distress—and this argues for counseling intervention.

Mogul (1979) described from a psychiatric perspective some of the tensions with which the women reentering the workforce must contend. Although primarily directed to the older woman entering the workforce after a substantial period at home, many of the same insecurities are internalized by other working women.

Women resuming outside work after an interval . . . have to struggle simultaneously with the realities of the work world, friction at home, and their own inner conflicts. The more a woman's sense of herself was grounded in her identity as a wife and mother, the greater the readjustment in her sense of self when she reenters the occupational world. The sense of femaleness, attractiveness, and lovability is often related to being dependent, and less competent than men, so that doubts about important parts of the self are stirred up as other parts are developed. To be aggressive and actively self-promoting— necessities in the school or work world—are characteristics to which (an older) generation of middle-aged women did not aspire in their youth. Since women primarily grew up to be those who nurture and give to others and are sensitive and vulnerable to real or imagined disapproval from people who are important to them, the sense of guilt and failure is almost unavoidable as they begin to do for themselves.

In order to change her lifestyle during her middle years without either too much guilt and inhibition or too much angry repudiation of her former life, a woman has the psychological task of testing and making room for new identities and new self-perceptions without entirely discarding old ones that had offered grounds for previous self-regard. It is helpful to have social and family support for these changes and also to have derived solid gratifications from the previous role. (p. 1140)

When considering the psychological factors related to women's entry into, adjustment to, and mobility within the workforce, other barriers also need to be addressed and considered. Spanard (1990) has classified those that women returning to higher education experience into institutional, situational, and psychosocial barriers. Such a classification can also be applied to other settings by thinking of institutional barriers as including such factors as sexism, job discrimination, location, accessibility, availability of day care and other support services; situational barriers as including home responsibility, lack of marketable skills, lack of money; and psychosocial barriers as including guilt feelings, a low opinion of the individual's abilities, opinions of others, attitudes, beliefs, and values.

In studying the effects of the Carl D. Perkins Act on the provision of vocational education and vocational guidance for special populations in several geographical entities, Herr (1987) found that in programs for single parents and displaced homemakers, the major issue that women faced was not securing training but rather gaining a sense of self-efficacy, the confidence that they could actually do what was expected of them in the workplace. This finding is consistent with that of Welborn and Moore (1985) in their work with displaced homemakers. As they reported,

often the displaced homemaker is in the position of not only actively needing and seeking employment, but also of being required to cope with a number of other issues, such as feeling out of control, feeling isolated from those segments of society in which she must now operate, feeling little sense of personal power, feeling a void where she once felt intimacy, and feeling a keen sense of disorientation as the emphasis on family is necessarily reduced as she prepares to go to work. (p. 104)

Whether or not women are described as *reentry women, displaced homemakers*, or by some other label, Gilligan (1982), Hotelling and Forest (1985), and others considered the possibilities that the two sexes experience dependence-independence and relationships differently. In the case of women, certain overreactions may occur that have implications for counseling in general. Hotelling and Forest described the condition as follows:

From Gilligan's perspective, a woman's development is restricted because she fails to realize that she must incorporate both self-care and care of others into her identity.

Many women may view this as an overwhelming task. Two responses, both of which are maladaptive, are the super woman phenomenon (an attempt to uphold extremely high standards both at work and home) and the male model (which requires one to excel at work only). The consequences of the first model are emotional and physical strain and overload; often the woman feels not only exhausted and confused but guilty if she does not perform all tasks perfectly. The second model, which defines self through separation, may result in a woman progressing in her career but ignoring her need for connection with others. The expectation to maintain autonomy and independence in a vacuum of human intimacy at work can be painful, confusing, and lonely to a woman who has learned that connection with others is essential. (p. 184)

Counseling of women in relation to work and career will take many forms depending on the education, motivation, and experience of specific women. Herr and Cramer (1996, pp. 541-542) have recommended that the goals (in abridged form) for reentry women should be to

- reinforce positive feelings about self-worth and ability to make a contribution in the workforce outside the home;
- provide any information that may be lacking about basic career decision making: personal assets and limitations, values and attitudes, the world of work, resources, and so on;
- assist in exploring changes in lifestyle that may be occasioned by first-time entry or reentry into the labor force;
- help clients understand the implications of full-time versus part-time work;
- prepare women to deal with possible discrimination, both overt and covert;
- provide specialized experiences, if necessary, in such areas as consciousness raising and assertiveness training;
- explore entry-level jobs with extant education versus possible jobs with additional education or training;
- provide a referral system for placement assistance and teach job-seeking skills; and
- provide follow-up and continuing support.

In addition to following these recommendations, counselors assisting women to deal with career-related issues probably will need to engage in other possible functions as well, such as networking, peer counseling, support groups, financial and personal counseling to deal with such issues as divorce or other major life changes, time management, and stress management.

Although being a woman constitutes a risk factor in relation to work and career, women are certainly at risk in other areas as well. Among these are violence, sexual abuse, and rape. Estimates of the number of women who will be a victim of rape are variable, ranging between 1 in 20 and 1 in 30. Certainly, crime statistics on forcible rape have suggested that this violence continues to increase across the nation. Of particular note is the reality that, "In the United States today, a woman is more likely to be physically assaulted, raped, or murdered by a current or former male partner than by any other assailant" (Carden, 1994, p. 545). Such violent wife abuse is frequently associated with or leads to miscarriage, abortion, drug and alcohol abuse, attempted suicide, physical disfigurement or disability, cognitive distortions, chronic depression, anxiety, and lower self-esteem. Battered women frequently show indications on assessments of behavior that would under other conditions suggest severely disordered psychiatric behavior including intense anger, confusion, paranoia/fearfulness, and pessimism. Some researchers (e.g., Walker, 1991) have suggested that the psychological status of the battered women is essentially that described in the *DSM-IV* as post-traumatic stress disorder.

Counseling and medical treatment for victims of violence, rape, and sexual assaults often need to be combined. Initial counseling of the victim or the family, depending on the age of the victim, needs to be designed to combat the negative effects of the experience. Among appropriate emphases are to

- reassure the victim of present safety;
- affirm that the victim has regained control of the situation;
- emphasize rapist or sexual abuser responsibility for the crime;
- help the victim conceptualize the experience through verbalization;
- encourage and support expression of feelings;
- acknowledge the traumatic nature of the experience;
- provide information regarding possible immediate and long-term effects (rape trauma syndrome); and
- use such counseling techniques as teaching victims to deal with adverse symptoms through relaxation sequences, thought stoppage, covert modeling, and other techniques (Sproles, 1985, pp. 15–16).

As one of the major forms of violence against women, according to the National Center for Prevention and Control of Rape of the U.S. Department of Health and Human Services (Sproles, 1985), the major effects of rape on the adult are brought about through

- inability to defend against the suddenness of the attack;
- intentional cruelty;
- the feeling of being trapped and unable to fight back; and
- physical trauma.

The resulting loss of control and heightened victim vulnerability lead to a rape trauma syndrome that can be divided into an acute (initial phase) and a long-term (reorganization) phase. The acute phase can last from a few days to several weeks. The typical symptoms are a wide range of emotional responses emanating from shock and disbelief. These responses can be demonstrated in an expressive way through anger, fear, and anxiety or in a controlled way through hiding one's feelings and seeming composed or subdued. After the initial phase, a reorganization phase may last for months or even years. In this phase a variety of complications may occur unless initial counseling or psychiatric therapy is available and effective. Such complications include a limitation on activities and general lifestyle, inability to feel safe, and aversion to all sexual activity. In addition to experiencing chronic depression, the victim may develop fears and phobias specific to the rape and then generalize the fears to symbols of the rape, such as fear of being alone, fear of men, and fear of sex. Counselors involved in the initial phase or in the reorganization phase need to develop not only treatment plans with the victim but also follow-up checks to assess the needs for referral or reinitiation of counseling. In many parts of the nation, rape crises centers have been implemented to provide such services as crisis intervention, counseling, advocacy and accompaniment, community education and prevention, and self-defense training (Harvey, 1985).

A final area we will identify here as a risk factor for women is depression. In general, clinical depression is twice as common in women than in men (Lobel & Hirschfield, 1984). The predisposing factors are not clear. Clinical depression can be associated with another psychiatric disorder, such as schizophrenia, or with alcoholism; it can be related to a physical illness such as a viral disease or endocrine disorder; or depression can occur without any intermediary disturbances. The reasons for the comparatively large amount of depression in women as compared with men may be genetic, sociocultural, hormonal, a function of diagnostic practice, or the fact that women are more likely than men to seek help.

Clinical depression usually is characterized by a set of symptoms that persist longer than 2 weeks and are manifested by a depressed mood or a loss of interest in usual activities. Symptoms may include appetite, weight, and sleep disturbances; hyperactivity or lethargy; anxiety; crying; slowed thinking; suicidal tendencies; and feelings of guilt, worthlessness, and hopelessness.

About 10 to 14 million people in the United States suffer from a diagnosable depression. Only about one half of these seek treatment. Treatment ordinarily includes a variety of antidepressant drugs and lithium, a combination of drugs and psychotherapy, or electroconvulsive treatment. When psychotherapy or counseling is used in combination with medication, or alone if the depression is mild or moderate, cognitive, behavioral, interpersonal, or short-term therapies may be used. In some cases, group, marital, and family therapies are useful. Cognitive/ behavioral therapies that focus on the depressed person's negative or distorted thinking patterns are increasingly used in clinical depression. They are discussed more fully in the next chapter, but the basic assumption of such approaches is that negative thought patterns lead to depressed feelings and behaviors. Thus the way to change the feelings is to change the thoughts.

Persons With Disabilities

Persons with disabilities are another major population at risk of psychological and economic vulnerability. "With the onset of a potentially disabling condition, an individual experiences both economic and psychic losses as he or she faces restricted choices. The individual may suffer pain, incur increased medical costs, lose income, and face societal prejudice" (Berkowitz & Hill, 1986, p. 1). Persons with disabilities are victims of social stigma, just as other populations suffer the effects of sexism, ageism, and racism.

Aside from persons of color in this nation, there is probably no group that has had to fight so diligently for dignity as persons with disabilities. The Rehabilitation Act of 1973 and the Americans With Disabilities Act of 1990 are among the significant legislative mechanisms designed to provide greater access to economic and social opportunity for persons with disabilities, to recognize their potential and actual contributions to the larger society, to acknowledge their significance as workers, family members, and citizens.

The terminology of disability is a bit confused. Some authors use the terms *disabled, handicapped,* and *persons with a disability* interchangeably (Campbell, 1985). Other authors approach the issue differently. Berkowitz and Hill (1986) defined disability as

. . . the loss of the ability to perform socially accepted or prescribed tasks and roles due to a medically definable *condition*. . . . In some relatively few cases, the condition leaves a person with some residual *impairments*, that is, some physiological, anatomical, or mental loss or abnormality that persists after the condition has stabilized. . . . In some cases, (again, relatively few) these residual impairments cause a person to have *functional limitations*. . . . As a consequence of these functional limitations (physical or emotional), some persons may perform their expected roles only with extreme difficulty; hence we classify them as being *disabled*. (pp. 4–5)

Thus the problem of having a disability is not simply that of being significantly unemployed and poor, although persons with disability are both significantly poorer and unemployed at a rate two or three times more than that of the nondisabled. Perhaps a more important matter, as suggested in chapter 4, is that a central issue for persons with disabilities is that of self-perception. How do persons with disabilities label themselves? What stereotypes from the able-bodied population do they internalize as valid about the inferiority, incompetence, or worthless of the disabled? Such attributions undoubtedly vary greatly, but as a burn victim who spent 6 months in hospitals and a long period of recuperation after that, I can testify to the reality that cosmetic injuries and burns of this magnitude quickly set you apart in your own mind from other people, cause you to feel profoundly different, inferior, and lonely, and leave a residual of malingering physical and psychological impairment that requires a long time to overcome.

Dunham and Dunham (1978) have taken a perspective on disability that is closest to the views in this book. They considered the disabled person to be structurally, physiologically, and psychologically different from a normal person because of an accident, disease, or developmental problem. A person with disabilities, they maintained, feels less adequate than others, either in general or in a specific situation. Absent such a view of self, a disability may not be a handicap.

Disability, then, may take one of several forms: *physical* (such as amputations, birth defects, cancer, heart problems, burns, deafness, blindness, multiple sclerosis, muscular distrophy, orthopedic deformities, spinal injury), *intellectual* (mental retardation, learning disability, brain damage, speech and language disorders), *emotional* (mental illness, substance abuse, alcoholism, obesity and other eating disorders) or *sociocultural* (limited English, victim of racial or ethnic bias, inadequate social understanding or skills). In an important sense, each of these categories represents a set of risk factors that can cause a disability to become a handicap and limit an individual's economic, social, and psychological well-being.

Given the differences in definition of persons with disabilities, it is difficult to be precise about the numbers of people involved. One method of identifying the magnitude of those with disabilities is to determine the number of people with a work disability. As Campbell (1985) noted,

According to the Census Bureau, there were 147.3 million noninstitutionalized persons 16 to 24 years of age in March of 1982. Of this working-age population, 13.1 million reported a work disability. There were 6.67 million disabled males, 41.5% of whom participated in the labor force. Unemployment of disabled males was 16.9% in contrast to 10.2% for the nondisabled. The disabled female population was 6.4 million with a labor participation rate of 23.7% and unemployment of 18.3%. Nondisabled females had an unemployment rate of 8.8%. . . . Disabled females in central cities are one of the most disadvantaged groups throughout the nation. Their earnings approximate only 42.1% of the mean earnings of disabled males. (pp. 15–16)

Campbell suggested that external influences affect the employment opportunities for persons with disabilities even when they are qualified by knowledge, skill, and motivation. These include environmental access, job conditions, personnel management practices, management attitudes and behaviors, employer relations practices, affirmative action efforts, law enforcement, and protection of rights. Embedded in such environmental influences are the effects of employment myths and stereotypes, the degree to which employers have attempted to modify their workplaces to accommodate the needs of disabled workers to function effectively, and apprehensions about the productivity of disabled workers.

Clearly, the unemployment rates of the disabled are much higher than those just reported. Many disabled people cannot or do not seek work, thus they are not counted when unemployment rates are calculated. Indeed, if we count the difference between disabled men who actually participate in the labor force (41.5%) and those who do not (58.5%) and then calculate the 16.9% unemployment rate on the first figure, the unemployment rate or, perhaps more precisely, the number of disabled men of working age who do not work, is close to 65% or more. Disabled people are considerably less likely to be employed full-time (8% for partially disabled men, 31% for partially disabled women), compared to the nondisabled population (86% for men, 49% for women). Median family income of the severely disabled was approximately half that of the income of the nondisabled (Daniels, 1985). Persons with disabilities, then, are themselves a minority who are at serious economic and psychological risk.

Given the wide variation in types of disability and the levels of their severity—mild, moderate, profound—it is not possible to describe here a major approach to working with persons with disabilities. Many of these persons will need a counseling emphasis on ego-building and strengthening of self-esteem. Some will need assertiveness training. Many will need advocacy, financial support, retraining, job skills, and placement within supportive, therapeutic milieus. Others will need ongoing medical services and support while they learn to use prostheses and other medically induced adaptations. Some persons with disabilities and their spouses or children will need family counseling, marital or couples counseling, and help in reassessing their sexual needs and how to deal with them. Others will need to develop crucial life skills for successful living within whatever functional limitations they now face—personal/social, routine survival, or occupational skills. Because a disability may, in fact, restrict or totally alter a life or career trajectory, individuals may need help to examine where in their developmental progress the disability has intruded, and then to find alternative ways to reach their goals within their available resources. They will need to redefine capacity and potential, not only loss and limitations.

Older Adults

An expression that is frequently used to describe the United States is the "graying of America." The United States is no longer a nation in which children and youth are the largest population groups. Currently one in five Americans is over age 55; and some 13% of the total population—more than 32 million people—are now over age 65 (Conner, 1992). Most of them are active and functioning well. Only 4% of men and 7% of women aged 65 and over in 1990 resided in nursing homes, homes for the aged, and similar institutions (Farley, 1996). The remainder were independent, living in their own home or with family. But in many instances, myths and stereotypes captured by the term *ageism* have restricted the productivity, potential contributions to society, and the feelings of well-being and acceptance for many older people.

Thus chronological age can be considered a risk factor for many, whether or not any other risk factors are present in their lives (e.g., disability, minority group membership). Both because of the growing number of people who are at or beyond conventionally defined retirement ages, and because of the growing understanding of the effects of ageism and other risk factors for these populations, counselors and psychologists are recognizing the need to provide counseling and related services and, indeed, to develop new therapeutic tactics to work with this population.

Like other population groups, some older adults also have

> distressing emotional problems they seem unable to solve by themselves—problems like depression, intense fears, anxiety, persistent anger, frustration, unrelieved loneliness. And others have occasional problems which are too much for them, especially grief and depression caused by the death of a loved one. (Sargent, 1980, p. 1)

Even under the best of circumstances, many older and retired people learn that they must come to terms with perceptions they and the larger society have come to believe or manifest toward older persons. Society's attitudes toward older adults have been less than benevolent (Offerman & Gowing, 1990), and they are often internalized. An older individual may feel that he or she is now on the shelf and less important than when he or she was fully engaged in the workforce or child rearing; that because he or she is not working and productive, he or she is parasitic and generally disapproved of; that living on a fixed income places him or her in a vulnerable position in case inflation runs rampant in the future; that he or she has entered the last stage of life and has to consider how much time is left; and that chronic illness and aging tend to go together and are likely to restrict freedom and independence in the near future. Theriault (1994) has described what he has termed *anxiety of the end*, which is stimulated in some older persons as they make the transition from work to retirement.

Because of the need to cope with the social stigma of ageism and the phenomena associated with aging just described, older people probably have more psychological problems than any other age group, with the possible exception of adolescents (Sargent, 1980). Although this statement is difficult to prove conclusively, there is relevant evidence to support it. Several observers have contended that a conservative estimate of those in the older age population who need mental health services is about 15%. Those who argue that this figure is overly conservative do so because a large number of the older population who have physical illnesses or impairments that are complicated by emotional reactions amenable to therapeutic intervention do not obtain mental health services. Estimates are that of those aged 65 or over who are living in the community, 5% are severely impaired in their psychological functioning, and a further 20% are moderately impaired. A final indicator of the needs for counseling and psychological assistance among the older population is the estimate that 25% of suicides in the United States are committed by people, particularly White men, over age 65, a figure that is higher than that for any other age group.

One of the issues that complicates delivering mental health services to older persons is that this population is not homogeneous in health, in attitudes, in financial means, or in other factors that affect their mental health. In gross terms, this population has been divided into the young old (65 to 74), old old (75 and over), and the oldest old (85 and over) (Conner, 1992). Each of these groups differs in the extent and severity of physical impairments and in the scope of the future they can contemplate. Given general actuarial estimates that a person turning 65 currently can anticipate another 14.6 years of life, the psychology of that perspective is different from that of the person who has already achieved 80 or more years and believes that they have exhausted the number of years allocated to them. In that sense, just as an aging population needs a continuum of community services from meals on wheels to chore and home maintenance services to home health care and adult day care to keep the person independent as long as possible and, finally, nursing homes and other residential services when that becomes necessary (Conner, 1992), it is likely that an aging population will need a continuum of mental health services that address the developmental needs of the aging population.

Older people do not avail themselves of mental health services for many reasons. Some do not trust "head doctors," and others feel that an individual should handle his or her own problems. Some feel that they do not deserve help or feel guilty or too worthless to receive help. Some do not know to whom to turn for help or feel they cannot afford it, even if it is covered by Medicare or other insurance. As a result only 4% of older adults are serviced by mental health centers, and few receive preretirement counseling.

As a result of such resistance to the use of counseling and mental health services, an array of nontraditional therapies has arisen in senior citizen and community mental health centers around the nation. These include such emphases as assertiveness training for the aging, widows groups and emeritus classes, adult day-care centers, creative aging workshops, peer counseling programs, behavioral approaches to therapy with the elderly, counseling and reassuring the dying (in or outside of hospices), and programs to facilitate the transition to nursing homes (Sargent, 1980).

Certainly, within the aging population, older workers and those considering retirement are major constituencies for counseling. As suggested in chapter 2, the demographics of the workforce are changing. The baby boom is over, and the number of adolescents and young adults entering the workforce is rapidly decreasing. Rather than finding ways to encourage older workers to retire and make room in the workforce for younger people, it is likely in the future that the emphasis will shift to finding ways to retain older workers and help them to remain productive. This will require redesigning jobs, educating employers or management about coping with the needs of or the myths about older workers, designing programs to retrain older workers or to find new placements for dislocated workers, and providing opportunities for older workers to engage in part-time as well as full-time work (Herr & Cramer, 1996).

Kieffer (1980) suggested some methods to assist older workers now on the job. Most of these are counseling-related processes. He advocated more effective performance evaluation programs; identification of alternative jobs or work arrangements in the same or related organizations; alternative job placements; development and improvement of counseling services for furthering a career or for retirement;

improvement or adaptation of systems for training, development, and promotion; updating of advisory services on pensions and fringe benefits; review of terminating procedures; and mental health counseling. Some older workers presently on the job are likely to be plateaued workers, persons who have reached the highest point in their organization to which they will ever progress. Tan and Salamone (1994) have suggested that such workers require a reassessment of their career goals and a refocus on related learning goals. These authors also recommended that counseling be provided to these plateaued older workers, including the "opportunity to deal with (a) loss of one's idealized career and personal goals, (b) anger concerning real or perceived negative circumstances or supervisory experiences, and (c) apprehension about the likelihood of future opportunities" (p. 300).

A final group we will mention here as important within the aging population are people contemplating retirement. Older people approach retirement with various feelings: apprehension, threat, eagerness, psychological malaise, surprise, anxiety, depression, or deliberation. Among the factors that seem to be involved in a positive transition to retirement are adequate income, voluntary rather than involuntary retirement, good health, specific plans, staying active, and a history of an orderly rather than a disorderly career (Herr & Cramer, 1996). Ultimately retirement is very much an individual matter that can be facilitated by counseling and by preretirement programs in industry.

Counseling for retirement can include many strategies. Dillard (1982) suggested teaching specific retirement lifestyles. Herr and Cramer (1996) advocated that counseling for preretirement and retirement should include (1) assistance in planning for and obtaining information about health, finances, housing, and other concerns related to daily living; (2) clarification of affective reactions to retirement; and (3) appropriate referrals to community agencies designed to deal with particular aspects of the aging. It is now estimated that about half of all large corporations offer preretirement programs for their older workers that vary across a continuum of narrow to broad content. Across such a continuum, the topics usually covered, starting with the narrow and expanding to the broadest or most comprehensive, include Social Security and Medicare, financial benefits and options, physical and mental health, leisure, legal aspects, employment, housing, community resources, options for employment after retirement, interpersonal relations, and life planning.

TRANSITION POINTS AS RISK FACTORS

The preceding sections of this chapter have dealt with the effects of various chronic or ascribed at-risk factors in populations served by counselors. This is certainly not a complete inventory of the factors that put people at risk. Other at-risk characteristics that have been only lightly mentioned are alcoholism and substance abuse, eating disorders, sexual orientation and preference, and violence in the family. Each of these areas deserves a fuller treatment than is possible here.

The other major perspective on risk factors that will occupy our attention in the remainder of this chapter is the growing literature that addresses the vulnerability of persons at key transition points in life.

Several terms tend to interact when we think of transition points as inducing risk. They include *transition, crisis, life events, stress, developmental,* and *situational.* It is useful to note that there are clear relationships between life events and physical and mental health. Such a concept is central in analyses of stress. In other words, stress is associated with life events or the accumulation of life events, and when stress rises to unhealthy levels or the body runs out of resources or is completely fatigued, physical or mental disease is likely to result. Life events are essentially points of transition that may occur as a part of normal and predictable developmental tasks, or they may be crises precipitated by unexpected and traumatic events. Sometimes transitions turn into crises.

As research on individual growth through the life span has unfolded over the past two decades, it has become apparent that each phase of life has its own developmental tasks that individuals need to master if continuous growth is to ensue without their progress being arrested or fixated at a particular developmental level. Throughout life, earlier themes or processes may be revisited as an individual moves through the transition from one stable period of life to another. Thus in terms of biological and cultural timing, many life events and transitions can be predicted and anticipated. Some examples of major transitions and life events from adolescence forward are listed in Table 6.1.

Obviously, not all of these transitions or life events will occur to one person. But, particularly if their likelihood is unanticipated, such transitions or life events can become crises when they are embedded in considerable turmoil, or when a particular developmental stage is disrupted or made particularly difficult. Such a circumstance can occur when transitions are thwarted by a lack of skills, knowledge, ability to take risks, physical resources, or social resources (Danish & D'Augelli, 1980).

A crisis can also unfold because transitions or life events have occurred too fast and with too much intensity for the individual to cope. This is what Slaikeu (1984) called *demand overload* and what led Holmes and Rahe (1967) to define as a life crisis the accumulation of life events totaling more than 350 Life Change Units a year as measured by their Social Readjustment Scale. As noted in the scale, life events are weighted in terms of their severity of stress. Experiencing an accumulation of 350 or more life change units in a year is likely to result in a life crisis. For example, on the scale, the death of a spouse is rated as 100 points and divorce as 73 points. At the other end of the scale, a vacation is rated as 13 points and minor violations of the law as 11 points. The rapid accumulation of these life changes increases stress and pushes many beyond their resources or ability to cope, thus precipitating a crisis.

Slaikeu (1984) reported that a transition or life event can precipitate a crisis if the timing of it is inconsistent with society's expectations. Not being settled in a career or being married at a particular age, being forced to retire too early, having children late in life, or becoming a grandmother at too young an age can precipitate a crisis because these situations call for changes in self-concept, identity, and use of time that the individual may be unprepared to make or finds unusually difficult to accommodate.

Beyond what might be called normal or predictable transitions or life events, an individual's development can be upset by situational life crises. These can strike virtually anyone at any time and usually are defined by such criteria as sudden onset, unexpectedness, emergency, potential effect on entire communities, danger, and opportunity. The categories of situation crises ordinarily considered are physical illness and injury, unexpected/untimely death, being a crime victim or offender, natural and man-made disasters, war and related acts, and situational crises of modern

Table 6.1 Major Transitions and Life Events

Graduation from high school	Adjusting to changes in children becoming
Going to college	young adults
Finding a first major job	Divorce of a child
Adjusting to a job	Dealing with responsibilities regarding aging
Breaking up with a girlfriend or boyfriend	parents
Breaking engagement to marry	Death or prolonged illness of parents
Selecting and learning to live with a	Setback in career
mate/partner	Financial concerns
Developing parenting skills	Dissatisfaction with goals achieved
Purchase of home	Promotion
Conflict between career goals and family goals	Marital problems
Adjusting to physiological changes of middle	Health problems
age	Empty nest
Change in physical living arrangements	Preparing for retirement
Conflict with grown children	Death of a spouse
Illness or disability	Awareness of loneliness
	Difficulty in adjustment to retirement

Note: From K.A. Slaikeu, *Crisis Intervention: A Handbook for Practice and Research* (Table 3.1, pp. 42–44), 1984, Boston: Allyn & Bacon. Copyright © 1984 by Allyn & Bacon. Reprinted/adapted with permission.

life (e.g., psychedelic drug experiences, economic setbacks, migration/relocation) (Slaikeu, 1984).

Such situational life crises are so intense that they challenge the individual's or family's ability to cope and to adjust. They may make life goals unreachable or even threaten life itself. They may precipitate a state of disorganization characterized by inability to cope and potential for long-lasting damage.

The concern about situational life crises in which violence and other forms of intense trauma are involved have spawned such relatively new terms as *post-traumatic stress disorder* and, as a response, *post-traumatic therapy*. Post-traumatic stress is most typically associated with reactions that occur to victims of violent crimes (including sexual abuse), hostages, combat veterans, prisoners of war, survivors of the Holocaust and their dependents, and refugee survivors of torture and violence. Post-traumatic therapy is a clinical approach that focuses on recent events, the coping skills and strengths of the victim, the realistic options available, and the misconceptions or self-defeating thoughts that interfere with rapid emotional healing (Ochberg, 1988; Widiger et al., 1996). The assessment procedure a counselor uses in crisis intervention needs to be sensitive to the possibility of post-traumatic stress disorder in the client. For example, it is common for the trauma of combat experiences or violent crime to be repressed and to lie dormant for years until reactivated by some other life crisis such as divorce or unemployment. Because of the possible residual feelings of guilt, shame, and low self-esteem and the clients' projections of danger and distrust on their children or spouses, post-traumatic therapy frequently needs to include the victims' immediate family and social group (Slaikeu, 1984). In addition, in the case of Vietnam combat veterans experiencing delayed forms of post-traumatic stress, group counseling with other veterans who have shared and understand the trauma they have mutually experienced may be an important therapeutic modality.

The post-traumatic stress syndrome can take a number of behavioral forms. Extended emotional vulnerability is one. Substance abuse is another. Interpersonal problems, unresolved grief and feelings of defeat, explosive violent behavior, social ostracism, and isolation as well as exceptionally vivid and persistent reexperiencing (flashbacks) of psychological trauma are all likely to be present and must be dealt with as manifestations of the underlying, unresolved stress (Rosenheck, 1985).

As just suggested, people who experience either developmental or situational crises are not pathological or mentally ill. They are people who typically have exceeded their levels of emotional resources or support systems to cope with a particular event or transition. Frequently, they are people who have reached levels of stress that finally produce exhaustion or other maladaptive responses. Using a stress paradigm proposed by Tubesing (1981), it is possible to suggest that all people are exposed to stressors of different types: overwork and fatigue, fear and hate, exposure and injury, hurry and tension, and expectations and pressures. When these stressors occur with too much intensity or in too great a quantity, the body protects itself or tries to maintain stability and balance by initiating the general adaptation syndrome that includes an alarm reaction, resistance or adjustment, and then exhaustion (Selye, 1976). Each initiation of the general adaptation syndrome uses up a portion of the body's adaptive energy, which is limited and cannot always be restored through rest. Continual fighting by the body against stressors can ultimately lead to such exhaustion that it begins to break the body down. As it does so, symptoms of distress may appear in the form of cardiovascular, emotional, gastrointestinal, arthritic, or other diseases. Thus the linkage between life events, stress, and physical or mental health is clear.

Because of the pervasiveness of stress and burnout and their predisposition to put people at risk, counselors are increasingly engaged in stress management and other interventions. One view is that such intervention should be holistic (Sparks, 1981). In this perspective, the appropriate treatment of stress includes attention to physical health, nutrition and exercise, relaxation techniques (e.g., meditation, progressive relaxation), biofeedback, yoga, listening to certain types of music, massage, controlled breathing, rational emotive therapy, cognitive restructuring, psychological education, social support, and action goal setting.

Slaikeu (1984) suggested other coping strategies that counselors might use in either developmental or situation crises. These include in vivo and systematic desensitization, group sharing or writing of experiences and feelings, coping imagery, calming imagery, assertiveness training, behavior rehearsal, thought stopping, rational emotive therapy, deep muscle relaxation, Gestalt empty chair technique, and outside readings.

We have emphasized here the types of transitions that are akin to crises, but transitions are a significant part of every individual's life, even though they may differ in their dramatic or visible characteristics. Schlossberg and her co-authors (e.g., Schlossberg & Robinson, 1996) have written a series of comprehensive treatments of the transition process that have ranged from the scholarly to the popular.

Schlossberg and her various associates have also made clear in their work that there are many terms of significance in transition processes. A major one is *change*. However we consider an individual transition in role relationships, at work, in loss, embedded in the process is change. Sometimes the change is planned, sometimes it is unplanned, sometimes it is represented by a nonevent, sometimes it is chronic. We might contend that planned change is the least troublesome to the individual because he or she is able to anticipate over time the decisions that must be made about, for example, attending college, choosing a particular job, or marrying. Transitions that are characterized by an unplanned change can be more difficult psychologically because spontaneous and involuntary decisions need to be made without the luxury of time to contemplate and weigh alternatives or the familiarity of cues and roles that provide support and security while the individual makes a decision. Such unplanned changes often are perceived by the individual as a loss of control, a function of random events that lie outside the individual and can overwhelm the person with the uniqueness in roles and decisions that shape the individual's life. Nonevents have similar characteristics in their emphasis on hopes unfulfilled. These are the situations in which the person did not receive the promised job, was denied access to an education program on which the individual had counted, the election that was not won, the marriage that did not occur.

Although not all transitions or their content are of this importance, they often carry elements of risk that can be particularly magnified by unplanned events and nonevents. Across the course of her books on transition, Schlossberg and her associates have developed many perspectives that underlie a framework for helping adults in transition. In particular she suggests that counselors must see adults as individuals who relate directly to transitions. To assist with these issues, Schlossberg has developed various paradigms by which to anticipate and conceptualize the transition process. In these perspectives, according to Schlossberg (1984), the transition itself must be examined in terms of its type, context, and impact, with the transition process considered in relation to how the person reacts to it over time. In addition, the individual's coping resources need to be examined to determine if they are assets or liabilities, resources or deficits, either intrapsychically or environmentally. Coping resources—the balance of the individual's assets and liabilities—need to be evaluated in terms of the variables characterizing the transition (e.g., event or nonevent, trigger, timing, source, role changes, duration, concurrent stress), variables characterizing the individual (e.g., personal and demographic characteristics, psychological resources, coping responses), and variables characterizing the environment (e.g., social support, options). (Schlossberg, 1994, p. 108)

In 1991, Schlossberg simplified her model and labeled it Your Steps in Mastering Change. This model was constructed around three major steps and the questions that undergird each step. The three major steps that counselors can use with clients are

1. Approaching Change, which really has to do with what kind of transition this is and how has it affected the client's relationships, roles, routines, assumptions;
2. Taking Stock, which has to do with helping the client assess his or her resources for coping with the transition. As such, the focus in this step is on what Schlossberg has identified as the four Ss: the individual situation, self, supports, and strategies; and
3. Taking Charge, which has to do with helping the individual strengthen coping resources and select appropriate coping strategies, develop an action plan, and increase a sense of the options available and one's control.

Such steps are adaptations of the steps of the decision making with which most counselors are familiar, although in this instance they are couched in the particular vocabulary of the transition process.

Clearly, counselors need to be aware that people in transition are people for whom change is likely to cause stress. Stress, in turn, needs to be viewed holistically and as the focus of counselor proactivity and outreach as stress prevention and management are implemented. In dealing with the issues surrounding developmental transitions and situation crises, counselors must be prepared to take their own medicine, monitor their own stress, and provide opportunities for personal relaxation and support.

CONCLUSIONS

As chapter 6 has discussed, risk factors for adults can be classified in many ways: as social, psychological, economic, or political; in terms of alcohol or substance abuse and their attendant codependencies; or in terms of such group characteristics as age, disability, sex, or minority group membership. Many forms of at-risk behavior in adults actually have their roots in the early life of the individual, and barring early identification and successful intervention, manifest themselves in late adolescent and in adulthood.

Many of the risk factors that place people in special populations or categories are dynamic, not fixed. On one hand, people who have never been at risk may be thrown into that category at certain points of crisis or transition in their lives; on the other hand, people who have been at risk on a long-term basis may, because of changes in social or political circumstances, no longer be considered to be at risk. What is apparent in either case, however, is that although people may evidence certain personal predisposing factors that make them more vulnerable to stress and other factors, being at risk is largely triggered by outside events. With rare exceptions, people at risk are not psychopathological. Rather they lack adequate psychological resources or support systems to cope effectively with the risk factors (social/historical/bias/transition/stress) with which they are confronted.

Chapter 6 has described a range of counselor responses that have been found to be effective or that have been recommended as appropriate for different types of at-risk problems. These responses range from primary prevention to intense clinical intervention, from advocacy and environmental redesign to psychoeducational models of skill development. Chapter 7 will elaborate on the assumptions and uses of many of these counseling techniques and describe others that are useful with people at risk and others not so classified.

Chapter 7

CHANGING CONCEPTS, PROCESSES, AND PRACTICES OF COUNSELING

THE PRECEDING CHAPTERS HAVE EXAMINED SEVERAL major environmental and ecological processes likely to shape the types of problems that clients will bring to counselors in the foreseeable future. Economic and occupational changes, shifting family structures, cultural diversity, and risk factors make people captive to the attitudes and knowledge associated with their place in externally defined social, political, cultural, or economic environments. The influence of these environments is ingrained in individual self-concepts, in feelings of self-efficacy, in behavior.

Against such a context, counseling and related therapeutic activities can be viewed as mechanisms that free people from the captivity of negative attitudes, obsessions, irrational beliefs, information deficits, and low self-esteem. In such a view, counseling and related interventions represent both release and purpose: opportunities to shed the shackles of self-imposed or environmentally imposed limits on self-worth, dignity, or ambition as well as processes by which to translate renewed feelings of confidence and competence into plans of action, risk taking, and growth.

There have been many analyses of the role of the counselor in contemporary society. In one analysis (Bellah et al., 1985), for example, the counselor is seen as a secular priest, one who has replaced the clergy and the church, and who assists people to pursue an elusive personal meaning as well as to find personal support. In other instances the counselor is portrayed as a kind of psychic mechanic who diagnoses and repairs trouble spots in individual behavioral systems. In still other perspectives, the counselor is viewed as a broker of information and as a confronter of self-imposed and inaccurate attributions about self and others. This focus is intended to help free people from restricting attitudes and belief systems. It connotes counselor proactivity and outreach through facilitating transactions between the individual and his or her environment, and through helping the client learn new skills, acquire

229

more accurate self-understanding, and feel less socially isolated. In this view the counselor is a sort of switching mechanism between the individual and the environment, an enabler of personal initiative and control, a maximizer of opportunity.

Any metaphor that can be conceived to describe the counselor's role in society rests upon and shapes conceptual models of counseling, the appropriateness of specific interventions and ethics, and the application of such processes within a possible range of populations and settings. Over the past century, the application of counseling to individual problems has continued to broaden and to be applied to a more comprehensive range of human problems in a more comprehensive range of institutions and settings. Counselors are increasingly taking their places as important elements of the mental health system of the United States. Their competencies are being acknowledged in state licensure and in federal legislation, and they are working closely with other mental health practitioners in the delivery of mental health services across the continuum of mental illness, problems of living, the promotion of wellness, and enhanced quality of life.

As we consider the changes in counseling over the past half century, it becomes evident that counseling is seen as important for virtually all people at some time or at several times during their lifetimes, not just for a small percentage of the population. The target populations for counseling are not only the severely emotionally distressed, on the one hand, or those choosing or adjusting to work, on the other; but the target populations also increasingly encompass those with individual needs for assistance at times of crisis, major life transitions, or periods of unusual stress or frustration.

In such contexts, counseling has become both a process that has worldwide utility and a process that is increasingly important in schools, community agencies, universities, workplaces, and independent practice. It has utility for children, youth, and adults. Those dealing with major life events, dislocated and underemployed workers, new immigrants and the culturally different, disintegrating and blended families, single parents, the terminally ill and their families, aging and senior citizens, those contemplating retirement, those considering reentering the workforce, those who have been abused or are codependents, those attempting to cope with major changes and life transitions, and those concerned with life enhancement and reduction of risk factors are the major but not the only populations for whom counselors will be increasingly important agents of support, change, education, growth, and development in the future. As the involvement of counselors with such broad population groups across the life span becomes more visible, counselors and counseling are likely to be more often seen by policymakers as being of central importance to achieving national goals of productivity, purposefulness, health, and happiness.

A major but largely unspoken issue in the national social rhetoric is that there are far fewer counselors available than there are persons who need their services. Estimates vary, but it is possible that not more than 10% of the children, youth, and adults for whom counseling would be helpful actually have access to or initiate contact with a counselor. The number of counselors available is not likely to increase dramatically in the foreseeable future in part due to economic issues and limited training capacity. Therefore, it becomes vital that current counselors and those in training become equipped with the most effective and efficient models of counseling concepts, processes, and practices now available in the profession.

In relation to these contextual elements in which counseling is embedded, this chapter discusses the changing conceptual paradigms that undergird counseling practice; the use of technology in counseling; the ethics of counseling; and emerging trends in counseling interventions.

CHANGING PARADIGMS FOR PRACTICE

As the application of counseling becomes more and more comprehensive in the settings where it is available and in the populations served, views are shifting with regard to how counseling should be conceptualized and practiced. Terms that might be used to summarize and describe such paradigm shifts, include *cognitive, constructivist, brief, planned, interdisciplinary, eclectic, educative, preventive*, and *technological*. In the following sections some of these concepts are examined.

The Cognitive Sciences in Counseling

Probably the major advance in counseling and psychology during the 1970s and 1980s was the concern of researchers and practitioners about cognitive phenomena—about what the person is thinking as well as what he or she is feeling and doing. This conceptual foundation for counseling continues to be of major importance in the 1990s and, in all likelihood, into the 21st century.

Tyler (1983) suggested that cognitive theories of behavior are replacing the dominance of such theories as associationism and behaviorism. In her view, cognitive theories can be sharply distinguished from the latter theories because

> first of all, they assume an active process of some sort, occurring in sequential phases, rather than the automatic linking of contiguous ideas or stimuli. Second, they postulate mental structures of some sort that impose form on input and control output. Third, they merge lines of research that have traditionally been separate, perception, memory, learning of skills, problem solving, and various others, incorporating the findings of experiments in these separate fields in their more inclusive formulations . . . the distinction between cognition and motivation is becoming blurred. Finally, many theorists are emphasizing the interdisciplinary aspects of the new cognitive science. (pp. 77–78)

The research underlying cognitive science takes many forms. Posner and Shulman (1979) suggested four major topics: (1) Representation—How does the mind represent either concrete or abstract concepts? (2) Laws or rules of thought—How do people process information? Do they follow rules of logic or psychology? (3) Products of the thought processes that emerge during problem solving—How do people make decisions? What are the elements of differences in decision-making styles? How do choice outcomes differ? (4) Individual differences in cognitive abilities—What differences in cognitive processes account for the differences revealed by intelligence tests and other assessments of cognitions?

The importance of cognitive science to counseling lies with the growing attention to how individuals process information within the framework of how they construct reality. All people develop symbolic maps or representations of what they perceive to be reality and, indeed, their personal identity or place within this reality. These representations are systems of meaning, attitudes, or belief systems by which an individual interprets and acts upon events and the perceptual cues or information that attends them. In such a view, what is meant by phenomenological or perceptual fields is the construction an individual gives to his or her experiences. Such constructions evolve over time and assimilate the mirroring of meaning that comes from parents, peers, and others.

Beck (1985) contended that a major commonality among systems of psychotherapy

> is the mechanism by which the specific therapy produces therapeutic results. There is considerable evidence accumulating that each of the effective therapies has an impact on cognitive processes. When measures of these cognitive processes show a shift from negative to positive, they are accompanied by a general improvement in depression and anxiety (p. 333).

Thus a cognitive approach assumes that the individual's primary problem has to do with his or her construction of reality—faulty assumptions, irrational beliefs, or misconceptions. The task of the counselor is to help the individual modify the inaccurate or maladaptive cognitions he or she holds about self, others, and life events.

As Beck suggested, most theories of psychotherapy are devoted to influencing the cognitive structures that trigger or sustain behavior. In this sense, it is difficult to find a clear beginning for cognitive behavioral approaches to counseling.

Beck and Rush (1988) indicated that in historical terms, cognitive therapy shows the confluence of three main sources of theoretical underpinnings: (1) the phenomenological approach to psychology, (2) structural theory and depth psychology, and (3) cognitive psychology.

> The phenomenological approach to psychology emphasizes the view of the self and the personal world as central to the determination of behavior. This concept was originally formulated in Greek stoic philosophy and in most recent times was evident in the writings of Adler (1936), Alexander (1950), Horney (1950), and Sullivan (1953). The structural theory and depth psychology of Kant and Freud, particularly Freud's concept of the hierarchical structuring of cognition into primary and secondary processes, was the second major influence. The third sphere of influence stems from developments in contemporary cognitive psychology. George Kelly (1955) is generally recognized as being the first to describe the personality in terms of personal constructs and to define the role of beliefs in behavior change. The cognitive theories of emotion of Magda Arnold (1960) and Richard Lazarus (1984), which assigned primary importance to cognition in emotional and behavioral change, also contributed to the theoretical structure of cognitive therapy. (p. 533)

Each of these methods and the theorists who proposed them helped to shape conceptions of how individuals formulate perceptions of reality and how these are ultimately misconstrued or require modification if the person is to develop a changed personal identity and restructure the attitude toward reality through which the world can be seen and dealt with in a different manner (Guidano & Lotti, 1985).

In describing the commonalities in the processes used by cognitive therapists, Hoffman (1984) contended that

> cognitive approaches . . . are included under directive therapy. The directive therapist endeavors to structure the situation as strongly as possible. His (her) function consists mainly in directly influencing the client's symptoms in order to effect necessary changes.
>
> In this sense, the manner of proceeding used by cognitive therapists is very similar to that employed by behavioral therapists. Both conduct a series of diagnostic interviews to obtain detailed description of the client's current difficulties. Subsequently, a synthesis of the problems is made, formulated in the therapist's respective theoretical language, which provides the client with an explanation for the emergence of his difficulties. The

therapist, in order to eliminate the target symptoms, gives precise instructions about the procedures during the sessions and for the time between. On the basis of the therapist's personal and professional authority, the patient commits himself [or herself] to adherence to these instructions.

In this sense, cognitive therapy, like behavior therapy, is to be understood as a technology which builds upon the findings of basic research concerning the part played by cognitive factors in the regulation of behavior, both in general and in the origin and maintenance of specific disorders, and which develops strategies of intervention whose effectiveness must be established through follow-up investigations. (p. 7)

The most typical contemporary attributions of the beginning of cognitive behavioral therapy tend to be the work of Ellis and the work of Beck. Ellis's work began in the 1950s (Ellis, 1958, 1962) and evolved from notions of rational psychotherapy into the system known as Rational-Emotive-Therapy (RET) and then, in 1993, as Rational-Emotive-Behavioral-Therapy (REBT) (Weinrach, 1996). Beck's work began in the 1960s as cognitive therapy.

In Ellis's view of RET, people's emotional disturbances are the main concern; that is, how they largely create their own normal or healthy (positive and negative) feelings, and how they can change them if they wish to work at doing so (Ellis, 1985). The theoretical perspectives on changing feelings are defined by the ABCs: A stands for activating events or experiences, activities "or agents that people disturb themselves about" (Ellis, 1985, p. 313). B stands for rational or realistic beliefs or irrational beliefs about the activating events that then lead to C, appropriate consequences, or IC, inappropriate consequences. More recently, Ds and Es have been added to the theory. D means disputing irrational beliefs, that is, detecting them, discriminating them from rational beliefs, and debating them. E stands for effective rational beliefs to replace irrational beliefs, effective appropriate emotion, and effective functional behaviors to replace disturbed emotions and dysfunctional behaviors.

"According to RET theory, people have almost innumerable beliefs (Bs)—or cognitions, thoughts, or ideas—about their activating events (As) and these Bs importantly and directly tend to exert strong influences on their cognitive, emotional, and behavioral consequences (Cs)" (Ellis, 1985, p. 315). Also according to RET theory, irrational beliefs (IBs) are those cognitions, ideas, and philosophies that sabotage and block individuals' fulfilling their basic or most important goals. These can be learned from parents, teachers, and others.

From the beginning of his approach, Ellis emphasized confronting and eliminating irrational beliefs and providing an educational approach to client needs (e.g., teaching clients self-help skills to apply in solving their own problems).

Ellis made many important contributions to the conceptualization of cognitive therapy, including the specification of basic irrational ideas many people accept as valid assumptions and to which their behavior is oriented to preserving or manifesting. According to Ellis (1962), such major irrational ideas include the following:

- You must—yes, must—have sincere love and approval almost all the time from all the people you find significant.
- You must prove yourself thoroughly competent, adequate, and achieving, or you must at least have real competence or talent at something important.
- You have to view life as awful, terrible, horrible, or catastrophic when things do not go the way you would like them to go.

- People who harm you or commit misdeeds rate as generally bad, wicked, or villainous, and you should severely blame, damn, and punish them for their sins.
- If something seems dangerous or fearsome, you must become terribly occupied with and upset about it and make yourself anxious about it.
- People and things should turn out better than they do, and you have to view it as awful and horrible if you do not quickly find good solutions to life's hassles.
- Emotional misery comes from external pressures, and you have little ability to control your feelings or rid yourself of depression and hostility.
- You will find it easier to avoid facing many of life's difficulties and responsibilities than to undertake more rewarding forms of self-discipline.
- Your past remains all important, and because something once strongly influenced your life, it has to keep determining your feelings and behavior today.
- You can achieve happiness by inertia and inaction or by passively and uncommittedly "enjoying yourself."
- You have to view things as awful, terrible, horrible, and catastrophic when you are seriously frustrated, treated unfairly, or rejected.
- You must have a high degree of order or certainty to feel comfortable, or you need some supernatural power on which to rely.
- You can give yourself a global rating as a human, and your general worth and self-acceptance depend upon the goodness of your performance and the degree to which people approve of you.

Weinrach (1996), in quoting the analysis of RET by Walen, DiGuiseppe, and Dryden (1992), suggested that there are six principles of RET theory:

(1) "Cognition is the most important proximal determinant of human emotion" (Walen et al., 1992, p. 15). This means that humans feel what they think. (2) "Dysfunctional thinking is a major determinant of emotional distress" (Walen et al., 1992, p. 16). Much of psychopathology is a result of dysfunctional thought processes (i.e., subscribing to irrational beliefs). (3) If emotional disturbance is largely caused by holding irrational beliefs, "the best way to conquer distress is to change this thinking" (Walen et al., 1992, p. 16). RET does this through cognitive, emotive, and behavioral interventions. (4) "Multiple factors," including both genetic and environmental influences, "are etiologic antecedents to irrational thinking and psychopathology" (Walen et al., 1992, p. 16). (5) RET "emphasizes present" rather than "historical influences on behavior" in large part because humans maintain their disturbance through repeated self-indoctrination (Walen et al., 1992, p. 16). Finally, (6) "beliefs can be changed, although such changes will not necessarily come about easily" (Walen et al., 1992, p. 16). Clients do not surrender their deeply held irrational beliefs without some resistance. (Weinrach, 1996, p. 326)

Weinrach also indicated that

what differentiates RET from other cognitive approaches such as those of Aaron T. Beck, David Burns, and Donald Meichenbaum is Ellis's emphasis on a particular kind of cognition known as evaluative beliefs. . . . In order for a client to be upset, he or she must first evaluate his or her beliefs about an event or thought and conclude that it is terrible or awful as compared to inconvenient or unpleasant. (1996, p. 326)

Other therapists have integrated the work of Ellis within other conceptions of cognitive science. An excellent example is the work of Krumboltz (1983). As a major theorist in his own right, Krumboltz has been instrumental in advancing and refining a social learning theory of career decision making (Krumboltz, Mitchell, & Gelatt, 1975; Mitchell & Krumboltz, 1984). Social learning theory, as an outgrowth of the general social learning theory of behavior proposed by Bandura, Adams, and Meyer (1977), assumes

> . . .that the individual personalities and behavioral repertoires that persons possess arise primarily from their unique learning experiences rather than from innate developmental or psychic processes. These learning experiences consist of contact with and cognitive analysis of positively and negatively reinforcing events. . . . Social learning theory recognizes that humans are intelligent, problem-solving individuals who strive at all times to understand the reinforcement that surrounds them and who in turn control their environment to suit their own purposes and needs. (Mitchell & Krumboltz, 1984, pp. 235–236)

Krumboltz and his associates described the categories of influences on career selection and the types of outcomes that would be predicted by social learning theory. The four categories of influences are

1. **genetic endowment and special abilities:** These include race, sex, physical appearance and characteristics, intelligence, musical ability, artistic ability, muscular coordination.
2. **environmental conditions and events:** These include number and nature of job and training opportunities, social policies, physical events, family characteristics, community and neighborhood emphases.
3. **learning experiences:** There are two major types of such experiences. *Instrumental learning experiences* (ILEs) are those in which antecedents, overt and covert behavioral responses, and consequences are present. Career planning skills and those of other educational and occupational performance tend to be learned through instrumental learning experiences. *Associative learning experiences* (ALEs) are those in which the learner pairs a previously neutral situation with some emotionally positive or negative reaction; examples are observational learning and classical conditioning.
4. **task approach skills:** These include such processes as problem-solving skills, work habits, mental set, emotional responses, and cognitive approaches.

The combined influences of genetic endowment and special abilities, environmental conditions and events, and instrumental and associative learning experiences lead to several types of outcomes. They include

- **self-observation generalizations (SOGs):** These are composed of overt or covert statements evaluating an individual's actual or vicarious performance in relation to some set of learned standards.
- **task approach skills (TASs):** These include cognitive and performance abilities and emotional predispositions for coping with the environment, interpreting it in relation to self-observation generalizations, and making covert or overt predictions about future events. Task approach skills of relevance to career planning, for example, might include such skills as value clarifying, goal setting, alternative generation, information seeking, estimating, planning, and related processes.
- **actions:** These include behaviors that reflect overt steps in a career progression, including such possibilities as applying for a specific job or training opportunity and changing a college major.

Krumboltz linked and explained individual-environmental transactions through the medium of learning, and particularly learning that is socially mediated by families, peers, or community representatives. It is within the context of social learning through modeling, reinforcement systems, information availability, and content that Krumboltz's theoretical views intersect with those of Ellis. Krumboltz (1983), for example, suggested that each person conceives a system of private rules that guide his or her decision making. These private rules are affected by the social learning influences previously described, and particularly by the self-observation generalizations and task approach skills that result. Within such outcomes, self-observation generalizations and perceptions of environmental conditions can be affected by irrational beliefs as they are described by Ellis. In Krumboltz's view, the irrational beliefs that can affect career decision making, and by extrapolation other problem solving, are those involving faulty generalizations, self-comparison with a single standard, exaggerated estimates of the emotional effect of an outcome, false causal relationships, ignorance of relevant facts, undue weight given to unlikely events, and self-deception.

Krumboltz contended that the content, character, and preservation of private rules of decision making and the irrational beliefs that sometimes infuse such rule-making systems relate to the reality that decision making is painful and can be associated with different types of stress: threats to self-esteem, surprise, deadlines, and absence of time. When such stresses are present, they are likely to lead to or be accompanied by impaired attention, increased cognitive rigidity, narrowed perspectives, and displaced blame.

The counseling techniques that Krumboltz proposed in his various books as effective in dealing with irrational beliefs, stresses, and inaccurate self-observation generalizations range across a wide array of options. Of importance are examining assumptions and presuppositions that underlie the expressed beliefs; looking for inconsistencies between words and behavior; testing simplistic answers for inadequacies; confronting attempts to maintain an illogical consistency; identifying barriers to stated goals; challenging the validity of key beliefs; building a feeling of trust and cooperation; thought listing; in vivo self-monitoring; imagery; career decision-making simulations; reconstruction of prior events; use of psychometric instruments; cognitive restructuring techniques to alter dysfunctional or inaccurate beliefs and generalizations; use of positive reinforcement and appropriate role models; use of films depicting problem-solving strategies; teaching belief-testing and self-monitoring processes; analyzing task approach skills and teaching those in deficit; study materials; cognitive rehearsal; narrative analyses; exploration bibliotherapy; and using computerized guidance systems to provide and reinforce problem-solving tasks and skills (Krumboltz, 1983, 1996; Mitchell & Krumboltz, 1984).

Beck, like Ellis, is considered by many to be one of the original founders of cognitive approaches to therapy. In Beck's view, a phenomenon like depression can be understood by integrating biochemical, psychological, behavioral, psychoanalytic, and cognitive perspectives. But from a cognitive perspective, Beck contended that depression arises from a cognitive blockage that interferes with the reception or integration of positive data (Beck, 1985). According to Beck, studies have shown that clinically depressed patients have impaired recall of favorable feedback, pleasant events, self-referent positive adjectives, or pleasant schemes in stories. They may selectively block out positive aspects of experience and attach much higher probabilities to mishaps occurring than do "normal" people. In cognitive therapy, Beck's approach emphasized providing a series of selected positive experiences and instructing a patient to write down experiences relevant to pleasure and mastery and to repeat them during the therapy sessions. In cognitive therapy, it is assumed that negative cognitive reactions occur in automatic and maladaptive ways. Thus this automatic thought sequence must be interrupted through coaching, reality testing, disproving the irrational conception, providing a series of selected positive experiences, and interjecting a more realistic perspective into the client's thinking.

Beck (1985) also interpreted depression in terms of a "cognitive future triad," the activation of three major cognitive patterns that induce the patient to see him- or herself and the future in an idiographic, negative manner:

> [The] first component of the cognitive triad concerns the patient's negative view of himself [or herself]. He [or she] sees himself [or herself] as deficient, inadequate, or unworthy, and he [or she] tends to attribute his [or her] unpleasant experiences to his [or her] physical, mental, or moral defects. . . . He [or she] regards himself [or herself] as lacking in those attributes that he [or she] considers essential for the attainment of happiness or contentment. . . .The second component of the triad is the patient's distorted interpretation of experience. He [or she] consistently construes experience in a negative way. He [or she] interprets his [or her] interactions with the environment as representing defeat, deprivation, or loss. . . . The third component of the triad consists of viewing the future in a negative way. The depressed patient anticipates that his [or her] current troubles will continue indefinitely. As he [or she] looks ahead, he [or she] sees a life of unremitting hardship, deprivation, and frustration. (pp. 156–157)

Beck's model assumed that the concepts that predispose people to depression originate early in life and derive from personal experiences, identification with significant others, and perceptions of the attitudes of others toward them. In Beck's view, cognitive therapy is technically eclectic and uses the entire range of current psychotherapeutic strategies from role-playing to marriage counseling and relaxation training. Other techniques include induced fantasy, labeling and relabeling, redefining goals, anxiety management training, reattribution, confrontation, homework, and graded positive experiences. The point at issue, however, is that each technique is chosen as a means of expanding the depressed person's perceived range of options and altering negative views of self, the world, and the future (Beck & Greenberg, 1984).

Burns (1980), a colleague and student of Beck's, translated much of Beck's work into a book directed to the lay public for self-monitoring and self-help. In it, many of Beck's premises are accented. A major concept that underlies this view of cognitive therapy is that whether the individual talks about anger, anxiety, depression, or other emotions, the individual creates these emotions by the meanings given to specific events. Thus the emotions that result in any situation are a function of the individual's thoughts or cognitions. Feelings or emotions result from the cognitions, labels, and meanings assigned to the event, not the other way around. Thus cognitive therapy is focused on helping individuals change the way they interpret or look at events to make them feel better and act more purposefully and productively.

To put Beck's approach in its simplest form, Burns (1980) presented Beck's thesis as follows:

> (1) When you are depressed or anxious, you are *thinking* in an illogical, negative manner, and you inadvertently act in a self-defeating way. (2) With a little effort you can train yourself to straighten your twisted thought patterns. (3) As your painful symptoms

are eliminated you will become productive and happy again, and you will respect yourself. (4) These aims can usually be accomplished in a relatively brief period of time, using straightforward methods. (pp. 3–4)

The therapeutic regimen in cognitive therapy rests, in a first dimension, on helping clients understand the foundation of their moods, anxieties, or depression and the direct linkage between their thoughts and their feelings; and teaching them how to interpret the automatic thoughts they tend to accept about themselves and their beliefs about how others feel about them. A second dimension is helping clients to understand and label the 10 areas of cognitive distortions that underlie their automatic thoughts and negative feelings. These 10 distortions are similar to but not the same as the irrational beliefs identified by Ellis. They include, for example, all-or-nothing thinking, overgeneralization, jumping to conclusions, and "should" statements. Once clients identify and understand these distortions, they are provided homework as well as techniques by which to interrupt and rebut negative feelings. Depending upon clients' needs, the counselor or therapist helps them to build self-esteem and eliminate feelings of worthlessness. In doing so, it is often necessary to help the client overcome the all-or-nothing perspective and overgeneralization of a problem and reduce it to a more manageable size and perspective. Doing so frequently involves the therapist and client in defining the real problem, breaking it down into its specific parts, and then applying appropriate solutions.

Other Cognitive Behavioral Approaches

Although it contains basic components of cognitive therapy, the work of Ellis and Beck does not capture the whole of the emerging cognitive behavioral treatments of anxiety, depression, anger, divorce, work adjustment, panic disorders, suicidal ideation, or similar mental health problems. Five other approaches include systematic desensitization (Wolpe, 1973), anxiety management training (Suinn, 1976), systematic rational restructuring (Goldfried, Decenteco, & Weinberg, 1974), stress inoculation training (Meichenbaum, 1985), and anger management (Novaco, 1976). Deffenbacher (1988) analyzed the basic premises of the first four of these approaches. In abridged form they can be discussed as follows using as a constant their treatment of anxiety.

- **Systematic desensitization** (Wolpe, 1973) incorporates the principle of reciprocal inhibition by arranging learning conditions in such a way as to pair a response that reduces (reciprocally inhibits) anxiety (usually relaxation) with an anxiety-arousing stimulus. Using a hierarchy of the low to high anxiety-arousing stimuli for the particular individual, the client is taught progressive relaxation techniques to counteract each level of anxiety until he or she is able to be exposed to the anxiety-producing stimulus either in imagination or in reality and still maintain a relaxed or comfortable approach to it. The types of anxieties that might be at issue here are test anxiety, math anxiety, or communication or social skill anxieties.
- **Anxiety management training** (Suinn, 1976) also uses relaxation and anxiety imagery but in a different format than in systematic desensitization. Anxiety management training helps the client to become aware of his or her internal cognitive, emotional, and physiological cues of anxiety arousal and to use these to initiate relaxation coping skills. The focus of this technique then is to train clients in pro-

gressive relaxation techniques on the one hand, and, on the other hand, how to recognize and respond to internal anxiety cues.

- **Systematic rational restructuring** (Goldfried et al., 1974) does not necessarily use relaxation techniques but rather focuses on the effects of cognitive processes, particularly irrational beliefs, in the creation of and continuation of anxiety relative to a particular type of performance such as speech anxiety. In this process clients learn about their dysfunctional cognitive beliefs, and they obtain help in applying methods of countering such cognitions and thereby reducing anxiety. Frequently clients try to counter irrational beliefs while anxiety-producing stimuli are visualized in some form of an anxiety hierarchy. The cognitive skills acquired are transferred to the anxiety situations encountered in the daily life of the client through homework.

- **Stress inoculation training** (Meichenbaum, 1985) is an active process involving both cognitive and relaxation coping skills. In this approach the client is also taught relaxation coping skills in relation to an anxiety-producing hierarchy in the area about which he or she is concerned such as math, test, or speech anxiety. Beyond the relaxation coping skill training, however, the client is taught cognitive coping skills related to restructuring of dysfunctional or irrational cognitions, task-oriented self-instruction, and self-reward and self-efficacy responses. The client rehearses the cognitive coping skills in role-plays, simulations, or imagery of circumstances in which the client will have to perform. Reinforcement and transfer of the skills to daily living is accomplished through homework assignments.

The applications of cognitive-behavioral therapy are not confined to individual counseling or therapy. Sank and Shaffer (1984) described the use of cognitive behavior therapy in groups. This program also includes a psychoeducational model by which the group participants are trained in coping skills. Although such models are discussed more fully later in this chapter, suffice it to say here that the categories or modules of skills used in this group program include relaxation, cognitive restructuring, assertion training, and problem solving. These four coping skills modules are seen as being pertinent, in selective terms, to group members or others experiencing depression, angry outbursts, job stress, headaches, and related problems.

Within the group process, other techniques have been used with the coping skills training. One of these is bibliotherapy, the reading of selected books that translate coping skills into self-monitoring and easily understandable formats.

Constructivism

Embedded in cognitive approaches to counseling is a concern about how individuals think about and label events, how they process information, how they learn to perceive cues around them, how they construct their belief systems in rational or irrational terms. In short, cognitive approaches, although they rarely use the precise terminology, are concerned about how individuals create meaning for themselves. In this sense, people are perceived as activists in constructing their own reality by the decisions they make and by those they avoid making.

This emphasis on individuals as *meaning makers* is central to constructivist approaches that are being rapidly incorporated into counseling, psychotherapy, and career interventions. Although there is not one definition of constructivism, in general this view suggests that human beings are not simply passive recipients of information, nor simply persons who share or receive one true reality that is external to them and capable of objective, quantitative analysis. In contrast to such a view, people are creators of a self or of personal constructs through organized patterns of meaning within a world of multiple realities. As proposed by Sexton (1997), constructivism places emphasis on a person's active creation and building of meaning and significance; constructivists view knowledge as an invented and constructed meaning system rather than a freestanding, stable, external entity (p. 11). Peavy, a Canadian psychologist, in discussing constructivism has contended that

> Language in its function as communication, especially metaphor, narrative, and conversation, is the means which humans use to construct realities and is central to the constructivist perspectives. It is because we all live out narratives in our lives and because we understand our own lives in terms of the narratives that we live out, that the form of the narrative is appropriate for understanding the actions of others. (Peavy, 1994, p. 32)

As we will discuss later in this chapter when we discuss new trends in career counseling, many authors have begun to incorporate into their counseling approach the use of client narratives and narrative analysis to identify themes in a client's life and to help them sharpen, reconstruct, and alter or rescript these narrative themes as they come to terms with the sense of meaning they seek in their lives (Cochran, 1997; Jepsen, 1996; Savickas, 1993).

Particular emphases in the constructivist approach can be seen in Peavy's (1994) application of this approach to career counseling. He drew implications (pp. 33–34) from his view of constructivist perspectives that include

- reducing the conceptual gap between career and life;
- placing meaning at the center of our conceptual space—meaning and personal constructs drive behavior (or "action" as we prefer to say), meaning making and construing replace, at least in part, emphasis on information processing and behavior change;
- construing persons as self-organizing authors of their own lives—always within historical and cultural contexts; and
- taking the epistemological stance that human realities, both personal and social are "negotiated"—that is, constructed and reconstructed. From our perspective, counseling and inquiry are both processes of reconstruction and closely resemble each other. The counselor is also a researcher inquiring into the meaning structures of the other's life world.

Peavy's observations about the implications of constructivist theory for career counseling certainly go beyond career intervention to the heart of psychotherapy and counseling more generally conceived. It is clear that many psychotherapists and many counselors are trying to modify their approaches to incorporate the belief systems about individual behavior, relatedness, and agency that evolve as our own cultural paradigms have moved from romanticism to modernism (with its emphasis on rationality, control, and individualism) to postmodernism (with its notions of multiple truths, relativism, and relationality). In the latter view, which undergirds much of constructivist theory, the emphasis in counseling is less on fixing and controlling things and much more on helping the individual to deal with and examine efforts to make meaning a central tenet of his or her lived experience. A modernist view, that which essentially has given birth to many contemporary approaches to counseling and to psychotherapy, has tended to "the unfortunate result of locating problems within the individual, a view that leads people who experience problems to conceive of themselves as having personal deficits rather than difficult interactional situations" (Kuehlwein, 1996). In one sense, we can argue that this book is about the latter rather than the former, even though it has not primarily done so systematically from a constructivist position.

Several things about emerging constructivist approaches are important to note. One is that many of the perspectives and many of the interventions inherent in cognitive behavioral approaches interact with constructivist approaches, although with different labels and language systems. As Kuehlwein has observed, there are strong constructivist threads running through the cognitive theories of Aaron Beck and others. It is within such a context that Neimeyer (1996) made the observation that

> it is worth emphasizing that constructivism is not a separate school of therapy, distinguishable from other schools, but a particular mind-set for approaching the work of therapy, whatever the therapist's theoretical orientation. Indeed, there are vigorous expressions of constructivism in clinical traditions ranging from the psychodynamic . . . and the humanistic . . . to the family systemic . . . and cognitive behavioral. . . . (p. 407)

Neimeyer, in both building bridges across approaches to counseling and psychotherapy through the perspectives on constructivism and attempting to clarify unique contributions of constructivism as a language-related and conversational-oriented system, has created a tentative taxonomy of process intervention in constructivist psychotherapy. His taxonomy included such verbal action-oriented intervention as empathizing, analogizing, accentuating, nuancing, dilating, constricting, contrasting, structuring, ambiguating, and weaving (p. 385). He believed that trying to specify such interventions can make constructivism more concrete and can lead to research that helps to consider the specific relevance of these practices to particular patterns of client construing in the service of restructuring and clarifying the personal realities of the client.

PSYCHOEDUCATIONAL MODELS AND PREVENTION

Another major trend in the present and the foreseeable future is the use of psychoeducational models and prevention. Although psychoeducational models and prevention of mental health problems are not precisely the same, they frequently overlap in form and substance if not always in purpose.

Models

Psychoeducational models are frequently linked to cognitive-behavioral or behavioral therapies, but that relationship is not absolute. Psychoeducational models tend to combine educational procedures, such as planned or structured curricula, didactic teaching, and specific content, exercises, and homework, with a range of psychological techniques, such as simulations, role-playing, behavioral rehearsal, modeling, feedback, and reinforcement. Basically psychoeducational models teach clients coping skills pertinent to dealing with current and future problems. Counselors in educational institutions, community agencies, business and industry, and independent practice are likely to use psychoeducational models either for treatment or for prevention of problems. Programs as diverse as career education, deliberate psychological education, stress management, decision-making training, anxiety or anger management, job-search strategies, parent effectiveness training, assertive training, social skills development, and communication skills each incorporate psychoeducational models and skills. In some instances they do so to provide clients skills that their problems in living affirm they need if they are to correct effectively some skill deficit implicated in their behavioral difficulties. For example, clients who have problems with anger may simply not have a behavioral repertoire from which to select behaviors likely to be more socially acceptable or interpersonally sound. Therefore, they are likely to use physical violence or intense verbal aggression that leads to education, job, or social maladjustment. The solution to this problem may be coping skills training by which clients can better understand what precipitates their anger and how they can exert more self-control in dealing with anger-producing situations, and learn communications, positive assertiveness, or other skills that allow them to express anger in a constructive fashion. In contrast, coping skills training or psychoeducational models may be used to prepare students or clients to anticipate certain types of problems and help them acquire needed skills when they face such problems, thereby reducing the surprise, novelty, or other stress-inducing emotions when a problem of a particular type occurs.

Some researchers have advocated structured learning approaches to teaching prosocial skills. For example, Goldstein, Sprafkin, Gershaw, and Klein (1980) argued that the research on adolescents indicates that three categories of behavior problems can account for most adolescent behavior disorders. These three categories are aggression, withdrawal, and immaturity. From a psychoeducational view, however, the important point is that each of these sets of problems can be related to some set of skill deficits. More conceptually, "Each type may be described in terms of both the presence of a repertoire of dysfunctional and often antisocial behavior and of the absence of a repertoire of prosocial or developmentally appropriate behaviors" (Goldstein et al., 1980, p. 5). Thus one approach is to diagnose the dysfunctional behaviors and try to remove them; another is to teach the desirable, functional skills under the assumption that the absence of such prosocial skills leads to dysfunctional behaviors, and that the presence of desirable skills will allow the individual to be more discriminating and able to choose from a range of skills appropriate to a certain type of occasion.

In describing the developmental tasks adolescents must face, Goldstein et al. (1980) suggested that love, sex, peer relationships, and school-related tasks are likely to require social skills, skills for dealing with feelings, skills for dealing with stress, planning skills, and related skill clusters. Each of these skill categories can be taught in a systematic, structured fashion. In addition, each of these skill categories is likely to be composed of a number of subskills that need to be acquired. For example, beginning social skills taught to a withdrawn or immature adolescent might include listening, starting a conversation, engaging in a conversation, asking a question, saying thank you, introducing him- or herself, introducing other people, and giving a compliment.

Psychoeducational models include different emphases, but they typically involve teaching of skills, homework and practice, and the use of audiovisual materials, simulations, or similar approaches.

> Thus, in the typical psychoeducational training session, skill-deficient trainees are shown examples of competent skill behavior, given opportunities to rehearse what they have seen, provided with systematic feedback regarding the adequacy of their performance,

and encouraged in a variety of ways to use their new skills in their real-life environment. (Goldstein et al., 1980, p. 13)

In the model proposed by these authors,

structured learning consists of (1) modeling, (2) role-playing, (3) performance feedback, and (4) transfer of training. The trainee is shown numerous specific and detailed examples (either live or on audiotape, videotape, film, or filmstrip) of a person (the model) performing the skill behaviors we wish the trainee to learn (i.e., modeling). The trainee is given considerable opportunity and encouragement to rehearse or practice the behaviors that have been modeled (i.e., role-playing) and provided with positive feedback, approval, or praise as the role-playing of the behaviors becomes more and more similar to the behavior of the model (i.e., performance feedback). Finally, the trainee is exposed to procedures which are designed to increase the likelihood that the newly learned behaviors will in fact actually be applied in an able manner in class, at home, at work, or elsewhere (i.e., transfer of training). (p. 15)

The application of psychoeducational elements as just suggested appears in different emphases in such approaches as microtraining and microcounseling, deliberate psychological education, employment readiness, and similar programs.

Prevention, Personal Competence, and Behavioral Promotion

Psychoeducational models can be used for remediation of skill deficits already apparent in the dysfunctional behavior of adolescents and adults or for the prevention of behavioral disorders likely to ensue in the absence of appropriate social, planning, and other skills. Such intervention strategies rest upon conceptualizations of mental dysfunctions as other than organic, as behavioral and learned, or, at least, as frequently preventable. Albee (1982), a major spokesman for a preventive rather than remedial approach to problems in living, suggested

If your purpose is to reduce the incidence of the different conditions or lifestyles we refer to as mental disorders . . . there are several strategies for accomplishing our purpose: the first of these is to prevent, to minimize, or to reduce the amounts of the organic factors that sometimes do play a role in causation (e.g., lead poisoning, brain damage from automobile accidents). . . . A second strategy . . . involves the reduction of stress . . . (p. 1046). Another area . . . involves increasing the competence of young people to deal with life's problems, particularly with the problems of social interactions, and the development of a wide range of coping skills. . . . Increases in support systems and self-esteem have been shown to reduce psychopathology (p. 1045). . . . Those who argue against the concept of mental illness do not deny the existence of behavior that can be called abnormal or pathological. They simply hold that abnormal behavior can be learned through perfectly normal processes—and what can be learned can be unlearned or prevented. (p. 1050)

Albee (1980) also argued that a competence model must replace the defect or illness model of mental disturbance. A competence model contends that individuals, youth or adults, have adaptive potential and competencies that can be enhanced by mental health professionals by strengthening individual coping skills, self-esteem, and social support systems.

From such a view, most of the problems that people bring to counselors are not pathological or organic. Rather they are matters of personal competence and the degree to which people have knowledge or skills that permit them to cope with or master the various developmental tasks, transitions, or crises they face across the life span. Personal competence can be seen in many ways. Gladwin (1967) suggested that competence includes the ability to utilize various alternatives in reaching a goal, an understanding of social systems of which one is a member, the ability to use one's resources, and effective reality testing. Personal competence can also be seen as a series of skills an individual either possesses or can learn through training. The acquisition of certain skills may generalize to facilitate the development of competence in other aspects of an individual's life (Danish, Galambos, & Laquatra, 1983). Some observers term these skills *life development skills,* and their content includes cognitive and physical skills; interpersonal skills such as initiating, developing, and maintaining relationships (e.g., self-disclosing, communicating feelings accurately and unambiguously, being supportive, and being able to resolve conflicts and relationship problems constructively); and intrapersonal skills (e.g., developing self-control, managing tension and relaxation, setting goals, and taking risks) (Danish et al., 1983).

Amundson (1989), a Canadian counseling psychologist, has suggested that "competence refers to a state of being as well as a state of doing. A competent person is one who has the capacity (or power) to adequately deal with emerging situations" (p. 1). Amundson's model of competence has eight components, and thus to be competent in, for example, almost any job demands some capability in (1) sense of purpose; (2) self/other/and organizational understanding; (3) communication and problem-solving skills; (4) theoretical knowledge and understanding of facts and procedures; (5) practical experience; (6) a supportive organizational context, which at minimum, has elements that allow people to achieve without wasting time and resources; (7) a support network that allows competent people to give and to receive help as part of maintaining their competency; and (8) self-confidence, including acceptance of oneself, the strength to learn from mistakes, and perseverance.

A preventive approach to counseling, whether group or individual, presupposes that the elements of personal competence, the skills needed to handle problems in living, and the behaviors on which relationship enhancement, marital harmony, or positive interpersonal relationships rest can be known and understood. Such a notion implies that the knowledge, attitudes, and skills central to life coping skills or to personal competence can be identified, used as the content of preventive structured learning or psychoeducational approaches, or as targets of other therapeutic interventions, and thereby learned, changed, or strengthened. These assumptions are implicit in psychoeducational models of the increasingly common counseling language of assertiveness training, anger management, stress inoculation, obesity or smoking control, decision-making training, or other forms of planned psychosocial development.

A rapidly emerging application of such conceptualizations is not simply the prevention of behavioral or mental health problems but, indeed, the promotion of mental or physical health. In somewhat simplistic terms, we can argue that primary prevention includes processes and activities intended to reduce the incidence of a disorder or the likelihood of its occurrence in a population at risk. Thus teaching parents who were abused as children effective parenting strategies and other skills that strengthen personal competence may reduce or eliminate the likelihood of these parents abusing their own children, children who under ordinary circumstances would be at risk of receiving such abuse. The intent, then, is to prevent or reduce the incidence of such abuse. By contrast, mental health promotion includes psychoeducational activities or other skill-development processes designed to increase people's sense of competence, coherence, and control so that they can live effective and satisfying lives in a state of social well-being (Perlmutter, 1982). In such a focus, the intent of the counseling or skill-development processes used is not only to prevent problems but also to enhance the quality of life. The latter approaches are found in such rapidly expanding domains as behavioral medicine, health psychology, and behavioral health. The term *behavioral health* has particularly come to mean approaches used by counselors and psychologists to help currently healthy people to maintain health and prevent illness and dysfunction (Goldstein & Krasner, 1987), and it has application in physical health (e.g., diet and stress management) as well as in work adjustment or what might be termed occupational health.

One of the potentially most wide-ranging applications of psychology in behavioral health is in school improvement and education reform. Among the many legislative initiatives concerned with education reform in the schools of the nation are those dealing with school health. Perhaps overshadowed by the many discussions of curriculum content, national academic standards, use of technology in learning, or the reorganization of schools, concerns about improving school health programs are gaining intense scrutiny at national and state levels. The rationale for such interests in improved behavioral health in schools is expressed well by Kolbe, Collins, and Cortese (1997) of the Centers for Disease Control and Prevention:

> The most serious and expensive health and social problems that afflict the United States today are caused in large part by behavioral patterns established during youth (e.g., tobacco use, high-fat diets, drug and alcohol abuse, violence, and sexual risk behaviors). Health problems spawned by these behaviors fuel unnecessary health care costs, and unattended health and social problems among America's young people seriously erode their health status, educational achievement, and quality of life. Young people who suffer from physical illness or injury, mental health problems, hunger, pregnancy, alcohol and drug use, or fear of violence are less likely to learn irrespective of efforts to improve educational methods, standards, or organizations. (p. 256)

Following on from this perspective, the authors argued that one of the most important functions of schools has always been to maintain and improve health, but the infrastructure available in schools has been restricted in its vision of improving the health of children to two or three components: health services, health education, and the health environment. The implementation of these components has traditionally been seen as the responsibility of the school nurse and the health educator/physical education teachers rather than in the more comprehensive terms now being advocated. For example, the Centers for Disease Control and Prevention, the American School Health Association, the Joint Committee on National Health Education Standards, the Council of Chief State School Officers, and related bodies have advocated a more comprehensive view of school health programs that in various perspectives embody eight interactive components (Kolbe, 1993):

1. health services;
2. psychological, counseling, and other social services;
3. health education;
4. nutrition services;
5. physical education and other physical activities;
6. the psychosocial and biophysical environment;
7. health programs for faculty and staff; and

8. integrated efforts of schools, families, and communities to improve the health of students and staff.

Such a model of interactive components is intended, among other purposes, to identify and involve professionals who can work collaboratively as members of the school's health team. Such perspectives lend themselves to other initiatives that argue that schools, particularly in urban areas, should be community centers that offer integrated social and health services, in a type of "one-stop shopping," not only for students but for their families and other community members as well. These views reflect the reality that the school is the single "institutionalized social program that directly touches the lives of virtually every American. Schools reflect the merging of cultures, values, and priorities of diverse citizens in their surrounding communities and society at large" (Short & Talley, 1997, p. 234). As such, schools should be seen as centerpieces of integrated communities, not as autonomous units. Schools in their content and purposes are also creatures of the metaphors by which they and their components are characterized by the larger society. Until now schools have been primarily equated with academic education, not with public health; problems of children have been conceptualized in educational and psychological terms, not as social and public health concerns. But as suggested in other chapters, terms of reference and metaphors change; and as they do so, they redefine how the practitioners of the content at issue are seen. Within these contexts, although it is not likely that current conceptions of school counselors will change dramatically, emphases on how their work can be conceived of in terms of behavioral health and in the prevention of health and social problems among students adds a new affirmation of their importance as well as a new challenge to how their role is conceptualized.

Whether in terms of prevention or enhancement, promotion or treatment, the approaches included in this section apply the findings of psychology to prevent certain behaviors from occurring by either developing, strengthening, or enhancing other behaviors. But behavioral health has come as well to refer to the use of counseling interventions in areas in which the problems brought to the counselor have physiological and stress-related components. One such growing relationship is that of career counseling and behavioral health.

EMERGING PERSPECTIVES ON CAREER COUNSELING

For most of its history, career counseling has not been seen as directly related to the reduction of emotional distress or to other aspects of mental health. Indeed, some observers have argued that career counseling and psychotherapy are separate processes. In such perspectives, career counseling has not been seen as a therapeutic modality but has been traditionally portrayed as more oriented to economic health, to the choice of an occupation, and to the development of prevocational skills and the preparation for work than to the reduction of stress and other factors that put many at risk of work pathologies or physical and mental illness. Such a view is slowly changing in the face of growing evidence that career counseling is critical to reconnecting unemployed and underemployed youth and adults to a sense of purposefulness and self-efficacy, and in so doing to a diminution of the stress-related side effects of hopelessness and despair.

The past two decades have seen a broadening of perspectives on career behavior, including those that center around the effects of work that do not enhance self-esteem, inappropriate person-job fit, and the multiple personal problems associated with unemployment and underemployment. In each case, research has demonstrated that a variety of life difficulties and mental health problems ensue when work life is unsatisfactory. Distress about work and, particularly, unemployment is associated with a range of personal and social problems.

Unemployment is not simply a social or economic crisis; it is virtually always a personal crisis for the person experiencing it. The meaning of unemployment is increasingly found not only in the economic corollaries of unemployment but also in the psychological, behavioral, and emotional corollaries of disrupted or confused meaning, identity, affiliation, and negative feelings of self-esteem that for the individual accompany this crisis (Herr, 1993). It is in this context that career counseling is seen to be a mental health modality when it is put at the service of the unemployed, the underemployed, and those with major adjustment problems. Dawis (1984), for example, contended that job dissatisfaction is related to mental and physical health problems including psychosomatic illnesses, depression, anxiety, worry, tension, impaired interpersonal relationships, coronary heart disease, alcoholism, drug abuse, and suicide.

Many other research studies have linked work and mental health. For example, Borgen and Amundson (1984), in a major study of the experiences of unemployed people from a variety of educational, cultural, and work backgrounds in Canada, contended that the experience of unemployment depicts an emotional roller coaster comparable in its effect and stages to those described by Kübler-Ross (1969) in the grief process associated with the loss of a loved one: denial, anger, bargaining, depression, and acceptance. Borgen and Amundson also suggested that unemployment brings with it a needs shift, as in Maslow's model of prepotent needs (which suggests that as needs at the bottom of a hierarchy are satisfied other needs emerge), and unemployment therefore involves tumbling down the hierarchy from need levels attained under previous employment to more primitive need levels that are dominant under unemployment. According to Maslow (1954), the categories of needs that emerge as lower levels of needs are routinely met, or taken for granted, begin with the most basic physiological needs, and then proceed to the safety needs (security, stability), to the love and belonging needs (relatedness), to the esteem needs (prestige, self-worth, recognition), and, finally, to the self-actualization needs (creative self-expression). Although people rarely attain the highest level of self-actualization in their work, it can be assumed that most people successfully employed will be able to attain needs beyond the most primitive physiological necessities and to meet needs for safety, love, belonging, and esteem. Thus Borgen and Amundson's research has suggested that whatever needs are attained in employment shift downward significantly under unemployment, as in Maslow's model of prepotent needs, and that the psychological reactions are those of loss as defined by the Kübler-Ross paradigm. There may also be feelings of victimization similar to those experienced by victims of rape, incest, disease, and crime. Such feelings include shock, confusion, helplessness, anxiety, fear, and depression (Janoff-Bluman & Frieze, 1983).

Borgen and Amundson's (1984) research further showed that unemployment is experienced differently by different groups of men and women who did or did not anticipate job loss, and by immigrant populations. The factors that vary among these groups and mediate the emotional reactions to unemployment include attachment to the job, social status, individual personality variables, financial situation, social support system, and future expectations.

In applying Borgen and Amundson's (1984) model to the situation when long-established plants closed, Hurst and Shepherd (1986) found similar emotional stages among workers anticipating job loss prior to plant closings. In such instances, the emotional roller coaster is likely to be prolonged as older workers remain while younger workers are laid off to pare down the workforce. Lopez's (1983) research also showed that groups varied in their reaction to job loss. Hurst and Shepherd further found that those employees most likely to experience prolonged depression are those few who are handicapped by physical, skill, and age barriers, and those with very low self-esteem. But as Hunt and Shepherd as well as Lopez found, even workers who do not experience clinical depression tend to experience "feelings of loss, sadness, resentment, and anger because of the end of the company, close collegial relationships, and a way of life for most employees" (Hurst & Shepherd, 1986, p. 404).

Borgen and Amundson's research (1984) highlighted what other theorists and researchers have observed in relation to the interaction of mental health and the state of the economy, unemployment, or related phenomena: such interactions are likely to include multiple variables, not simply unidimensional relationships. Different people experience economic downturns and unemployment differently, and mental health outcomes can be precipitated by factors in the environment (sociogenic) as well as factors within individuals (eugenic) (Berg & Hughes, 1979). Thus there are questions of social causation, social selection, precipitating factors, and individual predispositions that have to do with how work and mental health are related. Brenner (1979) attempted to clarify the differences among some of these concepts. For example, physical or mental health are not unitary concepts. Some people react to stress in physical terms (e.g., cardiovascular disease, cirrhosis, hypertension, chemical dependency, early death), others in behavioral terms (e.g., aggressiveness, violence, spouse abuse, child abuse), and still others in psychological terms (e.g., depression, anxiety). Thus precipitating factors in the environment (e.g., a plant closing, losing a job) can cause different reactions among people (e.g., physical, behavioral, psychological) depending on individual predisposing factors to stress.

The links between unemployment and other individual or social costs are complex. In their review of studies of the social and private costs of unemployment, Liem and Rayman (1980) indicated that

> prolonged unemployment is commonly a serious threat to health and the broad quality of life. These costs, furthermore, are borne not only by individual workers, but also by their families and communities. . . . [Further,] there is good evidence that losing one's job can increase health risks, exacerbate chronic and latent disorders, alter usual patterns of health-seeking behavior, and exact numerous other social and interpersonal costs. (p. 1116)

Unemployment, underemployment, job dissatisfaction, and problems in the workplace spill over into other parts of an individual's life. This has been found to be true in other nations as well as in the United States. For example, Kieselbach and Lunger (1990), in reporting on their research in Germany, suggested that the major psychosocial problems experienced by the unemployed sample they studied (and the percentage who experienced the problems) include

- problems with partner (47%);
- accusations leveled by family (47%);

- excessive alcohol consumption (44%);
- difficulties contacting others (39%);
- problems looking for work (36%);
- trouble with the government's labor office (33%);
- loss of status (33%); and
- crisis of self-esteem (25%) (p. 192).

Among the specific problems found in the research literature to be associated with unemployment and economic decline are first admissions to psychiatric hospitals, a rise in infant mortality rates, increased deaths from cardiovascular and alcohol-related diseases, a sharp increase in suicide rates, greater demand for mental health services due to increased psychological impairment (Brenner, 1973), threats to the structural interdependence between the family and the workplace (Kantor, 1977), stress in the children of unemployed parents (such as moodiness at home, new problems in school, strained relationships with peers) (Liem & Rayman, 1980), and digestive problems, irritability, and retarded physical and mental development as well as child and spouse abuse, and juvenile delinquency (Riegle, 1982). The ripple effects of unemployment touch not only the individual who is unemployed but also all parts of the system of which he or she is a part. Each person involved commonly manifests a wide range of physical, emotional, and social stresses and strains. In chapter 2 a more detailed discussion of unemployment and its effects was presented.

Much more could be said about these matters, but suffice it to say here that the stress reactions and stress-related physical and psychological diseases that accompany problems of work adjustment, work choice, and the exit from work bring career counseling directly into the realm of the emerging movement in behavioral health and, more broadly, behavioral medicine. Flowing from earlier work in psychosomatic medicine and studies on alcohol in the workplace, behavioral medicine is a broad interdisciplinary study of scientific inquiry, education, and practice concerned with health and illness or related dysfunctions (e.g., essential hypertension, cholesterolemia, stress disorders, addictive smoking, obesity). Behavioral health is usually considered a subspecialty within behavioral medicine, which is specifically concerned with the maintenance of health and the prevention of illness and dysfunction in currently healthy persons. Behavioral health conceptualizes health-related activity in overt behavioral terms in much the same way as is true of perspectives on the developmental tasks underlying career behavior and the transitional elements of performance, understanding of the affective context in which work is played out, being able to work with others, and being able to implement self-discipline, loyalty, and career mobility. Many of the techniques in behavioral health are also those used in career counseling: behavior therapy, cognitive restructuring, psychosocial skills training, family counseling, stress inoculation, and stress management.

Career counseling approaches in or out of business and industry can provide dislocated workers, unhappy workers, maladjusted workers, and underemployed workers information, support, encouragement, or skill-building approaches that can facilitate hope and reduce feelings of being a social isolate and unworthy. Skill-building approaches can deal directly with such matters as anger management, assertiveness, planning, interpersonal competencies, and openness to constructive supervision. These approaches educate people regarding choice and emphasize personnel development, not only personnel management. Their availability and implementation are not just matters of occupational choice and adjustment; rather they also help people to create reality and make meaning for themselves within the context of work and career. The latter are directly related to behavioral health.

Newer conceptions of career counseling embody the reality that personal adjustment and work adjustment exist in a symbiotic relationship. The workplace becomes an environment in which both positive and negative, healthy and unhealthy, good and bad outcomes are stimulated, and an environment in which the conflicts, thwarted aspirations, and emotional baggage from an individual's life outside the workplace that are brought into it filter and shape his or her life as a worker. Undoubtedly there will be increased conceptualization of career counseling, career assisting, and career intervention in the future as a complex blend of development and remediation, of education and skill facilitation, and of therapeutic modalities increasingly concerned with the economic life of the individual and expressed in more multidimensional and holistic terms.

As theory and research on career behavior have matured, they have acknowledged both the complexity of influences upon and the psychological characteristics of career choice and adjustment throughout the life span. In so doing, credence has been given to career counseling as a therapeutic modality that goes beyond dispensing and discussing information. Crites (1981) suggested that as insights from client-centered and psychodynamic approaches are applied to career counseling, choice problems are viewed as essentially personality problems. Therefore, the assumptions that guide the provision of career counseling need to be considered in relation to personal adjustment counseling or psychotherapy.

Brown (1985) pushed the interaction of career counseling and personal counseling even further than Crites. Brown, who defined career counseling "as the process of helping an individual select, prepare for, enter, and function effectively in an occupation" (p. 197), viewed career counseling "as a viable intervention with clients that [sic] have rather severe emotional problems." In particular, Brown distinguished between clients who have intrapsychic (cognitive or emotional) problems and those who work in a nonsupportive, stress-producing environment that may cause symptoms that seem to be intrapsychic, mental health disorders rather than functions of poor personal-work environment fit. Obviously, how the counselor makes such distinctions will determine whether the therapeutic approach focuses upon intrapsychic changes, as in personal counseling and psychotherapy, or on altering the work environment, choosing another work environment through career counseling, or assisting the individual to manage the stress induced by such an environment. Such a view obviously extends both the range of problems likely to be addressed by career counseling and the settings in which career counseling should be offered. Viewing career counseling in such ways provides almost an inevitable connection to behavioral health.

Increasingly, models are being formulated that extend the conceptions of career counseling in new and more comprehensive ways, including addressing the relatively unique needs of particular populations. These models have become more specific in their view of the types of career counseling that should be implemented in different settings. In some cases, these new models of career counseling are emerging because the concept of career itself is changing and the work relations of persons and institutions have been significantly altered. For example, Rifkin (1995), in his book *The End of Work: The Decline of the Global Labor Force and the Dawn of the Postmarket Era*, has suggested that the global economy is undergoing a fundamental transformation in the nature of work that will lead to the steady and inevitable decline of jobs. He argued that because of the productivity of computers, robots, telecommunications, near workerless factories, and virtual companies there will be too few jobs to absorb the large numbers of workers displaced by the new technologies and too few hours of work to occupy fully those who do have a job. Even so, he contended that it is no longer necessary for everybody to work to produce the things we need. Therefore, more people will turn to volunteer efforts and to efforts in the world of nonprofit organizations to provide services and other activities not provided by the private corporate sector or governmental agencies. As such a possibility becomes a likelihood, how will career counseling respond? Will career counseling increasingly attend to counseling about opportunities for volunteer work and other activities in the nonprofit sector that are different from the customary counseling about jobs?

A somewhat different question is raised by the current widespread restructuring of corporations and the downsizing of their workforces. In these cases, it is not simply that people are being displaced by corporate restructuring but that there are fundamental shifts in how corporations get their work done. For example, as Handy (1994) has suggested, corporations now rest in the middle of several concentric rings. In the center of these rings is the corporation primary or core workforce. This is the portion of the workforce that will have a relatively long relationship to the corporation, receive benefits, and be afforded training and security. This relatively small core of permanent workers will be augmented by a second concentric ring consisting of a large cadre of temporary or contingent workers whose particular services are purchased only when they are needed. Many of these contingent workers will be full-time; many others will be part-time. The issue to be dealt with, however, is that these workers are not likely to have the health and retirement benefits available to the permanent, core workers, and perhaps even more disconcertingly, they are not likely to have a sense of institutional identity. They will be "serial workers" across institutions for specified periods of time and for specified and limited purposes. How should they be counseled? Should the focus be on how they can become members of a permanent core work group or on how to reduce their work identity and find their gratifications and fulfillment in the nonpaid periods of their life? Or should we help these persons become entrepreneurs, salespersons of their own skills as essentially self-employed brokers of their time and skills? The third concentric ring around the corporation of today is populated by outsourcing, contract firms. In this instance, the corporation, rather than having particular kinds of specialists in their permanent, core workforce, instead outsource different work functions to firms that specialize in those functions. In such instances, a corporation may decide not to have its own advertising staff, maintenance staff, or employee assistance group. Instead, it contracts with local companies to provide such services without putting their employees on the corporate payroll. This reduces the costs of overhead and of employee housing as well as of health and other social benefits. Again, however, it changes the questions to which career counseling is applied in ways similar to the changes in questions applicable to contingency workers—and it also changes the metaphors and conceptions of the images workers should have of themselves and the skills they need.

In the latter context, the book *The Career Is Dead—Long Live the Career. A Relational Approach to Careers*, by Hall and associates (1996), provided views of the emergent career pattern of workers that are different from much of contemporary career development theory. Because of the many changes in traditional organizational careers, a new form of career—the protean career—is emerging, according to Hall and his associates. The protean career, driven more by the individual than by the organization, is characterized by frequent change and self-invention and motivated by the desire for psychological success rather than by externally determined measures of success. As contended by Hall et al.,

> organizational and social cultures have changed enough so that people no longer expect—or, in many cases, want—a long-term career within a particular organization; more likely, they think, if I can't get to the top or make a big financial killing, I might as well do what I really want to do. . . . As we approach the 21st century, then, our career focus has shifted inward. The driving questions are now more about meaning than money, purpose than power, identity than ego, and learning than attainments. (1996, pp. xi, xii)

The new status quo for workers is characterized as "continuous learning and feeling continuously on the edge, off balance" (p. 315). In such circumstances, the new psychological career contract includes terms such as "training, growing, individual responsibility, empowerment, performing, and working hard. . . . [Further,] the career is no longer to be entrusted to the organization; it is managed by the employee, and employees value this new personal control over their lives" (p. 316). Hakim (1994) described this new contract as one in which employees have to adopt a new mind-set: that of being self-employed, of not working for but with a company.

Undoubtedly the perspectives of Rifkin (1995), Handy (1994), and Hall and associates (1996) are accurate analyses of some segments of the workforce now and more so in the future. But there also are other models of shifting perspectives of career counseling that are noteworthy. Hershenson (1996), for example, has formulated a model using systems approaches as the bases for new applications of career counseling to the various dimensions of the person and of the environment that relate to specific components of work adjustment as the targets for intervention. In his view, subsystems of the person include work personality, work competencies, and work goals. Elements of the work setting include the organizational culture and behavioral expectations, job demands and skill requirements, and rewards and opportunities. Components of work adjustment include work role behavior, task performance, and work satisfaction. In such a view, work adjustment involves complex interactions between the subsystems in the person and the work setting. Although space does not permit the detailing of specific work-related issues in each of the subsystems, suffice it to say that these are issues of the person's self-concept as worker, work motivation, work-related interpersonal skills, work competencies, task performance, and understanding and being able to act on work-role expectations and other facets of work-personality/work-setting interaction. According to Hershenson, the career counselor or career guidance specialist will focus on the relation between the person and the work setting, and attempt to evaluate and to isolate subsystems to which interventions will be directed.

Another example, not unrelated to the concerns about work adjustment problems expressed by Hershenson, is an attempt by Herr (1997) to illustrate the growing acknowledgement that career and personal counseling must fuse if selected work adjustment problems are to be dealt with effectively. This fusion occurs on a continuum from choice, indecision, and situational concerns to change, indecisiveness, and personal concerns as portrayed in Figure 7.1. A fundamental notion in this figure is that career counseling, as it is evolving, is increasingly seen as a continuum of intervention foci rather than a single focus. Such a view suggests that different career counseling emphases have relevance for different career problems, much as Hershenson's (1996) systems-based approaches suggest that different elements of the work personality or elements of the work setting need to be seen as the targets of interventions. A view of career counseling as a continuum of intervention is reinforced by Super's (1993) view that there are really different kinds of counseling, situational and personal, and that these are not dichotomous but rather on a continuum. He further elaborated the point to suggest that situational counseling has

> . . . subspecialties that focus on differing types of situations (career, family, etc.) and personal counseling, in which the focus is on individuals whose problems are based primarily on their own approach to and coping with situations, not on factors in the situations they encounter. In accepting this dichotomy, one should not actually treat it as a dichotomy, but as a continuum of which there are extremes. (p. 135)

Figure 7.1 illustrates some of the elements that characterize a continuum of career counseling emphases by using the content of the National Career Development Association's (1985) "What do career counselors do?" perspectives and by reflecting the continuum notion of Super as well as the enlarging view of career counseling discussed throughout this chapter and chapter 2.

MENTAL HEALTH COUNSELING AND BEHAVIORAL MEDICINE

Although it may seem somewhat radical to some readers to connect career counseling and behavioral health, or to portray a fusion of career and personal counseling, it is less difficult to connect mental health counseling and behavioral medicine. As observed by Nicholas (1988), "today's 10 major causes of death, in rank order, beginning with the highest, are heart disease, malignant neoplasms, stroke, accidents (other than from motor vehicle accidents), influenza and pneumonia, motor vehicle accidents, diabetes, cirrhosis of the liver, arteriosclerosis, and suicide" (p. 69). At least 7 of these 10 causes of death are directly related to lifestyle, personal behavior, and personal choices. Thus mental health counselors, as practitioners concerned with behavioral change, have major roles to play in the prevention and remediation of behaviors that put an individual's health at risk and in promoting those behaviors that promote health and wellness.

Nicholas suggested that from the beginnings of the professional identity of mental health counseling, practitioners have been committed to the promotion of well-being. Citing the interdisciplinary background of behavioral medicine, Nicholas advocated the work in medical sociology of Antonovsky (1979) who proposed the term *salutogenesis*—the origins of health—as the counterpoint to *pathogenesis*—the origins of sickness—thereby prompting mental health counselors to concern themselves primarily with the question of what keeps people healthy rather than the question of what makes people sick.

Within the above context, then, Nicholas (1988) suggested that there is a conceptual convergence between behavioral medicine and mental health counseling in their joint emphases on

Figure 7.1 Perspectives on a Continuum of Career Counseling Foci

Choice Indecision		Change Indecisiveness
Career counseling - - - - - - - - -	Fusion of career and personal counseling	Reconstructive focus on reframing past experiences Reinterpreting ego identity and meaning. Deciding and acting upon ways to replot career pathways.
Educational Supportive Problem solving Conscious awareness	Enable the individual to identify and use resources available to help cope with life.	

- Conduct individual and group counseling sessions to help clarify life/career goals.
- Administer and interpret tests and inventories to assess abilities, interest, etc., and to identify career options.
- Encourage exploration activities through assignments and planning experiences.
- Utilize career planning systems and occupational information systems to help individuals better understand the world of work.

- Provide opportunities for improving decision-making skills.
- Assist in developing individualized career plans.
- Teach job-hunting strategies and skills and assist in the development of resumés.
- Help identify available career paths in a firm and its requirements for advancement.
- Clarify with workers their marketable, transferable, elastic work skills and where they might be applied.
- Assist in the identification of work personality, work competencies, and work goals.

- Help resolve potential personal conflicts on the job through practice in human relations skills.
- Teach stress reduction, anger management, assertiveness, communication skills.
- Help clients develop emotion-focused coping strategies to manage the emotions aroused by stressors and therefore maintain affective equilibrium.
- Teach clients how to monitor stressors and engage in positive problem solving.
- Assist in understanding the integration of work and other life roles.
- Provide retirement planning.
- Teach advancement strategies.
- Help individuals to improve their fit with their work role.
- Clarify elements of personal job satisfaction in relation to the organizational culture, behavioural expectations, and job demands.

- Provide support for persons experiencing job stress, job loss, career transition.
- Provide opportunities for displaced workers to vent their anger and their feelings about personal concerns.
- Provide problem-focused coping by which to actively change the self and develop a more satisfying work situation.
- Provide job-separation counseling.
- Provide referral for substance-abuse treatment.
- Provide family counseling.
- Assist in modifying irrational career beliefs.
- Address underlying issues which lead to work dysfunctions.

Situational   **Personal**

Note: From "Career Counseling: A Process in Process," by E. L. Herr, 1997, *British Journal of Guidance and Counselling, 25*(1), Figure 1, p. 91. Copyright © 1997 by British Journal of Guidance and Counselling. Reprinted with permission.

. . . (a) a conceptual shift away from pathogenesis toward salutogenesis; (b) the assumption of personal responsibility for one's health; (c) an integrative, holistic view of health and the recipients of health care; and (d) prevention as one of the full-range of health care services. (p. 73)

It is also useful to note that the model proposed by Nicholas illustrates a continuum of interventions as suggested earlier in this chapter. He contended that on the end of the continuum concerned with tertiary prevention or the modification of risk factors associated with premature death, there is an array of chronic illnesses that is likely to precipitate mental health issues as well as behavioral issues to which counselors can respond. The areas in which such tertiary prevention is appropriate include stroke, heart disease, cancer, diabetes mellitus, epilepsy, spinal cord injuries, asthma, bronchitis, emphysema, and chronic pain as well as treatment compliance and social support. At the other end of the continuum is the role of the counselor in providing primary prevention and promoting optimal health. In this context, the counselor may be in a support role to a physician or work alone to create the coping skills and insights associated with preventing risk factors implicated in disease. Thus counselors may provide individual or group approaches designed to help people implement weight management, smoking cessation, aerobic exercise, stress management, appropriate alcohol use, social support, or adherence to a regimen leading to optimal health.

Nicholas's (1988) perspectives have received support from Palmo's (1996) analysis of the identity of the Mental Health Counselor (MHC). Palmo suggested that a major distinguishing characteristic of the MHC is "the emphasis on a developmental model of counseling and therapy within an overall prevention scheme, with a . . . focus on promoting healthy development of coping capacities and on using environmental forces to contribute to the goal of wellness . . ." (Hershenson & Strein, 1991, pp. 250–251). According to Palmo, what this means is

> that the MHC examines clients' concerns as a part of the normal developmental issues and crises faced by most people as they progress through daily living experiences. The client is not viewed as "sick," but rather, as an individual who must learn more effective coping mechanisms in order to function appropriately and gainfully within society. (Palmo, 1996, p. 56)

SYSTEMATIC ECLECTICISM

Cognitive psychology, constructivism, expanded models of career counseling, psychoeducational models, and the use of such approaches for both prevention and treatment have spawned a further emerging trend in counseling, that of differential treatment or systematic eclecticism. Fundamentally, such a model of counseling assumes that specific treatments or counseling approaches are effective for some purposes and not for others, and that clients come to counselors for many different reasons. Rather than assuming that the same treatment or approach is useful for all people, the counselor tailors the counseling response to the unique needs of an individual client. In this view, counselors will ideally be trained in a repertoire of treatments—such as individual, group, psychoeducation, self-monitored based on scientific analyses of their effectiveness under certain conditions and for specific purposes. As the counselor and the client define the goals of the counseling relationship and clarify the reasons the client has come for counseling, one assumption of systematic eclecticism is that the counselor can implement the most powerful or relevant approach.

Systematic eclecticism does not suggest that the counselor should flail about for treatments in a random way. Rather, it suggests that it is possible to think of counseling approaches and client outcomes as a matrix of possible interactions. Some counseling approaches or treatments will be more effective for certain purposes and not for others. The validity of such an assumption is at the heart of attribute-treatment research that examines the degree to which outcomes from treatment become more positive the more consistent they are with the personal characteristics of the client. As an example of this type of research, Nelson and Roberge (1993) examined the relationship between personality types as measured by the Myers-Briggs Type Indicator (MBTI) and the preference of college students for selected career services, including both interactive (e.g., workshops, counselor assessments, advising) and noninteractive interventions (computerized assessments, career readings, educational catalogues and directions). The results indicated that the student subjects indicated preferences for interventions that were consistent with their psychological type. As might be expected, extroverted students were most satisfied with interventions that were interactive; introverted students preferred noninteractive approaches; sensing-intuitive students did not differentiate among intervention types.

The scientific problem, given the complexity of factors that brings people to counseling, is how precise the matching of treatment and outcome might be. A further problem is the likelihood that counselors can be trained equally well to implement a large range of treatments or interventions. Traditionally counselors have been trained in counseling approaches that are essentially theory bound: psychodynamic, client-centered, behavioral, cognitive-behavioral. Systematic eclecticism, however, suggests that each of these theory-bound approaches has utility for certain purposes to achieve certain client outcomes. But systematic eclecticism also suggests that no one theory-bound approach has all the answers to all the client needs that are brought to counselors. Therefore, counselors should be trained across theoretical domains to learn about the most effective contributions of each in order to apply such approaches systematically and scientifically.

Systematic eclecticism as a structure for conceiving counseling interventions rests upon another notion as well. It is, in essence, that most clients who come to counselors do not have one problem, they have several. People may need help, for example, with behavior, emotions, nutrition, and problem solving, not only one of these, if they are to overcome their problems in living. This view of the multiple dimensions of client problems is the basis for such models of counseling as multimodal therapy (Lazarus, 1981).

The assumptions of systematic eclecticism, differential treatment, or multimodal therapy are giving rise to other terms as well. For example, the tendency for counselors to use whatever approach is technically useful and practical regardless of theoretical orientation has been labeled *pragmatic technical eclecticism* (Keat, 1979), *eclectic psychotherapy* (Norcross, 1986), and *adaptive counseling and therapy*—an integrative eclectic model (Howard, Nancy, & Myers, 1986). The momentum that eclectic approaches to counseling now have was suggested more than a decade ago by the research of Smith (1982), who reported that about two thirds of the counselors queried indicated that the primary movement or trend was toward some form of eclectic approach. Although the terms used varied (e.g., *multimodal,* 19%; *creative syn-*

thesis, 17%; *emerging eclecticism,* 17%; *technical eclecticism,* 9%), the hybridization or combining of previously discrete approaches to counseling seems to be advancing rapidly. Current figures continue to suggest that over 60% of practitioners consider themselves eclectic in their approaches to the conduct of counseling (Lazarus, 1993; Mahoney, 1991; Norcross, 1993). As Seay and Seay (1996) have suggested,

> model dependency appears to have ended. Counselors are more free to use a wide variety of techniques drawn from diverse models. A counselor who claims allegiance to one of the humanistic models of counseling may be found using systematic desensitization or cognitive restructuring. . . . By the same token, it is not at all unusual to find behavioral therapists engaging in cognitive restructuring or affective focusing. . . . (p. 89)

Brief Therapy

As new configurations of counseling are advocated and a continuum of treatment, prevention, and mental health promotion is advanced and refined by theorists and researchers, an underlying concern in the field is the problem of scarce resources and their effective use.

Sometimes the argument about scarce resources takes the form of deploring the large counselor-student ratios in school counseling across the nation. Or sometimes the argument centers around the imbalance or shortcomings in federal expenditures for different types of mental health services. As an illustration, Grossman (1981) estimated that 96% of federal expenditures for all forms of health care are for treatment and only 4% for efforts in prevention. Yet as indicated elsewhere in this chapter, other data suggest that 50% of all deaths can be attributed to an unhealthy lifestyle in which 7 of the 10 leading causes of death are behaviorally determined and could be reduced by the appropriate application of counseling techniques for prevention and for the promotion of wellness.

Sometimes the resource argument relates to the needs in the population for mental health services and the lack of availability of mental health practitioners to serve such needs. Estimates are that 15% (Kiesler, 1980) to 35% (Dohrenwend et al., 1980) of the population is in need of mental health services in any given year. Myers (1996), quoting available data analysis and selected sources, estimated that almost one third of older persons have mental health problems that warrant professional intervention. Using the conservative estimate of 15% of the population means that approximately 33 million people need some form of mental health service. Kiesler's analyses (1980) of mental health service availability suggested that if all the available licensed and certified psychiatrists and psychologists were to provide psychotherapy on a full-time basis, offering it three times a week to each client, they could provide such a service to only 2% of those needing it. When we add to this estimate the growing number of clinical mental health, nationally certified, and professional counselors being licensed to practice in many states, the pool of mental health providers is larger than estimated by Kiesler. Nevertheless, using the assumptions on which his estimates are based, it may well be that the pool of mental health resources available can at best meet only 5% to 10% of the needs for such services.

An important question in relation to estimates of needs for mental health services is whether it is necessary to provide counseling or psychotherapy three times a week to meet the mental health needs of those who have a need for such services. One approach might be to demystify mental illness and mental health into the behavioral deficits or competencies on which they rest and then to identify the range of mental health responses available to treat or prevent mental health problems, on the one hand, and to promote mental health on the other. In addition, however, there is a stimulus to search for brief therapies that may address mental health problems with more precision and efficiency than has often been achieved in the past.

Some evidence has suggested that brief therapy can be helpful to many clients (Cummings, 1977) and that targeted brief therapy (Cummings, 1986) will be increasingly required to meet the needs for mental health services. Of particular interest here are the findings of Cummings and Follette (1976) with regard to the cost-effectiveness of psychotherapy as a way to reduce the utilization of medical services. They found, for example, that one psychotherapy session only, with no repeat visits, can reduce medical utilization by 60% over the following 5 years, and that a 75% reduction in medical utilization over a 5-year period can be achieved for patients initially receiving two to eight psychotherapy visits (brief therapy). In an 8-year follow-up study of patients involved in psychotherapy within a health plan, results reinforced earlier findings that reduction in medical utilization occurred as a "consequence of resolving the emotional distress that is being reflected in the symptoms and in the doctors' visits" (Cummings & Follette, 1976, p. 716).

Cummings (1977), in other studies designed to summarize the cost-effectiveness of psychotherapy in reducing the need for medical services and, particularly, the utility of brief therapy, found several interesting results. One was that rather than increasing the intensity or frequency of psychological services for the most interminable or difficult clients, the commonly accepted remedy has become to see these clients at spaced intervals of every 2 or 3 months as a way of maximizing both cost- and therapeutic effectiveness. Beyond these findings, however, Cummings (1977) reported that

> . . . when active, dynamic, brief therapy is provided early and by psychotherapists who are enthusiastic and proactive regarding such intervention, it is the treatment of choice for about 85% of the patients seeking psychotherapy. . . . By providing such brief therapy, it makes economically feasible the provision of long-term psychotherapy to the approximately 10% of the patients who require it for their treatment to be therapeutically effective. . . . Therapeutically cost-effective programs can be developed for groups with such problems in living as alcoholism, drug abuse, drug addiction, chronic psychosis, problems of the elderly, and severe character disorders. (p. 717)

Various authors have described brief therapy in different ways and as appropriate for different settings. For example, Fuhriman, Paul, and Burlingame (1986) discussed eclectic time-limited therapy in a university counseling center. They indicated that the model they developed was conceived for pragmatic rather than theoretical reasons. Their initial concern was the stress that results for potential clients, staff members, and referral agencies from incessant, growing client waiting lists for services. The eclectic brief therapy model they conceived included several elements that other brief therapy models seem to hold in common: (1) time limitation on amount of therapy provided, (2) specific, restricted, and focused goals, (3) expectation-sharing between therapist and client about the time limitations and the goals to be achieved, (4) more directive therapeutic intervention, and (5) selection of appropriate clients. They overlaid these five elements on the developmental model of the helping process outlined by Egan (1985). In essence, this model begins with an intake session, ends with a concluding session, and has eight sessions in between.

A particularly important part of implementing brief therapy or time-limited approaches is identifying clients who can profit from this focused and brief approach. In the counseling center described by Fuhriman et al. (1986), clients who are severely depressed and require medication, who experience anger as the main affect, who are borderline or actual psychotics, or who suffer from an organic mental disorder are excluded from this approach. Those who are excluded are referred to other treatment modalities or time-unlimited approaches. Thus the intake session is vital to ensuring that the time-limited therapy is likely to be effective. It is useful to note that the standard format includes one 50-minute session per week for 10 sessions. The client problems seen as amenable to time-limited therapy include mild to severe anxiety; ambulatory disorders; concerns of identity, independence, and career choice; problems resulting from absent or disruptive relationships; and lack of success in educational pursuits. Within this array of problems, there are a variety of individual treatment possibilities, ranging across client-centered, psychodynamic, behavioral, and cognitive-behavioral methodologies. It is possible within the parameters of a time-limited approach to use group approaches, including marriage therapy, rather than brief individual therapy.

Eclectic time-limited therapy as portrayed in this model allows counselors to work from their own theoretical orientations while observing the overall goals prescribed for the delivery of services (e.g., 10 sessions, a problem-solving and focused approach). From this vantagepoint, eclectic time-limited therapy is different from other approaches to brief therapy that are both more theoretical in their orientation and more prone to focus on specific psychological issues such as "separation and individuation, dynamic conflict between present and past and unconscious and conscious, decisional conflict, and dysfunctional and maladaptive behaviors" (Fuhriman, et al., 1986, p. 229).

Another approach to brief therapy is solution focused. Basile (1996) reviewed solution-focused brief therapy and made many important observations about brief therapy in general. For example, Basile suggested that brief therapy is a different way to think about and approach therapy. In essence it is a form of therapy that uses as few sessions as possible to develop a satisfactory solution; it is intentionally designed to make the most of limited contact. Basile reported that in one study the average number of sessions in solution-focused brief therapy was five. Further, Basile quoted the Budman and Gurman (1988, p. 6) observation that "the goal [of brief therapy] is to help the client achieve maximum benefit with the lowest investment of therapist time and patient cost, both financial and psychological."

In discussing solution-focused brief therapy per se, Basile suggested that a prime characteristic of such an approach is the emphasis on focusing on what is positive, that is, on strengths, problems, and solutions. In this view,

> solution-focused brief therapists do what the name suggests: they focus clients on solutions to their problems rather than on the problems themselves. . . . Unlike problem-focused therapies, the direction of treatment is shifted away from problems to what clients want to happen or want to be different in their lives. (Basile, 1996, p. 3)

According to O'Hanlon and Weiner-Davis (1989, p. 1) solution-focused brief therapy "focuses on people: competence rather than their deficits, their strengths rather than their weaknesses, their possibilities rather than their limitations."

Basile suggested that a number of interventions tend to be specific to solution-focused therapy. Among them are intentionally using the first session immediately to create a working alliance, understand the complaint, and create an expectation for change by shifting the client's attention from the past to the present and the future. In addition, counselors tend to focus on motivating the client to do something different rather than to keep doing more of the same unhelpful behavior. Clients also are encouraged to consider *exception questions* designed to identify when the problem is not occurring and what the client has done to become problem-free; *miracle questions* designed to elicit the client's perceptions of how they would know a problem was solved and what would be different; and *scaling questions* by which they rate their clinical issues from 1 (the worst) to 10 (the best). These allow the counselor and client to set priority goals for treatment, to monitor progress, and to determine how to improve the situation.

The steps that summarize the elements of the solution-based brief therapy model according to Basile (1996, pp. 8, 9) are to

- foster the development of a therapeutic or working alliance;
- assess the client's motivation for change;
- establish a goal for treatment;
- use presuppositional and solution-focused language;
- search for strengths, solutions, and exceptions;
- connect and stay connected with your client's sense of humor;
- be pragmatic; and
- stay on track: brief therapy moves slowly.

Time-Limited Therapies and Crisis Intervention

It is also important to acknowledge that briefer therapies are the treatments of choice in crisis intervention. When people experience major traumatic episodes, natural disasters, drug overdoses, and other similar phenomena, brief therapy can serve to reduce the likelihood of more pervasive or chronic problems. Small (1971), for example, reported that brief psychotherapy has prevented or decreased the need for rehospitalization of schizophrenic patients, decreased the acting out of suicide threats, restricted and minimized the effects of a full-fledged mental disorder, and served as a procedure for saving life in severe depression. Crisis intervention using brief and focused therapy and counseling in such situations can result in a decrease in pain, a shortening of the period of disturbance, and a greater awareness of other possibilities and resources in an individual's life by which purpose and control can be restored.

There are many different models of crisis intervention; some are psychodynamic in origin, others are behavioral or insight-oriented. Crisis intervention continues beyond the immediate traumatic episode that precipitates or attends the actual crisis. Although estimates of time involved vary, crisis intervention as a form of brief therapy usually takes anywhere from 1 to 6 weeks as the client regains equilibrium and control of the coping skills important in dealing with the factors that triggered the crisis (e.g., marital breakup, intense emotional experience, loss of a loved one, abrupt unemployment, acute illness, drug overdose).

In crisis work, counselors are typically more active, directive, and goal oriented than in noncrisis situations. "Since time is short, therapists become active participants in assessing the difficulty, pinpointing immediate needs, and mobilizing helping resources. In some situations, crisis counselors give advice and initiate referrals to help a person 'make it through the night' " (Slaikeu, 1984, p. 79). Although various authors have recommended different process models, the salient steps in crisis intervention, according to Slaikeu, are to

- make psychological contact (e.g., invite client to talk, listen for facts and feelings, summarize and reflect facts and feelings, make empathic statements, communicate concern, encourage catharsis, physically touch or hold, bring calm control to an intense situation);
- explore dimensions of the problem (e.g., inquire about needs, the precipitating event, lethality, the status of present inner and social resources, the immediate future, impending decisions);
- examine possible solutions (e.g., ask what client has done thus far, explore what client can do now, brainstorm possible actions together, help the client to redefine the problem and possible solutions);
- assist in taking concrete active steps (e.g., give advice, refer, mobilize other resources, act on the person's behalf, control the situation to ensure that the person is safe); and
- follow up (establish a procedure to follow up and maintain contact with the client to assess progress and to reinforce the use and availability of resources) (p. 87).

Crisis intervention or brief therapy is sometimes called *psychological first aid*. Within this context, Slaikeu has proposed three subgoals: providing support, reducing lethality, and providing linkage to helping resources. Earlier, Pasewark and Albers (1972) suggested that crisis intervention involves three main areas: (1) establishing or facilitating communication with the person in crisis and with others who are significant (e.g., family members) or who can be of immediate help (e.g., suicide prevention teams, medical personnel); (2) assisting the individual or family in perceiving the situation correctly and concretely with respect to the meaning of the events at issue and their possible outcomes; and (3) assisting the individual or the family to manage feelings and emotions openly and comprehensively.

Obviously, there is much overlap between crisis intervention and brief or time-limited therapy. Counselors in many different settings will find such techniques important in their direct service delivery to clients, in their provision of consultation and in-service to other potential caregivers in the community (e.g., clergy, teachers, policy makers, attorneys, hospital emergency room personnel, managers or supervisors in the workplace) and in their supervision of peer-counseling mechanisms (e.g., telephone hot lines).

PROGRAM PLANNING OF COUNSELING AND RELATED SERVICES

Implicit, if not explicit, in systematic eclecticism and in psychoeducational approaches to counseling described here is the concept of planned approaches to intervening in client behaviors either on a preventive or a remedial basis. In other words, rather than waiting until a client with a demonstrated problem arrives in the counselors's office, planned approaches allow the counselor to reach out and to be proactive in relation to the likely needs of potential clients. Such approaches are particularly useful in the prevention of certain types of problems or in the promotion of health and wellness. Examples are programs in managing or reducing stress, developing problem-solving skills, managing anxiety more consciously and with more control, assuming personal responsibility, gaining an internal locus of control, and increasing feelings of power or reducing feelings of powerlessness. These programs involve planned application of the skills of interpersonal communication, anger management, assertiveness, decision making, values clarification, and relaxation. They represent developmental content designed to equip clients with the attitudes, knowledge, and skills by which they can anticipate, plan, and act on a variety of personal, psychological tasks. They also often serve as support mechanisms for persons engaged in significant transitions in their lives.

Planned approaches in counseling can be designed specifically to modify risk factors, as described in chapters 5 and 6, that predispose certain individuals or groups to develop psychopathology or problems of living. The content of such programs might include promoting social competence and coping in children and adults, facilitating infant development, and providing systematic parent training to reduce instances of child abuse and to create environments that foster healthy growth and development. These approaches involve a body of content that is psychological in nature, is designed to address some set of life skills, and embodies various techniques of learning (e.g., identifying the target behavior, modeling appropriate strategies, giving homework, providing practice and feedback).

Planned approaches not only reflect important content but are useful in describing the likely results of counseling, group work, or other therapeutic approaches. Rather than arguing that if a school, or community agency, or independent practitioner offers a specific, defined set of services the effect on clients will probably be positive, planned approaches identify the outcomes or results to be achieved. The intervention strategies can vary in relation to the intended outcomes, but a counseling program can be evaluated and held accountable for the results it achieves and the difference it makes, not on whether or not certain functions are in place. Planned approaches in any setting endeavor to specify clearly the ends sought and the specific methods by which such ends will be realized.

Planned approaches in counseling systematically link theory and practice and increase the application of the scientific knowledge of human behavior and what is known about the effectiveness of counseling interventions under specific conditions. When a program has a clear set of outcomes to be achieved, there are likely to be many processes or interventions that can be implemented to achieve selected individual outcomes. Focusing on the contents of specific program outcomes, and then determining what process (or processes) is likely to be effective in achieving them, is different from providing every person the same intervention or set of interventions whether or not they are relevant to the needs to be served or to the outcomes sought. It is in this context that the perspectives of attribute-treatment interaction, differential treatment, multimodel therapy, or systematic eclecticism combine with processes such as that of psychoeducational approaches to provide the content for program planning.

The impetus toward planned programs in counseling has been particularly evident in schools, colleges and universities, and career counseling programs in business and industry. For example, in school counseling for at least the past two decades there has been a press to make school counseling programs more specific in the results they intend to achieve and in the ways they hope to achieve them. In a major report on school counseling in the United States about 20 years ago (Herr, 1979), major emphasis was given to the then-emerging trend to apply "systems thinking" to guidance and counseling programs in the school and to create planned programs. Examples of the outcomes to be expected from such systematic problems were identified as

1. statements of program goals and behavioral expectations for students that lay a base for a clearer national definition of how guidance and counseling integrate with larger educational goals;
2. clarity about expected outcomes from guidance and counseling with their contributions distinguished from those of other aspects of education;
3. clear rationale for the provision of guidance and counseling at elementary, middle and junior, and senior high school levels as part of an articulated program from kindergarten through grade 12;
4. the basis for identifying the counselor competencies necessary to achieving each of the outcomes assigned to programs of guidance and counseling and, as such, a knowledge base for designing both preservice and in-service preparation for school counselors;
5. a conceptual framework for considering not only guidance and counseling as processes but also as curriculum; and
6. a conceptual structure for aligning the goals of guidance and counseling with those of education and for delineating the guidance responsibilities of teachers, parents, community representatives, administrators, and school counselors (pp. 117–118).

These perspectives have been incorporated into conceptions of school guidance programs—not just school guidance services—by the American School Counselor Association (1984). Specifically, in a major school counselor role statement related to career guidance, this professional organization asserted that professional school counselors *develop* and *manage* their guidance programs to ensure career development assistance to all students, particularly to those who will begin their work-centered life upon completion of high school. They will also collaborate in the development of other programs designed to assist students' successful transition from school to work, such as vocational education and apprenticeship programs. Throughout this document and others from the American School Counselor Association, there are similar expectations that school counselors will engage in planned programs as major intervention strategies.

A further explicit example of the need for such planned approaches to counseling programs in schools was affirmed by the Commission on Precollege Guidance and Counseling (College Entrance Examination Board, 1986, pp. 5–6) when it recommended the following actions as priorities for schools:

1. establish a broad-based process in each local school district for determining the particular guidance and counseling needs of the students within each school and for planning how best to meet these needs;
2. develop a program under the leadership of each school principal that emphasizes the importance of the guidance counselor as a monitor and promoter of student potential, as well as coordinator of the school's guidance plan;
3. mount programs to inform and involve parents and other members of the family influential in the choices, plans, decisions, and learning activities of the student; and

4. provide a program of guidance and counseling during the early and middle years of schooling, especially for students who traditionally have not been well served by the schools.

Although statements about planned programs of counseling in colleges and universities are less apparent than is true in schools, such programs, particularly in career development and placement, have clearly become more planned and systematic. In university centers concerned with career development, planning, and placement, placement of students into majors or jobs is no longer seen as an event but rather as a process in which various types of information, skills, and attitudes need to be developed. Thus many career guidance activities are sequenced throughout the college experience to bring the college student to a point of maturity and decision making that can culminate in effective placement. In such situations, universities are seen as interacting systems of academic departments, experiential opportunities, and career specialists that can by systematic planning be brought to bear on student career development through career advising, career counseling, and career planning; through courses, workshops, and seminars that offer structured group experiences in career planning, job-access skills, decision making, and related topics; and through group counseling, individual counseling, placement programs, peer counseling, and computer-assisted career guidance (Herr, Rayman, & Garis, 1993).

Business and industry have also become increasingly conscious of planning programs of human resource development, employee assistance programs, career development, and other areas of importance to counselors. The intent in these efforts is to assist workers to become more productive, reduce job dissatisfaction, combat substance abuse, and plan their career mobility and informal or formal education. Because of the costs involved as well as the potential long-term value to workers and to employers, such employee counseling and development programs need to be comprehensively planned in their design and implementation. Gutteridge (1986), using the language of industry, reinforced such a point when he stated that "human resource management is comprised of four distinct yet interrelated job systems: organizational design, human resource (manpower) planning, career development, and control and evaluation" (p. 53).

Leibowitz, Farren, and Kaye (1986) argued that comprehensive, systematic career development programs have become essential to maximize employee productivity and meet the human resource needs of organizations. To that end, they developed a change and planning model to install career development systems in industry that includes 12 principles or tasks grouped into four categories: Needs: Defining the present system; Vision: Determining new directions and possibilities; Action plan: Deciding on practical first steps; and Results: Maintaining the change. These categories or stages roughly parallel those proposed by Herr and Cramer (1996) as appropriately applied to the design of comprehensive programs of career development in schools, colleges and universities, workplaces, or agencies:

1. develop a program philosophy;
2. specify program goals;
3. select alternative program processes;
4. describe evaluation procedures; and
5. identify milestones (crucial events) that must occur for program implementation.

The basic set of assumptions on which rests the viability of planned programs, whether psychoeducation, prevention, career, or eclectic, includes the following:

- Individuals can be equipped with accurate and relevant information translated in terms of personal development level and state of readiness.
- Individuals can be assisted to formulate hypotheses about themselves, the choice points that will be in their future, and the options available to them.
- Individuals can be helped to develop appropriate ways of testing these hypotheses against old and new experiences.
- Individuals can be helped to come to terms with the personal, educational, and occupational relevance of what they already know or will learn about themselves in the future.
- Individuals can be helped to see themselves "in process" and to acquire the knowledge and skills that will allow them to exploit this process in positive, constructive ways.
- Individuals acquire feelings of personal competence or power from self-understanding and the ability to choose effectively.

Still within the rubric of planning is the development of programs such as Life Skills Training (Gazda & Pistole, 1986). Although it might just as easily be described in the earlier section on psychoeducational models in this chapter, skills training represents a systematic and planned program for sharing psychological knowledge and expertise. The focus of the program, according to Gazda and Pistole, is on "the kind of behavior-based psychological learning needed to help people cope with predictable developmental tasks" (Adkins, 1985, p. 46, as quoted in Gazda & Pistole, 1986) that occur throughout the life span. In particular, the Life Skills Training model draws from a developmental taxonomy of generic life skills based upon seven areas of human development: psychosocial, physical-sexual, cognitive, moral, vocational, ego, and affective. In turn, the Life Skills Training program is composed of developmental families of life skills including such areas as interpersonal communication/human relations; problem solving/decision making; physical fitness/health maintenance; and identity development/purpose in life.

After identifying, together with the client, the gaps in knowledge or the skills deficits to be addressed in either individual or group counseling, a five-step training model is implemented. The steps include, in a flexible sequence, (1) didactic instruction, (2) leader modeling of skills or the use of videotaped models of skills being demonstrated, (3) demonstration using simulations to allow the clients to practice the skills in a controlled environment using role-play or paper-and-pencil responses, (4) the use of skills in personally relevant interactions with others in real situations, and (5) transfer of training to enable spontaneous use of the life skills in dealing with problems on a day-to-day basis.

As suggested in each of the examples cited in this section, counseling and related processes, particularly those focused expressly on psychoeducational and deliberate skill development, whatever the setting, are planned and systematic events, not random events. Many examples of such programs are available to be adapted from the professional literature and from commercial sources. Much more of such program development is likely to be seen in the future.

COMPUTERS AND COUNSELING TECHNOLOGY

As the previous sections of this chapter have suggested, counselors are inexorably becoming applied behavioral scientists and program planners. They are also becoming technologists. For the past two decades or more, various technologies have been developed to extend or reinforce the counselor's potential to effect behavioral change in clients. Depending upon the specific point in time at issue, new counseling technologies have included the application of gaming, audio-video processes, simulations, films, assessment centers, problem-solving kits, self-directed inventories and programmed resource material, and, perhaps most comprehensively, computer-person interactive systems designed to facilitate client behavior rehearsal and exploration, information retrieval, assessment, planning, simulation of likely outcomes of action, and treatment. The latest technology to augment counseling, and particularly career counseling, is the Internet.

Implicit in the preceding observations is the notion that advanced technology as described in chapter 2 has implications not only for affecting the lives of clients. It also continues to promise new tools, new conceptual models, and new ethical dilemmas for counselors. Of particular concern in this regard are the effects of computers and the Internet in counseling.

Computers in Counseling

Mainframe, mini, or micro computers have been to many counseling, guidance, and mental programs what electricity has been to the light bulb, a source of energy that gives form and substance to many types of interventions impossible without such energy. Many metaphors have implicitly or explicitly been applied to explain the effects, potential and actual, of computers and related technology on individual personal and career development, mental health, decision making, or information retrieval and analysis. In some instances, the computer has been cast as a mind multiplier, as a way of compounding an individual's vision about possible futures in which she or he can engage, or as the pathway to such futures and the risks or investments associated with different behaviors. In other instances, the computer has been conceptualized as a prosthesis, a replacement for a specific individual's disabilities or limitations that enhances mobility, communication, or problem solving, thereby expanding an individual's development. Beyond these roles, computers have been conceived of as forecasters of possibilities, organizers of time, schedulers, and information retrieval devices. They have been used for assessment and diagnosis, for psychophysiological measurement and biofeedback, for behavior observation and assessment, for statistical and visual analyses of data, for motivation of children, for administrative support of counseling programs (billing, financial management, budget preparation, maintaining databases, word processing), for telecommunications (Romanczyk, 1986), for consultation on emotional crises (Hedlund, Vieweg, & Cho, 1987), and for intervention with psychiatric patients (Matthews, DeSanti, Callahan, Koblenz-Sulcor, & Werden, 1987).

Within such possibilities, computers have been found useful in extending the capability of counselors in managing client or student development information; monitoring medication usage by psychiatric patients; record keeping; assessment or test scoring; helping people develop a predictive system about opportunities available to them, creating a personal profile of their strengths, and developing job-seeking skills; and guiding individual decision making. In social terms, the information and the images that computers can provide have the potential to neutralize the differences or deficits in experiences that characterize the life opportunities of different people as these are related to socioeconomic background, race, sex, or disabling condition; to alter decision-making patterns; and even to alter human identity (Mruk, 1987).

Perhaps more importantly, computer-based technology potentially empowers individuals to have an internal rather than an external locus of control. It says, however indirectly, "You can choose, you have options, you can make connections between the present and the future." In this sense, computers both provide information as the fuel for decision making and say, in figurative terms, to the chooser, "You can control how you will participate in education, training, work, or life." Thus computers not only help to educate people for choice but also represent a tool by which an individual is enabled to choose uniquely, as an independent person who is encouraged to impose a planning structure upon possible behavioral scenarios rather than let behavior fluctuate randomly at the whim of external forces.

As such, computers have inexorably redefined the content, the time spectrum, and the characteristics of the intervention strategies appropriate to influencing the personal and career development of different groups of people. Although many of the uses of computers in personal and career development are still promises, not actualities, they have required that counselors increasingly become technologists. As technologists, counselors have been stimulated to think as applied behavioral scientists and as program planners; as professionals who can use computers as part of an integrated set of elements that extend the capabilities of counselors, not replace them; as specialists who recognize that the personal and career development of individuals and groups is multidimensional and requires differential treatments. Although many of the questions to be confronted in the incorporation of advanced technology in the workplace or in counseling are theoretical and abstract in nature, the computer, and its effect on the profession of counseling, is no longer an abstraction. It is a tool, a form of technology, that fits not in an absolute sense but in a relative way into some conception of program, some formulation of goals, some pattern of methodology. It is a powerful tool capable of overwhelming and overshadowing the very elements it is designed to promote; to an unprecedented extent, the medium is a very important component of the message, which has implications for ethical issues, professional standards, counselor preparation, and professional development (Herr & Best, 1984). Viewed in somewhat different terms, the use of computers and other forms of technology has made it important for individual counselors and the profession to come to terms with, at the least, recognizing the meaning of technology in personal or career development, identifying the counselor's role in technology, encouraging appropriate preparation of counselors in the use of technology in personal and career development, and paying attention to the ethical issues and problems generated by technology (Herr, 1985).

The Meaning of Technology in Personal and Career Development

As discussed in chapter 2, technology is applied science. The technologies affecting personal and career development flow from theoretical conceptions of behavior, empirical validation of such conceptions, assumptions about interventions in such behavior, and finally empirical verification of the effects of such interventions. Technology is neither hardware nor, indeed, software.

> The objective of technological discoveries as well as of their applications is information. . . . High technology is not a particular technique, but a form of production and organization that can affect all spheres of activity by transforming their operations in order to achieve greater productivity or better performance, through increased knowledge of the process itself. (Castells, 1985, p. 11)

Applied to personal, educational, and career development, computers and technology are valuable to the degree that the outcomes they facilitate are appropriate to the program planning or counseling outcomes to be achieved. An isolated computer sitting in a room removed from the mainstream of a counseling program is unlikely to affect significantly the development of students or clients unless the information it is capable of providing is relevant to the types of behavior change a counseling program intends to promote and is systematically integrated into a program of behavioral change. The presence of the computer must affect the organization and the process of career counseling, guidance, or psychotherapy if the applied scientific potential it represents is to influence systematically the resulting personal or career development of clients.

Therefore, counselors must be proficient in those approaches—such as differential treatment, multimodal approaches, and systematic eclecticism—that reflect the need for and the structure of multiple intervention. Counselors must learn to view the use of computer-assisted approaches to individual development as part of a plan, as one of the treatments of preference, not the only, or even the preferred, approach for all counseling programs. In so doing, they must demystify technology, understand its uses and abuses, and reduce the propensity to imbue technology of any kind with a spirit and life that it does not have.

Computer Applications

As already suggested, many computer applications are possible in counseling and in psychotherapy. Three will be briefly discussed here in terms of their utility.

Computerized career guidance systems. Perhaps the most well-known computer applications are computer-assisted programs of career guidance, which have been in development and use for nearly 30 years. Each day, they serve thousands of users (Sampson & Reardon, 1990). Over 30 major projects to apply computers to career guidance have occurred in the past 20 years, although not more than six to ten major systems are in operation. Those systems that do survive have become increasingly comprehensive in their coverage and in their incorporation of content that emanates from the work of major theorists. For example, the DISCOVER II Program, offered by the American College Testing (ACT) program and created originally by Rayman and Harris-Bowlsbey (1977), incorporates Super's developmental stages, Tiedeman and O'Hara's decision-making model, the data-people-things paradigm of the *Dictionary of Occupational Titles,* and the Holland personality-work environment typology. In the modular approach to the various elements of self-analysis inquiry into occupational and educational opportunities and decision-making processes, people can assess interests, aptitudes, and values; compare input to job requirements, occupations, and programs of study available; determine their location on a world-of-work map; and engage in various decision-making exercises and other forms of inquiry. The SIGI system (the System of Interactive Guidance and Information), developed by the Educational Testing Service (Katz, 1980), focuses on the interaction of values and decisions. In this system people engage in a dialogue with the computer as they examine their values and identify and explore options, receive and interpret data, and practice decision making (Katz, 1993).

Several other major systems (e.g., GIS, CHOICES, CECIL) have similar purposes. Within the broad arena of computerized guidance systems, there are at least eight in America that are primarily concerned with job matching (Botterbusch, 1983). The basic purpose of each of these systems is to match a client's vocational characteristics (or profile) with the requirements for specific jobs. One of the fundamental purposes of employment counseling and, more specifically, of vocational evaluation has been to help a person find a job that requires or relates to what he or she can do. The availability of computer technology has not changed the goal. It has, however, made the goal more attainable, included a larger pool of information to be considered in decision making, and synthesized the interaction of different forms of data with one another so that the likely consequences of choices can be more fully considered. Each of the computer systems just discussed has multiple purposes related to job matching. Although the systems do not cover each of the five purposes usually considered under the rubric of job-person match, they tend to accommodate several of these purposes: conducting job searches for placement, identifying skills from previous jobs that relate to present job conditions and requirements, and providing occupational information, support for decision making, and identification of education/training needed or available as related to various jobs.

A variety of studies have assessed the effectiveness or utility of computer-assisted career guidance systems compared to more traditional career counseling interventions or to other computer-assisted systems. Among the findings are that computers cannot replace professional counselors, but when combined with counselor-delivered career counseling, the combined treatments produce stronger effects than either component alone (e.g., Garis, 1982; Glaize & Myrick, 1984; Niles & Garis, 1990).

Gati (1994), after a comprehensive analysis of four categories of problems and dilemmas of computer-assisted career counseling, suggested that these are also shared by career counselors who do not use computer-assisted career guidance systems. These dilemmas include (a) the fact that all career-related information, including that provided directly by counselors, may be subject to unintentional selection and presentation biases; (b) the need to elicit both aspirations and compromises from clients; (c) the need to provide all of the relevant, but only the relevant, information needed by a client; and (d) the need to evaluate the quality of the counseling whether it is augmented by a computer-assisted career guidance system or delivered by a counselor only. Further, Gati recommended several important procedures for counselors using computer-assisted career guidance systems. These include designing diagnostic pre-screening procedures regarding who should be encouraged to use the available computer-assisted career guidance systems, when, and which system(s); actively monitoring the client's dialogue with the computer-assisted career guidance system and assessing with the client his or her decision-making style; discussing, integrating, and interpreting with the client the information received from the computer-assisted career guidance system, thus making it more meaningful to the client (p. 54).

Computerized personal counseling. The use of computers in personal counseling has been described as one of the most controversial issues in mental health

(Sampson, 1983), partly because of the ethical issues involved and partly because of stereotypes about the amount of interpersonal respect, understanding, and love required in a counseling relationship. Nevertheless, various approaches to the use of computers in personal counseling and psychotherapy are apparent, and such applications are growing.

According to Wagman (1984), there are two general ways to develop a computer-assisted personal counseling system. The first is to design the computer software to model the behavior of the counselor in responding to a client, and the second is to model the computer's intervention after a particular technique of counseling. Several systems have been developed to incorporate one or both models. One of the aspects of computer-assisted counseling programs is the provision of absolute privacy to an individual, who can seek information and assistance without revealing the problem or question to another human being. As these counseling systems become more sophisticated, ethical issues become more complex.

Sampson (1986) has drawn important distinctions between computer instruction in support of psychotherapy and computer-assisted psychotherapy. Computer-assisted instruction (CAI) in support of psychotherapy involves the use of computer technology to facilitate the human interaction between the psychotherapist and the client. Computer-assisted psychotherapy involves the direct and exclusive provision of psychotherapeutic services to the client by the computer. The latter, for technical reasons (e. g., the state of the use of natural language and artificial intelligence), is less advanced than the former. As Sampson suggested, computer-assisted support to all clients is not equally feasible. For example, such an approach is likely to be inappropriate

> . . . for individuals when emotional, cognitive, and/or neurological factors severely limit the capacity to perceive, process, and respond to CAI. For example, individuals who are experiencing motivational difficulties related to a major depression, who have a poor reading ability related to intellectual capacity, or who have an impairment in short-term memory as a result of a closed head injury, are not likely to profit from CAI as an adjunct to psychotherapy. These individuals tend to need the high degree of structure available from conventional psychotherapy. (Sampson, 1986, pp. 4–5)

Sampson also discussed the conditions under which some clients may be able to use stand-alone, self-help CAI software to facilitate behavior change or when CAI is most useful in conjunction with counselor intervention in the provision of psychotherapy. In the latter sense, Sampson also discussed the ways in which CAI can be used as an adjunct to psychotherapy. Examples include its use as an orientation to psychotherapy, as an assessment tool for standardized tests and immediate computer scoring, as a second opinion in diagnosing or classifying the etiology of the client's problem, as an aid to intervention by providing the client examples of cognitive distortions and ways to exercise alternative cognitions (about which the computer could provide feedback), or as a method to simulate or model desirable skills that the client might imitate and practice. Undoubtedly, many other such applications will emerge in the future.

One precursor of the future is the use of a computer for consultation for emotional crises. Hedlund, Vieweg, and Cho (1987) described the use of a proposed computer-assisted evaluation and treatment program for senior enlisted medical corpsmen on nuclear submarines where physicians or psychiatrists are not available. The psychiatric component is intended to provide evaluation and treatment of emotional/behavioral emergencies for nonexperts or paraprofessionals (the medical corpsmen). The system functions as follows.

When a crew member is referred for some type of emotional or behavioral problem, the corpsman uses a highly structured paper-and-pencil interview guide, the Groton Interview Schedule (GIS), to obtain specific information about the problem involved. Whatever information is obtained, including the corpsman's physical examination results, any available collateral information, and any other observations, is entered into a microcomputer. The corpsman is then able to obtain a computer-generated Patient Summary that provides a probable diagnosis, along with a listing of all related symptoms. From this Patient Summary, specific changes or corrections may be made to the data already entered, and the corpsman may obtain treatment suggestions. After initial emergency treatment, the corpsman may modify the patient's database directly through the Patient Summary or by completing GIS data collection, which may have been impossible initially, for additional (or more complete) diagnostic and treatment suggestions. Four references/glossaries (Emergency Treatment Principles, a Diagnosis and Treatment Glossary, a Medications Glossary, and a Glossary of Psychiatric Terms) are available to the corpsman interactively and in hard copy at any time during the assessment-treatment procedures. The diagnostic concepts follow those of the *Diagnostic and Statistical Manual of Mental Disorders* (APA, 1980, 1987, 1994). Treatment suggestions for each psychiatric diagnostic category were adduced from standard texts and expert opinion. A single psychotropic medication for each major problem area (e.g., anxiety, depression, psychotic symptoms) is stocked on the submarines for use by corpsmen as suggested by the diagnostic and evaluation computer system.

Computerized psychological testing.   Alluded to previously is the use of computers for test administration and scoring. Such processes may occur in immediate conjunction with the process of counseling or psychotherapy or simply as an administrative procedure in support of, but distant from, the actual counseling with a client. Nevertheless, computer-based test interpretations are becoming increasingly important in counseling and in psychology. Such applications include computerized adaptive testing that tailors the difficulty of a test to the test taker's ability level. This approach depends upon having a large bank of test items to measure a particular psychological trait that are precalibrated to assess people with different levels of ability or other characteristics (Weiss & Vale, 1987). There are also computer-based test interpretations that rest on systems of knowledge that can be applied to patterns of test scores, thereby providing narratives, profiles, classifications, diagnoses, and suggestions for treatment as well as hypotheses about the client to be pursued in counseling and second opinions that can aid the client and the counselor in psychological decision making. These are so-called expert systems. Obviously, computer-based test interpretation systems can score tests rapidly, accurately, and in large volume, and, where required, can engage in data reduction important for research purposes and for the creation of new tests or test forms.

In broad terms, *computer-based test interpretation* refers to the automation of a set of prespecified rules for use in analyzing, interpreting, and assigning certain qualities to a response or response pattern (e.g., test score, profile pattern) (Harris, 1987). Implicit in this observation, however, are concerns that the quality of the data used in developing software becomes paramount to successful computer applications, as do the training and expertise of test users. These, in turn, affect the accuracy of interpretative output, speed of interpretation, and validity of explanations or classifications (Eyde, 1987).

The Internet in Counseling and Career Interventions

The Internet in its simplest description is the linking of computers at individual sites through existing computer networks around the world to create an international network of information sources and other processes (e.g., group conferences, directories, job listings, on-line counseling, chat rooms). This large number of computer sites and networks when linked together act as though they were one huge mainframe. Originally the Internet allowed users to access text only, but with the recent application of hypertext cards to networked computers and the development of a new Internet protocol, the worldwide web was created and visuals (pictures, graphics, charts) and sound as well as text are now available on an individual user's computer monitor through the Internet (Bolles, 1997).

The Internet to date has been used in counseling primarily for purposes of job search and career-related issues. There are also examples of career counseling being done through e-mail over the Internet (Sherman, 1994). The types of support for job seekers on the Internet, aside from those emerging on-line opportunities for career counseling and career advice, are electronic bulletin boards of job listings, many of which are free, and commercial on-line services (e.g., America Online, CompuServe, Delphi, Prodigy). These commercial services usually charge both a monthly and an hourly usage fee, but they provide such career-related services as career areas with job listings and other features; employer databases by which to research employer characteristics, products, and locations; and opportunities for networking with other users.

According to Bolles (1997), the Internet can be helpful to job hunters or career changers as a place to

1. search for job vacancies or job listings provided by employers;
2. post your resume so potential employers can review it;
3. get some job-hunting help or career counseling;
4. make contacts with people who can help you find information, or help you get in for an interview, at a particular place; and
5. find information or do research on fields, occupations, companies, cities (p. 7).

In addition to describing the career-related capability of the Internet, Bolles also provided the caveats that are relevant to each of these categories of information. For example, there are more than 11,000 sites that report job vacancies on the Internet. Even with some of the excellent search engines (e.g., American Job Bank), it is hard to sort that many jobs and locate the appropriate sites. Many, although certainly not all, are computer-related jobs and as historically been true in using the classified ads, 80% of jobs available are never listed by employers. A similar problem exists with posting a resume on the Internet. A relevant employer must find it, be willing to read and download it, and follow up—but most employers do not search the Internet for resumes. They obtain them in other, more conventional ways. Nevertheless, the Internet is and will become a source of particular types of career-related information that a counselor can help a client seek for and use. Among the possibilities emerging for counselors through the use of the Internet, as identified by Sampson, Kolodinsky, and Greeno (1997), are

- videoconferencing as a possible alternative to the traditional face-to-face employment interview conducted on college campuses;
- using e-mail to respond to specific individual questions about a variety of mental health issues; in this case, the individual frames a problem and a mental health professional responds with information, recommendations for action, and possibly a counseling referral;
- facilitating bulletin board discussion groups that allow counselors to consult with other professionals about specific types of client issues;
- marketing counseling services both on-line and at a geographic site, with an electronic screening interview provided to determine if counseling should proceed;
- delivering counseling services by two-way videoconferencing processes, e-mail, using computer-assisted instruction, moderated discussion groups;
- delivering self-help psychoeducational resources;
- providing counselor supervision and case conferencing; and
- assisting in research and data collection.

Because of the primitive nature, rapid development, and newness of the Internet as a counseling tool, there is an obvious potential for problems associated with the use of the information highway for counseling purposes. Among these, according to Sampson et al. (1997), are

- ethical issues (confidentiality, validity of data delivered via computer networks, inadequate counselor intervention, misuse of computer applications by counselors, lack of counselor awareness of location-specific factors that may affect clients, equality of access to Internet and the information highway by less affluent clients and those who do not have ready access to the Internet, privacy concerns related to counselor-client interactions, credentialing of persons purporting to offer counseling or career advice on the Internet); and
- relationship development issues. How restricting is counseling provided to clients at remote locations through the videoconferencing or other forms of electronic communication? What are the types of clients and circumstances under which counseling via videoconferencing is appreciated?

Thus computers and the Internet offer increased client access to information and to career and mental health counseling, but they also pose challenges to ethical standards for the counseling profession.

Promoting Ethical Standards

The forms of technology, including computer-assisted career guidance or counseling systems and the Internet, that currently are available to influence client development are not benign. They carry with them the potential to harm or to help individuals. As such, they become the focus of ethical dilemmas and the impetus for revised ethical standards.

Because of space limitations, the discussion on ethical issues in this section will focus on the ethical issues related to using computers and the Internet to deliver career services. There are at least two types of dilemmas in dealing with such issues.

One has to do with the nature of ethical issues related to computers primarily, and then by extrapolation to other counseling interventions and goals including the Internet. The other has to do with whether there are both common and unique ethical issues related separately to different types of counseling interventions. Although these distinctions in emphasis may be more apparent than real, they do differ in whether we focus principally on the ethical issues in the use of computers in the delivery of career services or whether we see computers as simply one of many career interventions that share common ethical issues confounded by some unique concerns related to the nature of the particular intervention.

If we assume that, regardless of the nature of the career intervention, there are ethical issues common to the delivery of career services, it is relatively easy to refer to the major ethical codes of the American Counseling Association, the American Psychological Association, or the International Association of Educational and Vocational Guidance, for example, and find categories describing the ethical responsibilities of counselors or psychologists. These categories tend to be familiar to most readers. They include such expectations as the following as found in the Code of Ethics of the American Counseling Association (1995).

- "Counselors and their clients work jointly in devising integrated, individual counseling plans that offer reasonable promise of success and are consistent with abilities and circumstances of clients" (A.l.c.). This point is further extended in the ACA Code of Ethics to career and employment needs of clients by stating, "Counselors work with their clients in considering employment in jobs and circumstances that are consistent with the clients' overall abilities, vocational limitations, physical restrictions, general temperament, interest and aptitude patterns, social skills, education, general qualifications, and other relevant characteristics and needs" (A.l.e.).

- There are many other ethical obligations for counselors included in the ACA Code of Ethics that relate to neither condoning nor practicing discrimination in working with clients; respecting their diverse cultural backgrounds; informing clients of the purposes, goals, techniques, procedures, limitations, potential risks, and benefits of services to be performed and other pertinent information; ensuring freedom of choice by clients; avoiding actions that seek to meet the personal needs of counselors at the expense of clients; respecting the client's right to privacy and affording him or her confidentiality as fully as it can be offered; maintaining accurate records of professional services and not releasing them to third parties unless permitted by clients; knowing and working within boundaries of competence and claiming only legitimately earned professional credentials; referring the client to another mental health provider who has the competencies required when a client needs levels or kinds of intervention that the counselor cannot provide; performing only those testing and assessment services for which training has been received and which are appropriate and relevant to particular clients; and respecting the client's rights to know the results of assessments, the interpretations made, and the bases for conclusions and recommendations.

In large measure, the Code of Ethics proclaimed by the American Counseling Association overlaps with the Ethical Principles of the American Psychological Association (1992). The APA's principles, for example, expect psychologists, counseling psychologists, and others to maintain high standards in their work; to recognize the boundaries of their particular competencies and the limitations of their expertise; to provide only those services and use only those techniques for which they are qualified by education, training, or experience; to demonstrate their integrity in the science, teaching, and practice of psychology; to uphold professional standards of conduct, clarify their professional roles and obligations, accept appropriate responsibility for their behavior, and adapt their methods to the needs of different populations; to accord appropriate respect to the fundamental rights, dignity, and worth of all people and the rights of individuals to privacy, confidentiality, self-determination, and autonomy; to contribute to the welfare of those with whom they interact professionally; and to be aware of their professional and scientific responsibilities to the community and to the society in which they live and work.

In broad terms, these ethical standards define the values, or moral compass, that guide the professional actions of counselors or counseling psychologists whatever their specialization, whatever the intervention in which they engage, and whatever the population they serve. Thus ethical standards provide a frame of reference within which counselors can ensure clients' equal access to career services as well as use of technology that is judicious and sensitive to clients' needs. Although originally constructed to guide the practice of counseling with individuals in the context of a dyadic or therapeutic alliance, as the technologies of counseling or guidance or career services have expanded through the years, ethical standards have expanded to incorporate group work, in some cases computers, and, in their next iteration in all likelihood, the Internet. Thus ethical standards are always works in progress, captives of the state of the art in counseling at the time of their most recent formulation, always in one sense chasing social and technological changes that have an impact on what and how counselors discharge their professional responsibilities.

We can argue that the ethical obligations of counselors to clients (e.g., for respect, dignity, confidentiality, disclosure, preventing harm, doing no harm) change very little, but the roles of counselors change as new technologies and scientific knowledge bases expand to modify what counselors do. It is here that we come to the unique ethical issues that arise from the use of specific interventions or technologies that augment the basic counselor-client relationship. There are many examples that might be cited in the use of interventions that are self-directed or that incorporate gaming or simulation strategies. But certainly two prominent areas that suggest particular possibilities for ethical issues or dilemmas arise in the current growth of computer applications in career services and in the emerging use of the Internet for the delivery of career information or career services. The latter is not yet reflected in any of the major ethical standards for counselors or psychologists at the time of this writing, but the former—the use of computers in counseling or in career services—is reflected in some ethical standards but not in others. For example, as recently as December 1, 1992, the *Ethical Principles of Psychologists and Code of Conduct* of the American Psychological Association did not explicitly address the use of computers. But not doing so does not reduce the obligations of psychologists to act in an ethical and competent manner. For example, Principle A: Competencies, states that

> In those areas in which recognized professional standards do not yet exist, psychologists exercise careful judgment and take appropriate precautions to protect the welfare of those with whom they work. They maintain knowledge of relevant scientific and professional information related to the services they render, and they recognize the need for ongoing education.

Such ethical principles are obviously good advice to counselors as well, but in addition, the Code of Ethics of the American Counseling Association (1995) has addressed directly computer technology used in counseling; and in Subsection A.12. states as follows:

a. *Use of Computers*. When computer applications are used in counseling services, counselors ensure that (1) the client is intellectually, emotionally, and physically capable of using the computer application; (2) the computer application is appropriate for the needs of the client; (3) the client understands the purpose and operation of the computer applications; and (4) a follow-up of client use of a computer application is provided to correct possible misconceptions, discover inappropriate use, and assess subsequent needs.

b. *Explanation of Limitations*. Counselors ensure that clients are provided information as a part of the counseling relationship that adequately explains the limitations of computer technology.

c. *Access to Computer Applications*. Counselors provide for equal access to computer applications in counseling services. (See A.2.a)

This section (A.2.a) in turn states that "counselors do not condone or engage in discrimination based on age, color, culture, disability, ethnic group, gender, race, religious, sexual orientation, marital status, or socioeconomic status." It is this language that addresses specifically the issue of equality of access in computer use but extrapolates to this specific intervention from an ethical legacy that counselors treat all persons, that they provide access to counseling services to all persons with the caveat that they do so with sensitivity to the characteristics of the client and to his or her potential cultural or gender differences from the counselor.

The International Association for Educational and Vocational Guidance (IAEVG) adopted its first ever set of Ethical Standards in Stockholm in August 1995. The basic ethical principles that guide the counselor's or career specialist's obligations to clients as seen through international lenses rest upon the same fundamental elements as have already been described in the ACA Code of Ethics and the APA Ethical Principles but the *IAEVG Ethical Standards* (1996) also explicitly cite the use of computers in several specific contexts. For example,

6. . . . Members of IAEVG. . . recognize that emerging techniques, e.g., computer-based testing or career guidance programs, require periodic training and continuing familiarity with the professional literature in administration, scoring and interpretation. . . .
7. Members of IAEVG promote the benefits, to clients, of new techniques and appropriate computer applications when research or evaluation warrant such use. The counselor/practitioner ensures that the use of computer applications or other techniques are appropriate for the individual needs of the client, that the client understands how to use the technique or process involved, and that follow-up counseling assistance is provided. IAEVG members further ensure that members of underrepresented groups have equal access to the best techniques available, to computer technologies, and to nondiscriminatory, current, and accurate information within whatever techniques are used.

In addition to the ethical standards of the ACA, APA, and IAEVG already cited, it is useful to note that ethical standards related to computer-assisted career guidance (CACG) systems have been established by the American Association for Counseling and Development (1988) and the National Board for Certified Counselors (1987) as well as other professional organizations. But as Sampson and Reardon (1990) have eloquently stated, such ethical or evaluative standards, although important and potentially useful, are effective only when counselors (1) are aware of the ethical and professional issues involved, (2) have an attitude of cautious optimism about the appropriate use of valid software, and (3) are provided with effective CACG counselor training opportunities.

As these perspectives on what major current ethical standards describe vis á vis the use of computers, equality of access, and, increasingly, the use of the Internet and other forms of electronic communications for the delivery of career services, the ethical issues, whether or not they are embodied in codes of ethics, suggest the following actions by counselors:

- Assure that the content of the computer program or, indeed, of the Internet site being used includes accurate, relevant, and timely information for the client or clients using it. When this fact is established, insure that all clients (regardless of gender, race, ethnicity, disabilities) have equal access to such technology.
- Implement efforts to address the needs of inadequately prepared users who are not at ease with using computer or electronic technology or who do not know what they need from the system. Assure that such clients can manipulate the system effectively in order to profit from its use.
- Provide opportunities to engage in follow-up after the counselee has accessed and experienced a system so that the information obtained can be personalized as well as scanned to make sure it is timely and accurate.
- Make use of less expensive ways to accomplish career services when they are found to be as good as or better than other forms of technology.
- Develop safeguards to insure that client privacy or confidentiality is neither violated nor vulnerable in the computer or Internet process in which the client engages.
- Make sure that any computer-assisted career guidance system or Internet use being implemented as part of a career guidance program provides appropriate and accurate information, does not violate practice and ethical standards, does not take decision making out of the hands of the client, and ensures in-depth career exploration.
- Create strategies by which CACG systems as well as other computer and Internet use are seen as tools that may or may not have relevance for particular clients, that are not to be seen as standing alone or independent of the goals and other elements of a career guidance program, and that require counselor monitoring and collaboration with clients about information located or options examined. Several available research studies have suggested that counselors have important roles in insuring that clients gain maximum benefits before, between, and after using CACG systems and that these counselor interventions differ at each of these times (Garis, 1982, Sampson et al., 1989).
- Explore the values that computers or Internet use are most likely to add to individual career counseling or other types of intervention (e.g., increased knowledge of information sources and occupational and educational options, opportunities to try out various career options by exploring the effects of selected variables or access to and outcomes of selected career options, opportunities to engage in a "virtual community" of persons who can be supportive or provide information about specific career issues).

The ethical issues surrounding electronic communications for the delivery of career services also suggest that conselors should be sensitive to the observations by some researchers (e.g., Johnston, Buescher, & Heppner, 1988) that there should not be wholesale use of computerized career guidance and information systems because they have not been subject to sufficient content or psychometric scrutiny. In particular, four types of issues are cited that can be conceived as constituting ethical issues. They include (1) psychometric issues, such as validity and reliability, sex fairness, and fakeability; (2) programming issues, such as flexibility, accuracy of information, technical difficulties, and readability; (3) technical-service issues, such as adequate service by producers when malfunctions or other problems arise; and (4) staffing issues, such as who monitors the computer, what is the counselor's role in relation to the use of the computer, what are staff attitudes toward access and use of the computer.

Sampson and Reardon (1991) have identified six problems related to the use of CACG systems that potentially embody ethical dilemmas for counselors and that to some degree overlap with the observations just cited from the work of Johnston et al. (1988). These six problems or issues are

1. **indiscriminate use of systems**: In essence, this problem includes the overuse as well as the indiscriminate or automatic use of CACG systems with all persons at the beginning of a career guidance process rather than using CACG systems in a deliberate, planned way to meet the unique needs, wants, or goals of the person seeking assistance. Such indiscriminate use of CACG systems assumes incorrectly that all clients have the same or similar needs, rather than unique needs that should be individually matched to the intervention used.

2. **proliferation of technology**: The issue here is not that counselors should use only one intervention or technology but rather that whatever is used should be planned and managed, should be appropriate for the organization and clientele for which it is to be used, and should be within the competencies of the client.

3. **inadequate implementation**: Basically, this issue relates to either the lack of planning by which to integrate CACG systems into a comprehensive program or the lack of counselor input into what systems should be purchased and for what purposes.

4. **inadequate training**: The major problem here is the lack of preservice and inservice training of counselors or paraprofessionals who manage the CACG system and the need for better materials and procedures for training support.

5. **inadequate evaluation of CACG services**: This issue is wide-ranging and deals with the impact of CACG systems on particular career counseling outcomes and on particular populations such as at-risk youth, minority group members, persons with disabilities, various adult populations, and/or clients with varying personality characteristics (e.g., Holland types). Such evaluative issues also have to do with the cost of computer technology and the continuous need to refine or replace it while yielding appropriate cost-benefit ratios.

6. **use of invalid, inexpensive CACG software**: This issue has to do with the possible widespread use of inexpensive, unvalidated, nonstandardized, career-related software. In essence, to the degree that such a problem exists, it obviously relates to several of the previous issues including inadequate training of counselors and seeing CACG systems as stand-alone or piecemeal interventions rather than as systematic and planned parts of a comprehensive career guidance program.

Such problems and issues undoubtedly vary across computer systems and the uses to which they are put. It is likely that in some CACG systems none of these issues or ethical dilemmas pertain, but in others they may be quite relevant; and at this early stage in the development of the Internet, all of these and others cited may be critical. Indeed, the Internet may be particularly vulnerable to other types of problems including widespread violations of copyright law and violations of privacy and confidentiality by forwarding to others e-mail messages by an individual without release to do so. That there is no monitoring of the credibility or accuracy of course content or other information placed on the Internet is another problem. Further, because the Internet is, in an oversimplified sense, a global network of computers that allows many millions of computer users to share and exchange information, ethical problems can be introduced at multiple sites and by multiple users. And such ethical problems can arise separately in connection with the use of electronic mail, transferring files, engaging in special discussion groups, navigating the resources available on the worldwide web, or engaging in chat rooms on special interest topics. For example, there are now 50 million web pages on the Internet with estimates of 30,000 new pages being added each day—which suggests that potential issues of information accuracy, confidentiality, and privacy are serious concerns.

In addition to the perspectives just cited about possible issues and ethical dilemmas that can occur in connection with computer systems in general, there are other issues of which counselors need to be aware that are associated more directly with a specific computer purpose, such as computer-based testing. In such cases, the negatives tend to be more idiosyncratic with regard to aspects of a particular instrument, interpretive program, or hardware configuration than with any inherent problems in the idea itself. Such issues include the near impossibility of group administration of computer-based testing because of the cost of multiple stations. Further, some programs are not user friendly; some instruments are so new and rushed to market so quickly that they provide inadequate validity and normative data; and erroneous or overly generalized interpretations are possible.

Implicit in the potential ethical issues identified here for computer use and, indeed, Internet use are those that more directly affect counselor training per se. Many counselors received their preservice education and training before the computer revolution. Thus their knowledge of computers has been gained largely through formal or informal in-service preparation; consequently it may be superficial and episodic rather than comprehensive and complete. Hence, several possible ethical issues related to the matter of counselor competence to use such systems in career services arise. An overarching one is that because the computer can produce an impressive-looking report, the counselor may assume without checking that the information provided is accurate and up to date or that it is operating within the parameters or context of what is known about career development. In the case of tests, again because the computer is producing impressive reports, the counselor may assume that there is no need to have an in-depth knowledge of the test, its underlying constructs, its psychometric strengths and weaknesses, and its appropriate interpretations, nor to integrate the results with everything else in the career development of the client. Such reliance on computer interpretations by counselors who do not possess sophisticated training in assessment can lead to simpleminded and possibly harmful practices. Although, as already noted, the Ethical Principles of the American Psychological Association as recently as 1992 did not discuss computers directly, as early as 1986, APA produced guidelines for computer-based tests and interpretations. This document outlines how computer usage in mental health fits into the general Ethical Principles provided by the American Psychological Association (such as the general principle "Psychologists shall limit their practice to their demonstrated areas of professional competence," and the specific computer application "Professionals will limit their use of computerized testing to techniques with which they are familiar and competent to use"). At the very least, the ethical obligation is to obtain training in the use of computer-assisted career guidance systems or in the use of the Internet and develop awareness of possible ethical dilemmas associated with them before using such techniques in superficial and potentially harmful ways. In addition, nine user responsibilities are offered (such as "Test performance should be monitored, and assistance to the test maker should be provided, as is needed and appropriate. If technically feasible, the proctor should be signaled automatically when irregularities occur").

There is an emerging concern about ethical research in the information age, particularly as it relates to the Internet. The implication is that researchers who study electronic communities or on-line communications are likely to find themselves increasingly using qualitative methods, changing their commonly used research tools, and adapting their research activities to these new electronic environments. In essence, each of the current capabilities of the Internet, from e-mail to chat rooms, poses its own research dilemmas concerning how to obtain informed consent; how to conceive respondents as owners of the materials they create; how to protect copyrighted material on the net; how to create a climate of trust, collaboration, and equality with electronic community members; how to negotiate researcher entrée into an electronic community; how to treat electronic mail as private correspondence not as research data unless express permission is given; and how to respect the identity of the research respondents in an electronic community, that is, how to protect or mask the origins of the communications and then communicate the results of the research to participants in the research (Schrum, 1995).

In essence, the ethical standards of professional organizations clearly suggest that in order to avoid ethical issues in career services, counselors must learn to view the use of computer-assisted approaches to career development as part of a plan, as one of the treatments of preference, but not as the only (or even the preferred) approach for all counseling programs. In so doing, counselors and, indeed, clients must work to demysticize technology, understand its uses and abuses, and reduce the propensity to imbue technology of any kind with a spirit and life that it does not have.

Further, counselors and clients need to remember that in relation to other career service interventions, the computer or the Internet as the medium is a very important component of the message, a component with serious implications for ethical issues, equality and quality of access, professional standards, counselor preparation, and research.

CONCLUSIONS

As much of the content of this book affirms, the roles of the counselor and of counseling are changing in contemporary society and are likely to change in the foreseeable future. Counseling has become an important method of dealing with mental or emotional disorder, decision making, stress management, the prevention of problems in living, and the promotion or enhancement of wellness and the quality of life.

Counseling, then, is increasingly important across the population spectrum of children, youth, and adults as well as in diverse settings, including educational institutions, workplaces, community agencies, and independent practice.

Within this wide range of people and settings, counseling must also serve diverse purposes. Counseling cannot be seen as a singular process but rather as a set of techniques and approaches that is dynamic in its substance and in its capability to be tailored to the specific needs of populations and settings. Chapter 7 has identified some of the conceptual models and interventions that are becoming standard elements of a counselor's professional repertoire and that enlarge the counselor's ability to differentiate treatments to match client needs. Inherent in such a notion is the likely reality that many clients will need multiple treatments, some of which counselors can provide and some that may come from other referral sources. For example, some clients will need one-on-one cognitive behavioral therapy, computer-assisted career guidance, training in nutrition or budget management, a redesigned job environment, and assistance with subsidized housing or transportation. The counselor alone will not be able to deliver each of these responses, but may instead address the multidimensional needs of the client by providing some responses in a differential treatment design or by serving as a broker of referral sources.

Although the range of possible counseling interventions in client behavior is likely to be larger than any given counselor can use effectively, several trends are changing how counseling is being conceptualized and delivered. These trends deserve to be considered fully by every counselor. Paradigm shifts arise from a fuller understanding of human behavior and from refinements in the application of technology to counseling.

Among the trends in counseling described in chapter 7 most likely to be pervasive in their effect on counseling are those that derive from applying advances in the cognitive sciences—insights into how people process information, connect thinking to feeling and doing, and link cognition to motivation—to methods of intervening in client behavior. The seminal work discussed in this chapter of such authors as Ellis in rational emotive therapy, Beck in cognitive therapy, Krumboltz in social learning and in describing the private rules of decision making, Burns in cognitive distortions, Wolpe in systematic desensitization, Meichenbaum in stress inoculation training, Novaco in anger management, and Suinn in anxiety management represents the ingredients of modified views and approaches to psychotherapy and counseling. These emphases on the cognitive structures that trigger or sustain behavior provide the substance for counseling approaches that, as compared to many earlier approaches, include more active participation between counselor and client in designing appropriate treatments, greater focus on client cognitions and how they might be changed, and the transfer of skills learned in counseling to daily living through homework and other exercises. Certainly, constructivist approaches that strongly assert that persons are active agents of their own meaning making are likely to transform views of clients as passive recipients of treatment, pursuing one external view of reality, into views of clients as collaborators in the dynamic search for relevance in a world of multiple realities.

Beyond the rapid and pervasive effects of cognitive behavioral approaches to individual and group counseling, but not necessarily independent of such perspectives, is the rise in the use of psychoeducational models for purposes of treatment, prevention, and promotion. These approaches combine educative and psychological methods to help people develop skills relevant to more effective coping or to management of different forms of behavior.

Other rapidly emerging trends in counseling include the linkages between career counseling and behavioral health and between mental health counseling and behavioral medicine. These connections, the format and content of such trends as psychoeducational models, and the increasing demands for mental health services in excess of available capacity, among many other factors, have combined to stimulate growing attention to the systematic planning of counseling programs; to brief or time-limited therapy; to new views of eclecticism, multimodal therapy, or differential treatment; and to the use of computers and the Internet in career counseling and psychotherapy. As such changes emerge, they subtly and profoundly alter the professional identity of counselors, expand the range of situations in which counselors must be sensitive to ethical dilemmas, and create new content to be assimilated into counselor training.

The challenges to counselors, theorists, and researchers to find new and increasingly efficient ways to provide counseling have not ended. Chapter 8 identifies additional recurring, emerging, and future challenges that promise to continue to affirm the needs and importance of counseling and to shape the ways by which such processes are defined, organized, and provided.

Chapter 8

RECURRING AND EMERGING CHALLENGES IN COUNSELING

PREVIOUS CHAPTERS HAVE IDENTIFIED FOUR MAJOR challenges that have shaped and will continue to shape significantly the expectations for and the content and practice of counseling for the foreseeable future. These challenges—the economic climate and the effects of advanced technology, changing family structures, growing pluralism and cultural diversity, and expanded perspectives on populations at risk—are both dynamic and comprehensive in their effects upon individual behavior. As such the elements of these challenges encompass many of the factors that precipitate or underlie the majority of problems brought to counselors.

In addition to the four major challenges that are at the heart of this book, other less encompassing but important challenges to counselors are also related to effects upon human behavior and counselor functions. The latter challenges tend to recur across time, are now emerging, or are only dimly perceived as future possibilities. Although these sets of recurring and emerging challenges may be more limited in the proportion of the population they affect than the four major categories of challenges previously discussed, they are also likely to have differential effects on counselors in schools, in colleges and universities, in community mental health centers or private practice, or in business and industry.

While attempting not to duplicate what has already been discussed in other parts of the book, the following sections of this chapter consider some more specific challenges, their temporal characteristics, the populations and settings most affected, and the substance of the challenges or problems at issue. The focus here is on recurring and emerging challenges. Chapter 9 will explore future challenges.

RECURRING CHALLENGES

Recurring challenges are those that tend to reappear under new guises as the national social, political, or economic environment changes. There is no attempt to address all such challenges here, but several seem sufficiently encompassing to note.

A major recurring challenge is the continuing national debate about the role of school counselors in a changing society. Because this debate affects many potential readers of this book, it will be given attention first. A second recurring challenge is the broader issue of the professional identification of counselors as compared with other mental health professionals. Within this challenge are played out the notions of history, language system, power, and other variables that affect how counselors, particularly clinical mental health counselors, are likely to be able to function in the future. A third recurring challenge has to do with contemporary views of testing or assessment and the recurring issues that emanate from such concerns, particularly in relation to culturally different clients. These three recurring challenges will be discussed in turn.

The Role of School Counselors

As the national rhetoric about educational excellence has proceeded in the spate of reports that have followed the National Commission on Excellence report, *A Nation at Risk* (1983), some 15 years ago, one group of professionals whose role often has been ignored, treated negatively, or debated as to new directions is that of school counselors. Some individuals both in and out of the counseling profession question whether school counseling is now obsolete or irrelevant. Others speak of its imminent demise and disappearance. Others address the need for a total restructuring of the school counselor's role around a results-based rather than a process-based model. Still others speak of the reality that however important school counselors are in helping children and adolescents resolve the litany of issues and decisions that accompany their development, the school counseling profession is still plagued by several basic issues (Paisley & Borders, 1995). These issues include the

> lack of control school counselors have over their day-to-day work activities and the development of their profession. The school counselor's role continues to be either explicitly or implicitly defined (if not dictated) by a number of sources [and people], few of whom have any background or experience in school counseling and who often provide somewhat contradictory direction. School counselors, for example, are [often] directly accountable to school principals and the school system's director of school counseling. . . . These two . . . supervisors may have very different agendas about the counselor's role in the school (p. 151). . . . The lack of control over one's professional life and destiny probably contributes a great deal to a second fundamental issue: the ongoing confusion and controversy about the appropriate focus for its practitioners (p.152). [The lack of control also contributes to two continuing philosophical role questions.] The first concerns their role in the delivery of a comprehensive developmental program . . . [although] despite its centrality to the profession . . . such a program has rarely been implemented; and the second philosophical role question being . . . debated is, "What is counseling in the schools?" A frequent response to this question is "school counselors don't do therapy." The distinction between counseling and therapy is never clear, and it often seems to have little relevance. (p. 152)

Those who question the role of school counselors seem to frame questions as dichotomies that yield either affirmative or negative answers. Typical questions are, Are school counselors obsolete or not? Relevant or irrelevant? Likely to survive or to disappear? However, given the complexity of the roles and functions of school counselors in diverse urban, suburban, and rural settings, variations in affluence in school districts and among those served, and variety in the need for mental health services in and out of schools, yes or no answers about the relevance and suitability of school counseling as a profession seem to oversimplify the factors involved. It might be possible to reduce the status of school counseling in a particular school district or school building to criteria that yield yes or no answers, but the status of school counseling across the nation is not so easy to describe in simplistic terms (Hayes, Dagley, & Horne, 1996; Herr, 1986).

If the question for the profession of school counseling is not one of simple survival as a visible entity in the school, what is the question? It is more nearly, What models of school counseling roles and functions are most likely to be effective under different conditions of student need, educational priorities, and availability of resources? Such a question does not address whether school counseling is worthwhile or effective. It does not treat school counseling as a singular process or set of functions to be uniformly applied in all settings. Rather, it suggests that school counseling can take on different forms and has different purposes given different assumptions about its values and priorities.

In this sense, school counseling has different types of relevance depending on the needs of the nation or of a particular school district at a particular time. Such a perspective also indicates that because different approaches to and organizations of school counseling can effect varied outcomes, the expectations of different groups of students, parents, teachers, administrators, policy makers, or others involved are likely to be described differently. Indeed, as social and economic conditions change in their effects on children and youth, new expectations for counselor functions will continually emerge and be given varying levels of priority.

Examples of relatively recent areas in which various constituents have expected counselors to intervene by offering identification of problems, treatment, or support are single-parent and blended families, chemical dependency and recovery from such dependency, grief and bereavement, adolescent suicide, child sexual abuse, children with learning disabilities, conflict resolution, and anger management. Of course, such foci for counselor involvement exist along with the traditional assumptions that school counselors will engage in preventive, developmental, or remedial efforts on behalf of curricular choice and planning for postsecondary education, career development, education for decision making, job search and access, the transition from school to work, personal adjustment, and other related areas.

Neither the emerging nor the traditional expectations of school counselors are necessarily inappropriate. In schools across the nation, counselors undoubtedly get involved with every one of these problem areas and many others. The problem for counselors in such circumstances is not whether they are relevant or whether they are wanted; rather, it is the need to clarify their priorities given varying resources and multiple sets of needs.

One very positive sign that school counselors are increasingly exerting their professional judgment about the priorities they should be meeting and their place in the school setting is found in *The National Standards for School Counseling Programs* developed over several years and adopted by the American School Counselor Association (ASCA) (1997). In the Executive Summary of the standards, ASCA answered the question, Why School Counseling Programs?

> The purpose of a counseling program in a school setting is to promote and enhance the learning process. The goal of the program is to enable all students to achieve success in school and to develop into contributing members of our society. A school counseling program based on national standards provides all the necessary elements for students to achieve success in school. This programmatic approach helps school counselors to continuously assess their students' needs, identify the barriers and obstacles that may be hindering student success, and advocate programmatic efforts to eliminate these barriers. (ASCA, 1997, Executive Summary)

In line with the increasing emphasis on results-based counseling programs that are discussed at several points in this publication, the American School Counselor Association has suggested that school success requires that students make successful transitions and that this outcome, in turn, involves the acquisition by students of the attitudes, skills, and knowledge essential to the competitive workplace of the 21st century. The areas of student development that underlie such student access are also the areas that school counseling programs must facilitate: academic development, career development, and personal-social development. These three broad areas encompass nine standards, each of which includes a list of student competencies or desired learning outcomes that define the specific types of knowledge, attitudes, and skills students will obtain as a result of an effective school counseling program.

The nine National Standards for School Counseling Programs (without the specific student competencies for each standard) by area are as follows.

Academic development
- Standard A—Students will acquire the attitudes, knowledge, and skills that contribute to effective learning in school and across the life span.
- Standard B—Students will complete school with the academic preparation essential to choose from a wide range of substantial postsecondary options, including college.
- Standard C—Students will understand the relationship of academics to the world of work, and to life at home and in the community.

Career development
- Standard A—Students will acquire the skills to investigate the world of work in relation to knowledge of the self and to make informed career decisions.
- Standard B—Students will employ strategies to achieve future career success and satisfaction.
- Standard C—Students will understand the relationship between personal qualities, education and training, and the world of work.

Personal/social development
- Standard A—Students will acquire the attitudes, knowledge, and interpersonal skills to help them understand and respect self and others.
- Standard B—Students will make decisions, set goals, and take necessary action to achieve goals.
- Standard C—Students will understand safety and survival skills.

These standards and the associated student competencies, implementation materials, and evaluation instruments available from the American School Counselor Association suggest that regardless of the particular emphasis or model of school counseling that is implemented by a particular school, there is a core of student knowledge, attitudes, and skills that should be basic outcomes of any school counseling program, that these can be measured, and that they are central to the mission of the school.

In essence, these observations suggest that some counselors may be asking the wrong questions. There is little evidence that school counselors are not wanted or are likely to become extinct as a profession. More positively, there seems to be considerable evidence that some observers view school counselors as quite relevant, even essential to achieving certain educational goals, but they are calling for new emphases in school counseling programs, more integrated services with other professionals, and more direct attention to the challenges to students from a multicultural, technologically sophisticated, and rapidly changing society (Hayes et al., 1996). A few examples of the many available national indicators of support for school counselors over the past 15 or so years follow.

The Carl D. Perkins Vocational Education Acts. The Carl D. Perkins Vocational Education Act of 1984 and the Carl D. Perkins Vocational Education and Applied Technology Act of 1990 have been designed to influence national and state educational initiatives, including funding curriculum development that integrates academic and vocational skills for vocational education and for academic students, advances the articulation of vocational/technical program from the secondary school into the community college and beyond, advocates comprehensive career guidance programs for all students, and promotes equity and excellence for minority students in relation to their opportunities in vocational education and in the occupational structure.

Both of the Perkins Acts are literally filled with support for the importance of career guidance and counseling in meeting the Acts' purposes. In many of their titles and sections, the Perkins Acts advocate the importance of career guidance and counseling roles in dealing with such issues as the problems of special needs populations, sex equity, career choice, information about new and emerging occupations, and many other matters of importance to vocational and nonvocational education students and to the economic development of the nation.

What is perhaps most important, the 1984 Carl D. Perkins Vocational Education Act required that career guidance or counseling functions should be discharged by professionally trained and certified counselors. Unless school counselors and others are aware that earlier vocational education legislation identified career guidance functions as important but did not require certified counselors to do them, they may not understand the importance of the language of the 1984 Perkins Act. Such legislative language affirmed that school counselors are relevant to students' choice of and success in vocational education, to the transition from school to work, and to the nation's economic development; and it described the specific functions of school counselors that are relevant to these goals.

As this book was being written, the U.S. Congress was debating the reauthorization of the Perkins Acts. Of concern was that several conservative special interest groups wanted to eliminate explicit provisions for career guidance and counseling and for school counselors, even though the 1984 Perkins Act had made them major emphases. In any case, funds will continue to be available to support such activities. Although the fate of this reauthorized bill had not been decided by the Congress, it was clear that persons both in the House of Representatives and the Senate were interested in strengthening the career guidance and counseling provisions.

In the Perkins Acts, whatever the reauthorization of 1998 ultimately concludes, the question is not whether school counselors are useful, worthwhile, or obsolete. Rather, the implied question is, What roles are important for them to play? The question to be debated, therefore, is not a dichotomous good or bad, but rather which functions under what conditions are priorities for school counselors if they are to be most facilitative of the educational goals for students supported by the Perkins Acts.

Although other subsequent federal legislation related to vocational education, the school-to-work transition, and economic development has not been as specific about the need for and the roles of professionally trained and certified school counselors as the Carl D. Perkins Act of 1984, that precedent has been established, and there have many instances in which school counselors have been incorporated in federal legislation, either explicitly or implicitly.

The School-to-Work Opportunities Act. On May 4, 1994, the U.S. Congress passed the School-to-Work Opportunities Act. Programs under this Act combine classroom learning with real-world work experience and fund the training of students in general job readiness skills as well as in industrial-specific occupational skills. The School-to-Work Opportunities Act provides incentives to high schools and community colleges to create programs in cooperation with business and to develop the academic skills and attitudes toward work that too many adolescents lack and that both educational and community agencies have neglected.

The School-to-Work Opportunities Act provides for a school-based learning component, a work-based learning component, and a connecting activities component. Although many elements of these components have relevance for the school counselor, it is particularly important that the Act makes career guidance in the school a central component. In Section 4, Definitions, the Act defines *career guidance* to mean programs

(A) that pertain to the body of subject matter and related techniques and methods organized for the development in individuals of career awareness, career planning, career decision making, placement skills, and knowledge of local, state, and national occupational, educational, and labor market needs, trends, and opportunities; (B) that assist individuals in making and implementing informal educational and occupational choices; and (C) that aid students to develop career options with attention to surmounting gender, race, ethnic, disability, language, or socioeconomic impediments to career options and encouraging careers in nontraditional employment.

Obviously these are the types of processes in which many school counselors engage and in which more could do so. In that sense, the School-to-Work Opportunities Act affirms the importance of these types of school counselor functions; it affirms the importance of considering career guidance a systematic program as has been discussed in chapters 2 and 7; it builds on many of the concepts found in the earlier Perkins Acts; and it responds to a variety of national reports and blue ribbon panel recommendations of the last 10 or 15 years. Many such reports and recommendations can be cited.

The Educational Testing Service report. *From School To Work* (Educational Testing Service, 1990) suggests that there are two difficult lifetime transition points:

into the workforce for adolescents and out of the workforce for older people. Given the rapid shifts in the American economy, currently the more difficult transitions are into the U.S. workforce. The report concluded that

> . . . the U.S. record in assisting these transitions is among the worst in the entire industrial world (p. 3). . . . School counselors are overburdened, and helping with job placement is low on their agendas. The U.S. Employment Service has virtually eliminated its school-based programs. Our society spends practically nothing to assist job success among those who do not go directly to college. On the whole, the answer to the question, who links school and work is "the young themselves, largely left to their own devices" (p. 3). . . . Most developed countries have highly structured institutional arrangements to help adolescents make this transition; it is not a matter left to chance. West Germany does it through the apprenticeship system, combining classroom work and on-the-job instruction. In Japan, the schools themselves select students for referrals to employers, under agreements with employers. In other countries, there is either strong employment counseling and job placement function within the school system or this function is carried out by a labor market authority of some type, working cooperatively with the schools . . . to be sure, there are some school systems [in the United States] that have good linkages to the work world, often found in the guidance offices of vocational education schools, or as the natural operation of cooperative education programs. But the general pattern has been one of doing a whole lot more to link high school students to college than to work. (p. 22)

Although this report is less flattering to school counselors than some of the other reports and legislation cited here, at least as it relates to the work of school counselors in career guidance, it does not see school counselors as irrelevant. The opposite is in fact the case. The report makes quite clear that the work of school counselors is extremely important to adolescents, but that the counselors are often burdened with so many diverse responsibilities that they are unable to focus on career guidance and job placement.

   U.S. Department of Labor report.   In 1993, Public/Private Ventures of Philadelphia, Pennsylvania, under funding from the Employment and Training Administration, U.S. Department of Labor, engaged in an extensive process to identify potential exemplary programs by conducting a comprehensive search of databases for materials related to career guidance for disadvantaged youth, particularly for reports containing evaluation information; by reviewing summaries of all programs identified by the Department of Education's National Diffusion Network; and by pursuing recommendations made by experts in the field. Four exemplary sites were identified, and the characteristics of these programs and their demonstrated success with their target populations were extensively studied and reported on in *Finding One's Way: Career Guidance for Disadvantaged Youth* (U.S. Department of Labor, 1993). The researchers found that in these programs in general, "drop-out rates declined while attendance, motivation, life skills, and future planning [by students involved] increased" (p. 33). Of particular interest to the discussion of counselor relevance were the findings that the exemplary programs were found to share several traits (described here in slightly abridged form).

- **Career guidance is not compartmentalized and targets youth in ninth grade or earlier.** Exemplary programs utilize an integrated sequence of career development activities (self-exploration, information gathering, hands-on experience, and decision-making components) rather than one-shot approaches occurring late in the school career (i.e., late adolescence). They are built in rather than added on and consist of activities tailored to the age and status of participants.

- **The connection between education and employment is emphasized.** According to the researchers, all programs visited seek to help students understand the relationships between their current status, their planned occupational futures, and their educational needs. They link education, knowledge, and skills to economic, personal, and social rewards. All four of the programs visited provide opportunities for youth to gain work experiences and reflect on these experience in a guided, controlled environment.
- **A limited caseload for counselors, advisers, mentors, or coaches allows for individualized attention.** They have low adult-to-youth ratios, and all four programs have mechanisms that provide for continuity of relationships between youth and individual members of the counseling staff; the programs assume that given the career development needs of the participants, easy and consistent access to counselors is critical. The delivery of the programs' other components is individualized to ensure both the quality of program content and youth's positive relationship with adult authority figures.
- **Coalitions linking programs to businesses, parents, and community agencies are fostered and developed.** Outreach to these partners helps ease the load of counseling and guidance and connects youth to the adult worlds of work, family, and civic responsibility. Adults outside school settings play particularly important roles in guiding youth's career decisions. Each constituency contributes to the delivery of the program and has a stake in its success.

National Commission on Secondary Vocational Education report. Because the report of the National Commission on Excellence in 1983 essentially neglected the role of vocational education and school counseling in achieving academic excellence, the National Commission on Secondary Vocational Education was created to correct that imbalance and to provide affirmation that school counselors are important to excellence in vocational education.

The commission's report, *The Unfinished Agenda* (National Commission on Secondary Vocational Education, 1984), was of particular importance to the discussion of the relevance of the school counselor in relation to vocational education. For example, with regard to overall function, the report suggested that "school counselor functions need to include cooperative activity with teachers, the use of group guidance techniques, computer-assisted guidance, comprehensive career information systems, and related methods designed to provide career guidance to all students" (p. 24). The commission also recommended that counselor-student ratios should not exceed 250 students per counselor and that systematic programs of interest and aptitude assessment, career planning, and occupational information designed to facilitate student curriculum choices should be available to all students. In the report, the commission further suggested that all students should be able to choose from a comprehensive set of course offerings across academic and vocational areas.

In broad as well as in narrower terms, the commission's report supported school counselors in roles beyond those of importance only to vocational education students:

> . . . inadequate student knowledge subtly but formidably constrains student access to vocational education. Students and parents need to be accurately informed about what

vocational education is, how it relates to their personal and career goals, and how it can be used to help them achieve their goals. One does not choose what one knows little about or is constrained from choosing by unexamined social attitudes.

We need comprehensive career guidance programs that will provide this information and remove some of the subtle status distinctions involving vocational education. Comprehensive guidance means counseling that is available to all students, covering all subjects, leading to all occupations.

We cannot achieve this goal of comprehensive guidance when counselors must deal, on the average, with 400 or more students. Nor can this goal be achieved unless counselors and teachers cooperate in new approaches to facilitate the career development of students, unless counselors expand their use of group techniques, computer-assisted guidance, comprehensive career information systems, and other methods designed to provide assistance to all students. Counselors must serve as a resource to integrate career guidance concepts and occupational information in the classroom. In addition, the amount of shared information between vocational educators and school counselors should be increased to reinforce the likelihood that counselors will effectively advise students to consider vocational education as an option. (p. 16)

The Carnegie Foundation for the Advancement of Teaching report. Another major national report dealing with federal rhetoric about educational excellence was the Carnegie Foundation for the Advancement of Teaching's *High School, A Report on Secondary Education in America* (Boyer, 1983). Unlike many others, this report was unequivocal in its support of guidance as a critical need. According to the report's conclusion,

> The American high school must develop a more adequate system of student counseling. Specifically, we recommend that guidance services be significantly expanded; that no counselor should have a caseload of more than 100 students. Moreover, we recommend that school districts provide a referral service to community agencies for those students needing more frequent and sustained professional assistance. (p. 306)

The report alluded to how busy school counselors are, to the multiple expectations others hold of them, to the lack of time to meet with all those who need to talk with them, and to the overloading of counselors with case loads of students of more than 600 to 1 in some schools. There was no implication in the report that counselors are obsolete, useless, or irrelevant. The plea throughout was for the expansion of guidance services not only to meet the needs of college-bound students for a more effective assessment and guidance program but also to meet the needs of students not going on to college:

> There is also an urgent need to help noncollege students figure out where they should go and what they should do. It is ironic that those who need the most help get the least. Frequently noncollege students get only snippets of information about job possibilities from family or friends or other students or counselors at school. It is unacceptable to focus our elaborate testing and assessment system only on those moving to higher education while neglecting the other 40 to 50% who even more urgently need guidance. (p. 134)

The report of the Commission on Precollege Guidance and Counseling. In 1984, the College Entrance Examination Board established a 21-person commission consisting of school counselors, professors, industrialists, and administrators in higher education (i.e., presidents, directors of student financial aid or of admissions). *Keeping the Options Open* (College Entrance Examination Board, 1986), the final report of this commission—the Commission on Precollege Guidance and Counseling—was published in 1986. In general, it was a study of how students receive information about the opportunities and financial aid available to them in higher education. The commission was concerned about how early and in what forms information must be delivered to students and their parents so as to have the greatest effect on their academic planning, preparation, and achievement. Of particular interest was how information and support were provided to children from racial or ethnic minority groups. Among other issues of concern to the commission were when and how children develop feelings of self-worth and confidence and who is involved, what the preconditions for choice are, what the specifics of transition from high school to college are, and what elements need to be included in guidance programs in secondary schools to help ensure that once students have been admitted to a college of their choice they will be able to anticipate and cope with the requirements of college adjustment (e.g., time management, loneliness, and separation from home).

In the commission members' dialogues in cities throughout the nation, one theme prevailed: School counselors are important in precollege guidance and counseling at each educational level from elementary school through junior high school and into senior high school. The roles of counselors in fostering feelings of confidence regarding academic readiness, curriculum choice, and planning for higher education are not the same at each of these levels, but in the aggregate, counselors at each educational level complement each other's efforts. The commission also found that in many places counseling is inadequate because too little is offered too late, and it is uneven for particular groups of students. Counselors should not be expected to do everything. Their role has been stretched so many ways that its essence is frequently lost.

It is important to note that the commission was cognizant that if greater numbers of minority children are to gain access to and succeed in college, effective counseling must begin at an early age, in the elementary school, and continue through high school. Although counselors are not the only individuals responsible for the effective academic planning and performance of children, they are key sources of information and support in this process. Ways must be found, therefore, to sharpen the counselors' role on behalf of such students' needs, to prepare students for their roles, and to reduce the unevenness in availability of guidance services across students and settings.

The report of the College Board's Commission on Precollege Guidance and Counseling was cited in the previous chapter in relationship to its strong statement in behalf of planning for guidance programs and in doing so on a building-by-building basis.

The National Association of College Admissions Counselors report. Somewhat similar to the work of the College Entrance Examination Board's Commission on Precollege Guidance and Counseling was the National Association of College Admissions Counselors report, *Frontiers of Possibility* (1986). The concern of this report was the quality of the college decision process for students and the role of counselors in that process. Among other things studied was the amount of time that the guidance staffs of schools spent on college counseling as a proportion of all of their activities, including personal and vocational counseling as well as noncounseling activities.

This report provided one of the most constructive perspectives on the contribution of the school counselor and counseling in the context of schooling:

Situated at the juncture of the academic and the personal lives of students, we found that the counseling office is central to the mission and life of the school. Looking more specifically at the college counseling process, we found that the counseling office is strategically located at the convergence of school, family, and societal aspirations. . . . There are several college counseling practices that are consistently associated with excellence, including a (college) guidance curriculum, networks of support, financial aid initiatives, and productive relationships with colleges. (pp. 49-50)

The report also described the college guidance curriculum as one that has an explicit sequence of activities designed to carry students through several years of high school experience. Accordingly, "the goals of the curriculum should include the enhancement of student self-esteem, the broadening of horizons and aspirations, and preparation to make sound decisions—especially decisions about college" (p. 39). The content of such a college guidance curriculum should include effective study skills, clarification of values, writing and speaking, testing, the application process, career exploration, information about colleges, financial aid, criteria for decision making, work internship opportunities with local businesses and social service agencies, special workshops for women dealing with college issues, SAT preparation, and career counseling and transition workshops focused on coping with the transition from high school to college or work.

In addition to these perspectives on the content of a college guidance curriculum, the report also identified the characteristics of effective college counselors, such as student advocate, effective manager, and effective leader. To discharge such roles, counselors need both a strong work ethic and political savvy. This report, as well as the College Board report, acknowledged that minority students as well as nonminority students must be encouraged to prepare for higher education. The United States must expand its pool of skilled and educated people to provide leadership, research, and enlightened citizenship to the economic, social, and political structures of the nation as it moves toward the 21st century. School counselors are vital components of that process.

The relevance of school counselors: some summarizing thoughts. As we review the diverse but supportive views of the importance of school counseling just cited, several perspectives emerge. Collectively, they suggest that, in a major sense, the future role of school counselors is based upon several pivotal concerns:

- the degree to which school counseling programs are systematically planned; tailored to the priorities, demographics, and characteristics of a particular school district or building; and clearly defined in terms of the results to be achieved rather than the services to be offered;
- the degree to which school counseling programs begin in the elementary school or in the secondary school—thus, the degree to which school counseling programs can truly be longitudinal (K to 12) and systematically planned around major developmental tasks and the knowledge, skills, and attitudes they comprise rather than confined to crisis intervention activities and quasi-administrative functions such as testing and scheduling;
- the degree to which school counseling programs are seen as responsible for the guidance of all students or for only some subpopulations of students such as those at risk;

- the degree to which school counseling programs include teachers, other mental health specialists, community resources, parent volunteers, and families as part of the delivery system;
- the degree to which school counseling programs are focused on precollege guidance and counseling, counseling in and for vocational education and the school-to-work transition, counseling for academic achievement, and counseling for students with special problems, such as bereavement, substance abuse, antisocial behavior, eating disorders, and family difficulties (single parents, stepparents, blended family rivalries);
- the degree to which counselors should be generalists or specialists, members of teams or independent practitioners, and proactive or reactive with regard to the needs of students, teachers, parents, and administrators;
- the degree to which counselors employ psychoeducational models or guidance curricula as well as individual forms of intervention to achieve goals;
- the degree to which the roles of counselors can be sharpened and expanded while at the same time not holding counselors responsible for so many expectations that their effectiveness is diminished and the outcomes they effect are vague;
- the degree to which school counselors have a reasonable student load, 250 or less, so that they can know these students as individuals and provide them personal attention; and
- the degree to which school counselors effectively communicate their goals and results to policy makers and the media both to clarify their contributions to the mission of the school and to enhance their visibility as effective, indeed vital, components of positive student development.

The Professional Identification of Counselors

Many of the dilemmas and concerns of school counselors have relevance to the evolving professional identification of counselors in other settings. Reflecting both a recurring and an emerging issue, the status of professional licensed counselors, clinical mental health counselors, mental health counselors, and other subsets of counselors (who have successfully obtained credentials as nationally certified counselors or licensure to provide independent counseling practice in a particular state) in comparison to other mental care providers is still problematic.

As a function of history, training, credentialing, and power, the mental health professions differ in their status, in their fee-setting ability, in their access to third-party payments, in the techniques they are permitted to use, in the clients they may serve, and in relation to each other. Such differences describe the fact that the mental health professions independently and collectively play out various caregiver roles frequently defined in legislative statutes or in governmental regulations. Therefore, what they are permitted to do and to whom becomes part of a sociopolitical process that is partly scientific and to a much larger degree political.

In comparison to psychiatrists, clinical and counseling psychologists, clinical social workers, and psychiatric nurses, professional counselors (outside of either a school base or a setting concerned with employment or rehabilitation) are relatively new arrivals on the mental health scene, particularly as independent providers of such services. As the functions they perform are seen as overlapping with those of the mental health practitioners who have earlier established their legitimacy in the provision of such services, issues of professional identity are frequently proxies for issues of economics and political power. In addition, as professional counselors lay claim to the legal sanction to obtain clients without either the referral of physicians or other mental health professionals (particularly psychiatrists and psychologists) or supervision by members of such groups, professional identification and competence as buffers against problems of territoriality and other assaults (legal, economic, political, ethical) need to be communicated and the access to clients refought across states and communities, through legislation, and with third-party payers (e.g., insurance companies) regarding procedures for paying insurance or mental health care benefits.

These issues have been discussed at length elsewhere (Herr & Cramer, 1987; Weikel, 1985; Weikel & Palmo, 1996). Suffice it to say here that professional counselors' search for professional identification and sanction is not unlike the struggles that counseling psychologists had to engage in for recognition and social sanction. Professional counselors and counseling psychologists have both evolved from roots in the guidance movement, from origins in the practice of counseling in schools and universities, and, particularly, from historical commitments to vocational guidance as a technique in which they had obtained considerable expertise. In their evolution, professional counselors and counseling psychologists have adapted many psychotherapeutic interventions, including psychotherapy, to the developmental and crisis needs of many in the essentially "normal" populations, perhaps better described as nonpsychiatric or nonpathological, with whom they have traditionally worked. As national mental health policies have increasingly shifted funding from institutional settings, particularly educational settings, to community settings, then to private practice, and now to such settings as health maintenance organizations (HMOs) and other forms of managed care, professional counselors, clinical mental health counselors, and counseling psychologists, particularly those who wish to engage in longer term and more in-depth procedures with children, youth, or adults than educational settings permitted, sought other settings, including independent practice, in which to employ their skills.

Part of the recurring professional identity problem for professional counselors, clinical mental health counselors, and counseling psychologists is the tension between the mental health services for which the society wishes to pay and the skills that professional counselors have and the goals to which they are committed. For example, as cited in previous chapters, the prevention of mental disorders and risk factors or the promotion of health and the quality of life or career issues have tended not to be targets of mental health funding. Mental health funds, including so-called third-party payments, tend to be focused on the treatment of severe emotional or behavioral problems—those classifiable within the taxonomy provided by the American Psychiatric Association in its *DSM-IV* or its previous editions, *DSM-III* and *DSM-III-R*. Such disorders often tend to be seen as more appropriately treated by psychiatrists or clinical psychologists whose skills and training have been oriented to the procedures and perspectives of the medical rather than the nonmedical setting in which professional counselors and counseling psychologists are usually trained.

The conflict between funding of treatment or the funding of prevention and the promotion of healthy behavior also gets caught up in the recurring debates about the nature of mental illness, problems in living, personal competence, and other areas of behavioral, psychological, or biological dysfunction that cause personal distress or impairment. As these definitions blur and move from the realm of biological causes to those predominantly explainable by faulty learning, psychological distortions, inadequate socialization, behavioral skill deficits, or related phenomena, the clamor for parity ensues among a wider group of mental health professionals than among those with primary allegiance to the medical setting, the medical model, or the "cure" of pathology. Such notions lie at the base of the recurring issues of professional identification that professional counselors face. These issues then become overlaid with questions of content and length of training, type and length of supervision, purpose, organizational affiliation, and related matters by which different groups of mental health practitioners might be differentiated.

The classic distinction between counseling psychology and clinical psychology promulgated by Super in 1955 continues to provide contrasting views of service delivery, values, and priorities relevant to the clients that different groups of mental health providers might serve, and to what purpose. According to Super's definition,

> *clinical psychology* has typically been concerned with diagnosing the nature and extent of *psychopathology*, with the abnormalities of even normal persons, with uncovering adjustment difficulties and maladaptive tendencies, and with the acceptance and understanding of these tendencies so that they may be modified. *Counseling psychology*, on the contrary, concerns itself with *hygiology*, with the normalities of even abnormal persons, with locating and developing personal and social resources and adaptive tendencies so that the individual can be assisted in making more effective use of them. (1955, p. 5)

The two "windows" or anchor points provided by the distinctions cited by Super on the clinical psychology versus the counseling psychology approach to mental health delivery are both subsumed in the original definition of the professional mental health counselor:

> The mental health counselor performs counseling/therapy with individuals, groups, couples, and families; collects, organizes, and analyzes data concerning clients' mental, emotional, and/or behavioral problems or disorders; aids clients and their families to effectively adapt to the personal concerns presented; develops procedures to assist clients to adjust to possible environmental barriers that may impede self-understanding and personal growth; utilizes community agencies and institutions to develop mental health programs that are developmental and preventive in nature; provides a wide variety of therapeutic approaches to assist clients, which may include therapy, milieu therapy, and behavioral therapy. (Palmo, 1996, p. 55)

This definition of the clinical mental health counselor shows a decided interest in the use of counseling (or psychotherapy) to promote self-understanding and personal growth, in development rather than pathology in behavior, in prevention, and in the use of psychoeducational models designed to build client strengths and teach them life skills as a major therapeutic tool. This view of the professional counselor is more likely to focus on helping clients achieve control over their lives than on excising pathology, on helping them deal with the emotional intensity of transitions and life crises than on restructuring personality, and on helping them master and maximize personal resources and strengths through growth and learning than on diagnosing and classifying symptoms.

As Hershenson and Strein (1991) have reported, mental health counselors are not primarily concerned about the client in isolation but about the environment surrounding the client that he or she has to cope with and master. The relationship of the client to home, work, and community becomes a major aspect of the approach by mental health counselors to treating their clients.

Models of professional identity are always simpler than professional reality, where distinctions are less clearly defined or sharply drawn between pathology and hygiology, between treatment and prevention, between being in crisis and in transition. Nevertheless, the recurring problem of counselor professional identity seems to be moving positively and constructively toward tentative resolution as professional counselors are increasingly eligible for state licensure and able to declare their purpose and their contributions to treatment, to education, and to prevention. These contributions serve populations that are chronically at risk, acutely at risk, or are in transition to a new lifestyle through career choice or environmental or family change. They also serve those who seek a level of mentally healthy behavior or wellness not yet attained. These perspectives, as they organize broadly held views of professional counselors, mental health counselors, and counseling psychologists, are likely to diminish the recurring problems of professional identity for counselors and, indeed, for other mental health professionals.

But as professional identity for counselors is improving across the nation where 44 states now provide licensure statutes to regulate counseling and to define its scope of practice in that state, there are still battles to be fought in many states in relation to eligibility of counselors for third-party payments and for acceptability as independent providers of mental health services. In essence, providers of health insurance, employers who provide self-insured plans of health benefits for their employees, Blue Cross/Blue Shield, government programs (such as CHAMPUS, Medicare, and Medicaid) and managed care organizations (e.g., HMOs, preferred provider organizations, and other similar managed care groups) have different qualifications for counselor practice. These often vary across states and even within states. In some states, licensed professional counselors can not receive reimbursement directly from third-party payers for the mental health services they provide. Instead they must be employees or subcontractors of community mental health agencies; in other states they must be providers accepted by a managed care organization referred to and supervised by a physician or a clinical psychologist. In other states, licensed professional counselors are not eligible at all for certain forms of third-party payment.

These issues of professional identity and the ability of licensed professional counselors to meet the criteria for eligibility for third-party reimbursement are continuously improving, but these issues are dynamic as changes in policy and legislation concerning mental health delivery, cost-effectiveness, managed care, and related issues unfold at state and federal levels. In some states and with some payers, licensed providers must receive certification. In other instances, some third-party payers and managed care providers do not consider counselors one of the "core providers" of mental health services nor do they consider counseling to be a uniformly qualified profession because of what counselors are licensed to do versus psychologists (for example) and because their titles vary from state to state; in essence, these third-party payers do not believe that the profession is defined consistently by its regulatory laws (Throckmorton, 1996). In these particulars the counseling profession must continue to refine its competencies and training, its research base about counselor effectiveness, the consistency of its credentials across the nation, and its public relations and political activism.

Testing and Assessment

Another of the recurring challenges to counseling is the use of testing and assessment. Some theorists have argued that the use of tests violates the principles on which a nondirective or collaborative relationship between counselors and clients is based. Perhaps more emphatic is the concern of many observers that testing is sexually or racially biased and, indeed, penalizes rather than facilitates the growth of specific groups of clients. Still others argue that the reasons for testing during this century have changed, and that the purposes and uses of testing in contemporary counseling approaches must change accordingly. The latter is a particularly important point because significant social processes like testing and assessment, or indeed counseling with which they are so interactive, do not exist in a vacuum. They are shaped by and must respond to political and economic forces as well as to new advances in knowledge about cultural diversity, mental or emotional distress, learning, career development, and other phenomena of concern to the users of tests and assessment.

Most counselors are familiar with these contentions about testing and their recurring nature. Therefore, because of space limitations, an in-depth analysis of each of these matters will not be undertaken. But it is important to acknowledge the continuing challenge that the use of tests represents, summarize a few of the major themes underlying such concern, and speculate about emerging trends likely to have an impact on the content and processes of testing and assessment.

Gordon and Terrell (1981) put the pro and con arguments for testing succinctly:

> Critics of testing argue from a sociopolitical context, and thus challenge the very purpose as well as the developed technology of standardized testing. Defenders of testing argue from a traditional psychometric context, with little or no concern for political or social issues. The arguments of the two parties cannot be understood and appreciated without reference to those contexts. (p. 1167)

Gordon and Terrell argued that the reasons for testing at the beginning of this century and for several decades afterward have changed and so must the purposes of testing. In their view, a meritocratic approach to testing designed to identify those few who deserve special attention is no longer viable in a period when the availability of human resources has increased. In response to changes in the social and political environment, the meritocratic selection of a few as a goal has given way to allocation of opportunities. The assertions of group superiority on the basis of test scores and the subsequent control of the opportunity and reward structure to retain low-status groups in some socially assigned position has given way to an attempt to democratize access to opportunity; thus the use of tests also should change. As understanding grows about the pluralism in and diversity of the effects of ethnicity, sex, race, and social class upon cognitive and affective structures, learning styles, motivation, and related matters, these should be reflected in purposes for assessment. Gordon and Terrell (1981) contended that

> The proper course of assessment in the present age is not merely to categorize an individual in terms of current functioning, but also to describe the processes by which learning facility and disability proceed in a given individual so that it is possible to prescribe developmental treatment if necessary. . . . The equalization of opportunity may require that intervention be responsive to the functional characteristics of the person to whom the opportunity is being made available. It must be determined where the examinee is in terms of function, how he or she got there, and how growth within the examinee's particular social and cultural environment can be enhanced. (p. 1170)

Underlying the concerns of both the critics and the defenders of testing, but not always well articulated, is the reality that any test, assessment, or other measurement procedure has many validities, not just one (Messick, 1995). In fact, it is not only the validity of the measure itself about which counselors must be concerned but rather the validities of the inferences from the measures that counselors make. Guion (1974) stated that, "the kind of validity statement we seek in any given measurement situation depends on the kinds of inferences we wish to make. This fundamentally is a value judgment" (p. 290). Thus however scientific or empirical the development of any measurement instrument may be, its probable multiple validities and the inferences that can be made from it bring both the test and the inferences into the area of values and social contexts. Frequently, then, those who argue for or against tests, are really arguing about the different validities or inferences that can be assigned to these tests. In essence, many of the controversies about standardized tests and other forms of assessment can be dismantled into issues that have to do with the constructive or predictive validity of tests on the one hand, and such issues as the utility of test information or, perhaps more precisely, the social functions of standardized tests on the other.

Haney (1981) studied the history of social concern over standardized tests and testing throughout this century. Although the content of the debate continues to change as more is known about the technical aspects of test construction and interpretation and about the behaviors being measured, Haney contended that social concerns about standardized testing tend to be as much matters of social and political philosophy as they are technical matters of scientific measurement.

Embedded in the ongoing debate about the social functions of testing is a major concern about test bias, particularly with regard to sex-related concerns and to whether members of minority groups are being inaccurately assessed or otherwise disadvantaged by the use of tests. But test bias, like other aspects of test content and use, is more than a singular issue. For example, as many experts have observed, test bias consists of at least the following elements: overinterpretation, sexism, content, differential validity, the selection model, the wrong criterion, and the testing atmosphere. These factors are often confounded by the cultural background of the student or client and of the counselor or clinician (Tseng & Streltzer, 1997).

Other observers argue that the main features of test bias lie in content, modality, and structure as well as in application and interpretation. Therefore, standardized tests are inappropriate for use with populations whose cultural, linguistic, economic, or social backgrounds differ from those in the majority culture for whom the test was designed and validated. Supovitz (1997) responded to these concerns by contending that a diverse society deserves a more diverse assessment system. Supovitz argued that

> of course standardized tests are biased. But it is not just standardized tests—any simple testing method is biased because it applies just one approach to getting at student knowledge and achievement. Any single testing method has its own particular set of blinders. Since the bias in testing is intrinsic in the form of assessment used, we cannot eliminate this problem simply by changing the questions asked. Rather we must ask the questions in many different ways (p. 34). . . . What we need are more experiments employing combinations of assessment approaches to arrive at an appropriate melding of test forms both economically feasible and robust enough to minimize the bias inherent in any single measure alone. . . . In the end, the larger, more intractable sources of disparities in student performance stem from broad social and educational inequities. . . . Within the realm of assessment the challenge . . . is to find the appropriate balance of a variety of assessment forms, so that students of different genders, from different backgrounds, and with different affinities can demonstrate their capabilities. (p. 37)

Cole (1981), Cronbach (1980), and other scholars of testing have differentiated between the technical aspects of test bias and the questions of proposed use of tests that are really ethical or policy questions. These scholars are concerned about whether or not a test accurately measures what it purports to measure. This is a scientific and technical question involving assessments of criterion-related or predictive, construct, or content validity, or, indeed, the more recent efforts to combine these three measures of validity into a broader understanding of the meaning of a particular score (Cronbach, 1980). In the latter view, the different types of information reflected in the various approaches to validating a test's accuracy are simply types of evidence that singly or in combination attempt to reduce the technical bias, the lack of accuracy in what is measured, the inappropriate interpretation of test scores, and the misranking of persons on the construct or content measured. But the concern of counselors and the public about test bias is not a technical matter. For the most part, it is a question of ethics or values. Simply stated, the questions are, Regardless of the technical validity or accuracy of the test, should it be used for the proposed purposes? What are the potential consequences of testing or the effects upon social values inherent in a particular type of test?

In essence, a test can be designed to predict accurately performance in some educational or occupational set of tasks. Indeed, it may accurately indicate that Whites or men are more likely to be successful than Blacks or women on these tasks. Thus in its predictive validity it is unbiased in its technical or psychometric qualities, but the social and ethical questions begin where questions of technical bias stop. The question arising in this example is, Should the test be used for selection purposes? If it is, Whites or men will continue to gain in access to opportunities, and Blacks or women will continue to be impeded in this quest. Is such a result ethical? Does it represent an appropriate social policy? Does the test accurately reflect the social history of the groups? For example, even though the test accurately differentiates the groups on the basis of their potential performance, it is not able to factor in the fact that Blacks and women have been penalized in their current performance on the basis of previous inferior educational opportunities, limited developmental experience, or lack of encouragement. What part should the causes of (the etiologies and the developmental factors that influence) different types of test performance play in using the test results? These are not issues of test validity per se but rather of policy, ethics, and values. They raise policy questions about "differently weighting" the characteristics of applicants to attempt to compensate for past social wrongs, or the use of quotas in selection of applicants. They also raise other questions of ethics or policy. For example, should tests be used to select or facilitate access to opportunity?

Anastasi (1985), after reviewing trends in psychological measurement over a 50-year period, extended to test developers and counselors the challenge that results from the interaction between the individual and the social contexts in which he or she has developed and in which tests are given. These two contexts may be dramatically different in cultural and in other terms. Different cultures provide different opportunities or reinforcements to learn or to implement different cognitive skills, form particular concepts, participate in logical analysis, or engage in abstract thinking. These cultural contexts are also likely to differ in the affective variables they reinforce relative to test performance and test taking generally. Counselors must understand and appreciate such differences and transform the information tests provide into what is relevant to the counseling purposes at hand—to modify and extend behavioral options not simply to classify people in fixed categories of high and low—and to the growing understanding of the effects of cultural diversity on test performance.

The recurring challenges to testing just specified are not likely to abate for the foreseeable future. Counselors will continue to need to understand and be able to respond to such challenges. But counselors also need to see the new possibilities in the use of and the purposes for testing. One of these is reflected in the growing need for informed personal excellence.

Since 1983, many reports have called for a renewed national effort to attain educational excellence. The impetus for this pursuit is the rapid application of advanced technology in the home and in the office, in government and in industry, in the armed forces and in education. According to this perspective, the technical requirements of new industrial processes and of international competition will set excellence in basic academic skills as a requirement for larger numbers of youth and adults than ever before. People lacking such knowledge and skills, those who are functionally illiterate, or those who possess other major academic deficits are likely to be left in the wake of technological applications to more and more occupations, workplaces, and settings. Thus educational excellence must surely embrace the teaching of basic academic skills to children and youth of different learning styles and motivations, to diverse populations of new immigrants, to adults who need retraining, and to those who have been on the margins of society with jagged work histories and assorted limitations on their ability to perform consistently and effectively in the workplace. Each of these groups will require different forms of educational excellence to equip them with the requisite skills and attitudes necessary to compete in an economic environment of rapid occupational change.

From an assessment perspective, however, educational excellence is an unattainable abstraction without personal excellence and the individual's ability to use fully the educational opportunities available. The mechanism pivotal to effective use of educational opportunities is accurate self-knowledge and intelligence about the individual's strengths and purposes. Such self-knowledge must, in turn, be embedded in the personal confidence that using the individual's skills or talents constructively will lead to meaningful and desired outcomes. Thus assessment cannot stand alone but must be integrated with other dimensions that provide motivation and direction to individual purposefulness. In the case of children and youth, such self-knowledge must be available as early as possible so that students can use it before making curriculum choices that restrict their future access to advanced education or occupational mobility. To assist students in making effective use of the educational reforms manifested in improved academic standards and courses, schools must help students acquire a base of personal information capable of providing purpose and direction to their schooling, and monitor their progress toward goals. In large measure, the vehicle for such personal information is a comprehensive testing program.

Within such a comprehensive testing program, in addition to monitoring academic progress in various clusters of academic skills (such as mathematics, science, and reading) and to flagging the need for remedial education where necessary, it is equally important to use assessment to help students decide upon and adjust their decisions about which academic patterns of coursework to pursue. This type of testing is important not only in pursuing educational or personal excellence but in career guidance as well. Curriculum decisions are not trivial. They are, in fact, intermediate career decisions. By their content, they open some doors and close others. The degree to which individual course selection includes mathematics and science determines whether or not an individual will enter specific college majors, which are also intermediate career decisions, or specific occupations or careers.

Thus within a comprehensive testing program there must be at least two major types of assessment: aptitude and interest. Aptitude assessment measures what is variously called *developed abilities* or *learning potential*. These are the individual traits that comprise maximum performance, potential for vertical mobility, competitiveness, and trainability at different levels of intellectual or cognitive rigor.

In interest assessment, the focus is not on maximum behavior but on an individual's typical behavior relative to those attitudes and preferences that mediate job satisfaction or feelings of similarity in values and goals with others in a workplace, occupational group, or curriculum. Related to interest assessment are values assessment and other measures of motivational direction. Whether the focus of such assessment is interests, values, or satisfaction, the content is not so much cognitive or performance-based as oriented to identifying preferences and the educational or occupational groups to which the individual's test scores are similar or bear resemblances. Such data help the individual to define goals, purposes, and settings in which performance aptitudes might be applied.

Aptitude assessment and interest measurement combine in various ways with other measures of career planning and decision making to help students or adults make informed choices, set personal standards, chart progress, determine areas of performance in which they are likely to succeed, and career fields in which they might feel comfortable. The self-knowledge from these assessments permits the student to approach educational opportunities and challenges with a sense of personal commitment and anticipation. It permits the student to view educational opportunities as avenues leading to personal goals rather than hurdles over which to leap without a clear sense of where the finish line is or what the rewards awaiting the student upon finishing the course are.

We have lingered over the notions of an informed commitment to personal excellence as fundamentally important to a national quest for educational excellence. This commitment is no less vital given the competitiveness of the international economy. In the corporate world there is also an increasing shift of emphasis from personnel management to personnel development. For broad national goals as well as for individual adults seeking a midcareer change or contemplating retraining, the assessment of occupational potential, personal preferences, and ability to choose becomes an important factor in facilitating employability, commitment, satisfaction, and goal direction.

In such views assessment procedures and testing are not simply classification devices. Rather they represent information resources by which clients can plan changes in their commitments, in the options they wish to pursue, or in other aspects of their environment. Such information is not seen as a static or fixed characterization of individuals but rather as a snapshot of a point in time of potential modifiability in goals and behaviors. This information can be used to educate people for choice and to celebrate diversity, not slot people into roles defined by some cultural criteria. Implementing different perspectives on testing and articulating its meaning to the public and, indeed, to clients will be a recurring challenge. So will the emerging trends to which testing and assessment will need to respond in the immediate future. For example:

1. As the United States continues to engage in school reform, workplace reorganization, and to redefine workforce education and development as well as school-to-work transitions, this nation, like several other nations (e.g., England) will place an increasing priority on the certification of competencies possessed by students and by workers. Employers are no longer satisfied to accept program completion as evidence of employability or occupational skill. Instead, competency certification at various levels and in different paradigms will be expected and assessment measures will be sought to provide such certification. Given the changing nature of the workplace, and the skills required to work with new industrial and business processes in technologically intensive environments and in collaborative work groups, we can expect that the certification of student or worker competencies will go beyond those of competitiveness, problem-solving ability, and resemblance or similarity to work groups, and include greater attention to competencies that underlie complementarity—that is, to the ability to facilitate the work of others and engage in group problem solving, to career motivation (e.g., career resilience, career identity, career insight), to personal flexibility and teachability, to elements of emotional intelligence (e.g., self-awareness and impulse control, persistence, zeal and self-motivation, empathy and social deftness) (Goleman, 1995), and to the skills of integrated planning (Hansen, 1997).

2. It is, of course, important to acknowledge that just as the workplace is changing and the needs for new forms of measurement and measures of newly important skills in the workplace are emerging, so, too, are the broad demands for assessment of progress toward national educational goals at local and state levels and the translation of these into individual competencies that can be measured (National Education Goals Panel, 1994). Many of these goals address measuring demonstrated competency in academic subject areas. Obviously, what is meant by demonstrated competency and how that might be best assessed (e.g., through portfolios and standardized content tests) is still arguable. But aside from such measurement issues, there are others that will challenge and require expansion of our contemporary assessment technologies. The goal stating that "by the year 2000, all children will start school ready to learn" is an example. What does *readiness to learn* mean per se? Do we have the appropriate measures? How do these connect with current clinical measures used for early identification of children at risk? The goal stating that "by the year 2000 all teachers will have the knowledge and skills to teach to an increasingly diverse student population with a variety of educational, social, and health needs" is another example. This poses an interesting competency assessment problem as the criterion variables change across different subgroups of Asian, African American, Latino, Native American, and other culturally diverse groups as well as by age, by educational level, by ability level, by knowledge domain, and by predictor variables describing different characteristics of teachers who are to achieve such competencies. A further example is the goal stating that "by the year 2000, every adult American will be literate and will possess the knowledge and skills necessary to compete in a global economy and exercise the rights and responsibilities of citizenship." This again poses a major set of competency assessment issues. Although we are generally competent to assess individual literacy, we have not yet brought closure to consensus on the knowledge and skills required to compete in a global economy or, indeed, to execute the rights of citizenship.

3. Within the notions of certifying competencies just noted, such perspectives extend to counselors as well. Growth in the ability to make such assessments has increased through the efforts of many researchers and professional organizations, including the National Board for Certified Counselors (NBCC) and the Council for the Accreditation of Counseling and Related Educational Programs (CACREP), but most of the certification approaches have been knowledge based, not performance based, at least as they relate directly to the impact of the counselor on clients. Therefore, if and when the issue of which mental health provider group is most qualified to provide specific services to clients arises because of credentialing competition or some other reason, the resolution of such concerns will need to be achieved in answers to more precise assessment questions, such as Who has the competencies that can be demonstrated in their accuracy, relevance, and effectiveness relative to client needs? What is adequate or proper training and how can it be assessed? What are the specific counselor competencies achieved by counselors-in-training from test and measurement courses as a part of the core preparation for professional counselors? How do these compare with those possessed by clinical and counseling psychologists (master's and doctoral levels)? How should counselor competencies differ in relation to the types of tests being used in counseling practice (e.g., the assessment and diagnosis of emotional disorders, the assessment and diagnosis of aptitudes, interests, career maturity)?

4. A further emerging challenge in testing is teaching the test. The practice of using tests as diagnostic instruments to identify developmental deficits or psychological traits or states of different forms of maximum behavior (as in aptitude tests or typical behavior as found in attitudes or interests) has a long and important history. Often we consider scores from these assessments as both fixed effects rather than as both fixed effects in some cognitive or behavioral areas and modifiable effects in other areas of more malleable individual characteristics that are susceptible to learning or the influence of culture on the learning of the individual. In these cases *teaching the test* means teaching persons why their answers to the tests they took were wrong and what is implied for them in learning or relearning certain types of behavior or knowledge. In such cases, depending upon their uses, tests can be interventions in their own right and the content for counselor-client collaboration. This is a different mentality about testing than the mentality that suggests the scores attained are absolute scores and therefore not susceptible to modification.

The concept of teaching the test is relevant to the observations by Healy (1990) and others that focus on helping clients develop self-assessment skills and on being true collaborators in the appraisal process. In particular, Healy has talked about four obstacles to such a shift in thinking about new counselor-client collaborative models of using appraisal data in career counseling. We have all heard them many times. They include

(1) casting clients as subordinates rather than as collaborators; (2) discounting self-assessment by favoring counselor assessments; (3) de-emphasizing the influence of contexts in clients' development; and (4) focusing on a single choice rather than on strengthening client decision making and knowledge for follow-through. (p. 214)

Such views are obviously impediments to empowering the client by giving him or her the assessment skills that can strengthen self-evaluation and decision making in ways suggested in the excellent book edited by Kapes, Mastie, and Whitfield (1994), through which the relationship between testing and counseling can be enhanced, not fragmented.

5. A final challenge, although not necessarily a new one, has to do with computer applications to testing. In one sense such applications have become commonplace, but such applications are also uneven in their use across settings, populations, and geographic regions. As discussed in chapter 7, computer applications to testing include the self-assessments embedded in computer-assisted career guidance programs, but they go beyond such applications to the administration, scoring, and interpretation of tests. We are finding increased use of computers for self-help programs of all kinds, including those purporting to provide personal counseling through expert systems that model counselor behavior in responding to a client's descriptions of his or her psychological dilemmas. The computer also is being used by some health personnel for consultation on emotional crises when and where psychiatrists, psychologists, or counselors are not immediately available.

Computer-based test administration and interpretation, like every other technique available to a counselor, can be both a boon and a bane. The positives include cost-effectiveness and, in the case of microcomputers, the provision of test information virtually instantaneously. In general, clients seem to enjoy the experience and to achieve as much self-knowledge as when paper-and-pencil tests are used. Further, no violence seems to be visited on the psychometric properties (such as validity, reliability) of accepted testing instruments that are computerized. The negatives of computer-based testing are more involved with the idiosyncratic aspects of a particular instrument, with interpretive programs, or with hardware configurations rather than with the idea itself. Group administration is obviously difficult, if not impossible, because of the prohibitive cost of multiple stations; some programs are not user-friendly; some instruments are so new and rushed to market so quickly that they provide inadequate validity and normative data; and erroneous or overly generalized interpretations are possible. Further, there is as yet little research to determine individual differences in client-machine interactions. If testing and assessment are to meet the challenges required by the tensions in their use between technical and social validities in the use of testing and by the emerging domains to which testing and assessments are expected to contribute definition and measurement, a major national research effort will be required.

EMERGING CHALLENGES

Because of the interplay between external events and people's feelings about themselves, the information they possess, and the knowledge and skills they have acquired, the content of counseling is, in some sense, always changing. Although underlying issues of lack of self-efficacy, misperceptions or mislabeling of events, inability to make commitments, stress, depression, anxiety, or uncertainty may be present in any problem brought to counselors, the precipitants of the counseling problem or its overt classification may change. Thus the fundamental elements of the problems counselors help clients solve may remain relatively constant, but the causes of the problems or the interactions between clients and economic, social, or psychological environments constantly undergo change.

Although it is not possible to consider all the emerging challenges of concern to counselors and clients, several deserve special note. They include AIDS, alcohol and substance abuse, and the importance of self-esteem, personal responsibility, and control as well as and the variety of issues associated with counseling for an older or elderly population.

AIDS

One of the most feared of contemporary health problems is AIDS. Although AIDS is caused by the human immunodeficiency virus (HIV), distinguishing between the two is important. According to Keeling (1993), it often takes some 8 to 10 years for persons who are infected with HIV to develop AIDS. Many people who have tested positive for HIV do not develop the symptoms that characterize AIDS for many years, and as new medications and treatments for the HIV virus and for AIDS become available it is likely that the time between being HIV positive and developing AIDS may grow. Indeed, it may be possible to prevent some persons who are HIV positive from actually developing full-blown AIDS symptoms as well as to better control AIDS symptoms.

As this is written, however, HIV continues to be a disease transmitted sexually or through blood products most often by sharing needles or by associated adventitious events. Recent research has shown that "a majority of new HIV infections in this nation are related to drug abuse—through sharing of contaminated drug injection paraphernalia, through sexual contact with an injection drug user, or through the transmission of HIV perinatally" to children (Leshner, 1997, p. 3). The latter is a particular problem because AIDS is now the fourth leading cause of death among women 15 to 44.

When a diagnosis of AIDS is given based upon the Centers for Disease Control criteria for AIDS (opportunistic infections, neurological disease, and wasting syndrome), AIDS is considered a terminal disease for which there is currently no cure. There is only prevention or a slowing down of the progression of the disease through combinations of medications. Prevention is typically viewed by medical authorities as either complete abstinence from sexual activity, monogamous sexual relationships with partners free from AIDS antibodies that signify the presence of the virus, the use of condoms to keep bodily fluids from being exchanged by sexual partners, or, in the case of intravenous drug users, not sharing needles. Indeed, the sharing of intravenous drug apparatus is seen as the most likely conduit of AIDS to the heterosexual population (Bridge, Mirsky, & Goodwin, 1988), although it is not uncommon for heterosexual persons to be infected by any partner who is HIV positive. In broader terms, the Centers for Disease Control and Prevention's semiannual *HIV/AIDS Surveillance Report* classified cases reported through June 30, 1997, by exposure category as follows: men who have sex with men 298,666 cases; injecting drug use 113,635 males, 41,209 females; men who have sex with men and inject drugs 38,923; hemophilia disorder 4,567; heterosexual contact 18,811 males, 35,760 females; blood transfusion 8,075; risk category not reported or identified 32,854 males, 11,823 females.

AIDS is also a highly emotional disease in respect to the fact that many of the public have overlooked current medical research suggesting that a person who tests positively for AIDS antibodies may not necessarily progress to the terminal and malignant disease itself nor to the AIDS-related complex (ARC). Obviously, however, testing positive for AIDS antibodies is a precondition for acquiring the symptoms and experiencing the degenerative course of the disease. The current primary uncertainties concern whether an individual who has the AIDS antibodies will also develop the disease, and if AIDS develops, how long it will take for the person to die as a result of the disease, particularly in view of the availability of new medicines that have been found to slow the progress of the disease down or cause it to go into remission.

The extensive media attention to the AIDS epidemic within the gay community and with users of intravenous drug apparatus poses major challenges to the counselor in any setting. For example, how does a counselor work with an AIDS victim who is by definition experiencing a terminal illness that will likely result in death in a foreseeable future of possibly months to perhaps 5 to 10 or more years? Or how does a counselor inform students about AIDS and its prevention? Or what responsibility does the counselor or psychologist have to notify an individual at risk for exposure to the HIV virus because of his or her relationship with a carrier of the virus, such as a significant other or a wife who the counselor knows is married to a client with AIDS? Are counselors, who help AIDS victims to practice stress management and other forms of health psychology, able to assist AIDS victims to slow the course of the disease?

Answers to the these questions are not yet clear or complete. Both the American Psychiatric Association and the American Psychological Association are developing policy guidelines to identify psychotherapists' responsibility for notifying individuals at risk of exposure to HIV (AIDS virus). The complexity of that responsibility has been debated in an important article by four attorneys (Girardi, Keese, Traver, & Cooksey, 1988). The thrust of their analysis of therapist responsibility is the degree to which the *Tarasoff* decision in California is applicable in the case of knowledge of an AIDS carrier. Essentially, in the classic case of *Tarasoff v. the Regents of the University of California* (1976), a patient confided to his psychologist his intention to kill his ex-girl friend, Tatiana Tarasoff. The psychologist notified the campus police of this threat but did not notify or warn Tatiana Tarasoff of the known and pending danger posed by his patient. The patient eventually brutally murdered Tatiana Tarasoff, and her parents brought a claim against the Regents of the University of California (employer of the psychologist). The question with regard to AIDS is whether a counselor or psychotherapist who knows that a client is an AIDS carrier should consider that person's sexual activity a "lethal threat" and thereby warn any known sexual partners. Thus in respect to the principal outcome of the *Tarasoff* decision, public policy in favor of protecting confidential communication must yield to the extent to which disclosure is necessary to avert danger to others. The application of this concept to the therapist's or counselor's responsibility in AIDS has not yet been clearly drawn by the courts, but it presages the complexity of the challenges the presence of AIDS holds for counselors.

Beyond the legal implications for counselors, AIDS also holds other concerns. For example, there is the question of the counselor's role in educating people about AIDS. One recommendation is that programs should stress behavioral strategies for preventing AIDS.

> The development of skills in decision making, assertive communication, stress management, and self-esteem will empower students to take control of their lives and practice

healthy behavior. . . . Students must understand that AIDS is a disease for which one chooses to put oneself at risk. (Sroka, 1988, p. 36)

One of the important findings about AIDS is that it is not only an immunodefective disease but also a neuropsychiatric disease. The HIV viral infection proceeds rapidly to the brain and begins to generate central nervous system manifestations. These include cognitive impairment (forgetfulness, poor concentration, confusion, slowed thinking) and motor symptoms (loss of balance, poor handwriting, leg weakness) as well as affective problems (depression). Among the treatments now being used, beyond those of treating the viral infection itself, are processes familiar to or available to counselors: stress management techniques, social support systems, and classical conditioning to combat depression, stress, and other psychosocial factors that make the AIDS victim more susceptible to secondary infections and other forms of physical vulnerability. Enough research is now available to suggest that there is a direct relationship between heightened stress and less effective performance of the immune system. There is also significant evidence that personal attitudes of "hardiness," willingness to fight against the disease by positive personal attitudes, and similar expressions of "control" may delay, it not prevent, the deterioration associated with many progressive diseases, including AIDS (Cohen & Adler, 1988; Glaser & Kiecolt-Glaser, 1988; Temoshok, 1988). These findings do not suggest that AIDS is acquired because of stress-induced problems; rather they suggest that psychological attitudes, positive or negative, influence the course of the disease. Counselors using cognitive behavioral therapy, stress and anger management, and related techniques are likely to provide important help to AIDS patients as they attempt to improve the quality of their life, reduce depression and anxiety associated with having the disease, and exert as much control as possible over the progressive deterioration expected.

Further, counselors are likely to come into contact with terminal AIDS victims and their relatives. In such instances, the role of helping the terminally ill and those who remain to work through the Kubler-Ross stages of loss is similar to that in the case of other terminal illnesses. These methods are discussed elsewhere in the book.

Finally, what makes AIDS an emerging challenge to counselors, although both HIV and AIDS have been known and of major concern to medical authorities, the general public, and counselors for more than 15 years, is the lack of systematic or routine training for counselors about HIV and AIDS in counselor education. When House, Eicken, and Gray (1995) surveyed 243 counselor education programs in the United States, they found that 40% of the programs included no AIDS training in their coursework. Of the 60% of programs indicating that they did provide training about HIV/AIDS, only 2% devoted entire courses to AIDS-related topics. Most of the responding programs that offered coursework in HIV/AIDS did so in courses on human sexuality. The remaining programs included a unit or other coursework on HIV/AIDS as part of a counseling course, practicum, or internship, or held workshops or symposia on HIV/AIDS. Hunt (1996) found somewhat similar results in a survey of CACREP-approved programs, of which 43 of 64 responded. About half of the counselor training programs that responded were providing some basic level of training and education related to HIV/AIDS. About one quarter of the programs offered an entire course, or a large part of a course, devoted to HIV/AIDS; another quarter offered a colloquium. Many of the other programs offered information on HIV/AIDS in courses on human sexuality or related coursework. Hunt also found in her research that few master's papers or theses were addressing HIV/AIDS issues but that some 44 (13%) of the counselor educators surveyed were engaged in counseling services for persons with HIV/AIDS.

What the House et al. and Hunt studies seem to indicate is that counselors will be exposed to AIDS-related issues into the next century regardless of the setting in which they work. To date, however, many counselors are being educated in programs in which they are not exposed to any training in HIV/AIDS topics or counseling practices, even though there seem to be models available in selected counselor education programs that could be adapted more widely. Such a goal will be an emerging challenge for both counselors and for counselor education for the next decade.

Alcohol and Substance Abuse

In other chapters of this book, alcohol and substance abuse were identified as major risk factors for different populations, conditions related to family violence, and the seedbed for children of alcoholics who themselves are likely to become alcoholics or to reflect other types of addictive or codependent behavior. The challenge for counselors regarding the prevention or treatment of alcohol and substance abuse is likely to continue into the future. Thus this challenge is described as an emerging one only in terms of the growing recognition of the magnitude of the problem.

The National Institute of Mental Health (Taube & Barrett, 1985), for example, has indicated that of all mental disorders, the most prevalent for men is alcohol abuse/dependence, and the third most prevalent is drug abuse/dependence. Using the very conservative figures of the 1980 census, 6.4% (10 million) of the population aged 18 and older experience substance abuse disorders. These figures include 7.8 million who abuse and are dependent on alcohol and some 3.1 million who use and are dependent on other drugs. Of admissions to inpatient psychiatric services in the United States in 1980, 22% of those entering state and county mental hospitals had alcohol-related disorders and 5% had drug-related disorders; 34% of the people entering Veterans Administration medical centers experienced alcohol-related disorders and 5% had drug-related disorders. Indeed, alcohol-related disorders represented the most frequent primary diagnoses among admissions to VA medical centers and state and county mental hospitals. In some contrast, affective disorders (e.g., manic episode, depression, dysthymia), followed by schizophrenia, were the most frequent reasons for admission to private psychiatric and nonfederal general hospitals, but within the latter, primary diagnoses for alcohol-related disorders still represented about 9% of all admissions. In other research, alcohol abuse was found to be the most common of 15 major psychiatric disorders with a prevalence rate of 11.9% for men and 2.16% for women and lifetime prevalence rates of 23.83% for men and 4.75% for women (Helzer, Burnham, & McElroy, 1991). Although not every person who abuses alcohol will become an alcoholic, some 5% to 10% of persons who drink will develop a drinking problem, including becoming an alcoholic. The research of Helzer et al. suggested that affective disorders, anxiety disorders, and conduct disorders (antisocial personality) are the three most common psychiatric disorders to be associated with alcoholism. Some 47% of alcoholics have a dual diagnosis, alcohol abuse and a second psychiatric disorder. Estimates are that the lifetime prevalence of major affective disorders among alcoholics is between 18% and 25%. In addition, some 20% to 90% of the alcoholic population experience depressed mood, sleep or appetite disturbance, or cognitive disturbance.

Alcohol is a drug, and it can be addictive. The use of alcohol, particularly drunkenness (being under the influence), is implicated in perhaps the majority of traffic accidents in the United States. It is also implicated in a range of interpersonal problems including child abuse, spouse abuse, and difficulties at the workplace. Overuse of alcohol is implicated in cirrhosis of the liver, which occurs six times more frequently among alcoholics than among nonalcoholics (95% of liver cirrhosis deaths are attributable to alcohol), heart disease, and other cardiovascular problems. In 1992, it was estimated that excessive alcohol consumption was directly related to 100,000 deaths. Alcohol-related homicide and suicide accounted for 11% and 8% respectively. Certain types of cancer that are, at least, partly attributable to alcohol, such as those of the esophagus, larynx, and oral cavity, contributed 17% of the deaths. About 9% are reflected in alcohol-related stroke (Doyle, 1996). Alcohol use is also related to symptoms of depression when people are not drinking (Parker, Parker, Harford, & Farmer, 1987).

The actual number of alcohol-related deaths is hard to estimate, but the true figure is likely to be close to 200,000 deaths per year. According to national polls, there are now about 28 million alcoholics in the United States, and 32% of homes have someone with a serious drinking problem. Put another way, one out of every five people who drink alcohol has a serious problem with its effects. According to the National Highway Traffic Safety Administration, in 1985 more than 22,360 people were killed in alcohol-related traffic accidents involving either primary drivers or pedestrians. This figure does not include all the people injured, the broken families, or those who suffer as a result of such accidents (Alcohol Research Information Service, 1987a). In addition, 1983 data from the U.S. Department of Justice on alcohol use among convicted offenders just before committing an offense indicated that the percentage of people convicted of violent crimes found to be using alcohol at the time of the offense was 54%; of people convicted of property crimes, 40%; of people convicted of drug traffic or possession, 29%; of people convicted of violating the public order, 64% (Alcohol Research Information Service, 1987a). In collective terms, the cost to the U.S. economy for alcohol problems was estimated by the Alcohol Research Information Service to be $128.3 billion for 1986. This amount included the costs of treatment, health support services, mortality, lost employment, reduced productivity, crime, social welfare, incarceration, and motor vehicle crashes.

Alcohol is a mood-altering drug and one that has been called "the most dangerous and debilitating of all the common drugs" (Glasser, 1984, p. 127). However, chemical dependency, or drug abuse, also includes a variety of other substances that cause their consumers pain and problems. These mood-altering substances include amphetamines, barbiturates, cocaine, inhalants, LSD, opiates, PCP, tranquilizers, marijuana, quaaludes, valium, and heroin. Tobacco and even caffeine might also be included in this list. All of these substances change physical, social, or psychological conditions in ways that stimulate, tranquilize, or energize behavior, or increase personal feelings of control for short periods. These drugs are both psychologically and physically addictive for regular users. They become psychologically addictive because the mood alteration that occurs feels good or gives sufficient pleasure to the user so that he or she wants to experience it as often or as intensely as possible. They are physically addictive because the body accepts them, integrates them into normal body chemistry, and begins to crave them in increasing amounts.

Alcohol and substance abuse are problems for all age groups, and they are a major concern for children and youth. In the most recent data released by the National Institute on Drug Abuse, Mathias (1997b) reported that 8th and 10th grade students increased their use of marijuana and tobacco in 1996 while 12th graders continued to use these two substances at generally the same level as in 1995. Marijuana appeared to be the most used drug by 8th, 10th, or 12th graders other than alcohol or cigarettes. These students also seemed to underestimate marijuana's effects. As reported by Mathias, clinical studies have shown that marijuana can have a host of acute and short-term effects including impairment of skills related to attention, memory, and learning as well as of complex motor skills such as those needed to drive a car. Clinical studies also indicated that regular marijuana users may have many of the same respiratory problems that cigarette smokers have.

Specific findings relating to current use of marijuana (defined as use within the past 30 days), increased from 9.1% in 1995 to 11.3% among 8th graders in 1996 and from 17.2% to 20.4% among 10th graders. These findings indicated that marijuana use has increased by 250% among 8th graders since 1991 and 150% among 10th graders during the same period. Of the seniors, 21.9% indicated that they had used marijuana in the past 30 days, and 4.9% reported smoking marijuana every day. Cigarette use also was on the rise for 8th and 10th graders and essentially stable for 12th graders. Current use for 8th graders was 21% and 30.4% for 10th graders. Some 34% of seniors used cigarettes. These figures can be contrasted with 25% of adults who reported current use of cigarettes. In terms of alcohol use, 9.6% of 8th graders, 21.3% of 10th graders, and 31.3% of 12th graders reported they had been drunk in the past month, with larger numbers reporting the use of alcohol in the past 30 days: 26.2% (8th graders); 40.4% (10th graders); and 50.8% (seniors).

Because alcohol and drugs are so widely available and adolescents are so susceptible to peer pressure, it is estimated that over 90% of high school seniors have tried marijuana and that many have tried other drugs such as cocaine and, particularly its smokable form, crack. Alcohol is believed to be the drug most widely abused by youth in binge drinking, particularly on weekends. Because adolescence is a period of considerable confusion about personal identity, career directions, sexuality, self-esteem, and many other matters, teenagers may decide to turn to drugs to mask their emotions and their insecurities as well as to feel a part of their peer group. Although it is very difficult in the early stages of drug use to separate the signs of normal fluctuations in adolescent behavior from those associated with incipient drug use, the signs likely to be present are increasingly secretive behavior, isolation, change in friends, depression or mood swings, change in interests or family involvement, school problems (grades, attendance), the presence of drug paraphernalia (pipes, rubber tubing, razor blades, cigarette papers), money problems, and physical symptoms (needle marks, changes in weight or dress patterns) (Krames Communications, 1987).

Half of all teenagers treated for alcohol and drug abuse started using alcohol by age 12 and marijuana by age 13. In a study conducted in 13 treatment centers in five states, it was found that many addicted teenagers have problems at home or at school. For example, 60% of the teens reported that someone else at home also abuses drugs or alcohol. Of the addicted teens, 45% of the girls and 35% of the boys reported having experienced physical abuse; 45% of the girls and 11% of the boys reported having experienced sexual abuse. About 11% of the girls and 25% of the boys who were addicted to alcohol or drugs were identified as suffering from learning disabilities; 30% of the girls and 10% of the boys had attempted suicide; 44% of the girls and 60% of the boys had been suspended or expelled from school; and 15% of the girls and 33% of the boys had been arrested. Other underlying problems found among the addicted teenagers included poor self-image, troubled relationships with parents, sleep disorders, and depression. Moreover, in most instances, the teenagers reported experiencing three or more of these problems (Alcohol Research Information Service, 1987b). This study advocated a multidimensional approach in which teenagers are treated for personal problems at the same time as they are treated for alcohol and drug abuse problems. They also need to be helped to acquire the social or job skills necessary to cope with life events after their chemical dependency is terminated.

Other researchers have suggested using *peer cluster theory* to understand why adolescents use drugs as well as how to provide treatment or preventive approaches (Oetting & Beauvais, 1986). Peer cluster theory suggests that "small subsets of peer groups, including pairs, dictate the shared beliefs, values, and behaviors that determine whether, when, and with whom drugs are used and the role that drugs play in defining cluster membership" (p. 17). From a treatment standpoint, the premise is that unless the influence of the peer cluster in determining adolescent drug use can be changed, there is little likelihood that the counselor can change the drug involvement. Thus the counselor may need to help the client dissociate from the drug-using group and strengthen ties with another peer cluster. Or the counselor may work directly with the drug-using peer cluster in applying techniques analogous to those in family or systems therapy in order to try to change collective reasons for drug use and to find alternative methods of filling the needs to which drugs are related. Further, in addition to working with the peer clusters that support drug use, it is important for the counselor to deal with whatever underlying psychosocial problems clients experience that sustain their drug use, such as needs for self-confidence or social acceptance, anxiety, unhappiness, social isolation, anger, or feeling blamed. Peele (1986) contended, in responding to the peer cluster theory, that society and, indeed, counselors

> . . . give children the competencies, values, and opportunities to find superior alternatives to drug use for relating to their world. . . . The mission of those concerned with adolescent drug abuse is to create a cultural climate that encourages children to value and to achieve independence, adventure, intimacy, consciousness, activity, fun, self-reliance, health, problem-solving capacities, and a commitment to the community. . . . There is no better antidote for drug abuse than adolescents' beliefs that the world is a positive place, that they can accomplish what they want, and that they can gain satisfaction from life. (p. 24)

From a preventive standpoint, the National Institute on Drug Abuse (Mathias, 1997b) has reported on the use of a 15-week Life Skills program that has been found to be effective with both White suburban students and with minority inner-city youth. In contrast to a conventional drug education program that provides students with information about drugs and the hazards of drug use, the Life Skills program has regular classroom teachers teach junior high school students skills to resist social pressures to use drugs and foster students' antidrug attitudes and perceptions. The program also teaches a range of social and personal skills that increase young people's ability to handle the challenges of adolescent life more effectively and reduce the likelihood that they will use alcohol and drugs. Follow-up studies of students participating in the Life Skills program showed significant reductions in both current drug use and intentions to use drugs. The studies also showed that those who participated smoked cigarettes and marijuana and drank alcohol significantly less often.

With respect to adult alcoholics, there are many treatment formats in which counselors are likely to be involved. Among them are brief inpatient treatment (approximately 30 days), day treatment programs, or halfway houses. Extended outpatient psychotherapy rather than brief counseling with alcoholics is believed to be an effective intervention, particularly with people who have neuropsychological limitations. Outpatient group counseling, counseling approaches that emphasize role-playing, behavioral rehearsal of appropriate actions in stressful situations that are known to contribute to relapses, and psychoeducational approaches targeted to helping alcoholics acquire new behaviors that improve interpersonal skills and self-efficacy each represent an important approach to counselor intervention for particular types of alcoholic clients, depending on whether or not they experience cognitive deficits or other neuropsychological problems (Clifford, 1986). In addition, family education and counseling, built around basic family systems concepts, is now a component of most alcohol treatment programs (Goodman, 1987).

Van Doren (1996) has suggested that within the context of intensive treatment, the chemically dependent client must be confronted about the denial of such dependence. In addition, the counselor must facilitate the client's recognition that specific personal concerns may be directly related to substance abuse. These personal concerns may include sexual abuse, depression, anxiety, poor self-concept, and poor interpersonal skills. These connections must be explored and dealt with as a way of preventing relapse to alcohol or other substance abuse following treatment. However, the primary focus for treatment must be the elimination of chemical dependency and the related health problems. These will require lifestyle changes by the client in order to develop new ways of coping without alcohol or other chemicals. Treatment is also likely to include participating in support systems including Alcoholics Anonymous and other self-help groups.

Before leaving the multifaceted challenges for counselors reflected in alcohol and substance abuse, two related phenomena need to be noted. One is the growing national concern for children of alcoholics, and the other is the related issue of codependency. Although problems of and approaches to dealing with children of alcoholics were discussed in chapter 3 and mentioned in other parts of the book, it will be useful to revisit this matter briefly.

Children of alcoholics. Current estimates suggest that there are approximately 12 to 15 million minor children of alcoholics and between 15 to 18 million adult children of alcoholics (Black, 1981), with in all perhaps as many as 34 million children of alcoholics (Black, 1986) now living in the United States. Estimates also suggest that 50% to 60% of alcoholics and up to 80% of cocaine addicts are children of alcoholics (Van Doren, 1996). Whether or not genetic connections or environmental factors are involved, research has found an array of negative outcomes associated with being raised by an alcoholic parent. These include being too self-critical, serious, responsible, and controlled. Such children may have difficulty with intimacy, honesty, and commitment. They may tend to ignore their own needs, possess a poor self-concept or low frustration tolerance, and experience poor academic performance.

They may experience a high incidence of depression, hyperactivity, emotional and behavioral disorders, sexual confusion, and a variety of somatic complaints. They may also have suicidal tendencies as well as tend to deny parental alcoholism, have family relationship problems and difficulties in trusting others, exhibit compulsive behavior (workaholism), and be chemically dependent themselves (Downing & Walker, 1987; Goodman, 1987; Van Doren, 1996).

The treatments proposed for children of alcoholics include family counseling and therapy, intensive group psychotherapy, support groups, and psychoeducational groups. The latter tend to focus on reducing feelings of isolation and decreasing denial; confronting denial and learning about alcoholism and codependency; and recognizing and recovering feelings. This final phase tends to include structured group exercises and group discussions of such topics as difficulties in trusting others, emotional awareness and expression, responses to the alcoholic, reactions to drinking, and valuing of personal needs (Downing & Walker, 1987). Lewis (1987) contended that counseling for young children who still live in the home with the alcoholic parent should concentrate on providing empathy and support and on developing coping skills useful in the current situation and in the future. The latter is likely to include helping them reach out to others, recognize and express their previously forbidden emotions, and possibly participate in a structured group that allows them to experience peer support and learn about substance abuse, families, feelings, and coping with problems and choices. There is also a growing body of self-help materials that younger children and adult children of alcoholics can use to try to understand and cope with their experiences.

Codependency. Implicit in the work with children of alcoholics already cited is concern about the notion of codependency. Codependents may be children, spouses, or other intimate partners of alcoholics who have behavior problems or exhibit violent behavior. Codependency, which has come to have different definitions, is best summarized as follows: "A codependent person is one who has let another person's behavior affect him or her, and who is obsessed with controlling that person's behavior" (Beattie, 1987, p. 31).

Thus codependents are not the primary victims of a life of mental disorder, substance abuse, or other behavior problems, but they are nevertheless victims in comprehensive ways. They are the caretakers of troubled people and get caught up in their problems. As Beattie (1987) suggested,

> . . . codependents are reactionaries. . . . They react to the problems, pains, lives, and behaviors of others. . . . Many codependent reactions are reactions to stress and uncertainty of living or growing up with alcoholism and other problems. . . . Codependency is progressive. As the people around us become sicker, we may begin to react more intensely. What began as a little concern may trigger isolation, depression, emotional or physical illness, or suicidal fantasies. . . . Codependency may not be an illness, but it can make you sick. And it can help the people around you stay sick. . . . Whatever problem the other person has, codependency involves a habitual system of thinking, feeling, and behaving toward ourselves and others that can cause us pain. Codependent behaviors or habits are self-destructive. (pp. 33–34)

Codependency, like other human behavior, is learned. Sometimes it is learned early in life; sometimes later in life. The roots of codependent behavior may come from religious interpretations or from socialization of nurturance in sex-related differences.

In general, codependent behaviors surface as the individual tries to cope with an environment where a significant other is troubled, ill, alcoholic, or a problem for him- or herself and others. In this context, children, spouses, friends, and parents take on self-protective adaptations that may become self-destructive if perpetuated beyond their time of primary usefulness. According to Beattie (1987, pp. 37–45), such self-protective adaptations may involve caretaking (e.g., thinking and feeling responsible for other people's feelings, thoughts, actions, choices, wants, needs, well-being, lack of well-being, and ultimate destiny); low self-worth (e.g., blaming themselves for everything); repression (e.g., being afraid to be authentic or to be themselves; pushing thoughts and feelings out of awareness); obsession (e.g., constant worry about minor things and about problems and people); controlling (e.g., trying to control events and people through helplessness, guilt, coercion, threats, advice giving, manipulation, or domination); denial (e.g., looking for happiness outside themselves and centering their lives around other people); poor communication (e.g., frequently having a difficult time expressing their emotions honestly, openly, and appropriately or asserting their rights); weak boundaries (e.g., letting other people continue to hurt them as they increase their tolerance of negative behavior from others); lack of trust (e.g., not trusting their feelings, decisions, or other people); anger (e.g., having a lot of anger but being afraid of it and of other people's anger); and sexual problems (e.g., reducing sex to a technical act or losing interest in sex).

Clearly, codependent behaviors take on many different patterns. Many people, probably millions, could be described as in some stage of codependent relationship in which they feel trapped, helpless, to blame. Undoubtedly, a major emerging challenge for counselors will be helping such people recognize their codependency, find ways to be responsible for themselves, not others, and adopt more personally healthy behavior. This involves helping a codependent to detach him- or herself from the intense involvement and, indeed, entanglement with the person with whom he or she has been codependent, and to come to terms with the reality that he or she cannot solve problems for others and that worrying about the situation will not change it.

Character, Personal Responsibility, and Self-Esteem

Self-esteem, personal responsibility, control. At the root of many of the emerging challenges discussed in this and in previous chapters, particularly in sections dealing with changing family structures and people at risk, are recurring allusions to self-esteem, personal responsibility, and control. In some sense, these terms are interactive. When individuals feel good about themselves, they are able to accept their characteristics, and systematically attempt to understand and improve selected ones; these people are likely to experience high self-esteem and to love themselves in healthy and wholesome ways. In such a scenario, people of high self-esteem are also likely to exhibit personal responsibility toward self and toward others. They are able to exert control over their lives.

Self-esteem can be defined in many ways. It is basically a judgmental process about an individual's personal worth. As Coopersmith (1967), one of the pioneer researchers on self-esteem, suggested, it is a judgmental process in which individuals examine their performance, capacities, and attributes according to their own personal standards and values and reach decisions about their personal worth. Ford (1987), in his application of the Living Systems Framework (LSF) to the notion that humans are self-constructing living systems, placed self-esteem within a broader notion of human governing functions composed of regulation, values, and evaluative thought. In particular, he noted that humans must regulate their internal functioning; their functioning in relationship to the environment, especially the interpersonal environment; and their functioning in the relationship between their internal states and environmental transactions. In his view, there are two methods for accomplishing these tasks: biochemical regulation and cognitive regulation.

In Ford's (1987) perspective, self-esteem falls within the category of cognitive regulation:

> Every problem-solving activity, decision, or choice requires selection from among options representing alternative goals or means for controlling behavior. This implies that there must be criteria for making such selections. Evaluative thoughts provide such criteria. . . . Three major kinds of evaluative thoughts have been studied. One kind is self-evaluative thoughts. Every behavior episode provides people with information about themselves. From such information people develop concepts and propositions about themselves as parts of their behavior episode schemata. These concepts and propositions are often termed the *self-concept* or *self-system*, of which self-evaluations are components. Self-evaluations of one's ability or opportunity to function as a causal agent are sometimes called *self-efficacy expectations, causal-attributions*, or *control beliefs*. Self-evaluations of one's self- or social acceptability are often termed *self-worth* or *self-esteem*. (pp. 31–32)

Further, according to Ford and Ford (1987) in a second volume describing these theoretical perspectives,

> . . . self-esteem refers to evaluations of one's personal and social worth, rather than to evaluations of one's competence. It may be constructed, in part, from evaluations of performance feedback. . . . Self-esteem appears to be significantly influenced by the actual or anticipated social evaluative feedback provided by others. . . . This has led some to propose that one's self-concept is largely a social product. . . . (p. 476)

Obviously, dealing with issues of self-esteem may involve the counselor with the application of cognitive behavior therapy as described in chapter 7. Because a lack of self-esteem frequently stems from an individual's negative evaluations of worth, such evaluations and the bases for them may need to be confronted and alternative ways to viewing him- or herself must be examined. Because self-esteem is so fundamental to an individual's way of viewing others, the world, and the utility of an individual's continuing to live and being purposeful, the counselor must create in his or her communication with the client a relationship that is characterized by caring, trust, understanding, honesty, sincerity, acceptance, liking, and interest. These relationship variables may sound so familiar to the reader that they are passed over lightly in the reading; the point is, however, that these kinds of interpersonal elements are precisely what has been missing from the client's life and have brought him or her to a lack of self-esteem or self-worth. These types of counseling variables are the healing ingredients by which people can be helped to self-disclose, exhibit trust in another, and communicate the feelings of pain and loneliness that underlie and presage dealing with problems of self-esteem. Frankl (1963) observed 35 years ago that the salvation of humankind is love. It is in loving and being loved that individuals find a sense of self-worth, self-respect, and dignity. The counseling relationship should help the individual to restore the ability to love and to feel capable of being loved.

Johnson (1986) indicated that "the human species seems to have *a relationship imperative*: we desire and seek out relationships with others and we have personal needs that can be satisfied only through interacting with other humans" (p. 1). Johnson extended the point to suggest that the basis for personal well-being is effective interpersonal skills. In his view, human development follows a pattern of expansion of interdependence with others; individual identity is built out of our relationships with other people; psychological health depends almost entirely on the quality of relationships with others. Johnson also contended that each of us needs to be confirmed as a person by other people.

> Confirmation consists of responses from other people in ways that indicate we are normal, healthy, and worthwhile. Being disconfirmed consists of responses from other people suggesting that we are ignorant, inept, unhealthy, unimportant, or of no value, and, at worst, that we do not exist. (p. 3)

In a world of loneliness, rapid change, discrimination, complex stressors, and psychological or physical abuse, many have never learned nor have been systematically exposed to interpersonal skills that allow them to develop self-worth, identity, or effective relationships with others. Thus their behavioral repertoire may be very limited in how to act in an interdependent world, or they may feel so limited in their internal locus of control, their ability to manage their lives, that they attribute everything that happens to them to fate or external control by other people. The sense of stress, powerlessness, frustration, and lack of personal worth that results may frequently be manifested in vandalism, aggressiveness, uncontrolled anger, violence, bullying, chemical abuse, and other self-destructive or antisocial acts.

Among those for whom life is a negative experience and relationships with others do not lead to feelings of personal confirmation or a sense of community, a major counselor role is to help in the acquisition of the basic interpersonal skills by which to initiate, develop, and maintain caring and productive relationships. These sets of basic skills include those listed by Johnson (1986, pp. 7-8) as relating to

1. knowing and trusting others;
2. communicating with other people accurately and unambiguously;
3. accepting and supporting oneself and others; and
4. resolving conflicts and relationship problems constructively.

The learning of interpersonal skills is typically accomplished by the application of a psychoeducational model such as that described in chapter 7. Whether implemented on an individual basis or in a group context, clients have to be helped to understand why the basic skills to be learned are important in alleviating the problems they are experiencing, what the basic components of the skills are, the need to practice such skills and get feedback about their progress in implementing the skill, and, ultimately, the persistence to make it an authentic part of their personal behavior. In implementing such a psychoeducational approach to interpersonal development, the counselor will have to use modeling, reinforcement, homework, and other techniques to sustain the client's motivation to learn these skills in order to alter the feelings of poor self-esteem and unworthiness that are central motivations for whatever self-destructive or antisocial behaviors are exhibited. Counselors obviously cannot change the world, but they can help people understand what they are experiencing and equip them with the skills by which they might become more positive about themselves and enhance their ability to gain access to and cope with interpersonal, family, and career opportunities that validate them as persons.

The elements of building self-esteem, according to Johnson (1986), which in essence become the goals of the counseling relationship, a psychoeducational model, or a cognitive behavioral approach, include the following in somewhat abridged form:

- Control your self-esteem through how you see yourself. Changing the way in which you think about yourself will change your self-esteem.
- Set your own standards for evaluating yourself. People with low self-esteem tend to be particularly susceptible to persuasion and too readily accept others' standards as their own.
- Set realistic goals. Do not demand too much of yourself.
- Modify negative self-talk and attributions. Individuals with low self-esteem tend to think in counterproductive ways and make negative statements to themselves. In essence, they do not take credit for the good things they do or talk to themselves in self-enhancing ways.
- Emphasize your strengths. Accept your personal shortcomings that you are powerless to change and work to change those that are changeable.
- Work to improve yourself. Efforts at self-improvement can be used to boost your self-esteem.
- Approach others with a positive outlook. Negativism toward yourself can result in negativism toward others. When you approach people with a positive, supportive outlook, you will promote rewarding interactions and gain acceptance (pp. 288–289).

The lack of self-esteem or effective interpersonal relationships, in addition to resulting in self-destructive or antisocial acts, may also be reflected in such emotional manifestations as shyness, anxiety, and a reluctance to risk. These and similar feelings restrict people from being who they want to be. The way to control such feelings is to take charge of behavior that will alter these feelings or stimulate action that is managed and self-directed. Every individual operates within the limits of time, resources, and other restrictions on what can be done. But the only limits on attitudes or purposeful behavior within whatever external constraints exist are those that are self-imposed. "Doing" changes attitudes. This perspective, too, becomes a major ingredient of building self-esteem. It is the essence of what Glasser (1984) called *control theory.*

The central notion of control theory is that regardless of how people feel, they have some control over what they do. The underlying perspective is that "Nothing we do is caused by what happens outside of us. If we believe that what we do is caused by forces outside of us, we are acting like dead machines, not living people" (Glasser, 1984, p. 1). Thus people have the opportunity to choose how they will feel and how they will react or behave in response to life's unfolding events. If individuals then want to change a total behavior, they must choose what to *do* and what to *think* differently. As they do so, their *feelings* about themselves, about the situation, and about others are also likely to change.

Much more deserves to be said about the promotion of self-esteem, personal responsibility, and control as a major emerging challenge for the foreseeable future. Space does not permit a fuller elaboration of these matters here. Suffice it to say that although the terminology has been used differently, much of the content of this book has been about the variety of ways counselors can add a personal dimension to an otherwise impersonal and, perhaps, hostile environment whether in the family, the school or university, or the workplace. As the counselor helps clients of any age to consider alternatives, sharpen values, deal with their individual quests for meaning or spirituality, understand more about their strengths and their possible application in social and work situations, and identify and learn the skills sets (e.g., interpersonal, problem-solving, communication) likely to permit them to live a more purposeful and productive life, the probable outcomes for clients are increased self-esteem, personal responsibility, control, and a sense of dignity. By helping clients to free themselves from the negative attitudes, pictures, and information deficits by which their previous existence has been shaped and stifled, the counselor, through personal caring, commitment, and expertise, is acknowledging the worth of the clients and their potential to alter the conditions that brought them to counseling. The efforts of counselors who understand and provide the conditions to enhance individual self-worth, positive self-attributions, and respect for self and others are powerful ingredients in combating the need for chemical dependency, sexual exploitation, child and spousal abuse, suicide ideation, and other self-destructive or antisocial behaviors. Building character, personal responsibility, and self-esteem is obviously a major emerging challenge for the future.

Counseling With Older Americans

It is probably fair to suggest that counselors and counseling psychologists have, for most of their history, been more identified with youth and young adult populations than with older Americans or the elderly. Indeed, as recently as 1984, a special issue of the *Counseling Psychologist* devoted to counseling with the aging indicated that people who are old or concerned specifically with matters of later life are basically a new clientele for counseling psychologists (Ganikos & Blake, 1984). In 1986, the American Association for Counseling and Development implemented a division particularly focused on adult development and aging concerns: the Association for Adult Development and Aging (AADA). In 1990, the first set of *Gerontological Competencies for Counselors and Human Development Professionals* (Myers & Sweeney, 1990) was developed to identify counselor competencies important to all counselors working with older persons. Although more comprehensive than can be treated effectively in the space available here, these competencies are available from the AADA and from an excellent article by Myers (1995). Among competencies identified for gerontological counselors are areas of knowledge and skill related to the human development of older persons and wellness-enhancing attitudes toward and empowerment of older persons: understanding of the characteristics of the settings, public policies, and the cultural factors affecting older persons; medication use and misuse; social services and other resources available to older persons; the multiple roles of counselors specializing in working with older persons (e.g., advocate, family consultant); and the approaches to appraisal and other interventions that have been found effective in counseling older persons. Partially based on the availability of these gerontological counseling standards, curricula recommendations, and related knowledge, the Council for the Accreditation of Counseling and Related Educational Programs approved a specialty emphasis in gerontological counseling within its community counseling emphasis.

Clearly, as these professional responses signify, the perspective that older persons are not a major constituency of counselors is changing as more insight is gained in research and theory about the variety of transitions and changes older Americans experience. As life circumstances change, so do identity, marital, and career issues. Life after young adulthood, like life in all other stages, is dynamic and filled with questions and uncertainties. The implementation of counseling responses to the needs of older citizens represents a major emerging challenge to counselors in the years ahead.

But the challenge of counseling with older Americans is not solely a matter of new and comprehensive insights about the needs of this population. It is also a function of demographics. Americans are a "graying" population. By 1985, older people outnumbered teenagers in the United States. Statistics available from the U.S. Administration on Aging that describe the older populations in the United States, as reflected in census data and other resources, will put the situation in perspective:

- Persons 65 years or older numbered 33.5 million in 1995. They represented 12.8% of the U.S. population, about one in every eight Americans. The number of older Americans increased by 7% since 1990 compared to an increase of 5% in the population under age 65.
- Since 1900, the percentage of Americans 65 years or older has more than tripled (4.1% in 1900 to 12.8% in 1995), and the number has increased nearly 11 times (from 3.1 million to 33.5 million).
- The older population is getting older. In 1995 the 65 to 74 age group (18.8) million) was eight times larger than in 1900, but the 75 to 84 group (11.1 million) was 14 times larger and the 85 years or older group (3.6 million) was 29 times larger.
- In 1995, persons reaching age 65 had a life expectancy of an additional 17.4 years (18.9 years for females and 15.6 years for males).
- In 1995, there were 19.8 older women and 13.7 million older men, or a sex ratio of 140.5 women for every 100 men. The sex ratio increased with age, ranging from 120 to 100 for the 65 to 69 group to a high of 257 to 100 for persons 85 and over.
- The older population will continue to grow in the future. The most rapid increase is expected between the years 2010 and 2030 when the baby boom generation reaches age 65. By 2030, there will be about 70 million older persons, and they will represent 20% of the population.
- Minority populations are projected to represent 25% of the elderly population in 2030, up from 13% in 1990.
- Half of all older women in 1994 were widows. There were nearly five times as many widows (8.5 million) as widowers (1.7 million).
- The majority (68%) of older noninstitutionalized persons lived in a family setting in 1994. About 30% (9.3 million) of all noninstitutionalized older persons in 1994 lived alone.
- In 1995 about 15% of older persons were minorities: 8% were Black, 4% were Hispanic, 2% were Asian or Pacific Islander, and less than 1% were American Indian or Native Alaskan.
- The median income of older persons in 1995 was $16,484 for males and $9,355 for females.
- About 3.7 million elderly persons were below the poverty level in 1995. Another 2.3 million or 7% of the elderly were classified as *near poor* (income between the

poverty level and 125% of this level); older women (14%) had a higher poverty rate than older men (6%) in 1995.

- One of every 11 (9%) elderly Whites was poor in 1995, compared to one fourth (25%) of elderly Blacks and about one fourth (24%) of elderly Hispanics. One half of older Black women (49%) who lived alone were poor in 1995.
- About 3.8 million older Americans (12%) were in the labor force in 1995. They constituted 2.9% of the U.S. labor force. Approximately half (54%) of the workers over 65 in 1995 were employed part-time: 51% of men and 63% of women.
- Of older persons over 85, 24% are in nursing homes or other institutions.
- Most older persons have at least one chronic condition and many have multiple conditions. The most frequently occurring conditions per 100 elderly in 1994 were arthritis (50), hypertension (36), heart disease (32), hearing impairments (29), cataracts (17), orthopedic impairments (16), sinusitis (15), and diabetes (10).

Within these statistics describing the older population there is obvious variance across many categories of concern. Not all older people have health problems or economic difficulties, Not all older people are lonely or alone. However, that does not mean that the elderly who do not fit such descriptions are without mental health issues related to identity, self-worth, employment, interpersonal conflicts, parent-child or grandchild concerns, or other topics that matter to them. There are also pre-retirement issues and issues of how to begin to taper off, which concern people from 55 to 65 years of age, that need to be addressed in counseling availability and response.

Given the size and variation of the older population and those around the age of 50 who begin to contemplate retirement and its attendant issues, the need for access to comprehensive counseling responses will be an increasing challenge. The Office of Technology Assessment (OTA) of the U.S. Congress (1985) stated that "a major challenge stretching well into the 21st century will be to maintain the health and functional ability of America's rapidly growing older population." Among the responses OTA recommends to meet the needs of the older population are programs designed to help older people acquire behaviors that promote health and thereby prevent or delay the onset of various chronic diseases (even at the oldest ages, the positive effects of such behaviors can be realized in relatively short time periods); supportive services and settings; workplace technologies that may improve performance, efficiency, and safety for many older workers; the use of telecommunications to enable older people to take advantage of new home-based work arrangements; and retraining of older workers to encourage continued employment or provide new employment possibilities. In one way or another, most of these recommendations have been addressed in other parts of this book with other populations. Thus, in essence, many of the counseling techniques or approaches described in chapter 7 and elsewhere are applicable to older populations. However, there are additional possibilities.

Waters (1984), for example, contended that in counseling with older clients "new knowledge must be acquired and although basic counseling skills apply across the life span, adaptations frequently must be made to meet special conditions or counseling needs that an older person may bring to the helping encounter" (p. 63). For example, "As people reach more advanced ages the basic goal of maintaining independence and control over one's life often becomes increasingly threatened and at the same time increasingly important to the individual" (p. 64). Within such a context, group work can be a helpful modality by which to assist older people to improve their social skills, discover resource sharing and increase self-esteem, reduce loneliness, facilitate catharsis, and discover commonalities with their peers. Such approaches might include preventive mental health or enrichment groups designed to enhance self-esteem and communication skills; assertion training groups to help with the improvement of interpersonal communications skills and direct expression of feelings to help older people cope with bureaucracies and significant others; retirement planning groups to help older citizens anticipate and adjust to retirement; and self-help groups for widows or widowers or other special populations of older citizens for whom support, sharing, and structured opportunities to communicate with other older citizens could be particularly useful.

Frequently, agencies for the aging, senior citizens groups, and counseling centers providing counseling to older citizens are using older people as peer counselors and group leaders. This trend is occurring for several reasons: a gross lack of counseling services for older people, an insufficient number of counselors trained in gerontological mental health issues, the high cost of providing traditional mental health resources to older citizens, and the reluctance of older people to avail themselves of mental health services because they think that doing so denotes a lack of ability to manage their own affairs or solve their own problems. On the more positive side, older people serving as peer counselors have a measure of instant credibility to other senior citizens because of their comparable age and experience; they also can serve as role models for other older persons in their willingness to be useful and other-directed. Regardless of the potential benefits of using older persons as peer counselors, it is also important to train them in effective listening skills and in other behaviors that will be of therapeutic use to others. Age itself is an insufficient criterion for selecting peer counselors. Systematic screening, training, and ongoing support are essential for using peer counselors at any age.

Waters (1984) suggested that some specialized counseling procedures are particularly useful with older people. The techniques Waters suggested, including life review, reality orientation, and remotivation, are additions to and not replacements for more general techniques useful with any age population.

Life review is a technique that focuses on the tendency of older people to engage in reminiscence and reliving the past. As a therapeutic device, this life-review process can help older people take stock of their lives, survey and resolve past conflicts about which they have been troubled, complete unfinished business, reintegrate past experiences, and think through how they want to use whatever time is left to them. Life review as a counseling technique for older citizens is consistent with the observation that throughout life the questions people ask have different orientations depending on where they are on a continuum of time from birth to death. For example, youth tend to orient their questions to the future; people in midlife are oriented to the present; older citizens are concerned about the past. Therefore, "Young people ask: Who am I becoming? People in midlife ask: Who am I? Do I want to remain this person for the time I have left? Old people ask: Who have I been? What has been the meaning of my life?" (Waters, 1984, p. 70). Life-review processes may help older people identify recurring themes in their lives, rediscover coping mechanisms they used at earlier times that may still be useful, and rediscover already developed skills that may be valuable now in different applications. Such a review may broaden the range of alternatives they might consider for the future.

Reality orientation as a therapeutic approach to working with older people is a technique designed to hold or reverse "the confusion, disorientation, social withdrawal, and apathy so characteristic of institutionalized elderly patients" (Waters, 1984, p. 71). At its simplest level, reality orientation reinforces the repetition and learning by older patients of the basic facts of their existence: their names, the place where they are living, date, time and day of week, or when the next meal or bath will be. Beyond these routine matters, the principle is to show personal respect to older patients and thereby provide social reinforcement in order to reduce dependency and deterioration.

Reality orientation as a technique is frequently an antecedent of *remotivation*, another technique used with older citizens. Remotivation is an attempt to get moderately confused elderly patients to renew their interest in their environment by engaging them in the objective features of everyday life. Using a structured program of discussion topics, pictures, music, and other stimuli, the elderly can be encouraged to focus on such matters as sports, gardening, pets, work, and how these topics relate to their former roles, functions, and likes and dislikes as ways to bridge their current status to the larger "reality" of their present and past lives.

Many other techniques may be especially useful in working with older citizens. For example, in milieu therapy elderly patients are encouraged to try new skills in a safe and supportive environment. Or analyses of support systems help older people identify support systems present in their lives, or those available to them if they learn certain accessing skills.

Sargent (1980) identified what he termed nontraditional therapy and counseling with the aging. Some of these methods have already been described briefly. In Sargent's view, such approaches to providing counseling services for senior citizens include assertiveness training groups, widows groups and emeritus classes, adult daycare centers (that allow the frail elderly to remain in their own or children's homes rather than nursing homes), new directions workshops for senior citizens, therapeutic efforts to facilitate the transition to nursing homes, creative aging workshops, and behavioral approaches to therapy with the elderly.

On balance, the nontraditional therapies Sargent advocated are in group formats and are skill-based in order to reduce the well-documented resistance of older citizens to use traditional mental health services and change their perceptions that being seen at the locations of mental health services advertises their distress or incompetence to handle their own problems. Nontraditional therapies are, nevertheless, responding to the magnitude and range of mental health problems many older citizens experience. Estimates by professional organizations such as the American Psychological Association are that at least 15% of the older population need mental health services. Other observers feel that such an estimate is much too conservative because of the combination of poor economic and interpersonal factors that put so many of the elderly at risk of significant emotional breakdown or decline. Other statistics that affirm the older citizens' needs for mental health services are the large number of suicides among people over age 65. According to Hayes (1997),

older adults take their own lives at the highest rate of any segment of the population—more than 50% more frequently than the nation as a whole. . . . According to the National Alliance for the Mentally Ill (NAMI), from 1980 to 1992 the suicide rate for persons age 65 or older increased 9%. Most striking was a 35% increase in the rate for those

between the ages of 80 and 84, [and] all but a handful of older persons who commit suicide are suffering from depression. (p. 6)

Given that the need for mental health services among the older population is great
and older citizens' resistance to availing themselves of traditional mental health services is high, one of the answers is to provide increased opportunities for therapeutic
activities in settings where senior citizens may come together but that are not themselves traditional sites for mental health services (e.g., day-care centers, long-term
care facilities, senior citizen centers, churches, housing settings, malls) (Myers &
Salmon, 1984).

To move from the notions of nontraditional therapies for older citizens to the
more traditional, several comments are in order. Because of the comprehensiveness
of the needs of older citizens, it is necessary to recognize that for some groups of
older citizens remediation or rehabilitation will be important; for others, preventive
approaches; and for others, educational or developmental orientations. In some
instances, the application of family theory and family counseling will be extremely
useful as an elderly parent is moving to an intact family of his or her child. The need
to look at the alterations of family dynamics and how such matters can be anticipated
and reduced in their effect upon the various family members will be helpful.
Similarly, family counseling is likely to become important in the situation when an
elderly parent is contemplating moving from either his or her home or the children's
home to a nursing home.

Whether traditional or nontraditional therapy is used with the older population,
several dimensions have been found from syntheses of the research literature to be
important considerations in counseling with the older population (Wellman &
McCormick, 1984).

- The relationship between the counselor and the client is important in the change
  process.
- Brief therapy is somewhat more successful than long-term therapy.
- Interventions that are experiential, participatory, and encourage a high degree of
  client involvement are more effective than more passive interventions.
- Cognitive/behavioral interventions tend to be effective.
- The success of treatment is related to the client's mental and emotional resources.
- Group interventions are helpful for those elderly who are not severely disabled.
- Although team approaches look promising, more research is needed with this
  modality.

One of the new groups to whom counselors will need to give particular attention
in the future is the children of aging parents. An increasing number of middle-aged
people are finding themselves in the situation of parenting their own children while
at the same time taking on a parental role for their elderly parents. Such a condition
can cause stress, anxiety, financial burdens, and uncertainty for all concerned. As a
result, a large and increasing need for help for the adult children of aging parents has
become apparent in the past decade, and its importance is likely to increase dramatically in the future. Frequently, a group format can be useful to help adult children of
aging parents to share their concerns with others experiencing the same circumstances. The counselor is likely to share information about the aging process to help
these adult children understand what is happening with their older parents as their

needs and behaviors are changing. Information is typically shared about the availability of community resources. Helpful books about the aging process are frequently identified and their use reinforced.

In most such situations, a group environment needs to be created in which these adult children of aging parents are able to examine their personal feelings of guilt, unfinished business, financial or communications problems with their aging parents and with their own children, and alternative ways of responding in the areas identified. These middle-aged parents/children are sometimes called the "sandwich generation" because their needs are sandwiched between those of their adolescent children, who seek increasing independence, and those of their aging parents, who are facing a loss of independence (Myers, 1988). Many people caught in these multigenerational responsibilities find themselves losing their own independence at a time in their life when they had anticipated freedom as their children leave home, as their career is well advanced, and as they have an opportunity to reestablish intimacy with their spouse. They lack role models for caring for aging parents while also maintaining their own quality of life. Role changes and role strains occur in unanticipated and frustrating ways and may in fact put the adult child and caregiver of aging parents at risk of ill health. When adult children have siblings, either near or distant to the aging parent, rivalries and tensions can arise about how contributions to the aging parents will be made and by whom.

Myers (1988) suggested that in working with adult children of aging parents counselors may engage in individual counseling, family counseling, or group work with any of the actors in the situation. Given the complexity of the interpersonal and family dynamics involved, it may be difficult to know clearly who is the client and whose needs are preeminent at different points in time. Within such circumstances, counselors need to help both adult children and their aging parents to achieve a balance between their needs, to identify future solutions, and to reestablish and maintain the level of emotional relationships and communication important to each of them.

As discussed briefly in chapter 3, another group of older persons needing counseling and other forms of support are grandparents raising grandchildren (Pinson-Millburn et al., 1996). Within the last decade, there has been a 40% increase in these households across the United States. According to Pinson-Millburn et al., the primary impetus for such situations are the increase of cases where dysfunctional parents who remain in the picture are unable or unwilling to nurture their own children because they are substance abusers; because they are victims or perpetrators of physical or sexual violence, or sufferers of emotional or neurological diseases that render them incapable of parenting; or because they may be HIV positive, enrolled in drug treatment programs, or incarcerated. Any of these circumstances can cause a grandparent to assume parenting responsibilities. Among other concerns, "these grandparents are faced with multiple problems: their own declining health, the incapacity of their children, and the possibility that their grandchildren could also be disabled or dysfunctional" (Pinson-Millburn et al., 1996, p. 548).

As counselors deal with the set of issues posed by both the grandparents who are raising their grandchildren and the grandchildren themselves, counselors will need to assess the needs of these two groups carefully. Among the interventions they are likely to find useful are providing outreach to the grandparents who are doing the caregiving, helping them link up with grandparent or family support groups, and teaching them the skills of parenting or stress management as well as how to access legal and social services available to them and how to help their grandchildren with their homework and study habits or related information. In addition, the grandparents are likely to need counseling about their own frustrations, lowered self-esteem, or anxiety occasioned by the circumstances in which they find themselves or which relate to their children's negative behavior and their feelings of ineffectiveness as parents to their own children, let alone their grandchildren. In some cases, school counselors will be able to provide this counseling; in other cases they will need to refer these grandparents to community mental health. It is likely that the grandchildren themselves will also need counseling about their situation. This might take the form of grief or bereavement counseling associated with the reality that even though their parents are still alive, as far as the child is concerned they are lost to him or her because of parental dysfunction. The children also may need help with stress management, drug and alcohol education, life skills training, support groups, and possibly access to after-school groups that are available to reinforce their physical, intellectual, and social development.

Many other trends reflect needs for counseling responses to aging populations that deserve to be mentioned but for which space is limited. One of these has to do with counselors working with older workers. Obviously, older and elderly workers are in the workforce. Although the number of such workers has been decreasing, that situation is likely to change because of the relative lack of young workers available to enter the workforce. Rather than continuing to encourage older workers to retire early, prior to age 65 or even 60, an increasing emphasis on retaining older workers is likely. Other factors that might reinforce this trend are federal legislation prohibiting age discrimination in the workplace, continuing efforts to reduce ageism and its stereotypical and demeaning effects upon older people, and, certainly, the economic aspects associated with proposals to raise the eligibility age to receive Medicare or Social Security benefits to age 67 or beyond. Aside from these factors, many older or elderly workers remain in the workforce beyond normal retirement ages for personal reasons such as income. But work also provides other important life satisfactions for older people that for many constitute reasons to continue in the workplace: status, personal achievement, social relationships, and the structure of time.

Older workers who remain in the workforce, retire from one career and return to the workforce in another part-time or full-time role, or who modify a long-time career pattern are likely to seek and benefit from counseling (Hitchcock, 1984). These people are likely to need counselor help to evaluate their strengths, interests, and transferable skills, and to learn how to cope with salary or age discrimination, how to market themselves, or how to implement job search skills. They may need assertiveness or communications training. They may profit from peer support or other therapeutic interventions designed to increase their self-esteem and their feelings of self-efficacy. In one analysis of the counseling needs of older workers (Herr & Cramer, 1996), it was suggested that depending upon the particular circumstances of an individual older worker, counselors may provide support in exploring possible retraining and other employment avenues; assisting individuals in accurately gauging their present state of motivation, the expectations they hold for future employment, and their perceptions of themselves as workers; helping the older worker determine whether he or she is seeking part-time or full-time employment and for what purposes, such as financial, to keep busy, for affiliation and identity, to make a contribution; and referring individuals to appropriate agencies or services where placement assistance may be available.

Smyer (1984), in noting the large amount of within-group variance in the development of biological and psychological variables among the older population, advocated three major counseling tasks with this population:

1. help the client differentiate normal aging from pathology;
2. help the client assess his or her resources and deficits; and
3. explore the reality of aging and its social consequences.

Sterns, Weis, and Perkins (1984) acknowledged a major concept that receives little attention in the literature: Most of the problems of older workers are not unidimensional; they are multidimensional. They also suggested that different personal needs require different forms of intervention. For example, using Blocher's model of human effectiveness (1966), they suggested that if the client's issue is mastery, an educational intervention is most appropriate; if coping, peer support; if striving, group counseling; if inertia, family therapy; if panic, individual counseling. Whether or not we agree with these particular problem/treatment interactions, the important issue is that the older worker or older client needs to be understood holistically, and treatments need to be matched to whatever set of needs the client has.

CONCLUSIONS

As suggested in other chapters, the content with which counselors deal is dynamic. The unfolding of social, political, and economic events creates new and different stressors, and these, in turn, are reflected in the anxieties, uncertainties, confusion, information needs, or the perceptions of self-worth and potential, accurate or inaccurate, that people bring to counselors. But the changing psychological, political, and economic environments within which people negotiate their identities, attempt to resolve personal and social conflict, or forge careers also affect the methodology and the professional identity of counselors.

In this chapter, several recurring challenges have been identified that reflect perennial concerns for counselors. They include the appropriate role of school counselors, the credibility and opportunities for professional counselors to deliver mental health services compared to those of other mental health providers (e.g., psychiatrists, clinical psychologists, counseling psychologists, marriage and family therapists), and the social implications of testing and assessment of individual differences. Each of these challenges surfaces regularly as a focus for debate and for new syntheses of concepts and purposes.

In part, the recurring challenges identified are affected by the emerging challenges described in the chapter. AIDS, alcohol and substance abuse, and the importance of self-esteem, personal responsibility, and control as well as the growth and needs of the aging population are neither new challenges nor challenges about which new insights have suggested much greater importance than was previously understood. AIDS, for example, is a terminal disease that did not affect Americans until two decades ago. Its presence has spurred threat, anxiety, probable changes in the sex habits of many Americans, and, potentially, a growing recognition of the part that stress plays in increasing the vulnerability of the immune system to hastening the course of HIV infection. These considerations, in turn, have reinforced the role that counselors can play in helping people deal with stress management and with other corollaries of the disease, including grief, bereavement, anger, and rejection.

Certainly, a second major challenge is the rapidly expanding knowledge of the destructive effects on personal health, social relationships, family integrity, and work productivity from alcohol and drug abuse. Although general knowledge of such effects is not new, the pervasiveness and the intensity of the effects of these substances has brought new levels of concern to policy makers, educators, employers, and the public at large. The victims of substance abuse and their codependents have come to be a more visible clientele for counselors in all settings. An emerging result of the AIDS epidemic and the widespread concern about alcohol and substance abuse is the dawning recognition in many sectors of the society that the basic antidote to such problems lies in personal responsibility, feelings of self-worth, control, and personal character. Helping people to deal with the emotional aspects and stress of AIDS and the problems represented by alcohol and substance abuse will be formidable challenges for counselors far into the future. In addition, however, counselors will increasingly be involved with helping people develop the attitudes and behaviors toward themselves and others that foster personal responsibility, acceptance of internal behavioral control, and related ingredients of mental health.

Finally, the shifting demographics of the American population to one which is, on average, becoming older and experiencing the wide-ranging needs for information, support, opportunities, and quality of life associated with the elderly constitutes a new frontier for counselors. Such challenges will require counselors to develop new techniques and modify existing ones as they work comprehensively with older citizens and their families, with those approaching retirement, and with those who create barriers for older persons through attitudes of prejudice and discrimination.

Chapter 9

FUTURE CHALLENGES FOR COUNSELING

A PERSISTENT THEME OF THIS BOOK, expressed in many different ways, is that counseling content, counseling processes, and counselors' and counseling psychologists' roles are shaped by events—cultural, political, economic, and social—external to the client. Such external events shape behavior as they are filtered through clients' perceptions, information processing, feelings of self-efficacy, and other intrinsic mechanisms by which possibilities are translated into actualities. How the client interprets and acts upon these external events becomes the content of counseling. Put somewhat differently, the term *psychosocial* is frequently used in the counseling literature to imply "that at all stages of the life cycle, healthy development represents an interaction among the individual and his or her psychological dynamics, and the larger social world in which the individual is living" (Kiunick, 1985, p. 126). Thus human development does not occur within a cocoon that is independent of the environmental influences within which an individual negotiates his or her identity, forges a career, and plays out the life cycle. The forms, directions, and substance of people's lives are interactive with political, social, and economic environments.

In addition to the contextual interactions that affect client's lives, cultural, economic, political, and social events also shape the content of counseling, the roles of counselors, and the interventions counselors are likely to use. What counselors do and how they do it, then, are interdependent with the characteristics and missions of the settings in which they work, the types of needs and at-risk factors that describe the populations whom they serve, and the focus of governmental regulations that guide their practice as well as the ripple effects from the external challenges to their clients' well-being, self-esteem, productivity, and purposefulness that serve as stimuli to the client's seeking counseling.

In the previous chapters, we have examined four major challenges and several recurring and emerging challenges that counselors need to consider and plan for as they look to the remainder of this century and the beginning of the next. Other future challenges tend to be more vaguely defined, more abstract in their possibilities than those discussed up to this point. These represent projections, estimates, and extrapolations that have been promulgated by individuals and groups who term themselves "futurists." Although not all the trends they foresee are directly relevant to counseling and counselors, they represent the future psychological, sociological, and organizational topography in which future clients will grow and develop and by which counseling and related mental health processes will be shaped, supported, and delivered.

The following sections discuss some of the future trends to which counselors will need to become increasingly alert and informed and to which they will need to be able to respond. The chapter concludes with specific recommendations for counselor function in the future.

PERSPECTIVES ON FUTURE CHALLENGES

In the first edition of this book, two futuristic perspectives were used as the frame of reference for the section on future challenges for counselors. They were the views of the future of American society into the 1990s and beyond forecast by Oxford Analytica (1986) and the megatrends described by Naisbitt in 1984 and Naisbitt and his group in 1986. Since that time there have been many additional projections about the trends that will potentially affect the quality of life, the organizational forms in which people will live and work, uses of technology, educational and occupational structures, and other aspects of life that will be the emerging sources of growth and mobility or stress and anxiety. These projections represent a bewildering array of possibilities, the complete treatment of which goes beyond the purposes of this book. Nevertheless, it is important to highlight some of these trends and their likely impact on counseling. In many cases, the themes represented are concepts that have had continuity across futurist observers over the last decade or so; in some cases the themes are very recent. In most instances, however, they are trends running out of the past into the future as scientific breakthroughs, political decisions, economic events, and organizational transformations weave their way into the social fabric and the consciousness of the nation, both collectively and individually.

In 1986, the research reported by Oxford Analytica suggested that there are eight themes of importance to the United States through the 1990s. In abbreviated and updated form, these are

1. **the resilience of the American dream:** In essence, is the vision of abundance, openness, and opportunity to which Americans have subscribed for 200 years in its twilight? The speculation is No, the American dream is not dying, it is being neutralized by the energy of the American enterprise system, by its adjustment to global and economic structural changes that are rapidly occurring, and by the continuing openness of the United States to immigration and to the absorption of immigrants into the mainstream of the United States. The levels of immigration into the United States are now essentially the same as the numerical peaks that occurred in the great immigrant waves between 1900 and 1910. But whereas the major flow of immigrants at the beginning of the 20th century was from Europe,

the current waves of immigrants are predominantly from Hispanic countries—Mexico and Central and South America—and from Asia.

2. **diffusion:** With the increasing waves of immigration and cultural pluralism, there is a growing likelihood of more fragmentation in politics, economic policy, and social characteristics; more deregulation of economic policies will continue to disperse power from governmental institutions to corporations and other private sector entities; special interest groups may incorporate much of the power formerly held by major political parties; federal government functions such as welfare, health, and educational provisions may be increasingly decentralized to state and local units and possibly not performed at all in some parts of the nation. Such circumstances may exacerbate the social contrasts among different population groups and intensify the poverty of people now captured in its web.

3. **precarious conservatism:** A deep stream of conservative values (e.g., reaffirmation of the importance of personal and family success, personal fulfillment, security over change) characterizes large segments of the American population, particularly those in the baby boom generation now approaching 50 years of age. This group—perhaps out of frustration, cynicism, anger, or sheer practicality—seems to reject ideas of "big government" and its ability to solve major social problems. As a result, there is a turning inward to personal achievement, local programs, and the importance of the family as antidotes to what are perceived as government extravagances, wrong national priorities, falling national prestige, and the excesses of the counterculture.

4. **europeanization:** As America matures and moves into the next century, it is expected to acquire certain characteristics Americans typically think of as European: smaller families are becoming the rule rather than the exception; the rural past of the United States is merging into the suburban and urban reality of contemporary America; religious belief, as in Europe, may become more personal and less collective. Similarly as was suggested strongly in chapter 4, in the United States regional differences in attitudes, resources, lifestyles, and occupations are becoming more visible. It is possible that those differences will be reflected in more clearly defined ethnic identities from region to region, differences in economic and political life, and divergent relationships with other nations or areas of the world: "The East will look to Europe, the Sunbelt to Latin America, and the West Coast to Asia and the Pacific rim" (Oxford Analytica, 1986, p. 334). Such trends may also be translated into the structural equivalent of "walled" cities in which special groups are likely to seek protection, security, and the companionship of those like themselves: senior citizens, students, ethnic minorities, young married couples, the wealthy retired. Such enclaves can potentially harden class lines and reduce social mobility.

5. **the household:** In previous chapters of this book analyses of the effects of the changing family structure in the United States were discussed. It was projected by Oxford Analytic in 1986 that the household, however it is defined, will become more central as a private world of support to develop and reaffirm values and to provide leisure and intimacy and, indeed in many instances, serve as a center of part-time work as telecommuting and other uses of technology will permit more working at home rather than going to an office or workplace at a physical distance from home. Although such possibilities have many positive outcomes, there is also the possibility that increased stresses and strains among family mem-

bers may arise as tensions develop from being so totally immersed in each other and the possibilities for which the household serves as the center: paid work, entertainment, religion.

A variation on the theme of the household frontier is the growing propensity by some corporations to increase the "home at work" as workers are treated more holistically, and as child care, health care, fitness programs, employer educational assistance programs, family counseling, and related initiatives are provided. As these employment-bound activities expand, and are implemented, they will blur the lines between home and work and personalize the work environment in new ways.

6. **high-risk and high-stress society:** A United States in major transition in values, opportunities, work, family structures, cultural diversity, and political and social institutions is also a society of potentially great stresses and strains within families, communities, and population groups. Although opportunities to choose may be greater for most, people are also likely to pay penalties for choosing wrongly or be traumatized into indecision or indecisiveness because of "overchoice" (Toffler, 1970). Clearly, stress in the workplace and in other aspects of life have become major components of daily life for many Americans. The stressors to which these people react take many forms: role conflict, uncertainty or inadequate knowledge about an event or events that require action or resolution, ambiguous roles, time urgency, inability to perform effectively the tasks demanded. Keita and Sauter (1992) have suggested that "psychological strain is quickly becoming one of the most prevalent, costly, and debilitating forms of occupational ill-health" (p. viii).

7. **limits of technological life:** As discussed in chapter 2 and elsewhere in this book, technology of many forms has pervaded American life. It has changed the content and processes of the workplace and the nature of the occupational structure. It has changed health care and altered personal longevity. Home entertainment, transportation, retailing and wholesaling, chemicals, agriculture and fishing, and manufacturing have each experienced dramatic modifications as technology has been adopted. But creeping into the national and international consciousness is ambivalence about some of the ethical and political dilemmas certain forms of technology pose (e.g., genetic engineering, acid rain, cloning of animals, the greenhouse effect) and about ecological disasters that have occurred when supertankers carrying oil sink and pollute pristine fishing grounds (e.g., the Exxon Valdez) or nuclear power plants experience a melt down (e.g., Chernobyl), contaminate a large geographic area, and cause major health problems for children and adults exposed to such contamination. Such disasters, however rare they may be, have sobered and frightened many persons in countries around the world about the price that needs to be paid for technological advances or international competitiveness. Such concerns—when added to the stresses and strains of individual worries about being swept up in a technological juggernaut that necessitates retraining, requires changes in personal identity, creates unemployment for some and underemployment for others, and potentially widens the gap between the rich and the poor and the skilled and the unskilled—create an environment that is intensely psychological in its influence on personal responses. Given such circumstances, it is likely that expressions of concern about the economic insatiability of investment in technology, as well as concerns

about whether the human price exacted by technological advancement is equaled or exceeded by the benefits derived, will be apparent at many levels of society.

8. **testing confidence:** As the United States moves through the multiple transitions just described, the levels of confidence about the future of the nation, whether its institutions are working properly, and the security of its place in the global economy are likely to ebb and flow. As this volatility occurs, the likelihood of blaming other nations, institutions, or elected leaders and the potential for internal conflict between subgroups of the population will be high. People will search for reassurance that existing problems can be fixed and that everything will ultimately come out all right.

As we consider each of these eight themes that were seen as relatively futuristic in 1986, it is likely that we will view many of them as descriptive of perspectives and tensions of today. Some of them clearly connect to other parts of this book and the major challenges for counselors discussed there. Even so, many of these themes continue to affect the future. So it is with the other set of projections that were used as a focus in the first edition of this book: the popular forecasts of Naisbitt in 1984 in his now classic book, *Megatrends: Ten New Directions Transforming Our Lives,* and Naisbitt and his group in 1986 in *The Year Ahead 1986; Ten Powerful Trends Shaping Your Future.* Just as with the trends as originally forecast by Oxford Analytica, so, too, have the *Megatrends* of the 1980s now become part of the American mentality. And as we will note next in this chapter, even though the megatrends cited in the 1980s are being replaced by megatrends forecast for the year 2000 and beyond, there are overlaps in how these transformations speak to the context in which job paths, educational content, and interpersonal circumstances are likely to be shaped and sustained. In some cases, these trends have been unfolding for 30 and more years, but their effects have only recently come to fruition. In other cases, the trends have evolved as the American society has taken on new characteristics and possibilities for personal action.

Megatrends

These megatrends (and, indeed, other futurist projections) represent a structure by which to classify and make sense of the enormous barrage of information that confronts each individual each day in the form of media—television, videos and films, newsprint. Megatrends and other futurist projections are dynamic because the world's political, economic, and social structures are constantly changing. For example, when Naisbitt and his associates developed their megatrends in the early 1980s and Oxford Analytica made their forecasts in the mid-1980s, the Cold War was still a reality; Hungary, Poland, the Czech Republic were still occupied by Soviet armed forces; the Berlin Wall still divided East from West Germany; there was still a Soviet Union; South Africa was still governed by an official policy of apartheid; the global economy was still in its infancy; personal computers were primarily a business tool, not a personal tool; and totalitarianism had just begun to give way in many parts of the world to a rising spirit of human rights and freedom. All of these have changed in the last decade and created new trends and new uncertainties. The megatrends identified by Naisbitt and his associates in the 1980s included the following 10 transformations:

1. from an industrial society to an information society;
2. from forced technology to high tech/high touch;

3. from a national economy to a world economy;
4. from a short-term to long-term (planning, rewards, visions);
5. from centralization to decentralization;
6. from institutional help to self-help;
7. from representative democracy to participatory democracy;
8. from hierarchies to networking;
9. from North to South (in regional differences in population and economic activity); and
10. from either/or to multiple options.

Most of these trends are a familiar litany to many counselors, and their implications for counseling content and planning are transparent. But what about megatrends for 2000 and beyond? "Megatrends do not come and go readily. These large social, economic, and technological changes are slow to form, and once in place, they influence us for some time—between 7 and 10 years or longer" (Naisbitt & Aburdene, 1990, p.12). The trends of the 1980s continue pretty much on schedule, according to Naisbitt and Aburdene, but they are now only part of the picture. Ten new megatrends are emerging that have a different emphasis and direction than those forecast for the 1980s and early 1990s. A new set of forces is coming into play.

As part of this chapter's analysis of future challenges for counselors, we turn briefly to the 10 megatrends (and related projections) that Naisbitt and Aburdene (1990) saw as the gateway to the 21st century.

1. **The global economic boom of the 1990s:** As has been discussed elsewhere in this book, the global economy is rapidly emerging as a major factor in the competitiveness of nations and in the demands for skilled workforces that are characterized by literacy, numeracy, teachability, flexibility, and commitment to life-long learning. In part because of its leadership role in the world economy, commentary on radio and television, as this is written, speaks of an economy that is in almost perfect balance and that is reflected in a stock market that has soared to record heights. The unemployment rate in the United States is now at 4.5%, the lowest in 24 years.

    The effects of the global economy appear in many guises. In a National Public Radio lecture on the program Alternative Radio on August 24, 1997, one of the authors of *Global Dreams. Imperial Corporations and the New World Order* (Barnet & Cavanaugh, 1994), cited statistics such as these: Of the 10 largest economies in the world, 51 are multinational corporations, not countries; the economic worth of Wal-Mart is greater than 161 of the nations of the world, although 30 countries do have larger economies; 500 million people around the world drink Coca-Cola each day; 1 billion Marlboro cigarettes are sold throughout the world each day; one third of the world's trade occurs within multinational corporations trading among their own units spread around the world; the income of the 447 billionaires in the world is larger than the poorest half of the world's population; and 30% of the world's population are underemployed or unemployed.

    Many of these astounding economic statistics are possible only because of the pervasive influence of technology on the restructuring of work organizations and workforces and on the interdependence of the world's economy. Through technology massive amounts of currency can be moved electronically overnight without regard to national boundaries, and work for a corporation can be done

at any location in the world and linked electronically with the central administrative unit wherever that entity is located. Major regions of the world are now
represented by free trade zones such as the European Economic Community,
the North American Free Trade Agreement, or the emerging Association of
South East Asian Nations. These have altered patterns of worker mobility and of
the content of work in the nations affected. As Naisbitt and Aburdene (1990)
suggested,

> The movement to global free trade is being driven by an alliance between telecom-
> munications and economics that permits you to deal with a business associate in
> Colorado as if you were across a table—sharing conversation and documents. . . .
> Telecommunications—and computers will continue to drive change, just as manu-
> facturing did during the industrial period. . . . We are laying the foundations for an
> international information highway system. In telecommunications we are moving
> to a single worldwide information network, just as economically we are becoming
> one global market place. (p. 23)

It seems clear that the future of the world's economy is to reduce national
economic sovereignty and to increase the interdependence of national
economies into a single organism, and that nations not able to participate in
such a world economic structure will find it difficult to maintain their national
economic growth and development.

2. **Renaissance in the arts:** Naisbitt and Aburdene (1990) predicted that as
   income and job quality increases for more and more Americans, there will be a
   "fundamental and revolutionary shift in leisure time and spending priorities"
   (p. 62). They suggested that as the affluent information economy has spread
   throughout the United States, Europe, and the Pacific rim nations, "the need to
   reexamine the meaning of life through the arts has followed" (p. 62). The
   authors cited as their data for such an observation the rapid growth in museum
   attendance, professional dance, leading music ensembles, visual arts, books sold,
   opera attendance, and other related factors that suggest an unprecedented liter-
   ary and cultural revival. In the wake of the end of the cold war, they argued
   that "much of humanity is free to ponder, to explore what it means to be
   human. . . . It is a spiritual quest, but its economic implications are staggering"
   (p. 63), not only in large cities but throughout the nation. The arts and sports
   are now in an intense competition for people's leisure time and dollars (p. 84).
   In addition to the income cities and corporations accrue from the arts boom per-
   vading the nation, a wealth of new career opportunities in music, acting, and
   dance as well as arts production, promotion, media, sales, and administration
   have occurred.

3. **The emergence of free-market socialism:** Socialism in many parts of the
   world, with its historic emphasis on centralization of power and on the primacy
   of the state, is giving way to the new importance of the individual. In part this
   transformation has resulted from the end of the cold war, but probably more so
   because of effects of technology and telecommunications, the attractiveness of
   participating in the global economy, the high cost of welfare-state socialist
   schemes, and the decline of union membership and its historical support in
   many nations' socialist parties. The result has been widespread attempts to reinvent socialism from centrally planned economies to economies that offer a wide

range of market mechanisms, privatizing the means of production and distribution, creating stock markets, deregulating, and letting markets set prices.

In short, the forms of socialism appearing around the world are shifting from economies run by governments to economies run by markets (Naisbitt & Aburdene, 1990, p. 96). As such economic transformations, reform, and restructuring are attempted, however, they can not occur without a growth in individual liberties, individual enterprise, individual responsibility and accountability. To do so, in Russia and in other former communist nations, has meant breaking the old social contract between the government and its citizens. That contract guaranteed every citizen at least a low wage job, subsidized housing, subsidized food, and free medical care if the individual did not criticize the state, and accepted the party and the state as absolute authority. When that contract is broken, individual opportunities can expand dramatically but so can unemployment; the quality of life can improve dramatically but so can the uncertainty of life; entrepreurship can increase but so can costs of food and housing and other processes. The rewards that accompany individual freedom, political pluralism, and the potential for personal achievement can also mean for some a new, and often different, struggle for shelter, food, and personal dignity.

4. **Global lifestyles and cultural nationalism:** Given the extent of contemporary travel, global telecommunication, television, and international trade, persons in countries around the world are consuming foods, music, and fashion from each other's nations and are creating international lifestyles. As the world embraces a global economy, it also embraces products that become "world brands." These include Coca-Cola, IBM, Sony, Porsche, McDonald's, Honda, and Nestlé, among others (Naisbitt & Aburdene, 1990, p. 119). Images of lifestyles in the United States and in other nations speed around the world at the velocity of light. Persons can "talk" to each other by electronic mail or fax almost as quickly as by telephone. McDonald's now has outlets in more than 50 countries. Kentucky Fried Chicken operates the world's largest fast-food restaurant in Beijing near Mao's tomb. Domino's Pizza delivers on motor scooters in Tokyo. Sushi bars are appearing in many U.S. cities, including those in which there are few Japanese residents. Cappuccino and Perrier are available and sought out not only in restaurants but also as part of the groceries we buy for home consumption. Clothing, jewelry, and shoes imported from Britain, China, Colombia, France, Italy, and Mexico become regular consumer items for U.S. customers. Films, television shows, and music are major American exports to countries throughout the world, just as Americans purchase music and watch films and television shows produced abroad.

English has become the language of the global lifestyle as well as of transportation, business, and diplomacy. At the same time, as international lifestyles are growing and apparent homogenization of food, fashions, music, and television are occurring, there is a countereffort in many parts of the world to preserve cultural uniqueness and identity whether the focus is religious, cultural, national, linguistic, or racial. This is certainly true in religion, particularly in Islamic nations such as Iran; it is true in nations where efforts to preserve and reinforce the language of a particular culture are apparent as is true in Catalan, Quebec, Singapore, and Wales. As Naisbitt and Aburdene (1990) observed, "The trend toward a global lifestyle and the countertrend toward cultural assertion represent the classic dilemma: how to preserve individuality within the unity of the family or community" (p. 153). At a different level, it is also the classic dilemma within the United States as the great richness of persons representing American pluralism seek both to find common cause with national goals and values and to preserve their cultural traditions and uniqueness.

5. **The privatization of the welfare state:** In many nations of the world, privatization of industries, airways, and other enterprises has replaced or is replacing state control of these enterprises. This trend has been very evident in Europe, including Russia and the Eastern European nations, as well as in Africa and the Americas, including Canada and other nations. Naisbitt and Aburdene (1990) indicated that as they were preparing their book more than 100 nations around the world were in the process of transforming governments that had been dominated by socialism and the welfare state to privatization of state enterprise and to private stock ownership. We see much the same phenomena in the United States, even though it has never been primarily a socialist or a welfare state in its orientation or in its control of enterprise.

    Among the examples of privatization underway in the United States are the railroads, the U.S. Postal Service, potentially Social Security, and other historically governmental functions. The current major example of such processes is the national movement toward getting people off welfare and into private sector jobs. Essentially all states are now implementing some form of workfare and jobs in an attempt to help former welfare recipients make the transition from public assistance to genuine employment and to self-determination and responsibility. This transformation of one of the major programs that emanated from the years of the New Deal during Franklin Roosevelt's presidency and the Great Society under President Lyndon Johnson has not been easy; nor will it be instantaneous because more than 11 million people are on welfare, some 90 percent of the adults on welfare are mothers with dependent children, and two thirds of welfare recipients are children under 18.

    Transition to workfare will need to occur over some period of time, jobs will need to be available for former welfare recipients, and support systems will need to be put in place so that the induction and adjustment to work are effective. There also will be those persons who will not be able to make such transitions and to take care of themselves, and they will continue to need some governmental assistance. Not only the United States but countries throughout the world will need to rethink the responsibilities of government to its citizens. The hope is that the transition from welfare to workfare will focus on individual needs rather than on classes of persons. Thus it is likely that what will emerge is "a tailored program to match individual strengths and needs, to have government in concert with the private sector respond to each individual, not to classes and groups and categories" (Naisbitt & Aburdene, 1990, p. 176). In reality, then, the basic shift in welfare reform, as it is in the move to privatization more broadly, is from central government to individual empowerment. Undoubtedly such moves will increase the need for more career counseling and for attention to the kinds of skills individuals need to achieve the types of empowerment sought by governments and by the legislation that promotes workfare rather than welfare.

6. **The rise of the Pacific rim:** Shortly beyond the year 2000 it is anticipated that Asia will comprise two thirds of the world's population; in contrast, Europe will

have only 6%. The nations of the Pacific rim, particularly the countries of the Asian Pacific rim, are advancing rapidly in economic and in educational terms. As Naisbitt and Aburdene (1990) attested, "Today the Pacific rim is undergoing the fastest period of economic expansion in history, growing at five times the growth rate during the Industrial Revolution" (p. 179). The resulting forecast is that the center for trade is and will shift increasingly from the Atlantic to the Pacific and that many of the cities of the Pacific rim—Hong Kong, Los Angeles, Seoul, Sydney, Tokyo, Vancouver—will replace much of the economic power now held by such cities as London, New York, and Paris. It also will be likely that many of the U.S. states, particularly along the Pacific rim, will find themselves increasingly oriented to Asia trade and to economic interactions principally with Asian Pacific rim nations. Although California, Oregon, and Washington State have long been the home of Asian immigrants and affected by the pluralism of Asian values and traditions, it is likely that such influences will intensify in importance. More and more of the jobs in these states will be devoted to trade with East Asian nations. And many Americans will work for organizations owned by Japanese, Korean, and Taiwanese firms. These nations had been increasing their investment in the United States dramatically until 1997, when South Korea, Thailand, and, to a lesser degree, Japan experienced major and unexpected problems because of bad loans by and corruption in their banking systems and their resulting difficulties in meeting foreign debt obligations. Even so, it is anticipated that because of the magnitude of Japanese investment in the United States, by the year 2000 approximately 1 million Americans will work for Japanese firms. Asian immigration and Asian workers assigned to the United States will continue to grow, as will the numbers of Asian students enrolled in American education. As these trends continue, abilities in speaking Asian languages as well as knowledge related to the economic, legal, and history of these countries will be increasingly valued. In addition, there will be growing needs for mental health services to be available and culturally responsive to both Asian immigrants and Asian workers.

7. **The 1990s: decade of women in leadership:** The reality of women as a minority in the workforce is over. Women are rapidly becoming a critical mass in many occupations that were nontraditional for women in the past, and either the proportions of women are even with men or are now a majority in many other occupations. About 80% of women with no children under 18 years of age are employed, and about 70% of women with children under 18 are employed. Women are rapidly becoming new business owners and entrepreneurs, and they dominate the occupations that are information based. As Naisbitt and Aburdene (1990) observed, women are now poised to become corporate and business leaders in large numbers. Many women possess the vision, commitment, and abilities to share power and to assume responsibility that new work organizations require in their corporate leaders now that organizations are dispensing with traditional power hierarchies, moving toward flatter structures and shared governance, and placing greater emphasis on internal communications and on treating workers holistically. These expressed values are often those that women executives believe in and are freer to express than men who have progressed through more bureaucratic, hierarchical, control-oriented, authoritarian work structures and organizations.

In newer, emerging forms of work organizations, as they are emerging, the primary emphasis has shifted from management that is devoted to controlling (and often micromanaging) all aspects of an enterprise to management that empowers workers to be the best they can be, to be flexible, and to be able to respond quickly to change. The latter is a more democratic and relationship-oriented management vision, and one in which leadership is less intrusive and coercive. It is also one in which the search for shared values and unity among employees and management, with respect and compassion for one another, are vital elements of the corporate culture. Earlier forms of more authoritarian management, centralized information, and top-down instructions were effective in assembly lines and much manufacturing work, particularly with a workforce that was less educated and more male dominated than is true today. The workplace and the workforce of today's information economy is different and requires new tasks and new leadership.

As we said earlier in this book, knowledge work has replaced manual work in occupation after occupation. The knowledge worker who uses computers as tools, who manages data and uses it to drive machines, and who troubleshoots problems and creates solutions, engages in work that predominantly involves "mental tasks," that is, tasks which are not performed on assembly lines and can not be managed as though they were. Because women dominate the occupations that comprise the information society—teachers, health care workers, data entry specialists, computer operators, financial services, marketing, advertising—they have acquired the skills, experiences, and education to provide leadership in many of these enterprises and for many workforces in those sectors. Some 45% or more of adult women are now college educated and are being paid for what they know as well as what they do. The emerging skills of leadership including loyalty, compassion, the ability to balance roles across career and family, the disposition to be a self-developer, and the capacity to earn respect as well as the capability of working with others and sharing power with an increasingly educated workforce are attributes that women have gained in abundance. As they have gained a critical mass in the professions and dominate in the occupations comprising the information society, the need for the talents they represent will grow at a pace that will disregard gender as an issue. In the interim, career counseling tailored to the unique needs of women and such phenomena as increases in self-help and support groups will grow in importance in the decades ahead.

8. **The age of biology:** As described earlier in this book, biology has increasingly become a preeminent discipline in its applications to the study of brain chemistry and the origin of various forms of mental illness, to biogenetic engineering, and to many other technological developments. Naisbitt and Aburdene (1990) argued that

> we are shifting from the models and metaphors of physics to the models and metaphors of biology to help us understand today's dilemmas and opportunities. . . . *Physics* furnished the metaphor that suggests: energy-intensive, linear, macro, mechanistic, deterministic, outer-directed. . . . Today, however, we are in the process of creating a society that is an elaborate array of information feedback systems, the very structure of the biological organism. . . . *Biology* is as metaphor suggests: information-intensive, micro, inner-directed, adaptive, holistic. (p. 241)

As biotechnology continuously expands its linkages to computers; to the design of new pharmaceuticals, vaccines, and medicines; to the mapping of the human genome (the 50,000 to 100,000 genes stored on the 23 chromosomes) to locate specific genes and their functions; to the understanding of persons who are genetically predisposed to certain diseases and to the creation of new and different treatments for them; to the use of genetically engineered organisms to control the insects that diminish the productivity of agricultural crops and to "eat" toxic chemicals and other pollutants; to create new strains of animals or fish that are resistant to infections or parasites to feed the world's population; to engineer plants so that they have the protein value of meat and animals so they can produce drugs and other biological products that are helpful to humans, it is clear that the quality of life will be improved for many persons, that the life span will be increased, and that a variety of ethical questions about the use of such information will require new knowledge bases and policies. The research needs and investment requirements to advance the contributions of technology will be huge, worldwide in scope; and many new technical occupations will emerge to administer, implement, and distribute the outcomes of biotechnology.

9. **Religious revival of the third millenium:** There seem to be unmistakable signs of revival in many religious traditions and in many parts of the world. Perhaps the growth of Islamic fundamentalism in much of the world is the most obvious. But certainly as the nations of the former Soviet Union and other nations previously under communist domination have become free and moved toward democracy, their people have returned to their historic churches and have signaled a hunger for religious books and training. Some argue that as the world approaches the year 2000 there is an unusual importance ascribed to the meaning of this transition to a new millenium as prophesied in the books of the Old Testament and, particularly, the book of Revelation in the New Testament. As a result, more persons of Jewish and Christian traditions have become more preoccupied and focused on the implications of religion and spirituality for their own life. Part of this phenomenon may be the reaction of persons who are experiencing the stresses and anxieties of living in a period of tremendous change and challenge. Many of them may feel that the promises of a better, more satisfying quality of life through science and technology is hollow and devoid of the feelings of inner satisfaction and peace they desire. As a result, they seek a haven, a place that is solid, or a person or a positive, active creative force that transcends human existence and reflects the Divine.

It is also true that, to the degree that constructivist theory (as described earlier in this book) is accurate, as persons engage in meaning making, in making the choices that define their own reality, they inevitably come face to face with their own destiny, with their own spirituality, with questions of their nature and importance, with questions about whether this life is all there is or whether there is an eternal life of the soul or spirit. In such quests for understanding of their personal meaning, persons look for reassurance, for personal validity, for faith in something beyond themselves, which they may find in New Age cults, humanism, or organized religious traditions. However they do it, many persons are seeking "a link between their everyday lives and the transcendent" (Naisbitt & Aburdene, 1990, p. 277). Thus counselors in all settings will in the future inevitably find greater need for attention to the quest for meaning and for spirituality—which tends to be associated with many of the issues of anxiety, malaise, discontent that bring persons to counseling.

10. **The triumph of the individual:** Following on the erosion of totalitarianism in an increasing number of nations of the world, Naisbitt and Aburdene (1990) contended, there is a new respect for individuals as the foundation of society and as the basic unit of change. Within this context, there is a growing emphasis on individual responsibility for what the individual does, for achievement, for improving the society.

As the power of states and of governments to control individual behavior, opportunities, and goals diminishes across the world, individual power to choose and to be responsible for individual choices grows. The individual no longer must be part of a faceless, anonymous collective, but the individual can choose to build and contribute to community. As the traditional institutional jobs in the Fortune 500 companies have decreased in number and have turned to outsourcing contracts and temporary workers to augment their permanent workforces, individual entrepreneurs have become increasingly important players in the global economy, in part because new technologies have extended the power of individuals to create new products, to communicate, to sell and export, to publish, to provide specific services in competition with larger organizations. In such contexts, "Computers, cellular phones, and fax machines [can] empower individuals rather than oppress them, as previously feared" (Naisbitt & Aburdene, 1990, p. 303). These machines have allowed many people to work in almost any geographic location they wish and yet be in virtually instantaneous communication with any site on earth. People of the future will not be required to live adjacent to their workplace and to aggregate in large cities. Indeed, many people will be able to make decisions based on their desired quality-of-life issues, perhaps live in rural areas outside of metropolitan areas, and engage in a variety of forms of self-employment, including being contractors for firms located in other parts of the nation.

Quite aside from issues of location or specific forms of employment, individual quests for spirituality, for uniqueness, for creativity and an enhanced quality of life are growing whether they are expressed in terms of a clean and safe environment or access to the arts or humane jobs in the workplace. Such themes tend to pervade many of the other future trends identified here. Although there are many persons in the world who have not yet enjoyed the individual power or its personal benefits that are becoming available more widely elsewhere, the trend toward greater emphasis on providing for more individual achievement, fulfillment, productivity, and purpose seems to be growing in the United States and around the world. There are certainly many challenges yet to be overcome—economic, political, bureaucratic—that work for conformity and sameness, rather than uniqueness and individuality. But these are eroding in favor of individuality and creativity.

Although we have used the 10 trends that Naisbitt and Aburdene (1990) have projected as the megatrends that will shape the beginning of the 21st century, there are many other perspectives by futurists for which our space does not permit a full examination. Nevertheless, it is worth acknowledging some of the trends represented by other futurists because they, too, will effect counselors and clients in a variety of ways. Examples of some of central themes of other futurists are identified in Table 9.1.

Implications for Counselors of Emerging Challenges

The perspectives of futurists and scholars about the projected changes in environments, institutions, technologies, economic and political processes, and other aspects of the psychological contexts 21st century Americans are likely to encounter could be extended into many volumes. However, the various sets of trends identified in this chapter and earlier are sufficient to make the point that has been reiterated throughout this book: the content of counseling and its importance is a function of political, social, and economic events in the larger society.

The effects of these events—whether psychological or literal—upon individuals shape the questions of self-efficacy, purposefulness, social value, access, and performance with which counselors must be prepared to deal. Counselors can not view these events in parochial, monocultural, or narrow ways. They cannot function effectively in a world of rapid and comprehensive change by possessing only a limited understanding of the contexts, images, events, or cultural traditions within which people negotiate their identity, security, and goals, and many find themselves at risk. Counselors must be able to help clients separate the general effects of events that occur around them from the specific effects of these events, if any, on themselves as individuals. Counselors must help clients anticipate the timing and the meaning of their experiences and of plans of action to modify or strengthen their ability to deal with such matters.

Further, counselors in all settings must be open to new metaphors about the needs for counseling, or the emerging content of counseling, or new ways to create and implement counseling strategies that respond to the emerging challenges facing their clients and that are ethical and effective.

Table 9.1   Examples of Future Trends by Selected Futurists

James (1996)	Kotter (1995)	Handy (1994)
• Smart work • Star Trek technology • Interdependence • Complexity and customization • Adaptability of mind and body • Miniaturization • The Internet • Doing more with less • Mastering new forms of intelligence • Profiting from diversity • Change • Flexibility • Jobs of the future will be mental, not manual	• Unconventional career paths • Away from the big and bureaucratic to the small and entrepreneurial • Speed and flexibility essential • Management giving way to leadership • Lifelong learning increasingly necessary for success • Globalization the key to markets and competition • Shifts from high volume to high value • More volatility and less job security	• The paradox of intelligence • The paradox of work • The paradox of productivity • The paradox of time • The paradox of riches • The paradox of organizations • The paradox of aging • The paradox of justice

As changes occur in the larger society—whether at the global level or in a local town or family—they tend to stimulate needs for new behavioral patterns and skills that hitherto had not been expected or sanctioned or needed. We find expression of these concerns in research and scholarship on views of behavior that go beyond the normative, the average, the conforming to such terms as *optimization of behavior, personal resilience, self-renewal, personal flexibility.* Whether in structured interventions, or in group or individual techniques, such behavioral paradigms emerge in the training and practice of counselors as new and important emphases in counseling. Attempting to promote optimal behavior, personal flexibility, resilience, or self-renewal is different in kind from providing remedial treatment for a particular phobia or anxiety. The former constructs are more forward looking and comprehensive.

In addition, when the focus of counseling is addressed to promoting individual empowerment and the notions of renewal, resilience, flexibility, and optimization, there are other constructs that tend to be involved as well, such as those termed *spirituality* and *dignity.* These, too, become metaphors to which counselors in the future will need to give more attention.

Finally, as counselors embrace and are empowered by new behavioral styles, as counselors understand and maintain awareness that individuals enlarge their attempt to derive meaning and purpose (indeed spirituality) from their life as they are provided more economic and personal freedom, counselors also need to discover, modify, and use techniques that are relevant to the content and purposes to be served in counseling. Often this requires that former definitions of counseling or psychotherapy or interventions be revisited and expanded and that these terms be invested with new metaphors, processes, and practices, and used across wider audiences. But also at issue is the awareness that as new counseling strategies and techniques unfold they frequently bring with them new ethical issues (such as are found with the use of the computer and the Internet in delivering career services). As these complex sets of factors—behavioral challenges from external environments, needs for remediation or optimization of behavior, the search for individual meaning and spirituality, the evolution of new techniques in counseling and the need to adapt ethical principles to such technologies—new emphases in counselor roles will continue to become visible in the decades ahead. The remainder of this chapter will briefly discuss some of the metaphors and elements comprising optimization of behavior, perspectives on human dignity and spirituality, and shifting emphases in counselor roles.

OPTIMIZATION OF BEHAVIOR

Chapters 5 and 6 of this book have focused on at-risk children, adolescents, and adults. The percentages of persons of all ages with clinical depression, intense stress and anxiety, substance abuse problems, tendencies toward violence toward others, and other behavioral styles that are antisocial present a bleak picture of human behavior and how it should be remediated. Frequently, issues such as the enormous impact of poor parenting, of child neglect and physical assault, and of living trapped in poverty and in decaying physical conditions seem almost insurmountable. But there are other paradigms emerging in which counselors are not solely focused on overcoming negative environmental and family situations or poor personal intrapsychic images. Rather they are encouraged to promote optimal or resilient behavior that supports individual strength to absorb negative life experiences and keep moving forward.

Seligman (1996), for example, believed that it is possible to prevent depression in children by identifying the signs of pessimism in children and teaching them the skills of optimism. In his view, optimism is the antidote to helplessness, which is the feeling that nothing the individual does matters. According to Seligman, the society is awash in an epidemic of pessimism that becomes entrenched in the minds of many children and leads to depressed mood, resignation, underachievement, and even unexpectedly poor physical health. Seligman suggested a variety of ways to promote optimism in children. Many are really variations on cognitive-behavioral therapy techniques, such as recognizing and acting on the negative thoughts that automatically cross an individual's mind at the times when he or she feels worst, recognizing that these automatic thoughts may not accurately reflect what is going on, challenging these negative explanations and generating more accurate ones when bad things happen, and not "catastrophizing" or overgeneralizing the negative things that happen but instead trying to bring them into perspective and into balance. Beyond these techniques, Seligman identified exercises for teaching skills of optimism to children, thus helping them to achieve mastery within their own tasks, to learn to make choices and to be interactive with others, and to attain readiness to take on, learn about, and master new activities rather than be coerced and rebuked for not doing so.

Rak and Patterson (1996) have advocated assessment techniques and strategies that promote resiliency in youths at risk. As described by these authors, "resiliency in children is the capacity of those who are exposed to identifiable risk factors to overcome those risks and avoid negative outcomes such as delinquency and behavioral problems, psychological maladjustment, academic difficulties, and physical complications" (p. 368). Within this context, Rak and Patterson have identified several personality, familial, and environmental variables that promote resiliency. These include such personal characteristics of resilient children as (a) an active, evocative approach toward problem solving, which enables them to negotiate an array of emotionally hazardous experiences; (b) an ability from infancy on to gain others' positive attention; (c) an optimistic view of their experiences even in the midst of suffering; (d) an ability to maintain a positive vision of a meaningful life; (e) an ability to be alert and autonomous; (f) a tendency to seek novel experiences; and (g) a proactive perspective. There are also family conditions that promote resiliency, that tend to contribute to buffering children in the wake of the stressors that place them in an at-risk category. These include

> (a) the age of the opposite-sex parent (younger mothers for resilient male participants, older fathers for resilient female participants); (b) four or fewer children spaced more than 2 years apart; (c) focused nurturing during the first year of life and little prolonged separation from the primary caretaker; (d) an array of alternative caretakers—grandparents, siblings, neighbors—who stepped in when parents were not consistently present; (e) the existence of a multiage network of kin who shared similar values and beliefs and to whom the at-risk youths turned for counsel and support; (f) the availability of sibling caretakers in childhood or another young person to serve as a confidant; and (g) structure and rules in households during adolescence despite poverty and stress. (p. 369)

Outside of the family, there are also supports in the environment that act as buffers for potential at-risk children. Prominent among these are role models, such as teachers, school counselors, supervisors of after-school programs, coaches, mental health workers, workers in community centers, clergy, and good neighbors. Clearly, the availability of caring and interested adults who encourage the child or adolescent to seek them out, use their mentoring, and thereby reject rejection is a critical issue in promoting resiliency.

A number of self-concept factors also appear to be important in providing at-risk youth buffers against stress and personal vulnerability. A major factor is the at-risk child's or adolescent's ability to understand him- or herself and define boundaries between him- or herself and the origins of long-term stressors like family psychological or physical illness, be expected or needed to engage in socially desirable acts of helpfulness that prevent other people in his or her family or community from experiencing distress, and have a feeling of confidence or faith that things will work out as well as can reasonably be expected.

In essence, the factors of personal characteristics and self-confidence as well as those of mentoring and support represent the points of influence to which counseling strategies should be aimed to promote resiliency in at-risk children. Such programs need to be seen as multidimensional. Just as Seligman advocated ways to teach children skills of optimism, Rak and Patterson advocated counseling strategies to reinforce individual resilience and teach and model behaviors by which the client's capacity to self-manage and cope with problems and stressors are strengthened. Included in such counseling strategies is the use of initiatives to enhance the child's or adolescent's self-concept, to provide them unconditional positive regard and positive reinforcement, to teach them conflict resolution skills, and to help them access peer support. Beyond the direct work with the child, counselors can provide individual and group consultation with parents to help with effective parenting strategies and better communications with their children, to set logical consequences for misbehavior rather then withholding love as punishment, and to help them find appropriate referral to community agencies dealing with health care, financial matters, and related needs. Further, the counselor in a school or a community agency setting can be very influential in communicating with and facilitating the work of mentors and other support persons to reinforce their roles in promoting resiliency for at-risk children.

Self-Renewal

A variation on optimization of behavior as a counselor strategy is that of promoting individual self-renewal. A major aspect of such a goal is to determine what behaviors or attitudes need to be renewed. One possibility is individual happiness. Until recently, psychological research has tended to focus more on negative emotions than on positive ones. But if unhappiness is correlated with suicide ideation, substance abuse, anxiety and depression, and excessive stress, personal happiness and joy have been found to be associated with such phenomena as mind-body healing, resilience, less prejudice, better interpersonal relations, better achievement in school and at work, and better coping with stress. Counselor promotion of the behaviors and skills that comprise happiness and helping persons to renew such positive emotions is another way to stimulate optimization of behavior.

According to the research of Myers and Diener (1997), four traits characterize happy people. First, happy people like themselves; they have positive self-esteem. Second, they feel personal control and empowered rather than helpless. Third, happy people are usually optimistic and positive thinking; they believe they can achieve what they set as goals. Fourth, happy people tend to be extroverted persons who reach out and interact positively with others whether they live alone or not, live in rural or metropolitan areas, work alone or with others. Persons' happiness may be dependent to varying degrees on their genetic makeup and on their socialization; however, happiness can be modified, and it can be renewed. Counselors can assist in such processes by helping persons rethink their priorities, find ways to increase their satisfaction from work and leisure, and strengthen their systems of social support and their interpersonal relationships as well as consider their involvement in religion, in volunteerism, or in other community activities that provide hope and purpose.

Although happiness and self-renewal are important aspects of optimization of behavior, so, too, is emotional intelligence. Goleman (1995) argued that the abilities that make up emotional intelligence should be taught to children, should be the subject of prevention programs and, certainly, of counseling. In his view, an expanded model of what it means to be intelligent puts emotions at the center of aptitudes for living. They are the mediating variables that allow individuals to pursue other cognitive forms of intelligence appropriately and effectively. In essence, emotional intelligence is a different way of being smart. As such, emotional intelligence includes self-awareness and impulse control, persistence, zeal and self-motivation, empathy and social deftness. Goleman contended that these are the qualities that mark people who excel in real life, whose intimate relationships flourish, who are stars in the workplace. These are also the hallmarks of character and self-discipline, of altruism and compassion.

Emotional intelligence can be taught by families, by schools, and by counselors. Helping children, adolescents, and adults label their emotions and develop less impulsive reactions to them is to increase emotional literacy. Indeed, some schools are teaching courses in emotional literacy. Other schools are more likely to teach courses in life skills, conflict resolution, anger management, more specific problem solving models (e.g., SOCS—Situation, Options, Consequences, Solutions), and other forms of curricula that help students to learn emotional self-awareness, manage emotions, harness emotions productively, improve empathy and sensitivity to others' feeling, read and interpret social cues, and handle relationships. Many counselors have engaged in providing such courses in the past under other labels, but the findings about the importance of the relationships between emotional intelligence and improved academic performance, reduced depression and violence, and more caring about others that result from emotional literacy courses provide a compelling rationale for emphasizing among counseling goals the skill development necessary to facilitate optimization (and renewal) of emotional intelligence behavior.

Covey (1989), in his now classic book *The Seven Habits of Highly Effective People. Restoring the Character Ethic,* included a number of principles of human effectiveness and of self-renewal. He saw the habits he espoused as a basic, primary internalization of correct principles upon which enduring happiness and success are based. He argued that these habits constitute a continuing process of renewal that helps an individual to consider his or her mental maps, perceptions of problems, character, and motives. In demonstrating these seven habits of effectiveness, individuals should

1. **be proactive:** This habit means that as human beings we are responsible for our own lives; our behavior is a function of our decisions, not our conditions. We can subordinate feelings to values. We have the initiative and the responsibility to make things happen.

2. **begin with the end in mind:** The essence of this habit is knowing our values, aspirations, center.

3. **put first things first:** This is self-discipline. The focus of habit three is that, "the successful person has the habit of doing things failures don't like to do. . . . They don't like doing them either necessarily. But their disliking is subordinated to the strengths of their purpose" (pp. 148–149).

4. **think win/win:** Habit four emphasizes the need to develop the frame of mind and heart that constantly seeks mutual benefits in all human interactions; it is based on the paradigm that there is plenty for everybody, that one person's success is not achieved at the expense or exclusion of the success of others.

5. **seek first to understand, then to be understood:** Habit five emphasizes empathy and patience as well as diagnosing before prescribing.

6. **synergize:** Habit six indicates that the whole is greater than the sum of its parts. The essence of synergy is to value differences—to respect them, to build on strengths, to compensate for weaknesses.

7. **sharpen the saw:** This is the essence of renewal, so that the other six habits can be possible. It means living a balanced life and expressing the four dimensions of our nature regularly and consistently in wise and balanced ways: physical (through exercise, nutrition, stress management); spiritual (through value clarification and commitment, study and meditation); mental (through reading, visualizing, planning, writing); social/emotional (through service, empathy, synergy, intrinsic security).

Hudson (1991) has also focused on issues of self-renewal for adults. It is his contention that society is becoming more adult centered after being youth centered for years. Within this context, adults are living longer and are in more need of periodic self-renewal than ever before. Hudson suggested that self-renewing adults are typically characterized by 10 traits, and that these traits, and the categories of skills identified, represent a frame of reference by which counselors can promote and facilitate self-renewal among adult clients.

Hudson's (1991) 10 traits or qualities of self-renewing adults, in significantly abridged form, are as follows:

1. They are value driven, committed to values and purpose. Renewal for them is the repeated revival of the central concerns of their lives within the changing contexts in which they find themselves (pp. 210-211).

2. They are connected to the world around them. They care and communicate. They network information, contacts, and resources.

3. They require solitude and quiet. They plan for introspection as well as for interaction and decision making.

4. They pace themselves. "They are not trying to sustain optimal performance at everything they do; rather they seek to be fully present and available for all the occasions of their life course" (p. 212).

5. They have contact with nature. They often find nature to be a dependable source of renewal.

6. They are creative and playful, active not passive. They pursue ways to express themselves.

7. They are adaptive to change. "Self-renewing adults are critical thinkers who sustain the abilities to gather information, evaluate, solicit opinions of others, and make both firm decisions and firmer redecisions" (p. 214).
8. They learn from down times. They do not live lives without stress, failures, mistakes, loss, and tragedy, but they learn from their disappointments, necessary losses, and down times.
9. They are always in training. They never stop learning.
10. They are future oriented. "They do not dishonor the past or the present, but they focus their lives on the 'not yet' and the 'What if?'" (p. 216).

Such a profile of the attributes or traits of self-renewing adults provides counselors the frame of reference by which to educate adults to the extant research on self-renewal, to the behaviors and attitudes they may want to emulate or set goals to develop.

Hudson's (1991) categories of skills "for sustaining integrity and self-renewal throughout the adult years" (p. 217) (with examples of how the skills are demonstrated) include

- **feelings:** "Maintains high levels of self-confidence and self-esteem. . . . Empathizes with and validates others" (p. 217);
- **thinkings:** "Distinguishes between trivial and significant problems. . . . Reflects upon sense of self and its personal life course" (p. 217);
- **doings:** "Perceives problems and evolves strategies for their solution. . . . Plans and feels responsible for making the future happen" (p. 218);
- **intimacy and relationship skills:** "Has parenting skills and provides an environment of love and learning for a family. . . . Seeks and maintains friendships that are mutually rewarding" (p. 218);
- **communication skills:** "Presents ideas and makes them convincing. . . . Accesses and networks necessary information" (p. 218);
- **team player skills:** "Fosters trust and cooperation. . . . Adjusts to and is curious about new conditions" (p. 218); and
- **change master skills:** "Is able to look at things from new perspectives. . . . Assumes responsibility for successes and failures" (p. 219).

Such skill sets related to self-renewal and personal mastery can become the content of counselor workshops for older adults dealing with preretirement issues or, indeed, the basis for assessment of older adults' needs and status. In any case, the skills identified here represent important content to use in counseling with adults who need help in initiating and implementing life/career planning.

Personal Flexibility

Implicit in optimization of behavior and in self-renewal is the need for personal flexibility. It is not possible for an individual to reach a state of optimized behavior or self-renewal unless he or she finds ways to learn, to acquire new skills, to see trends with fresh perspective, to be willing to be flexible in responding to the political, social, economic, and organizational changes that affect individual behavior. In a multicultural world, it is not possible to conceive of personal flexibility as an absolute set of behaviors that can be defined independent of history or culture or government policy or forms of work or other social organization. Such an observation suggests that counseling for personal flexibility is likely to have different nuances and content in different societies and that counselors operating between or across cultures must be trained in multicultural counseling techniques and be sensitive to varying interpretations of personal flexibility, the behaviors that comprise it, and applications of personal flexibility that are likely to arise in the worldviews of persons from different cultures.

With due respect to how cultural differences may alter any particular model of personal flexibility proposed, there are a number of knowledge and behavioral emphases common to most of the industrialized nations that seem of relevance to facilitating personal flexibility. These are reflected in Table 9.2.

The concept of counseling for self-renewal or for optimization of behavior adds new expectations for counselor behavior and the metaphors on which such counseling is based. The same is true when the subject is facilitating personal flexibility. Counseling for personal flexibility is likely to fuse personal and career counseling for many persons. Because counselors typically operate at the intersection between individuals and their environments, at the point where negative transactions between the client and different aspects of their environments need to be analyzed and reinterpreted and new sets of attitudes and behaviors developed that allow the client to chart new directions, new perceptions of counselor roles are likely to emerge. In such circumstances, as counselors promote personal flexibility, they are likely to be seen as brokers or maximizers of opportunities; as interpreters or translators of the relationships between education, training, or retraining and their implications for different career pathways and different career outcomes; as support persons by which clients can acquire insight into their own stereotypes and irrational beliefs that have acted as brakes on their personal mobility and freedom of action; as stimuli to their use of strategies by which to increase their feelings of power and self-efficacy; as personal coaches or trainers by which clients can learn skills (e.g., assertiveness, anger management, decision making, conflict resolution, stress reduction) that increase their internal locus of control of the attitudes or behaviors they display in a particular situation and that, in general, facilitate growth in their emotional intelligence; as mentors who provide feedback and advice about specific tasks or perceptions of tasks with which the individual is coping; as persons who are sensitive to the grief and mourning experienced by those whose cultural identity has been lost in their migration from one community, region, or nation to another; and as enablers of personal initiative and control. In these changing dimensions of counselor roles, counseling for personal flexibility is likely to be active, collaborative, and goal directed.

Because a lack of self-esteem impedes personal flexibility and frequently stems from negative evaluations of worth, such evaluations and the bases for them may need to be confronted (by, for example, using cognitive behavioral theory) and alternative ways of viewing the self examined. Self-esteem is fundamental to personal flexibility, to an individual's way of viewing others and the world as well as the utility of continuing to live and to doing so purposefully. In dealing with self-esteem issues, the counselor must create in his or her communication with the client a relationship that is characterized by caring, trust, understanding, honesty, sincerity, acceptance, liking, and interest. These relationship variables may sound so familiar to the reader that they are passed over lightly. The point is, however, that these interpersonal elements are precisely what has been missing from the client's life, and their lack has brought him or her to a lack of self-esteem or self-worth. These types of

Table 9.2   Elements of Personal Flexibility

Basic academic skills

Adaptive skills
   Problem solving
   Handling evidence
   Analytic ability
   Implementation skills
   Human relations
   Learning skills
   Coping skills
   Employability skills (e.g., self- and career management)
   Work context skills

Transfer skills
   Deal with change
   Self-assessment skills
   Learning to learn
   Taking self-initiated actions
   Understanding skill elasticity

Mobility skills
   Job seeking and job getting
   Interviewing skills
   Resume preparation

Entrepreneurial skills
   Managing innovation and change
   Visioning future applications and opportunities for skills and services
   Time and resource management

Career motivation (London & Stumpf, 1986)
   Career resilience
   Career insight
   Career identity

Competence (Amundson, 1989)
   The capacity or power to deal with emerging situations
   Sense of purpose
   Self/other/organizational understanding
   A support network and a supportive organizational context
   Self-confidence
   Communication and problem-solving skills
   Theoretical knowledge and understanding of facts and procedures
   Practical experience

counseling variables constitute the healing ingredients by which people can be helped to self-disclose, exhibit trust in another, and communicate the feelings of pain and loneliness that underlie and presage dealing with problems of self-esteem.

Another aspect of promoting personal flexibility is related to an individual's relationships with other people; psychological health depends almost entirely on the quality of relationships with others. Johnson (1986) contended that each of us needs to be confirmed as a person by other people. According to him,

> Confirmation consists of responses from other people in ways that indicate we are normal, healthy, and worthwhile. Being disconfirmed consists of responses from other peo-

ple suggesting that we are ignorant, inept, unhealthy, unimportant, or of no value, and, at worst, that we do not exist. (p. 3)

In a world of loneliness, rapid change, discrimination, complex stressors, and psychological or physical abuse, many have never learned nor have been systematically exposed to positive interpersonal skills that allow them to develop self-worth, positive individual identity, or effective relationships with others. Thus their behavioral repertoire may be very limited in how to act in an interdependent world, or they may feel so limited in their locus of control—their ability to mange their lives—that they attribute everything that happens to them to fate or external control by other people.

Counselors obviously cannot change the world, but they can help people understand what they are experiencing, equip them with the skills by which they can become more positive about themselves, and enhance their ability to gain access to and cope with interpersonal, family and career opportunities that validate them as persons and increase their personal flexibility.

Much more deserves to be said about the promotion of self-esteem, personal responsibility, and control as major challenges for the foreseeable future. Suffice it to say that although the terminology is used differently by different authors, the counselor of the future must be prepared to help clients of any age consider alternatives, sharpen values, deal with their individual quests for meaning or spirituality, understand more about their strengths and their possible applications in social and work situations, and identify and learn the skill sets (e.g., interpersonal, problem solving, communication) likely to permit them to live a more purposeful and productive life and one of increased personal flexibility.

As the counselor addresses other elements of personal flexibility (as described in Table 9.2) with different clients, other techniques for dealing with career issues, transitional concerns, crisis interventions, inadequate support systems, anxiety, and uncertainty will be useful for particular purposes. On balance, counseling for personal flexibility can be conceived as having three emphases: *remediation*, that is, assisting persons in the cases where a lack of the elements necessary for personal flexibility has put them at risk at points of transition, unemployment, or underemployment; *prevention*, that is, counseling adolescents and adults to anticipate the importance of and providing ways to acquire the elements of personal flexibility; and *optimization*, that is, providing clients the counseling support and reframing of life opportunities by which they can apply their personal flexibility to higher levels of self-actualization, clarity of meaning and purpose, pathways of personal excellence, and more effective relationships with others.

HUMAN DIGNITY: A RATIONALE FOR COUNSELING

Although dignity in many ways implies optimization of behavior, it goes beyond that perspective and deserves greater emphasis then in the past as a rationale for counseling at any level. Indeed, we could argue that counseling in this nation arose and has continued to be important precisely because it is a process committed to the facilitation of human dignity.

As any history of the counseling profession will attest, counseling in this nation arose approximately a century ago, in the midst of the industrial revolution, to facilitate greater economic and social justice for immigrant populations coming to this nation from many countries around the world and for persons migrating from the rural areas of the United States to its cities to find economic opportunity. Social reformers, settlement house workers, and other groups concerned with human rights were making strong efforts to have workers viewed not as chattels of industry but rather as persons of dignity with a right to determine their own destinies. It was from these groups of sensitive and committed persons that early counselors emerged. Indeed, this prizing of and concern for human dignity has been at least an implicit raison d'être for the provision of counseling in this nation, however any particular theory or conceptual model of counseling intervention may portray it.

As in the complex conditions that spawned counselors and counseling 100 years ago, counselors today find themselves caught up in new challenges that can create barriers to or assault human dignity in both direct or indirect ways. As we come to the eve of the 21st century and review the characteristics of the 20th century, it is apparent that we live in a world that continues to struggle between conflicting desires to either degrade or enhance human dignity. As we view the daily news and witness the "ethnic cleansing" in Bosnia or Afghanistan, the neo-Nazi anti-Semitic terrorism in Germany, the human rights violations and exploitation of child laborers or political prisoners in many nations, or personally observe the effects of racism, sexism, or ageism in our country as well as the homelessness, poverty, addiction, and violence on our streets we wonder and despair about what we do and what we allow to be done to others and the impact of these processes on human dignity.

The contemporary challenges to individual dignity and, therefore, to counselors are embedded in much of the content of this book. We have talked about four major challenges in this book. Each of these is in transition, although each adds to the collective stimuli that are changing behavioral metaphors and psychological structures, and each adds to the social structure changes that are transforming the ways in which individuals negotiate their personal identity, live out their self-concept, and come to terms with their perceptions of human dignity or its lack.

The first major challenge to clients and to counselors identified here includes but is not limited to transformations in the economic and social opportunity structures of the nation as these have been increasingly affected by the growing global economy, the international economic competition it reflects; job dislocations due to corporate downsizing; continuing problems of unemployment and underemployment; rising educational requirements for emerging occupations; the pervasive incorporation of advanced technology in the home, classroom, and workplace; and the stresses that occur when the rhythm and output of technology get beyond human capabilities to cope and to control. Such dynamics have affirmed that, in large measure, the economic problems of the world are not technical problems, but human problems; they stimulate situations in which persons caught in the throes of economic competition, organizational downsizing, and rapidly changing requirements for work desperately seek ways to maintain their feelings of self-worth and personal dignity.

A second major challenge with implications for the acquisition and maintenance of human dignity is related to changing family structures and shifting child-rearing practices; to single parenting and its potential corollary of economic vulnerability, loneliness, and lack of personal support; and to the gender revolution and the accompanying tensions as new types of relationships between males and females are forming in the home and the workplace.

The third challenge has to do with the growing pluralism of races, languages, ethnicities, cultural traditions, belief systems, and the generalized aspirations for equal opportunity and a better quality of life for all as well as the lingering problems of understanding, acceptance, and integration of persons whose cultural and racial backgrounds are different from those of majority groups. The fourth challenge concerns the changing definitions of at-risk populations, those who need extra support and help in rebuilding their feelings of meaning and purpose and of being persons of dignity.

Given this brief analysis of some of the circumstances in which the quest for human dignity falters, it is interesting to find that the term *dignity* is not often found in the counseling or psychological literature. It is not often found in indexes to texts or journals, although the term *dignity* is sprinkled through counseling language, organizational bylaws, and statements of professional purpose. In such contexts, dignity is seen as an end state, an ideal, a goal to be sought through counseling. Dictionary definitions of dignity speak of worth, value, honor, self-respect, distinction. They also speak of the process of dignifying another, of enabling, honoring, glorifying, raising, lifting. Thus counseling can be defined as a process of dignifying another, of manifesting respect for another's value or significance, of helping persons get beyond the internalization of the indignities that environments impose on them in the form of victimization, oppression, insensitivity—so that they can move to the freedom of accepting, being responsible for, and acting on their personal significance and potential. In these perspectives, to have dignity is to have personal power, self-respect, security, freedom to choose, purpose, a sense of meaning or spirituality, and optimism.

Flowing from these definitions has come a vocabulary in counseling that has spoken primarily of the elements of dignity rather than of dignity itself. These elements include self-esteem and self-worth, cultural pride, positive identity, internal locus of control, personal agency, personal goals, resilience, insight, self-actualization. These are words that celebrate pluralism and strength, not homogenization and deficiency. The professional literature has talked more fully about the symptoms that arise when persons do not feel a sense of dignity: anxiety, depression, loneliness, violence, low self-esteem, powerlessness, identity diffusion or confusion, anger, incivility, depersonalization, oppression, and vulnerability. As such, these symptoms have become the targets of counseling interventions whether directed at individuals or systems.

Stripped of its formality, then, dignity means essentially that each individual is significant, to be valued, important. These conditions are inherent in human heritage and in human rights. In this sense, dignity is a moral term, a moral imperative that is inherent in human personhood. Indeed, the civil rights movement in this nation for the past 50 and more years was and is a struggle for personal significance, for personal inclusion, for personal dignity. So have been the women's movement, the Gray Panthers movement, and the fights for such legislation as the Americans With Disabilities Act of 1990.

It is such contexts, and those of the major challenges for clients and counselors explored in this book, that suggest that at its core the counselor's role is to dignify his or her counselees. Whatever population he or she serves, in whatever setting, the counselor's role is to acknowledge and respect human dignity, promote and develop it, and recognize in all that he or she does that dignity is not a function of a particular skin color, race, ethnicity, gender, physical or mental wholeness, income level or education; it is a characteristic that underlies humanity and humanness. Without feelings of dignity, it is unlikely that any individual can attain his or her full potential as a human being. Without personal dignity, it is difficulty to grant it to others, to take personal responsibility for our actions, to gain a sense of agency or self-efficacy, to find alternatives to violence as an appropriate strategy to gain what we seek.

Thus when persons appear in counselors' offices, regardless of how the presenting problem is labeled, they are often there because they lack a feeling of dignity, of significance, of importance, of value to others. They are experiencing the claustrophobia of an environment that denies them life chances or creates images of achievement and social credence that they perceive to be unattainable or for which they do not possess the strategies to pursue. These feelings do not arise from pathology or genetic deficiencies, but from transactions with environments, systems, and individuals that have marginalized these persons, depersonalized them, reduced their self-esteem, created identity confusion, blunted their goals, and stimulated anxiety or anger or other emotional, psychological, or behavioral results.

SPIRITUALITY

As we consider the future challenges for counselors in a changing world society, including the importance of achieving the goals of optimizing behavior, facilitating personal flexibility, or validating human dignity, it seems clear that issues related to attaining personal meaning and security in an environment in flux are pervasive. Within such contexts, it is understandable that there seems to be renewed attention to personal spirituality, faith, and religion as issues for clients and for counselors. Covey (1989) has contended that among the four dimensions of adult renewal—physical, spiritual, mental, and social/emotional—an individual needs to be focused on the spiritual, as reflected in value clarification and commitment, study and mediation, if he or she is to enjoy a healthy balanced life.

Certainly, as many persons consider, spirituality is a core concept, a centering mechanism, a place of commitment to values. It is an aspect of the self to which an individual may retreat to meditate about and to identify sources of timeless truth and commitment. For some individuals, such commitment is found in great literature or music that, each in its own way, expresses spirituality and faith; other persons find spiritual nurturance in nature; still others find their spiritual essence in churches, temples, mosques, and synagogues. Thus individuals find spiritual renewal differently, but it is increasingly seen as an intense human need if people are going to find purpose, peace, and empathy for the needs of others. Covey (1989) argued that, "Peace of mind comes when your life is in harmony with true principles and values and in no other way" (p. 298). Other researchers seem to agree.

Myers and Diener (1997), for example, in examining the research findings about actively religious people, found that such people are much less likely to become delinquent, to abuse drugs and alcohol, to divorce, and to commit adultery, and that they also report greater happiness than those not religiously active. These authors also found that happiness and life satisfaction rise with strength of religious affiliation and frequency of worship attendance and that among the elderly one of the best predictors of life satisfaction is religiousness. Further, those with strong faith are less vulnerable to depression then their nonreligious counterparts and more likely to recover greater happiness after suffering divorce, serious illness, or unemployment.

Hansen (1997), in her model of Integrative Life Planning, suggested six critical tasks as central to career development and to decision making: (1) finding work that needs doing in changing global contexts; (2) weaving our lives in a meaningful whole; (3) connecting family and work; (4) valuing pluralism and inclusivity; (5) exploring spirituality and life purpose; and (6) managing personal transitions and organizational change. Of particular attention here is her emphasis in critical task 5, exploring spiritually and life purpose. In her review of the literature related to this topic, she found that concepts of spirituality were important in the work of many prominent theorists in psychology and counseling, including Viktor Frankl, the creator of the theory of logotherapy; Carl Rogers, the initiator of client-centered counseling; and Abraham Maslow, the advocate of the idea of prepotent needs and self-actualization. These theorists and many others—Carl Jung, Gordon Allport, Rollo May, Adrian Van Kaam—differed in whether or not they embraced organized religion, and if they did, they differed in the religious tradition they embraced. But they each agreed that humankind was characterized by its search for wholeness, for meaning, for purpose, and, as a reflection of each of these, for spirituality.

Stronger connections between spirituality and its related concepts and their more obvious presence in counseling theories in the future seems to be likely. Although such connections between spirituality and psychology or the mainstream of counseling or psychotherapy have not been central topics in these fields in the past, the historic barriers to such integration seem to be slowly dissolving as the practice of scientific inquiry and the practice of faith are beginning to build bridges and acknowledge that each may be complementary to the other and, indeed, that each has a significant contribution to facilitating human development, human healing, and human purpose.

CHANGING EMPHASES IN COUNSELOR ROLES

Throughout this chapter and, indeed, the earlier chapters of the book, implications that challenge counselors to add new techniques and redefine or expand their roles have been identified. These challenges to counselors do not imply that what they have been trained to do or have done is wrong or inappropriate. Rather, they suggest that new metaphors for counselors, new forms of counseling content, new knowledge of human behavior, and new consequences of person-environment transactions create situations that are dynamic, constantly changing. They require the counselor to be a constant observer, learner, and strategist as he or she experiences the client behaviors that result from interactions with other persons and with the other elements of their environment.

Clearly, counselors have passed the tests of commitment to service to others and to adapting their procedures and practices to the challenges with which they have been confronted in the past century. As we enter the 21st century, there will be new challenges and new needs for the applications of counselor skills to new problems, new populations, and new settings. Examples of these challenges and needs are as follows:

- Given the growing pluralism of the United States, increasing needs for counselors to be bilingual, sensitive to cross-cultural needs, and more fully representative of underserved populations are apparent.
- As traditional values and behavioral anchors erode, many persons feel adrift and stressed and find difficulty in defining personal norms that are secure and satisfy-

ing. Counseling will be an increasingly valuable sanctuary and a process by which to sort out such feelings, clarify individual meaning, establish personal reference points, and develop plans of action.

- In the midst of shifting values on the centrality of work and its security for many people as well as a rise in attention to family values, counseling will be an important mechanism to help persons clarify their commitment to family-work role integration, personal fulfillment, and career paths that allow accommodation of parenting and family achievement.

- As special groups of citizens—senior citizens, students, ethnic minorities, persons with disabilities, young married couples, the wealthy retired, the frail elderly, persons of alternative sexual orientation—become more visible and more vocal in their special needs, counselors will need to be more conscious of the special problems of these groups and the strategies that can be implemented to provide services tailored to them.

- In workplaces where attempts are made to create more holistic responses to workers, to provide them "more home at work," counselors will be central ingredients of such corporate strategies as child care, health care, fitness programs, employer educational assistance programs, family counseling, and orientation and support for the geographic transfer of family units and their adjustment to new regional or national cultures.

- As corporations continue to downsize their permanent workforces to a small primary core of personnel augmented by temporary employees and outsourcing, counselors will be vital elements in the processes of interpreting changing structures and skill requirements, of helping employees understand their options within the workplace, and of helping temporary employees identify new forms of career paths as well as their assets (e.g., variety, comprehensive learning about organizations) and their potential liabilities (e.g., minimal institutional identity, minimal health and other benefits, and job insecurity).

- Persons who are highly stressed and unable to deal with the rapidity or magnitude of change or the shifting social and value systems currently occurring in the United States and in other nations are likely to be major consumers of mental health services of all kinds, including counseling.

- As the ripple effects of advanced technology affect the exploration of work, education and lifelong learning, work adjustment and retraining, and unemployment and underemployment, counseling is likely to be important in helping people deal with their hopes for and skepticism about technology, their technophobia, their views of the lifestyles and habits generated by technology, and their worries about the limits that technology will impose on their future.

- In a world dominated by daily media analyses of natural and political turmoil, terrorism, failing institutions, and internal conflicts among subgroups of the population, counselors will have important roles in helping people identify the sources of the ambivalence, ennui, and uncertainty they experience, the steps they can take to create a more manageable environment, and the areas in which they can exert personal control.

- Counselors in all settings will need to understand the influences on at-risk behavior in populations they serve and design strategies by which to reduce the frequency or minimize the effects of such behavior through education, prevention, and initiatives that can increase the positive mental health climate created by families, schools, and workplaces.

- As individual empowerment and optimization of behavior become more fully articulated as counselor strategies, counselors and clients will engage in more collaborative definitions of problems and needs for treatment. Clients will participate more actively in their own treatment and the use of homework and self-directed materials to augment and perhaps accelerate the insights and planning gained from counseling. In such contexts and in others, counseling must be facilitative and collaborative, a maximizer of opportunity, not a cold and distant evaluator and interpreter.

- Counselors in the 21st century are likely to be situated in more settings and likely to continue to expand the comprehensiveness of the populations they serve. In addition to their traditional roles in remediation of behavior and attitudes and prevention of mental health problems, counselors will be increasingly concerned with client needs for self-renewal, optimization of behavior, personal flexibility, and spirituality and meaning.

- As the pervasive effects of technology in the workplace and in the larger society change the nature of work and possibly limit the number and types of jobs available, counselors will need to help persons affected by such changes to find alternative forms of satisfaction and identity, beyond work, in community and social service.

- The rapidity of change, unemployment and underemployment, and cross-cultural and cross-national mobility will create more conditions in which clients will experience grief and mourning about lost opportunities, lost aspirations, and lost cultural identity to which counselors will need to be sensitive and therapeutic.

- The language of counseling will continue to change the metaphors for and role descriptions of counselors, including those concerned with mentoring, coaching, supporting, collaborating, and brokering. In most instances, with most clients, counselors will play multiple roles. This reality is a reflection that most clients will have multiple problems, not single problems, and frequently counselors will have multiple roles to play in working with clients including, increasingly, being part of a team of helping professionals, not simply the sole provider of services,

- In a world in which rapid and pervasive psychological strain debilitates people's physical and psychological resources, counselors will need to help clients interpret the meaning of various situations for themselves and find ways to be renewed psychologically and spiritually.

- As social boundaries between ethnic groups and other minority/majority groups as well as gender roles blur and become more permeable, new tensions and uncertainties arise for many persons. In such circumstances, counselors will need to help persons learn conflict resolution and about cross-cultural differences, shared aspirations, and ways to live effectively in culturally diverse environments.

- New technologies will increasingly be applied to augment counselor roles that go beyond computer-assisted career guidance systems and computerized test interpretations to greater use of computer analyses of individual mental health problems, counseling at a distance through interactive computers, telecommunications technologies, and the Internet. Counselors will need to understand the increasingly complex ethical issues related to these technologies and act in accord with relevant ethical principles.

- Because of the continuing intensity of immigration to the United States, particularly from the Asian nations, there will be growing needs for counseling and other mental health services to be accessible and culturally responsive to Asian immigrants and workers.
- Career counseling tailored to the unique needs of women moving rapidly into management and executive roles in the workforce as well as needs for counselor facilitation of self-help and support groups will rapidly increase in the decades ahead.
- As the discoveries of biology are reflected in new medical processes that increase the longevity of life, new demands on counseling for senior citizens coping with questions of career, quality of life, and security will arise.
- Counselors in all settings will in the future inevitably find greater need for attention to the quest for meaning and for spirituality, which tends to be associated with many of the issues of anxiety, malaise, and discontent that bring persons to counseling.
- In a world of rapid and comprehensive change in the 21st century, counselors must be able to help clients separate the general effects of events that occur around them from the specific effects of these events, if any, on themselves as individuals.

Two decades ago, Walz and Benjamin (1979) suggested seven emerging behavioral and social consequences or areas of change that had particular meaning for counselors. They saw these as "beacons of future developments and as priorities which may be instrumental in shaping future counselor roles and functions" (p. 8). Many of these consequences or areas have become increasingly pertinent images as the past 20 years have unfolded. Among them are the following—with some updated commentary by the author of this book.

- **Individuals will place an emphasis on role before goal.** The essence of this image is that in a society with the intense psychological quality of contemporary America, individuals are increasingly likely to give primary priority to finding themselves as human beings and seeking to clarify their own personal identity before identifying their goals or professional identity. Such a perspective seems to be consonant with the growing development of self-help materials and groups, the quest for lifelong learning opportunities, and the attention to personal fitness and control that seem to describe many people in the American society. Issues of role integration, blurring of sex-related division of labor or education, and balance in family life, leisure, and commitment to work each suggests that many Americans in the 1990s are intensifying their attention to who they are, who they want to be, and how to exert as much control as possible given the instability of a changing world.
- **Hostility, polarization, and aggression will become more commonplace.** Many occasions can be cited to suggest that hostility, polarization, and aggression are only slightly below the surface in many localities and present dangers in some urban areas. Gang wars, racially inspired violence, and other forms of prejudice and discrimination symbolize the psychological economic realities with which many Americans live on a daily basis. They reflect feelings of need to protect "me and mine," to fend off perceived incursions by other groups into what is already a fragile economic situation, and "to do unto others before they do unto me." For

many swept up in such environments, counselors will be engaged, on the one hand, in conflict resolution and, on the other, in dealing with people whose priorities are personal satisfaction and survival rather than contributing to a more abstract common good or even achievement as defined in broad social terms.

- **Knowledge will become the most eagerly sought-after resource of the future.** As suggested in many parts of this book, the United States is in transition from an economy and an occupational structure based on industrialization and the production of goods to one based on the generation, distribution, and application of information. Some 65% of jobs in the American workforce now deal with information as a major aspect of the work content. Obviously, then, the wedding of science and technology, which is a central aspect of the American economy, has also made knowledge, trainability, ability to retrieve and use information, and lifelong learning essential elements of work access and mobility. For those not interested in or prepared to deal with these realities, opportunities for work will shrink in demand and in reward. The role of counselors as specialists who help people with educational planning—that is, with analyzing and engaging in retraining programs, with anticipating needs for remediation of skill deficits, and with keeping career options open as long as possible through deliberate choices of curriculum and course content—will increase not only in schools but also in other contexts.

- **The transitional dynamics in personal and social change will increase in importance.** American society, like most societies in most of the world's nations, is in the process of transforming its social and economic institutions and its national metaphors. Change swirls through society and pervades all systems, from the macrolevel to the microlevel, with which individuals interact. Although this comprehensiveness of change is inevitable and, indeed, in a conceptual sense understandable, it also generates feelings of stress, anxiety, and uncertainty as well as information deficits in individuals and organizations. Thus counselors increasingly need to be able to understand and interpret change processes, the characteristics of intervention in crises and transition, and the procedures for planned choice and planned change.

- **Attitudes and values in relation to work will change.** Two decades ago, Walz and Benjamin (1979) and many others assumed that the midterm future would bring an increasingly jobless society, that within 20 years 15% of the population would be able to provide all the necessary goods and services for the total population. As this book is being written, we are through the midterm future that Walz and Benjamin were projecting in 1979; and instead of becoming a jobless society, we are seeing a continuous decrease in unemployment. The 4.5% rate at the beginning of 1998 is one of the lowest since World War II. There seems to be (as described in chapter 2) a continuing movement from agriculture and manufacturing to service; and there is lower unemployment but higher underemployment, with those who are unemployed tending to have the jagged employment histories and multiple problems that require comprehensive remediation. The United States has a new and less dominant role in the global economy, but one that creates growing employment opportunities for workers; and the demographics of a smaller youth cohort entering the labor force permits other population groups (e.g., immigrants, women, older people) to find employment with less competition than is true in a time of a population bulge. It remains clear, however, that changes in attitudes and values in relation to work as well as in the content of work available will be major issues for counselors as they deal with youth in the process of exploration and preparation for work, with adults contemplating retraining and midcareer change, with dislocated workers who are unemployed because of structural changes in their work, with women intending to reenter the workforce, with dual-career couples deciding on how to synchronize the best opportunities for each partner, or with immigrants trying to gain entrance into the American workforce.

- **Depersonalization will be a common response to viewing the future.** Depersonalization in the face of change can take many forms. One is acting as though it will not affect the individual personally and therefore does not require planning for change. Depersonalization might also mean withdrawing into an insular existence with an individual's interpersonal contacts limited to people who share his or her views. Counselors in a depersonalized world need to help people find relationships between external events and personal plans of action that are as accurate as possible and that reinforce personal control. In the case of other forms of depersonalization, counselors can help people to connect with self-help, support systems, and volunteer opportunities that allow them to reach out, be less insulated, and gain increased sensitivity to the needs and aspirations of other people for communication and social interaction.

- **Future images act to control present behaviors.** Walz and Benjamin suggested in 1979 that an individual's view of the future "can have a direct effect on how one behaves in the present" (p. 13). That insight has been reinforced in the past 20 years as the growth of cognitive psychology has acknowledged that feelings and actions follow an individual's thoughts about a situation. Therefore, if individuals believe that they can master the challenges of the future, they are likely to attempt to understand the emerging trends and opportunities as the bases for personal plans. If they think that the future is frightening and beyond their ability to cope, they are unlikely to plan for it. Such people are likely to seek immediate, short-term gratification rather than longer term gain and to behave as though life were a function of external control and fate rather than a context in which they can maximize an internal locus of control or develop an evaluative center from which to define opportunities for choice and personal action. In such situations counselors will need to be able to teach people about planning, about the relationships between the future images they hold and current behavior, and about general coping skills that can be used to anticipate and deal with both potential problems and potential opportunities in the future.

In response to the seven topical areas of change, Walz and Benjamin (1979) identified, they suggested four roles counselors could play in "helping individuals to create a future that is positive both for the person and for society" (p. 15). The four roles, in paraphrased form, are

1. **facilitator of caring and sharing:** Counselors can help people strengthen their own sense of self-worth and the need to achieve that self-concept through expressing their interdependence and through caring for and sharing with others.
2. **facilitator of life transitions:** Counselors increasingly will be called upon to assist individuals understand and acquire the skills by which to move in and out of different life roles and activities.

3. **broker of vital information:** Counselors will be sought out as "resource linkers," as professionals who can help people locate, interpret, and use information and data relevant to their specific needs and interests and who can help them implement a systematic decision-making process.

4. **facilitator of change:** Counselors can assist people to "acquire the skills of effective change agents, to be authors of change rather than passive or frantic responders to it. Specifically, they can help their clients to develop criteria for identifying when a change is needed, to learn a process for making the change happen, and to develop guidelines for determining whether the change is a successful and adequate response to their particular needs and wants" (p. 17).

We can use other terms such as *maximizer of resources* or *broker of opportunity* or *facilitator of self-actualization* to describe images to which counselors might aspire. However, when combined with the array of central challenges portrayed in this book—the effects of advanced technology and a changing economic climate, a shifting family structure, rising cultural diversity, and growing concerns about at-risk conditions among youth and adults—the essence of the counselor roles projected by Walz and Benjamin 20 years ago (facilitator of caring and sharing, life transitions, and change; broker of vital information) continues to have currency as the content of a metaphor counselors can embrace as they turn their gaze to the 21st century.

CONCLUSIONS

The projections of social and economic trends likely to unfold in the next decade and beyond incorporate many dynamics that are likely to affect the types of problems clients bring to counselors and the interventions counselors use to respond. These future challenges for counselors are diverse in their content and, in some cases, vague; but they are rooted in the multiple social, economic, and political transformations that the United States is now undergoing. These changes are likely to have different effects on different groups in the society, although the timing and the intensity of the impact of such changes are not predictable. Even so, the comprehensiveness of the social, economic, and political trends described in this chapter and, indeed, in the earlier chapters of this book are of such magnitude in their effects on individual choices, behavior, and needs for knowledge and skills that counselors cannot dismiss their potential impact or be encapsulated within limited models of individual-environment transactions. Counselors must develop for themselves a "meta-language" of likely change in the various environments their clients occupy (education, family, work, social, leisure, training), an understanding of how people may be affected by such changes, and perspectives on the remedial, prevention, and optimization strategies most likely to assist clients choose the best of the options available to them.

Counselors must also be attentive to the constant refinements and reformulations of the possible interventions in client behavior they might use for different categories of presenting problems, and to the changing insights into behavior that continually emerge. Both the repertoire of treatment-problem interactions and the available conceptualization of different expressions of behavior are dynamic. They change as understandings of stressors, risk factors, physiological deficits, or psychosocial influences change. New interventions emerge as research on cognitive structures, value systems, and information processing mechanisms is linked to experimental evidence showing how and under what conditions these structures, systems, or mechanisms can be modified.

Perhaps, in the last analysis, the ultimate challenge to counselors will be that of continuing self-definition as professionals, commitment to lifelong learning so as to hone and add to their competencies constantly, and the willingness to read widely and experience life fully in order to stay current with the trends and conceptual models that signal the need for and the processes of behavioral change. The future will require that counselors sharpen their professional self-concepts as applied behavioral scientists, as technologists, as program planners, as facilitators of caring and sharing, and as maximizers of opportunity for others. Counselors of the future will need to think much more conceptually about the outcomes and results they can and do achieve rather than confine themselves to implementing a set of processes and services without a clear sense of the behavioral outcomes they intend to produce. In the future, counselors will need to give more attention to who they are and the influence they have as professionals in a nation of growing pluralism, changing family structures, shifting work conditions, and technostress as well as in a society abundant in risk factors and conditions that create personal vulnerability.

REFERENCES

Ackerman, N. (1958). *The psychodynamics of family life*. New York: Basic Books.

Adams, A.V., & Mangum, G. (1978). *The lingering crisis of youth unemployment*. Kalamazoo, MI: Upjohn Institute for Employment Research.

Ahrons, C.R. (1979). The binuclear family: Two households, one family. *Alternative Lifestyles, 2*, 499–515.

Albee, G.W. (1980). A competency model must replace the defect model. In L.A. Bond & J.C. Rosen (Eds.), *Primary prevention of psychotherapy: Vol. 4. Competency and coping during adulthood* (pp. 75–104). Hanover, NH: University Press of New England.

Albee, G.W. (1982). Preventing psychopathology and promoting human potential. *American Psychologist, 37*, 1043–1050.

Alcohol Research Information Service. (1987a). *Monday Morning Report, 11*(24), 2.

Alcohol Research Information Service. (1987b). *The Bottom Line on Alcohol in Society, 8*, 3.

Alexander, J.A., & Harman, R.L. (1988). One counselor's intervention in the aftermath of a middle school student's suicide: A case study. *Journal of Counseling and Development, 66*(6), 283–285.

Alter-Reid, K., et al. (1986). Sexual abuse of children: A review of the clinical findings. *Clinical Psychology Review, 6*, 249–266.

American Assoication for Counseling and Development. (1988). *Ethical standards*. Alexandria, VA: Author.

American Association of Retired Persons. (1994, October). Barriers to raising grandchildren. *AARP Bulletin, 35*(9),3.

American Counseling Association. (1995). *Code of ethics and standards of practice*. Alexandria, VA: Author.

American Psychiatric Association. (1980). *Diagnostic and statistical manual of mental disorders* (3rd ed.). Washington, DC: Author.

American Psychiatric Association. (1987). *Diagnostic and statistical manual of mental disorders* (3rd ed., rev.). Washington, DC: Author.

American Psychiatric Association. (1994). *Diagnostic and statistical manual of mental disorders* (4th ed.). Washington, DC: Author.

American Psychological Association. (1986). *Guidelines for computer-based tests and interpretations*. Washington, DC: Author.

American Psychological Association. (1992). *Ethical principles of psychologists and code of conduct*. Washington, DC: Author.

American Psychological Association. (1993). *Guidelines for providers of psychological services to ethnic, linguistic, and culturally diverse populations*. Washington, DC: Author.

363

American School Counselor Association. (1997). *The national standards for school counseling programs*. Alexandria, VA: Author.

American School Counselor Association. (1984). *The school counselor in career guidance: Expectations and responsibilities* (Role Statement adopted in 1984). Alexandria, VA: Author.

Amundson, N.E. (1989). *Competence: Components and development*. Unpublished paper, University of British Columbia, Department of Counselling Psychology, Vancouver, Canada.

Anastasi, A. (1985). Some emerging trends in psychological measurement: A 50-year perspective. *Applied Psychological Measurement, 9*(2), 121–138.

Antonovsky, A. (1979). *Health, stress, and coping*. San Francisco: Jossey-Bass.

Aponte, H. (1982). Introduction. In M. McGoldrick, J.K. Pearce, & J. Giordano (Eds.), *Ethnicity and family therapy* (pp. xiii-xiv). New York: Guilford Press.

Arrendondo, P. (1992). Promoting the empowerment of women through counseling interventions. *Counseling and Human Development, 24*, 8, 1–12.

Ashley, W.L., Cellijni, J., Faddis, C., Pearsol, J., Wiant, A., & Wright, B. (1980). *Adaptation to work: An exploration of processes and outcomes*. Columbus: Ohio State University, National Center for Research in Vocational Education.

Atkinson, D.W., Morten, G., & Sue, D.W. (1979). *Counseling American minorities*. Dubuque, IA: Wm. C. Brown.

Avioli, P.S. (1985). The labor-force participation of married mothers of infants. *Journal of Marriage and the Family, 47*, 739–745.

Ballantine, M. (1993). A new framework for the design of career interventions in organizations. *British Journal of Guidance and Counselling, 21*(3), 233–245.

Bandura, A. (1982). The psychology of chance encounters and life paths. *American Psychologist, 37*(7), 747–755.

Bandura, A., Adams, N.E., & Meyer, J. (1977). Cognitive processes mediating behavior change. *Journal of Personality and Social Psychology, 35*, 125–139.

Barnet, R.J., & Cavanaugh, J. (1994). *Global dreams. Imperial corporations and the new world order*. New York: Simon & Schuster.

Barnett, E.R., Pittman, C.B., Ragan, C.K., & Salus, M.K. (1980). *Family violence: Intervention strategies*. Washington, DC: U.S. Department of Health and Human Services, Office of Human Development Services.

Barnlund, D.G. (1975). *Public and private self in Japan and the United States*. Tokyo: Simul Press.

Basile, S.K. (1996). A guide to solution-focused brief therapy. *Counseling and Human Development, 29*(4), 1–10.

Bassi, L.J. (1996). Skills and the education level of U.S. workers. *Looking Ahead, 18*(1), 16–18.

Beattie, M. (1987). *Codependent no more: How to stop controlling others and start caring for yourself*. New York: Harper/Hazelden.

Beck, A. (1985). Cognitive therapy, behavior therapy, psychoanalysis, and pharmacotherapy: A cognitive continuum. In M.J. Mahoney & A. Freeman (Eds.), *Cognition and psychotherapy* (chap. 14). New York: Plenum Press.

Beck, A., & Greenberg, R. (1984). Cognitive therapy in the treatment of depression. In N. Hoffman (Ed.), *Foundations of cognitive therapy: Theoretical methods and practical applications* (pp. 155–176). New York: Plenum Press.

Beck, A., & Rush, A.J. (1988). Cognitive therapy. Foreword to Section V. In A.J. Frances & R.E. Hales (Eds.), *Review of psychiatry: Vol. 7* (pp. 533–537). Washington, DC: American Psychiatric Press.

Bellah, R.N., Madsen, R., Sullivan, W.M., Swidler, A., & Tipton, S.M. (1985). *Habits of the heart: Individualism and commitment in American life*. New York: Harper & Row.

Benedict, R. (1934). *Patterns of culture*. New York: New American Library.

Bennett, B., & Reardon, R. (1985). Dual-career couples and the psychological adjustment of offspring: A review. *School Counselor, 32*(4), 287–295.

Bennett, S.K., & Big Foot-Sipes, D.S. (1991). American Indian and White college student preferences for counselor characteristics. *Journal of Counseling Psychology, 38*(4), 440–445.

Berg, I., & Hughes, M. (1979). Economic circumstances and the entangling web of pathologies: An esquisse. In L.A. Ferman & J. Gordus (Eds.), *Mental health and the economy* (chap. 2). Kalamazoo, MI: Upjohn Institute for Employment Research.

Bergin, A.E. (1985). Proposed values in guiding and evaluating counseling and psychotherapy. *Counseling and Values, 29*, 99–115.

Berkowitz, M., & Hill, M.A. (1986). *Disability and the labor market: An overview.* Ithaca, NY: Cornell University, ILR Press.

Bernes, K., & Magnusson, K. (1996). A description of career development services within Canadian organizations. *Journal of Counseling and Development, 74*(6), 569–574.

Black, C. (1981). *It will never happen to me.* Denver: Medical Administration Company.

Black, C. (1986). An interview with Claudia Black. *Changes, 1*(4), 4–18.

Bland, R., & Orn, H. (1988). Family violence and psychiatric disorder. *Canadian Journal of Psychiatry, 31*, 129–137.

Blocher, D.H. (1966). *Developmental counseling.* New York: Ronald Press.

Bloom, M. (1996). *Primary prevention practices.* Thousand Oaks, CA: Sage.

Bolles, R.N. (1997). *Job hunting on the Internet.* Berkeley, CA: Ten Speed Press.

Borgen, W., & Amundson, N. (1984). *The experience of unemployment: Implications for counselling the unemployed.* Scarborough, Ontario: Nelson Canada.

Botterbusch, K.F. (1983). *A comparison of computerized job matching systems.* Menomonie: University of Wisconsin-Stout, Stout Rehabilitation Institute, Materials Development Center.

Bowen, M. (1978). *Family therapy in clinical practice.* New York: Aronson.

Boyer, E.L. (1983). *High school: A report on secondary education in America.* New York: Harper & Row.

Brenner, M.H. (1973). *Mental illness and the economy.* Cambridge, MA: Harvard University Press.

Brenner, M.H. (1979). Health and the national economy: Commentary and general principles. In L.A. Ferman & J.P. Gordus (Eds.), *Mental health and the economy* (chap. 3). Kalamazoo, MI: Upjohn Institute for Employment Research.

Brenner, M.H. (1987). Economic change, alcohol consumption, and heart disease mortality in nine industrialized countries. *Social Science and Medicine, 25*(2), 119–132.

Bridge, T.P., Mirsky A.F., & Goodwin, F.K. (Eds.). (1988). *Psychological, neuropsychiatric, and substance abuse aspects of AIDS: Vol. 44. Advances in biochemical psychopharmacology.* New York: Raven Press.

Bridges, W. (1996). Leading the de-jobbed organization. In F. Hesselbein, M. Goldsmith, & R. Beckhard (Eds.), *The leader of the future. New visions, strategies, and practices for the new era* (pp. 11–18). San Francisco: Jossey-Bass.

Briere, J. (1984, April). *The effects of childhood sexual abuse on later psychological functioning: Defining a post-sexual-abuse syndrome.* Paper presented at the Third National Conference on Sexual Victimization of Children, Children's Hospital National Medical Center, Washington, DC.

Brinkerhof, M.B., & Lupri, E. (1988). Interspousal violence. *Canadian Journal of Sociology, 13*(4), 407–434.

Brislin, R.W., Lonner, W.J., & Thorndike, R.M. (1973). *Cross-cultural research methods.* New York: Wiley.

Bronfenbrenner, V. (1979). *The ecology of human development.* Cambridge, MA: Harvard University Press.

Brown, D. (1985). Career counseling: Before, after, or instead of personal counseling? *Vocational Guidance Quarterly, 33*(3), 197–201.

Browne, A. (1987). *When battered women kill.* New York: Free Press.

Bruner, J. (1986). *Active minds, possible worlds.* Cambridge, MA: Harvard University Press.

Budman, S.H., & Gurman, A.S. (1988). *Theory and practice of brief therapy*. New York: Guilford Press.

Buell, F. (1994). *National culture and the new global system*. Baltimore, MD: Johns Hopkins University Press.

Bureau of Labor Statistics, U.S. Department of Labor. (1994). *Employment and earnings*. Washington, DC: U.S. Government Printing Office.

Bureau of Labor Statistics, U.S. Department of Labor. (1996). *Occupational outlook handbook, 1996-97*. Washington, DC: U.S. Government Printing Office.

Burns, D.D. (1980). *Feeling good: The new mood therapy*. New York: Signet.

Cabral, A.C., & Salomone, P.R. (1990). Chance and careers: Normative versus contextual development. *Career Development Quarterly, 39*, 5–17.

Campbell, J.R. (1985). Approaching affirmative action as human resource development. In H. McCarthy (Ed.), *Complete guide to employing persons with disabilities* (pp. 14–30). Alberton, NY: National Center on Employment of the Handicapped, Human Resources Center.

Carden, A.D. (1994). Wife abuse and the wife abuser: Review and recommendations. *The Counseling Psychologist, 22*, 4, 539–582.

Carl D. Perkins Vocational Education Act of 1984, Pub. L. No. 98-524.

Carl D. Perkins Vocational Education and Applied Technology Act of 1990, Pub. L. No. 101-392.

Castells, M. (1985). High technology, economic restructuring, and the urban-region process in the United States. In M. Castells (Ed.), *High technology, space, and society* (chap. 1). Beverly Hills, CA: Sage.

Centers for Disease Control and Prevention. (1995). Suicide among children, adolescents, and young adults. *Morbidity and Mortality Weekly Report, 44* (15), 289–291.

Centers for Disease Control and Prevention. (1997, September 25). *HIV/AIDS surveillance report*, 1–2.

Cheatham, H.E. (1990). Empowering Black families. In H.E. Cheatham & J.B. Stewart (Eds.), *Black families. Interdisciplinary perspectives* (pp. 373–394). New Brunswick, NJ: Transaction.

Chew, C. (1993). *Tech-prep and counseling: A resource guide*. Madison: University of Wisconsin, Center on Education and Work.

Chilman, C.S. (1980). *Adolescent sexuality in a changing American society: Social and psychological perspectives*. Washington, DC: U.S. Department of Health, Education, and Welfare.

Christensen, C.P. (1985). A perceptual approach to cross-cultural counseling. *Canadian Counsellor, 19*(2), 63–81.

Clark, L.A. (1987). Mutual relevance of mainstream and cross-cultural psychology. *Journal of Consulting and Clinical Psychology, 55*(4), 461–470.

Clifford, J.S. (1986). Neuropsychology: Implications for the treatment of alcoholism. *Journal of Counseling and Development, 65*(1), 31–34.

Coates, J.F., Jarratt, J., & Mahaffie, J.B. (1990). *Future work. Seven critical forces reshaping work and the workforce in North America*. San Francisco: Jossey-Bass.

Cochran, L. (1997). *Career counseling. A narrative approach*. Thousand Oaks, CA: Sage.

Cohen, N., & Adler, R. (1988). Immunomodulation by classical conditioning. In T.P. Bridge, A.F. Mirsky, & F.K. Goodwin (Eds.), *Psychological, neuropsychiatric, and substance abuse aspects of AIDS: Vol. 44. Advances in biochemical psychopharmacology* (pp. 199–202). New York: Raven Press.

Cole, N.J. (1981). Bias in testing. *American Psychologist, 36*(10), 1067–1077.

College Entrance Examination Board, Commission on Precollege Guidance and Counseling. (1986). *Keeping the options open: Final report*. New York: Author.

Committee for Economic Development. (1985). *Investing in our children, business, and public schools*. New York: Author.

Compas, B.E., Connor, J., & Wadsworth, M. (1997). Prevention of depression. In R.P. Weissberg, T.P. Gullotta, R.L. Hampton, B.A. Ryan, & G.R. Adams (Eds.), *Enhancing children's wellness* (pp. 129–174). Thousand Oaks, CA: Sage.

Conner, K.A. (1992). *Aging America: Issues facing the aging society*. Englewood Cliffs, NJ: Prentice-Hall.

Constantine, L.L., & Constantine, J.M. (1973). *Group marriage: A study of contemporary multilateral marriage*. New York: Macmillan.

Cook, E.P. (1985). Sex roles and work roles: A balancing process. *Vocational Guidance Quarterly, 33*(3), 213–220.

Cooney, J. (1988). Child abuse: A developmental perspective. *Counseling and Human Development, 20*(5), 110.

Coopersmith, S. (1967). *The antecedents of self-esteem*. San Francisco: Freeman.

Copeland, E.J. (1983). Cross-cultural counseling and psychotherapy: A historical perspective, implications for research and training. *Personnel and Guidance Journal, 62*, 10–13.

Covey, S.R. (1989). *The seven habits of highly effective people. Restoring the character ethic*. New York: Simon & Schuster.

CPC Foundation/Rand Corporation. (1994). *Developing the global workforce—insights for colleges and corporations*. Bethlehem, PA: College Placement Council.

Crites, J.O. (1981). *Career counseling: Models, methods, and materials*. New York: McGraw-Hill.

Cronbach, L.J. (1980). Validity on parole: How can we go straight? In W.B. Schrader (Ed.), *New directions for testing and measurement: No. 5. Measuring achievement, progress over a decade*. San Francisco: Jossey-Bass.

Cummings, N.A. (1977). The anatomy of psychotherapy under national health insurance. *American Psychologist, 32*(9), 711–718.

Cummings, N.A. (1986). The dismantling of our health system: Strategies for the survival of psychological practice. *American Psychologist, 41*(4), 426–431.

Cummings, N.A., & Follette, W.T. (1976). Brief psychotherapy and medical utilization: An 8-year follow-up. In H. Dorken and Associates (Eds.), *The professional psychologist today: New developments in law, health, insurance, and health practice*. San Francisco: Jossey-Bass.

Cyert, R., & Mowery, D. (1987). *Technology and employment*. Washington, DC: National Academy Press.

Daniels, S. (1985). Attitudinal influences on affirmative action interpretation. In H. McCarthy (Ed.), *Complete guide to employing persons with disabilities* (pp. 31–46). Alberton, NY: National Center on Employment of the Handicapped, Human Resources Center.

Danish, S.J., & D'Augelli, A.R. (1980). Promoting competence and enhancing development through life development intervention. In L.A. Bond & J.C. Rosen (Eds.), *Primary prevention of psychotherapy: Vol. 4. Competence and coping during adulthood*. Hanover, NH: University Press of New England.

Danish, S.J., Galambos, N.L., & Laquatra, I. (1983). Life development intervention: Skill training for personal competence. In R.D. Felman, L.A. Jason, J. Mortisuqur, & S.S. Farber (Eds.), *Preventive psychology: Theory, research, and practice* (pp. 49–66). Elmsford, NY: Pergamon Press.

Davis, D.D. (1986). *Managing technological innovation*. San Francisco: Jossey-Bass.

Davis, R. (1981). A demographic analysis of suicide. In L.E. Gary (Ed.), *Black men* (pp. 179–196). Beverly Hills, CA: Sage.

Dawis, R.V. (1984). Job satisfaction: Workers' aspirations, attitudes, and behaviors. In N.C. Gysbers (Ed.), *Designing career counseling to enhance education, work, and leisure* (pp. 275–302). San Francisco: Jossey-Bass.

de Tocqueville, A. (1969). *Democracy in America* (J.P. Mayer, Ed., and G. Lawrence, Trans.). New York: Doubleday.

Deffenbacher, J.L. (1988). Introduction: The practice of four cognitive-behavioral approaches to anxiety reduction. *The Counseling Psychologist, 16*(1), 3–8.

Deming, G. (1996). A decade of economic change and population shifts in U.S. regions. *Monthly Labor Review, 119*(11), 3–14.

Dohrenwend, B.P., & Dohrenwend, B.S. (1974). Social and cultural influences on psychopathology. *Annual Review of Psychology, 25*, 419–452.

Dohrenwend, B.P., Dohrenwend, B.S., Gould, M.S., Link, B., Neugebar, R., & Wunsch-Hitzig, R. (1980). *Mental illness in the United States: Epidemiological estimates.* New York: Praeger.

Dohrenwend, B.S., & Dohrenwend, B.P. (1979). Class and race as status-related sources of stress. In S . Levine & N . Scotch (Eds.), *Social stress.* Chicago: Aldine.

Downing, N.E., & Walker, M.E. (1987). A psychoeducational group for adult children of alcoholics. *Journal of Counseling and Development, 65*(8), 440–442.

Doyle, R. (1996, December). Deaths due to alcohol. *Scientific American.*

Draguns, J.G. (1981). Counseling across cultures: Common themes and distinct approaches. In P.B. Pedersen, J.G. Draguns, W.J. Lonner, & J.E. Trimble (Eds.), *Counseling across cultures* (chap. 1). Honolulu: University of Hawaii Press.

Draguns, J.G. (1985). Psychological disorders across cultures. In P. Pedersen (Ed.), *Handbook of cross-cultural counseling and therapy* (pp. 55–62). Westport, CT: Greenwood Press.

Draguns, J.G. (1996). Humanly universal and culturally distinctive. Charting the course of cultural counseling. In P.B. Pedersen, J.G. Draguns, W.J. Lonner, & J.E. Trimble (Eds.), *Counseling across cultures* (4th ed., pp. 1–20). Thousand Oaks, CA: Sage.

Drucker, P.F. (1981). *Toward the next economics and other essays.* New York: Harper & Row.

Drucker, P. (1993). *The post-capitalist society.* New York: Harper Business Books.

Dryfoos, J.G. (1997). The prevalence of problem behaviors: Implications for programs. In R.P. Weissberg, T.P. Gullotta, R.L. Hampton, B.A. Ryan, & G.R. Adams (Eds.), *Enhancing children's wellness* (pp. 17–46). Thousand Oaks, CA: Sage.

Duberman, L. (1975). *The reconstituted family: A study of remarried couples and their children.* Chicago: Nelson-Hall.

Dunham, J.R., & Dunham, C.S. (1978). Psychosocial aspects of disability. In R.M. Goldenson (Ed.), *Disability and rehabilitation handbook.* New York: McGraw-Hill.

Dusenbury, L., & Falco, M. (1997). School-based drug abuse prevention strategies: From research to policy and practice. In R.P. Weissberg, T.P. Gullotta, R.L. Hampton, B.A. Ryan, & G.R. Adams (Eds.), *Enhancing children's wellness* (pp. 47–75). Thousand Oaks, CA: Sage.

Dyrenfurth, M.I. (1984). *Literacy for a technological world.* Columbus: Ohio State University, National Center for Research in Vocational Education.

Education Commission of the States. (1985). *Reconnecting youth: The next stage of reform.* Denver, CO: Author.

Educational Testing Service. (1990). *From school to work.* Princeton, NJ: Author.

Egan, G. (1985). *The skilled helper.* Monterey, CA: Brooks/Cole.

Ekstrom, R.B., Goertz, M.E., Pollack, J.M., & Rock, D.A. (1986). Who drops out of high school and why? Findings from a national study. *Teachers College Record, 87*(3), 356–373.

Elliot, D.C. (1994). *Youth violence: An overview.* Boulder, CO: Center for the Study and Prevention of Violence.

Ellis, A. (1958). Rational psychotherapy. *Journal of General Psychotherapy, 59,* 35–39.

Ellis, A. (1962). *Reason and emotion in psychotherapy.* Secaucus, NJ: Lyle Stuart and Citadel Press.

Ellis, A. (1985). Expanding the ABCs of Rational-Emotive Therapy. In M. J. Mahoney & A. Freeman (Eds.), *Cognition and psychotherapy* (chap. 13). New York: Plenum Press.

Etaugh, C. (1984). Effects of maternal employment on children: Implications for the family therapist. In S.H. Cramer (Ed.), *Perspectives on work and the family* (pp. 16–39). Rockville, MD: Aspen Systems.

Evanoski, P.O., & Tse, F.W. (1989). Career awareness program for Chinese and Korean American parents. *Journal of Counseling and Development, 67,* 472–474.

Evans, R.I. (1985). Psychologists in health promotion research: General concerns and adolescent smoking prevention. In J.C. Rosen & L.J. Solomon (Eds.), *Prevention in health psychology* (pp. 18–33). Hanover, NH: University Press of New England.

Eyde, L.D. (1987). Computerized psychological testing: An introduction. *Applied Psychology: An International Review, 36*(314), 223–235.

Family Service America. (1984). *The state of families, 1984-85.* New York: Author.

Farley, R. (1996). *The new American reality. Who we are, how we got here, where we are going.* New York: Russell Sage.

Feather, N.T., & O'Brien, G.E. (1986). A longitudinal study of the effects of employment and unemployment on school-leavers. *Journal of Occupational Psychology, 59,* 121–144.

Federal Bureau of Investigation. (1981). *Uniform crime reports for the United States.* Washington, DC: U.S. Government Printing Office.

Federal Bureau of Investigation. (1983). *Crime in the United States.* Washington, DC: Author.

Federal Bureau of Investigation. (1984). *Crime in the United States* (1983 uniform crime reports for the U.S. Department of Justice). Washington, DC: Author.

Fenell, D.L., & Weinhold, B.K. (1996). Treating families with special needs. *Counseling and Human Development, 28*(7), 1–10.

Ferandez, M.S. (1988). Issues in counseling Southeast Asian students. *Journal of Multicultural Counseling and Development, 16,* 157–166.

Finkelhor, D. (1979). *Sexually victimized children.* New York: Macmillan.

Finkelhor, D. (1983). Common features of family violence. In D. Finkelhor, R.J. Gelles, G.T. Hotaling, & M.A. Straus (Eds.), *The dark side of families: Current family violence research.* New York: Sage.

Fiske, A.P. (1991). *Structures of social life. The four elementary forms of human relations.* New York: Free Press.

Flaim, P.O., & Sehgal, E. (1985). Displaced workers of 1979–1983: How well have they fared? *Monthly Labor Review, 108,* 3–16.

Fong, M.L. (1995). Assessment and *DSM-IV* diagnosis of personality disorders: A primer for counselors. *Journal of Counseling and Development, 73*(6), 635–639.

Ford, D.H. (1987). *Humans as self-constructing living systems: A developmental perspective on behavior and personality.* Hillsdale, NJ: Erlbaum.

Ford, D.H., & Ford, M.E. (1987). Humans as self-constructing living systems. In M.E. Ford & D.H. Ford (Eds.), *Humans as self-constructing living systems. Putting the framework to work* (pp. 1–46). Hillsdale, NJ: Erlbaum.

Forrest, D.V. (1990). Understanding adolescent depression: Implications for practitioners. *Counseling and Human Development, 23*(1), 1–9.

Fox, J.A. (1996). *Trends in juvenile violence.* Washington, DC: U.S. Bureau of Justice Statistics.

Framo, J. (1976). Family of origin as a therapeutic resource for adults in marital and family therapy: You can and should go home again. *Family Process, 15,* 193–210.

France, M.H., & McCormick, R. (Eds.). (1997). First Nations Counselling [special issue]. *Guidance and Counselling, 12*(3).

Frankl, V.W. (1963). *Man's search for meaning* (Rev. ed.). New York: Washington Square Press.

Frazis, H.J., Herz, D.E., & Horrigan, M.W. (1995). Employer-provided training: Results from a new survey. *Monthly Labor Review, 118*(5), 3–17.

Fromm, E. (1962). *Beyond the chains of illusion.* New York: Simon & Schuster.

Fuhriman, A., Paul, S.C., & Burlingame, G.M. (1986). Eclectic time-limited therapy. In J.C. Norcross (Ed.), *Handbook of eclectic psychotherapy* (pp. 226–259). New York: Brunner/Mazel.

Fujimura, L.W., Weis, D.M., & Cochran, J.R. (1985). Suicide: Dynamics and implications for counseling. *Journal of Counseling and Development, 63*(10), 612–615.

Galambos, N.L., & Garbarino, J. (1983). Identifying the missing links in the study of latchkey children. *Children Today, 12,* 2–4, 40.

Ganikos, M.L., & Blake, R. (1984). Guest editor's introduction. *The Counseling Psychologist, 12*(2), 13.

Gardner, H. (1983). *Frames of mind. The theory of multiple intelligence.* New York: Basic Books.

Garfield, R. (1980). The decision to remarry. *Journal of Divorce, 4,* 1–10.

Garis, J. W. (1982). *The integration of a computer-based system in a college counseling center: A comparison of the effects of DISCOVER and individual counseling upon career planning.* Unpublished doctoral dissertation, Pennsylvania State University, University Park.

Garreau, J. (1981). *The nine nations of North America*. New York: Avon Books.

Gati, I. (1994). Computer-assisted career counseling: Dilemmas, problems, and possible solutions. *Journal of Counseling and Development, 73*(1), 51–56.

Gazda, G.M., & Pistole, M.C. (1986). Life skills training: A model. *Counseling and Human Development, 19*(4), 1–7.

Gerwin, D. (1981). Relationships between structure and technology. In P. Nystrom & W.H. Starbuck (Eds.), *Handbook of organizational design* (chap. 1). New York: Oxford University Press.

Getz, H.G. (1987). Family counseling. In C.W. Humes (Ed.), *Contemporary counseling services, applications, issues* (chap. 10). Muncie, IN: Accelerated Development.

Gibson, E.J. (1982). The concept of affordances in development: The renascence of functionalism. In W.A. Collins (Ed.), *The concept of development: Vol. 15. The Minnesota Symposium of Child Psychology* (pp. 55–81). Hillsdale, NJ: Erlbaum.

Gibson, J.J. (1979). *The ecological approach to visual perception*. Boston: Houghton Mifflin.

Gilligan, C. (1982). *In a different voice*. Cambridge, MA: Harvard University Press.

Gilmartin, B.G. (1977). Swinging: Who gets involved and how? In R.W. Libby & R.N. Whithurst (Eds.), *Marriage and alternatives: Exploring intimate relationships* (pp. 161–185). Glenview, IL: Scott, Foresman.

Ginzberg, E. (1982). The mechanization of work. *Scientific American, 247*(3), 66–75.

Girardi, J.A., Keese, R.M., Traver, L.B., & Cooksey, D.R. (1988). Psychotherapist responsibility in notifying individuals at risk for exposure to HIV. *Journal of Sex Research, 25*(1), 1–27.

Glaberson, W. (1990, October 4). One in four young Black men are in custody, study says. *The New York Times*, p. B4.

Gladwin, T. (1967). Social competence and clinical practice. *Journal for the Study of Interpersonal Processes, 30*, 30–38.

Glaize, D.L., & Myrick, R. (1984). Interpersonal groups or computers? A study of career maturity and career decidedness. *Vocational Guidance Quarterly, 32*, 168–176.

Glaser, R., & Kiecolt-Glaser, J. (1988). Stress-associated immune suppression and acquired immune deficiency syndrome. In T.P. Bridge, A.F. Mirsky, & F.K. Goodwin (Eds.), *Psychological, neuropsychiatric, and substance abuse aspects of AIDS: Vol. 44. Advances in biochemical psychopharmacology* (pp. 203–215). New York: Raven Press.

Glasser, W. (1984). *Control theory: A new explanation of how we control our lives*. New York: Harper & Row.

Glazer-Malbin, N. (1978). Interpersonal relationships and changing perspectives in the family. In H.Z. Lopata (Ed.), *Family factbook* (1st ed., pp. 9–24). Chicago: Marquis Academic Media.

Glenwick, D.S., & Mowery, J.D. (1986). When parent becomes peer: Loss of intergenerational boundaries in single-parent families. *Family Relations, 35*(1), 57–62.

Glick, P.C. (1984). American household structure in transition. *Family Planning Perspectives, 16*(5), 205–211.

Goldfried, M.R., Decenteco, E.T., & Weinberg, L. (1974). Systematic rational restructuring as a self-control technique. *Behavior Therapy, 5*, 247–254.

Goldstein, A.P., & Krasner, L. (1987). *Modern applied psychology*. New York: Pergamon Press.

Goldstein, A.P., Sprafkin, R.P., Gershaw, N.J., & Klein, P. (1980). *Skill-streaming the adolescent: A structured learning approach to teaching prosocial skills*. Champaign, IL: Research Press.

Goleman, D. (1995). *Emotional intelligence*. New York: Bantam Books.

Goode, W.J. (1970). *World revolution and family patterns*. New York: Free Press.

Goodlad, J.I. (1983). *A place called school: Prospects for the future*. New York: McGraw-Hill.

Goodman, R.W. (1987). Adult children of alcoholics. *Journal of Counseling and Development, 66*(4), 162–163.

Goodman, W.C., & Ilg, R.E. (1997). Employment in 1996: Jobs up, unemployment down. *Monthly Labor Review, 120*(2), 3–18.

Gordon, E.W., & Terrell, M.D. (1981). The changed social context of testing. *American Psychologist, 36*(10), 1167–1171.

Gottfredson, G.D., Gottfredson, D.C., & Cook, M.S. (1983). *The school action effectiveness study: Second interim report, Part I.* Baltimore, MD: Johns Hopkins University Center for Social Organization of Schools.

Granrose, C.S. (1985). Anticipating the decision to work following childbirth. *Vocational Guidance Quarterly, 33*(3), 221–230.

Gray, K., & Herr, E.L. (1995). *Other ways to win: Creating alternatives for high school graduates.* Thousand Oaks, CA: Corwin Press.

Grossman, J. (1981). Inside the wellness movement. *Health, 13,* 10–15.

Guerin, P. (1976). *Family therapy: Theory and practice.* New York: Gardner Press.

Guerney, B.G., Jr., Vogelsong, E., & Coufal, J. (1983). Relationship enhancement versus a traditional treatment: Follow-up and booster effects. In D.H. Olson & B.C. Miller (Eds.), *Family studies yearbook* (Vol. 1, pp. 738–756). Beverly Hills, CA: Sage.

Guidano, V.F., & Liotti, G. (1985). A constructivistic foundation for cognitive therapy. In M.J. Mahoney & A. Freeman (Eds.), *Cognition and psychotherapy* (chap. 4). New York: Plenum Press.

Guidubaldi, J., & Cleminshaw, H. (1985). Divorce, family health, and child adjustment. *Family Relations, 34*(1), 35–41.

Guion, R.M. (1974). Open a new window. Validities and values in psychological measurement. *American Psychologist, 29*(5), 287–296.

Gutteridge, T.G. (1986). Organizational career development systems: The state of the practice. In D.T. Hall & Associates (Eds.), *Career development in organizations* (pp. 50–71). San Francisco: Jossey-Bass.

Hadlock, P., Hecker, D., & Gannon, J. (1991). High technology employment: Another view. *Monthly Labor Review, 114*(7), 26–30.

Hafen, B.Q., & Frandsen, K.J. (1986). *Youth suicide: Depression and loneliness.* Evergreen, CO: Cordillera Press.

Hakim, C. (1994). *We are all self-employed.* San Francisco: Berett-Koehler.

Haley, J. (1976). *Problem-solving therapy.* San Francisco: Jossey-Bass.

Hall, C.S., & Lindzey, G. (1957). *Theories of personality.* New York: Wiley.

Hall, D.T. (1996). Implications: The new role of the career practitioner. In D.T. Hall & Associates (Eds.), *The career is dead—long live the career. A relational approach to careers* (pp. 314–336). San Francisco: Jossey-Bass.

Hall, D.T., & Associates (Eds.). (1996). *The career is dead—long live the career. A relational approach to careers.* San Francisco: Jossey-Bass.

Hall, D.T., & Mirvis, P.H. (1996). The new protean career: Psychological success and the path with a heart. In D.T. Hall & Associates (Eds.), *The career is dead—long live the career. A relational approach to careers* (pp.15–45). San Francisco: Jossey-Bass.

Handy, C. (1994). *The age of paradox.* Boston, MA: Harvard Business School Press.

Haney, W. (1981). Validity, vaudeville, and values. A short history of concerns over standardized testing. *American Psychologist, 36*(10), 1021–1034.

Hansen, L.S. (1997). Integrative life planning. *Critical tasks for career development and changing life patterns.* San Francisco: Jossey-Bass.

Hare-Mustin, R.T. (1983). An appraisal of the relationship between women and psychotherapy: 80 years after the case of Dora. *American Psychologist, 38,* 593–601.

Harper, F.D. (1981). Alcohol use and abuse. In L.E. Gary (Ed.), *Black men* (pp. 169–178). Beverly Hills, CA: Sage.

Harrington, M. (1962). *The other America: Poverty in the United States.* New York: Macmillan.

Harris, W.G. (1987). Computer-based test interpretations: Some development and application issues. *Applied Psychology: An International Review, 36*(314), 237–247.

Harvey, M.R. (1985). *Exemplary rape crisis programs, a cross-site analysis and case studies.* Rockville, MD: U.S. Department of Health and Human Services, National Center for the Prevention and Control of Rape.

Hawkins, J.D. (1997). Academic performance and school success: Sources and consequences. In R.P. Weissberg, T.P. Gullotta, R.L. Hampton, B.A. Ryan, & G.R. Adams (Eds.), *Enhancing children's wellness* (pp. 178–305). Thousand Oaks, CA: Sage.

Hayes, L.L. (1997). Suicide rate among older Americans remains unchecked. Recognizing risk factors essential to prevention. *Counseling Today, 40,* 6, 6.

Hayes, R.L., Dagley, J.C., & Horne, A.M. (1996). Restructuring school counselor education: Work in progress. *Journal of Counseling and Development, 74*(4), 378–384.

Hayes, R.L., & Hayes, B.A. (1986). Remarriage families: Counseling parents, stepparents, and their children. *Counseling and Human Development, 18*(7), 1–8.

Hayghe, H. (1986). Rise in mothers' labor force participation includes those with young children. *Monthly Labor Review, 109,* 43–45.

Healy, C.C. (1990). Reforming career appraisals to meet the needs of clients in the 1990s. *The Counseling Psychologist, 18,* 214–226.

Hedlund, J.L., Vieweg, B.W., & Cho, D.W. (1987). Computer consultation for emotional crises: An expert system for "nonexperts." *Computers in Human Behavior, 3*(2), 109–128.

Helgesen, S. (1996). Leading from the grass roots. In F. Hesselbein, M. Goldsmith, & R. Beckhard (Eds.), *The leader of the future. New visions, strategies, and practices for the new era* (pp. 19–24). San Francisco: Jossey-Bass.

Helzer, J.E., Burnham, A., & McEvoy, L.T. (1991). Alcohol abuse and dependence. In L.N. Robins & D.A. Rieger (Eds.), *Psychiatric disorders in America.* New York: MacMillan.

Henkin, W.A. (1985). Toward counseling the Japanese in America: A cross-cultural primer. *Journal of Counseling and Development, 63,* 500–503.

Hernandez, D.S. (1993). *American's children: Resources from family, government, and the economy.* New York: Russell Sage.

Herr, E.L. (1978). *Work-focused guidance for youth in transition: Some implications for vocation education research and development.* Occasional Paper No. 43. Columbus: Ohio State University, National Center for Research in Vocational Education.

Herr, E.L. (1979). *Guidance and counseling in the schools: Perspectives on the past, present, and future.* Falls Church, VA: American Personnel and Guidance Association.

Herr, E.L. (1982). Career development and vocational education. In H.F. Silberman (Ed.), *Education and work* (pp. 117–139). Chicago: University of Chicago Press.

Herr, E.L. (1984). Links among training, employability, and employment. In N. Gysbers (Ed.), *Designing careers: Counseling to enhance education, work, and leisure* (pp. 78–105). San Francisco: Jossey-Bass.

Herr, E.L. (1985). International approaches to career counseling and guidance. In P. Pedersen (Ed.), *Handbook of cross-cultural counseling and therapy* (pp. 3–10). Westport, CT: Greenwood Press.

Herr, E.L. (1985). The role of professional organizations in effecting the use of technology in career development. *Journal of Career Development, 12*(2), 176–186.

Herr, E.L. (1986). The relevant counselor. *The School Counselor, 34*(1), 6–13.

Herr, E.L. (1987). *A case study of the impact of the Carl D. Perkins Act in Pennsylvania.* Washington, DC: U.S. Department of Education.

Herr, E.L. (1990, August). *Counseling for personal flexibility in a global economy.* Plenary paper presented at the XIVth World Congress, Counseling in a Global Economy, of the International Association of Educational and Vocational Guidance, Montreal, Canada.

Herr, E.L. (1991). *Guidance and counseling: A shared responsibility.* Alexandria, VA: National Association of College Admissions Counselors.

Herr, E.L. (1993, October). *The crisis of unemployment.* Plenary paper presented at the International Conference on Unemployment and Counseling, Eotvos Lander University, Budapest, Hungary.

Herr, E.L. (1995). *Counseling employment-bound youth*. Greensboro: University of North Carolina at Greensboro, ERIC-CASS.

Herr, E.L. (1997). Career counselling: A process in process. *British Journal of Guidance and Counselling 25*(1), 81–93.

Herr, E.L., & Best, J. (1984). The family as an influence on career development. In S.H. Cramer (Ed.), *Perspectives on work and the family* (pp. 1–15). Rockville, MD: Aspen Systems.

Herr, E.L., & Best, P.L. (1984). Computer technology and counseling: The role of the profession. *Journal of Counseling and Development, 63*, 192–195.

Herr, E.L., & Cramer, S.H. (1987). *Controversies in the mental health professions*. Muncie, IN: Accelerated Development.

Herr, E.L., & Cramer, S.H. (1996). *Career guidance and counseling through the life span: Systematic approaches* (5th ed.). New York: HarperCollins.

Herr, E.L., & Long, T.E. (1983). *Counseling youth for employability: Unleashing the potential*. Ann Arbor: University of Michigan, ERIC/CAPS.

Herr, E.L., & Niles, S. (1988). Values in counseling: Three domains. *Counseling and Values, 33*(1), 4–17.

Herr, E.L., & Pinson, N. (Eds.). (1982). *Foundations for policy in guidance and counseling*. Falls Church, VA: American Personnel and Guidance Association.

Herr, E.L., Rayman, J.R., & Garis, J.W. (1993). *Handbook for the college and university career center*. Westport, CT: Greenwood Press.

Herring, R.D. (1990). Attacking career myths among Native Americans: Implications for counseling. *The School Counselor, 38*, 13–18.

Hershenson, D.B. (1996). Worth adjustment: A neglected area in career counseling. *Journal of Counseling and Development, 74*(5), 442–446.

Hershenson, D.B., & Strein, W. (1991). Toward a mentally healthy curriculum for mental health counselor education. *Journal of Mental Health Counseling, 13*, 247–252.

Herskovits, M.J. (1948). *Man and his works*. New York: Knopf.

Hesselbein, F., Goldsmith, M., & Beckhaard, R. (Eds.). (1996). *The leader of the future. New visions, strategies, and practices for the new era*. San Francisco: Jossey-Bass.

Hilton, M. (1991). Shared training: Learning from Germany. *Monthly Labor Review, 114* (3), 33–37.

Hitchcock, A.A. (1984). Work, aging, and counseling. *Journal of Counseling and Development, 63*(4), 258–259.

Hodgkinson, H.L. (1985). *All one system: Demographics of education—kindergarten through graduate school*. Washington, DC: Institute for Educational Leadership.

Hodgson, M.L. (1984). Working mothers: Effects on the marriage and the mother. In S.H. Cramer (Ed.), *Perspectives on work and the family* (pp. 40–55). Rockville, MD: Aspen Systems.

Hoffman, N. (1984). Cognitive therapy. Introduction to the subject. In N. Hoffman (Ed.), *Foundations of cognitive therapy* (pp. 1–20). New York: Plenum Press.

Hofstrede, G. (1992). *Cultures and organizations: Software of the mind*. London: McGraw-Hill.

Holland, J.L. (1966). *The psychology of vocational choice*. Waltham, MA: Blaisdell.

Holland, J.L. (1973). *Making vocational choices: A theory of careers*. Englewood Cliffs, NJ: Prentice-Hall.

Holland, J.L. (1985). *Making vocational choices: A theory of vocational personalities and work environments* (2nd ed.). Englewood Cliffs, NJ: Prentice-Hall.

Holmes, T.H., & Rahe, R.H. (1967). The social readjustment rating scale. *Journal of Psychosomatic Research, 11*, 213–218.

Horner, D., & Vandersluis, R. (1981). Cross-cultural counseling. In G. Olthen (Ed.), *Learning across cultures*. Washington, DC: National Association of Foreign Student Advisors.

Hosie, T.W., West, J.D., & Mackey, J.A. (1993). Employment and roles of counselors in employee assistance programs. *Journal of Counseling and Development, 71*, 355–359.

Hotelling, K., & Forest, L. (1985). Gilligan's theory of sex-role development: A perspective for counseling. *Journal of Counseling and Development, 64*, 183–186.

Hough, R.L., Landsverk, J.A., Karno, M., Burnham, M.A., Timbers, D.M., Escobar, J.I., & Regier, D.A. (1987). Utilization of health and mental health services by Los Angeles Mexican Americans and non-Hispanic Whites. *Archives of General Psychiatry, 44*(8), 702–709.

House, R.M., Eicken, S.E., & Gray, L.A. (1995). A national survey of AIDS training in counselor education programs. *Journal of Counseling and Development, 74*(1), 5–11.

Howard, G.S., Nancy, D.W., & Myers, P. (1986). Adaptive counseling and therapy: An integrative, elective model. *The Counseling Psychologist, 14*(3), 363–442.

Hudson, F.M. (1991). *The adult years. Mastering the art of self-renewal.* San Francisco: Jossey-Bass.

Huey, W.C. (1987). Counseling teenage fathers: The maximizing a life experience (MALE) group. *The School Counselor, 35*(1), 40–47.

Hull, D.M., & Pedrotti, L.S. (1983). Meeting the high-tech challenge. *VOCED, 58*(3), 28–31.

Hunt, B. (1996). HIV/AIDS training in CACREP-approved counselor education programs. *Journal of Counseling and Development, 74*(3), 295–299.

Hurst, J.B., & Shepherd, J.W. (1986). The dynamics of plant closings: An extended emotional roller-coaster ride. *Journal of Counseling and Development, 64*, 401–405.

Ibrahim, F. (1984). Cross-cultural counseling and psychotherapy: An existential-psychological approach. *International Journal for the Advancement of Counselling, 7*(3) 159–170.

Ibrahim, F., & Herr, E.L. (1987). Battered women: A developmental life-career counseling perspective. *Journal of Counseling and Development, 65*(5), 244–248.

International Association for Educational and Vocational Guidance. (1995). *IAEVG Ethical Standards* (1995). Stockholm, Sweden: Author.

Isenstein, V.R., & Krasner, W. (1988). *Children at risk.* Rockville, MD: National Institute of Mental Health, Mental Health Studies and Reports Branch.

Ivey, A.E. (1986). *Ethics and multicultural therapy: An unrealized dream.* Unpublished manuscript, University of Massachusetts at Amherst.

Jackson, L.A., Jr. (1987). Computers and the social psychology of work. *Computers in human behavior, 3*(314), 251–262.

Jackson, M.L. (1987). Cross-cultural counseling at the crossroads: A dialogue with Clemmont E. Vontress. *Journal of Counseling and Development, 66*(1), 20–23.

James, J. (1996). *Thinking in the future tense. Leadership skills for a new age.* New York: Simon & Schuster.

Janoff-Bluman, R., & Frieze, I. (1983). A theoretical perspective for understanding reaction to victimization. *Journal of Social Issues, 39*, 1–17.

Jepsen, D.A. (1996). Relationships between developmental career counseling theory and practice. In M.L. Savichas & W.B. Walsh (Eds.), *Handbook of career counseling theory and practice* (pp. 135–154). Palo Alto, CA: Davies-Black.

Johnson, D.W. (1986). *Reaching out: Interpersonal effectiveness and self-actualization.* Englewood Cliffs, NJ: Prentice-Hall.

Johnson, F.A. (1981). Ethnicity and interactional rules in counseling: Some basic considerations. In A.J. Marsella & I.B. Pedersen (Eds.), *Cross-cultural counseling and psychotherapy* (pp. 63–84). New York: Pergamon Press.

Johnson, W.R., & Skinner, J. (1986, June). Labor supply and marital separation. *American Economic Review,* 455–469.

Johnston, J.A., Buescher, K. L., & Heppner, M. J. (1988). Computerized career information and guidance systems: Caveat emptor. *Journal of Counseling and Development, 67*, 39–41.

Jones, E.E., & Thorne, A. (1987). Rediscovery of the subject: Intercultural approaches to clinical assessment. *Journal of Consulting and Clinical Psychology, 55*(4), 488–495.

Josephson, G.S., & Fong-Beyette, M.L. (1987). Factors assisting female clients' disclosure of incest during counseling. *Journal of Counseling and Development, 65*(9), 475–478.

Judson, H.F. (1985). Paradoxes of prediction. The shape of science to come. *Science, 6*(9), 32–36.

Kalafat, J. (1997). Prevention of youth suicide. In R.P. Weissberg, T.P. Gullotta, R.L. Hampton, B.A. Ryan, & G.R. Adams (Eds.), *Enhancing children's wellness* (pp. 76–124). Thousand Oaks, CA: Sage.

Kantor, R.M. (1977). *Work and family in the United States: A critical review and agenda for research and policy*. New York: Russell Sage.

Kapes, J.T., Mastie, M.M., & Whitfield, E.A. (1994). *A counselor's guide to career assessment instruments* (3rd ed.). Alexandria, VA: National Career Development Association.

Karno, M., Hough, R.L., Burnham, M.A., Escobar, J.I., Timbers, D.M., Santanna, F., & Boyd, J.H. (1987). Lifetime prevalence of specific psychiatric disorders among Mexican Americans and non-Hispanic Whites in Los Angeles. *Archives of General Psychiatry, 44*(8), 695–701.

Katz, M. (1980). SIGI: An interactive aid to career decision making. *Journal of College Student Personnel, 21*(1), 34–40.

Katz, M.R. (1993). *Computer-assisted career decision making*. Hillsdale, NJ: Erlbaum.

Kazdin, A.E. (1987). *Conduct disorders in childhood and adolescence*. Newbury Park, CA: Sage.

Keat, D.B. (1979). *Multimodal therapy with children*. Elmsford, NY: Pergamon Press.

Keeling, R.P. (1993). Commentary: Educating and counseling about HIV in the second decade. *Journal of Counseling and Development, 71,* 306–309.

Keita, T.P., & Sauter, S. (1992). *Work and well-being: An agenda for the 1990s*. Washington, DC: American Psychological Association.

Keith, P.M., & Schaefer, R.B. (1985). Role behavior, relative deprivation, and depressions among women in one- and two-job families. *Family Relations, 34*(2), 227–233.

Kelly, G.A. (1995). *The psychology of personal constructs*. New York: Norton.

Kempe, R., & Kempe, C.H. (1984). *The common secret: Sexual abuse of children and adolescents*. New York: Freeman.

Kieffer, J.A. (1980). Counselors and the older worker: An overview. *Journal of Employment Counseling, 17*(1), 8–16.

Kieselbach, T., & Lunger, A. (1990). Psychosocial counseling for the unemployed within the framework of trade-union-oriented work. *Journal of Employment Counseling 27,* 191–207.

Kiesler, C.A. (1980). Mental health policy as a field of inquiry for psychology. *American Psychologist, 35,* 1066–1080.

King, Martin Luther, Jr. (1963). *Strength to love*. Philadelphia: Fortress Press.

Kipnis, D. (1997). Ghosts, taxonomies, and social psychology. *American Psychologist, 52*(3), 205–211.

Kiunick, H.Q. (1985). Disability and psychosocial development in old age. *Rehabilitation Counseling Bulletin, 29*(2), 123–134.

Kleinman, A. (1980). *Patients and healers in the context of culture*. Berkeley: University of California Press.

Kleinman, A. (1988). *Rethinking psychiatry: From cultural category to personal experience*. New York: Free Press.

Kluckhohn, C. (1962). *Culture and behavior*. New York: Free Press.

Kluckhohn, F.R., & Strodtbeck, F.L. (1961). *Variations in value orientations*. Evanston, IL: Row, Peterson.

Knaub, P.K. (1986). Growing up in a dual-career family: The children's perceptions. *Family Relations, 35*(3), 431–437.

Knouse, S.B., Rosenfeld, P., & Culbertson, A.L. (Eds.). (1992). *Hispanics in the workplace*. Newbury Park, CA: Sage.

Knowles, M. (1977). The adult learner becomes less neglected. *Training, 14*(9), 16–18.

Kolbe, L. (1993). An essential strategy to improve the health and education of Americans. *Preventive Medicine, 22,* 544–560.

Kolbe, L.J., Collins, J., & Cortese, P. (1997). Building the capacity of schools to improve the health of the nation. A call for assistance from psychologists. *American Psychologist, 52*(3), 256–265.

Kotter, J. (1995). *The new rules: Eight business breakthroughs to career success in the 21st century.* Boston: Harvard Business School Press.

Krames Communications. (1987). *Chemical dependency: Kids and drugs.* Daly City, CA: Author.

Krumboltz, J.D. (1979). Social learning theory of career decision making. In A.M. Mitchell, G.G. Jame, & J.D. Krumboltz (Eds.), *Social learning and career decision making* (pp. 19–49). Ranston, RI: Carroll Press.

Krumboltz, J.D. (1983). *Private rules in career decision making.* Columbus: Ohio State University, National Center for Research in Vocational Education.

Krumboltz, J.D. (1996). A learning theory of career counseling. In M.L. Savickas & B. Walsh (Eds.), *Handbook of career counseling theory and practice* (pp. 55–80). Palo Alto, CA: Davies-Black.

Krumboltz, J.D., Mitchell, A., & Gelatt, H.B. (1975). Applications of social learning theory of career selection. *Focus on Guidance, 8*(3), 1–16.

Kubler-Ross, E. (1969). *On death and dying.* New York: Macmillan.

Kuehlwein, K.T. (1996). Interweaving themes and threads of meaning making. In H. Rosen & K.T. Kuehlwein (Eds.), *Constructing realities: Meaning-making perspectives for psychotherapists* (pp. 371–412). San Francisco: Jossey-Bass.

Kukla, R.A., & Weingarten, H. (1979). The long-term effects of parental divorce in childhood on adult adjustment. *Journal of Social Issues, 35,* 50–78.

Kuttner, R. (1990, January 8). A toast to the Cold War's end—with a shot of reality. *Business Week, 3140,* 21.

La Fromboise, T., Foster, S., & James, A. (1996). Ethics in multicultural counseling. In P.B. Pedersen, J.G. Draguns, W.J. Lonner, & J.E. Trimble (Eds.), *Counseling across cultures* (4th ed., pp. 47–72). Thousand Oaks, CA: Sage.

Lauver, P.J., & Jones, R.M. (1991). Factors associated with perceived career options in American Indian, White, and Hispanic rural high school students. *Journal of Counseling Psychology, 38*(2), 159–166.

Lazarus, A.A. (1981). *The practice of multimodel therapy.* New York: McGraw-Hill.

Lazarus, A.A. (1993). Tailoring the therapautic relationship, or being an authentic chameleon. *Psychotherapy, 30,* 403–407.

Lee, C. (1988, January 15). *Cross-cultural counseling: Pitfalls and promise.* Paper presented at the NCDA 75th Anniversary Conference, Transformation in Work and Workers, Lake Buena Vista, FL.

Leibowitz, Z.B., Farren, C., & Kaye, B.L. (1986). *Designing career development systems.* San Francisco: Jossey-Bass.

Leininger, M.M. (1985). Transcultural caring: A different way to help people. In P. Pedersen (Ed.), *Handbook of cross-cultural counseling and therapy* (pp. 108–115). Westport, CT: Greenwood Press.

Leonards, J.T. (1981). Corporate psychology: An answer to occupational mental health. *Personnel and Guidance Journal, 30*(1), 47–51.

Leshner, A.I. (1997). NIDA responds to the changing dynamics of the AIDS epidemic. *NIDA Notes, 12*(2), 3.

Leung, S.A. (1993). Circumscription and compromise: A replication study with Asian Americans. *Journal of Counseling Psychology, 40*(2), 188–193.

Levine, E.S., & Padilla, A.M. (1980). *Crossing cultures in therapy. Pluralistic counseling for the Hispanic.* Monterey, CA: Brooks/Cole.

Levinson, R.W., & Haynes, K.S. (Eds.). (1984). *Accessing human services: International perspectives.* Beverly Hills, CA: Sage.

Levitan, S.A., & Johnson, C.M. (1982). *Second thoughts on work.* Kalamazoo, MI: Upjohn Institute for Employment Research.

Lewin, K. (1951). *Field theory and social science: Selected theoretical papers.* New York: Harper.

Lewis, D.O. (1985). Special diagnostic and treatment issues concerning violent juveniles. In L. Roth (Ed.), *Clinical treatment of the violent person* (pp. 145–163). Rockville, MD: U.S. Department of Health and Human Services, National Institute of Mental Health.

Lewis, J. (1987). Children of alcoholics. *Counseling and Human Development, 19*(9), 1–9.

Lewis, S., & Cooper, C.L. (1983). The stress of combining occupational roles and parental roles: A review of the literature. *Bulletin of the British Psychological Society, 36*, 341–345.

Lichter, D. (1988). Race, employment hardship, and inequality in American nonmetropolitan south. *American Sociological Review, 54*, 436–446.

Lichtman, R. (1978). Jobs and mental health in a social context. *Center Magazine, 11*(6), 7–17.

Liem, R., & Rayman, P. (1980). Health and social costs of unemployment. *American Psychologist, 37*(10), 1116–1123.

Linton, R. (1945). *The cultural background of personality*. New York: Appleton Century.

Lion, J.R. (1985). Clinical assessment of violent patients. In L. Roth (Ed.), *Clinical treatment of the violent person* (pp. 1–12). Rockville, MD: U.S. Department of Health and Human Services, National Institute of Mental Health.

Lipman-Blumen, J. (1975). A crisis framework applied to macrosociological family changes. Marriage, divorce, and occupational trends associated with World War II. *Journal of Marriage and the Family, 27*, 889–902.

Lipset, S.M. (1963). *First new nation*. New York: Basic Books.

Lobel, B., & Hirschfield, R.M.A. (1984). *Depression: What we know*. Rockville, MD: National Institute of Mental Health.

Locke, D.C. (1986). Cross-cultural counseling. In A.J. Palmo & W.J. Weikel (Eds.), *Foundations of mental health counseling* (pp. 119–137). Springfield, IL: Charles C Thomas.

Locke, D.C. (1990). A not so provincial view of multicultural counseling. *Counselor Education and Supervision, 30*, 18–25.

Locke, D.C., & Parker, L.D. (1994). Improving the multicultural competence of educators. In P.B. Pedersen & J.C. Carly (Eds.), *Multicultural counseling in schools. A practical handbook* (pp. 39–58). Boston: Allyn & Bacon.

London, M.E., & Stumpf, S.A. (1986). Individual and organizational career development in changing times. In D.T. Hall & Associates (Eds.), *Career development in organizations* (pp. 21–49). San Francisco: Jossey-Bass.

London, P. (1964). *The modes and morals of psychotherapy*. New York: Holt, Rinehart & Winston.

Long, T.J., & Long, L. (1981). *Latchkey children: The child's view of self-care*. Ann Arbor: University of Michigan, ERIC/CAPS. (ED 211 229)

Long, T.J., & Long, L. (1983). *Latchkey children*. Ann Arbor: University of Michigan, ERIC/CAPS. (ED 226 836)

Lonner, W.J., & Ibrahim, F.A. (1996). Appraisal and assessment in cross-cultural counseling. In P.B. Pedersen, J.G. Draguns, W.J. Lonner, & J.E. Trimble (Eds.), *Counseling across cultures* (4th ed., pp. 293–322). Thousand Oaks, CA: Sage.

Lopez, F.G. (1983). The victims of corporate failure: Some preliminary findings. *Personnel and Guidance Journal, 61*, 631–632.

Lopez, F.G. (1987). The impact of parental divorce on college student development. *Journal of Counseling and Development, 65*(9), 484–486.

Louis Harris & Associates (1981). *Families at work: Strengths and strains* (General Mills American Family Report, 1980–81). Minneapolis, MN: General Mills.

Lucal, B. (1995). The problem with "battered husbands." *Deviant Behavior: An Interdisciplinary Journal, 16*, 95–112.

Lyons, D., & Luker, B, Jr. (1996). Employment in R & D intensive high-tech industries in Texas. *Monthly Labor Review, 119*(11), 15–25.

Maccoby, M., & Terzi, K. (1981). What happened to the work ethic? In J. O'Toole, J.L. Scheiber, & L.C. Woods (Eds.), *Working: Changes and choices* (pp. 162–171). New York: Human Sciences Press.

Macklin, E.D. (1980). Nontraditional family forms: A decade of research. *Journal of Marriage and the Family, 42*(4), 175–192.

Mahoney, M.J. (1991). *Human change processes.* New York: Basic Books.

Marsella, H.A. (1980). Depressive experience and disorder across cultures. In H.C. Triandis & J.G. Draguns (Eds.), *Psychopathology handbook of cross-cultural psychology* (pp. 237–289). Newton, MA: Allyn & Bacon.

Martin, L.R. (1993). Guidance and counseling in various societies: Structures and development, problems and solutions. *International Journal for the Advancement of Counselling. 16*(3), 245–264.

Maslow, A.H. (1954). *Motivation and personality.* New York: Harper & Row.

Massachusetts Institute of Technology, Quality Institute for Minorities Project. (1990). *Education that works: An action plan for the education of minorities.* Cambridge, MA: Author.

Matarazzo, J.M. (1980). Behavioral health and behavioral medicine: Frontiers for a new health psychology. *American Psychologist, 35,* 807–817.

Mathabe, N.R., & Temane, M.Q. (1993). The realities and imperatives of career counseling for a developing South Africa. *Journal of Career Development, 20*(1), 25–32.

Mathewson, R.A. (1955). *Guidance policy and practice* (Rev. ed.). New York: Harper.

Mathias, R. (1997a). From the 'burbs to the hood' . . this program reduces students' risk of drug use. *NIDA Notes, 12*(2), 1, 5–6.

Mathias, R. (1997b). Marijuana and tobacco use up again among 8th and 10th graders. *NIDA Notes, 12*(2), 12–13, 19.

Matthews, T.J., DeSanti, S.M., Callahan, D., Koblenz-Sulcor, C.J., & Werden, J.I. (1987). The microcomputer as an agent of intervention with psychiatric patients: Preliminary studies. *Computers in Human Behavior, 3*(1), 37–48.

Maynard, P.E., & Olson, D.H. (1987). Circumplex model of family systems: A treatment tool in family counseling. *Journal of Counseling and Development, 65*(9), 502–504.

McCubbin, H.I., Joy, C.B., Cauble, A.E., Comeaw, J.K., Patterson, J.M., & Needle, R.M. (1980). Family stress and coping: A decade review. *Journal of Marriage and the Family, 42*(4), 124–141.

McDermott, J.F., Jr. (1980). Introduction. In J.F. McDermott, Jr., W.S. Tseng, & T.W. Maretzki (Eds.), *People and cultures of Hawaii: A psychocultural profile.* Honolulu: University of Hawaii Press.

McFadden, J. (in press). Stylistic model for transcultural counseling. In J. McFadden (Ed.), *Transcultural counseling* (2nd ed.). Alexandria, VA: American Counseling Association.

McGoldrick, M. (1982). Ethnicity and family therapy: An overview. In M. McGoldrick, J.K. Pearce, & J. Giordano (Eds.), *Ethnicity and family therapy* (pp. 3–30). New York: Guilford Press.

McGoldrick, M., Pearce, J.K., & Giordano, J. (Eds.). (1982). *Ethnicity and family therapy.* New York: Guilford Press.

McLanahan, S.S., & Sandefur, G.T. (1994). *Growing up with a single parent: What hurts, what helps.* Cambridge, MA: Harvard University Press.

Mechanic, D. (1985). Health and behavior: Perspectives on risk prevention. In J.C. Rosen & L.J. Solomon (Eds.), *Prevention in health psychology* (chap. 1). Hanover, NH: University Press of New England.

Meichenbaum, D. (1985). *Stress inoculation training.* New York: Pergamon Press.

Messick, S. (1995). Validity of psychological assessment: Validation of inferences from persons' responses and performance as scientific into score meaning. *American Psychologist, 50,* 741–749.

Millett, S., & Kopp, W. (1996). The top 10 innovative products for 2006. Technology with a human touch. *The Futurist, 30*(4), 16–20.

Minshall, C. (1984). *High-technology occupational trends.* Columbus: Ohio State University, National Center for Research in Vocational Education.

Minuchin, S. (1974). *Families and family therapy.* Cambridge, MA: Harvard University Press.

Mirvis, P.H. (Ed.). (1993). *Building a competitive workforce: Investing in human capital for corporate success.* New York: Wiley.

Mitchell, A. (1983). *The nine American lifestyles: Who we are and where we are going.* New York: Warner Books.

Mitchell, L.K., & Krumboltz, J.D. (1984). Research in human decision making: Implications for career decision making and counseling. In S. Brown & R. Lent (Eds.), *Handbook of counseling psychology* (pp. 238–280). New York: Wiley.

Mogul, K.M. (1979). Women in midlife: Decisions, rewards, conflicts related to work and careers. *American Journal of Psychiatry, 136*(9), 1139–1143.

Monnhan, J., & Klasson, D. (1982). Situational approaches to understanding and predicting individual violent behavior. In M.E. Wolfgang & N.A. Weiner (Eds.), *Criminal violence* (pp. 292–319). Beverly Hills, CA: Sage.

Moskowitz, R., & Warwick, D. (1996). The job outlook in brief, 1994–2005. *Occupational Outlook Quarterly, 40*(1), 2–41.

Moynihan, D.P. (1964). Morality of work and immorality of opportunity. *Vocational Guidance Quarterly, 12*, 229–236.

Mruk, C.J. (1987). The interface between computers and psychology: Toward a psychology of computerization. *Computers in Human Behavior, 3*(314), 167–180.

Munoz, R.F. (1982). The Spanish-speaking consumer and the community mental health center. In E.E. Jones & S.J. Korchin (Eds.), *Minority mental health* (pp. 362–398). New York: Praeger.

Murphy, G. (1947). *Personality.* New York: Harper.

Murray, H.A. (1938). *Explorations in personality.* New York: Oxford University Press.

Murray, H.A., & Kluckhohn, C. (1956). Outline of a conception of personality. In C. Kluckhohn (Ed.), *Personality, nature, and society* (2nd ed., pp. 1–26), New York: Knopf.

Murray, M.E., Crierra, N.G., & Williams, K.R. (1997). Violence prevention for the 21st century. In R.P. Weissberg, T.P. Gullotta,, R.L. Hampton, B.A. Ryan, & G.R. Adams (Eds.), *Enhancing children's wellness* (pp. 105–128). Thousand Oaks, CA: Sage.

Myers, D.G., & Diener, E. (1997). The science of happiness. *The Futurist, 31*(5), 1–7.

Myers, J .E. (1988). The mid/late life generation gap: Adult children with aging parents. *Journal of Counseling and Development, 66*, 331–335.

Myers, J.E. (1995). From "forgotten and ignored" to standards and certification: Gerontological counseling comes of age. *Journal of Counseling and Development, 74*(2), 143–149.

Myers, J.E. (1996). Gerontology: Mental health and aging. In W.J. Weikel & A.J. Palmo (Eds.), *Foundations of mental health counseling* (2nd ed., pp. 128–136). Springfield, IL: Charles C Thomas.

Myers, J.E., & Salmon, H.E. (1984). Counseling programs for older persons: Status, shortcomings, and potentialities. *The Counseling Psychologist, 12*(2), 39–53.

Myers, J.E., & Sweeney, T. (1990). *Gerontological competencies for counselors and human development professionals.* Alexandria, VA: American Counseling Association.

Naisbitt, J. (1984). *Megatrends: Ten new directions transforming our lives.* New York: Warner Books.

Naisbitt, J., & Aburdene, P. (1985). *Re-inventing the corporation.* New York: Warner Books.

Naisbitt, J., & Aburdene, P. (1990). *Megatrends 2000.* New York: Simon & Schuster.

Naisbitt, J., & the Naisbitt Group. (1986). *The year ahead 1986: Ten powerful trends shaping your future.* New York: Warner Books.

Nathan, P.E. (1985). Prevention of alcoholism: A history of failure. In J.C. Rosen & L.J. Solomon (Eds.), *Prevention in health psychology* (chap. 3). Hanover, NH: University Press of New England.

National Alliance of Business. (1984). *A nation at work: Education and the private sector.* Washington, DC: Author.

National Association of College Admissions Counselors. (1986). *Frontiers of possibility* (Report of the National College Counseling Project). Burlington: University of Vermont.

National Board for Certified Counselors. (1987). *Code of ethics.* Alexandria, VA: Author.

National Career Development Association. (1985). Consumer guidelines for selecting a career counselor. *Career Development, 1*(2), 1–2.

National Center for Health Statistics. (1986a, July 18). *Monthly vital statistics report; advance report of final natality statistics, 1984.* Hyattsville, MD: Public Health Service.

National Center for Health Statistics. (1986b, September 25). *Monthly vital statistics report; advance report of final divorce statistics, 1984.* Hyattsville, MD: Public Health Service.

National Center for Health Statistics. (1987, June 3). *Monthly vital statistics report; report of final marriage statistics, 1984.* Hyattsville, MD: Public Health Service.

National Center for Health Statistics. (1995). *Vital statistics of the United States.* Washington, DC: U.S. Government Printing Office.

National Commission on Excellence. (1983). *A nation at risk.* Washington, DC: Author.

National Commission on Secondary Vocational Education. (1984). *The unfinished agenda.* Columbus: Ohio State University, National Center for Research on Vocational Education.

National Education Goals Panel. (1994). *Data for the national education goals report: Vol. 1. National data* (pp. 8–11). Washington, DC: U.S. Government Printing Office.

National Occupational Information Coordinating Committee. (1988). *The national career counseling and development guidelines.* Washington, DC: Author.

Neimeyer, R.A. (1996). Process interventions for the constructivist psychotherapist. In H. Rosen & K.T. Kuehlwein (Eds.), *Constructing realities. Meaning-making perspectives for psychotherapists* (pp. 371–412). San Francisco: Jossey-Bass.

Nelson, L.S., & Roberge, L.P. (1993). The relationship between psychological type and preference for career services. Implications for career development strategies. *College Student Journal, 27*, 313–321.

Neugarten, B.L., & Neugarten, D.A. (1987). The changing meanings of age. *Psychology Today, 21*(5), 29–34.

The new jobless. (1988, May). *World Press Review, 35*(5), 46.

The next step: 25 discoveries that could change our lives. (1985). *Science, 6(9),* 2–3.

Nguyen, S.D. (1985). Mental health services for refugees and immigrants in Canada. In T.C. Owan (Ed.), *Southeast Asians' mental health: Treatment, prevention, services, training, and research* (pp. 261–282). Washington, DC: U.S. Department of Health and Human Services, National Institute of Mental Health.

Nicholas, D.R. (1988). Behavioral medicine and mental health counseling. *Journal of Mental Health Counseling, 10*(2), 69–78.

Niles, S., & Garis, J.W. (1990). The effects of a career planning course and a computer-assisted career guidance program (SIGI Plus) on undecided university students. *Journal of Career Development, 16*, 237–248.

Norcross, J.C. (Ed.). (1986). *The handbook of eclectic psychotherapy.* New York: Brunner/Mazel.

Norcross, J.C. (1993). Tailoring relationship stances to client needs: An introduction. *Psychotherapy, 30*, 402–403.

Norton, A.J., & Miller, L.F. (1992). Marriage, divorce, and remarriage in the 1990s. In U.S. Bureau of the Census, *Current population reports* (Series P-23, No.180). Washington, DC: U.S. Government Printing Office.

Novaco, R. (1976). Treatment of chronic anger through cognitive and relaxation controls. *Journal of Consulting and Clinical Psychology, 44*, 681.

O'Connell, M. (1991). Late expectations: Childbearing patterns of American women for the 1990s. In U.S. Bureau of the Census, *Current population reports* (Series P-23, No. 176). Washington, DC: U.S. Government Printing Office.

O'Hanlon, W., & Weiner-Davis, M. (1989). *In search of solutions: A new direction in psychotherapy.* New York: Norton.

O'Brien, S. (1980). *Child abuse: A crying shame.* Provo, UT: Brigham Young University.

Ochberg, F.M. (Ed.). (1988). *Post-traumatic therapy and victims of violence.* New York: Brunner/Mazel.

Oetting, E.R., & Beauvais, F. (1986). Peer cluster theory: Drugs and the adolescent. *Journal of Counseling and Development, 65*(1), 17–22.

Offerman, L.R., & Gowing, M.K. (1990). Organizations of the future. Changes and challenges. *American Psychologist, 45,* 95–108.

Office of Technology Assessment, U.S. Congress. (June, 1985). *Technology and aging in America* (OTA Report Brief). Washington, DC: Author.

Office of Technology Assessment, U.S. Congress. (1988). *Technology and the American economic transition: Choices for the future.* Washington, DC: U.S. Government Printing Office.

Ogilvie, B., & Daniluk, J. (1995). Common themes in the experiences of mother-daughter incest survivors: Implications for counseling. *Journal of Counseling and Development, 73*(6), 598–602.

Olson, D.H., Russell, C.S., & Sprenkle, D.H. (1980). Marital and family therapy: A decade review. *Journal of Marriage and the Family, 42*(4), 239–259.

Olson, D.H., Sprenkle, D., & Russell, C. (1979). Circumplex model of marital and family systems: Cohesion and adaptability dimensions of family types and clinical application. *Family Relations, 35*(1), 53–56

O'Neill, G.K. (1983). *The technology edge: Opportunities for America in world competition.* New York: Simon & Schuster.

O'Reilly, C.A., III, Chatman, J., & Caldwell, D.F. (1991). People and organizational culture: A profile comparison approach to assessing person-organization fit. *Academy of Management Journal, 34*(3), 487–516.

Osipow, S.H. (1982). Counseling psychology: Applications in the world of work. *The Counseling Psychologist, 10*(3), 19–25.

O'Toole, J. (1977). *The reserve army of the underemployed.* Washington, DC: U.S. Office of Career Education.

Owan, T.C. (Ed.). (1985). *Southeast Asians' mental health: Treatment, prevention, services, training, and research.* Washington, DC: U.S. Department of Health and Human Services, National Institute of Mental Health.

Oxford Analytica. (1986). *America in perspective: Major trends in the United States through the 1990s.* Boston: Houghton Mifflin.

Paisley, P.O., & Borders, L.D. (1995). School counseling: An evolving specialty. *Journal of Counseling and Development, 74*(2), 150–152.

Palmo, A.J. (1996). Professional identity of the mental health counselor. In W.J. Weikeln & A.J. Palmo (Eds.), *Foundations of mental health counseling* (2nd ed., pp. 51–72). Springfield, IL: Charles C Thomas.

Parham, T.A., & McDavis, R.J. (1987). Black men, an endangered species: Who's really pulling the trigger? *Journal of Counseling and Development, 66*(1), 24–27.

Parker, D.A., Parker, E.S., Harford, T.C., & Farmer, G.S. (1987). Alcohol use and depression symptoms among employed men and women. *Brown University Digest of Addiction Theory and Application, 6*(4), 48–51.

Parker, W.M., Valley, M.M., & Geary, C.A. (1986). Acquiring counselor knowledge for counselors in training: Multifaceted approach. *Counselor Education and Supervision, 26*(1), 61–71.

Parsons, T. (1951). *The social system.* Glencoe, IL: Free Press.

Pasewark, R.A., & Albers, D.A. (1972). Crisis intervention: Theory in search of a program. *Social Work, 17,* 70 77.

Peabody, D. (1985). *National characteristics.* Cambridge, England: Cambridge University Press.

Peavy, R.V. (1994). A constructivist perspective for counseling. *Education and Vocational Guidance Bulletin, 55,* 31.

Pedersen, P.B. (1978). Four dimensions of cross-cultural skill in counselor training. *Personnel and Guidance Journal, 56,* 480–484.

Pedersen, P.B. (1981). Triad counseling. In R. Corsini (Ed.), *Innovative psychotherapies* (pp. 840–855). New York: Wiley.

Pedersen, P.B. (1990). The multicultural perspective as a fourth force in psychology. *Journal of Mental Health Counseling, 12,* 93–95.

Pedersen, P.B. (1991). Multiculturalism as a generic approach to counseling. *Journal of Counseling and Development, 70,* 3–14.

Pedersen, P.B. (1994). *A handbook for developing multicultural awareness* (2nd ed.). Alexandria, VA: American Counseling Association.

Pedersen, P.B., Draguns, J.G., Lonner, W. J., & Trimble, J.E. (1996). Introduction: Priority issues of counseling across cultures. In P.B. Pedersen, J.G. Draguns, W.J. Lonner, & J.E. Trimble (Eds.), *Counseling across cultures* (4th ed., pp. vii-xvii). Thousand Oaks, CA: Sage.

Pedersen, P.B., & Marsella, A.J. (1982). The ethical crisis for cross-cultural counseling and therapy. *Professional Psychology, 13*(4), 492–500.

Peele, S. (1986). The cure for adolescent drug abuse: Worse than the problem. *Journal of Counseling and Development, 65*(1), 23–24.

Pennsylvania Department of Education. (1986). *Adolescent suicide.* Harrisburg, PA: Author.

Pennsylvania Department of Education. (1987). *Achieving success with more students: Addressing the problem of students at risk.* Harrisburg, PA: Author.

Perlmutter, F.D. (1982). New directions for mental health promotion. In F.D. Perlmutter (Ed.), *Mental health promotion and primary prevention* (chap. 1). San Francisco: Jossey-Bass.

Perry, L. (1982). Special populations: The demands of diversity. In E.L. Herr & N.M. Pinson (Eds.), *Foundations for policy in guidance and counseling* (pp. 50–69). Falls Church, VA: American Personnel and Guidance Association.

Personick, V. (1985). A second look at industry output and employment trends through 1995. *Monthly Labor Review, 108*(11), 26–41.

Phillips, D. (1985). The Western effect: Suicide and other forms of violence are contagious. *The Sciences, 25,* 32–39.

Pinson-Millburn, N.M., Fabian, E.S., Schlossberg, N.K., & Pyle, M. (1996). Grandparents raising grandchildren. *Journal of Counseling and Development, 74*(6), 548–554.

The politics of unemployment. Europe hits a brick wall. (1997, April 5). *The Economist, 343*(8011), 21–23.

Ponterotto, J.G., & Casas, J.M. (1987). In search of multicultural competence within counselor education programs. *Journal of Counseling and Development, 65*(8), 430–434.

Ponterotto, J.G., Casas, J.M., Suzuki, L.A., & Alexander, C.M. (1995). *Handbook of multicultural counseling.* Thousand Oaks, CA: Sage.

Posner, M.I., & Shulman, G.L. (1979). Cognitive science. In E. Hearst (Ed.), *The first century of experimental psychology.* Hillsdale, NJ: Erlbaum.

Protti, R., Shulman, N., & Kirby, S. (1985). *Microelectronics and human resources.* Symposium on Microelectronics and Labor, conducted at the National Institute of Occupational Research, Tokyo.

Pryor, R.G.L., Hammond, B., & Hawkins, T.L. (1990). New tasks, new visions: Employment counseling in Australia. *Journal of Employment Counseling, 27,* 160–170.

Pryor, R.J., & Ward, R.T. (1985). Unemployment: What counselors can do about it. *Journal of Employment Counseling, 22*(1), 3–17.

Rak, C.F., & Patterson, L. (1996). Promoting resilience in at-risk children. *Journal of Counseling and Development, 74*(4), 368–373.

Ramey, C.T., & Ramey, S.L. (1993). *At risk does not mean doomed.* Washington, DC: National Commission to Prevent Infant Mortality.

Rayman, J., & Harris-Bowlsbey, J. (1977). DISCOVER: A model for a systematic career guidance program. *Vocational Guidance Quarterly, 26*(1), 4–12.

Reich, R.B. (1983). *The next American frontier.* New York: Times Books.

Reich, R.B. (1987). *Tales of a new America.* New York: Vintage Books.

Reisman, D. (1961). *The lonely crowd.* New Haven, CT: Yale University Press.

Restoule, B. (1997). Providing services to Aboriginal clients. *Guidance and Counselling 12*(2), 13–17.

Reynolds, D.K. (1980). *The quiet therapies: Japanese pathways to personal growth.* Honolulu: University of Hawaii Press.

Rice, K.G., & Meyer, A.L. (1994). Preventing depression among young adolescents: Preliminary process results of a psychoeducational intervention program. *Journal of Counseling and Development, 73*(2), 145–152.

Richman, L.S. (1994, August 22). The new worker elite. *Fortune, 130*(4), 56–59, 62, 64, 66.

Riegle, D. W., Jr. (1982). Psychological and social effects of unemployment. *American Psychologist, 37*(10), 113–115.

Rifkin, J. (1995) *The end of work. The decline of the global labor forces and the dawn of the postmarket era.* New York: Putnam's.

Ritook, M. (1993). Career development in Hungary at the beginning of the 90s. *Journal of Career Development, 20*(1), 33–40.

Robins, N., Locke, B.Z., & Regier, D.A. (1991). An overview of psychiatric disorders in America. In L.N. Robins & D.A. Regier (Eds.), *Psychiatric disorders in America. The epidemiologic catchment area study* (pp. 291–327). New York: Free Press.

Robinson, B.E., Rowland, B.H., & Coleman, M. (1986). Taking action for latchkey children and their families. *Family Relations, 35*(4), 473–478.

Robson, B.E. (1987). Changing family patterns: Developmental impacts on children. *Counseling and Human Development, 19*(6), 1–11.

Rochell, C. C., & Spellman, C. (1987*). Dreams betrayed: Working in the technological age.* Lexington, MA: Heath.

Roe, A. (1956). *The psychology of occupations.* New York: Wiley.

Romanczyk, R.B. (1986). *Clinical utilization of microcomputer technology.* New York: Pergamon Press.

Roscak, T. (1986). *The cult of information: The folklore of computers and the true art of thinking.* New York: Pantheon Books.

Rosen, H. (1996). Meaning-making narratives: Foundations for constructivist and social constructionist psychotherapies. In H. Rosen & K.T. Kuehlwein (Eds.), *Constructing realities, meaning-making perspectives for psychotherapists* (pp. 3–54). San Francisco: Jossey-Bass.

Rosen, H., & Kuehlwein, K.T. (Eds.). (1996). *Constructing realities, meaning-making perspectives for psychotherapists.* San Francisco: Jossey-Bass.

Rosen, J.C., & Solomon, L.J. (Eds.). (1985). *Prevention in health psychology.* Hanover, NH: University Press of New England.

Rosenheck, R. (1985). Malignant post-Vietnam stress syndrome. *American Journal of Orthopsychiatry, 55*, 166–176.

Ross, E.R., Baker, S.B., & Guerney, B.G., Jr. (1985). Effectiveness of relationship enhancement therapy versus therapists' preferred therapy. *American Journal of Family Therapy, 13*(1), 11–21.

Roth, L.H. (Ed.). (1985). *Clinical treatment of the violent person.* Rockville, MD: U.S. Department of Health and Human Services, National Institute of Mental Health.

Rumberger, R. W. (1987). The potential impact of technology on the skill requirements of future jobs. In G. Burke & R.W. Rumberger (Eds.), *The future impact of technology on work and education* (chap. 5). New York: Falmer Press.

Rumberger, R.W., & Burke, G. (Eds.). (1987). *The future impact of technology on work and education.* New York: Falmer Press.

Russell, D.E.H. (1982). *Rape in marriage.* New York: Macmillan.

Saari, C. (1996). Relationship factors in the creation of identity. A psychodynamic perspective. In H. Rosen & K.T. Kuehlwein (Eds.), *Constructing realities, meaning-making perspectives for psychotherapists* (pp. 141–165). San Francisco: Jossey-Bass.

Sagestrano, L.M., & Paikoff, R.L. (1997). Preventing high-risk sexual behavior, sexually transmitted diseases, and pregnancy among adolescents. In R.P. Weissberg, P.P. Gullotta, R.L.

Hampton, B.A. Ryan, & G.R. Adams (Eds.), *Enhancing children's wellness* (pp. 76–104). Thousand Oaks, CA: Sage.

Sampson, J.P. (1983). An integrated approach to computer applications in counseling psychology. *The Counseling Psychologist, 11*(4), 65–74.

Sampson, J.P. (1986, April 4–7). *The use of computer-assorted instruction in support of psychotherapy.* Paper presented at the annual conference of the British Psychological Society, University of Sheffield.

Sampson, J.P., Jr., Kolodinsky, R.W., & Greeno, B.P. (1997). Counseling on the information highway: Future possibilities and potential problems. *Journal of Counseling and Development, 75*(3), 203–212.

Sampson, J.P., Jr., Peterson, G.W., & Reardon, R.C. (1989). Counselor intervention strategies for computer-assisted career guidance: An information processing approach. *Journal of Career Development, 16*, 139–159.

Sampson, J.P., & Reardon, R.C. (Eds.). (1990). *Enhancing the use and design of computer-assisted career guidance systems.* Alexandria, VA: National Career Development Association.

Sampson, J.P., Jr., & Reardon, R.C. (1991). Current developments in computer-assisted career guidance in the U. S. A. *British Journal of Guidance and Counselling, 19*(2), 113–128.

Sampson, J.P., Jr., Reardon, R.C., & Lenz, J.G. (1991). Computer-assisted career guidance systems: Improving the design and use of systems. *Journal of Career Development, 17*, 185–194.

Saner-Yiu, L., & Saner, R. (1985). Value dimensions in American counseling: A Taiwanese American comparison. *International Journal for the Advancement of Counselling, 8*, 137–146.

Sanik, M.M., & Mauldin, T. (1986). Single-versus two-parent families: A comparison of mother's time. *Family Relations, 35*(1), 53–56.

Sank, L.I., & Shaffer, C.S. (1984). *A therapist's manual for cognitive behavior therapy in groups.* New York: Plenum Press.

Sardi, Z. (1982). *The psychological aspects of immigration to Israel.* Paper presented to the International Round Table for the Advancement of Counselling, University of Lausanne, Switzerland.

Sargent, S.S. (Ed.). (1980). *Nontraditional therapy and counseling with the aging.* New York: Springer.

Satir, V. (1964). *Conjoint family therapy.* Palo Alto, CA: Science and Behavior Books.

Savickas, M. (1993). Career counseling in the postmodern era. *Journal of Cognitive Psychotherapy, 7*, 205–215.

Schlossberg, N., & Leibowitz, Z. (1980). Organizational support systems as buffers to job loss. *Journal of Vocational Behavior, 17*, 204–217.

Schlossberg, N.K. (1984). *Counseling adults in transition, linking practice with theory.* New York: Springer.

Schlossberg, N.K. (1994). *Overwhelmed: Coping with life's up's and down's.* San Francisco: Jossey-Bass.

Schlossberg, N.K., & Robinson, S.P. (1996). *Going to plan b: How you can cope, regroup, and start your life on a new path.* New York: Simon & Schuster.

School-to-Work Opportunities Act of 1994, Pub. L. No. 103-239.

Schrum, L. (1995). Framing the debate: Ethical research in the information age. *Qualitative Inquiry, 1*(3), 311–326.

Seay, T.A., & Seay, M.B. (1996). The role of theory in the practice of mental health counseling: History and development. In W.J. Weikel & A.J. Palmo (Eds.), *Foundations of mental health counseling* (2nd ed., pp. 73–104). Springfield, IL: Charles C Thomas.

Segall, M.H., Dasen, P.R., Berry, J.W., & Poortinga, Y.H. (1990). *Human behavior in global perspective. An introduction to cross-cultural psychology.* New York: Pergammon Press.

Sekaran, U. (1986). *Dual-career families: Contemporary organizational and counseling issues.* San Francisco: Jossey-Bass.

Seligman, M.E.P. (1996). *The optimistic child.* New York: Harper Perennial.

Selvini, M., Palazzoli, M.S., Boscolo, L., Cecchin, G., & Prata, G. (1980). Hypothesizing—circularity—neutrality: Three guidelines for the conductor of the session. *Family Process, 19,* 3–12.

Selye, H. (1976). *The stress of life.* New York: McGraw-Hill.

Sennett, R. (1977). *The psychology of society: A selected anthology.* New York: Vintage Books.

Sexton, T.L. (1997). Constructivist thinking within the history of ideas: The challenge of a new paradigm. In T.L. Sexton & B. Griffin (Eds.), *Constructivist thinking in counseling practice, research, and training* (pp. 3–18). New York: Columbia University, Teachers College.

Sgroi, S. (1982). *Handbook of clinical intervention in child sexual abuse.* Lexington, MA: Lexington Books.

Shanhirzadi, A. (1983). Counseling Iranians. *Personnel and Guidance Journal, 61,* 487–489.

Shapiro, S. (1987). Self-mutilation and self-blame in incest victims. *American Journal of Psychotherapy, 16,* 46–53.

Shelton, B.K. (1985). The social and psychological impact of unemployment. *Journal of Employment Counseling, 22*(1), 18–22.

Sherman, D. (1994). The job complex. *Journal of Career Planning and Employment, 55*(1), 30–32, 62–63.

Short, R.J., & Talley, R.C. (1997). Rethinking psychology and the schools. Implications of recent national policy. *American Psychologist, 52*(3), 234–240.

Shupe, A., & Stacey, W. (1987). *Violent men, violent couples.* Lexington, MA: Heath.

Silberman, H.F. (1994). Research review of school-to-employment experience. In A.J. Pautler (Ed.), *High school to employment transition: Contemporary Issues* (pp. 61–72). Ann Arbor, MI: Prakken.

Silverstein, L.B. (1991). Transforming the debate about child care and maternal employment. *American Psychologist, 46* (1), 1025–1032.

Simon, R.I., & Burton, G. (1990, January 8). What did I learn in the 1980s? A poorly educated labor force may cost the U.S. dearly. *Forbes, 145*(1), 103–104.

Slaikeu, K.A. (1984). *Crisis intervention: A handbook for practice and research.* Boston: Allyn & Bacon.

Small, L. (1971). *The briefer psychotherapies.* New York: Brunner/Mazel.

Smith, D. (1982). Trends in counseling and psychotherapy. *American Psychologist, 37*(7), 802–809.

Smith, E.M.J. (1983). Ethnic minorities: Life stress, social support, and mental health issues. *The Counseling Psychologist, 13*(4), 537–579.

Smyer, M.A. (1984). Life transitions and aging: Implications for counseling older adults. *The Counseling Psychologist, 12*(2), 17–28.

Snygg, D., & Combs, A.W. (1949). *Individual behavior.* New York: Harper.

Sommer, R., Barnes, G., & Murray, R. (1992). Alcohol consumption, alcohol abuse, personality, and female perpetrated spouse abuse. *Personality and Individual Differences, 13*(12), 1315–1323.

Sowell, T. (1994). *Race and culture: A worldview.* New York: Basic Books.

Spanard, J.M.A. (1990). Beyond intent: Reentering college to complete the degree. *Review of Educational Research, 60*(3), 309–344.

Sparks, D. (1981). *Helping clients manage stress: A practical approach.* Ann Arbor: University of Michigan, ERIC/CAPS.

Spokane, A. (1989). Are there psychological and mental health consequences of difficult career decisions? A reaction to Herr. *Journal of Career Counseling, 16,* 19–24.

Sproles, E.T., III. (1985). *The evaluation and management of rape and sexual abuse: A physician's guide.* Rockville, MD: U.S. Department of Health and Human Services, National Center for Prevention and Control of Rape.

Sroka, S. (1988, April 27). Planning effective AIDS-education programs. *Education Week,* p. 36.

Staples, R. (1982). *Black masculinity.* San Francisco: Black Scholar Press.

Steinmetz, S.K., & Lucca, J.S. (1988). Husband battering. In V.B. Van Hasselt, R.L. Morrison, A.S. Bellack, & M. Hersen (Eds.), *Handbook of family violence* (pp. 233–246). New York: Plenum Press.

Stern, D., McMillan, M., Hopkins, C., & Stone, J.R., III. (1990). Work experience for students in high school and college. *Youth and Society, 21*(3), 355–389.

Stern, G.G., Stein, M.I., & Bloom, B.J. (1956). *Methods in personality assessment.* Glencoe, IL: Free Press.

Sterns, H.C., Weis, D.M., & Perkins, S.E. (1984). A conceptual approach to counseling older adults and their families. *The Counseling Psychologist, 12*(2), 55–61.

Straus, M.A., Gelles, R.J., & Steinmetz, S.K. (1980). *Behind closed doors: Violence in the American family.* New York: Anchor Books.

Streib, G.F., & Beck, R.W. (1980). Older families: A decade review. *Journal of Marriage and the Family, 42*(4), 205–224.

Stroman, S.H., & Duff, E. (1982). The latchkey child: Whose responsibility? *Childhood Education, 59,* 76–79.

Studies target teen pregnancy. (1986, March). *Guidepost, 28*(14), 1, 16.

Sue, D., & Padilla, A. (1986). Ethnic minority issues in the United States: Challenges for the educational system. In *Beyond language: Social and cultural factors in schooling language minority students* (pp. 34–72). Los Angeles: California Department of Education.

Sue, D., & Sue, S. (1987). Cultural factors in the clinical assessment of Asian Americans. *Journal of Consulting and Clinical Psychology, 55*(4), 479–487.

Sue, D.W. (1981). *Counseling the culturally different.* New York: Wiley.

Sue, S., Akutsu, P.D., & Higashi, C. (1985). Training issues in conducting therapy with ethnic-minority-group clients. In P. Pedersen, *Handbook of cross-cultural counseling and therapy* (pp. 275–280). Westport, CT: Greenwood Press.

Suinn, R.M. (1976). *Manual: Anxiety management training (AMT).* Fort Collins, CO: Rocky Mountain Behavioral Sciences Institute.

Sundal-Hansen, L.S. (1985). Work-family linkages: Neglected factors in career guidance across cultures. *Vocational Guidance Quarterly, 33*(3), 202–212.

Super, D.E. (1955). Transition: From vocational guidance to counseling psychology. *Journal of Counseling Psychology, 2,* 3–9.

Super, D.E. (1985). Career counseling across cultures. In P. Pedersen (Ed.), *Handbook of cross-cultural counseling and therapy* (pp. 11–20). Westport, CT: Greenwood Press.

Super, D.E. (1993). The two paces of counseling: Or is it three? *Career Development Quarterly, 42,* 132–136.

Super, D.E., & Sverko, B. (1995). *Life roles, values, and careers. International findings of the work importance study.* San Francisco: Jossey-Bass.

Supovitz, J.A. (1997, November 5). From multiple choice to multiple choices. A diverse society deserves a more diverse assessment system. *Education Week, 34,* 37.

Tan, C.S., & Salomone, P.R. (1994). Understanding career planning implications for counseling. *Career Development Quarterly, 42,* 291–301.

Tarasoff v. Regents of the University of California, 17 Cal. 3d 425, 131 C.R. 14 (1976).

Taube, C.A., & Barrett, S.A. (1985). *Mental health, United States 1985.* Rockville, MD: U.S. Department of Health and Human Services, National Institute of Mental Health.

Taylor, R.L. (1990). Black youth: The endangered generation. *Youth and Society, 22* (1), 4–11.

Tedder, S.L., Scherman, A., & Sheridan, K.M. (1984). Impact of group support on adjustment to divorce by single, custodial fathers. *AMHCA Journal, 6*(4), 180.

Temoshok, L. (1988). Psychoimmunology and AIDS. In T.P. Bridge, A.F. Mirsky, & F.K. Goodwin (Eds.), *Psychological, neuropsychiatric, and substance abuse aspects of AIDS: Vol. 44. Advances in biochemical psychopharmacology.* New York: Raven Press.

Theobald, R. (1966). Cybernetics and the problems of social organizations. In C.R. Deckert (Ed.), *The social impact of cybernetics* (pp. 46–61). New York: Simon & Schuster.

Theriault, J. (1994). Retirement as a psychological transition: Process of adaptation to change. *International Journal of Aging and Human Development, 38* (2), 153–170.

Throckmorton, W. (1996). Mental health counselors and third-party reimbursement. In W.J. Weikel & A.J. Palmo (Eds.), *Foundations of mental health counseling* (2nd ed., pp. 283–311). Springfield, IL: Charles C Thomas.

Toffler, A. (1970). *Future shock*. New York: Bantam Books.

Toffler, A. (1980). *The third wave*. New York: Morrow.

Toffler, A. (1990). *Powershift, knowledge, weatlh, and violence at the edge of the 21st century*. New York: Bantam Books.

Tomlinson, J. (1991). *Cultural imperialism*. Baltimore, MD: Johns Hopkins University Press.

Tracey, P.E., Wolfgang, M.E., & Figlio, R.M. (1985). *Delinquency in two birth cohorts: Executive summary*. Washington, DC: U.S. Department of Justice.

Training for jobs. (1994, March 12). *The Economist, 7584,* 19–20, 26.

Triandis, H.C. (1972). *The analysis of subjective culture*. New York: Wiley.

Triandis, H.C. (1985). Some major dimensions of cultural variation in client populations. In P.B. Pedersen (Ed.), *Handbook of cross-cultural counseling and therapy* (pp. 21–28). Westport, CT: Greenwood Press.

Trimble, J.E., Fleming, C.M., Beauvais, F., & Jumper-Thurman, P. (1996). Essential cultural and social strategies for counseling Native American Indians. In P.B. Pedersen, J.G. Draguns, W.J. Lonner, & J.E. Trimble (Eds.), *Counseling across cultures* (4th ed., pp. 177–209). Thousand Oaks, CA: Sage.

Tseng, W., & Streltzer, J. (Eds.). (1997). *Culture and psychopathology. A guide to general assessment*. New York: Brunner/Mazel.

Tubesing, D.A. (1981). *Stress skills: A structured strategy for helping people handle stress more effectively*. Duluth, MN: Whole Person Press.

Tugend, A. (1986, June 18). Suicide's "unanswerable logic." *Education Week*, pp. 15–17.

Turkington, C. (1983). Lifetime of fear may be legacy of latchkey children. *APA Monitor*, pp. 14–19.

Tyler, L.E. (1983). *Thinking creatively: A new approach to psychology and individual lives*. San Francisco: Jossey-Bass.

U.S. Bureau of the Census. (1980). *1980 census*. Washington, DC: Author.

U.S. Bureau of the Census. (1991). *Current population reports* (Series P-60, No. 174). Washington, DC: U.S. Government Printing Office.

U.S. Commission on Civil Rights. (1978). *Consultation on battered women: Issues of public policy*. Washington, DC: U.S. Government Printing Office.

U.S. Department of Education. (1991). *Combining school and work: Options in high schools and 2-year colleges*. Washington, DC: U.S. Government Printing Office.

U.S. Department of Education/U.S. Department of Labor. (1988). *The bottom line: Basic skills in the workplace*. Washington, DC: U.S. Department of Labor.

U.S. Department of Labor, Employment and Training Administration. (1993). *Finding one's way: Career guidance for disadvantaged youth* (Research and Evaluation Report Series 93–D). Washington, DC: Author.

U.S. Department of Labor, Employment and Training Administration. (1995). *Skills, standards, and entry-level work. Elements of a strategy for youth employability development*. Washington, DC: Author.

U.S. Department of Labor, Secretary's Commission on Achieving Necessary Skills. (1991). *What work requires of schools*. Washington, DC: Author.

Vachon, R.A. (1987). Inventory-2 future for individuals with work disabilities: The challenge of writing national disability policies. In D.E. Woods & D. Vandergoot (Eds.), *The changing nature of work, society, and disability* (chap. 4). New York: World Rehabilitation Fund.

Vaizey, J., & Clarke, C.F.O. (1976). *Education: The state of the debate in America, Britain, and Canada*. London, England: Duckworth.

Van Doren, D. (1996). Mental health counseling and alcohol and other drug abuse. In W.J. Weikel & A.J. Palmo (Eds.), *Foundations of mental health counseling* (2nd ed., pp. 249–257). Springfield, IL: Charles C Thomas.

VanZijl, J.C. (1985). *Multicultural counseling: Mission impossible.* Paper presented at the International Round Table for the Advancement of Counselling, Lund, Sweden.

Vincent, J.P. (1980). *Advances in family intervention: Assessment and theory* (Vol. 1). Greenwich, CT: JAI Press.

Vondracek, F.W., Lerner, R.M., & Schulenberg, S.E. (1986). *Career development: A life-span developmental approach.* Hillsdale, NJ: Erlbaum.

Vontress, C.E. (1976). Racial and ethnic barriers in counseling. In P.B. Pedersen, J.G. Draguns, W.J. Lonner, & J.E. Trimble (Eds.), *Counseling across cultures.* Honolulu: University of Hawaii Press.

Vontress, C.E. (1986). Social and cultural foundations. In M.D. Lewis, R.L. Hayes, & J.A. Lewis (Eds.), *An introduction to the counseling profession* (pp. 215–250). Itasca, IL: Peacock.

Wachowiak, D., & Bragg, H. (1980). Open marriage and marital adjustment. *Journal of Marriage and the Family, 42,* 57–62.

Wagman, M. (1984). Using computers in personal counseling. *Journal of Counseling and Development, 63*(3), 172–176.

Walen, R., DiGuiseppe, R., & Dryden, W. (1992). *A practitioner's guide to rational-emotive therapy* (2nd ed.). New York: Oxford University Press.

Walker, L. (1984). *The battered woman syndrome.* New York: Springer.

Walker, L.E. (1979). *The battered woman.* New York: Harper Colophon Books.

Walker, L.E. (1991). Post-traumatic stress disorder in women: Diagnosis and treatment of battered women syndrome. *Psychotherapy, 28*(1), 21–29.

Wallerstein, J.S. (1980). The impact of divorce on children. *Psychiatric Clinics of North America, 3,* 455–468.

Wallerstein, J.S. (1984). Children of divorce: Preliminary report of a 10-year follow-up of young children. *American Journal of Orthopsychiatry, 54,* 444–458.

Walz, G.R., & Benjamin, L. (1979). *A futuristic perspective for counselors.* Ann Arbor: University of Michigan, ERIC/CAPS.

Wasserman, I.M. (1984). A longitudinal analysis of the linkage between suicide, unemployment, and marital dissolution. *Journal of Marriage and the Family, 46,* 14–22.

Watanabe, A.M. (1984, March 20). *Influences of microelectronics on education and training programs and career guidance in Japan.* Paper presented at the annual convention of the American Association for Counseling and Development, Houston, TX.

Watanabe, A.M., & Herr, E.L. (1993). Career development issues among Japanese work groups. *Journal of Career Development, 20*(1), 61–72.

Waterman, J., & Lusk, R. (1986). Scope of the problem. In K. MacFarlane, J. Waterman, S. Conerly, L. Damon, M. Durfee, & S. Long (Eds.), *Sexual abuse of young children* (pp. 3–12). New York: Guilford Press.

Waters, E.B. (1984). Building on what you know: Techniques for individual and group counseling with older people. *The Counseling Psychologist, 12*(2), 63–74.

Watts, A.G. (1981). Introduction. In A.G. Watts, D.E. Super, & J.M. Kidd (Eds.), *Career development in Britain* (pp. 1–8). Cambridge, England: Hobson's Press.

Watts, A.G. (1994). Occupational profiles of vocational counselors in Europe. *Journal of Counseling and Development, 73*(1), 44–50.

Watts, A.G., Dartois, C., & Plant, P. (1988). *Educational and vocational guidance services* (Education Policy Series 2). Sittard, Netherlands: Presses Interuniversitaires Europeans Maasricht.

Watts, A.G., Guichard, J., Plant, P., & Rodriquez, M.Z. (1993). *Educational and vocational guidance in the European community* (pp. 44, 45). Brussels, Belgium: Commission of the European Communities.

Watts, A.G., & Herr, E.L. (1976). Career education in Britain and the U.S.A.: Contrasts and common problems. *British Journal of Guidance and Counseling, 4,* 129–142.

Watzlawick, P., Beavin, J.H., & Jackson, D.D. (1967). *Parameters of human communication: A study of interactional patterns, pathologies, and paradoxes.* New York: Norton.

Watzlawick, P., & Weakland, J.H. (Eds.). (1977). *The interactional view.* New York: Norton.

Wegscheider, S. (1981). *Another chance: Hope and health for the alcoholic family.* Palo Alto, CA: Science and Behavior Books.

Weikel, W.J. (1985). The American Mental Health Counselors Association. *Journal of Counseling and Development, 63*(7), 457–460.

Weikel, W.J., & Palmo, A.J. (Eds.). (1996). *Foundations of mental health counseling* (2nd ed.). Springfield, IL: Charles C Thomas.

Weinrach, S.G. (1996). Nine experts describe the essence of rational emotive therapy while standing on one foot. *Journal of Counseling and Development, 74*(4), 326–331.

Weissburg, R.P., Gullotta, T.P., Hampton, R.L., Ryan, B.A., & Adams, G.R. (Eds.). (1997). *Healthy children 2010: Establishing preventive services: Vol. 9. Issues in children's and families lives.* Thousand Oaks, CA: Sage.

Weiss, D.J., & Vale, C.D. (1987). Adaptive testing. *Applied Psychology: An International Review, 36*(3,4), 249–262.

Welborn, A., & Moore, S.S. (1985). Counseling displaced homemakers. In D. Jones & S.S. Moore (Eds.), *Counseling adults: Life cycle perspectives* (pp. 103–107). Lawrence: University of Kansas.

Wellman, F.E., & McCormick, L. (1984). Counseling with older persons: A review of outcome research. *The Counseling Psychologist, 12*(2), 81–96.

West, J.D., Hosie, T.W., & Zarski, J.J. (1987). Family dynamics and substance abuse: A preliminary study. *Journal of Counseling and Development, 65*(9), 487–494.

Westermeyer, J. (1985). Mental health and Southeast Asian refugees: Observations over two decades from Laos and the United States. In T.C. Owan (Ed.), *Southeast Asians' mental health: Treatment, prevention, services, training, and research* (pp. 65–90). Washington, DC: U.S. Department of Health and Human Services, National Institute of Mental Health.

Westermeyer, J. (1987). Cultural factors in clinical assessment. *Journal of Consulting and Clinical Psychology, 55*(4). 471–478.

Whitaker, C.A. (1977). Process techniques of family therapy. *Interaction, 1,* 4–19.

White, R.M. (1990). Technology and the independence of nations. In H.E. Sladovich (Ed.), *Engineering and human development* (pp. 5–11). Washington, DC: National Academy of Engineering.

Whitemore, H. (1988, January 10). We can't pay the rent. *Parade,* pp. 4–6.

Whitman, D., Thornton, J., Shapiro, J.P., Witkin, G., & Hawkins, S.L. (1988, January 11). America's hidden poor. *U.S. News and World Report,* pp. 18–24.

Widiger, T.A., Frances, A.J., Pincus, H.A., Ross, R., First, M.B., & Davis, W.W. (1996). *DSM-IV sourcebook* (Vol. 2). Washington, DC: American Psychiatric Association.

Wijers, G.A., & Meijers, F. (1996). Career guidance in the knowledge society. *British Journal of Guidance and Counseling, 24*(2), 185–198.

Wilcox-Matthew, L., & Minor, C.W. (1989). The dual-career couple: Concerns, benefits, and counseling implications. *Journal of Counseling and Development, 68,* 194–198.

Wilson, J.W. (1985, March 11). America's high-tech crisis: Why Silicon Valley is losing its edge. *Business Week, 2883,* 56–67.

Wilson, K.L., Zurcher, L.S., McAdam, D.C., & Curtis, R.L. (1975). Stepfathers and stepchildren: An exploratory analysis from two national surveys. *Journal of Marriage and the Family, 37,* 526–536.

Wolpe, J. (1973). *The practice of behavior therapy* (2nd ed.). New York: Pergamon Press.

Worell, J. (1980). New directions in counseling women. *Personnel and Guidance Journal, 58,* 477–484.

W.T. Grant Commission on Work, Family, and Citizenship. (1988, January). *The forgotten half: Noncollege youth in America* (An interim report on the school-to-work transition). Washington, DC: Author.

Yiu, L. (1978). *Degree of assimilation and its effect on the preference of counseling style and on self-disclosure among Chinese Americans in Hawaii.* Unpublished doctoral dissertation, Indiana University, Bloomington.

Yoshioka, R.B., Tashima, N., Chew, M., & Murase, K. (1981). *Mental health services for Pacific Asian Americans.* San Francisco: Pacific Asian Mental Health Research Project.

Zablocki, B. (1977). *Alienation and investment in the urban commune.* New York: Center for Policy Research.

Zane, N.W.S., Sue, S., Hu, L., & Kwan, J.H. (1991). Asian American assertion: A social learning analyses of cultural differences. *Journal of Counseling Psychology, 38*(1), 63–70.

Zinner, E.S. (1987). Responding to suicide in schools: A case study in loss intervention and group survivorship. *Journal of Counseling and Development, 65*(9), 499–501.

INDEX